LETTERS OF
HEINRICH AND
THOMAS MANN,
1900 — 1949

# WEIMAR AND NOW: GERMAN CULTURAL CRITICISM

*Martin Jay and Anton Kaes, General Editors*

LETTERS OF
# HEINRICH AND THOMAS MANN, 1900–1949

*Edited by* HANS WYSLING

Translated by DON RENEAU

*with Additional Translations*
*by* RICHARD *and* CLARA WINSTON

UNIVERSITY OF CALIFORNIA PRESS

BERKELEY    LOS ANGELES    LONDON

First published as Thomas Mann and Heinrich Mann, *Briefwechsel 1900–1949*, edited by Hans Wysling. Letters of Thomas Mann © 1968 Katja Mann, Kilchberg and © 1984, 1995 S. Fischer Verlag Gmbh, Frankfurt am Main. Letters of Heinrich Mann © 1965, 1984 Aufbau-Verlag Berlin and Weimar. All rights reserved S. Fischer Verlag Gmbh, Frankfurt am Main.

English translation by Don Reneau © The Regents of the University of California, 1998.

English translations from *The Letters of Thomas Mann, 1889–1955*, edited and translated by Richard and Clara Winston © 1970 by Alfred A. Knopf Inc. and Secker and Warburg / Reed Consumer Books. Reprinted by permission of the publishers.

Foreword © 1998 Anthony Heilbut.

This book has been published with the assistance of a translation grant from Inter Nationes, Bonn.

University of California Press
Berkeley and Los Angeles, California

University of California Press, Ltd.
London, England

© 1998 by
The Regents of the University of California

Library of Congress Cataloging-in-Publication Data

Mann, Thomas, 1875–1955.
    [Correspondence. English. Selections]
    Letters of Heinrich and Thomas Mann / edited by Hans Wysling ; translated by Don Reneau ; with additional translations by Richard and Clara Winston.
       p.   cm. — (Weimar and now ; 12)
    Includes bibliographic references and index.
    ISBN 0–520–07278–2 (alk. paper)
      1. Mann, Thomas, 1875–1955—Correspondence.   2. Mann, Heinrich, 1871–1950—Correspondence.
3. Authors, German—20th century—Correspondence.   I. Mann, Heinrich, 1871–1950.   Correspondence.
Selections.   1998.   II. Wysling, Hans.   III. Title.   IV. Series.
PT2625.A44Z485   1998
   833′.912—dc20                                  96–38461
   [B]                                                CIP

Printed in the United States of America
9  8  7  6  5  4  3  2  1

*The publisher gratefully acknowledges the contribution provided by the Literature in Translation Endowment of the Associates of the University of California Press, which is supported by a generous gift from Joan Palevsky.*

# CONTENTS

# LIST OF ILLUSTRATIONS

# FOREWORD

There are few parallels to this remarkable collection of letters. The James brothers' correspondence may come to mind, but their geniuses and vocations were famously dissimilar. This was emphatically not the case with Thomas and Heinrich Mann. For many years they were the chief rivals for the crown of German letters: in 1913 D. H. Lawrence acknowledged the received wisdom that, along with Jakob Wassermann, they were the "artists in fiction of present-day Germany." Letters between such exalted rivals would be compelling even if they did not address all the major issues of their time, cultural and political. But their real fascination is psychological. Robert Musil dreamed of a novel in which "the world of emotions" would incorporate "the world of ideas." In these letters, as in the best of Thomas Mann's fiction, ideas and emotions become inseparable. Literary aesthetic, political platform, military strategy, the proper tendency of German culture—all these become ciphers for a sibling rivalry of mythic proportions.

They were once so famous. In 1929 Thomas became the first German to receive the Nobel Prize for literature since his country's defeat in the Great War; a year later *The Blue Angel*, a cinematic adaptation of Heinrich's novel *Professor Unrat*, became a worldwide sensation. Thomas would remain a literary star during his exile in America. He became the most famous émigré author as much for his fierce attacks on the Nazis (and, later, on the phenomenon known as McCarthyism) as for his best-selling novels. He had so transcended his literary origins that during World War II Roosevelt thought of naming him the head of postwar Germany. Critics like Georg Lukács and Theodor Wiesengrund Adorno were such fervent admirers that he quipped that their theories were latent in his texts, that he had virtually dreamed them up. Meanwhile at Harvard, Harry Levin taught a popular course, "Proust, Joyce, and Mann," while F. O. Matthiessen identified him as the great voice of cultural humanism.

But tastes change. Both brothers lived to see their reputations plummet. Levin, to Thomas's chagrin, renamed his course "Proust, Joyce, and Kafka." Heinrich spent his last years in Hollywood, waiting unsuccessfully for the movie studios to hire him. By the late 1980s he was forgotten by most American readers, and his brother was remembered primarily for *Death in Venice*. In recent years, new translations as well as the publication of his frankly homoerotic diaries have stimulated a new interest in Thomas. But Heinrich's books remain almost impossible to find.

These letters afford the most intimate view of Thomas outside the diaries. They will also introduce American readers to his formidable brother. Besides the light they shed on politics and culture, the letters illuminate the great and steady theme of all literary lives: how, in good times and bad, to keep writing.

—⁂—

The Mann brothers were superbly positioned to chart the decline of one class and the rise of another. Their father was the town leader of Lübeck, as civic-minded as he was rich. But the family business declined on his watch, and after his early death at fifty-one, the brothers found themselves in reduced circumstances. Senator Mann's class, the Bürgertum, had adhered to older values that were crushed by a juggernaut of bourgeois nationalism and new-fangled capitalism. In part out of loyalty to that class, the young Heinrich briefly edited a reactionary, anti-Semitic "rag" (in Thomas's words, though he provided an occasional short essay), *The Twentieth Century*. By rights, the Mann brothers should have remained conservative. When they moved to the left, their critics dismissed them as traitors to their class, indeed as secret Jews.

Their childhood had been privileged and inbred, so rarefied that Thomas quietly fantasized himself a prince traveling incognito through the city streets. Yet isolation from the masses left both brothers with a sense of marginality. Outsiders tended to find them excessively formal and self-effacing, the most melancholy of elitists. Very early Thomas began to identify with society's pariahs, Jews and gypsies. With another outlawed group, homosexuals, he found an enduring affinity.

Sibling tensions between the brothers were exacerbated by their different sexual orientations. Heinrich was an unabashed heterosexual, introduced as a teenager to the local brothels by his uncle Friedel. But at fourteen Thomas fell in love with a classmate, Armin Martens, an unrequited love that would find immortality in his story "Tonio Kröger" and would become the model for a lifetime of ardent if unfulfilled desire, expressed circuitously in his fiction. In 1929 he wrote that his first notions of desire could be found in that story, and at seventy-eight he wrote that no event, in a lifetime of strong emotions, had been as powerful. Somehow Heinrich found out about his brother's love troubles and with adolescent callousness wrote a friend that Tommy simply needed an inexperienced young girl to resolve all this "nonsense."

I argue in *Thomas Mann: Eros and Literature* that Thomas's sense of passion was directly informed by his homoeroticism, and that his experiences invariably ended in disappointment and rejection. Like Tonio Kröger, he would never win over the "commonplace" folk, that is, ordinary young men who could barely understand him much less return his love. By far the most dramatic correspondence in this collection, the letters of December 1903 when Thomas condemns Heinrich's work *tout court*—its vocabulary, narrative momentum, cold-hearted attention to a shallow psychology—needs to be read in the light of his failed relation with Paul Ehrenberg, "that central experience of my heart." While Thomas sweats heart's blood in pursuit of a literary transcendence, Heinrich keeps turning out glib fables of cut-rate decadence. Or so Thomas asserts in a confusion of critical principle and a broken heart.

It is enthralling to see Heinrich deal with his rival. He continues to act the role of protective older brother, clearly alarmed by Thomas's volatile nature and thoughts of suicide. But he also feels obliged to defend his own literary procedure. He never forgets Thomas's plaintive desire for a laurel wreath, only one allowed to a family.

Yet, as Wysling shows, there were numerous parallels in their early works. Both favored as their heroes isolated figures whom they scorned more than they loved. Both were uncannily alert to the workaday phenomena of fin-de-siècle Germany. They were two of Nietzsche's finest students, but curiously it was the initially apolitical Thomas who was less impressed by Nietzsche's grandiloquent notions of a superman—perhaps because he loved blond beasts only too well—and more receptive to the philosopher's skepticism, as articulated in his critique of Wagner and Bayreuth.

Both were obsessed with a preferred sister whom they would be equally ruthless in exploiting for literary purposes after she had died. Heinrich's favorite was Carla, the family actress, a bourgeois bohemian, and he would stun his relatives, though not Thomas, when he turned her suicide into a play and subsequently married the lead actress. Thomas's relations with the aggressively conventional Lula (a bohemian bourgeois?) were yet more astonishing. According to his son Golo he viewed her as his "female self." We know that Armin Martens courted her as may have Paul Ehrenberg. In *Doctor Faustus* the Ehrenberg character is killed by a woman based on Lula (the novel also includes a dramatization of Carla's suicide). In *Die Geliebten*, a novella he contemplated writing during the Ehrenberg years and later folded into *Faustus*, the heroine Adelaide is not based on Lula but on Thomas himself; his notebooks combine first- and third-person narrative. Adelaide's husband is based on Heinrich, perhaps because Thomas didn't know other heterosexuals well enough; perhaps because his brother symbolized the world's opposition to the so-called nonsense that Adelaide—and he—regarded as love.

Heinrich's condemnation of his brother's marriage to Katja Pringsheim may have expressed a residual anti-Semitism. Thomas had scarcely sold out to bourgeois convention, and Heinrich was an unconvincing bohemian. (Katja found him "the strangest man I ever met." During close to fifty years, they never graduated from "Sie" to "du.") But he may have understood something else, particularly after Thomas admitted that his choice of conventional happiness was strenuously willed and a bit disingenuous. Among this book's treasures is Heinrich's 1913 review of *Death in Venice*, in which he discovers in Aschenbach, his brother's surrogate, an instance of "death-in-life." So much for connubial bliss.

With all their similarities, the literary Manns were not easily confused. As Wysling observes, Heinrich's satires earned him the reputation of a political prophet, even though he feared that agitprop, along with Marlene Dietrich's legs, might be his only claims to fame. Their critic friend Hermann Kesten observed that Heinrich was wiser and Thomas deeper. Heinrich was initially more facile but in the end less ambitious. A Francophile, he declined to become an essayistic novelist in the German manner; he left intratextual commentary to Thomas. Nor was he a linguistic athlete; he agreed with Montaigne that language should be enriched, not expanded, and he deplored the German weakness for compound words. Heinrich's style is distinguished by his smuggling of rhetorical and analytical judgments into fictions that consist of rapid scene changes and highly charged dialogue. His work is invariably theatrical, and its greatest flaw is melodrama. Those who prefer it to Thomas's admire its "spontaneity"—though Heinrich later came to agree with Thomas that he had written far too much, far too quickly. Ultimately Thomas would survive as the greater artist, and his own political prophecies, initially unwitting, more a question of mood and atmosphere than of ideological design, have proved to be more resonant.

Up to 1914 their letters express anxieties about finances and the merry-go-round of fame. Heinrich liked to assume a magisterial note, as if he were above the fray. Yet his letters to his mother reveal that Thomas's success offended his *amour propre*. Both men feared that they had been superseded by young radicals who preferred Whitman to Nietzsche, cabaret to opera. In a despairing letter shortly before the war, Thomas dismisses each of his famous works as fatally inadequate. He, they, won't last.

Thomas's support of the German military during the Great War has been widely condemned, not least by the author himself. But at the time it was shared by almost every German-speaking intellectual. Heinrich was a very rare exception. Though he was entitled to condemn his fellow writers for their *trahison des clercs*, his attack in the famous Zola essay was specifically ad hominem. How else could Thomas read the opening words with their depiction of a burnt-out boy wonder but as a personal affront? Heinrich had published his self-doubts, his deepest fear that he was a lapsed wunderkind. His immense *Reflections of a Nonpolitical Man* became a means of answering an unnamed "you," with whom he had temporarily broken relations.

The book devastates the smug Puritan confidence of democrats, French and American alike, with the German—read Heinrich—figured to be the worst of all. But there is a more personal subtext. At the end, Thomas declares that democracy will mean the triumph of hearty macho men, of "husbands and fathers" over the "nervous exceptions" whose habitat once was German culture in all its musical, apolitical glory. By 1918 Thomas had fathered five children—Heinrich, only one. And yet the book suggests he was profoundly unmarried, thrilled by the prospect of soldiers finding love among themselves, away from their wives and families. In a book filled with allusions to Germany's great writers—himself emphatically included as a symptomatic product of the culture—Thomas's final troubadour is Hans Blüher, author of *The Role of Eroticism in Male Society*. This detail gives a special poignancy to Heinrich's unmailed letter when he reveals that he understands all too well Thomas's "ethos" (the allusion to "ethos" recalls the 1903 debates over passion).

That unmailed letter would have made a powerful conclusion to a Heinrich Mann novel. The tables are turned, and the person whom you've spent years fighting declares you intellectually and aesthetically irrelevant, the author of a few, small, solipsistic books.

At first in the war's aftermath, Thomas believed that Heinrich's victory was complete. He felt himself persona non grata among the radicals; he was not gladdened by the support of conservatives, most of whom he considered philistines. Worse, Heinrich was outselling him, and he briefly retreated into the sphere of domestic idylls, the novella *Herr und Hund*, and a poetic sequence addressed to his infant daughter Elisabeth, as if any work more challenging was beyond his strength.

But resuming *The Magic Mountain*, which he had abandoned early in the war, renewed his spirit. Even before the brothers reconciled in 1922, he had begun to join Heinrich behind the barricades. As early as 1921, in an unpublished essay on the Jews, he attacked the nascent "swastika-nonsense" then invading Munich. The next year, moving with his typically slow pace, he made a transition from Nietzsche to Whitman, inspired by the American poet's homosexual verse. In his audacious speech on the German republic, addressed to an audience of young conservatives, he envisioned a Whitmanesque democracy of loving comrades, a frankly sexual form of liberation. This argument expressed both his own desires and his belief that German men were fundamentally homoerotic; it was a left-wing version of Hans Blüher's thesis. But few were convinced by his attempt to crush the swastika with a calamus. Conservatives were horrified, leftists bemused.

Yet for the rest of the decade the Mann brothers were Germany's greatest defenders of secular humanism against the Nazi threat. As something of a tourist attraction himself, Thomas joked that Hitler's anti-Semitism would ruin Munich's chances for tourism. As German correspondent for *The Dial*, he was among the first to introduce American readers to what still seemed a local nuisance, Hitler and his band. By 1930 the Nazis were calling left-liberals "Thomasmänner."

During this period Heinrich consolidated his role as "the Hindenburg of the Left," the warrior with the longest, most honorable record. His invitation to Thomas to lead the German academy—impractical in the extreme!—can be read as an attempt to assert the dignity of German culture. Unfortunately the grand old men he wished Thomas to join included a Jew, Max Liebermann, who would have been doomed under Hitler, and Gerhard Hauptmann, Thomas's sometime friend and rival—and the model for the character of Peeperkorn in *The Magic Mountain*—who would become a Nazi supporter.

Along with many observers, the brothers had begun to read their story in mythic terms. Every five years they greeted each other's birthdays with public addresses, overcoming a never dormant tension by emphasizing the other's exemplary behavior. The myth was clearly a public one, heuristic and maieutic: if they could unite in defense of the republic, so could all other men of goodwill, no matter how steeped in traditional culture. In 1929 Heinrich announced Thomas's Nobel Prize on the radio as if it had saluted his *engagement* as much as his art.

But while Thomas's career flourished with *The Magic Mountain*, the great novella *Disorder and Early Sorrow*, and the first two Joseph novels, the decade leading up to 1933 was disastrous for Heinrich, reaching its abysmal worst in the pseudo-Catholic reveries of *Mother Mary* (translated into English by Whittaker Chambers, the future scourge of Heinrich's Marxist comrades!). As Wysling observes, Thomas's 1930 review of Heinrich's *Die große Sache* is unusually severe, taking back as much as it gives. But note the one development Thomas applauds—the hero's sudden attraction to a younger man. As in his later commendations of American gay writers, Thomas had a perpetual soft spot for this theme.

In the first years of exile, Thomas was uncharacteristically quiet about the Nazis in public, though his diaries express his hatred of them and their supporters—including, in one diary note, Gerhard Hauptmann. He was silent in part because he feared that discovery of his diaries would threaten his reputation, and perhaps his life: the first book the Nazis burned was by the homosexual activist Magnus Hirschfeld (whom Mann had once despised but, as he grew more liberal, came to admire), and the Nazis had been gay-baiting his children since 1926. Moreover his Jewish publisher Gottfried Bermann-Fischer argued that he must not forfeit his German readership. His eldest children Erika and Klaus were militant anti-Nazis: *Die Sammlung*, edited by Klaus, was the earliest magazine of the émigré opposition. They were infuriated by their father's capitulation to the market. But Heinrich endorsed it. Better, he thought, to have at least one Mann before the German public, and since the Joseph novels were so vividly philo-Semitic, they might do some political good.

By 1935 Thomas was finding it impossible to keep still, and essays like "Europe, Beware!" nearly gave him away. After his February 1936 letter to Eduard Korrodi, a Swiss critic, in which he identified himself with all of Hitler's opponents—Jews and Marxists alike—there was no turning back. At the end of the year, his letter to the dean of the University of Bonn, who had revoked his honorary doctorate, made him overnight Hitler's foremost literary enemy. Indeed from now on the Manns could be seen as the First Family of Anti-Fascism, with Klaus and Erika composing attacks as eloquent as anything written by their father and uncle.

Happily the pressures of exile served to consolidate the old men's talents. During the 1930s, between political essays, they wrote perhaps their best novels: Heinrich's *Henri Quatre* and Thomas's Goethe novel, *Lotte in Weimar*. Typically both made a political myth out of history. Heinrich's subject was a French monarch; Thomas's, the imperious lord of German literature. Heinrich remained Thomas's best reader; when he saluted *Lotte*, Thomas admitted that it contained the essence of what he knew about love. The world might find him an unfeeling monster, but he could trust Heinrich to read the novel—and its author—with more sensitivity.

Thomas had moved to America in 1937 and would become a citizen in 1944. In private, he condemned émigrés like Heinrich who remained in Europe as irresponsible. In public he fought hard for them and was overjoyed when Heinrich, accompanied by Golo, reached America late in 1940. By the next year both brothers were settled in California. For the first time in ten years, they could play the birthday game. But while the last event had drawn a huge crowd in Berlin, this was attended by a few refugees at the home of the émigré screen-writer Salka Viertel. In Christopher Hampton's uninformed *Tales of Hollywood*, Thomas's speech is satirized as a last gasp of old-world pomp. In fact, with its argument for a desperately needed "banality of goodness," and for the retirement of Nietzschean irony, it effectively predicted Hannah Arendt's famous work and, perhaps, went beyond it. The seventieth birthday address is another of this book's highlights.

During the 1940s Heinrich's fortunes were as bleak as Thomas's were grand. His years at the sufferance of Hollywood moguls placed him, as Thomas said, at "the devil's mercies." He couldn't get an American publisher for his new novel or autobiography; indeed, for nothing more than a seventieth birthday salute to his brother. In a replay of *The Blue Angel*, he had married a much younger bar girl, Nelly Kröger. Their public spats and her evident instability precipitated a scandal, embarrassing Thomas and Katja so much that they regarded her subsequent suicide with equanimity. "Where has my love gone?" Heinrich wondered in his 1945 tribute to Thomas, a reference both abstract and specific.

By now Thomas was a frequent source of financial support, as well as Heinrich's only advocate of note. He had also become, as Heinrich told Erika, the more radical brother, thoroughly alienated from Heinrich's leftist friends. In 1943, when émigrés like Brecht and Paul Tillich insisted that the Germans were inherently anti-Nazi, and that Hitler was a capitalist excrescence imposed from above, Thomas replied that anybody who remained in Germany was implicated in Hitler's crimes. But he didn't absolve the émigrés. Good Germany and bad Germany were hopelessly intermingled, and he had them both within himself: a formulation Heinrich felt worth an entire career in letters. (On September 9, 1944, Kurt Weill wrote his wife, Lotte Lenya, that the Thomas Manns were "two very sweet old people, wise, humorous, intelligent and far superior to all those intellectual refugees of the Brecht crowd.")

As a final insult from an unsympathetic fate, Heinrich died shortly before he was scheduled to return to East Germany. While he feared becoming a propaganda tool of the government, he also hoped to recover some of the authority that he had lost in translation. His death came in March 1950, ten months after his nephew Klaus's suicide. This was a period when Thomas, after incurring the publicly expressed hatred of Brecht and Alfred Döblin, received humiliating criticism from American conservatives. His local representative attacked him in the U.S. Congress; both *Time* and *Life* mocked his behavior as "The Way of the Dupe." Heinrich's loss only added to his sadness.

He lived long enough to see a new generation turn against him, partially for his so-called betrayal of the homeland, partially for his sheer prominence: he was simply too much in the way, the dominating father who must be slain. In his last months he was reminded of the much earlier rivalry with Heinrich. That one, at least, he intended to retire.

Time would determine the superior artist. While he admitted that he had a note more German and Italian—and it would seem, thanks to Whitman, more American—Heinrich's Gallic voice was uniquely powerful. Quoting Goethe's answer to those who put him up against Schiller, he wrote, "The Germans should be lucky to have two such boys," artists whose grasp had extended beyond national borders until they embodied both German culture and—in Goethe's patented phrase—"world literature."

Their literary fates remain uncertain. Heinrich has recently been attacked by cultural conservatives like Marcel Reich-Ranicki, ostensibly for his uneven production—though his few advocates still celebrate his intellectual vigor and transparent prose. Thomas's reputation has suffered from the difficulty involved in reading his lengthy though beautifully ordered periods and contending with his maddeningly allusive wit. Some of us hope that he can be seen as a profoundly erotic artist, worthy of comparison with Proust and Kafka, and more explicitly political than either.

Under any circumstances, the courage and stamina, the ability to work into old age despite personal tragedies and vicious criticism, remain to inspire and challenge all those who share a Mannian commitment to the word. Their story becomes all the more accessible, thanks to Don Reneau's excellent translation. He captures the bite and animus of an occasionally overwrought Thomas and the magisterial sadness of his equally complex brother.

*Anthony Heilbut*

# INTRODUCTION

## 1

"Being brothers—it means being youngsters together in a respectable provincial nook of the fatherland and making fun of that respectable provincial nook; it means sharing the freedom, irreality, essential purity, the absolute Bohemia of youth. And then, individually, but always in the context of an organic bond and in mutual intellectual reference, it means growing older, maturing into a life approached with the same radical irony as before, maturing, above all, through work, which, though meant as the product of absolute Bohemia, turns out to have been inspired by life, to have been performed in its service, and thus to represent a moral force. Being brothers, the way we are brothers, however, also means remaining profoundly faithful to that irrealistic lightheartedness of old. It means combining with the irony of early times that bashful excitation inspired in us by the vastness of the real world, which is partly intellectual but partly still the response of the provincial child. And, in especially stirring moments of things come true, things unbelievable from the childhood perspective, it means each of us finding our way out of our individual existences, finding our way back together and smiling, saying to each other, if not with our voices, then the more so with our eyes, saying, 'Who would have thought it?'"

In his address honoring Heinrich's sixtieth birthday, Thomas Mann delivered with painstaking fidelity a sketch of the path they had trod together. What bound him irrevocably to his brother in emotional terms was the memory of that "irrealistic" youth: their childhood shared in dreamy abandon in the paternal house on the Beckergrube in Lübeck, and those months in Palestrina and Rome, which they, with no ties or commitments, had idled away in absolute freedom. Neither the first intrusions of reality—early fame, love and marriage, the need for self-assertion against society and tradition, the need to preserve and establish oneself in life—nor all the later "hardening" of reality was able to sully the memory of the purity of their childhood life. Even the estrangement of their quarrel, the decline into narrow partiality that prompted Thomas to attack in his brother those very things that troubled him within himself, proved transitory compared to the shared experience of childhood. From the "childhood perspective," the conflict was finally not credible; their childhood emotion emerged undamaged—it could be seriously disturbed for years at a time, but it was not to be killed.

Beckergrube: that was the site of early dreams, of a fairy-tale happiness, and also of the first attempts to seek a way to the self through play, to conjure whole worlds, like magicians, out of thin air, to divide up the roles, and thus remain master of the story. In their memoirs, both brothers spoke of fairy-tale books read to the children by their mother once upon a time; Andersen's fairy tales were there, the fairy tales of the brothers Grimm, and then that huge brown book with the gold decoration and the illustrations by Doré: the sophisticated fairy tales by Perrault. And among them as well was the old book of mythology by Nösselt; it had Pallas Athene on the cover and once served the mother in her own lessons in mythology. The fairy tales offered the boys a chance to experience that dreamy abandon, a state of untethered floating, the suspension of space and time. Outside, things could buffet one as they might, but all distraction, Heinrich recalls, "died away as I read too many books and I could not recite the names of the houses on the street." Fairy-tale books! Thomas Mann maintained his loyalty to the "primal simplicity of the fairy tale" into old age; he believed he had found it again in Wagner's myths, in the young Siegfried, in Tannhäuser's Venusberg temptation, but also in the wondrous nocturnal realm of *Tristan und Isolde*. Like Heinrich, but more penetratingly and profoundly, he imbued all his works with fairy tales and myths; at bottom, he was always only telling fairy tales: the Sleeping Beauty story in *Royal Highness*; the fairy tale about one upon whom fortune smiles in *Felix Krull*; or, in *Joseph*, the story of the son who left home to find a kingdom. Royal dreams and divine games—they made up his childhood, and it is to these that the aging writer thinks back when he reports of elevated feelings and exaltations.

Then there was Heinrich's puppet theater—Hanno played with it, as did the title character in "The Dilettante." Heinrich, who would have liked to become a painter, made some of the sets himself; the children added figures made of porcelain, papier-mâché, and biscuit dough—the baboons, dachshunds, and setters that Thomas loved to outfit "with silk saddlecloths made out of patches from his sisters' reserves." Later, in a look back at his life, he would write, "There is no sharp boundary in my memory between children's games and the practice of art." For him, artistic talent is "the childlike preserved." Certainly, the play-drive is combined with intellectual maturity, "the infantile, the game, acquires dignity," but, in the inmost recesses of the artist, that which is both childlike and childish, that which is playful, remains intact.

It is also in play that children discover the freedom of standing above it all, the superiority of being master of the story. It gives them power and promises them effectiveness. From the remove of a superior perspective, they look down on the papier-mâché heads, which never play anything but themselves and which, spellbound within the shell of their own formulaic individuality, are forever restricted to a single angle of vision on the world. Those who are free and superior, however, know all perspectives. They are agile, manifold, while the figures are rigid and one-sided. Those who are able to adopt various standpoints, to see from all perspectives, are the richer ones. They raise themselves above the isolation of the individual and choose from the entire range of the possible: they carry within themselves "the seed, the beginnings, the possibility of all capabilities and activities." In their dreamy experimentation with all standpoints, the brothers anticipated the experience attributed later on to Krull, who never rested content with his own individuality "but was always striving, like an actor, toward the other." With this comes the first shudder of alienation, of the loss of identity, as well—who am I then, if I am aware of so many roles within myself? And, in a blend of reluctance and eagerness, they transpose the illusory character of the game onto life itself: they learn to experience, like Krull, "the illusory aspects of life and the world."

The time of childish self-assurance in their theatrical experiments passes quickly. Early literary efforts revolve about the instability, the perplexity, of the ego. Driven by relentless self-reflection, the ego becomes increasingly painfully conscious of its own questionable nature, though not, however, without becoming equally conscious of the questionable nature of the world. "Haltlos"[1] is then the title of Heinrich Mann's autobiographical story of 1890: "The black flood of carping and contempt, to which youth is already subjected by endless self-reflection, introspective analysis, and conclusions drawn about the external world, engulfed him, submerging every hope." This ego no longer has any "resolve of its own," no "striving that is secure in its direction"; it does no more than become increasingly accustomed to "its own internal embitterment, self-contempt, and contempt of the world." "To stand opposed to the common run of daily life as something other, something quite alien, harboring an interior world known only to himself, always kept anxiously concealed—that had flattered him." Thomas Mann followed in 1895 with the story "Walter Weiler"—it appeared later, reworked, under the title "The Dilettante"—the story of an unstable dreamer and do-nothing who ultimately founders on the "disgust inspired in me by life—my life—by 'all that' and 'the whole thing.'" The heroes of both novellas are outsiders who distrust and disdain the world they live in. Like Wellkamp—from Heinrich's novel *In einer Familie* (1894)—both suffer from a "sickness of the will": "In our present time, which is pointlessly critical and incapable of straightforward action, only extraordinary characters will be entirely free of this psychological sickness, which subjects its victims to an inward emotional degeneration, a degeneration of the self-critical impulse into increasingly feeble refinements, while it cripples more and more their ability to guide their actions in accord with their better judgment. Among more delicate natures, those predisposed from the outset to reflection and emotional dilettantism, the sickness of the will often leads to a complete loss of initiative. Self-criticism takes on such a form of manifold virtuosity that it renders the victim incapable of making the simplest decision, and his life is lost to the vacillations of an everlasting perplexity."

All that remains to help the ego gain a certain sovereignty over itself and its surroundings is the "taste for the psychological" and the "pleasure of seeing through people." Both the dilettante and Andreas Zumsee, the hero of *Berlin: The Land of Cockaigne*, depend

1. As in *Haltlosigkeit*, instability, in the preceding sentence.

upon it—and it is the pleasure of expression, the ecstasies of the artistic, that will later be the experiences of Tonio Kröger and Mario Malvolto. But psychological awareness lays waste to the vitality of emotional warmth; aestheticism is to be had only at the price of forfeiting participation in life: the "power of the intellect and the word, which sits smilingly on its throne above mute, unconscious life" secures nothing more than superiority in a vacuum. The artist is isolated, capable neither of compassion nor of action. Moreover, his analytical drive turns inward on his own ego. Tonio Kröger, according to a notebook entry as early as 1899, is quite simply destroyed "by his psychological awareness"; Mario Malvolto (in "Pippo Spano," Heinrich's 1905 artist story) becomes a clairvoyant jester of the self and thus falls victim to his "neurasthenic hypersensitivity." What remains is a blend of desire and contempt directed against the external world, against those who are harnessed to the ordinary, against the "well-wrought type" that knows nothing of the "lonely refinements" of Tonio and Mario. There also remains an existential disgust directed against "all that" and "the whole thing," and against the artist's own ego and its impotent failure in the world.

"Tonio Kröger" and "Pippo Spano" were written only after the stay in Italy, which once more created the closest of relations between the prodigal sons. After Beckergrube, now came Palestrina and Rome, via Torre Argentina 34. Both brothers recalled those years, 1896 to 1898, in their memoirs. "We lived as few Germans do," wrote Thomas, "through a long, scorching, Italian summer, in a little town in the Sabine Hills—Palestrina, birthplace of the composer. The winter, with its alternation of cutting tramontana and sultry sirocco days, we spent in the eternal city, taking rooms of an old woman who had a flat with stone floors and straw chairs in the via Torre Argentina. We made arrangements with a little restaurant named Genzano—I have looked for it since but could not find it—where we got good wine and capital *crochette di pollo*. Evenings we went to a café, played dominoes, and drank punch. We made no friends. If we heard German spoken we fled. We regarded Rome as the refuge of our irregularity, and I, at least, lived there not on account of the south, which at bottom I did not love, but quite simply because there was still no room for me at home." Their monthly allowances, plus a favorable exchange rate, offered them "economic freedom, the power to bide our time. If we did not want too much we could do what we wanted—and we did. My brother, who originally meant to be an artist, sketched a great deal, while I, in the reek of endless 3-centesimi cigarettes, devoured Scandinavian and Russian literature and wrote. The successes that gradually came my way rejoiced me but did not surprise. My attitude toward life was a compact of indolence, bad civic conscience, and the sure and certain feeling of latent powers." "I see him," wrote Heinrich, "by my side, both of us young [ . . . ]: with no ties—one would have said, not knowing how much pitiless obligation one destined to produce literature his whole life long bears with him as a young man wherever he goes. It was harder than the memory of it I can conjure today. Later on, the state of anticipation would have been unbearable. We needed all the hardiness of our youth to withstand it."

They read and talked, quite likely primarily about Nietzsche—it is not by accident that Adrian Leverkühn's conversation with the devil was set in the stone salon in Palestrina. And they wrote. Heinrich, a whole series of stories—"Das Stelldichein," "Ein Verbrechen," "Doktor Biebers Versuchung"; Thomas, "The Dilettante," the satire "Little Lizzy" ("it was among the first of my things that impressed you"), then "Tobias Mindernickel," the story of another T.M. who, like the dilettante, succumbs to his disgust with life. In hours of leisure, they drew illustrations and wrote text for the *Bilderbuch für artige Kinder*: "Seventy-five artworks from the hand of a master, among them, twenty-eight color illustrations and forty-seven copperplate prints, accompanied by sixteen highly artistic poems and many textual remarks of a content both morally instructive and amusing, gathered together and published conscientiously and with especial moral consideration for maturing German youth"—as Viktor Mann reported on the project in his family chronicle. Heinrich, however, sat down daily for weeks on end to pen-and-ink sketches, an "endless series of pictures, which we called 'The Life Work,' and the actual title of which was 'The Social Order.' And these pages, which we glued together into a long, thickly rolled frieze, really did depict human society in all its types and groupings, from the kaiser and the pope to the lumpenproletariat and beggars—there was nothing left out in this *trionfo* social pyramid; we had time and amused ourselves as we could." In moments of particular bravado—Thomas Mann thinks back on it in his letter of February 18, 1905—they planned together "a kind of Gipper-novel [ . . . ], which was originally supposed to have the song 'Der Omnibus fährt *durch* die Stadt' for a leitmotif. And at the end it was supposed to be the omnibus that drove Biermann to prison." Well, the Gipper-novel came to nothing, but Biermann went into *Buddenbrooks* as Hugo Weinschenk. A collaborative work à la Goncourt? The brothers seem, in fact, to have been considering it: "As we were still in the first half of our working lives," wrote Heinrich in his book on his life and times, "my brother and I shared with each other the same secret thought. We wanted to write a book together. I spoke first, but he was already prepared for it." Thomas commenced the writing of the novel at the end of October 1897, in Rome. At the same time, Heinrich Mann was writing the first lines of his "novel of the fashionable set," *Berlin: The Land of Cockaigne*: "I was overtaken by my talent on the Via Argentina in Rome in 1898, and I didn't know what I was doing. I thought I was writing a pencil draft, but produced the nearly finished novel."

*Buddenbrooks* and *The Land of Cockaigne*. The differences in temperament, approach, and objective are already clearly evident by now. *Buddenbrooks*, despite the richly abundant presence of the external world, encompasses the most personal experiences of the writer, experiences, to be sure, which he attempted to undermine philosophically in his drive toward self-definition: Schopenhauer's nihilistic metaphysics; the certainty that space and time are to be regarded as deceptions of maya; that life and the world have an illusory character; Nietzsche's unmasking psychology and, above all, his analysis of the decadent artist who loses himself neurotically in roles and no longer represents or establishes values.

A nihilistic aestheticism, that is, which would have liked to limit its perception of the world to the phenomenological but is not quite certain whether nihilism itself should not be understood as an aestheticist phenomenon. In a letter to Heinrich, Thomas Mann quoted two lines from Platen:

Dem frohen Tage folgt ein trüber,            A cheerless day succeeds a glad one,
*Und alles hebt zuletzt sich auf.*            *And, finally, all is canceled out.*

"This general canceling out of things," he added, "is a thoroughly melancholy, but also radically comforting thought. The world is as nothing—" Against all that, then, is Tony's will to life, her indestructible childlikeness.

Heinrich's novel is much less philosophically freighted, but for that the more energetic in its social criticism. While Thomas Mann released himself to a melancholy and ironic preoccupation with the problematic of his ego, his brother turned his satirical power against the "apish" pretense of an urban society grounded only in appearance. To narrate once again the *comédie humaine*, to push the human carnival, by exaggerating its social characteristics to the point of the grotesque and macabre—that is the goal of a combative moralism and a radicalism of truth, which seeks to preserve itself in destruction, even if it has nothing to offer in return but itself and its rebelliousness. Nietzsche here as well. For Heinrich, Nietzsche was above all an anarchist, his work the dynamite that would explode all rigidified conventions. "At the time," wrote Heinrich in a later essay on Nietzsche, "it seemed to be a justification of ourselves; we understood it, including its extravagances, in terms of our own intellectual inclinations. We were happy to place our trust in the individualist—of which it offered an ultimate example—in the opponent of the state, who would more likely be an anarchist than a devoted citizen of the 'Reich.' In 1890 and the following years, this was an attitude of personal independence. We prepared ourselves in this way for our own accomplishments, and Nietzsche was extremely welcome to us as a philosopher. At the pinnacle of his ideal society, he put the proud intellect—and why should that not be us?" Such may already have characterized Heinrich's thinking as he scribbled away at his "life's work" and waited; in *Cockaigne*, the writer Köpf adopts a similarly reserved attitude: he sees through the bustle of society but contents himself in the anonymous role of a spectator.

The different intentions of the authors are reflected in their heroes: Hanno Buddenbrook's erotic dream world of music and metaphysics proves incapable of life; it is secure only in death. For the sake of the dream, he arrives at a renunciation of the world. Andreas Zumsee, in contrast, would resort to opportunistic means to make of himself a hero in the world. He believes he is capable of manipulating it. In reality, however, it masters him: he is its product and, ultimately, its victim.

Thomas Mann, delicate and unstable, secures for himself his dreamy freedom, first of all, in "Indian passivity," and his intellectual freedom in evasive irony; turned back, laden with the past, he would ultimately press beyond fairy-tale romanticism into the realm of the mythic, to find security in myth and, at the same time, in the retelling of the myth, a freedom that was both tenable in its own right and relevant to life. Heinrich, no more stable himself, assumes the activist role. He turns his critical dialectic outward, gives himself over to ideological and utopian anticipations, and, by way of an extravagant dynamism, propels psychology and satire into the realm of prophecy. Both seek to free themselves in their work and believe that the writer's task, in view of the rigidities of established orders, is to open up the unrestricted sphere of the possible. What Heinrich said of his brother's first work applies also to *Cockaigne:* "This was the energetic manner of a new beginning, to liberate himself from the temptations of his not yet settled disposition."

If one looks generally at the childhood and youth of the brothers, what predominates despite all the obvious differences in temperament is what they have in common. Both attempt to preserve for themselves in art that which could have been lost in the normalcy of the bourgeois order: the game of a thousand and one possibilities, an unconstrained cast of mind. They experience themselves equally as destined and exceptional, as the "delicate children of life" and as the elect. Exterior motifs confirm points of particular inner sensitivity: each is equally subject to the tensions between the German and the foreign, the bourgeois and the artistic, the healthy and the sick. As a twenty-year-old, Heinrich Mann goes "home to Italy" and leads from then on a life of Zarathustran wandering; in *Zwischen den Rassen*, a book of bitterness and melancholy, he depicts in Lola a person for whom belonging to a people and a race becomes a problem. Thomas Mann displays the same tension in Tonio Kröger and Paolo Hofmann. Compared to Heinrich, he may seem to be settled and bourgeois, but scarcely any other writer sends his trains and caravans into such adventurous, impassable terrain as he. Both are extra-bourgeois through their calling, and for both that calling is strangely allied to sickness. It "creates a critical opposition to the world, to the average in life, disposes one to rebellion and irony against the bourgeois order, and offers its man the refuge of a free mind." What Thomas Mann called the "sickness of my youth" is the impotence of the reality-shunning dreamer, who looks upon the world of the secure and the dumb with a mix of hate and envy, contempt and desire. Like Heinrich, he raises himself in his work above the "cynical character flaws" of the time, thus gaining for himself the illusory consciousness of election, which is escape and grace wrapped up in one.

2

Heinrich was the older brother. In a picture from early childhood, he is sitting apart from his siblings in a chair, an absent, haughty expression on his face and a book on his knee. That is how the young Prince Albrecht, Klaus Heinrich's oldest brother, is depicted in the "Fürsten-Novelle": "He appeared unchildlike and extremely reserved, shy for reasons of embarrassment and proud due to a lack of grace." Klaus Heinrich simply has no choice but to accept it when Albrecht refrains once for several years from speaking a word to him, "without there having been a specific conflict between the brothers." The incident is autobiographical, Erika Mann explains, having recently given a fresh account of it: delicate, vulnerable, in need of love, and "full of a miserable scorn for the whole affair," in a constant state of self-defense against the meanness of life, Thomas was weaponless against the cool arrogance of his brother, who was probably subject, at bottom, to the same sort of princely anxiety as he. Like Klaus Heinrich, he endured mutely the sometimes wrenchingly painful outbursts of his older brother—they stemmed from the extreme sensitivity of those whose destiny takes shape early and who find it hard living within their "austere, difficult, passionate loneliness."

The young Thomas no doubt suffered on account of the superiority of his brother. To Thomas, the "fraternal constellation" was fate, a thorn in the side, and a spur to his ambition. His work appears, in the first instance, under the sign of self-assertion. No matter where he wanted to go, it seemed that the other was always already there; it was only his own special tenacity and his ambition to do better that kept him from being stifled. He was always late; he was always slow; but just before the finish line, he overtook the other and when finally he was done, it was his work that counted. The result was that the older brother was filled with envy and jealousy, and he complained that he had been plundered by the younger one. When Thomas pointed out reproachfully, at the time of their quarrel, that the "fraternal constellation" had led Heinrich to color everything personally and inspired him to excesses, Heinrich, in an unmailed letter, responded with blunt clarity: "From all that I see, you have underestimated your significance in my life as far as natural feeling is concerned, and overestimated in terms of intellectual influence. The latter, negative in form, you have suffered one-sidedly. You must accept this truth; it is not mere invective, like all of those phrases, more akin to pathos than ethos, in your letter. As for me, my sense of myself is that of a thoroughly independent existence, and I experience the world, not from within a fraternal constellation, but simply on my own. You do not disturb me."

Thomas Mann would not have chosen to assert the same. Not long before he died, he referred in a letter to the great shadow that had been drawn over the whole of his life, which had filled him with a sense of "chariness." "My basic attitude toward him and his somewhat formidably intellectual work was always that of a little brother looking up at the elder. It is expressed autobiographically in *Royal Highness*, where Klaus Heinrich says to his brother, the grand duke: 'I have always looked up to you because I always felt and knew that you were the more distinguished and superior of us two and I am only a plebeian compared with you. But if you deem me worthy of standing at your side and bearing your title, *and representing you to the people*, although I do not consider myself so very presentable and have this hindrance here with my left hand, which I must always hide—then I thank you and am yours to command.'" The letter concludes, however, with a further admission: "But it was an indescribable shock to me, and seemed like a dream, when shortly before his death Heinrich dedicated one of his books to me with the words: '*To my great brother,* who wrote *Doctor Faustus.*' What? How? He had always been the great brother!"[2] Thus once again, for the last time, the "fraternal constellation" colored the meaning of the words.

A look at the early works is instructive. The first years of Thomas Mann's creative accomplishments are marked by signs of admiring emulation. To do the same as his brother, to do it better than he does, is the primary objective of all his efforts. This extends even to the choice of models. As early as 1893, he writes an essay about Heinrich Heine, the "Good," in the school newspaper, *Der Frühlingssturm*. Heine's aestheticism reinforced in both brothers that feeling of a "scarcely definable superiority," which from the beginning separated them from bourgeois society and its subservience to pseudo-norms. Heine's technique of disillusionment anticipated in many respects the unmasking psychology of Nietzsche: "It was the 'pathos of distance' toward the majority of our fellow pupils, which everyone knows who has ever read Heine at fifteen in the fourth form made up his mind about people and the world," writes Thomas Mann in 1896 in "Wille zum Glück."

His first prose sketch, "Vision" (1893), was dedicated to Hermann Bahr, whose "nervous romanticism" had also had its effect on Heinrich Mann. By way of Bahr, Heinrich found his way to the Goncourts, to Barbey d'Aurevilly, Huysmans, Maeterlinck, and Bourget, and in the stories "Das Wunderbare" (1896), "Das Stelldichein" (1897), or yet again in "Doktor Biebers Versuchung" (1897), he yielded to doctrines clearly recalling Bahr's mysticism. (Bahr's sketchbook, *Fin de siècle*, which pushed decadent mysticism to the point of sophisticated excess, was banned in 1890.)

The sense for the inexplicable and mysterious, nourished by Bahr, found in E. T. A. Hoffmann an opportunity for further development and exercised a decisive influence on Heinrich's story "Das gestohlene Dokument" (1897). Thomas Mann followed closely behind with the story "The Wardrobe," a "story full of riddles," modeling it, even to the point of details, on "Don Juan," one of Hoffmann's *Fantasy Pieces in the Style of Callot*. It takes over that "curious incident that befalls a traveling enthusiast": like the secret door in Hoffmann, the wardrobe's false burlap back mediates between the gray sobriety of the hotel room and the dreamy, death-imbued wonder world of fairy tales. It was probably Hoffmann as well from whom Thomas Mann adopted the intoxication motif, which he uses from then on in all his works to indicate the line demarcating the limits of the real: Albrecht van der Qualen has a little glass of cognac; Thomas Buddenbrook smokes his Russian cigarettes; Hans Castorp drinks himself into the precipitous abandon of his Walpurgisnacht but also into the mythical depths of his snow dream; Krull indulges to excesses in cups of mocha before he allows himself to be drawn by Kuckuck into his panerotic, cosmic visions.

Before their involvement with Hoffmann, the two brothers had already made the acquaintance of the most sensational of all the magicians of romanticism, Richard Wagner.

2. *Großer Bruder* means both "big brother" and "great brother."

Notes from his music are to be heard rising in nearly all of Heinrich's early works. In his first novel, *In einer Familie*, he borrows Wagner's Hörselberg music to swell Wellkamp's love and raise it into the realm of the adventurous; and in *Die Göttinnen* (1903) he proves himself a follower of d'Annunzio's lead as a lover of Venice, the city of Tristan. While Heinrich later strayed to Puccini and Donizetti, Thomas Mann remained true to the master of his youth: Krull's dream world is as full of "billowing swells" and "resounding peals" as Hanno's early dreamy escapades. At nineteen, he read Nietzsche's critique of Wagner; at twenty-five, all critical scruples to the contrary, he lapsed into a disturbing attack of pubescent eroticism, a "Wunderreich der Nacht" renewed. In his letter of March 7, 1901, he suggested how completely indivisible music and metaphysics, Wagner and Schopenhauer, seemed to him at the time. (The insights into Schopenhauer's "conception of universal eroticism," that shudder of the mystical adept upon learning what is "in store" for him, is, to be sure, an experience that he does not share with his brother, one that belongs to him alone. And precisely this experience has a constitutive significance for his life's work; from the "sweet sleep" of his somnambulant heroes, he has all of the dream worlds rise—this runs in a generous arch from Thomas Buddenbrook through Hans Castorp to Joseph and Felix Krull.)

Whether Thomas Mann would have found his way on his own to Nietzsche or whether, here too, his brother prepared the way, we do not know. Heinrich knew *Zarathustra* by the time he was twenty; he read the critiques of morality in 1894. In that same year Thomas Mann noted his first Nietzsche quotation, from *Beyond Good and Evil*, and acquired in 1895 volume eight of the large octavo edition (containing the Wagner texts and the poetical works) which had just appeared; further volumes followed.

It is certain, in contrast, that his attention was drawn by his brother to Paul Bourget. Heinrich dedicated his first work to the French conjurer and conqueror of *décadence*. Shortly thereafter, Thomas Mann preserved the first fruits of a reading of Bourget in his notebook. To be sure, he claimed his distance quickly: as a collaborator on the periodical *Das Zwanzigste Jahrhundert*, under Heinrich's editorship from April 1895 to the end of March 1896, he remarked occasionally on Bourget's *cosmopolis* and on national sentiment in general; but he did not regard it as a viable force for the future, understanding it instead as a "literary taste." For Heinrich, collaboration on this nationalist periodical may have been an experiment; having been influenced by Bourget, he wanted to conduct it, at least, in an unambiguous attitude. For Thomas Mann, the "silly little paper," which his brother would soon be editing "somewhat reluctantly," was scarcely more than a welcome opportunity to earn some money and thus secure himself a little external freedom. (That Thomas Mann, incidentally, also published his first novellas in periodicals to which his brother had already gained entrance is noted only in passing. "Gefallen" appeared in 1894 in M. G. Conrad's *Gesellschaft*; "Der Wille zum Glück" in 1896 in *Simplicissimus*.)

In this general regard, it must not be overlooked that from the very beginning Thomas Mann also developed a thoroughly independent taste in his selection of models.

He read the Russians—Tolstoy above all others—the Scandinavians, the North German Fritz Reuter. Heinrich's taste, on the contrary, was oriented one-sidedly toward the French; after Bourget came Flaubert, Balzac, Hugo, and Zola.

What Thomas Mann studied in his brother's work more than anything else was the art of quoting. Heinrich Mann is a master of allusion. For his first novel he chose the constellation of *Elective Affinities*—Goethe's work is named in a conversation; he submerges the seduction scene in the Venusberg music. And the story "Das Wunderbare" is inspired by *Tannhäuser*; in addition to which Heinrich conjures the subterranean Venetian world from Eichendorff's *Marmorbild*. "Magic mountain" comes from Eichendorff: Nietzsche repeats it in *The Birth of Tragedy*. In "Doktor Biebers Versuchung," finally, Heinrich alludes to Flaubert's *Temptation of Saint Anthony*; Antonius Bieber, the doctor in the clinic for nervous disorders, sits down to the piano at a critical moment and plays—from *Tristan und Isolde*. Hanno's dreamy interludes at the piano; the enchanted park from the "Fürsten-Novelle," and, there, the prince's children with their game of life and death; Gabriele Eckhoff as a little fairy-tale queen by the fountain and then at the piano: it is all already there in Heinrich—the Wagner cult, *Jugendstil*, and the fin de siècle. But Heinrich's stories have not lasted; they are lacking in that final quality, the metamorphosis, the animation of the material, which alone makes the writer.

Out of Heinrich's casual technique of allusion, Thomas Mann developed a genuine art of composition. He not only refers in passing to figures and situations known from world literature but, moving well beyond that technique, bases whole stories on preexisting plot patterns. These patterns also make possible that narration among the spheres, that "art of combining," in which voices from all times are to be heard resonating within each other. Fairy tales and Hoffmann's version of "Don Juan," together with the Albrecht van der Qualen plot, make up the narrative texture of "The Wardrobe." "Tristan," as well as the "Fürsten-Novelle" and "The Blood of the Walsungs," is modeled on a Wagnerian myth. In the early "Krull," the fairy tale of fortune's child, Goethe's *Dichtung und Wahrheit*, and Manolescu's memoirs of a confidence man are woven in and through each other. In *Death in Venice* and then in *The Magic Mountain*, Thomas Mann uses motifs from classical myths for the first time as structuring elements—the extent to which this practice was inspired by Heinrich Mann's *Die Göttinnen* or "Mnais," the story of 1906, is not known. What is obvious is only that he sets off on his journeys to Hades at precisely the same time his brother published the story "Rückkehr vom Hades" (1906).[3]

Meanwhile, he appears also to have contributed some to the sophistication of Heinrich's compositional art. While the sounds of Puccini (from *La Bohème* and *Madama Butterfly*) in *Die Jagd nach Liebe* and *Schauspielerin* serve only to underlie specific scenes, the whisperings of Goldoni, Beaumarchais, Donizetti, and Verdi in *The Little Town* are coordinated compositionally in a most artistic way. At the same time that Thomas Mann is

3. "Return from Hades."

working out his fairy tale of the royal children in a fashion similar to the *Meistersinger* comedy, using reminiscences from Bang's "Hoheit" and Heinrich Mann's "Contessina" and sending notes from *The Magic Flute* and sounds from the Psalms drifting across the whole, Heinrich Mann is creating a *commedia dell'arte* that can stand on its own apart from Hofmannsthal's iridescent cabinet games.

In the use of biographical and documentary sources, the brothers had long been equals. In the drive for "realization," they draw on whatever could conceivably be useful in lending a realistic character to the fictional world. Thomas Mann relies on his sister Julia's reports, sometimes without changing a word, to match Tony's fortunes to his Aunt Elisabeth's biography. In 1910, in reference to Krull's South American trip, he borrows excerpts from his mother-in-law's travel diary. ("The use of experiences has been everything to me, and invention out of thin air unimportant: I have always considered the world more ingenious than my genius," he jotted in one of his early notebooks, obviously pleased to be able to appeal to Goethe on this point.) And Heinrich, under the nearly jealous eyes of his brother, describes Lola's childhood according to memories written down by his mother. Like *Buddenbrooks*, his works had also to endure being branded romans à clef.

The practice of borrowing copiously from reality is presumed to lend historical works in particular the character of authenticity. To be able to supply *Fiorenza* with faithfully realistic details, Thomas Mann studied Burckhardt, Villari, and Vasari, making use of what he could in countless excerpts; at the same time he collected visual materials and visited art exhibitions until, finally, his "hunger for the real" drove him to Florence itself. Likewise Heinrich. The bundle of notes among his posthumous papers pertaining to *Die Göttinnen* shows that he not only read "productively" d'Annunzio, Henri de Régnier, and E. T. A. Hoffmann, but drew in addition upon a long list of historical sources and illustrative works—he found even his Baedeker useful. In biography and history, the artist can find, as Tonio Kröger says, "the raw material out of which, with bland and serene mastery, he creates the work of art."

The brothers' intellectual closeness becomes even more visible when one compares not only their techniques but the themes, motifs, and characters found in their work. It is fascinating to see how the conversation conducted in the letters is continued in the books. Thomas Mann's works in particular teem from early on with open and secret borrowings, with memories, allusions, and veiled revelations. *Cockaigne*, for example, stimulated him in a hundred different ways. A few instances will suffice. When Tonio Kröger sets the emotionality of his northern homeland off against the *bellezza*, he does so in words similar to those already spoken by Claire Pimbusch. Heinrich characterizes Türkheimer as a "Renaissance man" and compares him with Cesare Borgia: the target of Tonio Kröger's outburst is therefore deliberately chosen. There is then a straight line running from James L. Türkheimer to Samuel N. Spoelmann in *Royal Highness*, who in the earliest notes to the novel, and with a similar aura of the Anglo-Saxon, was to have been called Davis. Schiller's "And so should the singer walk with the king, they both are exalted among earthly things" was quoted already in *Cockaigne*. Türkheimer's wife is resurrected in Mme Houpflé; fortune's child Andreas Zumsee finds a successor in Felix Krull. (On his way to the top Zumsee is compared to a fairy-tale prince, and his "happy self-consciousness" and his "happy naïveté" are mentioned repeatedly. The dandy and Pulcinella motifs and the whole thematic concern with illusion are already present here, although they appear in Thomas Mann with more philosophical depth—he had already wanted to import Schopenhauer's "veil of maya" into the social novel, plans for which he began making shortly after *Cockaigne* appeared and later abandoned to Gustav von Aschenbach.) Incidentally, Zumsee is also compared to Tannhäuser; Hans Castorp's Hörselberg experiences surpass and deepen those of his predecessor. But that is all far from imitation by this point; it is, at most, a kind of demonstration: You see what can be made of such themes? Since *Buddenbrooks*, Thomas Mann had the feeling of being the greater writer.

Heinrich, for his part, referred increasingly to his brother's motifs. In his story "Der Unbekannte" (1906), he picks up the Tonio Kröger problematic. *The Blue Angel* recalls the satirical school chapter in *Buddenbrooks*. Diederich Heßling's experiences in the military derive from Thomas Mann's own time in the garrison—which he had also used himself around 1913 in "Krull." Many characters repeat themselves in variations: Gugigl resembles Permaneder; Erneste in *Zwischen den Rassen* succeeds Sesemi Weichbrodt—and the model for both is Thérèse Bousset, the owner of Mühlentor boarding school in Lübeck. It is not always possible to say with certainty which brother was the first to take up a theme or motif: much simply lay in the air, available to both, and what seems to be a borrowing proves to be common property. They were especially prone in the early period to mutual variations of the *décadent;* but, while Heinrich strips him of everything heroic—as evidenced by Wellkamp, Claude Marehn, and Arnold Acton—Thomas Mann creates a "hero of weaknesses," who lives in an attitude of "nevertheless," and wins greatness by overcoming the obstacles in his path.


3


Tensions are unavoidable, and, because the brothers knew each other so well, the blows struck home. It began in the *Fiorenza* period. The occasion was Heinrich Mann's Renaissance trilogy *Die Göttinnen*, which was published at the end of 1902 by Langen. In March 1903 Thomas Mann reviewed Toni Schwabe's novel, *Die Hochzeit der Esther Franzenius.* He praised the author's language, "a quiet and sincerely animated language, one gently elevated, which in extraordinary moments touches the sober pathos of the Bible. A tender forcefulness of effect is achieved, which, to describe it more precisely, is roughly the opposite of the bellows-poetry that has been arriving here for some years from the beautiful land of Italy. There are occasional places in Storm where, without the slightest linguistic extravagance, the mood suddenly thickens, where one closes the eyes and feels how the melancholy tightens the throat." Tonio Kröger says something similar; but Thomas

Mann's remark about "bellows-poetry" is directed against the ardor in Heinrich Mann's style enkindled by d'Annunzio (and Balzac). "What I wanted to say is this: We poor plebeians and tschandalas, we who suffer the derisory smiles of the Renaissance men for revering a feminine cultural and artistic ideal, we who believe as artists in pain, in experience, in profound depths and the suffering of love and who confront beautiful superficiality a touch ironically: it must most likely be from us that the most remarkable and interesting work is to be expected from woman *as artist*, indeed, that she someday will rise among us to leadership and mastery. [ . . . ] There is nothing in that, what stiff, cold pagans call 'the beautiful.'"

It had been brewing for some time beneath the surface. In 1901, the year of their stay together in Italy, Thomas Mann had probably learned more details of Heinrich's Italy novel, and it was then that he began conceiving in his notebooks the character of the neurasthenic Renaissance enthusiast, who, by the name of Albrecht or Eugen, was supposed to have appeared in the novella *Die Geliebten* and, later, the maya novel. Albrecht was depicted as "that Nietzschean type . . . who is constantly taking a stand for life, for beauty, dumb instinct, and power," but who, meanwhile, "is sitting on horseback with a parasol." In Albrecht, Thomas Mann attempted to caricature all that belonged at the time to what, in *A Sketch of My Life*, he called "the fashionable and popular doctrines" of Nietzsche's philosophy: "the cult of the superman, the easy 'renaissanceism,' the Cesare Borgia aesthetics, all the blood- and beauty-mouthings then in vogue." Now, *Die Geliebten* was never written, nor was *Maja*; but the pathos of the neurasthenic worshiper of power was resurrected from the notes of 1901–1902 twice: first in Axel Martini, "who, with consumption glowing in the cheeks, kept on shrieking: 'How stark and beautiful is life!' and, nevertheless, went cautiously to bed at ten"; and in Helmut Institoris, who glorified the Italian Renaissance as a time "that 'reeked of blood and beauty,'" but who is "delicate and nervous" and spends most of his time in sanatoriums.

*Die Göttinnen* was a true Dionysian orgy, even if Heinrich Mann repeatedly qualified his fascination with a life of profligacy and himself exposed his cult as "Renaissance hysteria." Tonio Kröger was the first to turn against life "as a vision of savage greatness and ruthless beauty," and with Savonarola Thomas Mann adopts the standpoint of an ascetic moralist in opposition to all life-affirming aestheticism. "I am a softhearted plebeian," according to a note of 1902, "in comparison with the refined, the cold H., but I am equipped with a great deal more lust for power. It is not by accident that my hero is Savonarola." Even though, in "Pippo Spano," Heinrich exposed the artist as a neurasthenic weakling and pretender, who lives "not from force, but from a will to force," Thomas Mann was not to be restrained from juxtaposing to the "aestheticist Renaissance Nietzscheanism" of his brother and to "d'Annunzio's insufferable pontification about beauty" his own pessimistic moralism. He remained focused on Heinrich's fascination, not on his critical consciousness. Thomas Mann's Tolstoyism put him on the side of Pascal and Meyer—"the epic air, the aroma of Faust, the cross, death, and the tomb": Dürer's *Knight, Death, and the Devil* was his sphere. In opposition to the "profligate aestheticism" of his brother, he represented from that time the "northern-moralistic-Protestant, *id est* German" world. "It was," Thomas Mann recalls in the Institoris chapter of *Doctor Faustus*, "the antithesis between aesthetics and ethics, which in fact largely dominated the cultural dialectics of the time and was to some extent embodied in these two young people: the conflict between a doctrinaire glorification of 'life' in its splendid unthinkingness, and the pessimistic reverence for suffering, with its depth and wisdom." There follows a sentence that characterizes the brothers' relations to each other as scarcely any other could: "One may say that at its creative source this contrast had formed a personal unity and only through time fell out and strove against itself."

The already open fissure grew larger on account of *Die Jagd nach Liebe*, as is evidenced, above all, by Thomas Mann's fulminating letter of December 5, 1903. The tensions began affecting the larger family circle as a whole. "If that had been the extent of it," wrote Julia Mann on November 20, 1904, to her eldest son, "that T. and L[öhr]s, like a large part of the reading public, sharply condemned your latest novel—but that you have turned away from your siblings, makes me feel *very sorry* for you. Hold with them, my dear Heinrich, send them a few friendly lines or reviews now and again, and don't let them see that you don't feel yourself to be as highly regarded by the literary world as T. is in the moment. [ . . . ] You are *both* divinely favored people, dear Heinrich—don't let your personal relationship with T. and the L.s be disturbed; how could a year and a half change it so drastically just because your last work didn't find general acclaim. But that has *nothing to do* with your family relationships!" Heinrich's sister Julia in particular refused to excuse him for portraying prominent Munich personalities in "too daring" a manner in his novel. Having assumed social obligations through her marriage to the banker Löhr, she became an ever more resolute representative of a bourgeois-puritanical standpoint.

External circumstances alone were enough to make Thomas Mann feel bound to his sister Julia. His marriage subjected him to social considerations and obligations. The times of "bohemian absolutes and independence" were over for him. Secretly, and precisely in relation to Heinrich, he experienced his own decision to marry as a kind of betrayal of that freedom that had kept him tied to Heinrich since the days in Rome and had long seemed to him the unqualified precondition of life as an artist: "I've not been free since of a feeling of constraint," he confesses just about a year after the wedding, "which in moments of hypochondria becomes very oppressive, and you will no doubt call me a cowardly bourgeois. But it's easy for you to talk. You are absolute. I, in contrast, have deigned to submit to my situation." Even in the engagement period, he had to a certain extent excused himself on account of his "bliss." "I did not 'win' it, it did not 'fall' to me—I have *subjected* myself to it: out of a feeling of obligation, a kind of morality, an inborn imperative, which I, because it is a move *away* from the desk, have long feared as a form of dissoluteness, but which, with time, I have learned to recognize as something moral. 'Bliss' is a service performed—the opposite of it is incomparably more comfortable; and I emphasize this, not because I assume anything like envy on your part, but because I suspect the contrary, that you look upon my new being and nature somewhat disdainfully." When, in "A Difficult Hour," he tells of how Schiller "had ceased to be an intellectual freebooter and occupied a position of civic dignity, with office and honors, wife and children," he is speaking from personal experience.

With that the battle lines were drawn. On one side stood Thomas and Julia, the—for all appearances—bourgeois siblings; on the other the bohemians, Heinrich and Carla. Turned to literary ends, these ties assume an incestuous form; the relationship between Claude Marehn and Ute in *Die Jagd nach Liebe* already points in this direction, but so does Heinrich's story of 1905, *Schauspielerin*, which likewise takes Carla as the model for its heroine. The same year, in his never completed "Fürsten-Novelle" (the preliminary work to *Royal Highness*), Thomas Mann depicts the Tristan-and-Isolde love between the fairy-tale children Klaus Heinrich and Ditlind but then devotes another story to the incest motif, so that on January 17, 1906, he can write Heinrich that a closer acquaintance with *Schauspielerin* shows "as you already gently suggested, that the work I did with 'The Blood of the Walsungs' was work already done to a certain extent." (As in the later work *The Holy Sinner*, the love between the exceptional siblings in "The Blood of the Walsungs" also springs from their "overgrown fastidiousness"; in their narcissistic arrogance Grigorß and Sibylla, like Siegmund and Sieglinde, know love only for their own kind, "the ecstasy of equal birth.") Heinrich's ties to Carla remained extremely close even beyond her death, as the play *Schauspielerin* (1911) and late letters to Karl Lemke demonstrate.

Over time, tension came from other sources. That Heinrich could not make up his mind to clarify his relationship with Ines (Nena) Schmied, a singer born in Brazil, disturbed Thomas Mann primarily because it only deepened the rupture between Julia and the older brother. His feeling was that the community of siblings from Beckergrube was sacred, that it belonged to the dream legacy of childhood. Whoever violated this ideal image transgressed against the "sense of family." In his letter of April 1, 1909, he reminds Heinrich of their togetherness in the paternal house in Lübeck. He felt similarly a year later about Carla's suicide, that it was a violation of "sibling solidarity"—in *A Sketch of My Life*, years later, he censured it as a "betrayal of our brotherly-and-sisterly bond," as unfaithful to "the guileless irrealism of our youth." Vice versa, manifestations of a true sense of family could literally move him to tears. When Heinrich defended *Fiorenza* against Kerr, he wrote to him, for example (November 11, 1913): "In my best moments I've dreamed for a long time of writing another big and faithful book about life, a continuation of *Buddenbrooks*, the story of the children, the five of us. We are worth it. All of us." And in the letter of October 15, 1905, we come, with no contextual preparation, upon the sentence "I am filled with the necessity of our holding together."

In the same year, he had read *The Blue Angel* and privately given vent to an entire list of reproaches, all of them directed against Heinrich's "undue facility" in working. "Anti-Heinrich" is written above the following outbursts in the seventh *Notizbuch:*

### Anti-Heinrich

> I consider it immoral to avoid the discomforts of indolence by writing one bad book after another.
>
> "Light artistic reading"—fine. If only it were not ultimately a *contradictio in adjecto!*
>
> It is the most amusing and frivolous stuff that has been written in German for a long time.
>
> Topsy-turvy! The pupil Ertzum turns in an essay, after he was made to sit in the corner before he began writing; cigarette sellers and café managers are pupils of the gymnasium professor: such as this is no longer to be counted "artistic license," but somewhat more, namely, belletristics that really goes to town. The book does not seem to be calculated to last.
>
> Eating oats must make one very frivolous—and very productive. But perhaps productivity is only a form of frivolity.
>
> Impossible things, so that one does not trust the eyes. Unrath cries in the concert hall: "In the corner!"!
>
> A god-forsaken version of impressionism. ("He aspired steeply.")

Not even the outbursts in *Freistatt* had such vehemence as this. Facility—that means, first of all, imprecise motivation. The longer it went on, the less Thomas Mann was able to suppress his vexation over the violent plot twists, the abrupt psychological shifts, the theatrical, indeed, cinematic exaggerations and convolutions in Heinrich's work. The irony in his letter to Heinrich (June 7, 1906) following his reading of *Stürmische Morgen* is now barely concealed: "A brilliant book once again, which displays all your best points, your gripping tempo, your famous 'verve,' the delightful precision of your language, your quite astounding virtuosity, a book to which one surrenders oneself because it clearly stems directly from passion." And in his letter of April 1, 1909, he reproves the "precipitous and strident fashion" that is part of his genius.

The reproach of "undue facility," however, refers as well to Heinrich's productivity in general. *The Blue Angel* was tossed off in the summer of 1904; Heinrich "took care of" *Die Jagd nach Liebe* in six months right after *Die Göttinnen;* Thomas Mann had not finished reading *Zwischen den Rassen,* and there lay "Die Branzilla" and, nearly simultaneously, *Der Tyrann* waiting for him. "Good God, you've finished something else already," in the words of the letter of June 7, 1907. By 1909 Heinrich was approaching his tenth novel, in addition to a multitude of stories, while Thomas Mann could look back on two novels and two modest collections of stories. "As for me," he wrote in 1906 for a periodical, "[writing] means gritting my teeth and slowly setting one foot in front of the other; it means exercising patience, lying idle for half a day, napping, waiting to see if it does not go better tomorrow with a rested head. To finish a longer piece, to remain true to what has once been undertaken, not to walk away from it, not to reach for something new, to be tempted by the blush of youth, all of that, given my style of working, requires in truth such patience—what am I saying!—such doggedness, obstinacy, such discipline and self-subjugation of the will as one can scarcely imagine and from which the nerves, you can take it from me, become strained to the breaking point." To his brother he confessed on February 6, 1908: "My style of working makes me rigid and apathetic." Here, too, he juxtaposes the effortlessness enjoyed by some with the lot of the ascetic living under the lash of his talent, taking time, valuing slowness despite pressure and doubt, in this way achieving perfection. In a letter to Katja of August 1904, there appear sentences that raise Flaubert to the status of sainthood (and Schiller, in "A Weary Hour," repeats them almost verbatim): "It effervesces only for ladies and dilettantes, for the easily satisfied and the ignorant who do not live under the pressure and the discipline of talent. For talent is nothing easy, nothing playful; it is not an ability to perform without more ado. At the root it is *necessity*, a critical knowledge of the ideal, an insatiability which creates and intensifies the ability it requires, and does so at the cost of some torment." And Spinell's statement, that a writer is a man for whom writing is more difficult than for anyone else, runs just as counter to undue facility as that "insatiability" that forbids Aschenbach to rest "content with easy gains and half-perfection."

Yet a further conflict became apparent in the early years: the conflict between the artistic creator and the moral man of letters. It is more complicated than those named so far, for Thomas Mann had to work through it, not only against his brother, but against himself. In this case the tension became internal discord.

Thomas Mann became accustomed early on in Nietzsche's school to seeing in the artist the actor and charlatan, the morbid "intermediary species" whose sensuous, aping talent is productive of nothing but imitation. In his critique of Wagner, Nietzsche condemned the "character deterioration" of the artist and prophesied the "rise in music of the actor." Wagner appeared to him as "*historio*, the greatest mime, the most astounding theatrical genius the Germans have had, our *scene-maker par excellence*." "The problem of the actor has troubled me for the longest time. I felt unsure (and sometimes still do) whether it is not only from this angle that one can get at the dangerous concept of the 'artist'—a concept that has so far been treated with unpardonable generosity. Falseness with a good conscience; the delight in simulation exploding as a power that pushes aside one's so-called 'character,' flooding it and at times extinguishing it; the inner craving for a role and mask, for *appearance*; an excess of the capacity for all kinds of adaptations that can no longer be satisfied in the service of the most immediate and narrowest utility." Such instincts, Nietzsche believed, would have formed most easily among the lower classes, who learned early on to conform and developed mimicry into an art, until, finally, the instincts generate "the actor, the 'artist' (the zany, the teller of lies, the buffoon, fool, clown at first, as well as the classical servant, Gil Blas; for it is in such types that we find the prehistory of the artist and often enough even of the 'genius')."

From a contrary perspective, Nietzsche also represented the artist as a knowing type. The morbid, neurotic disposition of the artist had refined and sharpened the senses. He was a psychologist and as such gifted with a will to truth, a radicalism, that could extend to the hateful and self-destructive. Yet at the time of "Tonio Kröger," Thomas Mann speaks of the writer's "psychological clairvoyance," of his being "sick of knowledge," both of them ruinous afflictions, and he repeats his curse of literature, of which he had already unburdened himself in his letter of February 13, 1901, to Heinrich: "Ah, literature is death! [ . . . ] I dread the day, and it is not far off, when I shall again be shut up alone with my work, and I fear that the egotistic inner desiccation and overrefinement will then make rapid progress." Still, Lisabeta comes to the defense of literature: "of the purifying and healing influence of letters, the subduing of the passions by knowledge and eloquence; literature as the guide to understanding, forgiveness, and love, the redeeming power of the word, literary art as the noblest manifestation of the human mind, the poet as the most highly developed of human beings, the poet as saint. Is it to consider things not curiously enough, to consider them so?" In the notes to the "Literatur-Essay" of 1909, this view seems to have triumphed. With an enlightener's passion, Thomas Mann himself now speaks of the "Spinozanist effect of literature," of the "release from passions through analysis," and sees the highest stage of development for the literary man in Schopenhauer's type of the saint: "The literary man," he writes in his essay "Der Künstler und der Literat," "is respectable to the point of absurdity; he is honest to the point of sainthood, indeed through his link to the prophets of the Old Testament, as one initiated in knowledge and charged with judgment, he represents in the highest stage of his development the type of the saint more perfectly than any sort of anchorite from simpler times."

Over and over in his works Thomas Mann played off the artist as dilettante against the ascetic moralist inclined to self-mortification. Christian Buddenbrook, with his practical jokes and dandy poses, is opposed to Thomas, who, with his iron discipline, clings fast to the role of the bourgeois. (They are both role players, and the two roles exist in reference to each other; it was not by accident that Thomas Mann once set down in a note, "Thomas = Greek didymos"—twin.) Savonarola struggles with the zeal of a monk against the pagan hedonism of Lorenzo—he has nothing but contempt for the jesterlike "little race of artists." In Krull, the artist reappears as jester and Protean nature; in Aschenbach, his counterpart, the literary man as saint. To be sure, neither of them represents his type purely: Krull remains a soldier and moralist through all his erotic adventures; Aschenbach falls from the heights of moral will to the deepest degradation.

Toward his brother, who had so much of the jester, libertine, and bohemian in him, Thomas Mann always adopted the position of the moralist and bourgeois. He does not shy from informing his brother reproachfully that his art is lacking in dignity, in that discipline, self-control, and slowness that characterize the work of van der Qualen and Aschenbach; occasionally, indeed, it appears as if he wants to push the role of the artist-jester entirely off onto Heinrich. "You know," he writes on February 18, 1905 (having just completed *Fiorenza*), "I think that you have lost yourself in another extreme in that you have become nothing more than just an artist—while an artist, God help me, must be *more* than merely an artist." A year later, he contrasts his *Friedrich* to *Cockaigne* and *Die Jagd nach Liebe* in similar terms: "What is essential is that anything I'm supposed to spend years with must possess, in itself, as object, a certain *dignity*. In the past few years, I have gathered a mass of remarkable material for a modern big-city novel, have experienced and suffered so much, that it could really become a considerable book. But I fear I no longer have the patience and (forgive me!) the modesty, to drag around for two or three years the burden of *just any* modern novel."

And variations on the reproaches reappear in the works. Tonio Kröger, "flung to and fro forever between two crass extremes: between icy intellect and scorching sense," as if he were the descendant of "a wagonful of traveling gypsies." ("The writer as adventurer," according to a note for the novella; "*typus* Henry. As a writer, one is adventurer enough internally. Externally, he should dress well, damn it, and behave like a respectable person!") Heinrich immediately understood "gypsies" as referring to himself—he probably took it as revenge for Siebelind, the sickly writer in *Die Göttinnen*. Right away, in *Die Jagd nach Liebe*, Heinrich himself has acrobats arrive in the "green wagon" of gypsies, and Ute, the actress, asks the most overbearing of the gaping bourgeois onlookers if he thinks his existence is more valuable than that of the people in the wagon: "You would be mistaken." But that is not enough. In his essay of 1905, he has Flaubert say, "whenever there are gypsies peering out of their green wagons outside the gates to my city, it stirs in me something fraternal." Aschenbach then feels obliged to counter: "Only the incorrigible bohemian[4] smiles or scoffs when a man of transcendent gifts outgrows his carefree prentice stage, recognizes his own worth, and forces the world to recognize it too and pay it homage, though he puts on a courtly bearing to hide his bitter struggles and his loneliness."

In fact, neither Heinrich's behavior nor his works were calculated to dispel Thomas Mann's bourgeois scruples. Nearly all the women who played a role in Heinrich's life were actresses or of the demimonde, often both—this is true of a long series of women, from Carla to Ines Schmied, Tilla Durieux, Ida Roland, and Maria Kanova, to Trude Hesterberg and Nelly Kröger. His friends, Wedekind, Steinrück, and all the others, were theater people, his models, from Heine to Wagner, markedly theatrical. "At the Theater" is the title of a long chapter in Heinrich's memoirs. His characters, too, are jesters, whether on the stage or in life. What Mario Malvolto says of himself can be read again in *Henri Quatre*. *Totus mundus exercet histrionem:* "Everyone his own jester. *Totus mundus*—." Jesters flourish just as much in *The Little Town* as in the Wilhelminian era. When Thomas Mann undertook to sketch the actor type of artist, the dandy à la Barbey d'Aurevilly in the *Confidence Man* novel—not yet knowing that he would create his counterpart in Aschenbach—he selected 1871 for Krull's birthday; the work was obviously conceived first as a sort of "anti-Heinrich." Only later did he decide to replace Heinrich's birth year with his own: introspection had shown him how much of the histrionic pulsed in his own blood.

Naturally, Thomas was aware that the dilettante-type came no closer to exhausting his brother's work than the "saint" did his own. Social criticism, the overall concern with so-

---

4. *Zigeuner,* gypsy.

ciety—the political element in Heinrich's writings—spoke clearly enough to the contrary. Antipathies had developed early on in this area as well, and they were intensified to such an extent during the years of the First World War that all artistic and personal tensions were forced into the background behind them.

### 4

When Thomas Mann first affirmed the apoliticism of the intellect, he did so under the influence of Nietzsche and the great German romantic tradition. Like Burckhardt, Nietzsche viewed the state and culture as antagonists. Politics—that was nearly synonymous with a betrayal of the intellect. Artists and intellectuals were obliged to raise themselves above the level of the existing order and social control and thus safeguard the absolute freedom of the intellect. The result, in Thomas Mann, was an aestheticism that looked down on all bourgeois conflicts of power and interest, asserting the superiority of the intellect by subjecting life to a radically ironic perspective.

*Buddenbrooks* was not at all a work of social criticism but was, like all of Thomas Mann's early writing, the product of his "pains attending to a problematic ego." The industrial revolution and the rise of the fourth estate play scarcely any role; the decline of a family does not illustrate a historical dialectic. At issue is not the evolution of a modern society, but the law described by Schopenhauer according to which excessive intellectual development always entails a decline in vital powers, such that—Thomas Mann concludes—only ordinary people are healthy and the genius is necessarily sick. The individual is located at the center, in this view, and society is pressed to the margins. What Thomas Mann writes on April 23, 1925, to Julius Bab about *The Magic Mountain* he could have said earlier of *Buddenbrooks:* "I am very much aware that social problems are my weak point and I also know that this puts me to some extent at odds with my art form itself, the novel, which is propitious to the examination of social problems. But the lure—I put it frivolously—of individuality and metaphysics simply happens to be ever so much stronger for me. Certainly the very concept of the novel implies 'novel of society,' and the *Magic Mountain* did become this to a certain extent, quite of its own accord. Some criticism of prewar capitalism comes into it, along with other things. But I grant you that the 'other things,' such as music and the meaningful interweaving of life and death, were much, much more important to me. I am German—don't think I use the word in the sense of undeserved self-praise and without some national self-doubt. The Zolaesque streak is feeble in me, and that I should have had to discuss the eight-hour day strikes me as almost a parody of the social viewpoint." The same is true, despite all the pains he later took, of *Royal Highness* and *Felix Krull*. In the strict sense, Thomas Mann never wrote a work of social criticism. He stemmed from Nietzsche, not from Marx. His "tastes and cultural traditions"—as he said himself in *A Sketch of My Life*—were "moral and metaphysical, not political and social."

It was otherwise with Heinrich. What he took from Nietzsche was a warrant for unbounded experimentation. Following his encounter with Bourget he tried out the nationalist standpoint, then unrestrained romantic mysticism in the fin-de-siècle stories; *Cockaigne* condemns late capitalist society with sarcasm, and soon after, *Die Göttinnen* indulges to the point of excess a Nietzschean cult of the Renaissance and beauty. But the political and the artistic follow so closely upon each other that it is tempting to see both as deriving from a fundamentally unstable aestheticism, which, however, is dynamic and agile in its workings. The early turn to social criticism is unmistakable, yet, however forceful the grip, it seems that *l'art pour l'art* is also what informs the political satire. But there then comes a turn that stands out in all the writings of 1905: arrogance, the consciousness of loneliness, hatefulness—all are to be overcome for the sake of participation in the humane. "This hater of the bourgeois," he acknowledges in his essay "Gustave Flaubert und George Sand" (1905), "is himself a bourgeois. It would be more remarkable if he were not. Good satires cannot be written except by those who had some kind of relationship to that which he sacrifices to ridicule: an apostate or one denied membership. It can be envy or disgust, but satire always deals in malicious collective feeling." Not only Flaubert was aware of that, but Tonio Kröger as well. George Sand, in her warm-bloodedness, has a liberating and purging effect on the cramped aesthete's arrogance suffered by monkish artists. The "power of her humanity" is capable, momentarily, of forcing the "idée fixe of art" from Flaubert's consciousness. "She wants him to acquiesce, finally, to his own goodness and tenderness, to embrace them, to take part in the love of the simple, to put something down on paper from his heart." And, as he reads one of her pieces, he recognizes that art, which to him "is looking away from, abstaining from life, is relentlessly opposed to humanity," can also be different, namely, "tied to life, benevolent toward all, easy for him who practices it." A way out of decadent alienation from life: what is expressed in Thomas Mann's letters to Katja is revealed in Heinrich's letters to Nena. On July 13, 1905, he attempted to defend himself in regard to his early works by saying, "that it would be dishonest, given a certain nervous and mental condition, to want to reproduce nature simply and straightforwardly. That only feverishness, grotesques, even violence are authentic and sincere." And he continues, "No love was available for me, and nothing that seemed to me worth loving. A shortage of tenderness caused me to maintain that only the sensuous mattered; and to maintain it the louder, the less I believed it inside."

In his case, too, what began with the most private concerns quickly manifests its effects on the general: the isolated intellect is to become capable of joining society, indeed, of directing society. While Thomas Mann moves very reluctantly toward society and politics, Heinrich turns ever more decisively away from Flaubert's aestheticism. Maupassant, Balzac, Hugo, Zola become his masters, and in his programmatic essays of 1910—it is "as if a man from 1789 were speaking"—he makes his profession to human rights: "Freedom: that is the totality of all the goals of the intellect, of all human ideals. Freedom is [ . . . ]

progress and humaneness. To be free means to be just and true, means to be these things to such a degree that inequality is no longer comprehensible. Yes, freedom is equality."

Thomas Mann had already begun nervously anticipating this development early on. On February 27, 1904, having just read Heinrich's story "Fulvia," he wrote to his brother: "Much more remarkable, strangely interesting, and, for me, still a little improbable, is the development of your worldview toward liberalism. [ . . . ] Strange, as I said, and interesting! It must make you feel quite unexpectedly young and strong? Really, I would understand your turn toward liberalism as a kind of consciously reconquered youthfulness, if it did not, which is more likely, simply signify the 'maturity of the man.' Maturity of the man! Doubtful whether I'll ever get that far. For one thing, I don't have much understanding of 'freedom.' It is for me a purely moral, theoretical concept, equivalent to 'honesty.' (Some critics refer to that in me as 'coldheartedness.') But I have no interest whatever in political freedom. Was the prodigious literature of Russia not created under enormous pressure? Would it perhaps not have been created at all without that pressure? Which at least proves that the struggle for 'freedom' is better than freedom itself. What is 'freedom' anyway? Just because so much blood has been shed for the concept, it has something uncannily *un*free about it for me, something directly medieval. . . . But I really have no business talking about this at all." In the same vein, he regards *Zwischen den Rassen* as the "fairest, the most seasoned, gentlest, and *freest*" of Heinrich's works, because it displayed "no single tendency [ . . . ] no narrowness, no glorification and mockery, no privileged something or other and no disdain, no partisanship in intellectual, moral, aesthetic matters—but instead universality, knowledge, and art." And this about precisely the novel in which Heinrich sought to demonstrate the "enormous goodness of democracy," its power "to awaken dignity, mature humanity, spread freedom."

His thoughts finally were beside the point, when, at the same time as *Royal Highness*, *The Little Town* appeared—that hymn of praise to democracy, in which the people become the main character and the piazza the stage: the performance is public life, the struggle of progress against the backwardness. The song "People, People We All Are," in the simultaneous reproach of Klaus Heinrich's teacher, Dr. Überbein, is a "lazy song," an "ordinary song." He loves the "exceptional case," the "majesty of the singular," and superior in his eyes to all humanity and congeniality is the pathos of distance, the challenge of greatness, of a mission. On the one hand, Thomas Mann complains that reviewers had unduly emphasized the novel's elements of political and social criticism, neglecting the intellectual and literary, the confessional aspect. On the other, he speaks of the "reconciliation of the aristocratic melancholy consciousness with *new* challenges, which one already at that time could have formulated as 'democracy.'" Bahr had seen in the novel a virtual "beacon of democracy"—"my brother," writes Thomas Mann to Kurt Martens on January 11, 1910, "a passionate democrat of the newest stamp (his latest novel is an extremely interesting topical work), was *delighted* with Bahr's interpretation of *Royal Highness*." In his *Reflections*, he openly admits, "that a profound reluctance had accompanied that turn toward the democratic, toward community and humanity"; he would not want "to deny that the book, notwithstanding its democratic didacticism" represented "a genuine orgy of individualism." His own love belonged now once again to the "aristocratic monsters."

Meanwhile, Heinrich had already begun to write *The Patrioteer: The History of the Public Soul under Wilhelm II*, as its subtitle explained. Heinrich had been documenting it since as early as 1906. It was the attempt "to put a quite contemporary time, comprehensively at least as regards the moral and political, into a single book"; and in retrospect Heinrich was justified in saying that, in terms of substance, stylistically, and particularly in his "observation of contemporaries," he anticipated several developments. The challenge of contemporary interest also occupied Thomas Mann; but he was still far from able to find a transition "away from metaphysics and the individual into the social." While the allusion to Heinrich is clear in a 1909 note for *Geist und Kunst*, that the practice of literature "along with political engagement can lead to an almost trivial, almost childish radicalism," he nevertheless confesses to his brother, in the letter of November 8, 1913, "my inability to find a proper intellectual and political orientation, as you have been able to do." His lot was "a growing sympathy with death, which is deeply inborn: my entire interest has always been captured by decay, and that is probably what prevents me from developing an interest in progress. But what blather is all this. It is awful to be weighed down by the misery of the time, of the fatherland, without anyone having the strength to lend it form. [ . . . ] Or is it lent form in *The Patrioteer?* I look forward to your work more than to my own. You are in better shape psychologically, and that remains the critical factor. My time is up, I think, and I probably should never have been allowed to become a writer. *Buddenbrooks* was a novel of the bourgeoisie and means nothing to the twentieth century. 'Tonio Kröger' was merely *larmoyante*, *Royal Highness* vain, *Death in Venice* only half-cultivated and false." (*The Magic Mountain*, which he had been writing since September 1913, was not enough to save him from such moments of despair.)

"Those who are destined to dry up early step out deliberately when they have scarcely entered their twenties, a match for the world," he was able to read two years later in his brother's essay "Zola." There was no shortage, meanwhile, of interest in the contemporary: in the first years of the war, he wrote his three essays on immediate events: "Gedanken im Kriege," "Frederick the Great and the Grand Coalition," and the letter "An die Redaktion des *Svenska Dagbladet*, Stockholm." He took up *The Magic Mountain* again, which was not, indeed, meant only to be a "novel about time," but a timely one in a political sense. But the material he had still to digest was not yet "ripe for play and composition." Thus it was that he forced himself—it was the end of October 1915—to undertake a general review of his intellectual foundations, "that laborious work of conscience, *Reflections of a Nonpolitical Man*," through which he hoped to relieve the novel of "the worst part of its brooding encumbrance."

The title alone shows that this, too, is an attempt to save the apolitical romanticism that Thomas Mann had taken over from Nietzsche. If the book tended toward one-sidedness, was frequently more polemic than self-examination and accounting, that is to be understood in the first instance as a reaction to the propaganda of the Entente, which was supported by German writers with Western inclinations: "the pacifism of the partisan writers, expressionists, and activists of the time got on my nerves just as did the Entente powers' Jacobin-Puritanical propaganda of virtue, and against it, I defended the tradition of a Protestant-romantic, non- and antipolitical Germany, which I felt to be the foundation of my life," he would write on February 8, 1947, to Hermann Hesse. What he wanted to defend was and remained intellectual freedom, an apolitical-aestheticist nonpartisanship; but, under pressure from without and considering the whole, he believed it possible to preserve it only through one-sidedness and partisanship. "I was always too much of an ironist to be truly self-conscious," according to a letter of October 1, 1915, to Paul Amann. In a later letter to Amann, he alludes to Lessing: "Whoever believes himself to possess the truth cannot be a lover of the truth. [ . . . ] I am so far from defining myself intellectually through my *écrits*, that it is much more accurate to see the literary treatment of my thoughts as the only secure means of getting rid of them, to move beyond them to other, new, better, and, quite possibly, utterly opposed thoughts—*sans remords!*"

Alongside the thought of progress, that of balance: "my position is in every way between the poles, in the middle—it is precisely in this, it sometimes seems to me, that I am German, that I am completely a man of the middle, a middling man." This in a letter of June 8, 1916, to Ernst Bertram. Decades later he would write: "I am a man of balance. I lean instinctively to the left when the boat threatens to tip to the right—and vice versa." Thus did he hold with Treitschke and Troeltsch and adopt the role of reactionary; and his writings occasionally give the impression that he wholeheartedly represented the crude patriotism of a chauvinist. That, on a deeper level, he had not given up his Erasmian versatility is evident from a letter of November 4, 1915, to Oskar A. H. Schmitz, who had just published his book *Das wirkliche Deutschland*: "Liberalism," Thomas Mann writes there, sounding like Settembrini, "liberalism as a matter of the heart describes my case completely."

A personal spur to obstinacy and one-sidedness, then, was his brother's Zola essay, a carefully camouflaged confessional piece, in which Heinrich represents the Wilhelminian Reich in the mask of Louis Bonaparte's France, and himself in the mask of Zola. The essay was, in many respects, a direct response to "Gedanken im Kriege." Heinrich did not content himself with a discussion of political technicalities but this time mounted an attack with the kind of irritability and animosity, honed on Nietzschean psychology, that was not at all unknown to his brother.

The essay appeared at the end of 1915 in *Die weiße Blätter*. Since Thomas Mann did not receive a copy by way of Heinrich, on December 31, 1915, he turned to Maximilian Brantl; he also wrote impatiently to Bertram on January 5, 1916. A little later he finally had Brantl's copy in hand, and when he returned it on June 18, 1916, he offered "a thousand apologies for the pencil marks. I began to erase them but feared only making matters worse. Besides, this article practically requires pencil marks; it seems that the choicest double entendres are not noticed by the majority of readers." (The copy with the marks and marginal notations has been preserved in Brantl's estate; the erasure marks, next to the second sentence, which Thomas Mann called an "inhuman excess" in a letter of December 31, 1917, are clearly visible.)

Thomas Mann felt deeply wounded by the essay. On January 15, 1916, he writes to Bertram: "I have read it and am myself surprised that it is directed almost more against me than against Germany." From that point on the positions taken in the *Reflections* are primarily aimed at his brother. "What I find outrageous," he notes in the tenth *Notizbuch*, "what disgusts me, is the secure virtue, the doctrinaire, self-righteous and tyrannical hard-headedness of the civilization literati, who [ . . . ] pronounce that every talent that does not swear an oath to democracy will necessarily atrophy. Then I would rather wither in freedom and melancholy than blossom and achieve happiness through a narrow-minded politics." And again: "Surrender to a doctrine might be a good sign at twenty. At forty-five it is decline, refuge." Once again, the first and last concern is the concept of freedom. "Freedom," he notes, "is an intellectual principle to the point of nihilism, and therefore cannot endure—longer than 100 years—as a *political* principle. All the less can it lay claim to absolute, eternal political validity at a time when the intellect itself is entering a period in which the need is for new forms of *connection*, not separation."

Heinrich had called in his essay for the opposite relation between politics and literature. "In his beginnings," he writes of Zola—again, as veiled autobiography—"he disdained the craft of politics, just as every literary man does. Now he saw clearly what politics in reality was: 'the field of passion on which peoples contend for their lives, and where the seeds of history are sown for future harvests of truth and justice.' Literature and politics had the same object, the same goal, and each must permeate the other if neither is to degenerate." And here he comes to the crux of his position: "intellect is action, carried out in the name of humanity; and thus is the politician intellect, and thus must the intellectual act!" "No, the intellectual does *not* act," Thomas Mann objects in a note. "The chasm between thought and deed, literature and reality, will always remain broad and open. [ . . . ] The intellectual works through effect, not action. If he mistakes this, if his passion draws him into the real, he winds up in a false element, where he looks bad, dilettantish, and clumsy, where, as a human being, he suffers harm and is forced to wrap himself in a false and unnecessary martyrdom in order to preserve himself as a tolerable figure. Effect is your domain, artist, not action."

Both Goethe and Nietzsche bolstered him in this attitude. From Goethe he noted the statement that a good artwork can, indeed, have moral consequences, "but to demand of the artist that he pursue moral objectives is to ruin for him his craft." The politicization of Nietzsche he termed a "disfigurement," for "the latter was an artistic individualist and loved the German nature only to the extent that it was non- and suprapolitical." It is not that the point for Thomas Mann was an *au-dessus-de-la-mêlée* attitude, but that partisan writers and political activists alike seemed to him to transgress against the essence of art, against freedom.

As before, he continued to believe it possible to describe Heinrich's activist posture as a species of literary aestheticism. "The inner aspects are not simple," according to one note, "I, the bourgeois, am intellectually more of a gypsy than the intellectual politician, and the latter more aestheticist than I, the aesthete—as Heinrich's *Patrioteer* is an eminently aestheticist work, if in a negative way." And in the *Reflections*, in the chapter "The Politics of Estheticism," he suggests for Heinrich's consideration that one can also "as a 'serving' social-moralist and herald of resolute love of mankind, remain an arch-aesthete." In a previous note, he summarily characterizes politicizing and moralizing aestheticism as "committing vice with virtue."

The quotations offered demonstrate clearly enough that Thomas Mann was almost more occupied with the psychology than with the political effectiveness of the novelist-politician. He was most deeply wounded when Heinrich's invectives referred to his existence as an artist, when he was accused of parasitism, of "overweening political ambitions," and of ambition quite generally. As early as the planned story "The Abject," he had wanted to turn a critical eye on the "disreputable psychologism of the time." Back then, in his disputes with Theodor Lessing and Kerr, he had demanded "respectability as velleity," and he derived Aschenbach's artistry from this velleity. Now, in the chapter "Against Justice and Truth," he defends himself against the "psychological meanness" of his own brother: "But psychology, of course, is the cheapest, most vulgar thing. There is nothing on earth in which dirt cannot be discovered and isolated by 'psychological analysis,' no action or opinion, no emotion, no passion. Just tell me what on earth psychology has ever been good for! Has it served art? Life? The 'dignity of man'? Never. It can only serve the hatred that dearly loves 'psychological commentaries,' because through them everything can be utterly compromised. Anyone who is not a hater must find 'psychology' the most superfluous achievement of recent times. What if I were to repay civilization's literary man in kind? If I were to meet him 'psychologically'? If I urged him to turn against himself this type of knowledge he is using against me, and to ask himself if politics is not a pretext? If he had the slightest tendency toward moral hypochondria, he would have to turn pale and become silent. But he has no tendency toward moral hypochondria—alas, no." To Thomas, Nietzsche's psychological sensitivity had long since been distorted into "oversensitivity" and the hatefulness of knowledge had turned into "insolence"—here, once again, Thomas was turning tendencies against which he had to struggle in himself outward, against his brother.

It is not only the psychological "infamies" that prevent him, in 1918, in his letter of January 3, from extending his hand to his brother. He *needed* the conflict with Heinrich in order to complete the *Reflections*. And during the writing of *Reflections* he himself was inclined to regard it as a "retreat maneuver of the romantic bourgeoisie." The technical aspects of the conflict he was already able to describe very calmly and fairly in a letter of April

18, 1919, to Karl Stecker: "I frankly do not believe in my superior rank and worth; I believe only in differences of temperament, character, morality, experience, which have led to an antagonism that may be regarded as 'significant' in the Goethean sense, an opposition of principles—but based upon a deeply felt fraternal bond. In me the Nordic-Protestant element is uppermost, in my brother the Roman-Catholic element. With me, accordingly, the emphasis is more on conscience, with him more on the activist will. I am an ethical individualist, he is a socialist. However this antithesis might be further defined and formulated, it reveals itself in the realms of intellect, art, politics—in short, in every relationship."

In contrast, he had not resolved his feelings on the issue of "brother hating," and even after the reconciliation of 1922 it would be a long time before the wounds were more or less healed. "Joyful, in fact, wildly shaken with emotion though I am," he writes, on February 2, 1922, to Ernst Bertram, "I have no illusions about the fragility and difficulty of the revived relationship. A decently humane modus vivendi will be all that it can come to. Real friendship is scarcely conceivable. The monuments of our dispute still stand." In 1922 he had *Reflections* published in an abridged edition; he chose not to insist on the more extreme formulations. Heinrich, for his part, had the most conspicuous bits cut from the new edition of the Zola essay in 1931. In his memoirs of 1945, he wrote in regard to the war years that it was his brother's nature to represent, not to condemn: "His conscience traveled a difficult path before it resolved against his country. All the more lavishly was his resolve requited, here with love, there with hate. He is an uncommon witness. And he is not lukewarm." He was quoting here the princess of Orange: "Never to err, by our Lord in Heaven, that is called lukewarm."

The brothers had traded charges of opportunism. Heinrich reproved Thomas Mann's propensity for following the mood of the moment in Germany; the latter regarded his brother as a fellow-traveler of and spokesman for Western civilization's literary man. Subsequently, they each qualified their positions, with the reconciliation demonstrating perhaps—at least Thomas Mann said as much—that brothers, after "especially stirring moments of things come true, things unbelievable from the childhood perspective," are capable of "finding our way out of our individual existences, finding our way back together."

## 5

The 1920s transpired under the sign of the "modus vivendi" of which Thomas Mann writes in his letter to Bertram. That the correspondence of these years is limited to a few travel greetings is explained not only by external circumstance that the brothers lived nearby each other and could visit when they wanted—which they did; the main reason is that the relationship of blind trust they had enjoyed from their childhood had been to a large extent spoiled. And both had meanwhile become prominent public figures. Following the war, Heinrich Mann's works enjoyed surprising success; *The Patrioteer* alone sold one hundred thousand copies in four weeks. Kurt Wolff published an edition of the collected works: Heinrich's early works were being discovered now. The trilogy—*Das Kaiserreich: The Patrioteer, The Poor, Der Kopf*—made him the premier writer of the Weimar Republic; some Germans saw in him the future president of the Reich. Politics surged all around him. In 1923 he was the first German guest of the Entretiens de Pontigny; he was received by Masaryk in 1924, by Aristide Briand in 1931.

Although he had been a "public man" for a long while already, Thomas Mann was occupied with the laborious intellectual process of developing a new relationship to politics. His brother's bold interventions were not his style. "Perhaps we may after all speak of a certain evolution toward one another: I feel this may have happened when I realize that the thought which truly dominates my mind these days is of a new, personal fulfillment of the idea of humanity," he writes on February 2, 1922, to Bertram. In July of the same year, he began writing his address "Von deutscher Republik," which he delivered for the first time some months later, in the fall, to his brother and a few friends. The *Reflections*, from this perspective, appeared to him "a wartime project that contains a good many peripheral matters which today seem untenable even to me. But only crude misunderstanding can convert the book's apolitical humanism into political reaction. A certain antiliberal tendency in its profession of beliefs can be explained by my relationship to Goethe and Nietzsche, whom I view as my supreme masters [ . . . ]. I have tried to convey my idea of humanity," he continues in a letter of March 1, 1923, to Félix Bertaux, "in the essay 'Von deutscher Republik,' which has been denounced as apostasy from Germanism and as contradiction of the [*Reflections*], whereas inwardly it constitutes the linear continuation of that work." Once more, his slowness is apparent: while Heinrich has already followed his utopian political impulse and embraced socialist democracy, Thomas Mann is still working out an approach to democracy in its bourgeois humanist form. Outward signs of success, meanwhile, were not lacking for him either: in 1926, three years after his brother, he was in Paris; in 1929, he was awarded the Nobel Prize, not for *The Magic Mountain*, but for *Buddenbrooks*.

Private rivalries persisted, as evidenced by letters in which the brothers defined their positions on the newly founded literary section in the Prussian Academy of Arts. Although Thomas counseled reserve, Heinrich took over the chair in 1931, thus acquiring the unofficial title of "president of the writer's academy." And when, soon after, Thomas was proposed as the successor to Max Liebermann as the president of the academy as a whole, then it was Heinrich who advised strongly against acceptance—with success, incidentally, for Thomas Mann was fundamentally ill-inclined toward institutionalized activity.

The aftereffects of the conflict are felt most clearly in Heinrich's roman à clef *Der Kopf* (1925). The "fraternal constellation" is also what defines the friendship of Terra and Mangolf, who stand here for Heinrich and Thomas. "We are divided"—this statement comes right at the beginning of the novel—"by a single word, which he worships: success." And later Terra will say: "'The reason for your misery is as clear as day. You are, against your better judgment, a great careerist. [ . . . ] You disdain too much, and that will harm you. I would rather hate. [ . . . ] I hate the successes you first must talk your conscience into.'" The scene is glaringly lit: "They looked ardently at each other, each prophetically filled with the entire truth of his life, and mortally coiled to fight for his truth." Mangolf achieves success in that he finds his niche in established society. Terra, in contrast, is the rebel, who spends himself in a struggle against inert convention. Both Terra and Mangolf are pronounced guilty: "We have both sinned through pride." Hubris, superbia, is the lot of both. He had not yet read *Der Kopf*, writes Thomas Mann on April 23, 1925, to Julius Bab, but "I [ . . . ] suspect that the principle of division of labor will be preserved between my brother and myself."

And Thomas Mann's private reservations remained intact. When, in 1930, he reviews *Die große Sache*, all the earlier reproaches are still there: the novel, he writes, "is loaded and overloaded with stimuli to such a degree that the pleasure it offers is always on the verge of turning into pain." He misses in this "painfully truthful witches' sabbath" that "epic goodness": "Just the tempo of the novel is merciless and breathless; [ . . . ] stimulated and spellbound by a style unequaled in its noble verve, a blend of sloppiness and brilliance, of current slang and high intellectual suspense, one is ripped from one whirlwind to the next to land benumbed from the topsy-turvy of vehemently farcical adventures and crass travesties, exhausted from laughing about their grand improbability and moved to tears by intellectual goodness." Those are the reproaches he already put forth in *Freistatt* and "Anti-Heinrich." Neither, however, are those from the time of *Reflections* lacking: "This social visionary, who is at the same time a social prophet, has seen the times accommodate themselves to the thorough-going social and political orientation of his talent. [ . . . ] Crisis, social upheaval and adventure, politicization to the marrow—there is no lack of life here, and the social novelist is in his element." He raises the problem of freedom anew: "As concerns republican society, there is no mortal enemy of freedom who could pour more scorn over it and depict it in a more slapstick fashion than occurs in this novel." Reality is "lent the exaggerated intensity of a farce by means of an aestheticism that reproaches the ordinary only with not being ordinary enough, thus lifting it into a surrealistic realm." And "this is all strictly disciplined, also in its jests and in its goodness, strict and painful, lonely in its sociability, knowing and unwitting, fascinating and hard to endure, moving and insulting—like what? Like genius." That was clear enough, and Heinrich was probably not so far along at the time that he could have made the concession he later offered in *Ein Zeitalter wird besichtigt:* "Often, in striving for completion, I have improvised; I put up too little resistance to adventure, in life and writing, which are one."

What brought the brothers together in the subsequent period was their common enemy. Heinrich Mann was expatriated earlier than his brother. He soon became one of the leaders of the Popular Front in France. Thomas Mann's final break with Germany came only in 1936; but after he had made his position clear, *he* became the intellectual leader of the emigrants. In the 1930s Thomas Mann went through what he called "the politicization of Mind." "We have all," he writes on April 8, 1945, to Hermann Hesse, "under severe pressure, experienced a kind of simplification. We have experienced evil in all its hideousness and in the process—it is a shameful confession—discovered the good. If 'Mind' is the principle, the power, which desires the *good*; if it is a sensitive alertness toward the changing aspects of truth, in a word, a 'divine solicitude' which seeks to approach what is right and requisite at a given time, then it is political, whether or not this epithet sounds pretty. It seems to me that nowadays nothing alive escapes politics. Refusal is politics, too; it is a political act on the side of the evil cause." This statement echoes what he had said in his address honoring Heinrich Mann's seventieth birthday in 1941: that the "totality of the humane" includes the political, that this totality is that of which the bourgeois intellect in Germany was ignorant. "It was the fateful error of this educated German middle class that it drew a sharp distinction between mind and life, thought and reality, and looked down in contempt on the sphere of the social and the political from the heights of absolute culture." It lacked that pragmatism of which a "feeling of benevolence toward life, commitment to life" consists: the mind's sense of responsibility for life. He admits to Heinrich in this address that he had recognized and comprehended the new situation of the intellect earlier than most: "you pronounced the word 'democracy' when the rest of us scarcely knew what to make of it."

Heinrich was also the driving force in the first years of exile. He wrote hundreds of articles concerning the issues of the day—for *Die Neue Weltbühne, Dépêche de Toulouse, Pariser Tageblatt*, and *Internationale Literatur.* "My goal in all of this is yours," he writes on May 25, 1939, to his brother, "the German revolt must come before the war. [ . . . ] By the end of the year Hitler must have been defeated." Thomas Mann followed with countless essays and speeches: "Europe Beware!" "The Problem of Freedom," "This War." And then came the radio broadcasts, "Listen Germany!" The historical causes ultimately responsible for leading Germany into war he attempted to analyze in *Doctor Faustus.*

Heinrich's dramatic flight to America brought the brothers back together. There were now scarcely any political differences between them. "Politically, I really do get along quite well with your father now," Heinrich is supposed to have said to Erika. "He is just a little more radical than I." "That sounded terribly funny," Thomas Mann commented, "but what he meant was our relationship to Germany [ . . . ], toward which he was less angry than I, for the simple reason that he knew the score earlier and suffered no disillusionment." On a personal level, too, the brothers had meanwhile grown somewhat closer. In 1938, when Heinrich finished his masterpiece, *Henri Quatre*, he dedicated it to his brother with the words "To the only one close to me." In another work, he added the dedication: "To my great brother, who wrote *Doctor Faustus.*" For *Joseph* and *The Beloved Returns*, he found good, wise words.

Heinrich Mann no longer attempted to gain a foothold in America, as his brother had done. In profound solitude, more and more absorbed in the past, he completed the works of his old age. "It may be that ultimately one's personal present retreats behind memories.

With no prior intention and scarcely knowing why, I've suddenly begun reading *Budden-brooks*," he confided to Thomas Mann on April 15, 1942. The latter did all he could to min-imize the distance resulting from his disproportionate success but was unable to prevent Heinrich's solitude from turning into real isolation. Thomas Mann depicted Heinrich's life at the time in his "Bericht über meinen Bruder." "Mornings, after having his cup of strong coffee, from seven generally until noon, he writes, continues producing imper-turbably with his old boldness and self-confidence, borne by his belief in the mission of lit-erature, which he has so often acknowledged in words of proud beauty; he carries on with his current work, still dipping his steel-nib in the inkwell, covering page after page with his utterly clear and distinctly formed Latin script—certainly not without effort, for the good is difficult, but nonetheless with the trained facility of a great worker." In the last paragraph he speaks of the fruits of Heinrich's exertions: "Here, then, is where the new works origi-nate, marked not by fatigue but by the stamp of his unmistakable spirit, and which will be heard of soon enough. The scenes of epic drama, shining with that special enamel radiance of historical coloration, narrating dialogically the life of the Prussian Friedrich—a sur-prising choice of subject; the novel *Empfang bei der Welt*, a ghostly social satire set every-where and nowhere at all; and yet another novel, about what I do not know. And above all (I think, above all) the fascinating memoir *Ein Zeitalter wird besichtigt*, of which lengthy ex-cerpts have been made available in Moscow's *Internationale Literatur* and an English trans-lation is already planned. It is an autobiography conceived as a critique of the epoch expe-rienced by its author; a work of an indescribably rigorous and cheerful brilliance, of naive wisdom and moral dignity, written in a prose style of such supple intellectual simplicity that it sometimes strikes me as the language of the future."

Neither was able to believe in a return to Germany. When Heinrich was called to East Berlin to assume the presidency of the Academy of Arts, he could not conceal his mis-trust: "It could be they want to show me off and announce that another has returned." He died before he could make the trip. "My brother took his leave easily, as far as one can judge," Thomas Mann reported on March 30, 1950, "a cerebral hemorrhage in his sleep, without a sound and without stirring. In the morning it was simply not possible to awaken him. His heart worked for yet another day, through what was decidedly an irretrievable loss of consciousness. It is, at bottom, a merciful outcome. For he wanted to believe in his move to Berlin and, at the same time, was deeply certain that the effort would be too much for him. He rests in peace following an active life, the traces of which will not be lost so quickly."

In his last novel, *Der Atem* (1949), Heinrich Mann spoke one last time to his brother. The dying Maria Theresia von Traun, baroness Kowalksi, says to her sister, the successful Marie-Louise, duchesse de Vigne, " 'Marie-Lou, do not hate me because I lived or because I am dying. I know that you hated me only by denying yourself—for we were sisters. [ . . . ] We vexed each other with our inability to change, but for all that I loved you, Marie-Lou, I loved you most when we were separated by our animosity. You know that. Don't you know that?'" Dreaming, she continues: "I was very young when you could already see in me that I would never make it to the Order of the Starred Cross. It annoyed you, although you already had plans to overtake me. [ . . . ] It annoyed you that I declined the competition, instead losing in spite of my resistance. Remember this until you accept it as final, success was your nature, not mine." Already beyond reality's pale, she adds, "Marie-Louise, ma soeur bien aimée, tu m'as vaincue et bien vaincue, est-ce là une raison pour me haïr? [ . . . ] If you have to be alone, then you'd be glad to be it with me, before it ends. Now we may love each other again. It was true from the very beginning, with all that lay in wait, we loved each other as well as we hated."

From the very beginning: resonating once more, for the last time, the memory of childhood, where that which determined both of their lives began: brotherliness, brotherliness as destiny.

*Hans Wysling*

# THE LETTERS

*Garrison Infirmary*
*Wednesday, October 24, 1900*

Dear Heinrich:

This is a letter of congratulations. So it's true that success is possible! There will probably never be a second printing in store for me (who knows what hidden difficulties lie slumbering in times to come), but the thought is still refreshing. I really did get a kind of fright when I heard the news. Two thousand copies in one and a half or two weeks! Warm congratulations and my wishes for things to continue so. Every fourteen days 600 marks, that really would be a very nice annuity. I, too, am beginning to believe in the little green house.

I'm also a little famous these days; but not *so* famous. Piepsam caused a stir in all directions. I've gotten letters of praise and offers of introduction, and even hear that enthusiastic writers are sending me their books in care of my editors. The consciousness of having had an effect is truly sweet; but it only intensifies the need to bring to the effectiveness a somewhat larger style.

As you see, I'm already disabled and, indeed, so severely that I was sent here on Sunday, after having been kept sick in quarters for eight days. The problem is with my right foot, which—something I never suspected—is a flatfoot, and has been badly aggravated by the parade march exercises. Let it be blessed a thousandfold in other respects, for, according to the young doctors, after eight weeks it will probably oblige Dr. von Staat to discharge me. All I have to do, they add in cunning confidence, is keep getting pains in it. They are two kind young people assisting the chief doctor and they stop by twice a day, know my work, and are always very courteous.

I am decidedly happier here in general than in the barracks. That it's boring is true, and I'm weak from all the time spent in bed; but Grautoff, who in these bad days has taken on the role of love's messenger between myself and freedom, keeps me well supplied with reading materials. I am even studying my Savonarola as if I were at home. The food is a little crude, but solid and good.

Everything possible will probably be done to keep me in the army. I'm supposed to rest now for a few days, and then get a kind of compress bandage, which is supposed to correct the alignment of my foot. Who knows if that will work and how long it will take. If I were healthy, I could already start living at home as of today. I have to inquire, cautiously and as the opportunity arises, as to how it would be received if I proposed getting private treatment.

How are things with you? I'm writing to Riva on the chance that you are still there, though I don't know. Mama wrote me recently that you were wanting to return to Munich right away. Why not? It's cool here, but otherwise not bad. My empty room is available for you to work in.

I'm very curious to see how my affairs here will turn out. The stupid fellow who declared me fit for service simply overlooked my foot. The people here are always very slow about retroactive discharges for the reason that they fear being forced to pay compensation. I think one has to waive everything of that sort in writing. Compensation in my case would amount to only about 500 marks anyway. But it would be lovely if it were possible as early as *this* spring for me to depart on my research trip to Florence!

Holitscher sends his greetings. He dedicated his *Vergifteter Brunnen* to me, and wrote me a very grateful letter concerning "The Way to the Churchyard." I have enlisted him to send a copy of the relevant *Simplicissimus* to Fischer and, at the same time, ask for news about *Buddenbrooks*. I still know nothing about the fate of that honorable family. Good tidings would be very pleasant for me at the moment. Fischer should simply take the book as it is. Of its literary success I am certain; commercially it will probably be closer to zero and my profit the same, although Mama recently gave me strict instructions to demand 1,000 marks.

Warm greetings, and write to me here.

Warmly yours, T.


*Garrison Infirmary, Munich*
*Friday, November 2, 1900 (All Souls' Day)*

Dear Heinrich:

Many thanks for your letters, both of which finally arrived in order, despite Dr. von Staat's lengthy attempt to prevent delivery, and for the card from Ferrara with the monument, which pleased me especially. The figure is very inspiring. Might you not be able to find a larger photograph of it and send it to me rolled up—to Herzogstraße, for this time it really is likely that I shall not be here much longer.

In principle everything remains the same with my feet. The sodium silicate bandages (a substitute for plaster) have been taken off and, since the inflammation has not yet gone down completely, they will now be treated once more with wet poultices. But they are built badly and will stay that way; and for that reason I now want to be released back to duty soon, so that the first exercises will promptly cause them to fail again. In fact, they want me to purchase—at a considerable sum—springy insole supports for flat feet or even specially designed footwear; but if I'm not directly forced, I shall not do so, for my belief is that whoever has limbs requiring the correction of some kind of apparatus is not fit for active duty, and I think I shall be able to have this view prevail. When? That, of course, I can't say; but it would be very nice if I were already free by Christmas, and then I really would like to move to Florence soon after, to read what I need to on the spot. But, unfortunately, things have not progressed that far as yet, and then there is the question of what I would do with the apartment and my furniture. That will be easily taken care of, however, once I'm moving around again in the plain coat of free man.

What you wrote about our relation to the public and our kind of success made me distinctly melancholy. It is true that the effect achieved is always fundamentally the wrong one, and successes are really only capable of gratifying one who is vain, which, fortunately, I am a little. But the way you describe the success of *Cockaigne* is surely not the nature of it. Among your readers there are, of course, curious schoolboys and shop clerks; but I don't think the primary appeal for the public consists so much in the erotic as in the satire and social criticism, for which readers in Germany are just now remarkably receptive. The purely artistic efforts are lost, naturally, but the social satirical remains a much more worthy effect than the sexual.

I'm not doing well at the moment, for my worries about *Buddenbrooks* seem only to have begun now that it is finished. Fischer wrote to me after he had read the first half, and therefore did not yet know anything. After a few bits of exaggerated praise and some criticism, he arrived at the conclusion that he would be very inclined to publish it if I were willing to cut the book down by half. He was so shocked himself by this villainous demand, that he immediately called it "monstrous" and nearly begged my pardon; but, as a publisher, that was what he had to say. The sad story is simply that the novel amounts to more than a thousand pages and would have to appear in two volumes, which, at 8 to 10 marks each and in current circumstances, would be really and truly unsellable. Nevertheless, I am insisting that the book appear as it is, for, wholly aside from the question of my artistic conscience, I simply do not feel that I have the strength to set pen to it once again. Only extreme exertion allowed me to finish it and now I want finally to be freed of it so I can occupy myself with other things. In my extensive reply to Fischer, then, I refused resolutely to cut the book, but showed myself to be very flexible and resigned in regard to everything else. As things are now, I'm prepared to sign any contract that merely preserves the appearance that I am not simply giving away the work of three years. I instructed him to draw one up that offers him security, more or less; that limits, conditions, or reassigns the royalties, and stipulates, for example, that a potential loss on his part will be compensated by me out of later royalties. But he is to put the book out as it is. There is a distinction, after all, between long and long-winded! Even today a two-volume novel is not an absolute impossibility! And then I said to him that this novel was by no means the last book I would ever give him, and that ultimately everything depended upon whether he—also as a businessman—believed a little in my talent and was willing, or not, to stand up for it once and for all. Now I must return to waiting patiently, until he has read the story through to the end and writes again. The situation is difficult, difficult and in danger of proceeding badly. It would be very sad if I were left sitting with the book; I can already feel how that would make it harder for me to continue producing.—Incidentally—now you are not the only one receiving abusive postcards. I got a rhymed one about Piepsam, saying that I'm obviously a guzzler myself and therefore should "leave off" with the "scribbling." How charming! Dr. Geheeb sent me a whole package of new publications from the press in consolation, along with the request that I cause another such pleasant scandal right away.

As to the question of whether it's a fifth or a sixth, I have already written very insistently to Mother, and your letter will probably do the rest. I'm simply rather positive that we are to receive fifths. After all, it would be senseless to operate among five people with sixths, and Mama wanted and initiated that same division.

I'll let you know when I change my address again. The time to come is likely to be very unpleasant for me, since I'll be back in training and have to make up a lot of exercises and, at the beginning, still have to sleep in the barracks. And I'm so weak from all the time in bed that I don't know how I'm supposed to manage it. If only they wanted to make an end of it and throw me out!

Warm regards, Your T.

TRANSLATION, WINSTONS

*Munich, Sunday, November 25, 1900*

Dear Heinrich,

Today at last I can get around to sending a word to you, although it must be brief and provisional, for I am dead tired.

I received your last letter at Herzogstraße just when I was temporarily on my feet again. Discharged from the hospital, I soon found myself back on the sick list once more, because my foot relapsed after the first few steps. After another week on my back under the most repugnant circumstances, I drilled for a few days and then reported sick again, partly because I really was, partly to make them release me. But nothing happened and since Wednesday I have been back on duty. This has its pleasant side, since today is the first Sunday in a long while that I've spent outside the infirmary, the most unhealthful and abhorrent place I have ever seen in my life. What will happen now is uncertain. Through Mama's intervention, I have consulted her doctor, Hofrath May. He has examined my foot and does not think I will be able to do my military service. Moreover, he knows both my captain and the chief medical officer personally, and when I have to report sick again—which will probably happen sooner or later, possibly as early as next week—he is going to intercede for me. I am firmly convinced that I will not serve out the year; but nobody knows how long the matter will drag on. Perhaps I shall be free next week, perhaps by New Year's, perhaps later. You see that with the best will in the world I can't tell you anything definite about my trip to Florence. Besides, I think that after my discharge I'll need a while to rest and recuperate; the way I feel now, I wouldn't like to climb aboard an express train. I wish I could make promises and give you clearer, more pleasing answers. But things are obscure and uncertain, and I have neither time nor strength to arrange them more satisfactorily. You will have to see how you make out with Florence, Riva, and your funds; I can't promise anything. But of course I shall send word the instant any change whatsoever takes place.

They are really giving your *Cockaigne* a grand sendoff. Grautoff told me about the new squib that links it to *Sternberg*.

Schaukal is a queer bird. He has also sent his works to me and his portrait with them: probably the result of his becoming acquainted with Lobgott Piepsam. Wiesskirchen is in Moravia, and I hear that Schaukal, who married rich, occupies some government post there. God knows what he sees in me, for it is obvious that he is much closer to you. Just leafing casually through his books, I found a good deal that was appealing; but in general I am a poor reader of verse, and my Tolstoyism already predisposes me to feel that rhyme and rhythm are wicked.

Nothing new yet about *Buddenbrooks*. The *König von Florenz* is resting, of course; but I have received *The Civilization of the Renaissance* and see that the two volumes contain some magnificent material. How is your *Duchess* going?

I hope I can soon give you good news about all pending questions.

Warmly, T.

TRANSLATION, WINSTONS

*Munich*
*December 17, 1900*

Dear Heinrich:

You see, all has turned out well—at least for the moment, and such problematical creatures as I am are prone to stick to the moment.

All that was needed, of course, was the establishment of a private and social relationship to the medical powers-that-be; I owe it to Mama's doctor, whom you know. He is friendly with the Medical Corps major and worked on him, so that now I have been declared unfit for infantry service and have been given a furlough in anticipation of my deferment's being confirmed by the highest authorities. I am allowed to wear civilian dress, and until my official departure from the regiment I need only show myself in the barracks every so often, in order to have my presence in Munich certified and the furlough extended. It is, as I say, merely a declaration of unfitness for the infantry and a deferment. What will happen next year—whether I shall then continue the gay and glorious soldier's life in the supply wains or the artillery—is in God's hands. I keep thinking I should be able to avoid it one way or the other. Couldn't I withdraw at the right moment to some medicinal baths or similar refuge? We'll have to talk about it. For in these two and a half months I have really had enough of the flurry of barracks and infirmary.

Good luck can never be complete, so just at this time the painful business of paying taxes had to come along and give me some temporary anxiety about my trip to Florence. But it will have to be managed and so it will be, as Fontane would say. I still don't know when, exactly. My deferment might come through by the year's end, but it might also drag on to the middle or even end of January. So perhaps I shall not start out before the beginning of February, and I imagine that two months, February and March, will do me quite well for Florence.

So you plan to do something else later on along the lines of *Cockaigne?* I believe Grautoff will tell you all about Sternberg. I know almost nothing—only that he is very fond of children and has set in motion one of those proliferating corruption trials Berlin is so proud of. Yes, I received Ewers's article, "A New Social Novel." A bit sloppily written, but it certainly must have gained buyers for your book. In general I imagine that its success is even greater than we know. Engels recently included the novel in his Christmas book list in the *Münchener Zeitung* among the books every self-respecting person must own. At any rate, the way has been beautifully smoothed for the *Duchess.*

If only I knew what is to become of *Buddenbrooks!* I feel certain that it has some chapters not everyone can write nowadays, yet I fear that it will be left on my hands. So far there is nothing of the *König von Florenz* but the psychological points and a formless dream: the rest is yet to come. The ambiguity of the title is of course intentional. Christ and Fra Girolamo are one: weakness become genius dominating life. Supreme moment: the *bruciamento delle vanità.*—Incidentally, all sorts of materials for stories are running through my mind now, so it is very possible that a volume of tales will be ready before the drama I have set my heart on.

I've forgotten two things: First, Grautoff asks me to tell you that the brochure about Sternberg he promised you *may* be out of print or banned. Otherwise you will receive it. Second: my Burckhardt is the seventh revised edition and it cost, in elegant format, twelve marks. "Revised" scarcely implies new material, and six lire is at any rate temptingly cheap.

I am tenderly cherishing my freedom. It will, of course, be even better when the day comes that I am finally and fully free. But one must be grateful, and in this sense: Dear God, hurray, hurray, hurray.

Did you receive the 100 marks? I have yet to hear anything about it.

Your T.


*Munich*
*December 29, 1900*

Dear Heinrich:

Warm thanks for the two pictures, the interesting Napoleon copper, and the very beautiful Murillo. I'm planning to get nice frames for both of them, with one for the Madonna that will allow me to keep it on my desk. I did the same this year as last, I believe: I have finally given up sending anything to you. And what would it be? Italy is a good place to send presents from; but the Frauentürme as an ink and sand set or something similar—that doesn't work so well.

Did you spend a pleasant Christmas with the Hartungens? Here it was very peaceful and nice; the Löhrs were all there, the food was good, and my escape scot-free from the dreadful business with Dr. von Staat left me feeling serene and happy. Today I was in uniform once more, to be designated "unfit for duty at the present time" and released back to the enlistment authorities. That means, presumably, that I will have to appear one more time before the Enlistment Commission, hopefully not much more than a formality, since, first, I am already a fairly old fellow and, second, I can "produce" as many attestations as the gentlemen could possibly want.

So my trip to Florence is now, thank goodness, only a question of money, whereby it unfortunately does remain a question. The two hundred and some marks for taxes, which Mother is intractably resolved upon deducting from my allowance for the coming quarter, turn me quite simply into a church mouse, and I don't know what is supposed to happen. For you, with your income from *Cockaigne*, it makes no difference; but it destroys me. Thank God I'm working again now, even though not on *Savonarola*, which I can only creep around in cautious silence, but on a new story of a bitter-melancholic character, and I hope to gain a little income in that way. Nor does the conscience allow one to go on recuperating for very long, since working without pen and ink is something one scarcely dares to call "work," even to oneself.

The Secession is once again holding a Copieen exhibition of Florentine Renaissance sculpture (della Quercia, Pisano, della Robbia, Fiesole, etc.): extremely interesting for me, because the busts offer such a pleasant way to get to know the type of people from that time. What all there must be to learn in Florence! If only I could get there, my soul's dearest dream would come true. I would have a good deal to say in the play, but I'm far from a sufficient mastery of the necessary externalities; and such material is not to be had from a couple of books.

I almost forgot: I shall probably experience my first trial shortly. Because Mr. Tesdorpf expressed the view in a letter to Mama that I had freed myself from military service by simulating infirmity, whereupon I dispatched a strongly spiced letter (finally! what good it did me!), the most malicious of my life, which so hit its mark (oh, to have talent!) that the old ass is now threatening to sue. Can I not calmly await that eventuality?

Let me hear from you again.

Warmly, Your T.


TRANSLATION, WINSTONS

*Munich*
*January 8, 1901*

Dear Heinrich:

I find nothing by Ewers. If the *Berliner Tageblatt* has gone and lost a manuscript of his, he can at least claim compensation, can't he? But *that* isn't what matters; rather, we must now settle my Florentine project. I sat down between two candles to work it out and am still pale from the effort. Here in Munich, you know, figures are largely meaningless to me, and so I managed hitherto to deceive myself hopefully and frivolously about the facts. Compelled to look them squarely in the eye, I find I must say with Vicco: "I'm all a-tremble!" The truth in its horrid nakedness is that after cashing what remains of my fifth, ignoring my civilian tailoring debts, ignoring the rent, and even apart from the allowance for Mama (which I cannot ignore), I shall have some 240 marks. "You ask— o please don't ask me, why!" Enough; that's how it is. The sheet of paper with its irrefutable sums lies beside me. To repeat them here sickens me. No extras in sight for the near future. What I am writing now will be too long for *Simplicissimus*, and won't be finished overnight in any case, and Fischer is silent about *Buddenbrooks*. The situation remains: 240 marks for a quarter of a year, and to try and travel on that would be insanity. Not only can I not come on the 15th or the 20th; I cannot come to Florence before April. I've had to come to terms with that these past few days, and I'm only sorry that I strung you along in a pleasant hope that completely lacked a solid basis. I could eventually swallow the postponement if it weren't for the awkward fact that spring is just when you want to come back up here again. I rather enjoy being in Munich in the winter, and would miss a good deal if I left now. There are all sorts of premieres; Richard Strauss is coming, Wüllner is coming; the programs of the Literary Society are in the offing; I can write stories and for the present read Burckhardt and Villari. So I'll get through the winter all right. Are you absolutely set on coming back by the beginning of April? I don't quite see what you want to be here for, and why you can't stay down there at least until May. If I had to spend two weeks or so alone in Florence after you left, I wouldn't mind. The moment you tell me that we can be together in Florence for the month of April, *I* shall be comforted, and you after all will manage to spend your time quite well in the company of the Hartungens and the *Duchess*. Incidentally, I realize that I ought to give you a more detailed explanation of my money problems, but it would be humiliating and pointless. Please, let me have your comments only on the possibilities for April.

Certainly, *Cockaigne* was highly praised by Leo Greiner in the *Münchener Zeitung*, and so was Holitscher's latest. Don't you receive the clippings from Langen? Dr. F. Grautoff sends you his regards. He likes your book very much, he says, but the publisher of the *Leipziger Neueste Nachrichten* won't permit an article on it.—Incidentally, the advertising is magnificent. I heard recently that there were notices about the book on the Variété's programs.—Does Langen mean to underwrite your studying in Paris? You certainly could manage that if you wanted to. How well looked-after you are, and how brightly your star is beginning to shine. Fischer is silent, as I said, and if I send him an inquiry I'll probably have the changeling shot right back to me. Suppose nobody wants the novel? I think I would become a bank clerk. These fits come over me sometimes.

Warmly, Your T.

*Munich*
*January 21, 1901*

Dear Heinrich:

Just the two enclosed clippings for today, which you can send back to me—there's no hurry—when you have a chance. The raving praises from the *Neueste* are, of course, by Grautoff. But the truth is that Piepsam inspired spirited good cheer with almost every sentence and met with continuous applause. That I read well pleases me especially, and I'm proudest of the fact that Director Stollberg (from the Schauspielhaus), who was there, seemed to have enjoyed it extraordinarily; he applauded demonstratively and reserved for me a special bow. Such a theatrical director is such an important power!

I also sent the clippings to Fischer. As regards *Buddenbrooks*, I'm beginning to have hopes. Holm, who has recommended repeatedly that I go ahead and move to Langen, reassured me again emphatically, at a gathering he held recently, that Langen would have nothing in principle against a two-volume novel. He also spoke very amicably and temptingly about how he would stand by my side in my financial dealings with Langen. As a result, I have recalled Fischer's attention to the matter, and can await his decision to drop me or not with more confidence than I had before.

Nothing more for this time. About Capus and the books in the days just ahead.

Warmly, Your T.


*Munich*
*January 25, 1901*

Dear Heinrich:

If no newspapers print excerpts of Capus, then the book will appear in March or April, otherwise only in the fall.

Rieger couldn't find the Yriarte books in his catalogues. I instructed him to find out about them; that, however, will take another couple of days.

The enclosed review of *Cockaigne* was written by Martens for *Die Zeit*. It was already set, but then was forced aside by another, by whom and of what sort I don't know. Aside from the audacious assertion that literary worth rises and falls with the *seriousness* of a work, it contains probably the most reasonable of all that has been said about the book.

I want to arrange things now so that—if I have money and no other obstacles are put in my way, for example, by the military authorities—I will depart around the 15th of March. Until then I'll no doubt be busy here in every way. Then we will be together for half a month in Florence, and at the beginning of April I can expect Grautoff to be there; he also wants to make the trip if he can manage somehow to come up with the means. If we could meet then in Venice afterwards, that would be *very* nice. If it is at all possible,

I would also like to see Ferrara and Bologna; perhaps on the return trip? Hopefully, we'll be able to do everything just as we desire.

Holitscher sends his kindest regards; he will give me the book on English art shortly and then I shall send it to you. Pardon my terseness. If I don't begin letters with a fast, businesslike tone, I dawdle around with it for three hours, and then the day is gone. Whereby I only finish anything anyway after finishing is no longer any fun. One gets much irritation and little joy from oneself, as human being and artist. Enough. Otherwise I would deliver even more such Joachim-Pamps adages.

Warm regards, till we meet.

Your T.

TRANSLATION, WINSTONS

*Munich*
*February 13, 1901*

Dear Heinrich:

I hope you have received the art book. Holitscher has sent it to you with his regards and best wishes for the progress of the *Duchess.*

Unfortunately I still cannot give you any information about the French books, the reason being that for the present I cannot show my face in Rieger's book shop. Some time ago, you see, on impulse and whatever the cost, I ordered the German edition of Vasari, and only afterwards learned from Grautoff that it is a book of so and so many volumes priced at easily a hundred marks, and moreover truly dull. Whereupon I naturally did not call on Rieger again. I hope you will find out what you need some other way, and I shall have a look at Vasari in the library, if I find it necessary.

Is all well with you? I go through ups and downs. When spring comes, I shall have behind me a terribly turbulent winter. Really dreadful depressions with quite serious plans for self-elimination have alternated with an indescribable, pure, and unexpected inner joy, with experiences that cannot be told and the mere hint of which would naturally sound like boasting. But these highly unliterary, very simple and vital experiences have proved one thing to me: that there's something sincere, warm, and good in me after all, and not just "irony"; that after all everything in me is not blasted, overrefined, and corroded by the accursed scribbling. Ah, literature is death! I shall never understand how anyone can be dominated by it *without* bitterly hating it. Its ultimate and best lesson is this: to see death as a way of achieving its antithesis, *life.* I dread the day, and it is not far off, when I shall again be shut up alone with my work, and I fear that the egotistic inner desiccation and overrefinement will then make rapid progress.—But enough! Amid all these alternations of heat and frost, exaltation and suicidal self-disgust, a letter from S. Fischer blew in telling me that come spring he wanted, first, to bring out a second small volume of my stories and then, in October, *Buddenbrooks*, uncut, probably in three volumes. I shall have my picture taken, right hand tucked into the vest of my dinner jacket, the left resting on the three volumes. Then I might really go down happy to my grave.—But no, it is good that the book is going to see the light after all. So much of what is characteristically my own is there that it really will define my profile for the first time—for our esteemed colleagues in particular. Incidentally, I have heard nothing about Fischer's terms, which will probably consist of cautious codicils in respect to remuneration.—As for the volume of stories, it will be a thin one meant to yield no more than a quick refreshening of my name and some pocket money. The contents will be: (1) "The Way to the Churchyard" (as the title piece), (2) "Little Lizzy," (3) "The Wardrobe," (4) "Avenged," (5) a burlesque that I am working on at the moment and that will probably be called "Tristan." (Isn't that something! A burlesque named *Tristan?*) And possibly also (6) A long-planned novella with the ugly but thrilling title "Literature." (*Illae lacrimae!*)

As of this moment it seems I shall leave for Florence on the 15th of March. It depends on whether I can finish up the things I must get done before that date, for I am quite sure I can raise the money, especially since I have Fischer's explicit assurance that he is "altogether not of a mind to drop" me. Of course I will let you know in good time. Let me hear how you are doing, for a change.

Warmly, Your T.

[Munich
*February 28, 1901]*

Dear Heinrich:

It is certainly looking more and more like nothing will come of the 15th either, but that I shall leave only after the first of April, if Grautoff is also traveling to Fl[orence], although I know quite well that this is being handled quite unwisely and that your influence would be the only proper one for me in the moment. *I cannot imagine that you are taking offense at my unreliability?* The promised confessions I shall leave or put off after all, first, because I'm unsettled and, second, because you are not likely to be in the mood to hear them right now. Sincere congratulations on the translation of *Cockaigne* into French! What fun that must be for you! In a word, you are flourishing, while inside I am really falling to pieces. At bottom I desire nothing more than a good case of typhoid fever and a satisfactory exit—although it is rather tactless to make you nervous with such statements.—So: it is not completely out of the question, but you cannot count on me managing to leave before the beginning of April.

Your T.

*Munich*
*March 7, 1901*

Dear Heinrich:

I would naturally have answered at once, but for about a week all the incoming letters got wedged in my mailbox so that when I peered through the grating, I saw nothing. Today when I opened it by chance, a heap of letters tumbled out at me, some of them important, including yours.

No, you can leave for Italy without the slightest worry that for the present I shall commit any "follies." There is a good passage in *Buddenbrooks* when the news comes that the ruined aristocratic landowner has shot himself, and Thomas Buddenbrook, with a mixture of thoughtfulness, mockery, envy, and contempt mutters under his breath: "That is the nobility for you!" This is highly characteristic, not only of Thomas Buddenbrook, and should serve to reassure you for the present. At the moment, too, I don't want to hear anything about the typhoid. It is all metaphysics, music, and adolescent sexuality— adolescence hangs on with me. Grautoff, too, was deeply concerned; but it is hardly acute and is taking root so slowly; at the moment there is so little practical reason to go through with it, that you may rest easy. Of course I cannot vouch for what may happen some day; and whether, for example, with that obsession for the "Wunderreich der Nacht" in my heart I could go through the next bout of military service, is a question that disturbs me myself. But meanwhile a good deal of water will be flowing to the sea, and we will be here together again.—First I'll spare myself any more detailed confessions because writing and analysis only deepen and exaggerate these things. And they are things that should not be exaggerated. What is involved is not a love affair, at least not in the ordinary sense, but a friendship, a friendship—how amazing!—understood, reciprocated, and rewarded—which (I candidly admit) at certain times, especially in hours of depression and loneliness, takes on a character of somewhat excessive suffering. According to Grautoff, I am simply going through an adolescent infatuation; but that is putting it in his own terms. My nervous constitution and philosophical inclination has incredibly complicated the affair; it has a hundred aspects from the plainest to the spiritually wildest. But on the whole, the dominant feeling is one of profoundly joyful astonishment over a responsiveness no longer to be expected in this life. Let that be enough. Perhaps one of these days I'll say somewhat more when we are talking.

I have just received your postcard too. Genoa is a good idea. If I should reach Florence before you go south, you will come there for a while, won't you?

I'll write about the book of fairy tales.

Warm regards!

Your T.

*Munich*
*March 25, 1901*

Dear Heinrich:

Happy birthday! Hopefully, you will spend it in good cheer and with the tickle of spring in your back. We are still far from spring. Not that it hasn't already been nearly summerly, but real winter has returned in the last few days, with frost and a foot of snow. I really don't have anything at all against it, for even in the cycle of seasons and the accompanying changes I always recognize that lack of fidelity and constancy I fear more than all else in *Läben;* but the result has been that that old fool of mine has gone over to outright mutiny, so that I've decided to bow to general sentiment and bring it to trial. I've already met with a dentist known for his dash, from whom I shall request a strong anesthesia so that everything at all doubtful can be "dug out." The execution is to take place in the next few days. Hopefully my procrastination has not overly complicated the case and hopefully the anesthetic will take effect more or less without a hitch. It is also desirable that the business not require too much time, first because of bits of writing that must be finished and then because my portrait is being done in oil at the moment and the picture must be ready before I leave. It's supposed to be a surprise for Mama, so don't let on.

Otherwise, perhaps because of the physical emergency, my mood is decidedly healthier than it was around the time of my last writing to you; aside, of course, from the unavoidable ups and downs.

| | |
|---|---|
| Dem frohen Tage folgt ein trüber, | A cheerless day succeeds a glad one, |
| *Und alles hebt zuletzt sich auf.* | *And, finally, all is canceled out.* |

(Platen)

This general canceling out of things is a thoroughly melancholy, but also radically comforting thought. The world is as nothing—

*March 27th*

I just couldn't continue; the fool hurt way too much. I'm very sorry that this will cause you to get this letter too late. And I don't want to continue philosophizing so that it can at least be mailed today.

The operation is now four hours behind me, and it went off surprisingly pleasantly. Instead of chloroform, my anesthesia was ethyl bromide, which is good for the stomach, but wears off very rapidly. The first two or three breaths were really painful, but they were quickly followed by a complete, deep unconsciousness of approximately two minutes, during which the doctor pulled out 4 or 5 roots at his leisure. I am still bothered a bit by the wounds, but am otherwise very content. The fool will now bring me neither sorrow nor joy. Too bad for it! But it didn't want things otherwise.

Yesterday I received another extremely flattering letter from Fischer and his editor, as well as the *contract*, which is not so terrible at all. The crux of the matter: *a royalty of 20% of the cover price of every copy sold*. Nearly splendid in itself. But then he owns everything I write for the next six years, *under the same conditions*, aside from dramas, for which a separate agreement would have to be made—(poetry and criticism are not of any importance in my case). If he reduces the 6 to 3 or 4 years, I'll sign. If he doesn't—finally I'll sign anyway. For when I consider the risk he is taking, out of apparently genuine enthusiasm, with the (now four-volume) *Buddenbrooks*, I feel quite at peace. Typesetting should begin next month, which will really make me sweat. But it appears that the time is now approaching when this work of three years' torment will begin to bring me satisfaction, contentment, and joy. Dr. Heimann wrote to me: "It is an outstanding work, honest, positive, rich. I admire the way the bent toward the satirical and farcical *not only does not disturb the grand epic form, but even supports it*." I'm particularly proud of this last sentence. So, grandness despite the waggery! For it was precisely grandness toward which my secret and painful ambition was constantly directed during the work. My respect for the book grew steadily with its quantitative proliferation, so that I was always demanding a higher style from myself. It is good that it commences so modestly and then, by the end, turns out to be so much more than just any novel, something quite different and perhaps not at all ordinary. Sometimes my heart races at the thought. Hopefully I won't be taxed later for excess.

Grautoff will probably have to put off his journey to Florence; but now Holitscher plans on making the trip, so that I will have company in any case. I am thinking of leaving between the 10th and the 20th of next month. Hopefully you're not planning to return here too early. It would be very nice if we could meet in Vienna.

That's all for today. So the letter can finally be sent.

Warm regards! T.

TRANSLATION, WINSTONS

*Munich*
*April 1, 1901*

Dear Heinrich:

No, I absolutely cannot come right away, although the *cinque-lire pension* is very tempting indeed. But, first, I have no money at all, secondly my new story and my portrait must be finished, and thirdly I am feeling much too good here at the moment. I go on being "negative" and ironical in my writing largely out of habit, but for the rest I laud, love, and live, and since spring has come besides, everything is simply one grand festival. If I leave, it will be over for the present and won't come again *this* way; we know how that is. I want to hold on to it to the last moment.—I am being painted, of course, by the good fellow to whom (assuming that one should not talk about fate all the time, but may also thank specific persons) I owe such an incalculable debt of gratitude. He is doing it because it is fun for both of us. When I'm in the mood sometime I'll tell you more about him, face to face. Incidentally, I shall dedicate to him either the volume of stories or a section of *Buddenbrooks*, which he has read and likes very well—whichever comes out first. I feel such boundless gratitude. My sentimental need, my need for enthusiasm, devotion, trust, a handclasp, loyalty, which has had to fast to the point of wasting away and atrophying, now is feasting—

But do you absolutely have to go to Naples? Can't you let that wait for another few weeks, or even drop it entirely for the present, especially since you don't even feel like going? It would be so fine if I could find you in Florence shortly after the middle of the month and we could spend a little while together there. Do let me know whether you can't simply remain there for the present, since you're enjoying it. I'll postpone sending the Baedeker until I hear.

As for Fischer's conditions, you must consider that after all you received quite a lot of cash right at the outset, whereas I shall see nothing at all until September 1902; only then (a year after publication) is the first statement due. If the edition sells out, I grant you, I shall be receiving two thousand, for the bookstore price will probably have to be around ten marks. But who is to say that even as many as 100 copies will be sold? Incidentally, I expected nothing better, and in fact nothing so good.

My postcard about the fairy-tale book has no doubt reached you from Levanto.

Today I again received a new book of Schaukal's. You too?

I'll get the money.

But once again: My plea is that you simply remain peacefully in Florence for an indefinite time. I'll arrive there around the 20th. After all, you do know Naples, and if you need it for a setting you can easily refresh your memory from photographs. Spare yourself the trip, and write that you are going to await my arrival in Florence.

Warm regards! Your T.


*Florence*
*May 7, 1901*
*Via Cavour I I II*

Dear Heinrich:

I spoke once again, as well as I could, with the teacher. The publisher is out of town for a few days, but will visit Papyria after his return. It is certainly advisable that you meet with him yourself and praise the book. P. is naturally not altogether certain what the issue is, although her goodwill is clearly manifest.

I am much in favor of this and would ask you outright to abbreviate your stay down south and come either here or to Venice (preferably here) as soon as possible. I am once again at an end. My last experiences in Munich and the change of scene are beginning to lose their effectiveness, and I am again suffering through very difficult hours. And I have only about 175 lire left—the days in Venice will be quite costly and, when I calculate in my return trip, it makes me weak.

I wrote to the Casa Kirsch, which is listed in Baedeker as a pension: two good rooms, each with a bed, for the 15th, *and perhaps sooner.*—And I wrote to Grautoff.

Miss Edith and Miss Mary send their greetings. The former would like to read your *Cockaigne.* When you saw her, she was waiting, inexplicably, for you to offer it to her. Miss Mary, whose birthday was day before yesterday and whom I presented with a little basket of candied fruit, has been a source of much pleasure. But now I think I'm becoming too melancholy for her. *She is so very clever,*[5] and I'm always dumb enough always to love the ones who are clever, even though I can't keep up over the long run. The weather has been rainy since yesterday.

So please write—immediately—just to say when I can expect you.

Your T.

Many thanks for the autograph, which gave me a terrific kick. It must be a photograph or something of the kind? Genuine, it would be invaluable!

*Munich*
*September 15, 1903*
*Konradstraße II pt.*

Dear Heinrich,

Here are the two tickets. The six-mark places were already sold out today, except for the last row, and of those at eight these are pretty much the last ones. For myself I bought a ticket only for *Hedda Gabler*, because there are two other premieres in the Schauspielhaus I want to attend.

One more thing. Richard Schaukal has published an article about me in the *Rheinisch-Westfälische Zeitung*, in which (emphasizing, incidentally, your "gift") he was so predictable as to have woven into it an attack on *Die Göttinnen*. Since I cannot know whether you won't someday see the paper, I want to assure you emphatically that I have never given the author reason to imagine that I could find any satisfaction in or in any way approve of a disparagement of your accomplishment, in particular in the context of something having to do with me. Since, beforehand, he called himself my "friend," as part of a practically amorous description of my person (he even speaks of my "fine, nervous nose"!), I share responsibility toward the public, at least to the extent that it reads

5. Italicized phrase in English in original.

the *Rh. W. Z.*, for this nonsense and am very tempted to communicate my indignation to the editors for publication. In any case, Schaukal can expect no especially cordial thanks from me for this friendly service.

With warm regards, T.


*Munich*
*[December 5, 1903]*
*Konradstraße II pt.*

Dear Heinrich!

Now once again I'm "a King as well," as the idler used to say, and, after having recently savored another round of the distress and affliction of work on a deadline, I can write you the letter I promised. It's not something I should subject myself to again; it's too horrible. It was, as I think I already told you, a contribution to the first issue of the *Neue Rundschau*, formerly the *Neue Deutsche R.*, which will appear under the new name in a more "artistic" format come January. Fischer and Bie extorted the promise from me in Berlin to deliver a manuscript by the 20th, and, despite contrary experiences, that seemed an easy thing to do. What I needed first of all in Munich was some rest. Then I got busy, pleasantly and enthusiastically, acquiring some furniture, and, finally, at the last moment applied myself—just like a Monday morning essay—to a study I had in my head. Oppressed by low barometric pressure, rushed, and utterly dispirited, I scratched it down on paper in eight days. When it was "finished," I clearly felt that it had gotten completely away from me, and I sent if off with a bad conscience in the definite expectation that it would be sent back, with derision and shame, as unsuitable. Now I've already dealt with the proofs and had a grateful letter from Fischer: he read the piece with great pleasure and indicated that it proved me a master of the sketch, and, by the way, that another printing of *Buddenbrooks* (copies 11 to 13 thousand) was underway as he wrote. It's always that way. I work with loathing and without the slightest satisfaction, send the garbage off in profound despair, and then come the letters, the money, the praise, the handshakes, the "adoration." Everyone finds pleasure in it, except for me. And that is unfair indeed. But perhaps it's in the nature of things.

You asked me about my trip to Königsberg. It went well enough. At the reading, in a very large and very full hall, I was more nervous than usual and, as a result, hoarse. But the applause was friendly and the newspaper reports very respectful. To see Ida again left a marvelous impression. She waited for me in the hall after the reading, with the people in whose home—as she stressed with that My goodness, child! look on her face—she has now worked for fifteen years. She is not much grayer than she was, but now without her teeth, and she spoke with her old howling voice and behaved toward me roughly as she behaved earlier toward Grandmama: with little eyes and a curtsy.—I visited Ewers straightaway in the office, and was at his house for dinner the day after. His wife, a little shabby, dull, and ordinary, didn't appeal to me greatly. They are handsomely, nearly opulently installed and seem to feel quite happy in K., while they couldn't complain enough about Leipzig and, especially, F. Grautoff. I found Ewers himself largely unchanged, just filled out and with a longer mustache. Unbelievable, how he has preserved the Lübeck in him. He said that he was planning a "fantastic novel"—with nearly a parody of a local accent. For the rest, he was nice, friendly and warm, on account of old memories. He regretted that I no longer write verse—as I used to in the old days when I was always delivering my poems on the "Sea" and the walnut tree to him for review—and he emphasized again that he wouldn't have recognized me, because I'd changed so much in the meantime. Well, well!—The main experience and highlight of the trip was my meeting with Gerhart Hauptmann, at a dinner at Fischer's in Grunewald. I was very far from prepared for the magic of his personality, the spell it actually casts. A luminous mind, thoroughly cultivated, deep and yet clear; a being dignified and gentle, soft and yet strong. He is quite specifically my ideal. That's what one could have become, had one not been "damaged," as Ibsen's little Üz says . . . His altruism, his wonderful humaneness, of which his latest play, *Rose Bernd*, is full yet again, actually does surround his person like a sacred aura.—There was also a good deal of Cockaigne-comedy. Brahm from the Deutsches Theater said literally: "Nu, Herr Mann, wie is' mit'n Schtiek? Schicken Se's mir! Wir brauchen junge Talente!"[6] The good soul! He'll take ample care not to put my lines on his stage! Thinks probably he can now count on achieving the effect on the more general population—and is mistaken. The success of *Buddenbrooks* is based ultimately on a misunderstanding. And, with that, to the main point, to your novel!

My impressions? They are not exactly very pleasant—which impressions, indeed, don't absolutely need to be. It didn't exactly make agreeable reading—which, indeed, however, is absolutely not necessary either. I struggled back and forth with the book, threw it aside, took it up again, groaned, complained, and then got tears in my eyes again . . . For days, in the lowest barometric pressure in a hundred years (according to the meteorologist), I went about in the agony your book caused in me. Now I know approximately what I have to say to you.

That I am not in agreement with your literary development—that must finally be said; preferably now, when as far as I know you have nothing of your own planned— and, anyway, it could hardly confuse you. What is admirable in this new novel certainly does not escape me. The depiction of Nymphenburg, the automobile trip, the novella by Kupferstecher, Claude's meditation on the Piazzale with its expression of absolute hopelessness: "Suffering itself is finally no longer interesting"—those are things that no one, quite simply no one at all in Germany can match you in. I put this at the outset,

6. Untranslatable dialect; literally: "Well now, Mr. Mann, how about a play? Send me one! We need new talent!"

thickly underlined. And yet: I'm convinced that such books as *Die Jagd nach Liebe* lie not only outside of German development—that would be no reproach—but also outside your own.

When I think back ten, eight, five years! How do you appear to me? How were you? A refined connoisseur—next to whom I seemed to myself eternally plebeian, barbaric, and buffoonish—full of discretion and culture, full of reserve toward "modernity" and historically as talented as could be, free of all need for applause, a delicate and proud personality for whose literary endeavors there would quite probably be a select and receptive public . . . And now, instead of that? Instead, now these strained jokes, these vulgar, shrill, hectic, unnatural calumnies of the truth and humanity, these disgraceful grimaces and somersaults, the desperate attacks on the reader's interest! The way the squabble operates, the chained-up waiter, Panier's engagement, the card duel, Frau von Traxi, all of these senseless and disreputable episodes in deceit—I read them and don't know you anymore. The psychological content of the work, the desire of weak artificiality for life, this desire that would gladly masquerade as amorous desire within the lonely and sensuous artist—how is it supposed to move, to work convincingly when not even an attempt is being made to come close to life, to observe and capture even the air or the inner impulse of this simple madcap? Everything is distorted, screaming, exaggerated, "bellows," "buffo," romantic in the bad sense; the false gestures of the representative of Christendom from the *Göttinnen* are there again and the overdone sensationalist psychology that goes along with them—even Ute, who could have become an immortal character, is spoiled through a lack of all measure, and finally one asks oneself how you could ever have ridiculed Possart's excessive devices in a book the title of which should have been: "Die Jagd nach *Wirkung*."[7]

Dear Heinrich, I'm speaking candidly and saying things that I've had on my heart for the longest time. It is, in my view, a greediness for effect that is corrupting you, if, indeed, after this book corruption must really be spoken of. You've talked too much to me recently of effect and success. You compared the ending of *Salome* to that of *Cavalleria* in terms of "effectiveness"; when I told you about *Royal Highness* you emphasized above all that the title would distinguish itself well in the shop window, while I, without wanting to be holy about it, had not until then even thought of the "shop window"; you formulated the difference between the two of us by saying that I was closer to popular German sentiment than you, that you "would have to make it with sensation" . . . What is that—to make it? Who is it that "makes" anything anyway? The extra printings of *Buddenbrooks* are a misunderstanding, which I'll say again, and aside from the few hundred people with a serious personal interest no one will trouble over all that I cherish and have planned. And I'm well aware that it isn't the success of *Buddenbrooks* that has done

7. Thomas Mann suggests that the more appropriate title for *Die Jagd nach Liebe*, or *Chasing after Love*, would be *Chasing after* Effect.

this to you—it would be stupid and ridiculous to assume that—but, earlier, the idea of the book as achievement, as quantity. Your anxiety, the result of your neurotic concern that you'll achieve less than I—I, whose conditions aren't exactly the easiest ones for work either—has turned into ambition. With hygienic discipline, of which I've never quite known whether I should admire or disdain it, you've trained yourself to work far beyond my capacities; your quantitative accomplishment over the last year sets a record, which to my knowledge no serious writer has ever equaled—but (forgive my being trivial!) it's not the amount that matters, and your "Wunderbare" amounts to much, much more than the *Jagd nach Liebe*; you've made yourself so healthy that you can work six hours a day, but what you produce is sick, not because it is itself pathological, but because it is the result of a distorted and unnatural development and of an addiction to effect that becomes you unspeakably badly.

If it became you better, if you actually felt comfortable and at home in this grotesque world of crude effects, you would seem more independent, prouder, more resolved. That you didn't hesitate to take Grautoff's impossible sham—Possart supposedly reacting to news of a death by leaving the room and returning with his face made up white—straight into your book has the effect of weakness and poverty. "Horseteeth," both as word and observation, doesn't come from you. The ludicrous use of the word "lightly" ("lightly offensive," "lightly silly") is not from you. Trifles, certainly, scarcely mentionable out loud. But it goes farther. In Riva, in the rowboat, we already had the beginnings of a conflict about this unpleasant subject. In the course of all kinds of philosophical and psychological disputes in which we each represented our opposed position, I had told you of my plan to write a novel called "The Loved Ones." In *Göttinnen* I found the psychological content of this conversation used in superficial and farcical ways; above all, however, I found the juxtaposition "the loved—the unloved" used repeatedly word for word as something established and in general use. In response to my objection that that would make my title impossible you omitted, so it seems, "the loved"; but with a kind of delayed naïveté, also not particularly becoming, you left in "the unloved"! In "Tonio Kröger," in opposition to the artist, as I understand him, there is "the commonplace." The story speaks of the "charmingly commonplace," of the "bliss of the commonplace." And in *Die Jagd nach Liebe* I find the expression "the commonplace" used repeatedly to designate the opposite of the artist. No more than petty stinginess jealously watching over its miserable treasures. All very good! But then you were capable of thinking of the rich man who takes from the poor man his only sheep; and I for my part would be too proud and too scrupulous to treat someone else's words, in which a whole view of things, a world of pathos and experience is expressed, blithely as public property. You've already assured me that you, of course, just as fully as I, carry within yourself the stuff of *Royal Highness*. And what should I do when one day in a new work you speak quite incidentally now and again of the "royal highness" of the artist? It would be pedantic to want to pursue the matter further at that point.

All of this goes over into the style. It is indiscriminate, flashy, international. I'm disregarding the undue facility of usages like the word "partially" as an adjective. But I find no trace of discipline, of resolution, of a bearing toward language. Alongside Gallicisms are Austrian-Bavarian colloquialisms. Alongside a precious "Ach! Ach!" comes something entirely lacking in style: "As if you had any idea!" Whatever produces an effect is called upon with no consideration for its appropriateness. Prenominal genitives, which are of Scandinavian origin, don't belong here. The simple epic "but" at the beginning of sentences, with no indication of logical opposition—which is likewise of Scandinavian origin—it doesn't belong here. And, finally, the effect of medically precise descriptions of illnesses, which are right for a realistic novel, is styleless in this book. Had you wanted to be consistent, you would have had to describe impossible, unknown illnesses, which, however, agitate the reader through sheer hideousness and "make it on sensation."

Ambition, naïveté, unscrupulousness—those are indeed qualities of the "artist," of the "pure artist" whose role you have taken on, and I wouldn't reproach you with them if I didn't know that they are so utterly foreign to your original being and nature. I preserve in my memory something you once said when we were talking about Fielitz and his relationship to his wife. "If *that* is being an artist," you said, "then I, in any case, am not one." No, you weren't one; rather something better, higher, purer. Now it's different. "I was neurotic," you said to yourself; "I want to be healthy, artistic, effective. Intellectuality is also a neurosis; I want to be wholly sensuous, wholly physical, I want to make an impression." And in six months you write *Die Jagd nach Liebe*, without thinking (or did you think it?) that with your hands you were creating a new genre of light, pastime reading, namely a light literature with all the achievements of modernity.

And you probably also want to be done with historical fiction. The overcoming of the historical probably belongs to your idea of the artist as well. I've heard from you that you were tired of the historical, that all that interests you now is what's completely modern, contemporary, and—oh, my God!—vital; while I am convinced that the historical novel is your own special preserve. *Göttinnen*—which, alongside jarring lapses of taste, contained examples of quite wonderful beauty—I defended not only against Schaukal. I referred to the grand contextual riches and the sensuous beauty of the work, above all, however, to its historical profundity, which, like an artistic tapestry, served as a foil to the farcical events. Since, however, there is not much beauty in *Die Jagd nach Liebe* and nothing historical—what's left?

What's left is the erotic, that is to say: the sexual. For sexualism is not eroticism. Eroticism is poetry, is that which speaks from the depths, is the unsuspected, all of which lends it its thrill, its sweet charm, and its secrecy. Sexualism is the naked, the unspiritualized, that which is simply called by its name. It is named by name a little too often in *Die Jagd nach Liebe*. Wedekind, probably the boldest sexualist in modern German literature, comes off sympathetically in comparison to this book. Why? Because he is more demonic. One feels the uncanny, the depths, the permanently questionable nature of sexuality, feels the suffering caused by the sexual; in a word, one feels the passion. But the utter moral nonchalance with which your people, once they've just touched hands, fall down with each other and make *l'amore* cannot speak to the better sort of people. This flabby lust without end, this perpetual smell of the flesh are tiresome, disgusting. It's too much, too much "thigh," "breasts," "loins," "calf," "flesh," and one fails to understand how you would want to start it all up again every morning when there was already a normal, a lesbian, and a pederastic sex act the day before. Even in the moving scene between Ute and Claude on the latter's deathbed, this scene that made me feel weak, that made me want to forget—even here Ute's inevitable thigh is in action, and it wasn't possible to conclude without Ute walking around the room naked! I'm not playing Frà Girolamo in writing this. A moralist is the opposite of one who preaches morality: I'm completely Nietzschean on this point. But only apes and other southlanders can ignore morality altogether, and where it has not yet become a problem, has not yet become passion, there is nothing but boring vulgarity. I'm understanding more and more the identity of morality and *intellect*, and revere a saying of Börne's that seems to me to contain an everlasting truth: "People," he says, "would be richer in intellect if they were more moral."

I've reached the end. Some of it came out harder than I intended and I would probably copy the letter in milder terms if it were not that I'm permanently afflicted by a kind of writer's cramp. May you then read the epistle as it is. I think you will not misunderstand me. I am, God knows, no born pamphleteer and must have *suffered* to have written a few pages like the ones you have here. Nor should you reproach me with having a naive trust in my own judgment, like the good Schaukal. I'm not at all without doubt. Perhaps if you save this letter and it comes to light one day, perhaps a later generation will find it amusing how a younger brother couldn't appreciate your greatness—perhaps. Meanwhile I've done my feeble best to find a historical parallel by means of which I was able in a certain way to rank *Die Jagd nach Liebe*. My taste for studying the Italian Renaissance has acquainted me indirectly with epics of the Quattro- and Cinquecento, with Boiardo, Luigi Pulci, the author of *Morgante*, and their like; it occurs to me that it wouldn't even be unpleasant for you if one added you to their ranks. They were farcical minds, quite great at inventing obscenities, pranks, and jokes. They never "softened the pains of the burdened," never "eased the tears of the fearful." They weren't writers, weren't seers and prophets. They were artists, and what they wrote was light reading of an artistic sort, a wild and colorful flight of adventurous, impossible, and obscene diversions. I shall name them whenever I defend your work against people who come believing they might belittle it.

A pleasant Christmas and a fruitful New Year!

Your T.

*December 5, 1903*

*On the back of the last page of the letter, Heinrich Mann scribbled barely legible notes for an answer with an ink pen. He crossed out the individual portions with a vertical line after having made his notes. We reproduce the draft literally line by line. The symbols mean:*

[ . . . ] *crossed out by author*

+ . . . + *inserted later by author*

{ . . . } *completed by editor*

*Upper half of sheet:*

on 1) the farcical does have a *somewhat* deeper basis. Closing scene with von Eisenmann. Claude *sees* it this way. *Disdain* of life.

II The *sexual* as a dreadfully simple thing. Matthacker. Only romantic, don't understand the demonic. Nana. Greatness. for me *greatness* is lacking: the hero is too weak, and the females are no Nanas, they also mean nothing, they do not embody the corruption of a Kaiserreich.

Exaggerated secrecy of phys. processes. "Befouling"

Morality—intellect, what's the point of emphasizing intellect to the point that one writes nothing but essays?

1) It seems the interiority is missed. And yet for me, when I think of the book, I see *only interiority:* as if no one were in it but Claude and Ute. Nothing else interested me here, all the rest is the flight of phenomena, [half unreal,] comical, raw, dirty, half unreal, wholly insufficient: [like the lonely individual] [so] like Cl.{aude} sees them, like I see them. Dissolute and unreal

+he dissipates his feelings on them+

are the others, not him, *nor his illness.* How often is his loneliness stressed and

*Continues at 2) below.*

We have absolutely the same ideals in us. You long for the health of the North, I for that of the South. Already in reference to T. Kröger I suggested to you that there's not only a blue-eyed commonplace.

The repetition of the word commonplace in the J.{agd} n.{ach} L.{iebe} was just possibly a kind of answer? [But I don't remember anymore. The fact is only that I'm a Chroniqueur.]

*Lower half of sheet:*

There are a differences of degree between us. I have so much

And I'm so much sicker.

more of gypsy artistry that I can't resist. I'm more Roman, stranger and less stable. I'm so much more in need of calm, of time to consider.

I'm afraid: if I stop, it's over with me. *Then money. I am thinking, when I talk about effect, *exclusively* about money. I [have a] claim my complete right to make fun of the [merely] vain to whom there's something in applause for its own sake. To me the indefinite noise of the people behind it ([Miss] Mrs. Browning) is all the same. I'm too well aware of the fact that fame would only be a widely disseminated mistake concerning my person; that they would clap without knowing for whom. Everything that Cl.{aude} and M.{atthacker} have to offer about this is serious to me! I know that I'm alone and would still be on a

---

2) the indifference of everything, except for Ute! It would have been styleless to treat all the rest with engagement, objectivity, and seriousness. I therefore regard the book's style, despite everything, as right. That doesn't mean, however, that the book +itself+ [as such] can't be unwarranted. Perhaps it is not at all right for a character like Claude to be a medium for an image of the world. The resulting image is too sick, vulgar, unbearable. That would mean, in other words, that I would quit writing altogether.

*Hygien{ic} discipline already *before* Buddenbrooks appeared.


*Munich*
*December 23, 1903*
*Konradstr. II pt.*

Dear Heinrich:

Warm thanks for your letter! There's a lot in it I could respond to, but the devil with it! We two do best when we're friends—certainly I do. My very worst hours are when I feel hostile toward you. Certain sarcastic remarks in my little review in *Freistatt* were in fact directed consciously at you; I must say that for the sake of the truth. But now I would like to know who it was who wrote you that about fanaticism and wild flattery. If I know him (or her) even distantly, I hold you duty-bound to tell me who it is. I have to know who is against me.

Soon I'll send two little studies, which, without shame, I prepared on commission for the money.

Warmly, T.


*Munich*
*January 8, 1904*
*Konradstr. II pt.*

Dear Heinrich:

The precipitate lines I recently sent you were sincerely well intentioned, for they represented the resolve to extend my *hand energetically, beyond all misunderstandings and confusions, to you, whom I know to be so far superior to myself in human refinement, in psychological purity and clarity.* But you must have misunderstood the slightly comical Biedermeier gesture with which I did it, *must have found them superficial and frivolous, because you couldn't have known that they were just me breaking loose from a long period of thinking*, musing, worrying, and brooding, from that unhealthy and enervating condition to which I only too easily succumb and that I so hate because it is unfruitful. But you know that I'm no good to dispute with; it's just as bad in writing as speaking. I'm not capable of isolating a train of thought, of carrying through a conversation artistically. I fall apart inside from hundreds into thousands of pieces, everything I know psychologically gets stirred up, surges up in my head, the complexity of the world overwhelms me, the knowledge that all ideas have an artistic value but no value as truth chokes me physically in my throat, I start trembling, I get a beating in my stomach (a peculiarity of mine, instead of the usual beating of the heart), my brain turns around on me, and if I don't want to go crazy on the spot I have to pull myself together and say "the devil with it!" That might be egotistical, but if you knew what kind of mental torment I've already endured for your sake and the sake of our relationship, if you knew what discipline and mortification a letter like my four-page one about your book signifies for me—whose "intellectuality" is probably just a corrective to the gloomy and sluggish musicality that was predominant earlier—then you wouldn't speak so severely to me. The first feeling that your last letter inspired in me was of a naive indignation, similar to the time you reproached me for egoistic indifference toward Mama *and Vicco, when I had already grieved and brooded myself sick over Mama, and all the while you were looking at pictures in Italy, when I myself* was much more terribly obsessed than I am now. Recently I got an unexpected card from Uncle Friedel, a picture postcard with a Baltic Sea steamer on it, and the message in somewhat distorted script: "Your book *The Buddenbrooks* has caused me much suffering. A sad bird, that fouls its own nest! Your uncle, Friedrich Mann." At first it affected me like a kind of comic stitch. Then I thought: "You fool! He doesn't understand, that is, that I have concerned myself with him better, longer, and more passionately than anyone else." A similar misunderstanding exists between us, and I am not saying that it's your fault. My best letters to you haven't been written—out of egoism, I admit it! For my organizational skills, unfortunately, bear no relation whatever to my ability to experience and perceive and given how painfully slow I am, if I wanted to write all of these good letters, my own things, which lag desperately behind my experience anyway, wouldn't progress at all—while maybe it is rather important that they do progress.

You are too severe and too dejected. What does the judgment of one artist about another ultimately mean! Yesterday Schaukal sent me a letter written to him by a young poet in Brünn, Hans Müller, the author of a book of poems that's supposed to be very good and is called, I think, *Die lockende Geige*. In the letter (it is ten pages long, *beautifully done, very casual, on Christmas Eve) is the following passage: "It is a shame to name Th. Mann and Knoop in the same sentence. Th. M. is the Christian journalist, not* as distant as you think from Watercloset's *Renate*, it's just that the Jew Wassermann is clever in a sophisticated way and therefore *dégoûtant*. Mann, in contrast, almost a bit comical in his 'coolness.'

*Buddenbrooks* is certainly a boring but, just for that reason, miserable book (think for a second about Goethe) and of the stories in *Tristan* I could write all of them—with the exception of 'Tonio Kröger'—" (Ah! there is one!—the Chr. editor) "in forty-eight hours. This feeling, however, is not one I may allow myself to have, otherwise it's all over with the 'bowing.' By the way, my story collection, *Die Rosen des heiligen Antonius,* will—I hope—prove this." A splendid youngster! And I wish that you found my things likewise boring, miserable, and journalistic: then we could be the best of friends—in the good times, at least, when one takes a rest from intellectuality and—"the Devil with it!"—returns to the world of Lübeck, the family, the humane. Only in this healthy ability to relax and, like Wagner, make Saxon jokes, is there the possibility of enduring the extraordinary existence of an artist.

"Beyond all harmless relationships"! Melancholy and nothing more! And even that "won't-let-it-count" in your personality! I do not believe that you've developed particularly happily and harmoniously (but who does these days? Me maybe?); I do believe that you are less called than you persuade yourself is the case to represent on earth that gloomy and dubious blend of Lucifer and a clown that one terms "artist," that you would give less often the impression of being pained, even tormented if this were the proper role for you, that you actually are too good, too refined, pure, modest, fastidious, and respectable for it, that you would probably show up better, more worthily, and beneficially with editions from the Insel-Verlag for exclusive aesthetic connoisseurs and lofty historical gourmands (among your melodious artistic expressions belongs "Ein Gang vors Thor" in *Die Insel*), that, finally, your own understanding and representation of your being and essence, as you conveyed it to me in your long letter, doesn't need to be just as objectively true as it is plausible and logically indisputable (you yourself, with proper skepticism, called it "my current justification of myself"):—but leaving that aside, that it all can be quite false—does it then mean a "won't let it count" of your "personality"?! Your personality! The conversation often turns to you these days at the Löhrs, where I have lunch twice a week. Then we sit there and all three of us pull very serious, almost suffering faces. Everyone offers some halfway clever little tidbit about you, for *and against, and then comes a brooding silence. Finally I say, "The case of Heinrich is namely one I can spend hours thinking about." "Me too," says Lula. "Me too," says Löhr. And, again after a pause, I say with oracular emphasis:* "That he can so occupy all three of us proves that he's more than all of us." This is reported word-for-word and shows my "haughtiness" in the most shameless light. You don't know how highly I regard you, don't know that when I grumble about you I always do it only in the unspoken assumption that next to you there's nobody else really in the running! It is an old prejudice of a Lübeck senator's son that I share, an arrogant Hanseatic instinct *with which I think I have sometimes made a joke of myself, that in comparison to us everybody else really is inferior.*

Haughty? No. I might be haughty toward all the other writers: but toward you I am certainly not. But, of course, you're being too severe again when you demand "dignity and modesty" from me. I have neither the one nor the other—I'm too pathological and too childish, too much the "artist" to have it. You are different. You would never, like Wagner, hurl a rival's score from the piano, but are the holy man of literature, who distinguishes between accomplishments and actions and would never be capable of an action like the one I committed in *Freistatt*. You characterize it, in an extremely elegant paraphrase, as vile—well! I could defend myself, could make reference to the passion of the intellect, which, if at all genuine, cannot by numbed by "flattery"; but I don't want to forsake my deed, but instead accept responsibility for it—I have worse things to forget. I want only to ask whether, in estimating the degree of my badness, the openness with which I admitted the "action," entirely without having to and contrary to your belief— whether you couldn't have *taken it a little bit into consideration and whether this openness hasn't earned me the right to know the name of the gentleman who informed on me to you and whom* I meanwhile am perhaps unknowingly having to offer my hand.

Should we close now? I think it would be well if we gave our relationship time to mature; things just are as they are, certainly nothing definitive. We are just the one and the other side of thirty, an age, that is, in which one easily regards as ethos what is merely pathos and is always inclined to believe in the inalterability of his position. Nevertheless, in my best moments, I feel myself capable of the most surprising changes of mind and *reactions. When I read you the first act of my* Fiorenza *dialogue, you praised the character Pico: now, the one who set down this Pico can't possibly be a completely witless and willful Nazarene, but must have* some sovereignty of his own. It is there, believe me! It is there in the form of my irony, which I turn more diligently against myself than against the whole rest of the world, *and which is gradually turning into a both vain and superior joy in my own dubious personality*. I'm now reading, actually for the first time, Heine's book about Börne and recently came across the following lines: "Psychologically remarkable in the investigation is the way the inborn Christianity in Börne's soul gradually rises to the surface, after having been suppressed for a long time by his sharp understanding and his gaiety. I say gaiety, *gaieté*, not joy, *joie*; the Nazarenes sometimes display a certain resilient good mood, a funny, squirrel-like cheerfulness—even charmingly capricious, even sweet, sparkling too—which, however, is quickly followed by an unyielding darkening of the spirit: they lack the majesty of pleasure-taking bliss, which is found only among the conscious gods."

You wouldn't believe what pleasure such as that affords me, although I should really find it irritating. I drew a thick line under it, wrote *Ecce ego!* in the margin, and was quite blissful.

Read my "Infant Prodigy" with this in mind as my motto; it seems to me a good example of Nazarene *gaieté*. I'm sending you both of the unassuming occasional pieces at the same time as this letter. The *N[eue] Fr[eie] Pr[esse]* has been withholding my author's copies for a long time and my copy of the *Neue Rundschau* is in Mother's hands. So I'm sending you the proofs of "A Gleam." Now I have to write an essay about Gabr. Reuter's new novel for *Der Tag;* but that's really supposed to be the end of frittering away my energies and I want to turn back to more serious things. What do you have planned?

Warm regards! Your T.


*Munich*
*February 27, 1904*
*Konradstraße II g.fl.*

Dear Heinrich:

Warm thanks for the story! I've read it twice with joyous interest, shall take it with me tomorrow to the Löhrs, and then, when I go to Polling, hand it personally to Mother. It is a brilliant little piece, strong, noble, masterly, and with that romantic conciseness of style that is so your own. Once again I thought that you really are the only one today who can still tell stories, adventures, proper "novellas," who has "something to say." And the quality that you quite justifiably ascribe to *Die Jagd nach Liebe:* namely, that anyone who has ever read anything of yours has to recognize you after the first two pages—"Fulvia" has that very markedly; it is genuine and consummate H.M. What I mainly admire is that you were able to combine the naive tone of the narrative (and the dialogue) with such linguistic distinction. The best part of the whole for me, which I'm raving about in the moment as characteristic, is the true-hearted narration of the bombardment of Vicenza. Another very good detail is that Raminga always lets her little dog lick her face; and quite wonderful the part: "until we also saw our eyes. How much turbulence must have taken place in them in this night, without our having seen it. Now they were still as ghosts."—I have an antipathy against the inversion following "how," which you're fond of using. I can't explain properly why the turn of phrase "How are you ridiculous!" which is precious and flat at once, that is, seems ugly. To be sure, "How you are ridiculous!" wouldn't work here either. It is also just a quite personal question of my taste. Much more remarkable, strangely interesting, and, for me, still a little improbable, is the development of your worldview toward liberalism, which also comes to expression in this work. Strange, as I said, and interesting! It must make you feel quite unexpectedly young and strong? Really, I would understand your turn toward liberalism as a kind of consciously reconquered youthfulness, if it did not, which is more likely, simply signify the "maturity of the man." Maturity of the man! Doubtful whether I'll ever get that far. For one thing, I don't have much understanding of "freedom." It is for me a purely moral, theoretical concept, equivalent to "honesty." (Some critics refer to that in me as "coldheartedness.") But I have no interest whatever in political freedom. Was the prodigious literature of Russia not created under enormous pressure? Would it perhaps not have been created at all without that pressure? Which at least proves that the struggle for "freedom" is better than freedom itself. What is "freedom" anyway? Just because so much blood has been shed for the concept, it has something uncannily *un*free about it for me, something directly medieval . . . But I really have no business talking about this at all.

I haven't gotten much done recently and have a very bad conscience about it, for I would have so much to do! A rather lengthy essay of mine appeared in *Der Tag*, ostensibly about Gabriele Reuter, but kept on a very general and personal level. (I don't have a copy of it at the moment.) That's really all, for I'm still stuck in the second act of *Fiorenza*. (The dialogue is supposed to appear in *Die neue Rundschau*.) It's a new and exciting time for me, little suited to quiet work. The *Buddenbrooks* printing is now at eighteen thousand, and the story collection now approaching three. First I have to get used to the role of a famous man; it *is* very thrilling. The newspapers harass me with their eagerness for contributions. *Die neue Fr[eie] Presse*, after futile telegrams, sent me their agent in person, offering 300 marks for something else like "The Infant Prodigy." My post has become singularly promiscuous. One day not long ago I wrote to Amsterdam, Malaga, and New York. Recently I opened the new Verein with a reading (art discourse from Tonio Kröger and "Infant Prodigy") and was much celebrated. Invitations to Breslau and Lübeck I've declined for the time being. I'm being introduced to society, at the Bernsteins, at the Pringsheims. The Pringsheims are a fulfilling experience. Tiergarten[8] with genuine culture. The father a university professor with a golden cigarette case, the mother a Lenbach beauty, the youngest son a musician, his twin sister Katja (her name is Katja) a wonder, something rare and precious, a creature the mere existence of whom outweighs the cultural activity of fifteen writers or thirty painters . . . Infatuation is speaking here, but this time it is one which, if I behave accordingly, could have immeasurable consequences of the most varied sorts. One day I found myself in the Italian Renaissance salon, with the Gobelins, the Lenbachs, the doorjambs of *giallo antico* and accepted an invitation to a grand ball. It took place at their home the next evening. One hundred and fifty people, literature and art. In the ballroom an unspeakably beautiful frieze by Hans Thoma. I sat next to the wife of Justizrat Bernstein (Ernst Rosmer). For the first time since the most recent printing I was in grand company and had to exert myself terrifically to make the proper impression. People circled around me, looked me over, had themselves introduced, listened to what I had to say. I believe I didn't do too badly. I have a certain princely talent for making an impression when I'm feeling reasonably alert . . . This was the evening I made the acquaintance of the daughter of the household, after having only seen her before, seen her often, long, and insatiably, and had only greeted her one time fleetingly as I entered. Eight days later I was there again, for tea, "in order" to return to her mother a book I'd borrowed. I met her alone. She . . . she called Katja down and the three of us chatted for an hour. They allowed me to contemplate the Thoma frieze at my leisure. I was treated with the prospect of a

8. Tiergarten is the district in Berlin where the Pringsheims lived.

luncheon invitation. Had I been fooling myself when I had sensed a willingness from the other side? No! Two days later, the youngest son, Klaus, the musician, was sitting at my place returning my visit. He brought me his father's card, who unfortunately was too busy to come see me himself. I had already met him fleetingly at the ball: an extremely pleasing young man, soigné, educated, charming, with North German features. One has no thought of Jewishness in regard to these people; one senses only culture. We chattered freely about art, about his music, his sister . . . That was six days ago. Since then nothing has happened. Nothing whatever has happened. It all lives only in my fantasy, but it is too daring, too new, too wild, too marvelously adventurous for me to want to drive it out so soon. The *possibility* has occurred to me and makes me feverish. I can think about nothing else. Humpty Dumpty fell down the stairs and still got a princess for his wife. And I am—chest out—I am more than Humpty Dumpty! The thing is so terribly complicated that I would give a lot to be able to talk it through with you in some quiet corner. I'll say this right away: it is idle to ask whether it would spell my "bliss." Am I striving for bliss? I am striving for life; and *in that* probably striving "for my work." Moreover: I am not afraid of wealth. I've never worked because I was hungry, have denied myself nothing in the last few years, and already have more money than I know what to do with. And to me everything transient is just a symbol. Whether I warm my feet in the evenings before an oil stove or a marble fireplace doesn't affect the degree of my comfort . . . But all this is getting too far ahead of myself. The point is to await events, and it probably doesn't even make sense to ask for advice, because in the end I'll let myself be carried along with them. Mrs. Pr. will visit her family in Berlin in fourteen days. The dinner invitation will probably come after her return. I hope to see Katja before that at the Bernsteins, where I'm supposed to give a reading soon. What will happen? Considered quite practically, I have, as I said, the impression that the family would welcome me. I am Christian, from a good family, have merits that precisely this family knows how to value . . . What will happen? Probably nothing. But is the possibility not a bewildering experience in itself?

Something else that concerns you. Forgive me that I've forgotten it till now! At the P.s' ball I met Albert Langen. He had himself introduced to me—who used to work in his office—and conducted himself almost obsequiously. We spoke of you. "If I may permit myself," I said, "to offer you a piece of advice, this is it: Hold fast to my brother and never let him go! *One* time he *did* have a great success." "I wouldn't think of it," he said. "I know why you say that. I've made serious errors in this regard, I know it. I wouldn't even think of letting your brother go!" It sounded very ardent and persuasive, and I'm telling it to you because you once expressed concern. You needn't worry at all.

Warm regards! T.

*Munich*
*March 27, 1904*

Dear Heinrich:

My congratulations will reach you a day late, but it's on your birthday that I'm writing them down, which I actually find much better. So, good health and success in whatever you undertake! You are planning to come here at the beginning of May? I was thinking of going to Riva in the middle of April so that we would still have fourteen days together there and could discuss a world of things. But I don't know anything definite and, in truth, it's becoming ever less likely. If the great issue of my life has *not* been decided by the middle of April (it could be decided any day), then I'll have to remain here to press on with it, and if it has been decided, then it will probably become really impossible for me to leave. In the moment, Katja is sick in the Surgical Clinic, whither I sent her a couple of beautiful flowers this morning, with the permission of the beautiful Lenbach Mama, who always smiles encouragingly whenever I refer simply to "Katja" in her presence. The way things stand presently, following all kinds of changes that cost me more than a little suffering, is so favorable that it perhaps could not be more so. I, who am otherwise of a truly Indian passivity, have mustered unbelievable initiative in word and deed and, in good moments, am full of confidence. Sometimes, admittedly, I also fear that my fantasy extends far beyond realities. Of course, I am completely unsettled, and I have no calm for work, nor the solitude it requires. Ah, life! life!

Warm regards! T.


*Munich*
*December 23, 1904*
*Ainmillerstraße 31 III*

Dear Heinrich:

Now that it's Christmas something simply has to happen, I can see that; all the same, I need your forbearance and understanding only too much. You will understand: current goings-on are so badly suited to letter writing, they cause me so much confusion and tension and exhaustion that I haven't been able to prevent you from getting the impression in the distance that I'd altogether given up fretting further about the utterly simple problem of our relationship and was simply living out my "bliss" with no thought of it . . . Now, that of course is nonsense. "Bliss" itself would have to be something somewhat less problematic for it to be able to behave that way, and I couldn't be as mistrustful of it as I am. Bliss is something absolutely different from what those who don't know it imagine it to be. It is utterly ill-suited to making one more calm, content, and free of scruples in life, and I expressly dispute its capacity to contribute to a light and cheerful attitude.

I knew that. I have never regarded happiness as something light and cheerful, but always as something as serious, difficult, and severe as life itself—and perhaps what I *mean* is life itself. I didn't "conquer" it and it didn't "happen" to me—I have *submitted* myself to it: out of a kind of feeling of duty, a kind of morality, an inborn imperative, which, since it constitutes a move *away* from the desk, I've long feared as a form of slovenliness, but which I've in fact learned with time to recognize as something moral. "Bliss" is a duty— the opposite of bliss is much more comfortable; and I emphasize that not because I'm assuming anything like envy on your part, but because I suspect, on the contrary, that you look upon my new being and nature with something approaching disdain. Don't do that. I haven't made things easier for myself. Bliss, *my* bliss is to too great an extent experience, movement, realization, torment, is too little related to peace and too much to suffering for it to become a constant threat to my art . . . Life! Life! It remains an affliction. And thus will it quite likely keep on motivating me to a couple more good books.

But to get a bit more objective—I do not know that you are able to put yourself entirely in my position. The point is to work myself, not always with the freshest of energies, into a whole new existential form, to become active to a degree I've never known before, to "be" altogether, while earlier it was only making impressions. I'm not doing badly at it, as it seems. People assure me that I've become much more worldly; and with my dress suit I'm now wearing a light gray velvet vest with silver buttons. I put this in as a symbolic point, so that I don't have to get too long-winded about it. Otherwise you won't even get the letter on the first day of Christmas . . . Once again, the point is to maintain a humane strictness about oneself, and often enough the whole of bliss eventuates in a clenched jaw. The last half of the courtship—nothing but tremendous psychological exertion. The engagement—also no fun, as you can believe. The absorbing efforts to become a part of the new family, to conform (as far as it goes). Social obligations, a hundred new people, to be on display, behave oneself. Berlin—a splendid adventure. Lübeck—a farcical and touching dream. And in between on a daily basis the fruitless and enervating ecstasies that are peculiar to this absurd period of engagement: all of this still being listed here to excuse my silence. You will understand; I couldn't do otherwise. Even solitude was not to be had. There is a superficial solitude as there is a superficial sleep. Only now is it slowly beginning to get a little better, calmer, more normal, less pressing. But I am so worn out that I'm seriously entertaining the thought of disappearing for eight to ten days after New Year's, to withdraw to Polling and do nothing but work and breathe erotin-free (?) winter air.

Now, before that comes Christmas, and it is truly a pity that you can't be here for it. It will be completely different and amusing this year. On the second day Mother, the Löhrs, Vicco, and Grautoff will go with me to the Pringsheims. Quite a singular constellation I've put together, isn't it?

But to the wedding you will come for sure! It's not to be at all fatiguing. Not even church vows (Katja doesn't want it), and dinner just among close family, in which, however, you must be present. I've long looked forward to introducing you to Arcisstraße; and everyone there is also excited to make your acquaintance. Your artistic accomplishments are very much appreciated and I haven't a moment's doubt that you, too, will find the new family thoroughly pleasant. So far everything has come off excellently. Mother is already called "Mama" by Katja and addressed informally as "du," and Lula is already so far along with Katja that she recently said to her on the street: "Good day, you little titlark!" And all the while no one even really knows what a titlark is.

So, once again, you absolutely must come to the wedding. It will be the end of January before the arrangements have all been made—so you'll already be here, I hope, before then. And if you want to do something very nice, write Katja a few lines before you come welcoming her as a sister-in-law. That is, I believe, the custom, and actually it's already a little late. But you can just disguise it as a Christmas or New Year's greeting or acceptance of the invitation to the wedding, or something. In any case, it would be a pleasant touch.

Well, that's the letter. Not much became of it; but I couldn't become either too detailed or too *difficile*, since once again I got started at the very last minute.

Regards to Dr. von Hartungen, whom I have likewise shamefully neglected. Till we meet!

Your Tommy


*Baur au Lac*
*Zurich*
*February 18, 1905*

Dear Heinrich:

This evening I'm finally finding a peaceful hour to thank you for the beautiful present that you, along with Carla, gave my wife (that word writes so nicely) and me for our wedding. You don't know the present yourself yet, but hopefully will see it quite soon at our place and may rest assured in advance that it really is very nice: tasteful, quite directly useful, and thus actually more pleasing than the showy appliance from Tiergartenstraße that stood next to it on the table. Has Mama already told you all about our wedding? She at least was there and, along with the Löhrs and Vicco, represented the family in fine style. The whole process had a singular and bewildering effect, and I was surprised all day long by what I'd done in real life, like a proper man. Can you imagine tearing the daughter from the hearts of her weeping parents and carrying her off into the distance as your wife? Nor was I, God knows, able to imagine it. And all of that is really still the consequence of our having conceived a kind of Gipper-novel back then in Palestrina, which originally was supposed to have the song "Der Omnibus fährt *durch* die Stadt" for a leitmotif. And at the end it was supposed to be the omnibus that drove Biermann to prison. But now it has truly happened that I can speak of a "novel of my life," as I did at the table after the reading in Lübeck when I said in a sincerely emotional tone of voice: "Some of you know that I am standing at a significant turning point in my external and individual life. I was accompanied as far as Berlin by the young woman who has consented to become my wife, and a whole new chapter in the novel of my life is set to begin, a chapter that was conceived in sweet infatuation and is now to be built of love, art, and faithfulness . . . " And the omnibus, it turns out, is the Hôtel Baur au Lac, where I'm presently living with Katja in grand style, with "lunch" and "banquet" and evenings in a dinner-jacket with waiters in livery who run in front of you and open the doors . . . Incidentally, this isn't bliss swaggering! Despite reassurances from all sides as to the salutary hygienic effects of marriage, my stomach isn't always in order and I therefore don't always enjoy a good conscience about this idler's life; I long not rarely for a bit more cloistered peace and . . . intellectuality. If I hadn't gotten something finished right before the wedding, namely *Fiorenza*, my spirits would probably be very bad. Once again I was tormented by it as never before and, despite all the precedents, this time I was mortally convinced of the justice of the doubts with which I sent the (much too thick) manuscript to Berlin. Then, freed of the daily plague, I resigned myself. It was a severe defeat, but should teach me something. Since as early as "Tonio Kröger" I have allowed the concepts "intellect" and "art" to blur too much into each other. I had reversed them and, in the play, set them off against each other. That led to this Solneß-crash, this fiasco of endeavoring to fill an intellectual construction with life. About-face! Back to the naïveté of *Buddenbrooks!*—Now it seems in this case too, insofar as it's possible, that a stunning success is developing. Fischer wrote me that Bie had characterized the play to him as "something quite special." That made me childishly happy, but all the same, I'm determined this time to stand resolute against public opinion and continue regarding the work as thoroughly unsuccessful from an artistic point of view. Psychologically there probably are a couple of places where it achieves an extreme, and I believe that, as a stylist, I did well with the piece. But it remains a hybrid. Well, you will see. And you? Things seem to be pouring from you. You seem to have found yourself utterly and to be wholly unfamiliar with such mistaken initiatives and psychological defeats . . . You know, I believe, that you have lost yourself in another extreme in that you have become nothing more than just an artist—while a writer, God help me, has to be *more* than merely an artist. We must each have, as neurasthenics, perhaps, a fatal proclivity for the extreme—which, however, may then again be our strength. Bahr, excellent as ever, recently defined "talent" quite simply as a penchant "to perceive extremely and express it yet more extremely."—I'm very excited about your "Schauspielerin," which must be about ready to appear as a book. Do you know, by the way, that you play a role in Preuschen's most recent book?

At the end of the month we are moving into our Munich apartment (Franz Joseph-Straße 2 III). It will be wonderfully pretty. And hopefully I will throw myself back into work there.

Katja sends you her nicest regards and thanks. See you in the spring!

Your T.


*Munich*
*October 15, 1905*
*Franz Joseph-Str. 2*

Dear Heinrich:

I'm using my Sunday afternoon, which I always spend quite alone here in the apartment, to write you a letter to accompany the documents I have ready for you.

To begin at the beginning, your parting lines, mailed here on the 3rd, reached my hands early in the morning on the 9th. Well, that's Munich. Young Herr Schmied's reading was supposed to take place a couple of days after that, so my attention was brought to that in time. I went to it and did not regret it. You are certainly right to attribute to him a nice talent. The samples he read—I assume you know them—were extremely charming, secure in their humor in a way that must certainly be rare for such tender years. I'm anxious to see what he'll do. I was told that in Berlin he gets out of bed at 6:00 in the evening and then carouses through the night, and that he is not fond of work in general. Since he is a neurasthenic, that could be worrisome. But, on the other hand, there's something good, light, in not taking oneself too seriously. Let us hope for the best for him and from him. I had myself introduced to him and expressed my sincere enjoyment. By now, as far as I know, he's already been back with you in Riva for a long time and will have told you everything. I'm still enclosing Gumppenberg's report, which is surprisingly friendly.

The other newspaper clipping, an essay by Salten about *Götz Krafft* (do you even know what that is?) was so funny that I'm passing the pleasure of reading it on to you as well. The quotations are priceless. Is he the only one who can write like that, the magician? Does Ompteda perhaps manage it? I presume to write an equally funny article about ten other darlings. Thank God I'm not a darling anymore! I am free. Most people who value *Buddenbrooks* now find *Götz Krafft* yet much more heartfelt. And what I've written since then, what I'm writing and shall write, will never get over three thousand. What a sigh of relief! How much fresher the air around me is getting!

Third document: the first draft of my farewell letter to Schaukal. Now he's exhausted my patience too. You'll be able to imagine how he did it and can glean details from the text. Please read it and send it back to me when it's convenient, at which time I would be pleased to hear a word of approval from you. I no longer have any desire to drag along such a silly friend.

*October 17th*

I was interrupted here Sunday after all and am only today getting around to finishing the letter, which has the advantage of allowing me to supplement it by yet two more documents: little Ehrenberg's engagement announcement, which I'm passing on to you separately, and a copy of the book edition of *Fiorenza*. I would really like you to read it sometime in context and tell me your impression. I can't believe in the *complete* worthlessness of the little work. As for minor technical dramatic mistakes that I didn't even attempt to avoid, my nose shouldn't be rubbed in them. And the anticultural tendency is ridiculous. A book, as I said, that is *written* as if it came from someone in Lorenzo's circles is never anticultural; and in all the critical places it is more than necessarily objective and not tendentious.

But I'm speaking of myself . . . How satisfied were you with the essay by Frau Wassermann-Speyer? I found it not stupid, if a bit confused and contradictory. In any case, finally someone who understands your manner and heritage somewhat and whose effect is therefore educational.

Should I also say a couple of words about your own most recent *Zukunft* contribution? Well, it was obviously a secondary matter, done without much passion, and a product of that need to work with which you are so blessed; and, as a linguistic creation, it bore (for me) the marks of undue facility a bit too obviously. Otherwise, of course, very good. The two girls (I know them) moving; Herr Schumann, despite being a conventional type, exercising a novel effect in the light of your style. If one *is* something . . .

Since the weather has cleared up, I'll have finished my Tiergarten story in the next few days; it's supposed to appear first in the January issue of *Die neue Rundschau* and will do no dishonor to the *Ryl. Highness* volume. Thank God I'm gradually becoming an artist again. This last year, the year of my engagement and marriage, was tormentingly unproductive. Now I'm settled in and working regularly. Distractions ("temptations"—I'm reading Saint Anthony—I've never read anything like it!) there will be aplenty: the birth of the child, the art trip, etc. But I hope to hold out well, especially since my health and mood since the massage treatment (which I repeat every now and again) are much less leaden than they've been in years. Well, that is more than enough! You'll not have material enough for a six-page response. I would like to hear what's keeping you busy, what you are writing. *I am filled with the necessity of our holding together.*

In that sense,

Your T.

*Munich*
*October 22, 1905*
*Franz Joseph-Str. 2*

Dear Heinrich:

Accept my warm thanks for your letter. I've fretted far too much about this work for such a letter not to offer me a wonderful release—a release to *tears*. In fact, it more than once forced tears of joy to my eyes. I read it to Katja, let her mother read it, had Jof read it at the Löhrs. He said: "This letter must be published, in honor of you and Heinrich." Lula said, "Take good care of it for *one day it will* be published. And by the way I always knew that *Fiorenza* would bring the two of you closer again." In a word, I am happy. Now let the others twaddle as they like. There's already a feuilleton that characterizes it as "the cold mental work of the north German T. M." Yet better ones are sure to come. Farewell, thanks again!

T.


*Munich*
*November 20, 1905*
*Franz Joseph-Str. 2*

Dear Heinrich:

Your letter was a great pleasure for me, especially the promised dedication. You actually do owe me one, since I dedicated a part of *Buddenbrooks* to you. I'm intensely curious about the "good reasons" that moved you to decide on the dedication, and thereby (not only thereby) about the story itself.

Concerning the domestic event you will meanwhile have been informed of the details by Mama or Lula. So it is a girl: a disappointment for me, I'll admit between us, for I had very much wanted a son and haven't stopped wanting one. Why? It's difficult to say. I feel that a son is more poetic, more of a continuation, a new beginning of myself under new conditions. Or so. Well, he needn't be done without. And perhaps the daughter will offer me a closer relationship to the "other" sex, of which I still, though now a husband, actually know nothing.

The birth, contrary to expectations, was quite terribly difficult, and my poor Katja had to suffer so cruelly that it was a horror scarcely to be endured. I shall never forget that day all the days of my life. I had a conception of life and one of death, but what that was—birth, that I didn't yet know. Now I know that it is just as profound a matter as the other two. Right afterwards, all was idyllic and peaceful (the opposite of the peace that follows a death), and to see the child on the mother's breast, who herself still had the effect of a sweet child, was a vision by which the birth (which lasted altogether nearly forty hours) was transfigured and sanctified. The little one, who in accord with her mother's wishes will be called Erika, promises to become very pretty. Occasionally I believe I see a bit of Jewishness coming through for a moment, which always puts me in a cheerful mood.

Now, with "Jewishness" I turn to the main point of this letter, which is actually a request. The request regards the manuscript that will be sent to you along with these lines: "The Blood of the Walsungs," a Jewish story, and for which I am asking your advice, practically your help. The story is to appear in the January issue of *Die neue Rundschau* and has already been typeset. Professor Bie, however, objects to the ending, the very last sentence with the foreign words, of which he fears that the average reader would find it crude; he's pleading to the skies for me to disclose the matter, for the sake of his gala issue, just as discreetly at the conclusion as I have done throughout the events of the story. He is certainly correct. The final ending never appealed to me either. But I would like not to end with the dash (you will see which one I mean), but had the need to bring all that follows to a head once more with a reply—and with the best of intentions I don't know how to do it better. That it is not a question of simply replacing the Jewish expression with a German one is clear. That would be nothing. But what to do? How would you close? If you have any idea at all—don't keep it from me! But it's rushed.—The mistakes in the manuscript, I think, don't distort the meaning and you will be able to correct them easily. I'm curious altogether to hear what you think of the story. It is meant for the *Royal Highness* volume.

Did you read that G. Frenssen received a 200,000-mark advance for his new novel? I'm going to pass on it. What is Frenssen? Nothing but a sign that literary culture has gradually advanced so far in Germany that even rural pastors from Holstein can write quite passable books. A phenomenon without any value as to his person. A good-natured poetical fellow who has even heard, as one sees from *Jörn Uhl*, of the "transvaluation of all values." Of serious artistry, fate, discipline, passion, there can be no talk whatever.— But my name is sometimes mentioned along with his . . .

Adieu. Write soon. T.


*Munich*
*December 5, 1905*
*Franz Joseph-Str. 2*

Dear Heinrich:

I want to let you hear from me once more before my trip (which will begin on the ninth) and, above all, to thank you for your good words about "The Blood of the Walsungs." What you say about the conclusion strongly reinforced my belief in this version: in the possibility and internal justification of it. And I'm also resolved to retain it for the book edition. For the *Rundschau* I want to substitute another one for it, to please Bie for all I care—which needn't be a bad compromise, for it is not absolutely necessary that the end be focused on "vengeance." Rather, there is such a wealth of motivation beforehand that it's conceivable for the story to end on four or five other points. I could, for example, say: "But Beckerath?"—"Oh, he ought to be grateful to us. His existence will be a little less trivial, from now on." That would be the "Royal Highness."—Bie is right insofar as Jewish expressions are falling somewhat out of style, which certainly doesn't rule it out for a concluding trump, but can also be avoided just as easily. You say: To sacrifice what is characteristic to propriety is kitsch. But one can also say: Art is precisely being as characteristic as possible without offending any stylistic sensitivity. And *beganeft* violates the style, that has to be admitted. Before the ending all such things are avoided, reworded, or disguised. Neither the word "Jew" nor "Jewish" appears in the story. A Jewish intonation is only suggested very discreetly a couple of times. Of Herr Aarenhold it is said that he "had been born in a remote village in East Prussia." *Beganeft* doesn't go with this type of ironic discretion, although it is thoroughly warranted psychologically. And the style is almost more important to me, in a non-moral way, than the psychology . . . I'm saying all of this only to justify my decision to give in to Bie for the *Rundschau*. In the book the version you supported so well will regain its rights.

What are you doing? I hear from Mama that you are busy with a new novel, the beginning of which is taken from Mama's memoirs. May I know what it's about? And how is your health? Recently I had another acute attack of my nervous dyspepsia and spent a wretched day in bed. But I am having these attacks more and more rarely, and the treatment I'm receiving from my specialist (massage, electricity; finally the rectum was electrified directly by a rubber hose inserted quite far in) have helped me very noticeably.

Katja is up again, at least for a good part of the day. She is feeding the little one herself, so she'll get a good start. Occasionally, when I wake up in the morning with a softly massaged abdomen and a tolerably fit stomach, and hear the child crying and feel a desire to work, I have a pervasive feeling of happiness such as I haven't known for twenty years.

I'm presently writing an article for *Die M. Neueste Nachrichten*, about "invention" and "animation" . . . Incidentally, how did you like my reply in *Die Lübecker Anzeigen*— if you received the paper? Harden, who had seen it reprinted somewhere, wrote praising it highly to my mother-in-law (he's been reading me since Wedekind drew his attention to me) and concluded: "Il ira loin—wenn er sich nicht verweichlicht."[9] Very good. The German yet better than the French.

What this *loin* might be—if the "if" (and it is not the only one) should turn out to be unwarranted? At times I harbor ambitious plans. What would you say, for example, to this: writing a historical novel called *Friedrich?* Since I was twice in Potsdam and Sanssouci, the figure has become excitingly familiar to me. And my last literary

---

9. "If he doesn't go soft."

experience was Carlyle's *Frederick the Great*, which recently appeared in an excellent German edition. A splendid book—even if his concept of heroism is essentially different from mine, as I already suggested in *Fiorenza*. To represent a hero as human-*all-too-human*, with skepticism, with *malice*, with psychological radicalism, and still as positive, lyrical, written from personal experience: it seems to me that that has simply never been done . . . The antagonist would be his brother (*the brother problem always appeals to me*), the prince of Prussia, who was in love with Voss, was a dreamer and came to ruin from "feeling" . . . Whether I'm not called to this task? I'm now thirty. It is time to begin thinking of a masterpiece. It is not impossible that after *Ryl. Highness* (which is child's play compared [to] the new plan) I shall clear the table completely and get busy with Friedrich. What do you say to that? Do you think it's possible?—

—The latest event in Munich is the naming of Hermann Bahr as the chief director of the K. Schauspiel. An interesting development! He promises to raise the Hoftheater to the level of the Burgtheater and yet higher, and is drawing up an exquisite program, with Euripides, Plautus, Kleist, Hebbel and—*Fiorenza*. It's a fact, I heard it. He's supposed to be inflamed by *Fiorenza* and it is to be one of his first premieres. Well, nothing gets eaten quite that hot. And for the moment it's only a private report; so far I've heard nothing from Bahr directly. Just now he's traveling around gathering fresh talent—which *Fiorenza*, admittedly, would need. I don't trust the information; but it really did give me a considerable shock. And just the fact the Bahr likes the play so much pleases me. No surprise, incidentally. Earlier on I learned a great deal from him.

So that's all I have to tell. Now it's your turn.

Warmly, Your T.


*Munich*
*January 17, 1906*
*Franz Joseph-Str. 2*

Dear Heinrich:

I still have to thank you for your Christmas present: for *Schauspielerin*—on the cover of which I read with raised eyebrows "6 to 10 thousand." Do all the pieces in this series enjoy such wide circulation, or is it just *Schauspielerin* that made it? That shouldn't surprise me, for it is an enchantingly entertaining book, which is just as good for the many as it is for us other ones. I admire it greatly, with the virtuosity of tempo that it has, though it also lingers carefully over the difficult, psychologically critical passages. I hadn't given it an adequate reading in the earlier newspaper installments; now my closer acquaintance shows me, as you already gently suggested, that the work I did with "The Blood of the Walsungs" was work already done to a certain extent, and done indeed very well and completely. Less a pity then that the story *will not appear*. I probably didn't tell you that? Well then, short and sweet: Returning from my December trip, I found the rumor already spreading here that I had written a passionately "anti-Semitic" story, in which I had compromised terribly my wife's family. What should I have done? I had a look at the spirit of my story and found that, in its innocence and independence, it was not exactly suited to dispel the rumors. And I had to acknowledge that I'm no longer free individually and socially. So I sent a couple of imperious telegrams to Berlin and succeeded in having the January issue of the *Rundschau*, which was all set to go, appear *without* "The Blood of the Walsungs." Fischer (from fear of Langen) assumed the costs of the new printing, which might not have been so severe at all. Enough, the people evaded their scandal and I, who had initially frothed a bit at the mouth, am now rather indifferent. *That* good the piece indeed wasn't, and what is of worth in it, namely the milieu depiction, which I really do consider very new, can probably be used sometime in another way. To be sure, I've not been free since of a feeling of constraint, which in moments of hypochondria becomes very oppressive, and you will no doubt call me a cowardly bourgeois. But it's easy for you to talk. You are absolute. I, in contrast, have deigned to submit to my situation.

The bad thing, primarily, is that considerations also force me—when I get so little finished anyway—to suppress the product of long weeks of scrupulous work. Now, in the absence of completely fresh renown, I take pleasure in the fact that *Fiorenza* is gradually becoming a success—truly, it is coming into favor. The second printing is out, which, as Fischer was probably correct in remarking, means as much for a play as the tenth printing for a novel. And now it is also being widely and extensively reviewed, which wasn't the case before, and nearly always with the suggestion that a well-financed theater has to venture a production. That, of course, is a questionable matter, which I most prefer to avoid altogether. Should Bahr seriously want to do it, then I'm not sure that I wouldn't simply say no. He is so hated by a large contingent of the press, has become such a political person, that I'm full of reservations. If "The Blood of the Walsungs" is anti-Semitic, then *Fiorenza* is anticlerical, and it is much too fragile to tolerate being drawn into partisan squabbles. I think, however, that the desire for such experiments will already have been driven out of my old master beforehand, if he assumes the post at all.

In Basel, where I'm going at the end of the month for two evenings of readings, I want to read the first act to the people myself (which I've never tried doing before). For the first, my own vocal abilities will do in a pinch. You are probably scoffing at all the traveling. But I can't help myself; I find the self-presentation fun and each time the change of air pulls me out of the intellectual stagnation to which I am inclined. The *tournée* Prague-Dresden-Breslau went altogether pleasantly and respectably. It seems to me sometimes that I, if I made an effort at it, could turn myself into a kind of Wüllner of the podium, a conqueror of scant means on the strength of my nervous elasticity. Once again I saw what a difference practice makes. In Prague I was still sweating and probably didn't make a good impression. In Dresden (where I had two hearty lunches at Aunt Elisabeth's and heard Strauss's *Salome* in the Hofoper—an extravagant enchantment, but that doesn't interest you)—in Dresden I took rather better command of the hall. And in Breslau, where in fact I was already tired, I was ridiculously successful. The newspapers published enamored descriptions of my person, so bold and secure was I at the podium. But one forgets it every time in the intervals between trips and I'll probably be sweating again in Basel.

Prague is beautiful beyond all expectations, at least the splendid palace district on the other side of the Moldau; and since the way there took me through the terrain of the Seven-Years' War, I traveled by day and looked attentively all around. "Friedrich . . ." my heart skips a beat when I just think of it. Yes, yes, it is now as good as certain that it should be my next novel. I'm not yet free for it. *Ryl. Highness* still needs to be done. But for a while now I've begun gathering nourishment, research materials, for the Friedrich novel, and I have moments of excited belief in it. Certainly I am directed to the material by ambition, but scarcely by any concern for popularity. What is essential is that anything I'm supposed to spend years with, must possess, in itself, as object, a certain *dignity*. In the past few years, I have gathered a mass of remarkable material for a modern big-city novel, have experienced and suffered so much, that it could really become a considerable book. But I fear I no longer have the patience and (forgive me!) the modesty, to drag around for two or three years the burden of *just any* modern novel. "My *Friedrich*"—that is something else. That is something one would be proud to bear; it is sustaining, fortifies one's stamina . . . What you say in your letter I read eagerly and thought a lot about. It's probably true that my "historical instinct" is not very highly developed (although I believe you underestimate the correctness of my "Schiller." I cannot persuade myself that it's possible to make formal advances without simultaneously augmenting one's skepticism. A formalist is already practically a symbolist, and that is what I mean to represent by "freedom." I have returned very strongly to Schiller, have studied him intensely. He was ultimately *nothing* but artist and therefore not at all objective, at least not so in his innermost self, just as little as Wagner was, who also indulged the pretense of all kinds of objectivity, while, however, being nothing but a great artist—and whom Schiller's need anticipated in the most astounding way. If you have Schiller's letters to Goethe with you there, have a look at the one of December 29, 1797, about the symbolic in art and the future of the opera. You won't believe your eyes). What I am capable of in the way of history, as I believe I've already shown in *Fiorenza*, is the *tone*. (Here the art historians wonder how I captured it so offhandedly, with a minimum of research.) But the tone by itself is almost spirit and, in any case, is atmosphere. It makes the music, it also makes, artistically speaking, the story; and objective historical psychology without subjective animation, it seems to me, is tedious and impossible—in particular in dealing with a great man for whom the main thing is just his—timeless—*greatness*. The real presumptuousness in my undertaking seems to me to be much less that I, the ahistorical subjectivist, want to write a historical novel, than that I, the lyricist, am endeavoring to represent *greatness*.

For that requires knowledge of greatness, familiarity and experience with greatness . . . Do I have these things?—I am myself aware that this undertaking has been preceded, though without any intention or plan, by much research and conceptual work. My reading, which for a long time now has consisted not of belles lettres but of biographies, memoirs, correspondences, has been aiming at it. From a study of the being of the artist I moved unawares into the study of greatness. My "Schiller" is a small, provisional proof, *Fiorenza* a somewhat larger one, of the success of these studies in the sphere of the heroic . . . No, certainly, the merit of the work, once it is done, will not lie in the sphere of the historical. But if I accomplish on a large scale what, so I hear, I've already accomplished on a small one: to make greatness palpable, to depict it intimately and in its vitality—then my pride would know no bounds.—Forgive the speech! These days I am in a state of feverish spirits and exaltation.

But things are going well for you? It was a pleasure to hear that your life is now being warmed by friendship and family. Certainly that will leave its traces in what you are now writing (which I'm longing to see). And, just watch, one day you will "submit" too.

How is your health these days? My whole problem with neurasthenia is becoming more and more localized in the stomach, which behaves increasingly sensitively the more cautious I become. So why not eat marzipan?

I'll send you the article, which, however, is not very significant, as soon as it appears.

Your T.


*Munich*
*January 22, 1906*
*Franz Joseph-Str. 2*

Dear Heinrich:

The *Simplicissimus* with your story in it came today and I read it immediately and eagerly. I want to give you my impressions right away. This strangely strange, profound thing, which conveys in its extreme self-containment and concentration, in its quick, strong, significant points, the tragedy of the genius as a schoolboy story—is in my eyes the most revealing and extraordinary piece you've written. This is admittedly the judgment of an interested party, one who is connected to the work by all of what is visibly expressed for the world in the dedication. This work is so near to me that I nearly experience it as my own, and *as* work it did become my own so quickly and easily that a single reading and a quick look-through would suffice for me to reproduce the order of the paragraphs out of my head. In a word: I do not take part in it; I *am* part of it, and where one is part of something there is probably no real possibility of judgment. Nevertheless, I feel confident in my view.

This doesn't count as a letter; you should simply receive my congratulations and thanks. After Basel I'll write again.

There's been no sign of Klösterlein as yet. I'm already pretty compromised at the *Rundschau*, my good nature having caused me several times to recommend impossibly inferior works. To do it again I would really have to believe in it.

Adieu. I'm trying to regain my feeling for *Ryl. Highness*, from which I was already completely estranged. And for *Friedrich* I really am already beginning to make notes. If only I could be more diligent and move a bit more noticeably off the starting point. But my working technique, which consists of perpetual hesitation, is no longer subject to change.

Katja returns your greeting most warmly. She is recovering too slowly. If we've become dispensable for the child by early summer we want to make the trip along the coast from Bremen to Genoa for its restorative powers. It's supposed to be the best one for such a purpose, and I can also use it.

Your T.

*Munich*
*March 13, 1906*
*Franz Joseph-Str. 2*

Dear Heinrich:

Many thanks for your letter. It did me a lot of good. I have experienced so much unpleasantness lately that I'm only now slowly beginning to get the best of it. Concerning Schaukal, I admit being intrigued that he's supposed to have simply done it without questioning his belief that it was good and right. But there are several reasons why I can't respond. First, I'm not healthy enough right now to fight it out. The article would require so much effort and so tax my nerves. You don't know what agony it is, the way I get so upset devising a polemic, get consumed by internal dissension. Then, of course, S[chaukal] would respond, saying that our quarrel really only started in reference to *Fiorenza* (while in truth I first became impatient when he sent me a fat manuscript for me to place at Fischer and then added a note that he "didn't like" the first two acts of *F[iorenza]* and the third he hadn't read). And then he would (I know him) produce my amiable and tirelessly grateful letters to him. No, I cannot do it, however much the article in the *B[erliner] T[ageblatt]* might possibly harm me. But that no one, no one among all the "friends" and "admirers," feels sufficiently alarmed to call a halt on this narrow-minded and self-righteous fop, that hurts me. You can't do it, for then the meaning would be: it's his brother. Enough, I'm forced to let it slide. Incidentally, I believe he will deny to himself that it was an act of revenge. He will imagine himself to have acted in a *bona fide* manner; while, of course, it is completely clear that he would have written the essay quite differently or not at all but for that letter from me. Wassermann (who is a master after all) he calls a Jewish journalist; but he hasn't yet said it publicly. And about your books, which he considers insolent hackwork, he's also kept silent in public. That *Fiorenza* is hackwork, and bad hackwork at that, he publishes in the *Berliner Tageblatt.* And the *brutal* part is that he *knows* how much pain the book caused me. Really, he deserves to be thrashed. But I cannot and don't want to do it.

I hear that you're also going to Dresden? How come? We're looking forward to your stay in Munich. At the beginning of May we're going to Venice for fourteen days. And shall then likely spend the whole summer with the baby and the help in the country somewhere. That will do all three of us good. I'm doing nothing at present but nourishing the Friedrich plan with research. In addition, I have to absorb a great deal of new stuff: just the military aspect, the *war.* But I feel confident I'll get a grasp of it.

Here it was already spring, but today below freezing.

Regards! T.


*Munich*
*March 21, 1906*
*Franz Joseph-Str. 2*

Dear Heinrich:

Warm thanks! Your article refreshed, stirred, and cheered me very much. It's the same way as with youngsters: Someone did that to me and my older brother comes and avenges it.

So, I find your article excellent. The only thing I would criticize on tactical grounds is that you gear it entirely to the word "pretentiousness" (in qu[otation] marks)—which, however, doesn't appear in Schaukal's review. If he replies he can start with that and will perhaps deny that he ever made the charge that you are rejecting. It's true it would be easy to contradict him, for his essay does in fact amount to the charge of pretentiousness; it's just that in your article the word has the unwarranted effect of a quotation. I took the liberty, provisionally, of omitting the quotation marks in the title and, in the first sentence adding "'literature' and"; namely: "in *Zeitgeist* pronounced *Fiorenza* by T. M. 'literature' and pretentiousness." Then, so we don't lose any time in relation to *Zeitgeist*, I sent the article to *Harden.* The relationships we both have with him, yours literary and mine personal, mean that he won't easily be able to say no. I can imagine that he will publish the article in *Notizbuch* as a letter. I asked for the proofs, if it gets that far, to be sent to me. Perhaps you'll already be here when they come.—

Mama writes that you're reading in Berlin? Perhaps in Dresden as well? Yesterday the Berlin critic Lublinski visited me and said that you have a fanatic following among the "rising generation" in Berlin. When are you reading there? I'm supposed to make an appearance here in the first week of April. It would be nice if you were still here for it.

Next Thursday is your birthday. Since you will probably be underway on that day, I extend my congratulations to you today.

Warm regards! T.


*Munich*
*June 7, 1906*
*Franz Joseph-Str. 2*

Dear Heinrich:

Lying to my right is a whole little stack of written matters that have accumulated in the last fourteen days. There's nothing from you in it; and nevertheless the debt represented by the little stack acquires its true weight only by way of my debt to you. I want to make quick work of it to start with; suddenly the little stack and my conscience will both be considerably lightened.

The days immediately following my return from Weißer Hirsch (and Berlin) I was dead tired and slept until noon. Then there really were four or five days feeling renewed and in the mood for work, and I didn't want to spend the vigor on letter writing. And then I was in for a stomach attack, which broke and reached its high point yesterday, punctually on my birthday. For about a week in such cases I wander around in a deep gloom, intellectually desolate, and neurasthenically unsocial, incapable even of reading and unsure what is to become of myself. It doesn't, however, amount to more than a night that I spend utterly sleeplessly, moaning, vomiting, and retching from intestinal nerve pains, suffering quite dreadfully. That was the night before last. The following day then I'm very weak and tender, transfigured to a certain extent; and then I slowly get back in gear. Thus today. And now I want to thank you for your *Stürmische Morgen*, which I was already reading in Weißer Hirsch—so eagerly and all at once like I've read scarcely any other book—and to which I've also devoted myself repeatedly since being back here.

A brilliant book once again, which displays all your best points, your gripping tempo, your famous "verve," the delightful precision of your language, your quite astounding virtuosity, a book to which one surrenders oneself because it clearly stems directly from passion. These four good pieces will increase your fame. That the one dedicated to me is still my favorite today is surely as it should be. I already assured you of how close I feel this story is to me. But right after that comes "Der Unbekannte."


*June 8*

You see, that's as far as I could go. I got so dizzy and nauseous from leaning over the desk that I had to stop.—So, then: I admire "Der Unbekannte" very much and fancy that few people will be able to treasure the piece as I, who sees and feels its most personal symbolism. Apart from the emotional content, it is so excellently done, prepared extremely skillfully, and made plausible. That was necessary; for the fact that the boy notices nothing and fails to understand to the point of such extremity is actually a bit improbable. But what does probability finally matter? The greatest things are improbable. (See Björnson on Ibsen in the last *Zukunft*.) And the repeated "The simplest things never occur to me" does a great deal to counter improbability. Incidentally—how stirring and genuine is the story as a whole! The relationship of the schoolboy (this schoolboy) to the world, to the goings-on in his parents' house! You had to do that once—that too. The details that were most enjoyable for me you know yourself; they are surely those which were also most enjoyable for you. In short—heartfelt congratulations!—Did you receive Langen's "March" prospectus? It lists sales and first printings for everything you've written! I'm doing miserably. The effect of Weißer Hirsch is more negative than positive. I don't tell anyone around here how bad and exhausted and used-up and dead and finished I feel. Without a wife and child things would go better and I'd be more indifferent. I'm tormented by the thought that I was wrong to allow myself to be attached and tied down. I already suspected at the time that it was with the *last* of my energies that I won my external happiness. Enough! I believe you don't like to hear such as that and also have a right to refuse it. You have served your artistic nature more strictly and faithfully and your creative egoism has no need to know that I, apparently the happier one, have for a long time had it incomparably harder than you. Enough, such gloomy phrases make me sick. All that one wants with such talk is to disturb others and draw attention to oneself. I put my hopes in the summer in Oberammergau.

Brieger-Wasservogel has written to me again. Did you definitely turn him down? He says that Wassermann, you, Hirschfeld, Salus, R[icarda] Huch, Toni Schwabe, etc. had agreed, on terms the same as mine. Don't we perhaps want to allow him after all to print something? I have yet to respond in any way.

We're leaving on the fifteenth for the country.

Warm regards, T.


*Munich*
*June 11, 1906*
*Franz Joseph-Str. 2*

Dear Heinrich:

Your sympathy does me endless amounts of good and, almost more so, the trust with which you are now introducing me to the important events in your life. I already knew of it, was deeply moved directly upon hearing the first inklings, and am moved anew now that I seek to orient myself to the psychological realities lying behind your words.

It seems to be a relationship quite similar to mine and Katja's at the beginning, despite all the differences between the two women and in the external circumstances. The two of you are agreed and feel secure (of each other and of yourselves)—that is already a more favorable state of affairs than ours back then. And there seem to be no lasting external obstacles. I see here a great chance for happiness—also for me; for it's not out of the question that you and your wife would live for at least part of the year in Munich, and that could result in a very nice, agreeably stimulating life together, as I dream it might be sometimes, when I find impressions of my wife's family alien, terrible, humiliating, enervating, debilitating. But your fiancée is a singer? For the public? Will it become a life of wandering? I don't know if I should wish that for you. For as desirable as I find a certain mobility, freedom, restlessness, and insecurity, and fear for myself that laziness and stagnation and softness might be the result of a comfortable and luxurious bourgeois existence—I do believe that I know from earlier on that you also have in you an ample portion of the sedentary and a need for bourgeois comfort. I'm thinking of the cheerful indulgence with which you enjoyed your apartment, your library, your comfortable and secure domesticity on Zieblandstraße.—Well, that will be as it may. I, in any case, am bound and have a gold ball on each leg—whether that bodes good or ill for me. (Grautoff has declared that he's making no progress here and that he's going to Paris for good in October, to live there as an independent literary artist and shine shoes if he has to. That might be a big mistake, and yet I will watch him go with a certain longing.) As for Eckerthal, then, I, who have just returned from taking a cure, can't consider it under any circumstances—unless, that is, a *physical* collapse ensues, which is not likely since I'm sleeping and eating well and it's only my dear soul that is stale to the point of lifelessness. In contrast, I welcome joyfully your thoughts of coming to Oberammergau in the summer. Do that indeed! We could discuss the future and get something of a grip altogether on life.—I'm setting great store on my stay in the country; it has got to revive my energies. How little is accomplished by a mere "conception"; one feels that only once one has lost the energy, the courage to work, the ability to find fun in it (in the case of a highly developed talent, a great insatiability and conscientiousness), has lost the willingness to assume the burden of the effort required, the loathsomeness of the phases, the hardship of the rhythm. *Friedrich, Maja*, the stories I would like to write could perhaps become masterpieces, but one consumes oneself in plans and fails at the beginnings. Kleist didn't write his Robert Guiscard and Hartleben his Diogenes. Terrible, terrible! Well, let us hope! Thanks again for your sympathy and warm regards.

T.

*Munich*
*May 27, 1907*
*Franz Joseph-Str. 2*

Dear Heinrich:

Thank you for your card. I'm glad that you've found an agreeable place to stay. It's true, the Grand Hôtel was a swindle—a pretentious dive. What a real *grand hôtel* is I just saw once again in Frankfurt, in the Frankfurter Hof: There one knows what one is paying for and does it with a kind of joyousness.—So, we were there and witnessed the sixth and, for now probably the last, performance of *Fiorenza*. We left on Thursday evening and were back here Saturday evening. The performance, as inadequate as it was by and large, did show me that the play as a play is far from impossible, as nearly everyone believed, and that whatever is contemplated in a lively manner simply also lives on the stage, whether it's "dramatic" or not. Of the actors only the cardinal was really good, but he was practically unsurpassable, a thoroughly cunning, piquant, and strange character. Lorenzo was miserable, which meant that the third act, in itself a hard test of patience, was severely marred. But the public's devotion was touching. After the second act I had to take the stage twice, and three times after the third, to acknowledge the persistent applause, the final time without the actors. Otherwise things also went well for us. A lady from the Rothschild family took us for a ride in her equipage, and after the theater we dined in their luxurious house. It was stupefyingly hot on the way home. Now I am tired, desirous of work, and rejecting all triumphs, readings, all personal appearances out of hand.—On the trip I began *Zwischen den Rassen*, which Langen sent me, and read it nearly the whole day yesterday, so that I'm already about two-thirds through it. The nicest part so far was the Gugigl episode with Arnold. More details when I'm finished. My God, when I *compare*\* it with novels that are otherwise being written by Germans today! So my family ambition is feeling very satisfied. What Busse, Hesse, and Simpel will have to say this time!

Warm regards!

T.

\*(and not only then! But if you want to enjoy your worth, you finally have to compare.)


*Munich*
*June 7, 1907*
*Franz Joseph-Str. 2*

Dear Heinrich:

Good God, you've finished something else already—and I'm not even finished with your last one; that is, I've long since read it through but that doesn't mean that it's quit occupying me. It grows with distance—as an artwork, for I may be excused for having read it primarily as a personal and confessional document—having torn through it or more precisely: having been torn along by it, often deeply moved. I can't be very coherent (we are breaking up our household here, now reduced really to complete disarray, and I'm writing with a fountain pen I'm not yet used to). But I do want to give you my impressions briefly. They can be summarized along the lines of saying that *Zwischen den Rassen* is—at least at the moment—my favorite of your works, the one I feel is closest to me—why? First off, as I said, as confession. You've never *shown* such surrender, and despite the considerable austerity of its beauty, this book acquires thereby something soft, humane, something indicative of surrender, which kept me for entire paragraphs in a state of irresistible emotion. But the real reason for its singular effect is probably more deeply embedded in it. It is so moving, I mean to say, because this book is the fairest, the most seasoned, gentlest, and *freest* of your works. There is no single tendency here, no narrowness, no glorification and mockery, no privileged something or other and no disdain, no partisanship in intellectual, moral, aesthetic matters—but instead universality, knowledge, and art. That inheres in the material; but the material was you. *Zwischen den Rassen* [Between the races]—it amounts to an "*Above* the Races," and since "race" is ultimately only a symbol, it leads finally to an "Above the *World*." In this sense, it seems to me, this book—your most humane, your softest book—is simultaneously the most sovereign and artistic of your works, and this simultaneity is no doubt the source of its great emotional power for me.

Thank you for the birthday card. The day left me feeling very friendly and festive. We're moving Monday or Tuesday: Seeshaupt, Villa Hirth. Whether I'll get something done on *Ryl. Highness* this summer? Frankfurt once again distracted, demoralized, and tired me terribly. But by the sea I want to do my best.

Will you come to visit us, perhaps from Polling, where you're going next?

Warm regards, also from Katja!

T.


*Seeshaupt*
*June 19, 1907*

Dear Heinrich:

I opened the enclosed business letter to you because it was addressed to "Seeshaupt, Villa Hirth." Please excuse me.

I believe you're also having better weather now. Do you want to come by for a visit? There is a good inn not far from us. I'm as diligent as possible and am at least working *regularly* again, even if my day-to-day energies don't go very far.

Mama had prepared a room for you; she was truly sorry. I also wrote to her that her assent had gotten lost. She, incidentally, is going to Munich only for one day, to visit Lula, if I understood correctly.

Warm regards from Katja too!

T.

*Seeshaupt*
*June 22, 1907*

Dear Heinrich:

Thank you for your card. I did receive the lion (recently), but I had to pay almost as much for shipping and customs as the whole thing cost.

Since Grautoff has been gone, I haven't really had any connection at all to the *Neueste*, especially since Busching has also left. Only with the feuilleton editor Grimm do I still have a fleeting acquaintance, and so I'll write to him and inform Ewers of the answer myself. I owe him a letter anyway.—"Very, very hard"? I read *Zw[ischen] d[en] Rassen* in three or four sittings, which for me is fast. And this, when I'm bored by all the new novels—to be sure, however, not on account of their "difficulty." I find the book, among other things, as entertaining as only your books are.

I work to the extent of my energies. But what small steps! Such *patience* is necessary! Such *doggedness!*—*Nord und Süd* took the "Versuch ü[ber] d[as] Theater" for 400 marks. It's also supposed to be sold in a separate printing.—Isn't Harden priceless?

T.

*Seeshaupt*
*July 5, 1907*

Dear Heinrich:

I've gathered information about health resorts: all the Brenner locations, which is no distance at all from Kuffstein, are over one thousand meters, that is, Gossensass, Brennerbad, Mattrai (?), Steinach. Otherwise Kohlgrub (before Ammergau) could be considered, but it's only nine or nine hundred and fifty meters. Have you meanwhile made your decision?

A question from me: Katja is a little lacking in intellectual stimulation, to which she is accustomed from earlier. She must be encouraged to start attending lectures again in the winter. For now I had the following idea. You, after all, are editing the German Flaubert for Müller. Has the translation of all the volumes already been assigned? Would you perhaps pass on to Katja one of the ones you took over? She would like to do it and would presumably do as well, in fact better, than the average. Can something be done there?

Best wishes for your health!

T.

*Munich*
*October 2, 1907*

Dear Heinrich:

I turned down Otto Eisenschitz for lack of material. He seems to be undertaking a kind of cabaret, and to appear personally there would probably be somewhat lacking in dignity. In any case, I would advise you to wait and see what comes of it and who else is involved.

Yes, a short time after you left the weather took on its seasonal cast, with evening fog, which lent the heathlike landscape a fantastic appearance. Since then it's been very warm, and the recent move was ghastly. For the last few days we've been living here on Arcisstraße with our suitcases half unpacked, waiting for our apartment to be put in order, which will hopefully be the case tomorrow. My head is full of worries about the play, for *Fiorenza* is *supposed* to be performed before the month is out—and, indeed, if all goes well, with an excellent cast, under Professor Hierl-Deronko, a big deal locally, as artistic advisor. Heine has taken over the role of the Prior and Lützenkirchen, Lorenzo. I'm making efforts to get the Frankfurt Giovanni, who was exemplary, for here. But the Künstlerhaus is supposed to be bad both acoustically and visually, and I'm also a little anxious about Falkenberg's Gobelinesque direction. And otherwise about the *length* of the performance. In any case, I would be enormously pleased if you could come. Maybe it will yet be put off until November after all—almost probably.

My mood for work under the prevailing circumstances is minimal. On Franz Joseph-Straße, with more solitude in my life, it will have to improve.

Katja sends her warm regards.

T.

*Munich*
*October 16, 1907*
*Franz Joseph-Straße 2*

Dear Heinrich:

I recently addressed a card to Riva—about Carla, that it turns out she definitely could not come and that I'm also wary, given the experimental character of the whole, to experiment as well in details. The performance, as I foresaw, has been put off until November. It becomes apparent, of course, that it takes time to get everything set up. By then you will probably be here anyway.—We had an interesting visit day before yesterday: from S. Fischer, publisher, who rushed over expressly to settle the royalties in regard to *K.H.* (which stands for both Klaus Heinrich and *Kgl. Hoheit* [royal highness]). I read a chapter for him and was offered very agreeable conditions: six thousand for the preprint and ten thousand in advance. To me this optimism doesn't feel quite right.—My congratulations on that heartening democratic experience. I don't begrudge it Dr. von Staat.

Warmly, T.


*Munich*
*January 15, 1908*
*Franz Joseph-Straße*

Dear Heinrich:

Many thanks for your card and the newspaper. The bit about d'Annunzio does have its nice side, but one has the impression anyway that the excitement inspired by love of nation is being exploited in a thoroughly vain way by this little bad Wagner imitator. Or don't you think so?—We were recently at Bernstein's, who told me a great deal about the trial. A half-hour after it started Harden said to him: "Well, we might as well quit!" That's how brazenly the tendency of the trial emerged from the start. Moreover, the cultural niveau is supposed to have been unbelievable. Bernstein considers the appeal hopeless.—Here it's still cold as can be. In *R[oyal] H[ighness]* I've now gotten, thank God, to the love story. But it still has major compositional problems. Warm regards from both of us.

T.


*Polling*
*February 6, 1908*

Dear Heinrich:

Right now, finally, I'm going to take time to thank you for your moving letter from Rome. I've been so up to my ears in Munich for the last while that I didn't get around to it. Now I'm here for five or six days. Then Katja is coming for one day and we'll make the return trip together. There's a hard freeze, and conditions for writing, even aside from the ink, are not very favorable. But I stick to it for two hours every morning at my desk and narrate a little bit further. How much longer? Everything always demands much more time and space than I thought. But it probably has to be that way. It's a piece where the narration is to a great extent an end in itself. And I believe that it never gets really boring. Nor, however, is it exactly highly entertaining.

I've read your letter several times deeply engrossed. Yes, Rome. I'd like to know how it would affect my spirits if I saw the old places again. Perhaps not at all. To myself I often seem really indifferent. My style of working makes me rigid and apathetic. The only thing that would keep one fresh is likely the opposite: improvisation and occasional poems.—It is so beautiful, what you write about the Spanish Steps. I'm sure I'll never be able to admire a set of steps that way. This ability to freely enjoy beautiful sights is no doubt the main thing for which you have to thank your "effortless youth." I don't have it; during those years in which one probably develops something like that I was quite likely mired too deeply in difficult subjective matters.—I never would have thought that Herr Dräge would still be there. Were you also in Genzano, where we always were? By the fountain at the Villa B. I wrote part of "Little Lizzy"; it was among the first of my things that impressed you.—I often dream of taking a trip to Rome someday with Katja. I do think after all that my experience of the change in times would be gratifying. One has, ultimately, "accomplished something." Hopefully I'll be doing that much better again after another ten years. Sometimes I think that, if my body holds out, I'll have my best times between fifty and sixty.—

The details of the trial Bernstein related to me, I've already lost track of a little. They were such "imponderables." In any case, the tendency as a whole was shameless. Bernstein had half of his questions disallowed by the presiding judge as "leading questions." Whereby the judge himself and the prosecutor used all available means to intimidate the witnesses. Elbe is supposed to have been pressured unmercifully (with all kinds of threats of exposure and scandals), and the prosecutor threatened Dr. Hirschfeld (who is himself homosexual) with "very unpleasant" questions in the case that . . . , etc. Harden's concluding statement, which is supposed to have been excellent, was garbled by the press; in particular, a brilliant attack on the press was unanimously omitted (with burning scorn, he addressed the journalists directly and on that occasion unsettled even the court). Grautoff, who was briefly in Berlin, visited Harden. He reportedly made a very broken impression, but then seems already to have regained his health sufficiently to write, and *just hasn't found the tone*. Siegfr. Jacobsohn is supposed to have asserted, "according to Stilke's (?) estimate," that the number of subscriptions to the *Z[ukunft]* have dropped from eighteen thousand to two thousand. His explanation is that the public got too close a look at Harden, and that's the worst part. I don't know how much of that is accurate. But I'm afraid that Harden's *power* (which is all his pride) has been broken by the trial—and he may not be able to get it back. He feels that and that's why he "hasn't found the tone." It is a pity.

And in Berlin the Werdandi-Bund has just been formed, and that, as Uncle Friedl would say "is the most scandalous" of all. Privy Councillor Thode, Wagner's son-in-law, sad to say, is the chairman, and in its first call to action the Bund has formulated in unbelievable German a most emphatic stand in favor of health and German feeling in art. It's the most disgusting thing one can imagine, and Nordhausen has already welcomed it joyfully [in] the *Neueste*. That Wagner's name is mixed up with it by virtue of that ass Thode could be vexing, but in the end it's quite right. It always does me good to realize what a ridiculous misunderstanding underlies Wagner's bourgeois popularity. Thank God, one finally has the true Wagner for oneself.

Have you read the essay about you in the *Neue Revue?* A schoolboy. The "gothic festival of spires rising in the heavy sea air" and the ["]dawning majesty reaching defiantly and dreamily for the heavenly azure." On the other hand, a Florentine paper, *Nuova antologia*, has suddenly and remarkably published an extensive review about me in which I'm described as "ingegno acuto ed anima sensibile e raffinata." It's just as well, then, if I don't join the Werdandi-Bund.

Your card has just come. As soon as I'm back in Munich, I'll get the document.—Yes, it is a good joke that Aram's critique and your essay are in the same issue. Those editors will see nothing more from me. The merest tact would have dictated in that case that they also save the beginning of my piece for the February issue. As of today (the 6th), by the way, I haven't yet received the February issue. Nor the fee. Never again.

We entertained for the first time recently (fourteen people) and it went off respectably.

Till we meet, T.


*Munich*
*April 29, 1908*
*Franz Joseph-Str. 2*

Dear Heinrich:

The weather is rainy but warm. Now, in any case, it won't get cold again so we're spreading our wings. We're thinking of leaving on the evening of the 2nd, staying a day in Verona (or Vicenza), and arriving in Venice on the 4th. A meeting in Bozen is thus probably not the right thing; we both prefer the ease of the overnight trip. It would be very nice if Ines came. With her and Carla we would then be quite a group. But I do believe that it's better for everyone to arrange for their own rooms, since it's not certain Carla will come, Ines is coming only for a few days, and I don't really know what kind of accommodations you want. In short, making the reservations is too complicated for me. We might not reserve at all. There will surely be something available.

I recently spoke with Langen in the theater. The plan is there, but the performance is uncertain and, in any case, is still a long ways off. I've done what I could as to recommending Ewers, and L[angen] assured me he's willing to remember him if things ever get serious.

Ah, so the "box of paintings" I was informed fourteen days ago was being sent by order of a H[err] Gustav Wolff by a shipping agent in Rome is from you. Wetsch now has it, and it was supposed to have cost 31.50 marks for transport. I asked the agent for an explanation but received no answer. So now we'll have it picked up and shall keep it for you.

From Harden in person. His spirits were lifted considerably by the outcome of the local trial, despite persistent sleeplessness. He doesn't any longer think that Eulenburg will appear in court at all. The case will be dragged out forever on account of illness, etc., or else Eulenburg will be let off. Isenbiel, in any case, is now in a mess. May things turn out deservedly badly for him. The Munich proceedings are supposed to have been very dramatic and the *bon juge* Meyer the opposite of the presiding judge in Berlin. Yes, Bavaria. Unfortunately, I wasn't able to get hold of Bernstein; otherwise I would have been there.

The Insel-Verlag hasn't sent it yet. Hopefully it will soon.

May your tooth problems come quickly to an end. Clear memories make me capable of compassion.

Warmest regards to Ines and you from both of us.

T.


*Munich*
*June 10, 1908*
*Franz Joseph-Str.*

Dear Heinrich:

I had really completely forgotten that the letter from Löhr began with birthday wishes. I sent it to you for the sake of convenience and only for that reason. Forgive me if it seemed otherwise.

I was quite worried by the news of your illness. Good, at least, that you have Hartungen there. I hope from my heart that your recovery comes more quickly than you think. Please keep me informed.

I was probably too impatient with the Fontane. It happens easily to me in regard to books I've loaned. I hope Ines isn't irritated. I console myself with the thought that Ines ended up buying herself a good book.

Katja got the slippers for you, from Tiez. Supposedly they're not very pretty, but neither were they expensive, so you can buy yourself a nicer pair soon in good conscience. There weren't any better ones to be found at the moment.

Before we move to Tölz we want to visit Lula in Starnberg. She is supposed to be exhausted and have aged, for which her pathetic little man is largely responsible, as I'm only now realizing; his favorite topics, as everyone knows, are war, cancer, and poverty. In short, Lula deserves much sympathy.—I'm working regularly and dying of boredom. Get well soon!

T.


*[Munich]*
*September 30, 1908*
*Franz Joseph-Str. 2*

Dear Heinrich:

Here you have Bie's answer. It is rather incomplete. In particular he doesn't answer my question about whether he can have your novel start *immediately* following mine, that is, in the June issue at the latest. Now you have to think over whether you want to submit your manuscript to him or not.

Won't you come over sometime in the evening? Thursday the Loehrs are coming by, and Saturday we're going to *Antony and Cleopatra*. Give us a call! Since the weather is nice, we could spend the afternoon on the Wiese.

Warm regards,

T.


*Munich*
*November 10, 1908*

Dear Heinrich:

So is the air really as dry in Nice as Nietzsche always claimed? I'm glad that you've finally gotten there and can form an opinion.—I'll go ahead and keep your manuscript, but I can't imagine that Bie wouldn't accept it eagerly.—Today was the discussion in the Reichstag. But I don't have great hopes for it, since the report has already been refused. An early telegram says that Bülow is supposed to have looked "grave *but vigorous.*"— *R[oyal] H[ighness]* is progressing rapidly just now toward its operatic conclusion.

Warm regards, from Katja too.

T.

*Munich*
*December 7, 1908*
*Franz Joseph-Str. 2*

Dear Heinrich:

I got a letter today from Fischer: He, Bie, and Heimann have come to the agreement that *The Small Town* is not suitable for publication in installments in the *Rundschau.* If it's of any value to you, Heimann should explain the decision in more detail. You probably won't want that, and I shall write Fischer in that sense. He, however, added the following to his rejection: "For me the matter is such that my press would be very pleased to take on your brother's works if it were to be his desire to transfer his future output to me. I would then, of course, bring out the present novel in book form."

So you have to think that over.

As Katja already wrote to you, I'm not in a letter-writing state. For the *N[eue] Fr[eie] Pr[esse]* I turned out a worthless little piece, on account of the 300 marks, which I need for Christmas presents. It begins like this:

"Tell you a story? But I don't know any. Well, yes, after all, here is something I might tell." And on it goes in that vein.

The Vienna excursion was really as fine as could be, given that someone actually said right to my face that people were much more looking forward to you. The major event was probably the half day with Hofmannsthal in Rodaun, by which I remain quite enchanted to this day. When he was reading to me from his comedy he wore a pair of glasses, just like you.

Neither my fatigue nor my nervous flutter is improved by the news that you are also doing poorly. Hofmannsthal was likewise completely at an end and incapable of work when I was in Vienna. It's remarkable how it is precisely the best who are all working at the edge of exhaustion. Hopefully you can finish your novel soon, in the significance and value of which I *firmly believe.* I wish I could believe half as much in *R[oyal] H[ighness]*, from which I anticipate a miserable fiasco. Well, I have all kinds of other things in reserve.

Warm regards, from Katja as well, and get well soon.

Today we were with Inez at Mama's for tea.

Please convey my regards to Herzog and my congratulations on the Schiller Prize. The edition is very, very nice. I'm already looking forward to the next volume.

T.

Harden is speaking here soon on "the political situation."

*Munich*
*December 22, 1908*

Dear Heinrich:

We are having a small Christmas gift sent to you today. Hopefully it is welcome and *suited*—specifically—to you. If not, it may be returned without hesitation.

All the best to you, and accept warm regards from Katja and,

T.


*Munich*
*December 27, 1908*
*Franz Joseph-Str. 2*

Dear Heinrich:

Your bonbonnière is delicious. Please accept the most sincere thanks in Katja's and my name!

Hopefully you are doing better. I wish the holiday season, with its irregularities, were over. The children were delightful, just as it says in books, when we were passing out presents. Now they are twice as unruly as usual. Hofmannsthal sent me his poems with a dedication for Christmas; that pleased me almost more than anything.

A Happy New Year!

T.


*Munich*
*March 25, 1909*
*Franz Joseph-Str. 2*

Dear Heinrich:

Warm congratulations on your birthday!

Since I can't yet send you *R[oyal] H[ighness]*, you'll have to make do with the new edition of *L[ittle] Herr Friedemann*, which has been somewhat expanded. "The Hungry" is a kind of preliminary study to "Tonio Kröger" and once appeared in *Die Zukunft.* "Railway Accident" I did recently for the *Neue Freie Presse.*

I hope you're doing tolerably well. Is *The Small Town* finished?

I've had to undergo another annoying massage treatment for my intestines. Otherwise I'm doing so-so and preparing several things: an essay, which is supposed to contain all sorts of contemporary criticism, and a story, which ideally would take up where *R[oyal] H[ighness]* leaves off, but have a different atmosphere and, I think, contain a bit of the "eighteenth century," so to speak. It seems to me altogether as if I were entering a new period, as Schaukal would say.

We expect Katja to deliver by the day and by the hour. God grant that it proceed smoothly. Katja sends her warm regards and congratulations.

Your T.


*Munich*
*April 1, 1909*
*Franz Joseph-Str. 2*

Dear Heinrich:

Your letter troubled me a great deal and affected me deeply—especially since my resistance is not very high in the moment. The seventeen hours with Katja were also a severe trial for me, and even now I'm quite incapable of concentrating properly to write about the Ines-Lula problem, as much as it's been on my mind since reading your letter. Let me say one thing primarily, which is that you are treating the matter in the precipitous and strident fashion that is part of your genius, but which is far too severe, too intellectual, too passionate for the small, real-life case called "Lula." For the sake of your own health and nerves, which truly are too valuable for you to let them be consumed by such trifles as these, I ask you sincerely to regard the affair more calmly, much more calmly! If Lula and Ines can't stand each other, that's not really so astounding, for they have really very different natures and clever people don't have to get gray hairs over such feminine antipathies. Lula can say that she, when she refused the invitation, no longer had any reason to regard Ines as your betrothed. She had heard that there was no such tie in the offing and so she said: "Either—or. If she's not his betrothed, then she's a stranger and has nothing to do with me." Things that aren't clear-cut she doesn't understand. And as far as the visit in the pension is concerned, Lula can appeal with complete justice to the fact that Katja didn't visit Ines either. Evidently, that's not proper, but no one gave it a thought, me either. Who's going to be so precise about things anyway! Start with yourself and ask yourself whether, in social matters—for example, in relation to my in-laws— you haven't always done exactly what you wanted! And Ines herself! Lula is a mass of weaknesses and willfulness, but that she is always five times more disciplined than Ines, about that—a thousand pardons!—there can be no doubt! No one took offense at Ines's behavior in Venice, in Munich, in Tölz; Katja and I, at least, have always accepted her just as she is. But that she has forfeited the right to be particularly critical from her standpoint, that I do find to be the case.* Be fair and distinguish the light from the shad-

---

*Katja's mother called on Ines three times to visit. She didn't come. That was, if you will, a serious affront. All right, she doesn't want to.

ows! How do you know, anyway, that Lula didn't want to come to Mama's that time? You never needed to find that out and shouldn't have found it out. Did Ines criticize Lula to you (the way she criticized me to Mama, that I had been ugly to her in Venice!)? I would find that almost as improper as Lula's refusal. Moreover, if she is no longer your fiancée, she has no right to set you and your sister at odds. Or does she believe that there's nothing left there to destroy? I have the impression that she was unfavorably prepared for Lula, that you had put too much in her head from the start about bourgeois propriety and narrowness. Poor, silly Mama is to blame for a lot of it; her behavior through the whole thing has been as clumsy as possible. It's not on account of her good services if things between Ines and us are not just as they are between Ines and Lula. That the birthday present was from her you will have learned in the meantime, and hopefully you were aware of a mild tendency to find the misunderstanding amusing. If Mama now finds out that you've sent it back, it will be a great pity, and there will be crying fits and two confused letters a day to you and us. Remember that she gets weaker and more prone to worry with each passing year! In your place, I would write her a very soothing letter!

It disturbs me to hear that you are reading *R[oyal] H[ighness]* in the *Rundschau*. I'm afraid that you're not in a state right now to take the game I set in motion there, in the sense of my book, with regard to our fraternal relationship in the way that it must be taken. If only it were not that the tone is even all too well captured there. How would it have been if you had said to Lula: "Listen, Ines is expecting you to repay her visit, you have to go"? Don't you think she would have gone? Somewhat less unfamiliarity and stiffness! Somewhat more frankness and behavior befitting brothers and sisters! I always find that brothers and sisters shouldn't be able to have such fallings-out at all. They laugh unmercifully or scream at each other, but they don't get into a dither and leave each other. Think back on Beckergrube No. 52! Everything else is secondary!— Well, that's probably enough of my all-too-good-natured babble; but there's some truth in it, believe me! Katja had a fever yesterday, which caused me a pretty fright. But it was nothing and everything is back in order today.

This morning, as I entered my room, the Zeppelin maneuvered over right in front of my window. The rooftops black with people, the whole city on its feet, great excitement. Impressive nevertheless.

Farewell, dear Heinrich, I hope to receive some more friendly lines from you soon: also about *The Little Town*. I think *Nord und Süd* will bite. Dr. Osborn, the new editor, is a cultured man.

Warmly, Your T.

Katja's delivery was very difficult and painful. With not much left to go resort had to be made to the forceps, because the child's heartbeat was becoming weak. The child is once again of Mucki's type, slender and somewhat Chinese-like. It is supposed to be called Angelus, Gottfried, Thomas.

*Munich*
*April 5, 1909*

Dear Heinrich:

Your letter was a great relief to me. My warm thanks for it and for the beautiful flowers, which were a genuine pleasure for Katja.—*Die Zukunft* really is a good magazine. Taine by Sänger and Merezhkovskii on Gogol. And I recommend to you the little article by Scheffler about G. Hirth in the back of the *Rundschau;* as something that is first rate here, but seems inane measured against Berlin's grand, ambitious, European standard. Day before yesterday I was in illustrious company: Mottl, Kaulbach, Knorr, Maffei, Speidl (adorned with all his medals). But, my God, how one's provincial reverence is disappointed on such occasions! If I had to depict such company, such a salon, my provincial's disappointment would always be there between the lines.

Warm regards, T.


*Munich*
*May 10, 1909*
*Franz Josef-Str. 2*

Dear Heinrich:

Things are not the best with me either, and I have therefore decided to bid farewell to the world and all the good things in life for three or four weeks and go to Bircher-Brenner, a hygienic penitentiary in Zurich that has become famous for its results. I'm leaving this evening.

I'm supposed to pass on the enclosed materials to you from Grautoff. Hopefully you'll let yourself be ensnared by his flattery.

Thank you for your card and warm regards. The family is well.

T.


*Zurich*
*June 3, 1909*
*Bircher-Brenner*

Dear Heinrich:

Many thanks for your letter. You are completely right about the Martini scene; I've had the same feeling from the start and still couldn't let go, don't want to cut it even now. In dealing with it myself, I always appeal to Ibsen, who gives his Skule such a scene with a poet ("The gift of sorrow"). The danger that this involves, drawing attention to the distinction between conventional and true majesty, I'm not so afraid of. The distinction is not made at all in the book, and I don't believe that a reader will find Axel Martini's majesty more real than that of Klaus Heinrich. It is just another form. But the bad thing is that it is *the* form that all the other forms of majesty symbolize, and now suddenly it itself appears, clad intellectually in the same irony that permeates the whole. The poet's envy for the young Weber I don't regard as false. For this type of envy and desire, within this (intellectually very self-contained) book, practically belongs to majesty. It must be considered that the tendency of the book, even if with a somewhat insidious didactic strain, is to point to *life* or at least to a compromise between majesty and life. The young Weber, as a representative of life, is an example of this insidiousness, and envy of him belongs absolutely to the humor of the whole. All the same: the scene is faulty. A couple of lively details will distract the average reader from it. We others will learn something from it; and thus might I allow the mistake to stand.

I'm leaving here on the 5th, headed directly home, in hopes of a lasting effect. There's so much work waiting for me there that I don't know where to start. Hopefully Tölz will bring me calm and resolve.

Till we meet! T.


*Bad Tölz*
*September 30, 1909*
*Landhaus Thomas Mann*

Dear Heinrich:

Your reading for the booksellers is today. I've thought a good deal about coming to Munich for it. But, first of all, Ines will probably be there, for whom a meeting with me would presumably not be pleasant; and then I'm not doing well, I'm stuck in my work, feeling forlorn and tired.

The mass in the cathedral moved me deeply yesterday. Today I'm cheered by the return of the lawyer. The whole reads like a hymn of praise to democracy, and one gets the impression that only a democracy of great men is possible. That's not true, but under the impression of your writing, one believes it. And one is inclined to believe too, under this impression, in the "righteousness of the people," although that is probably even less true, unless, that is, "the people" is replaced by "time" or "history." I have my doubts, for example, as to whether "the people" will do justice to this book when it comes out; but I do definitely believe that one day it will garner much attention. Besides, who knows? Maybe that's already destined for the present. It has much in it that is contemporary in a lofty and progressive sense. I'm very curious about the effect it will have—actually much more curious than about the same question in regard to *R[oyal] H[ighness]*.

Warm regards, T.

*Munich*
*October 23, 1909*
*Arcisstraße 12*

Dear Heinrich:

So as far as we can tell we'll leave Wednesday evening and be in Milan on Thursday. Please reserve two one-bed rooms (or possibly one with two beds, if that's more economical).—Katja thanks you a thousand times, provisionally through me, for the extremely lovely picture book.

Most warmly, T.


*Munich*
*December 12, 1909*
*Franz Joseph-Str. 2*

Dear Heinrich:

Well we've arrived back happily after some active weeks. There was much unexpected excitement for me in Berlin—and on account of *Fiorenza*, which was suddenly supposed to be performed by the Akademische Bühne, while I've been as good as agreed with Reinhardt since the summer. Well, there was much protesting and weighing and conferring, and finally I held a reading for the students, who had gone to great expense, in the Kroll'sches Opernhaus, which was nearly empty because in the rush no one thought to lower the price and everyone had naturally returned their 6- to 12-mark tickets. A really wild story in its details.

Herewith two clippings. The *Echo* so you can see how Servaes has changed and for the eagerly awaited Busse. He leaves no room for hope, but within this hopelessness he turns out to be an almost sympathetic figure, serious and sad. You would appeal more to him. Otherwise nothing else worth reading has come. How do you find Bahr? Wassermann, whom I saw in Berlin, promises a *long* essay for the spring, in installments—political, aesthetic, and covering all aspects.—Please send the two excerpts along *to Mama*.

Ewers writing about you is actually surprisingly nice, with an obvious sensitivity for the magnitude of the matter. Now I want to read the *L[ittle] T[own]* over again less hurriedly.

How are you?

Warm regards from Katja too.

T.

*Munich*
*December 18, 1909*
*Franz Josef-Str. 2*

Dear Heinrich:

I'm sending you, as printed matter, an Italian article to read about *R[oyal] H[ighness]*. I didn't understand very much of it, not even the title. Perhaps you would give me a rough explanation of its standpoint.

I'd also like to take this opportunity to ask you the following. In Nice we spoke about the present state of your finances and the particular disadvantages it poses in precisely your current circumstances. If you are bored and the climate in Nice is not agreeing with you and a shortage of money is preventing you from traveling on, to Palermo, for example, or Africa, and doing so in an appropriate style—in short, if a couple thousand marks would help you get through this break in your work more pleasantly, then I can't stand by without asking you to share a bit, without giving it a second thought, in the economic fruits of *R[oyal] H[ighness]*. This proposal was already on the tip of my tongue in Nice, but I thought *The Little Town* would help you out. Now it really does seem that the publisher's ineptitude has wasted a lot of potential. For a book as contemporary as this one, as timely in the highest sense, a much more serious, even political, publicity program needed to be undertaken. And from my side, I've done so well this year that I can painlessly do without a couple thousand marks. You could spend it as befits your convenience, without having worries about paying it back. Please, if this would be of use to you, let me know right away.

Warm regards. T.


*[Munich]*
*December 21, 1909*

Dear Heinrich,

The collar pouch is from us and we hope it's welcome. Best wishes and regards from both of us,

T. and K.


*Munich*
*December 30, 1909*

Dear Heinrich:

Many thanks for the *Pester Lloyd*, which, along with the previous one *and* a review from the *B.Z. am Mittag* (received today), I'm passing on to Mama. The *Lloyd* is really very acceptable, indeed gratifying. There's no doubt that you are altogether mistaken when you talk of a "fiasco." It *cannot* be any but a purely commercial, wholly apparent one. Something like that never gets ignored, that's impossible. It's too solid and too lofty for that. I recently spoke to Heymel—no luminary, but listening to him is listening to an entire circle. He talks about you as people in his sphere really only talk about George (or used to talk, for G. has come in for very sharp criticism lately, which will hopefully do him good). These externalities are just happenstance. I have to hope that one can have them without being an idiot and I'm convinced that you can also have them any day. But their absence mustn't confuse you about your real effect.

T.


*Munich*
*January 10, 1910*
*Franz Josef-Str. 2*

Dear Heinrich:

Enclosed are two texts that needn't be returned. Of the lead article in the *Frankfurter [Zeitung]* I'm properly proud. If the Schickele plan is serious, you should absolutely take part so that the political message comes directly from you. The *L[ittle] T[own]* is much more above average than *R[oyal] H[ighness]*. Incidentally, Jaffe told me that he did a good business with the *L[ittle] T[own]* over Christmas.

I'm gathering, noting, and studying for the confessions of the confidence man, which will probably become my strangest work. Working on it surprises me sometimes at the things I'm finding in myself. But it is unhealthy work and not good for the nerves. Perhaps that is why Kerr really has succeeded now in enervating me and disturbing my work. In the *Tag* he'd already spit a couple of times in my direction. Now, in an essay about Shaw, he's smuggled the following sentence into the *[Neue] Rundschau:* "He does not boast like your *middling novel-makers. Any eccentrically neurasthenic clerk or old sanatorium patient who one day takes to writing novels is going to depict himself in a high social position and cover up his Achilles tendon* [sic] *in fiction.*" How do you like that? Naturally no one notices it but me, but that's precisely what's refined about it. If he'd even just left the word "social" out and written "in a high position," Bie would have noticed something and cut the sentence. I have to confess that it made me very ill for days. I have no psychological use for enemies and certainly not for such a disgusting sort of enmity as that; I'm not prepared for it. But if ever he really takes a stand, attacks me in a way that can be generally understood, then he'll fare worse in the polemic with me than he did with that poor Sudermann.

Warm regards! T.

*Munich*
*January 26, 1910*
*Franz Josef-Str. 2*

Dear Heinrich:

So the *B[erliner] T[ageblatt]* is a worthy little paper after all. True that Monty Jacobs is not quite equal to the task, but he didn't miss *everything*, and it remains remarkable that it would be left to this paper to publish something warm and positive. Political orientation probably does predispose one to an understanding of certain things or at least to sympathy for them.—I likewise gave the Sauer essay to Mama to read. You did receive it? It is very fine, even if she considers the two books much too exclusively from an artistic standpoint. Approximately the opposite of Bahr. And I gave Mama the article by Frost in *Die Zukunft*. Satisfied as she was, she found it "somewhat pompous," with a certain justice, it seems to me. The most significant bit must be the passage where she celebrates you as a depicter of the time, of modernity. I've sensed something similar as well and told you so, when I alluded to that certain affinity with Reinhardt. In any case, the fact of the article in *Die Zukunft* is very, very gratifying.

Concerning *R[oyal] H[ighness]*, I've not gotten to see much of an encouraging nature since Bahr. Criticism is decidedly ill-inclined to consider the book as whole, to take it quite seriously, and I have the impression that the success—in the higher sense—of yours is much greater. Even those most well disposed have doubts about the comic ending; the "austere happiness" reminded someone of Sudermann. The whole thing, or at least the second half, is being taken for a bit of carnival fun, a view for which I am probably somewhat responsible since I characterized it as an "epic jest" in the initial blurb. The review by the Literarhistorische Gesellschaft in Bonn is truly touching; but not even the gentle, knowledgeable scholar who wrote it believes in the "solution of the insoluble." I'm gradually coming not to believe in it myself. The ending probably is a bit popularly skewed— as is ultimately the ending of *Zwischen den Rassen*. Fundamentally, of course, Überbein is right; and one who was already planning a *Friedrich* before *R[oyal] H[ighness]* probably never fully believed himself in "austere marital bliss." Which doesn't prevent one from believing in it in a practical sense.

Your letter about Kerr did me a great deal of good and helped further my digestion of that disagreeable morsel. The whole thing is now forgotten.

Warm regards from Katja too.

T.

*Munich*
*February 17, 1910*

Dear Heinrich:

May the two *mille* be of some assistance. The "larger expenses" were probably swallowed up by *le Gâté* [?]? What you say about the Insel-Verlag really impresses me. It goes to show that he regards you highly and believes in you. I hear only enthusiastic praise for *The Little Town*. Everyone pronounces it your best book—and it's the last thing you wrote. Soon, properly rested, you'll begin again.—Once again, I can't get started and find a hundred excuses for it. What I have is the psychological material, but there's a hitch in the plot, in the narrative details. And I have to be careful that I don't lose control of it and that it doesn't happen again that story material turns into a novel. I'm reading Kleist's prose to get a proper grip on myself and after "Kohlhaas" was furious with Goethe, who rejected him on account of his "hypochondria" and his "contradictory spirit." His "Verlobung in St. Domingo," a fine example of narrative art, Goethe ignored to death, while the drama, *Toni*, which *Körner* made of it, he received warmly and read at court, even designing a set for it. This for your Goethe-Voltaire chapter.

Best regards, from Katja too.

—T.

*Munich*
*February 20, 1910*

Dear Heinrich,

My hearty congratulations for your strong, beautiful letter in *Die Zukunft*. The person to whom it is addressed . . . is in my opinion not altogether worthy of it and incapable of sharing your belief and verve. That simply makes your words the more necessary, and they will have a most fortunate effect on the impact of your book. Are you not slowly returning to your big essay? It certainly looks that way. My best wishes and regards!

T.

*Munich*
*March 16, 1910*
*Franz Josef-Str. 2*

Dear Heinrich:

Enclosed are your trophies, which brought me great pleasure. Heartfelt congratulations! Thus it is. As soon as *Der Tyrann* was staged, it became worth the effort to write articles about it; not before. Hopefully Reinhardt will now follow suit.

As a result of righteous indignation of a wholly non-egoistic sort, I've gotten involved in a public polemic with an abject fool (Carla's former critic Lessing), which has not yet come to an end and has completely reduced me to nervous hand-wringing.

I was also blessed with another little joy. One of Katja's brothers ran into the Schmied siblings at a ball for Reinhardt's theatrical school in Berlin. Ines's brother introduced himself to Katja's brother as an "intimate friend" and admirer of yours, adding that the former should convey to me the opinion that I had written an extraordinarily shallow and bad novel by the name of *Ryl Highness.* Response: "You must tell him yourself. I refuse to carry out the errand." But it reached me anyway through a third party. If the young Schmied was drunk, that excuses him stating the opinion, but not the opinion itself—which, therefore, must be that of your fiancée and those in your circle altogether. The best thing about us has never been our friends.

Warmly, T.


*Munich*
*March 20, 1910*
*Franz Josef-Str. 2*

Dear Heinrich:

I should be sorry if I caused you even temporary distress through my quite trifling stories—how ashamed I am that I allow them to distress myself. Of my two "enemies," the one is a poor simpleton, the other nothing but a silly babbler. That I let myself get involved with the former one at all was finally only the result of a desperate need for something to do. The secret truth is that I couldn't get going on *The Confidence Man;* the torment of idleness caused me to lash out, of that I'm quite conscious myself, only further exhausting my energy. Now I have to see how I can regain some of my vigor. You should have all the facts of the matter, if the April 1 *Liter[arisches] Echo* is available. Otherwise you wouldn't understand the circumstances leading up to it.

The Reinhardt matter is very problematic. Only a couple of weeks ago I finally got him to sign the *Fiorenza* contract with Fischer, which provides for a 1,000-mark fine if the contract is broken. I almost suspect that the only reason the fox is bringing up *Der Tyrann* is to find a good way to get rid of his obligations to me and to Fischer, in that he's hoping that I'll protest the excessive shortening of the play and pull out. If a tolerably normal theater evening is to be made of it, *Fiorenza* must literally be shortened by half. That is what happened in Frankfurt and here. So if it is cut by so much that another one-act play can follow it, then there's absolutely no sense left in talking about a performance of the play—instead, the evening's program would have to read something like "Scenes from *Fiorenza* and *Der Tyrann.*" That too would be quite lovely, only it would be something other than what was originally planned, and I don't know if "Scenes from *Fiorenza*" would allow the play's intentions to be clearly communicated. I actually like more and more the idea of having the two pieces performed together;* I just ask myself whether it wouldn't harm both of them and have to tell myself that Reinhardt's claim, that otherwise he wouldn't be able to find a place for *Der Tyrann*, is only an empty phrase. Any couple of one-act plays from Strindberg would do to fill out the evening.—To correspond with R. about such questions is impossible. I will speak to him, however, in the summer when he comes here to perform and I want to arrange everything with him then. Perhaps you will also be there. *Fiorenza* is not scheduled until next season.

Warm regards! T.

Please send me your story!

*The responsibility would be less, the event the more extraordinary.

*Munich*
*March 25, 1910*

Our warm congratulations to you on your birthday!

from T. and K.

*Munich*
*June 16, 1910*
*Franz Josef-Str. 2*

Dear Heinrich:

Congratulations! For it must be a happy outcome. So how much do the payments amount to? Producing two volumes in five years will not, I think, be difficult for you, especially since story collections also count. Moreover, it is under such circumstances that the best things are produced.

Fischer gave me his answer: "The Frankfurt portion amounts to 10 percent, related operating costs to me likewise 10 percent." That is, of course, considerably less than in your case. But then it's probably all been set in consideration of the regular monthly payments.

For your quick repayment of the 1,000 marks I am very grateful. If your monthly payments are high enough, you might decide to take care of the rest in installments every three or six months. I think that would be the method I most prefer. Incidentally, allow me to stress that there's no hurry in repaying the first 2,000 marks. In my letter to you in Nice I offered you that amount for as long as you like. So this really concerns only 3,000 marks.

Katja sends her best regards. She's doing well.

Warmly, T.

*Tölz*

*August 4, 1910*

Dear Heinrich:

The photographs of Carla's body just arrived. Mama was once again overcome by her grief and it was very difficult to calm her. The bad thing is that Mama is tormented by her suspicion that she is burdening us with her mourning—a senseless notion and, since assertions to the contrary don't help, one that only makes things worse with time. Mama is constantly wanting to get away, but doesn't herself know where to. I'll be glad when you're here. On Saturday, Katja's mother and cousin are coming for the day. Mama doesn't want to see anyone, which I understand, and will accompany Aunt E[lisabeth], who's leaving, as far as Munich on that day. She also wants to go to Polling, to pick up a few things. Then on Sunday or Monday we're expecting you. It would probably be best if you went with Mama to Polling and made the trip here with her.

We're all miserable. It is the most bitter thing that could happen to me. My sense of sibling solidarity makes me feel as if Carla's act also calls our existence into question, as if it loosens our anchor. At first I was always saying to myself: "One of us!" What I meant by that I understand only now. Carla didn't think of anyone else, and you say: "So that was wrong too!" But still I can't help feeling that she was wrong to separate herself from us. She had no feeling of solidarity when she did it, didn't have the feeling of our common destiny. She acted, so to speak, *in violation of a silent pact.* It is inexpressibly bitter. I hold myself together in front of Mama. Otherwise I'm nearly always crying.

The main point of this letter is to ask you to visit Lula before you come to us. You do her an injustice, and, in my opinion, you relinquish some of your self-respect when you take *one of us* for an ordinary philistine. No one of us can be that. If you let this opportunity pass, there arises the danger that the break between you and Lula will become something just as definitive as Carla's death, yes, become something quite similar to Carla's death. I am appealing to your mind and to your heart, and would be very disappointed if you came without having spoken to Lula.

Warmly, T.

TRANSLATION, WINSTONS

*Bad Tölz*

*August 7, 1910*

*Landhaus Thomas Mann*

Dear Heinrich:

After writing you a long letter, I set it aside because I realized that with the present state of your nerves it would probably do more harm than good. And so I'll simply let you know that we are expecting you. Your letter contains much that is feverish and objectionable, much that must be strictly and firmly dismissed. I hope that talking it over will be more profitable than further correspondence, which with us always tends to take too literary a turn. Mama is not returning here until Tuesday or Wednesday. It would be a kindness if you made the trip with her.

With warm greetings from us both,

T.

*Tölz*
*September 18, 1910*

Dear Heinrich:

Many thanks for your card, and also for the piece by Kerr. Did you read in the *[Neue] Rundschau* about his gallant life in all quarters of the globe?—Only recently, when Ida ihr Pinger was here, did I notice that the book of fairy tales you gave the children is *Der Kinder Wundergarten*. I spent a whole evening reading it.—So the comedy is finished and delivered? Congratulations! Reinhardt, incidentally, is still in Munich; I saw him fleetingly following the really splendid Mahler symphony. The Confidence Man inches slowly forward.

Warmly, T.

Kind regards from me too, and many thanks for the *Weltspiegel*.

K.

*Tölz*
*October 5, 1910*

Dear Heinrich:

Thank you for your card! The Fontane, however, I found very feeble.

The enclosed proofs from the Franz Moeser, Nachf. publishing house were already here when we returned from Munich. We spent eight days moving, intermittently taking part in many theatrical doings. A breakfast at Reinhardt's was genuinely interesting.

Tomorrow we have the christening, which is also the occasion for the family coming to stay. Hopefully we'll have you here again (perhaps with Richter) in the second half of the month.

Warmly, T.

*Munich*
*November 16, 1910*
*Mauerkircher Str. 13*

Dear Heinrich:

I received your telegram in Weimar and saw immediately that in that case it wouldn't work. There is absolutely no way for me to wait until the twenty-first. I have to produce two newspaper pieces by December 8th, which, since I've not even begun them, will be finished just in time anyway. But I did hear that the Neuer Verein wants to produce at least *Der Tyrann*, and if the three are successful on the 21st, which I certainly expect, then it is probable that Reinhardt will take them over. Then I would still have the chance to see them in Berlin. I got back from Weimar this morning, where I enjoyed truly touching hospitality in the Vitzthum household. He is now a Kammerjünker and Knight of St. John, and has also gotten a bit fat, but is otherwise quite the same. All my impressions of petty court life (from stories and what I saw) exactly confirmed my intuitions in *R[oyal] H[ighness]*. There was no harm in not having been there before. Moreover, I was deeply impressed in a historical sense. What strikes one there at every turn—especially the touching scenes in the parlor, which amounts to their holy of holies—is something so much more kindred than the silly Munich tradition in painting.—Kind regards and my warmest wishes! Do send word soon, won't you!

T.


*Munich*
*November 24, 1910*
*Mauerkircher Str. 13*

Dear Heinrich:

All I know about what happened in Berlin comes from three newspapers: the *[Münchner] Neueste [Nachrichten]*, the *B[erliner] T[ageblatt]*, and the *Frankfurter [Zeitung]*—which is to say I am *un*informed, for they say nothing about the response, about the public's attitude, and the ignorant stuff they do provide is of no help. I would have liked to have had a rough sense of how the afternoon went. *Der Tag*, from which I might have gotten something of that sort (for Kerr at least knows approximately what it's all about) wasn't available. I spent the 21st regretting that I couldn't be there. But it just wasn't possible. You are still in Berlin and will stop in Munich before you go on to Vienna or southward?

With warm regards, from Katja too,

T.

*Munich*
*December 23, 1910*

Dear Heinrich:

Please take note of the enclosed text. I sent my photograph because I found the list praiseworthy.

You are being performed one evening after the other in Berlin now. That must give you a feeling of pride.

We enjoyed Christmas Eve with Mama and Vicco. Hopefully our gift suits you at least to some extent.

T.


*Munich*
*January 26, 1911*
*Mauerkircherstr. 13*

Dear Heinrich:

I've just spoken with Löhr. The result is negative. Such a deal diverges too greatly from the normal type of transaction at the B[ayerischen] H[andelsbank]. Their business is limited to Bavaria. So I think Hartungen should try to contact an Austrian bank.

The impact of your political proclamation naturally proves mixed. The *B[erliner] T[ageblatt]*, from what I hear, printed an excerpt from "Geist und That" amid praise and assent. The *D[eutsche] Tageszeitung* is about like Uncle Friedel's Maria: "the most scandalous of the lot." That's also the paper that declared that I understood no more of princedom than a German prince from the ghetto. Bahr's statement, by the way, I found quite cheap and stale. A mind like his easily succumbs to the trivial in regard to "humanity."

I returned from my trip truly gratified. It was strenuous, but offered much of a stimulating and informative nature. Very remarkable, for example, was an afternoon at Frau Stinnes's in Mühlheim-Ruhr. Likewise, however, Münster in Westphalia, which is quite a surprise, a deeply Catholic city with markedly North and Low German inhabitants and full of traditional beauties. Modern beauties are limited to the large glass-paintings by Melchior Lechter (a Münster native) in the museum; the colors really do surpass everything of their sort, even Sainte-Chapelle in Paris. Utterly wonderful.

Katja couldn't decide to leave home. She had had a slight case of the flu and was still doing somewhat poorly. She would be grateful if you would arrange a translation (French) for her to do, perhaps something from the Müller Verlag. Please think about it now and again.

Lublinski recently died of a stroke. Lessing published an obituary in the *Die Schaubühne* of such liberal mendacity it could make one sick. He doesn't fail to mention that I had revealed my "astoundingly meager humanity" back then and he characterizes the affair between him and myself as "still not settled."

Warm regards, T.

*Munich*
*March 24, 1911*
*Mauerkircherstr. 13*

Dear Heinrich:

Just when I was asking myself where I might get hold of your address quickly enough to be able to congratulate you on your fortieth birthday, your letter arrives and saves me all the searching. So, my warmest congratulations—to which Katja adds her own! At this stage in your life you will be looking back with satisfaction at the proud and bold work you have produced so far and feel yourself to be at the height of your craft and development; you will be much thought of with great respect on this day. We read your latest, "Die Rückkehr vom Hades," with great pleasure. It is something from the sphere of *The Little Town*—in its ethereal operatic beauty.

I haven't accomplished anything of note in the last few months. My indisposition, which dragged on longer than usual and really got me down, was supposedly an irritation of the appendix, but ultimately was probably just the expression of a momentary exhaustion of the central nervous system. The aftereffects are still with me and my progress on the *Confidence Man* is wretchedly slow. It might be that I'll have to consent to a few weeks of Zurich (Bircher-Brenner) after all.

I'm very curious about your three-act play. Are you getting it properly in shape for the stage? Arrangements in Berlin for my *Fiorenza* have been shamefully bungled until now. I've written an offended letter and now await explanations.

How did you like the *Pan*-Jagow affair? I didn't like it particularly, for it seems to me that the Cassierer couple played a rather unfortunate role in it. Acquaintances of ours have seen how Durieux "entangled" Jagow in the theater. Sympathies in Berlin are supposed to be on Jagow's side, and so it is probably public opinion that sustains him. Kerr's first political action is to be regarded a failure.

We're planning a Dalmatian trip in May—if life and health allow it. When are you coming to Germany?

Warm regards! T.

*Tölz*
*October 3, 1911*

Dear Heinrich:

Many thanks for your play! I believe our departed one would find it beautiful and good.

These rainy days were hard to endure, and we were already thinking of packing up. Now we've taken heart and resolved to stay a bit longer.

Are you going to give Mama the play to read? I would like to know if it's all right to talk to her about it.

Warmly, T.


*Munich*
*February 17, 1912*

Dear Heinrich:

The state of Katja's health is making very slow, barely noticeable progress. She is in the Ebenhausener Sanatorium, to get the rest she needs and is also being treated with serum injections, for which she comes to Munich from time to time. She will presumably not be allowed to stay in the city for very long at present, but will have to remain at the institute until we undertake our annual trip and can move out to Tölz. The sanatorium stay involves substantial extraordinary costs, and you know how stressed our budget is anyway—a consequence of the whole style of our life. I therefore have no choice but to ask you seriously and urgently now that we're so pressed to give somewhat more thought than previously to the repayment of the money you owe us. For—if my calculations are not entirely wrong—you are now a man of roughly 10,000 marks annual income; your economic situation is therefore much more favorable than mine, since you are alone, don't have four children, nor four servants, a country house, and a 5,000-mark apartment in the city. Given some effort it would have had to have been easy for you, in monthly or quarterly installments, as I proposed, to have taken care of the major portion of your debt by now. Admittedly, it's never easy to pay debts. From numerous experiences with quite different kinds of debtors, I know that it must be hard, even when one probably could, and especially when one feels justified saying to oneself: "He doesn't need it." But I do need it. Our household is so arranged that Katja's annuity is too little by far to cover expenses and I personally have to earn a considerable amount if we want to manage. Well, recently I've earned very little; what I'm working on in the moment is interesting but not lucrative, and until *The Confidence Man* is published I'll have little income to speak of. My reserves are depleted except for what I've unwisely lent out to various persons, and if those who owe me money don't make a bit of an effort I simply won't be able to pay the rent come April 1. Then I would have to turn to Fischer for an advance, which would not be pleasant for me, for he's going to have to wait a long time yet for a big manuscript. I'm reluctant to approach my father-in-law, both for reasons of my self-esteem and because his business is going badly, his funds are mainly tied up in the collection, and it would possibly cause him embarrassment. That I'm also running this risk with you I consider out of the question; otherwise I wouldn't admonish you. So please accept this request and attend to it!

Warmly, T.

TRANSLATION, WINSTONS/RENEAU

*Munich*
*April 2, 1912*
*Mauerkircherstr. 13*

Dear Heinrich:

The 500 marks arrived in order yesterday. Many thanks. They are very welcome. I have conveyed your greetings and good wishes to Katja. She writes cheerful letters and already feels much better. The doctors up there say that her case is not serious but tedious. She will have to stay in the mountains six months—and should certainly have gone up long ago. The injection treatment (which Dr. Ebenhausen advised against) caused extensive nervous damage. I couldn't stop her because the idea was that it would avoid the long separation from the children.

Things are rather hard for me now, but aside from a few days of illness I have never entirely stopped working, and I hope *Death in Venice* will be finished before I go to Davos (beginning of May). It is something very singular at the least, and although you won't approve of it as a whole, you won't be able to deny certain felicities. An archaizing chapter in particular seems to me successful. The story will be published first in a limited edition by Hans von Weber, in a deluxe format.

I am looking forward to your play with extraordinary eagerness. Dr. von Jakobi, who visited recently, told me something about it.

Warm regards! T.


*Munich*
*April 13, 1912*

Dear Heinrich:

Cassirer sent to you "in care of" me 399.91 marks in royalties, Neues Theater Frankfurt a/M. Should I keep it? In that case, many thanks!

T.

*Munich*
*April 27, 1912*
*Mauerkircherstr. 13*

Dear Heinrich:

Forgive me for not answering your letter until today. I could not get to it at once. In addition to the usual afternoon correspondence I now have the regular reports to Katja.

Congratulations on the completion of the play! I wish I could say the same for my novella, but I can't find the conclusion. Perhaps I'll have to wait for the change of air in Davos in mid-May to help me along. My vitality is extremely low right now.

The military: My recollections of it are quite dreamy and hazy, mostly intangibles, matters of atmosphere that can't really be transmitted as facts, although I shall be able to bring it all into the penitentiary episode in *The Confidence Man*. My chief memory is the sensation of being hopelessly cut off from the civilized world, subject to a terrible, over-powering external pressure; and in connection with that, feeling an extraordinarily enhanced enjoyment of inner freedom—when, for example, in the barracks, while cleaning my rifle (which I never learned how to do properly) I whistled something from *Tristan*. But I suppose the patrioteer would not react that way. Even if he is averse to bourgeois attitudes, he would necessarily succumb completely to the spirit of this isolated world, as I saw the other conscripts doing. Does he *want* to be freed? Then let him do as I did and from the start seek a connection to the civilian world, with whose help he can free himself. I took refuge behind Mama's doctor, Hofrat May (whom I have used in *The Confidence Man* as Health Councillor Düsing), an ambitious ass who was friendly with my chief medical officer. In the regiment you scarcely come into contact with the chief medical officer; you're dependent on his subordinate, the junior medical officer, who examines you and sends you to the "infirmary" (the barracks sickroom for light cases) or to the hospital, or else orders you back to duty, etc. This medical officer was extremely coarse with me. "Who are you, what do you want," was his tone. During examinations, which I most respectfully insisted upon, he made outrageous speeches and would say, for example, that he had to light a cigar or else he would faint (from disgust). The result was "Back to duty. Enough. Dismissed." Dr. May, however, talked with the chief medical officer, who sent for me right on the drill ground and had me up to his room for examination. He seemed unable to find anything definite, but declared that I was to continue on duty only "for the present"; he would see what could be done. "With *that* foot . . ." After a few days an infirmary aide took a print of my foot on charcoaled paper. I had been treated in the hospital for "inflamed flatfoot," but the print showed that there could be no question of a flatfoot. Now, however, the chief medical officer came paper in hand to the infirmary where I was waiting, and where the medical officer was also present. The scene was marvelous and most appropriate for your novel. The chief medical officer, cap on his head, enters with aplomb, plants himself in front of the medical officer, and gazes bleakly and severely at the latter's cap. The medical officer, who is used to associating with him as a colleague, snatches off his cap in astonishment and stands at attention. Thereupon the chief medical officer shows him the paper, speaks to him in a low voice, and commands him to see something that isn't there. The medical officer blinks alternately at his superior, at me and at the paper, and agrees, clicking his heels. From that moment on he was exceedingly polite to me and treated me as a gentleman. He knew I had higher connections. A few weeks passed because of official formalities; then I was on the "outside." Most amusing example of corruption. Generally it is considered very difficult to get out once you're in.

In contrast, there was a case of idiotic severity which made a great impression on me right at the start. In other companies of one-year volunteers, infirmary cases (not hospital cases, that is) were allowed to take to their beds at home after the first fourteen days of illness (which are spent entirely in the barracks). Our captain forbade this. One soldier fell sick in the evening and next morning ran a temperature of 104 degrees, so that he was quite unable to make it to the barracks. He went through the illness at home and when he recovered brought a certificate from his doctor. For "punishment" he was confined to the barracks for a very long time—months, I think, which is very hard on these one-year volunteers. He had to sleep in the squad room, etc. Crazy. But the captain wore an expression of immense pride on such occasions. "My company," he used to say, "is going to be a company of *soldiers*." And as a matter of fact the company was called the Iron Eleventh. Another item for you. In connection with "squad room," I just remembered an incident: Someone was actually released as unfit because he announced to the Chief Reserve Commission that he was homosexual. Couldn't you weave that in?

But now with the best will in the world I can't write further. I leave for Davos in the middle of May.

Warmly, T.

*Davos*
*June 8, 1912*

Dear Heinrich:

Warm thanks for you letter and my warmest congratulations on the success of your play with Cassirer!

In regard to Ewers steps are being taken, even if I don't expect much to come of them. Is there even an opening? And if so: many people want to come to Munich. But I will write him concerning whom he should approach.—I'm thinking of leaving on the 17th and, after two days in Munich, going on to Tölz. Hopefully you'll come keep me company there?

Warm regards from both of us. T.

*June 14, 1912*
*Arcisstr. 12*

Dear Heinrich:

Arrived yesterday evening, and spoke immediately this morning on the telephone
with Frau Schäuffelen (who is more active than her slightly half-witted husband), praising E. very highly as a journalist. She will write to the *Augsburger [Abendzeitung]*. E.
should do that as well, enclosing articles and mentioning my name. I've already instructed him. If any position at all is free, or one becomes free, he will now at least be
strongly considered. I turned to Frau Sch. because she's a meddler, who likes to have
her fingers in all the pies.

Tomorrow or Sunday I'm leaving for Tölz.

Warmly, T.


*Bad Tölz*
*July 17, 1912*
*Landhaus Thomas Mann*

Dear Heinrich:

Thank you for the money, which came today. I read your play in a single sitting and
with great pleasure right after I got it. Is it true that the Munich Hoftheater has already
agreed to produce it? It could do no better. Something just of that sort it can perform
very well right now. I'm very much looking forward to that evening; it is all but assured
of a good reception. Your personal acquaintance with the actors, and their respect for
you, will be a help in rehearsals.

When can we expect your visit this year? While Mama is still here? She's thinking
of staying until August 1, but she would probably let herself be persuaded to agree to
a couple more weeks: at least until August 15, when the young Dr. Frank from Paris is
coming for a few days. I'm hoping for Katja's return in the beginning of September; it
is not yet a certainty. Then for the next while we'd like not to have visitors. But in October you would be welcome once again. You could also be here the same time as Frank, or
in the time between his departure and Katja's arrival. Think it over.

Warm regards! T.

*Munich*
*November 3, 1912*
*Mauerkircherstr. 13*

Dear Heinrich:

I'm sending you the two issues of the *Rundschau* with my novella, in case you're interested in seeing where the beginning, which I read to you that time, was headed.

My head is now better (I was really getting desperate)—and so we would be pleased if you came over again one evening. On the 10th I'm leaving for a few days and Katja is going to Berlin on the 15th for two weeks. Perhaps you'll give me a call so we can agree on an evening.

Warm regards, T.


*Munich*
*November 17, 1912*

Dear Heinrich:

Many thanks for the 300 marks. Do tell me sometime, please, how much you've paid back so far. I neglected to keep track of the payments. Harden sends his regards to you. He said he would have enjoyed seeing you. We were with him almost till morning after his two-and-a-half-hour talk. In all his falseness and passion he was once again fascinating. Regardless of politics, he remains one of the most remarkable of our contemporaries. And if one thinks of "character" not so much in moral but more in aesthetic terms, in the sense of a figure, of someone playing a picturesque role—then he is also a character. He swore he was going to make his influence with Reinhardt count, so that *Fiorenza* would finally be performed. Well, yesterday I got a telegram from Moissi saying that the rehearsals were set for the coming week. (Yet again.)

Best regards from both of us. T.


*Munich*
*January 16, 1913*
*Mauerkircherstr. 13*

Dear Heinrich:

Many thanks for the money. I now have the Berlin adventure behind me. (The premiere was on the 3rd and today's is the fifth and, I believe, last performance.) It was trying, and left a bitter taste in my mouth. A fundamentally flawed performance: slow, tediously realistic, with a wretched cast but for Wegener and Strichen, which all but obliterated the sense. The public was nevertheless very attentive (Prince August Wilhelm at the head) and there was sufficient applause for the good Winterstein to bring me out on the stage twice at the end. The press the following day with few exceptions was very bad. And on the day after that Kerr! He managed to exceed all my expectations. Enclosed is his article. Read it carefully, it's worth it, and then please send it back to me. It could be that I'll still need it.

I hear from Herzog that your *première* is being put off ? What are your plans for the immediate future?

T.


*March 25, 1913*

Dear Heinrich:

I made a mistake: I wanted to ask whether you could dine here with us and Vicco on the 27th, that is, your birthday, not tomorrow. Call soon so we can let Vicco know.

T.


*Bad Tölz*
*November 8, 1913*
*Landhaus Thomas Mann*

Dear Heinrich:

Fischer writes to me that he can't determine at the moment whether Austrian law would permit a translation into Czech this soon. According to the Bern Convention, a work becomes free when no translation has been made ten years after its publication in the original language.—It seems, therefore, that the people are right. *Cockaigne* had probably also been around for longer than ten years when it came out in Czech. At most one could appeal to the publisher's sense of decency, and I'll give that a try, because I once had a good experience with it in America.

How are things going with you and the *Patrioteer?* I'm often altogether melancholy and tormented. There are too many worries: the civic-humane ones and the intellectual ones, about myself and my work. Katja coughs and really needs to be going again already. Eißi seems to have inherited the tendency from her, inclines disturbingly to bronchial catarrhs and looks bad. And I'm far too indebted: 10,000-mark advance, 70,000-mark mortgage, and then some more for the property. If only my energy and desire to work were equal to it. But inside: the constant threat of exhaustion, exaggerated scruples, fatigue, doubt, a lingering pain and weakness, so that every attack shakes me to the core; and on top of that comes my inability to find a proper intellectual and political orientation, as you have been able to do; a growing sympathy with death, which is deeply inborn: my entire interest has always been captured by decay, and that is probably what prevents me from developing an interest in progress. But what blather is all this. It is awful to be weighed down by the misery of the times, of the fatherland, without anyone having the strength to lend it form. But that is probably just part of the misery of the times and of the fatherland. Or is it lent form in *The Patrioteer*? I look forward to your work more than to my own. You are in better shape psychologically, and that remains the critical factor. My time is up, I think, and I probably should never have been allowed to become a writer. *Buddenbrooks* was a novel of the bourgeoisie and means nothing to the twentieth century. "Tonio Kröger" was merely larmoyante, *Royal Highness* vain, *Death in Venice* only half-cultivated and false. There you have my latest realizations, consolation for the little hour of one's death. That I write to you like this is of course utterly lacking in refinement and tact, for how are you supposed to respond? But it's written now. Warm regards, and please excuse me.

    T.


*Bad Tölz*
*November 11, 1913*
*Landhaus Thomas Mann*

Dear Heinrich:

For your wise and gentle letter I thank you from my heart. I've made work for you with my scarcely honorable lamentations, and you have done good, high-minded work, as always.

In my best moments I've dreamed for a long time of writing another big and faithful book about life, a continuation of *Buddenbrooks*, the story of the children, the five of us. We are worth it. All of us.

You will have heard of Uncle Friedl's excess. It kicked up more dust than he could have imagined. A bunch of newspapers have seized upon it for their own purposes, the liberal ones by making fun of Uncle, which is also not my intention, and the conservative-anti-Semitic ones—for I'm a Jew now—by taking advantage of it to vent their scorn at me and moving to expel the book from literature as a roman à clef. All of that has also been taxing my nerves.

I can't tell you at the moment whether we are still able to invite you to visit. The situation is uncertain. Tomorrow I'm accompanying Katja to Munich for another examination and to find out whether she'll be sent away. She'll go only upon the doctor's direst orders. In the evening I'm giving a reading in Stuttgart. When I'm back I'll let you know what happened.

    Warmly, T.

*Munich*
*January 7, 1914*
*Poschingerstr. 1*

Dear Heinrich:

A storm of "practical affairs," as von Aschenbach would say, have kept me so long from thanking you for your Christmas presents. I've now moved into the house with the children—without Katja, whereby half of the pleasure has naturally gone to the devil.

Your play, which I read as soon as the holidays were over, is an exceedingly beautiful work, of wonderful economy in composition and dialogue. Personally, of course, I have a weakness for the old marquis, who, incidentally, cuts a really good figure; but the part with the greatest literary significance is surely the third act, with the concisely and exhaustingly rendered return of the heroine and the fine scene with the academicians. I can't think but that on the stage the play will have a grand, indeed enrapturing effect.

Oppenheimer's picture is less dear to me than others. The little head in the exhibit at Tannhauser's seemed to me better and more interesting. Have you seen mine? It is drawn badly and the lines are faddish, but it is a characteristic likeness nonetheless.

I'm often asked of late: "*Is* your brother actually married now?" So I answer: "I don't think so, for if he were I would probably have heard of it."

My travels begin again on the 18th: to Zurich, Lucerne, St. Gallen, and then to France. It earns a bit of money.

God grant that I soon find my way back into my story, the beginnings of which are quite good. My study so far is just splendid.

Warm regards! T.


*Bad Tölz*
*July 30, 1914*
*Landhaus Thomas Mann*

Dear Heinrich:

Above all, warm congratulations on the completion of your big work. The fact doesn't fail to make an impression on me, despite the threatening nature of the international situation.

We received news of a mobilization order this afternoon. A denial did indeed follow shortly after, but one has the impression that it won't be maintained for long. We've just heard that telephone and telegraph connections to Munich are going to be blocked in a few hours, since they have to be kept free for military needs. Things have never gone this far during our lifetime. I would very much like to know your reactions. I have to say that I feel shaken and confounded by the terrible weight of reality. I was optimistic and skeptical until today—one's temperament is too reasonable for the monstrous to be regarded as possible. And I still incline to the belief that it will be pushed only to a certain point. But who knows what insanity can seize Europe once it has been pulled into the fray!

Of course I will be at your disposal on August 12, and would make the trip to Munich a day early to be able to be at the office at 10:00 A.M. Perhaps, however, events will make the trip necessary even earlier. Should Vicco get his marching orders, it would obviously be desirable to be there for him before he goes, for him and Mama.

Warm regards to you and your wife!

T.

*Bad Tölz*
*August 7, 1914*
*Landhaus Thomas Mann*

Dear Heinrich:

If you stick to your plan of being married in Munich on the 12th, you'll have to forgive my not coming. For the present, it appears, there is no question of calling up the older classes of the Landsturm. So after having acted as witness for good old Vicco at his wedding and bidden him goodbye (we sent Katja's brother off to war as well), we have returned here and for the present want to await developments. The train connection with Munich is extremely bad; the ride takes four hours, and presumably this will go on for weeks. In these circumstances, and since any friend or acquaintance, Brantl, Herzog, or anyone else can replace me (Klaus Pringsheim would also be happy to fill in), I would be grateful if you will excuse me from the witnessing. But perhaps you will postpone the wedding for a little while?

I still feel as if I'm dreaming—and yet suppose I should be ashamed that I didn't think it possible and didn't see that the catastrophe was bound to come. What a visitation! What will Europe look like, inwardly and outwardly, when it is over? I personally have to prepare for a total change in our material circumstances. It is fairly certain that if the war lasts long, I shall be what is called "ruined." So be it! What would that signify compared with the upheavals, especially the large-scale psychic upheavals, which war must necessarily bring? Shouldn't we be grateful for the totally unexpected chance to experience such mighty things? My chief feeling is a tremendous curiosity—and, I admit it, the deepest sympathy for the execrated, indecipherable, fateful Germany which, if she has hitherto not unqualifiedly held "civilization" as the highest good, is at any rate preparing to smash the most despicable police state in the world.

Meanwhile I am trying to work. What luck for you that you have just finished. I must take comfort in the fact that my task is also not completely divorced from what is happening.

Warm greetings—to your wife too, T.

*Bad Tölz*
*September 13, 1914*
*Landhaus Thomas Mann*

Dear Heinrich:

It's bad for me that I got so involved financially right before the war broke out; without the war everything would have gone fine, but now it's doubtful. Of course my earnings are nil, the allowance from my father-in-law has had to be reduced by half, Fischer can only pay a small portion of the advance he promised, the country home in Tölz is unsalable for the present, and I have to come up with considerable payments on it by October. It is as good as certain—and I haven't the slightest objection to it—that I shall have to arrange my material life on a much narrower basis after the war; for now the question is how I maintain a tolerable footing until the time comes when the now superfluous real estate holdings can be sold. I have to calculate precisely and draw on whatever I can possibly have.

Now, you have also inherited 2,000 marks from Emma Gramman, which is precisely the sum I let you have a few years ago for as long as you wanted. Would it be possible for you to decide to return it to me now? I know well that you too have to suffer, but, in the final analysis, you weren't counting on the inheritance and in general I'm justified in saying that you have it easier anyway than I—who simply cannot adapt my household to prevailing circumstances overnight. There's no sense in going through all the numbers for you. Enough. You can be certain that I wouldn't turn to you with this request if I didn't have to.

Warm regards! T.


*Handwritten draft of an answer on the back of the letter of September 13, 1914*

[*Munich, September 1914*]

Dear Tommy

As soon as the money comes from Dresden, I'll send you 1,000 marks. I'm not in a position to diminish my funds entirely; these 2,000 marks were met, when we recently got the news, with a sigh of relief from both my wife and myself. For I'm quite well aware of your situation, but you, I think, do not recognize mine.

Allowances subject to cuts are not something I can count on, and now no one is paying what they owe me. Cassirer, whose fortune has been "nearly ruined," has been paying only a pittance since the war—as long as he at least pays that, we shall live on it and Mama's quarterly allowance. The few thousand marks in the bank are a reserve intended to relieve us of worry for a time no matter what happens. My work will be just as little suited after the war as now. So hopefully you'll not doubt that this is all I can do.

*Munich*
*September 18, 1914*
*Poschingerstraße 1*

Dear Heinrich:

Half the sum also offers me a certain relief. I would only like to reassure you that I didn't make the request without considering your position. But in ultimate terms: what can happen to you? You have no children, no obligations. The worst that can occur amounts to an extreme reduction. We have already reached that stage—within the compass of what, unfortunately, is already established. But for us it has more a moral than practical significance; it doesn't make that much difference, and if we can't pay, then we'll live through the wildest things. That too would be appropriate to the times; but, because everything would be lost in a bankruptcy, the economic reasons are sufficient motivation to do whatever is possible to avoid it.

In any case, my deepest thanks that you are doing what you can. I don't share your pessimism about your work and its future in Germany. Rather, I think you are being most unfair to German culture. Your fame has been climbing steadily these past ten years. Can you really think that as a result of this great, fundamentally decent, and in fact stirring peoples' war, Germany would be so set back in her cultivation or ethos that she could permanently reject your gifts?

Warm regards! T.

*Handwritten draft*

## ATTEMPT AT RECONCILIATION

*December 30, 1917*

Dear Tommy,

Your article in the *B[erliner] T[ageblatt]* was read in my presence. I don't know whether it occurred to the other listeners, but to me it seemed, in individual passages, to have been addressed to me, nearly like a letter. Therefore I believe I have to answer you, if without the detour through the press and for the sole purpose of saying to you how unjustified is your reproach of fraternal hatred.

In my public statements, there is no "I" and therefore neither is there a brother. They are broadly aimed, without regard—at least this is how I want it—for me, for my civic position, my advantage or disadvantage, and apply solely to an idea. Love for humanity (in political terms, European democracy) is certainly the love of an idea; but one who has sought to embrace the world will have tested his emotional mettle often enough in a narrower range as well. "Goodness of man to man" is what the play demands, for which I offered my warmest sympathy to the author Dehmel immediately after I saw the dress rehearsal. I am aware that I have gained [?] certain things from this goodness in the course of my life, and know of cases in which I imparted more often than received it. I have followed the whole of your work with the best of wills to understand it and sympathize. I have been aware all along of the antagonism in your spirit, and if your extreme position on the war surprised even you, I was able to foresee it. This knowledge has not prevented me from frequently loving your work, or, more often, from searching into it, from repeatedly praising or defending it in public, or, when you doubted yourself, from consoling you as my younger brother. If I got almost nothing of all that in return, I have not let it grieve me. I knew that for you to stand securely you required this self-circumscription, needed even to repel the other. And thus have I always overcome your attacks without great difficulty—they extend from the time of a paper by the name of *Freistatt* into your most recent book—and never retaliated, or only retaliated a single time, when it was no longer a matter of the personal, of literary preference or intellectual disputatiousness, but a matter of the most universal urgency and danger. In my protest entitled "Zola" it was that I stepped forth against those who, as it necessarily appeared to me, were pressing themselves to the fore for the purpose of causing harm. Not only against you, against a legion. Instead of a legion, there remain today only a few desperate men; your own writing is melancholy—and your final argument would be the mere reproach of fraternal hatred? I can swear, if not prove, that it does not apply to me. I have never acted out of such a feeling—and my actions were precisely contrary to it when I sought a rapprochement even at a time when it seemed hopeless. Our notification of the birth of our child was not well received. Perhaps my present explanations will fall on more welcoming ears. That would be possible if your most recent indictment was dictated by pain. Then you might realize that you needn't think of me as an enemy.

Heinrich

TRANSLATION, WINSTONS/RENEAU

*Munich*
*January 3, 1918*

Dear Heinrich:

Your letter comes at a moment when it is physically impossible for me to reply properly. I must start a fourteen-day trip which I curse and for which I am scarcely in the mood, but I have to go through with it. However, I wonder whether there would be any sense in trying to compress the mental torment of two years into a letter which would have to be much longer than yours. I believe you implicitly when you say that you feel no hatred for me. After the eruptive release of the Zola essay, and considering the way everything stands with you and for you at the moment, you have no reason to. The phrase about fraternal hatred was in any case rather a symbol for more general discrepancies in the psychology of the Rousseauite.

If I troubled you, you naturally troubled me a great deal more; that was in the nature of the thing, and I, too, honestly did what I could. To this day I praise at least two of your books, in the teeth of everyone else, as masterpieces. You forget or conceal how often you, with the "justification of passion," mercilessly abused my simplest and strongest feelings before I reacted with so much as a sentence. Of course, that statement is not meant just personally, any more than any of yours. The fraternal constellation does indeed color everything personally. But the things you permitted yourself in your Zola essay and expected me to take—no, I have never done or expected a living soul to take. And when after the truly French spitefulness, slanders, and slurs of this brilliant piece of hackwork, whose very second sentence was already monstrously excessive, you imagined you could "seek a rapprochement" although it "seemed hopeless"—this demonstrates the frivolity of a man who has "sought to embrace the world." At the time, incidentally, my wife wrote at length to yours, a delicate and warm letter, and received effronteries in reply.

It is not true that my conduct during the war has been "extreme." Yours was, and moreover to the point of being wholly detestable. But I did not suffer and struggle for two years, neglect my dearest projects, sentence myself to silence as an artist, probe, compare, and manage to keep going, just to answer a letter which (understandably) exudes triumph, sees me at the head of "a few desperate men" searching for last-ditch arguments, and concludes that I need not regard you as an enemy. Every line of your letter was dictated by moral smugness and self-righteousness. Don't expect me to fall sobbing upon your breast. What lies behind me was a galley-slave's work; all the same, I thank you for the knowledge that I now stand less helplessly exposed to your zealot's sophism than in the days when you could hurt me to the quick with it.

You and yours may call me a parasite if you like. The truth, *my* truth, is that I am none. A great bourgeois artist, Adalbert Stifter, said in a letter: "My books are not poetic creations alone; as moral revelations, as human dignity preserved with austere seriousness, they have a value which will last longer than their poetry." I feel I have the right to repeat those words after him, and thousands whom I helped to live—although I did not recite the *contrat social*, one hand on my heart and the other in the air—*recognize* that I have this right.

Not you. You cannot see the right and the ethos of my life, because you are my brother. How was it that no one, not Hauptmann nor Dehmel nor Harden, that advocate of preventive war to whom you now pay visits of homage, referred the invectives of the Zola article to himself? Why was all of its rending polemic aimed at me? The fraternal constellation drove you to this. Take Dehmel, who sent me thanks and congratulations from the trenches for my first war article in the *Neue Rundschau*. You can be as cordial and intimate with him as you please at dress rehearsals and he with you in return, for though you are radically different intellectually you are not brothers and therefore there's room enough in the world for both of you.—Let the tragedy of our brotherhood unfold.

Sorrow? It is bearable. One grows hard and apathetic. Ever since Carla killed herself and you broke with Lula for life, such ruptures are nothing new in our family circle. This is not the kind of life I care for. I despise it. But one must live it to the end, as well as one can.

Farewell. T.


*Handwritten notes and outline of a reply*

psych. of the Rousseauites.

"masterpieces"

"abused feelings"

frat. constellation.

brilliant hackwork. Likewise.

ethos—10 mil. corpses,

    hand, heart, air

    your letter more pathos than ethos

spitefuln. slanders slurs

the 2nd sentence

frivolous zealot

delicate, warm—insolence

extreme—detestable behavior

suffered and struggled, probed, compared, *managed to keep going,* (what's the point?)

moral smugness and self-righteousness *exudes triumph*

sad fate, to labor two years over the results of an exchange of opinion.

parasite?

thousands whom I helped to live. Vain and cowardly

adolescents


*Not sent*

    *Munich*

    *January 5, 1918*

    Dear Tommy,

In the face of such embitterment I ought to keep silent and accept the "break for life" in the spirit in which it is offered. But I don't want to neglect anything. I want to do what I can to help you see things more fairly, later, when all this has past. To a letter that betrayed no consideration or anything of the sort, but only arrogance, I ought to dictate to my wife an appropriate answer. But I never break with a person in principle and forever. I let things depend on whether the other person also does his part to arrive at a reconciliation. Such is the nature of my zealous frivolity.

It was not arguments that I wanted, not even four pages worth—and it is with deep regret that I learn that a single expression of opinion on my part has required you to spend two years working out your answer. I think I will leave your book unread, unless consideration for my reputation inclines me otherwise—not out of disrespect, but because I desire a polemical connection to you less than the other, the natural one. From all that I see, you have underestimated your significance in my life as far as natural feeling is concerned, and overestimated it in terms of intellectual influence. The latter, negative in form, you have suffered one-sidedly. You must accept this truth; it is not mere invective, like all of those phrases, more akin to pathos than ethos, in your letter. As for me, my sense of myself is that of a thoroughly independent existence, and I experience the world, not from within a fraternal constellation, but simply on my own. You do not disturb me. For example, if you were ever to write something other than nonsense about French actions and qualities, I would be sincerely pleased. But you—if I should decide to declare my allegiance to old Prussia, do you know what you would do? You would throw the notes for your *Friedrich* in the fire.

"*In inimicos,*" you said, twenty-two years old and sitting at the piano on via Argentina trenta quattro, turned with your back toward me. That is how it has stayed for you; but you are still young and I may still dissuade you before it's too late, for it wasn't good for you like that and will become ever less so. Stop understanding my life and behavior in reference to yourself; it is not appropriate and both would be literally the same without you. The 2nd sentence of "Zola" has nothing to do with you, and the few pages further on that apply to you as well as to others would still be the same or similar if there were only the others. Of these others, some of them have meanwhile changed their minds and I am once more their friend. I never break with a person in principle and forever.

Self-righteousness? Oh, no—far more likely, rather, a feeling shared with those others who, like me, know how much all of us, the art of our generation and its cast of mind, are responsible for having allowed the catastrophe to come. Probing and struggle have defined the experience of a few others besides yourself, if more modestly; what they have as well is regret and a new strength for action: they're not just "managing," which is not worth all the trouble; not just "suffering" for the sake of the self, this furious passion for your own ego. It is to this passion that you owe the production of a few narrow but resolute works. To it you owe as well your complete lack of respect for others, particularly for those who don't measure up to your standards, you owe that "contempt" that sits more easily with you than any other, in short, the inability to grasp the real earnestness of another person's life. You are surrounded by insignificant extras playing the role of the "people," as in your hymn of praise to the "Royal Highness." Extras have a fate, even an ethos?—Your own ethos—who tells you that I have mistaken it? I have always been aware of it, have respected it as a subjective experience, as you, and when I have met its representation in a work of art, I have not burdened it overlong with my doubts as to its value for humanity. If I, however, dare to express an ethical will of my own, how does it appear to you? In the image of a buffoon's swaggering, of a brilliant hack. You poor thing!

The inability to grasp the real earnestness of another's life ultimately gives birth to monsters—thus you find that my letter, which was a gesture of simple friendliness, breathes triumph! Triumph over what? That everything "stands" well for me in the moment—namely, a world in rubble and 10 million corpses underground. Now that's justification! That indeed promises satisfaction to the ideologue! But I am not the man to tailor the misery and death of peoples to the fancies of my mind, not I. I do not believe that the victory of one thing or another remains worth the words to mention it when people are perishing. After these last, utterly horrific events, whatever humanistic gains can be made in the future will taste bitter and sad. I don't know if anyone can "help" his fellows "to live"; but let our literature, at least, not aid them toward death!

Now they continue to die. But you, who approved of the war and continues to approve of it and accuses me—I had a play performed, which was no simple rhyme of impotence to the terrible present, and the first of all things with which I endowed the tormented characters was a belief in a better future—but you, who therefore finds my attitude completely detestable, you, God willing, will have forty more years to examine yourself, if not merely "to manage." The time is coming, I only hope, in which you will learn to see people, not shadows, and, then, that you will see me.

H.


TRANSLATION, WINSTONS

*Munich*
*January 31, 1922*
*Poschingerstr. 1*

Dear Heinrich,

With these flowers accept my warm greetings and best wishes—I was not allowed to send them to you earlier.

Those were difficult days that lie behind us, but now we are over the hill and will go on better—together, if you feel as I do.

T.

*April 19, 1922*
*z. Z. Überlingen/Lake Constance*
*Resort Hotel*

Here we are. Outside the snow beckons to winter sports; we decline. Otherwise it is all very pretty. We send our warm regards. Till we meet!

Heinrich and Mimi


*Postcard*

TRANSLATION, WINSTONS

*Amsterdam*
*October 20, 1922*

Greetings from the land of Spinoza. I am staying with friendly people and resting at last here; thanks to the amiable smallness of the country, most of the cities I must visit can be reached from my headquarters in Amsterdam. Have experienced a world of things in these ten days. After the great Berlin adventure (they consider me some sort of campaign speaker for Ebert; politics is foaming around me) came an episode in Hanover, then Düsseldorf; Duisberg with an impressive tour of the Rhine port; then Cleve, where I visited the big insane asylum. In Nymwegen, on the border, I had a curious literary conversation with a young Chinese who with great delicacy advocated the social ethics of Confucius against European individualism. He is studying phonetics in Leipzig and was about to leave for London over the holidays. I have not yet seen much of Amsterdam, shall be visiting the Rijksmuseum in the afternoon and taking the train to Utrecht for the evening lecture.

T.


TRANSLATION, WINSTONS

*Munich*
*February 17, 1923*

Dear Heinrich,

I needn't tell you that German lecture tours scarcely pay nowadays. I have just been in Dresden for 50,000 marks, which the impoverished association had received as an ad hoc gift, and I would have come out in the red if I hadn't stayed in a private house and hadn't needed to go to Berlin anyhow, so that the lecture at least covered the cost of the trip. If you ask 30,000 marks per evening for a cluster of cities, you won't make enough to compensate for the fatigue. On the other hand, I hardly think that the clubs can afford more. Ask 40,000 per evening for a start. I am going to Augsburg in the near future for 25,000, the arrangement having been made some time ago.

Our Frenchmen are behaving brilliantly. They seem determined to give the lie to everyone in Germany who urges moderation. One hears that the news about the Ruhr is not exaggerated but, instead, lags behind the truth. The anger is terrible—deeper and more united than that which brought on Napoleon's fall. There is no predicting the outcome. And the unfortunate part of it is that a French retreat, desirable though that would be, would signify the triumph of nationalism in domestic politics. Must the better side of Germany really be forced into this dilemma? Germany was completely malleable in 1918, but the others, who were convinced that they were so much better, have shown little capacity to learn.

Warm regards and wishes! T.


*Vienna*
*Hotel Imperial*
*April 1, 1923*

Dear Heinrich:

I am really sorry that the turmoil of our recent departure caused me to forget to congratulate you on your birthday. I'm making up for it now in the Easter spirit, wishing you a good, productive year. I have warm regards to convey to you from Schnitzler, with whom I had lunch here day before yesterday, in the company of Auernheimer, a proper literary type. I'm living here like Wilhelm before the fall and in Budapest, where I'm going tomorrow, there will likely be more of the same. I'm traveling to Prague on the night of the 5th and 6th, and hope to see Mimi. Yesterday I enjoyed an excursion by automobile to Semmering, which I had not yet seen. Today I'm visiting Hofmannsthal in Rodaun.

Till we meet! T.


*Bozen*
*October 17, 1923*

Warm greetings from the new Italy! We have relentless sun and go drinking every evening with Hauptmann, who really is a good old man. Thank you for helping teach those bad, unbridled children a thing or two. May God awaken reason in them with time! Till we meet.

T. K.

*London*

*May 6, 1924*

Dear Heinrich, a fond greeting from the adventurers. It makes me very happy to see remarkable Amsterdam with its black houses again. We had a good passage from Vlissingen and were amiably welcomed here. So we'll dine this evening with Galsworthy, Wells, and Shaw. Strange. Till we meet.

T.

And from Katia, the warmest regards.


*Dresden*

*November 16, 1924*

Dear Heinrich, warm regards from my trip in the company of *Abrechnungen*—I find them very entertaining and refreshing!

T.


*Munich*

*December 11, 1924*

*Leopoldstr. 59*

Dear Tommy,

It was with pleasure that we received your book, and our deepest thanks for the thoughtful gift. Mimi is obviously well supplied now, and can read for weeks. Then I hope to get to it. The writer of this big work must feel happy and relieved to see it finished. I'm still in the depths of my own, but the next months should see an end to it.

All the best, till we meet. H.


*Piraeus*

*March 18, 1925*

Dear Heinrich, Greetings to you and Mimi from Greece. It really is quite remarkable to look down from the Acropolis on Salamis and the sacred strait. Ultimately it is the beginning of all of us, and it makes one wish that the Persians might always be defeated over and over again.

T.

*Munich*
*April 22, 1925*
*Poschingerstr. 1*

Dear Heinrich,

It was a great moment yesterday afternoon when your novel was delivered here. Many thanks for the present! Katja got busy with it first but I also hope that in the next few days I can begin absorbing it in order to possess it. We are going to Florence in the first half of May; and at the beginning of June to Vienna, where a performance of *Fiorenza* is planned. Either before or somewhere in the middle, we'll surely get together again.

Warmly, T.


*St. Gilgen*
*August 24, 1925*

Dear Heinrich, We were in Aussee for two days, where Wassermann has some property with a wonderful landscape, and we send greetings from our midday stop on the way to Salzburg, where we want to hear some music. The V. Hugo essay was extraordinarily beautiful!

T.

Warmest regards to you and Mimi,

from your Katia


*Arosa*
*May 17, 1926*

Dear Heinrich, Greetings to you and Mimi from wild primal nature. We had endless snow, and now it's raining, which is probably supposed to suggest progress. But Katja is recovering slowly, and I'm letting my dry, hot head hatch all kinds of things.

T.


*Hotel Europejski*
*Warszawa*
*March 15, 1927*

Dear Heinrich,

Truly late, only toward the end of my stay here, am I managing to report that your censorship protest was received with great enthusiasm when I read it at the Academy session (I made a special effort) and was unanimously accepted for publication. One small editorial change was requested, affecting only the sentence referring to bookstores. It was seen as too obliging and the proposal is that it be cut.

*Danzig*
*the 16th*

It took a long time for me to get a letter to Katja and these lines finished. The stay in Warsaw was demanding, but truly heartwarming. I hadn't dreamed even in the slightest of such a reception. I'll have to tell you about it in person.

Warm regards! T.

*Kampen a/Sylt*
*August 19, 1927*
*Haus Kliffende*

Dear Heinrich and Mimi, Greetings from sea to sea! The charms of this island are chaste and meager and turn one's thoughts to grog. But we are amenable and the children more than that.

Till we meet! T.

Most warmly, K.

*August 23, 1927*
*Hôtel de l'Océan (at present)*
*Biarritz*

Dear Tommy,

Ponten writes me that he and W. Schäfer have nominated you for the presidency of the Academy. That is cause enough for congratulations, since most of the voters, except for a few in Berlin, would probably want you. Thus, from a personal angle, all would seem to be perfectly in order—for me, too, for you know as well as I do myself that your honors and successes do not upset me. And besides, sometimes I pick up a few crumbs from them myself. "German literature is ruled absolutely by the Mann family," I read in *Comoedia*.

But here I must raise issues of a technical sort, for I, as a member of the Academy, am myself involved in the matter. It is always dangerous to commit oneself collegially to an organization. There can, even without my doing anything, be conflicts. Conceptions of the goals of an association among colleagues always diverge too widely. Nevertheless, it surprises me that Ponten and I, however straightforward we believe our exchange of views concerning the Academy to have been, could have completely and utterly misunderstood each other. Now it is clear to me what he wants. He wants, first of all, that the president not be a Berliner, but, rather, that the chairman of a Prussian academy be a resident of southern Germany. Further, he finds it desirable to have a bigger name at the head than the current president. That seems to be all.

I thought that I had explained emphatically that I want much more. I have nothing against W. von Scholz, as such. That he does nothing is what I dislike. There is no limit to what can be done for the Academy, which at present has nothing but the name, and carries no weight. When we were called upon to draft a program, I presented as comprehensive a one as was possible for a single person at a given time. Yours would have been no less noteworthy. My conclusion is that all of these programs, or what comes of them through majority vote, should also be implemented, and that by the new chairman himself.

That is why the first requirement is that he live in Berlin. Equally imperative is that he devote, for years to come, the larger part of his work efforts to the tasks of the Academy. To raise money, and to raise it continually, to struggle for its public prestige, and, to the extent possible, to make it a power in the state—this can only be done by a considerable force, and one which is oriented toward the practical. If I assume you to be such a force, still I cannot believe that you would be prepared to allow your own work to suffer relative to so many other tasks.

Where the proper person is to be found, I don't know; but even if no one else knows either, the search for such a force would remain the only important point in the moment. If such a person exists among the writers outside the Academy, he should be brought in for the sake of the cause. The one chosen does not have to be named president right away; the statutes in this regard could be changed. An academy in the course of formation, which must first of all demonstrate to skeptics its right to existence, is much more in need of a director or general secretary who works and receives an income for it than all manner of prestigious representation. (The secretary of the overall Academy, who might otherwise come to mind, has probably not convinced you either that he would be on our side.)

The issue involved is of enormous proportions. German literature has perhaps its only opportunity to achieve the social status proper to it. That is possible above all only if the Academy is conscious of itself as the highest executive organ of the literary mind as such. All the weight must be on the profession and its way of thinking. Attention must not be distracted by a specially favored dignitary at the top. Internal differences of rank should not be emphasized. I would remind you that the French Academy has no president.

We might wind up with a decision to keep the president, but put an executive director in a position subordinate to him. But then authority would rest with the formal president and the actual executive would have none. When the latter, however, for example, negotiated with the ministry, he would require the support of the Academy's direct mandate. He would have to enjoy its trust. Then would the position of a president superior to him become superfluous on its own. As for the director, he might be just barely respectable as a literary talent. At issue is not individual honor, but utility to literature.

Individual honors do not help literature; that has been proved most painfully. We even had an Olympian, which as a title surely exceeds president. The state of literature remained a sad one. When the new republic wanted to commend itself culturally, it was eager to celebrate G. Hauptmann. Result: employers' representatives in the Provisional Economic Council voted against the fifty-year copyright; for, in their view, preferential treatment is due the booksellers, not the writers.

That would be all; hopefully, it is said here in a way that others would also have to understand it. But I'm not saying it to others. I'm saying it only to you. You can use it as you like, can speak to others in this spirit in case I have succeeded in winning you over to it, and can act accordingly yourself, in case the effect of my words extends that far. If not, that's fine as well—personally, I mean, in regard to my understanding of your behavior. I shall not find fault with it and would be glad if you found no fault with this step of mine. Admittedly, I could be easily alienated from the issue, for I would no longer expect anything from an academy that limited itself to honors and, instead of seeking to establish itself as significant, depended upon the significance of individuals.

That does not mean that I would resign my membership or even voice my opposition. As your brother, I could not afford to without inspiring unwarranted suspicions.

I shall not answer Herr Ponten for the time being. You shall certainly have an opportunity soon to tell him yourself that I would naturally agree with your decision, in case we choose not to search out a chairman (or, my preference, director) on the basis of a comprehensive program of action. As simple and urgent as it appears to me, it is possible that it is quite remote for most of those involved. Perhaps German writers, even once gathered together in an academy, do not yet understand their task. It is also to be feared that the good businessman my plan presupposes is not to be found among writers, even given the best of intentions; or that the members of the Academy, his employers, will fail to unite; or that he will prove ineffective or even abuse his position.

I've considered all the things that could go wrong, and if just one of them does, everything listed here as desirable would be in vain, even if you wanted it. I can guarantee nothing. The easiest thing is for you to accept, for me to agree. As long as I have questions, however, as to whether greater, more general advantages couldn't be achieved after all, I am obligated to make my judgment known. Given the situation, you were precisely the only one to whom I could do that.

We are leaving Biarritz in a few days. We'll see you in September.

With warm greetings from us to both of you.

Heinrich

*Kampen a/Sylt*
*August 29, 1927*

Dear Heinrich,

Your splendid letter has made me see quite clearly how wrong I was to carelessly accept Schäfer and Ponten's proposal. Soon after I said yes, which was more of a "Well, if I must," than anything else, this carelessness struck me as a mistake, if only because this move comes hard on the heels of the one I subscribed to, exactly as if the first had been the planned prelude for the present one. But I easily let myself be taken by surprise on the telephone, if only to shake free, and Ponten is a follower who is perpetually troubled by my literary existence and overcompensates by a blindly zealous friendship. In one respect, to be sure, the aims of these gentlemen are not so remote from yours: A more significant name at the head of the Academy, even if placed there only for decorative purposes, might help the cause—even financially. For this reason it was regrettable that Hauptmann dropped out of consideration from the start, due to the clumsiness of the Ministry, although he wouldn't have been the man you are looking for, either. But I wonder whether this man exists at all among German writers. You would be the one, if you had the time. Fulda probably would have the time; he has no quality, but he shows a certain competence. The only trouble is that his kind of competence corresponds to his quality: his point of view is unspeakably trivial compared with yours. He thinks of representing professional interests and no more—which seems to indicate that after all, the question of quality in this appointment had better not be entirely excluded. In any case my candidacy is nonsense, for the reasons you have cogently set forth. I shall write as much to Ponten and Schäfer and ask them to withdraw their nomination. What prompted me to agree temporarily and conditionally was not ambition, not at all, but rather the habit of putting myself at the disposal of others, "If you think so, fellows"; in other words, it was a kind of modesty. Our mutual professional standing, the relationship of yours to mine, is a ticklish matter in itself—"ticklish" being another one of those careless expressions. But in spite of your joke that sometimes you pick up a crumb or two from my successes, you know me well enough, I think, to know that I don't let myself be fooled. With me it always comes down to that "If you think so, fellows"; but many fellows don't think so at all, and I am only too inclined to regard them as right and to be contemptuous of the others. I won't go into the question of hypochondria, and to what extent it opens one's eyes to the truth.

This is a uniquely beautiful and exciting place. I can't work at anything major, but there is always something to do, of course. We too shall be returning to Munich toward the middle of September. Then we can confer again, and primarily I must hand over to you 150 marks, a fee from the *Tagebuch*, which I accepted for you because it was addressed to Poschingerstraße.

Warm regards—see you soon. T.

*August [probably Sept.] 6, 1927*
*Munich*
*Leopoldstr. 59*

Dear Tommy,

Following a journey from the ocean over the Pyrenees to the Mediterranean and through Switzerland, I found your letter waiting for me today and thank you for your friendly reception of mine. Oddly enough, your unqualified withdrawal leaves me feeling more uneasy than before. For, as you know, it has seemed to me extremely dubious from the outset whether my demands could be understood, let alone fulfilled. For that, it would have been necessary for the current president to have distributed our draft program for deliberation. As it stands, however, no one is even informed of it.

You will be able to tell from Ponten's answer whether he has any idea of the intended change of course. For myself, I can approach Schickele, whose interests in the Academy I know, with the proposal. But the time set for the election is too soon, and how could everything possibly be reorganized so quickly. If it does finally amount to a choice between two names, tendencies, and residences, for example, between Scholz and you, then I would simply vote for you.

Till we meet! Heinrich

*Carbon copy of a letter*

*Munich*
*April 18, 1931*

Dear Heinrich:

I'm very grateful for your letter. It encouraged me to give the draft statutes another thorough going over. Before I go into them in the context of what you wrote, I would like to briefly recapitulate the story of my contact with Dr. Huebner and my first fleeting acquaintance with the new charter.

During the celebration at the Academy, Huebner expressed his desire to confer with me about Academy matters. Since I had little time, I proposed meeting at Pelzer's for lunch the following day, and there at the table Huebner had me look through the draft statutes. Naturally I didn't do it very precisely. The draft was not yet entirely in order from a purely logical perspective and Huebner marked a few passages to which I drew attention. My interest was essentially concentrated on the paragraph that details the tasks of the literary section. That didn't look bad. Collaboration on legislative issues in the area of belles lettres seemed quite tolerable and even more so participation on the examination boards for German and historical textbooks, a point that was obviously incorporated thanks to the statement you made following your election to the chair. I took note of the draft and then we moved on, since from the outset the conversation had turned primarily on the question of the presidency and since that was clearly the reason Huebner had wanted to speak to me in the first place.

Huebner told me that Liebermann, above all on account of his advanced age and failing hearing, had declared himself through with holding office, and that precisely among the painters this news was greeted with some enthusiasm, because it meshed with a desire in those circles for a change in the presidency. At the same time he laid out for me the idea that for the next three years, including 1932, the Goethe year, a writer should be president of the overall Academy, as, indeed, the statutes also characterize as desirable a fair rotation among the three sections. The thought was not new to me, for I knew that Minister Becker had already been considering the same thing. As presumptive president, Huebner named Hauptmann, and we deliberated over whether he would accept the post, even though it would require him to move his residency to Berlin.

On the same evening or the next one—I'm not sure anymore—I then spoke to you and, operating under the impression of what you told me about Liebermann, tried to reach Huebner by telephone before I left Berlin.

I wasn't successful and then wrote to him from Munich asking if he could possibly ease my mind concerning certain scruples that had since occurred to me in regard to Liebermann. My personal and artistic respect for him, I wrote, would prevent me absolutely from ever taking part in a movement that sought anything like his involuntary resignation. As a member of the literary section I would obviously have to welcome the plan to make a writer president, but the precondition for my approval was that Liebermann's desire to leave office was an established fact, and I implored him to speak to me plainly about the matter. I received in response the letter which I sent to you and in which I believed myself to have found a sufficient guarantee on the loyalty issue.

It was thus not entirely correct—let me just express this—when you responded to Liebermann's question, concerning how you knew of the existence of an intrigue against him, by saying: "Huebner spoke with my brother." It was you, in fact, who informed me of an intrigue, and only then did I tell you of my conversation with Huebner. I'm not sure that "intrigue" is the right expression here. I don't yet see the interest that is supposed to be motivating the people in the ministry to work to topple Liebermann. It is obviously more the painters who want to get rid of him, and there might be personal and internal political reasons for that. I can't quite believe that the plan to have a writer as president is being pushed by the bureaucrats as a way to do away with Liebermann. I'm credulous enough to believe that the plan itself is primary. I miss the motivation for malicious intentions. In any case, I'm sticking to my standpoint, in which I believe myself to be in agreement with the entire section, that the implementation of the rotational plan should be accomplished with complete consideration for the honorable Liebermann. I can't imagine that such consideration would not also prevail in the impending elections if Liebermann should run again. If things work out differently, however,

I don't see how that could redound to the dishonor of us writers. We would have a clear conscience.

I've dealt with this matter first because it has preoccupied me most from a humane perspective. Now to the statutes, which, after giving them a close study, I can't regard as gloomily as you do, although I'm glad that their acceptance has been delayed, for I'm certain that they can be improved. But can things go on with the Academy as before? Haven't we all seen that something must be done toward its consolidation, toward an enhancement of its effectiveness? This obviously applies not only to the writers; attitudes seem to be similar in the other sections, for Grimme already wrote me a long time ago about the severe crisis affecting the entire Academy, in which, to be sure, the literary section played the major role. That was after the departure of the Kolbenheyer group and Hesse. Did we not reject the Schäfer people's woolly plans concerning a non-Prussian Academy and their constant agitation against "Berlin"? Is it not—I ask myself and would like to ask you too—actually to be welcomed if the activity of the individual sections, and thus the literary section as well, is carried over to the expanded senate and thus treated within a tighter framework? When I recall how our general meetings went with the non-resident members, Ponten, Kolbenheyer, Halbe, etc. there on expense allowances, and when I further consider that Doeblin reciprocated their jealousy—the Berliners didn't come to the section meetings either, but whatever happened was the doing of three or four minor sorts—then it is difficult for me not to see a kind of progress in the new working organization.

What you see developing is an academy of bureaucrats with no influence. I, however, don't yet see how the new order is supposed to paralyze us anymore than has previously been the case and why it has to turn us into bureaucrats. According to the draft charter, the literary senate is composed of six writers selected from among its members by the section itself. Then there is the third secretary of the Academy, who is Loerke, another writer. Then there is a literary scholar called by the minister, Petersen, and, as the ninth member, the theatrical director. That makes up nine votes, which, as far as one can foresee, would be tolerably compatible in intellectual-artistic matters. On the other side are two bureaucrat votes, namely Amersdorfer's and that of the lawyer. Is the ratio as bad as your letter would have me regard it and, of course, as it can be regarded temporarily? What would make us dependent, like Mussolini's people? And we're not going to be paid. The election of the senators, that is, the working members, requires confirmation by the curator: that, if it is up to me, is to be eliminated. It's not logical. Since elections to the section are free, the ones to the senate must also be free and mustn't be conditioned on any approval. For the rest, however, the closest inspection of the new charter fails to reveal to me any mechanism that would bureaucratize us. I already mentioned at the beginning that the stipulation of our obligations was characterized more by a willingness to meet us halfway than an inclination to restrain us. That Doeblin managed to get a protection of artistic freedom included is highly satisfying, although one could have considered it subsumed in the general protection of belles lettres defined under # 1. But collaboration in the textbook examination boards is a greater success, and it also seems to me worth noting that it needn't be the officials who authorize expert reviews in the area of literature and the theater, but that the section can also resolve to initiate them. You are yourself chair of the literary senate. Why should you, in this position, be yet less influential than the chair of the section? Those who are nonresident but full members—of whom the majority, in particular for understandable reasons the non-Germans, have behaved completely passively until now—should be called once a year to a general meeting, and otherwise as needed by well-founded motion from among the members. All who are at all interested will therefore take part in these meetings, thus preserving the relation between the section and the senate. What someone said to you about eliminating travel and expense allowances I regard as untenable, and that must absolutely be opposed. There's no reason for it, and the new statutes fail to give any justification for not continuing to underwrite travel expenses.

You see, dear Heinrich, that even under the influence of your letter I don't manage to perceive in the draft statutes an attack on the independence and potential effectiveness of the Academy. If reactionaries are elected in Prussia, if the skies over Germany as a whole continue to darken, then the future of the Academy as such is uncertain, and a different charter could do nothing to change that. But I just can't see what it is in the statutes that's supposed to make us into academicians of reaction and leave us pliant and unpaid. One might fear that the issue of pay would almost pose a danger in its own right, and Ricarda Huch did in fact declare that she would withdraw if such a measure were adopted. Otherwise, obviously, you couldn't be more right in saying "a million for the Academy versus the hundred million that others are getting," and of course the statement must be included in the memorandum the section is drafting to represent its specific demands. I have to confess that in the moment I have no further proposals for such a memorandum other than the concerns I've raised here against the draft statutes. God help me if I've been struck blind! Perhaps it's possible to see things more completely and correctly in Berlin than I am able to, but I can only say what I see. With warm regards,


*June 15, 1931*
*Bad Gastein*
*Salzburger Hof*

Dear Tommy,

I wish we could be together a few days this summer. I read your address again in the Kiepenheuer brochure, and the feeling of warmth it gives me is the cause of the wish.

It is no doubt difficult to arrange; we each have our separate plans. I want to have my daughter with me in July—not in Gastein, but preferably in a place that's not so high and has more woods. Did Attersee (near Salzburg) have woods? We were there together, I think in 1896.

Managing it from the perspective of work in particular is naturally a lot to ask. I mention it just in case such a change in the first half of July would make sense for you. I heard (from Golo, in Paris) that you probably won't make your trip to the sea before the middle of August. Personally, I would like to be at the Baltic in August. We could also meet on your return trip. If everything falls through, we will hopefully be in Berlin for a somewhat more extended period in October. I assume that you will be coming. The plenary session of the section will probably also consider whether it can join the International Federation of Professional Writers' Organizations. I have my doubts, as interesting as the founding of the Federation in Paris was. The French had taken the matter in hand with judicious enthusiasm. Their precise opposite is represented by contemporary Italians. They were incapable of sticking to the point even for a moment, and whenever they spoke for more than two minutes it became a propaganda speech for their great despot. One of them tried every time to clap, but had to give it up because no one joined in.—I had, incidentally, a conversation with Briand.

Most warmly, H.

*May 31, 1932*
*Berlin-Wilmersdorf*
*Trautenaustr. 12*

Dear Tommy,

I am deeply touched by the pleasure you're finding in my book. It makes it worthwhile.

I share your opinion that overt barbarism will be unable to prevail in this country. Its half successes and the on-going threat it poses hamper our activity sufficiently as it is, and require us to devote considerable energy to merely holding off the worst. In the process one sees what really ought to be going on!

Brüning, who is strong personally only as an extreme product of religious education, represented something great and remarkable after all in his recent public appearance before the foreign press. On the chair's other side, the nuncio spoke of "international goodwill"; on this side, Brüning exclusively of his concern for the unemployed. That's the precise reason for his current downfall, and the vested interests continue their approach at a steady gait.

Likewise was the election of the president of the Academy determined by mediocre interests, if not by envy of their betters. I'm enclosing the few lines, which naturally couldn't stop what had long since been in the cards. Please give them back to me.

Our section will never be able to prevail in the senate as long is it doesn't have the same number of representatives at the ministry as the two others. But what will the next minister be like?

Warmly, H.

June 2, 1932
Berlin-Wilmersdorf
Trautenaustr. 12

Dear Tommy,

The enclosed text is by Alfons Paquet. The congenial man recently deplored the brutalization of the atmosphere—it was on the day after the fight in the Landtag—so passionately that none could help being moved. It was resolved that a protest be composed; not even Mrs. Huch opposed it. Now, however, the text doesn't seem exactly to the point, and I scarcely expect it to have any effect.

Therefore I'm asking you for advice. Should we pursue the matter, or communicate our doubts to Paquet? Do you want to make changes and additions? If the affair interests you sufficiently, then perhaps you will come to an agreement on the wording with Paquet, Frankfurt a.M., Wolfgangstr. 122.

Otherwise, please, simply pass the draft on to Loerke, whom I have already informed. After you, the other members will probably have to be consulted as to whether they will sign.

Warmly, H.

November 1, 1932
Pension Stern
Kurfürstendamm 217
Berlin W 15

Dear Tommy,

I was very happy to hear from you and hope that you are in good health and working well. Just yesterday I received photographs of you, through Dr. Fiedler of Altenburg, a religion teacher who is supposedly going to be sacked on the basis of the Versailles Treaty. As for myself, I'm now issuing my final word on nationalism—and beyond that on the national fatherland. It has forfeited all rights, and there is no longer any justification for holding back. *Die neue Rundschau*, which is willing to risk publishing it in December, cut nothing from my personal statement, unfortunately, however, most of its concrete justification, the failures of principle on the part of the bygone republic.

A meeting of the Academy with Provisional Minister Lammers was scheduled. Now, however, our Mr. Grimme has reappeared. It is uncertain with whom we are to deal in the future. Everything is uncertain. In order to bring about a decision, individual intellectuals will have to file their statements against the national state and in favor of a supranational one. It won't work otherwise, but in that way it would work. For such a weak and wretched state would not be able to maintain for long a course running opposed to the resolve of those disposing over intellectual resources. Beyond this—for the moment, just between us—I would be in favor of closer ties among republican intellectuals for the purpose of providing a kind of oversight over the coming second republic. An upper chamber, so that intellectual weaknesses will not so easily spell the ruin of the republic: we must make efforts in that direction and already begin laying the groundwork.

I will be very happy if the novel I will soon be sending you wins your approval. Of course we must not allow ourselves to say: what can a novel mean in present circumstances? Rather, we must believe that the chaos in reality can also be subjected to order, like a novel.

Warmly, H.


*November 26, 1932*
*Berlin W 15*
*Kfdamm 217*
*as of Dec. 1: Fasanenstr. 61*

Dear Tommy,

Your letter will remain the most beautiful and best that I shall get to read about my book. I thank you. In every moment of my life you were the one closest to me, and you are that once again here.

What you don't like in my novel I also would not have done that way earlier. But if I consider fully the creatures of the present moment, the most complete ones, I mean, then I always run up against crime. It has become a power, human and social, which we are just now learning to recognize, and its influence on the survivors, like Bäuerlein, is what perhaps proves the most. I did write the novel quickly, but I didn't dash it off, and when I got to the part about Berlin, I was troubled by severe reservations. The self-contained idyll of the first chapters had been left behind and the novel lost its overview of life—the resolution, as you say. Only, Marie preserves her inner definition, and that is how she gets through. That is the meaning, if the book has one. If your word "religious" were applicable to these characters, that would be the best. Moreover, I listen to the reactions of some readers, who say that they respect this novel more than my previous ones. But I find it better not to think too much about the question of actual worth. This one won't be perfect either; it is simply what I was capable of.

It was possible to learn a remarkable amount from Hauptmann during the week devoted to honoring him. He looked as if he represented solely what he is, no longer having any idea of what he has done, especially not of how great it is. His pride comes to expression not only in modesty, but in something approaching resignation. And he is so healthy and cheerful—this man with whom I had breakfast and then that same afternoon shared champagne mixed with red wine. And then in the evening I sat with Michael Kramer, a truly and authentically religious figure!

What we have done was right, because it corresponded to our calling. No one is more justified, or even as justified, in thinking that as you are yourself during the work on your world-historical novel. As far as I know of it or can foresee, this work will raise you to your proper height, for you were destined to become more comprehensive at every stage—from the parental home to humanity; I would know no reason not to have complete faith in it. I do, without knowing the work. You yourself will ultimately accept and assimilate your reservations, as if they belonged to the work.

That is primarily what I wanted to express. Furthermore, great success will come afterward; you deserve it and I am always especially proud of it, next to the satisfaction I take in things that you have accomplished.

Something else altogether. The essay I hope you will soon read in *Die neue Rundschau* is not meant as literature, just barely as an intellectual achievement. It is a practical experiment. Will even a small number of thinking people want to promote the formation of a French-German federal state and regard a concerted effort in that direction as responsible and worthwhile? Privately I am well aware that experience since the Treaty of Verdun (856, I think) speaks without exception against it, especially recent, on-going experience. But I also know that this experiential chain will someday come to an end, if not a good end, then the worst. The best thing would be to break it off and begin new, 856. Since a new beginning runs counter to all experience, it can only come from above, as the *diktat* of thinking people. So the first thing would be our resolution and statement of principle. Enormously difficult, certainly no utopia; and just as remote as today only the rational can be.

The Academy now has its Hauptmann prize, four to five thousand marks annually, which is, anyway, the highest German award. After the grandiose honors extended Hauptmann and the impression that they made, we will try again in places where we have so far gotten nothing. Of course only Jewish bankers donated, by no means the Rhine industrialists, although they did respond to our invitation to tea. Sahm, in Berlin, is of the same ilk; he is tranquilly allowing the Lessing Museum to be auctioned off and its holdings scattered. For the athletic festivities in 1936, two and a half million have already been allotted. A nation, as far I understand the issue, consists more of past than of present and it is mistaken to term oneself a nationalist and at the same time display utter indifference to the tending of the past, which is called culture. That would make it possible for the nation to cultivate two specious myths simultaneously, such as those you identified.

A speech in honor of Gobineau, the father of all error—I raised all possible objections to it. If people want it anyway, I'll see then what there is to do.

When are you coming here again?

All the best, to you and yours. H.


*January 29, 1933*
*Berlin W 15*
*Fasanenstr. 61*

Dear Tommy,

Here is a report of the last meeting of our section senate. It was concerned with the Hauptmann endowment. The draft of the statute appears to have been written in the ministry primarily by young Zierold, the chief administrative advisor. You will receive a copy through the Academy. Present at the meeting were Fulda, Döblin, Molo, Loerke, Benn, and myself. Two important points inspired objection, the one from everyone, the other from three of the voting members present.

1) the draft provides that of the five members of the Hauptmann endowment committee only two be members of the Academy. We all objected: in that case it is not the Academy's prize. It is stated in the introduction of the draft, however, that the endowment will be given over to the Academy—or something to that effect; I don't have the precise wording in front of me.

It is to be anticipated that the public will identify the prize as a prize from the Academy. It is we who will bear responsibility for the selections made, while in reality we could be outvoted. It changes nothing if we are allowed to select two of the other three judges. These two outside writers will not be an integrated part of our group; there is thus the danger that they will be prejudiced toward us and resist agreement in principle—especially the "critic," who is supposed to be one of the additional judges. There is nothing to do but accept the fifth judge, a representative of the ministry, since that is also the source of most of the money. In the meeting no need was found for numbers three and four, the ones we select, unless, that is, the state mistrusts its own academy. Why does it trust instead two academy members plus two other writers, *whom we select ourselves?*

Zierold did not explain that to me. He warned us against proposing a change in the two to three ratio. If the ratio were to be reversed, then the minister would presumably demand the right to confirm our decisions; that would be even more undesirable.

I don't know what is more undesirable. If, however, we want to accept neither of the two limitations, neither the minister's right to confirm nor being outnumbered, then there is nothing left for the section to do but refuse the endowment. Two of us could be judges, but it would no longer be the Academy's prize. Of course nobody is thinking of refusing the endowment—at least not as long as there is hope of reaching an agreement with the ministry. I could see a way out in reducing the number of judges to three, two of us and one from the ministry. Moreover, that would simplify the work; having to persuade outsiders, particularly in the emergency committee that is supposed to have the right to nominate candidates, would only be an impediment anyway.

2) Now I come to the other controversial point. Here we disagree among ourselves, for it has to do with one's assessment of Hauptmann. Döblin's is markedly low; he spoke in terms of a "millionaire," who, furthermore, isn't worth five cents more than others. He maintained that the overvaluation of an individual brings no benefit at all to literature, that it is nothing but a celebrity cult. The opposite, it seems to me, is obvious. You and I think differently than Döblin about Hauptmann's work, but that is not the issue; the issue is whether literature and the section should diminish him, or whether, rather, it shouldn't take advantage of his great status for its own purposes. It has been a very long time since the arts had three such prestigious old men, Liebermann, Strauss, and Hauptmann. We mustn't allow ourselves to take positions against our own.

Something else argues in the same direction. The republic has set up Hauptmann as its literary exponent; the right treats him as an enemy, Fechter naturally as well. If we refuse him the distinctions provided for in the draft statutes, then whom are we serving? Obviously the cultural reactionaries, whom we have not given up fighting in a manifesto. A more or less reactionary minister could even grant our wish, for it would be his. Zierold hinted at this to me, expressing his surprise that such a proposal as this one against Hauptmann would come from us. What he meant was that our section counts on the whole as leftist.

I think he is completely right and I also spoke in the meeting against pushing Hauptmann aside. Döblin, however, has emotion in his favor and didn't hesitate to use it to convince Fulda and Molo. With these three votes (Benn is not in the senate and therefore has no vote) it was decided to propose to the ministry that Hauptmann have no more rights in regard to the endowment named after him than a sixth prize judge. To be removed from the statutes would be: his position as chairman, assuming he is present, and his veto power concerning recipients of the prize.

My understanding of my role as chairman is that I don't disregard majority decisions but execute them; otherwise I would not have been justified in accepting my selection. In any case, it seems to me imperative that a decision of such importance as this one be concluded only on the basis of the vote of all members of the senate. Your opinion is not yet known, nor that of Ricarda Huch. So I am asking that you make it known as soon as possible. Our next, and probably final, consideration of the two points detailed here is set for February 6.

Most warmly, H.

*February 9, 1933*
*Berlin W 15*
*Fasanenstr. 61*

Dear Tommy,

Your letter was very effective at the last meeting. We are now for Hauptmann having special rights. On the other issue, we will persist in our attempt to keep for ourselves four of the six seats in the prize judge collegium. I did my best to support acceptance of the endowment even if we are not successful on that point.

After considering further drafts, the efforts of Molo, Fulda, Benn, and Döblin, the manifesto against cultural reaction has been put off until a time when there is more promise of success. Now, however, I suddenly received an announcement of a congress, entitled "The Free Word," and appearing on the letterhead, along with Einstein's, is also my name. But the sole organizer is in reality the third, Mr. R. Olden, and the whole thing is brazenly unauthorized. I have demanded that Olden remove my name. If that doesn't happen, I will renounce it publicly, although reluctantly. For four weeks we conscientiously considered the issue in the Academy, and now someone is launching the action at the worst possible time and involving me—but you as well—in it. You are named in the program as "prospectively" delivering the opening address.

I assume that you have as little knowledge of this as I had, or that, perhaps three months ago, a nonbinding conversation with you also took place. In any case, I would like to implore you not to cooperate with the ambitious Olden in any way. Your participation would undermine, first, the Academy's position and, then, mine as well, and you yourself would be pointlessly involved in a failure. The best thing that remains possible would be a ban on the congress. But perhaps it will be permitted, to show how ineffective our opposition has become by now.

I would be grateful if you would send word about this.

Most warmly, H.


*April 15, 1933*
*Nice (A.M.)*
*Hôtel de Nice*

Dear Tommy,

I found out where you are staying from Madame Bertaux and am sure you would like to know where I am as well. From the same source I hear that your parents-in-law are not being allowed to leave. A professor between eighty and ninety—and I just read in the Catholic paper *La Croix* of a scene with Göring. Sweating and trembling, this scoundrel protested against suggestions that he wanted to root out "the intellectuals." There is still the hope that the bandits have a guilty conscience after all. Their lies and crimes are getting to be too much for them.

The characterization of my own situation by the head of the political police was that I "would not be given a pardon." And in fact they did impound my bank account in Berlin and have seized my Munich apartment. I wrote to Viko concerning an attempt to save it, but he doesn't even answer. He is threatened and will be feeling afraid.

The worst part is that the world is basically inclined to believe that it is all just a move against communism. Only the persecution of the Jews disturbs the picture, which would not otherwise be unwelcome. I will attempt to explain the truth. What is there left to lose? Garwin, in the *Observer*—utterly enraged, like all the English—is of the opinion that the Nazis are in for severe tests, and, indeed, before long. I have no judgment on that, but those who have remained contentedly uninvolved could finally be in for it.

My warm greetings to you and yours. H.

*April 21, 1933*
*Nice (A.M.)*
*Hôtel de Nice*

Dear Tommy,

Many thanks for your detailed letter. Of course I will name no names.

I read your essay on Wagner in *Europe* with the greatest admiration. What you confront there once again falls under the central category of "rabble versus mind" (*La canaille contre l'esprit*, I'm obliged to say now, for I will have to live from writing French articles)—and that is the fundamental theme of this so-called revolution. It turns out that we are the aristocrats.

When it's over, won't we—revive, as Häusser, no, Possart said. It's more like whoever is still around will have to consider his position on Bolshevism. For it, after all, is probably the most likely successor.

Berliners arriving here look suddenly ten years older. One probably does oneself.

On which of France's coasts do you want to be this summer? I'm very cautious about money. But if it is at all possible, I would like to see you!

Warmly, H.

*May 12, 1933*
*Nice*
*Hôtel de Nice*

Dear Tommy,

Your letter came at the right moment. I was just in the process of taking an apartment here. I want to delay that now, preferring first to come to Bandol instead.

Would you be so good as to find out the best price for which I can have a room facing the sea, above all with sun and if possible with a bath and toilet? The season has just barely begun and if there are as few travelers there as here it must be possible for 50 francs for room and board, especially if I stay about as long as you.

It truly pleases me that Mr. and Mrs. Pringsheim managed to escape after all. You have the good fortune of being with your wife and children, which is a great deal. I'm sure I shall find you bearing up courageously, which is the attitude we must maintain. It is sometimes difficult for me, especially when my energy for work suffers. But things must go on.

Please telegraph me tomorrow. Then I'll come Monday, assuming the post I'm expecting has arrived; otherwise Tuesday.

Warmly, H.

*October 8, 1933*
*Hôtel du Louvre*
*Nice (A.M.)*

Dear Tommy,

I find your positive impressions soothing and they make me truly happy. Hopefully you have found there the best possible substitute for your Munich surroundings; and later you shall have them back, if that's what you want. The word has been making the rounds, even here, that the German transport blockade will remain in force for two years. One asks: why? And no one knows the answer. But this general assumption that it will last that long could end up having a suggestive effect. The only trouble is that the war is anticipated by the end of two years.

That nice protestation of peace by the good old soldier Goering! Germany and France have no reason whatsoever, etc. Why then the whole seizure of power? They have a lot of fear as to the consequences. Their second string, for example, Frank II, doesn't yet get the picture and is still issuing statements about Germanic law (which has never existed, just as little as the Aryan race). He says: what benefits the German people (he means: his gang) is just and what harms it, unjust. That justifies in advance every future invasion, every annexation; but the Leipzig trial is also justified in that way. There is between the worthy president and the concentration camp sadists a community of interest, as only a bad cause can produce. Leipzig is the facade, Oranienburg, Dachau, and similar little places represent a view of the same building from the rear. I'm less astonished by the semi-respectability that continues to be preserved in the courtroom than by the inescapable similarity to the camp.

Meanwhile your attorney will have reported to you. Let it be favorable! So he thinks the house could be saved? Very nice; but even without that events would seem to secure its eventual return.

Poor S. Fischer has opened his season after all with Hauser and a dedication to Goering. If only the Jewish God doesn't take offense! But then they're all enlightened. Which seems to be the ultimate cause of all misfortune.

I'm atoning somewhat for my brisk activity during the summer, which, with our visits and other things, was an unexpected gift.

Things will get better, then I shall decide about my next place to stay. For now, my book has not yet come out and, beyond that, this familiar city seems so harmless to me.

I'm very much looking forward to your first volume, which must be about to appear. If not, please send news again anyway! I may assume that Erika is enjoying success, as usual.

Warm wishes and greetings, to you and yours, H.


*October 17, 1933*
*Hôtel du Louvre*
*Nice (A.M.)*

Dear Tommy,

Your book just arrived here. It looks very nice, and the organization, the chapter headings, everything that immediately strikes the eye, are enticing. However, I will put off the reading until next month; then I hope to have my head freer. In the moment it is somewhat burdened and I manage to read only for an hour evenings in bed. For your book, that would not be right.

I'm glad that it appeared so punctually, and thank you for your dedication, which mirrors my sentiments exactly.

Does the withdrawal of "Germany" cause you concern? Or does the nation's imminent round of unanimous applause disturb you? The remarkable aspect remains always the same: everyone sees through the swindle, and only the Germans are barred knowledge of it, although they actually do know it. "Who is being deceived here?" Enough, the world wants to be deceived. It goes along obediently with every dramatic turn on the part of the two dictators; the others don't want to resolve anything on their own in the League of Nations, won't carry through with the threatened sanctions, but instead tolerate the arms' buildup and even enter into treaties about it. These grand foreign policy deeds will be paid for dearly by the poor Germans, domestically. Once all have declared themselves national socialists, only then will a droll chattering of teeth commence.

Will you write to me what you are learning there? My greetings to you and yours.

Warmly, H.

*November 3, 1933*
*Hôtel du Louvre*
*Nice (A.M.)*

Dear Tommy,

My warm, deeply felt congratulations on your great success! It naturally means much more than it otherwise would; the better Germany has bestowed it upon you and upon itself. At the same time you are enjoying good fortune with three of your children at once, and that is a great deal in these times. Please tell Erika, Golo, and Bibi how pleased I am for them.

You were right in every respect, including the material, to have the book appear in Germany. The German success will extend its effects further and stimulate sales in America. That is no doubt more fruitful than publishing in Amsterdam and, just for that reason, being banned in Germany. If I could, I would do exactly the same. That is: conduct the struggle against those in power internally. Unfortunately, I can work only from without, if, for that, more directly.

I am now able to state that Germans who accidentally run across an article of mine are beside themselves with passion. They write to me "on the knees of the heart" as Kleist—who unfortunately would be right with them today—expressed it. But all the warnings I've been issuing now for years have found no echo other than the standard national socialist threats and insults. What is one to conclude? That the Germans really "needed" this hard lesson?

The French edition of *La Haine* has, I think, appeared; the German *Der Haß* is at hand. I will send you both as soon as I have copies. The impact, to repeat your two words, should be "deep" in Germany and "far-reaching" in the rest of the world. Opposed to that is the fact that only a few in Germany, at the cost of much effort and danger, will be able to read it. Among the great nations, however, only France's ideas about Germany are precise and well-grounded. All the Anglo-Saxons feel around until their fingers bump into some obvious detail. They don't want to know any more, in order to be able to remain "amenable to agreement," as you put it. For that reason the first book that expresses the painful truths in context hasn't yet even found a publisher in England. The good Feuchtwanger will intervene personally in London.

What I mainly want to say: the Germans themselves, if only they were still permitted to, now finally want to see and to learn. We must always remember how many of the "internal" Germans, yet more than those of us here on the outside, are being subjected by the country's demoralization to suffering of the most immediate sort. We, in any case, would be doing them wrong were we to renounce all ties with the country, which is wretched, to be sure, and, just as certainly, is allowing scoundrels to draw the world's abhorrence down upon it. If these scoundrels then go so far as to murder Torgler, then their accounts will be settled all the more quickly; they are already intolerably overdrawn. Accessories who see the end coming are now slinking off to the side, like the high-minded Spengler. It suddenly became clear to him that "stupid youngsters" are not capable of conducting politics. For now, he says only "stupid youngsters." As an agent of heavy industry, which he always was, he is not allowed to go any farther. But his like, all that calls itself German nationalist, is meanwhile experiencing a degree of embitterment that is no less than that of the Marxists. They, too, like the latter, are being removed from all, public and private, economic positions. The regime is provoking not only the better Germany to opposition, but also part of the other Germany that's not come off well—not even the SA is exempted. They were recently assembled on Alexanderplatz, but then they suddenly began singing: "If from Hitler we get no bread, then we'll beat him till he's dead!"

A popular table grace goes as follows:

Our dear Hitler, be our guest!
If what we had were only half your best!
Under Brüning and Papen,
We still ate sauerbraten,
Under Hitler and Goering
There's nothing but herring.

A banker, whose impressions were conveyed to me indirectly, is convinced that the authorities will at all events last through the winter, but definitely not any longer. The betting is on a military dictatorship. It is to be assumed that a Communist uprising will precede it. Schleicher is supposed by no means to be ill, but holding himself ready. Will it perhaps be possible to talk to him? But even with him only personally at most. A regime of generals can have no ultimate right to existence save preparation for war. Not to be foreseen is where and when the real renewal will begin. No question but that it must be preceded by a long and difficult period of inner cultivation on the part of Germans. They have never been enraptured by anything but orders from without. But history knows only two classes of nations now: the one has struggled for and won freedom and self-determination; for the other there remains much suffering and much to do. It will not make it easier for Germany if it goes on impoverishing itself intellectually, a process augmented now by the exodus of "Aryan" professors. Those remaining are convincing themselves and their Hitler that they can annihilate the whole of humanity with a bacterial culture—which is nonsense medically. If one finds oneself believing in that, then it's only all the more revealing. Moreover, 88 "writers" have announced their support for the Führer—now, when it would be smarter not to do it. But "she doesn't notice it at all," as one of Claudius's old sisters says of the other.

November 4. I already wrote too much yesterday—news, which is fresher when you get it yourself there, and thoughts, which are obvious anyway. Your business with the book guild reminds me of my own. Herzog, who offered me a licensed edition of my novel *Ein ernstes Leben*, seems since then more to have bungled than to have ordered the matter with Zsolnay. The Zsolnay Press *has authorized such licensed editions for nearly all of my novels and thereby received a part of the profits. This really has to be even easier to arrange with him now, since my books are selling only outside of Germany, and not really even that.—I assume that your business causes you to speak occasionally with Herzog. Would you be so good as to ask him if there's still any interest and where, given such a simple matter, the problem lies?* He wrote me confusingly about "publisher's rights," which surely is not the issue. We all know, after all, what a "license" is.

If Beermann is keeping you in his clutches, he still has some justification for it, and the success also gives him some right. Concerning Zsolnay, I can only say that he is the cowardly traitor most of his long-term friends and business partners are now becoming acquainted with. All the trouble that's come down upon my head has not yet moved him to a single word; on the contrary, I know from third parties who placed futile orders for my books with him that he refuses to deliver them to Germany. He could probably do so quite easily; for I know nothing of an actual ban and they are supposedly being displayed in bookstore windows in the workers' districts. But Zsolnay is obviously trying to save the remainder of his publications for Germany by abandoning me. The publisher's rights, however, he holds firmly in his hands, as is evident from his negotiations with Herzog. I would take them away from him if I were to win the approval of the *international court that exists for such purposes. Is it in Bern? Or is it the League of Nations' court in The Hague? I don't want to put you to too much trouble; but perhaps simply as a matter of course somebody in your circles there could inform you as to my chances? Please don't speak about this to Herzog, for then Zsolnay would find out.*—I hope to hear again soon about your experiences and impressions.

My warm greetings to all of you, and best wishes from Frau Kröger.

H.


*November 18, 1933*
*Hôtel de Nice*
*Nice (A.M.)*

Dear Tommy,

In three evenings I read your "Prelude" and now have the desire to let you know that it offered me my greatest reading experience since—when? I don't know.

I often convinced myself, when I still had my library, that Anatole France had a remarkable familiarity with the angels, with their story, their relationships to God and humanity. You have your own exegesis, even your own "doctrine," if I understand correctly, and it reaches grandly, deeply into the distance and then back again to you and to us. It is this universality that I admire and revere, including of course the enormous research work, during which your view matured and made such vivification possible. I have a particular feeling for the eager earnestness in the tone of your dialectics, behind which there appears humor and even travesty, and behind that earnestness once again.

And all of it, incidentally, is markedly—Catholic. Catholic skepticism, which is profound. Where Protestantism ceases, there begins simply unbelief. My own intellectual experience is not so broad that I am justified in the assertion, but I have the feeling that a culture conceived in terms of complete coherence issues in the same unity as old, unified Christianity.

Reflections on the "Descent into Hell" could lead who knows where? It was a pleasure to hear that someone in Germany termed your book a legacy of the former bourgeoisie, or something similar. What we have today is called National Socialism and the contrast between it and the "former bourgeoisie" is similar to that between abstract and concave. The truth is that they have broken with culture no less than with civilization, and are hopping about on their own in the traditionless desert of the present.

Sales of your book will now continue to be vigorous, and that means more every day the way everything else looks there. The easy triumph by way of the plebiscite will oblige them to further deeds, the final of which would be war. But if no one wants it? And, above all, if it is known about too long in advance! It is already too well known by now how dictatorships function. The passive resistance undertaken by the democracies is perhaps the right thing after all? I'm just asking for now. Things could also turn out such that Germany will have to fight its Thirty Years War alone against itself. It started it most eagerly.

The democracies must last until the regime collapses. The danger is that they get subverted prematurely. In this connection I remind you of the visit you had in September from a young man named Robert Aron. That evening he got married. And he works at Gallimard. But he publishes a fascist "new" newspaper. That's how they are: they take money from a publisher whose main author is the Communist Gide and are themselves fascists. Are Jews and fascists. Have to have a look at republican refugees even on their wedding day, let them speak their minds, but don't let on what they are, fascists. We must always be more careful! I heard about your Swiss tour. Certainly you may undertake it, but be careful with everyone you meet!

You received my two books. My warmest greetings to you and the others. Frau Kröger asks to join in that sentiment.

Most warmly, H.


*Küsnacht/Zurich*
*November 18, 1933*

Dear Heinrich,

I can thank you for your book, in both versions, only in a few inadequate words today. Katja is ill (a female matter, not serious, but probably the signal more of limited activities in the future), and so my responsibilities are greater than usual.

In the French edition I had already read much that was new to me, and reread pieces that were familiar; but when the German version arrived, it laid hold of me for another entire afternoon and evening, until I had raced through it from A to Z, breathlessly, so to speak, the great introductory essay included—which is how it absolutely must be read. It is not even the original version, in this case, and yet it is only from it that one becomes aware, at least it is so with me, of all the tension and charged passion that fill the book: making "contact" with it is quite a lot like touching something electric; it gets into your nerves, blood, and muscles, and it gets the reader in its "grip," like a powerful contraction that doesn't let up until the end. That was my experience, and I am convinced that it will be confirmed a thousandfold, in both outrage and enthusiasm. Outrage will try to take advantage of the way the book's analytical aspect is occasionally a matter of appearance and form, raising the highly moral pamphlet into the reaches of the unreal. *If the document in the Petit Parisien is counterfeit, then it is truly real.* Similarly here. And these crushingly condemnatory essays will remain forever a document of the most tremendous sort, a document of German shame and honor.

As to your recent question, I still have no response, in particular nothing regarding the international court. I haven't yet spoken to anyone in a position to offer information. I'm interpellating Herzog. He seemed distressed by the likelihood that nothing would come of a licensed printing by the book guild, because Zsolnay could not be legally held to make payment. I didn't press the matter further. Perhaps I'll take Rascher into my confidence; I'm negotiating with him anyway concerning a volume of essays.

Best wishes! Many thanks from Katja for the inscription. Since Sanary she has spoken of you often, with great fondness and affection.

T.


*December 25, 1933*
*11, rue du Congrès*
*Nice (A.M.)*

Dear Tommy,

Every evening, propped up in bed, which affords the maximum of attention, I read a few pages of your book; for racing through and putting it quickly behind oneself would be pointless here. I can recall no other book that would have offered so much to contemplate and admire. I do not know the origin of the account—it seems to me to be made up of a series of revealed mysteries—although I have to tell myself that it is the literary continuation of often meager sources. Rich writing, probably your richest; and the most alluring part of it is precisely its derivation from historical circumstances that were thought familiar to all, though each learns from you that he knew nothing about them and that the human past made present is yet more fabulous than he might ever have wished.— Enough. I shall be busy with the book for a long time yet and be grateful to you every evening.

Present-day Germany could learn from you that the uttermost in intellectuality, one knows not how and where, transforms itself into mysticism—or, in other words, that mysticism is something to be thought. But if present-day Germany could learn that much, it would not be the Germany of the present day.

You have there, no doubt, aside from your work, the relief of other distractions. Here I have little of that, and over time memories tend to grow more difficult rather than less. In the summer we had yet new impressions to assimilate, and even did it together. Hopefully, that will happen again.

One thing I know, and that is that I do not wish to return, nor even if I could, and not even if all of this were over. For I would no longer trust the people that it really is over.

I read the play by Bruckner; you probably saw it there. It struck me as excellent and true.

I heard about Golo that he has gotten himself very well established in St-Cloud. In my own case, a member of parliament is supposed to speak to the minister, but nothing will come of it; one must first become French. Golo will also have to decide.

You are probably all together for the holidays. To you and likewise to Katja, I wish the best of health, also that there are good surprises in store for both of you in 1934, in any case, that life will become easy, or nearly easy. Nothing better, for myself either, comes to mind.

Most warmly, H.


*January 25, 1934*
*11, rue du Congrès*
*Nice (A.M.ᵉˢ)*

Dear Tommy,

Many thanks for your letter; it always makes me very happy. Personal letters: do you still write many otherwise? I actually exchange them only with Paul Graetz, who has become a success in film in London; and he was the typical Berliner, could have held on there in the theater—such exceptions are made—but decided he'd rather struggle through in English.—Only one German stamp comes my way, when the press agent of the Circus Busch writes me without indicating his name.—I know of a particularly good story, of a man named Balder Olden, just as "Aryan" as the name, counted for a nationalist, took part in the fighting in Africa, could no doubt be right in the middle of Goebbels's "Reichskultur"; but in London he wrote a novel in English against the Third Reich, for no other reason than to remain honest. I would bow down before something like that.

You know, of course, that the German PEN Club has been founded in London. The address for membership declarations is Dr. Rudolf Olden (brother of Balder), 13 Manson Place, Queen's Gate, London S.W. 7. I hope that this organization will serve to get us League of Nations passports.

I especially wanted to express my happiness and congratulations regarding Golo's piece in *Die Sammlung*. Very remarkable, the scientific armor—and the bold talent that breaks through it.

Then the painful news I received first from you: Wassermann is really dead? And what is the meaning of "collapse"? Was he suffering from the loss of his previous status? It is to be feared that he no longer knew what for and for whom. Nor could his income have been any more, as is now usual, than a third of what it was. And if, on top of all that, one has already been ill for a lengthy period . . .

Your book has now passed thirty thousand copies, at least there's that: the great exception. And they won't dare close the German market to you, if you remain firm. I say that with no guarantee; ultimately everything is chance. But in what different stead everyone, including Wassermann and even myself, would have been had the intellectuals become conscious of their strength, and in particular of their intellectual duty, like the pastors. One gets to know them differently now than was ever to be hoped for. They convey the view of Christ and also of Luther. There are surprising things to be heard of people these days, but not only distressing ones.

I continue the writing on my great king, whom they at bottom didn't like and finally became utterly fed up with, like all the good ones. To be sure, they are very attached to those who "lead" them toward abomination. Unfortunately, I'm in the obscure beginnings of the novel; it will take a long time still. Nevertheless, I have already received one payment: it won't last any longer than the work itself; but to have a secure future in addition to everything else, today that would be demanding too much. *Der Haß* has had the effect that an American and a Parisian periodical have simultaneously indicated an interest in learning from me how intellectual freedom can be destroyed. That's something I could tell them. And today I asked the director of *Dépêche*, a government paper, whether I, as a foreigner, might report on the personal experience of a change in systems. For it is getting to be time. And one always wants to make oneself useful.

Warm wishes to you and yours. Please write me soon,

H.

*March 5, 1934*
*11, rue du Congrès*
*Nice (France)*

Dear Tommy,

It's nice that you're in Arosa; the air there must be invigorating. I, too, often think of the mountains, because I haven't been to Gastein since 1932.

You wrote to me on January 30th, and it was all of deep interest to me; nevertheless

I didn't answer for such a long time, but neglect is not the reason. I always had a lot of work, including some business, but otherwise nothing at all. No excursions into the world, nearly no familiar faces: only the indispensable strolls and the calm that is so necessary. It's getting like a monastery here. My novel is a work of several years; I have to have enough of them. In terms of its essential nature it would even be "the whole" and the final summary. Only I don't know whether I can keep at the novel and keep "it" up for that long. It is necessary to have confidence in the continuation of things, not to mention of oneself. "In terms of making something that lasts, fame is no laughing matter," said Flaubert and the pure bourgeois epoch. He also had seven years' time for a book then and never doubted the permanency of the world. I don't either, incidentally. It always comes back to its senses. Meanwhile, I work more than was otherwise usual, facing into the void, but can remember that as a beginner I quite likely expected still less from the outside world. Back then all the time to become pleasantly disillusioned still lay in the future. Today the only thing left that matters, the only thing that ultimately does matter, is not to have cheated oneself. I would be happy if things turned out for me as they did for you with *Joseph*. These tales of Jacob have a great calm about them, time is annulled, both for the generations of actors and for him who writes. This is what attracts me most today.

Incidentally, I have decided to devote a first volume of the novel to the youth of my king, and with that I am somewhat advanced. As for you, I assume and hope that you are allowing yourself a bit of freedom and recuperation. The third volume is not to appear until 1936? So you are allowing some time for reading tours. Those must have been encouraging impressions. I hope that the essay volume appears soon, with Wagner but also with "Freiheit und Vornehmheit";[10] no other two concepts belong so much together, and precisely what has the least prospect of success at present is to persuade an enslaved people of its nobility. Nothing that's going on or being attempted has any prospect; that doubtless remains the case, even when one doesn't know otherwise what might happen. Since I don't believe in the war, the most likely outcome appears to me to be the quick economic collapse of the dictatorships. They "graze" and are corrupt; no one ever anticipated anything like this. I only hope that this assessment proves true before the remaining democracies are turned fascist. In France that will take a good while, in my opinion. The countryside will continue to hold on to the republic for a long time; only Paris appears to be somewhat unstable. It was never any different: once the *Ligue* (1576), then Boulanger. Paris is always opposed to the countryside. It's remarkable: many republicans work against dissolving parliament because the countryside could return an overly strong representation of the left: that would result in an uprising in Paris.

The French, according to our friend Bertaux, are no smarter, but in the end more

---

10. Or "Freedom and Distinction"; a portion of the essay was published as "Goethe and Tolstoy" in *Essays of Three Decades*.

moderate than others. Or have become so, one must add: as the result of rich experience. Assuming further developments, I still see here promising the best chance to be left in peace. The smaller countries wouldn't offer me any personal security. In Switzerland my book was recently banned for a few days, obviously in response to pressure from Berlin. In Amsterdam they detained Heinz Liepmann, who had just come from the camp, and he will be fortunate if he is not extradited. Universal terror is on the rise for the time being; this country is the only one on the continent that remains closed to it; but there are certain intensifications that could take place, whereupon one would not want to be found with an old German passport. In short, I'm taking the first, nonbinding steps toward eventual naturalization. If things go that far, it would in any case take years and by then it would perhaps no longer be necessary or would come to nothing on its own. I say to myself what the ear doctor says to elderly people: "You will go deaf, but you won't be around to notice it."

Swiss citizenship would certainly be the right thing for you. Whoever is still around after the much longed-for change will become German again the very same moment. It also appears that, as long as your case is being processed, you don't have to live there; you mentioned Florence for next winter. Do you think, given more precise consideration, that you would feel comfortable there? It seems certain that too much, in particular the deceitfulness of everything that's happening there, would remind one precisely of what one wanted no part in. As for the thrift question, however: did Schickele write you about the house he rented here? A villa outside the city, ten rooms, a view of the mountains, and an unbeatable rent. I don't know if they've already moved in; only young Hans visits me.—Moreover, my judgment is colored by the fact that I would like to live in the same city with you. Couldn't we at least get together first this summer? Mountains gladly; just not so gladly expensive Switzerland. Wouldn't you like to get to know the Pyrenees? They are grand and so peacefully archaic. You can still get those transparent penholders there that our parents brought us back from resort towns. If I were to hear from you that you were not disinclined, then I would regret it less that Zurich is out of the question for me before summer—and then hardly likely. I have put off everyone wanting me to lecture until the beginning of summer; but it's a question of my work and of other circumstances as well whether I really will undertake anything. And the last year has sooner dampened than stimulated my desire to travel. The only thing I would really like to see is your house in Zurich: it is supposed to be so pleasant. I hope that all of you, especially Katja, to whom I send my best regards, will have a really fine spring following a winter that surely also brought its beauties.

I have that information from one of your visitors, Mr. Klaus Pinkus. And also that the more cautious sorts in Berlin are now beginning to justify themselves—for whatever happens. On the other hand, I also hear from Communists who are working more confidently than ever. And Oranienburg is no longer a camp for Marxists: now there's no one there but mutinous SA members. In Berlin SS and SA have exchanged gunfire. The ruins are crumbling; but only Schacht can be counted on; he'll get it done.—Otherwise, I also wanted to ask whether you have any information about "Dr. Paul Aron" of Paris, whom I took to be a fascist, although he came for a look at us in Sanary. Now he's writing me enthusiastically—but take care whom you trust. And I wanted very much to ask you to have a copy of "Tonio Kröger" sent to me: my lady friend Kröger wants to read it.

Most warmly, H.

*April 19, 1934*
*11, rue du Congrès*
*Nice (A.M.es)*

Dear Tommy,

Tagger was just here and now, finally, I know what was wanted of me in Zurich. Hartung had telegraphed and arranged for a telephone call, without, however, indicating the purpose. I prefer (because of the previous suspicious matter) not to have anything to do with calls, so instead I wrote express: open to anything, just not coming there. Now Tagger says to me that your efforts were behind the call; all the more painful, then, is my forced immobility. Unfortunately, I can't change it. If I had given in to the eight or ten invitations I received to travel this winter—even to America—there would be hardly a sentence written of my novel. As it is, however, I'm on the second third and hope to complete it after the summer break. This break is my next goal; I'm working steadfastly toward doing nothing. It's time for it: my last break was exactly two years ago. Forgive me, then, my apparent indolence and please let Hartung know as well that there was no failure of goodwill! I truly would have liked to see you. When could it be? In July? Beforehand I would undergo treatment at a spa. For some time together I propose then the coast in the southwest, from Biarritz to Arcachon at the farthest: there good weather is a certainty. Do you prefer a little place with villas, or a big one with hotels? Around here we would know more people, but Sanary again? Please write me what you think, and my warm regards to both of you.

H.

*May 13, 1934*
*11, rue du Congrès*
*Nice (A.M.es)*

Dear Tommy,

This year I have to hurry with my congratulations: you want to celebrate your fifty-ninth in another place altogether. My wish for you is that your extraordinary novel trilogy brings you further pleasure in peace and security. In my opinion this is a worthy goal, at least for the present—and not always only that breathless agitation and stimulation customary in "dynamic" places. It is your inestimable privilege to have time. But since you no doubt already know how things are to proceed, my wish to you need only be that a new work will become clearer and more agreeable on the summer ocean between here and America. For my part, I can offer the observation that one finds commensurate pleasure in a work only once its true sense emerges clearly. That point is where I have now happily arrived, but in a state of dreadful overexertion and with a great longing for a resort in the mountains. In practical terms, however, the way things stand just now makes it better for me to finish another main chapter before my summer holiday; and, despite the fatigue, I unfortunately also feel compelled to do it. One should finally learn to be patient and calm.

My refusal to travel to Zurich I truly regretted only once I read in your letter how disappointed you were. It didn't make me happy to stay away, that you can believe. And on top of that I now have to worry whether we'll be able to meet someplace between July and September. Will your trip leave you some time toward the end of the summer? I would be very happy. Since we parted, my closest company by far has been the characters in my novel—as it probably should be. But once a year it could be different. In the Hotel Bandol an older, somewhat hard-of-hearing man, Dr. Oscar Levy, sat occasionally at our table; he lived in Cannes for the winter and made the trip faithfully by bus so we could spend the evening together. He was patient and devoted, not to mention worthy in his own right. In contrast, the business with Schickele has proved difficult and thorny; it will be hard to continue it.—Rather moving news has come from Arnold Zweig in Palestine. I could only answer him by saying that our mother didn't come two thousand years ago, but around 1860 from Brazil; yet if I wanted to "return home" there, how much would I still recognize? Besides, so I said, it is one of our primary tasks to show that we, self-reliant as always, can live our lives respectably to the end, whether here or there. A bad, thankless country, which we had to leave, we don't need either.

You write that you are gratefully breathing the air of the Western world, and that is actually the best, the happiest of what I read from you. My wishes that your entire year might glow with that feeling, and that I might celebrate your sixtieth with you!

Greetings to Katja. And my highest regards to the great Erika. Tonio and your inscription touched Frau Kröger deeply and she extends her thanks.

Warmly, H.

*June 27, 1934*
*11, rue du Congrès*
*Nice (A.M.)*

Dear Tommy,

I heard that you've arrived back: I want to be quick to thank you for your news from the middle of the ocean. Since then I saw on the *first page of the New York Herald that the most eminent living man of letters*[11]—is you; and I thought with pleasure of the face of the vain old Shaw. Hopefully the trip was pleasant and agreed with both you and Katja.

I got a request from Hartung that I write something for Paris so that Ossietzky will be awarded the Nobel Peace Prize. Unfortunately, I had to respond that, as far as I know, there is nothing to be done in Paris. Wouldn't the best idea be for you to make use of your rights as a Nobel Prize recipient to formally nominate the peace martyr Ossietzky?—My particular wish would be for you to take the opportunity to make Kolbenheyer an impossibility in Stockholm. For there is the threat here (I don't know if it's very serious) of the Hitler regime receiving international literary recognition. It is supposed to be pursuing it ardently. Perhaps you can find out whether your intervention is advisable.

Gustav Hartung's address, incidentally, is: Mottafarm, Brissago (Tessin).

I'm giving up my apartment on June 30 and going to the mountains for a rest: where precisely I will write to you.

My warmest regards in the meantime. H.

*July 2, 1934*
*Cauterets (Htes Pyrénées)*
*Pension Les Edelweiss*

Dear Tommy,

This is where I am staying, and in addition to the name of the pension, the waterfalls and strolls in the woods are also reminiscent of Gastein.—Pallenberg! That affects me more than all the new abominations in Berlin. What is Massary's address? I hope to hear good things from you soon.

Warm regards to both of you. H.

*Küsnacht/Zurich*
*Schiedhaldenstraße 33*
*July 5, 1934*

Dear Heinrich,

Your card came today, which gives me the chance to thank you for your letter of June 27th, which was here to greet us when we arrived. The idea about Ossietzky is excellent; but the prize is awarded in Oslo, not Stockholm, and I have neither nominating privileges nor any other connections to the committee. Certainly, it is correct to

11. In English in original.

approach them with the idea, but will they accept it? In general, other countries are little inclined to give the gang running the German government the called-for box on the ears. Things are a little different with a literary prize. In this case I can write, astounded and incredulous, to Prof. Böök, the academician who holds the decisive vote—sincerely incredulous; because I cannot imagine that anyone seriously wants to present the internationally unknown, utterly boring Kolbenheyer to the world. From what I know, unfortunately, Hermann Stehr's prospects are better—which, of course, would also be unfortunate and annoying. I don't really know what is possible along these lines up there. It is only too likely, given the impression made by recent events, that the inclination to award the prize to Germany has fallen off. Since I unfortunately know what is *not* possible, I've suggested Hermann Hesse, some of whose work I like very much, and who represents a sympathetic instance of German extra-Germanism.

I was also appalled and filled with sadness by Pallenberg's death. I assume that Massary has meanwhile returned from Vienna to Bissone on Lake Lugano. We telegraphed our condolences to the Franks in Sanary. Newspapers reporting on the accident inside that wretched territory describe him as that "disgusting Jewish clown who held nothing sacred"—to prevent there being any sense in which things "German" would fail to contradict, in the sharpest terms, the world of normal decency and humanity. What is to come of all this? The answer lies more or less in the most recent bloody obscenities. This incredible mess will take its course according to the law with which it began, and we may be convinced that it will end according to the same law.

America was a tremendous lark—which perhaps suggests both what impressed me and what I found superfluous about it. It cost me four weeks, which, in regard to my third volume, I honestly could not afford. Still, I'm reluctant to regret the trip, for there was something worthwhile and good in harvesting so many years of sympathy, which is abundant and growing. More than once I heard from people, young and old, that it was "like a dream" to have me standing before them in reality; and it was all a dream for me as well. I felt very wistful, standing up at the "testimonial dinner" on June 6th at the Plaza Hotel (300 guests, the whole of literary Manhattan, with the mayor at the lead) to express my thanks. Ten days in New York filled and overfilled with social obligations are, of course, too little to gain any precise insight, but in terms of pure atmosphere my impressions were hopeful. Anything is possible in the future, also a Soviet America, but psychologically the people seemed to me healthier and happier than they are at home, by no means as hysterical, and Roosevelt is a *good man*[12] in the Anglo-Saxon sense of the word; that much is certain. It is dictatorship that he is pursuing as well, of course, but no doubt sincerely in the interest of democracy. From prosperous sorts I heard repeatedly that the revolution would have come for sure without him. I didn't meet him, incidentally, but

12. In English in original.

only the mayor of New York, La Guardia, who also invited us to a parade—an Italian half-Jew from the negro-Jewish neighborhood of East Harlem, the most amusing and comically sly physiognomy I ever encountered. He has, in addition, a Swedish adoptive son, and serves perfectly to represent the gigantic city with its chaos of races, languages, and human types. It is the only true metropolis in the world, and could even absorb us, I think, as it has already visibly absorbed George Groß. It is possible to become an American, and perhaps one should.

You were the cleverer one, spending the time working. Your essay on democracy, in your sense, had a marvelous attitude about it, and I can't tell you how curious I am about the king novel. Have you made good progress?

Warm wishes for your recovery! T.


*September 6, 1934*
*121, Promenade des Anglais*
*Nice (A.M.)*

Dear Tommy,

We've not heard from each other for a long time. You are probably engrossed in your third volume; following the summer holiday I've now found my way back into my first.

The immediate occasion for writing is a request from the actor Paul Graetz; he would like to have a role in your Joseph film. It is also certain that he deserves it, in both artistic and humane terms. He accepted exile out of honesty; other Jews used their popularity to avoid it. In London he has broken into film during the past year. He appeared in *Jud Süss, Blossom Time*, and several others. I know from an uninvolved director that proposing him for a role entails no risk. He would certainly be considered by King Vidor as well, if you would put in a word for him—in particular given the large number of parts and character parts that would be appropriate for him.—So. I wanted to have passed that on.

I don't yet have an apartment for the winter. If it's possible I'll go back to the rue du Congrès. What do you hear there about the prospects of Germany's chosen one? The KPD perpetually regards itself as just a hundred yards from the goal; that must be a nice feeling, but that's all it amounts to.

Warm regards to you and yours. H.

*Küsnacht-Zurich*
*Schiedhaldenstraße 33*
*September 11, 1934*

Dear Heinrich,

I was set to write you too, on account of your admirable essay in *Die Sammlung* about our accursed German colleagues. I read it with a sense of profound agreement, and, as far as I can tell, it caused a stir among the Swiss as well. German intellectuals, professors, and writers will be the last to concede what wretched nonsense it all has been; they will have to "stick with it" the longest, for having committed and prostituted themselves so miserably. Ordinary people are obviously much farther along. We're getting a lot of visitors from the Reich just now; some who had disappeared entirely are reappearing, aged, their voices lowered, shocked by what they are learning here about conditions at home. That the regime is already rotting from within, with deluded belief and enthusiasm both in full decline—all reports are agreed on that. The complete change of mood within the student body is being widely confirmed, and, indeed, at least in Munich, confirmed in public by the Nazi students' letter to *Der Stürmer.* The paper was banned for that reason, not because of some insult to Masaryk. The buffoon at the top, yakking away about millennia, is being guarded like no Romanov ever was—with air defenses and heavily armed soldiers present wherever he appears, and still there are supposed to have been four assassination attempts in July. Perhaps it is still too soon. But the question, "How long yet?" dominates every private conversation, from what I've heard, as well as, unfortunately for good reason, the other question: "What then?" What has long since been judged despicable survives, for now, because there is nothing, or nothing yet visible, capable of taking its place—which is no secret even to the regime. Unfortunately it also lives on because of the misery and general helplessness in the world at large, which supplies a serviceable foil. With Russia and Italy enduring privation, France in sorry shape, and America facing chaos, it is good in the end to have something resembling order— that's the worst of it and what allows it to go on. The attitude of the German masses, if I see the situation correctly, is one of fatalistic anticipation, a waiting for the catastrophe, which can indeed appear at any moment from any number of angles. My wish would be that the nightmare of the Reich be done away, with Bavaria going to Austria, and Germany freed of politics. Goethe said simply: "The Germans must be transplanted and dispersed through all the world, like the Jews, to develop fully the goodness that is in them to the benefit of all the nations." It is good to read Goethe's conversations now (the image of the "dismissive one" works very nicely in your essay). But I'm also reading widely in the old *Briefe eines Unbekannten* (Alexander Viller) in the moment. In 1870 he wrote: "I am so sick of this singing, phrase-mongering people that I have involuntarily broken all of the thousand ties that bind me to Germany." Yes, yes.

Whether I shall be able to arrange anything for your friend Graetz is doubtful.

Everything I know about the plans for the film I learn myself from the newspapers; I've not heard a word about the director or about casting directly from the company, and although they have hinted that I'm to "supervise direction," I do not have the impression that I will have any influence. I simply signed the option contract, somewhat hastily, since Reinhardt and Werfel are planning a big Old-Testament spectacle of their own, and I have to fear that the Londoners will respond by jumping ship. Business dealings are being conducted by telegraph. I have now—it's already been a number of days— posed certain questions in a letter, and simply have to wait and see if I get a reply. Perhaps then I could proceed in reference to Graetz.

Unfortunately, I'm not at all immersed in my third volume, but instead busy with "incidentals." I don't know whether it's because I had had enough of that world, or because failing over the long run to respond as a critical consciousness to the constant din of politics eventually starts to violate my sense of honor as a writer. In short, for weeks I have been making elaborate preparations for a polemic against the Third Reich—only then to let it drop again for the moment. If I do get started on it, it will be very extensive, a matter of months, perhaps many months, at the expense of the novel, which is already delayed; and which many see as oppositional, as resistance in its own right. It makes me sorry to neglect it. I also ask myself whether such a frontal attack is really my forte, since everything of the essence is obvious by now, and has been expressed elsewhere, most brilliantly by you, and even in the papers. We need not fear that anyone is fooled by this miserable affair. It also seems as if it's almost too late to make an explicit and extensive statement against what has already been refuted time and again. In short, I vacillate, a thoroughly enervating state, incidentally; to husband my time I get busy with some third thing, something neutral. I'm writing a kind of expanded feuilleton to round out the volume of essays: "Voyage with Don Quixote," in which I'm weaving a description of an ocean voyage into notes about the novel. That entertains me for the present, and by the time it's finished perhaps I'll know better what I want to do.

Good for you that your novel is growing. I look forward to its appearance. I'm now reading the proofs of your nephew Klaus's *Flucht in den Norden;* I find it charming.

Warm regards! T.


*September 20, 1934*
*121, Prom. des Anglais*
*Nice (A.M.)*

Dear Tommy,

Just a thank-you for your nice long letter. It's hard for me to find my way out of the atmosphere of the novel just now. At the end of the month I will have to make the leap and set to work on an article; otherwise no distractions. It is understandable that you would like to digress from your major work into a personal statement. Ultimately, however, you will probably put it off. One can also write an obituary on the Third Reich when it is over. Then as well, to be sure, I would ask: what for? We are thoroughly acquainted with it and the knowledge of the phenomenon will be preserved to the world even against its better nature. Once dead, then fundamentally so. Of Napoleon III, Rochefort, who had fought against him for eighteen years, already said: *Cet imbécile de qui personne ne parle plus.* How much truer that will be of an overthrown Hitler. My next effort will be to try to say to the rest of the world through a French newspaper that perhaps all that's lacking is its moral support for Germany to think better of it. Instead, other countries are inclined to repeat Germany's experience, after its complete failure. That is the scandal. With your permission, I will make use of the information in your letter. I relied solely on you for a detail I cited about Goethe in *Die Sammlung*. I hadn't known that he feared assassination. I knew only that the nationalists of those days also tended to commit murder. Your positive opinion of the essay pleases me greatly.

A lecture trip to Prague is causing me considerable agitation. It is supposed to earn money, precisely too much for me to have been justified in declining. But 1) chasing down the necessary papers and 2) the 40-hour train trip, or an airplane, which, however, may only be Italian. Where does one end up otherwise—this understood both literally and locationally. Better not to mention this yet; it's only anxiety that makes me say it, and because in the end I'll probably not make the trip anyway.

My warm regards! H.

*Küsnacht-Zurich*
*Schiedhaldenstraße 33*
*December 13, 1934*

Dear Heinrich,

I offer for your amusement the little piece enclosed, which recently appeared as a feuilleton in the *Neue Zürcher Zeitung*. I'm using it to conclude an essay volume, which will also contain the Wagner essay I described to you, the Goethe speech, and other affronts, and which Bermann indeed wants to bring out in February. If the volume is not banned it will be the best proof yet that the reins are trailing at home. I'm also enclosing a report from the *Baseler Nationalzeitung* on a very encouraging gathering. It took place four weeks ago and I participated—if with reservations. Pacifism, since the wolves have started preaching it, finds itself in a somewhat questionable situation. For that same reason, I did not in any way speak in opposition to the military preparedness of peace-loving peoples.

We have heard and read much about your honored and successful stay in Prague, and we saw the pretty picture with Goschi; you must have been happy to have had her there for your embrace. I heard in Basel that you had agreed with a student group there to deliver an address. Would that you came! The Zurich Schauspielhaus, which, incidentally, is seriously considering putting on your *Madame Legros* again, would also be more than a little pleased. What should prevent your coming? The events surrounding Die Pfeffermühle, which you perhaps heard about, mustn't blacken too much your image of Swiss conditions. It was a prank, and there were personal motivations in the background. The officials conducted themselves admirably, and Erika's guest appearance in Zurich proceeded triumphantly to its conclusion. Now she is on her way with her troupe to Prague, and we will probably meet her there; for I'm going to take up your traces from there again in January, going on to Vienna and Budapest, where I haven't been in years.

When is your Henri novel coming out? The volume about his youth must be finished any time now, and I have a great desire to see it. I hope I'm correct, imagining that your health is good, and that you are in good spirits altogether and busy with the final parts of your book.

And our return to Germany? What do you make of the prospects? Not that I'm in a hurry, personally—on the contrary, I'm not much tempted to live among those thrill seeking ignoramuses, who have soured life for so long for the likes of us. And yet, "waiting," in the sense of the old fervor, returns now in a ceaseless hoping and praying that the rogue regime at home will be delivered to its merited end sooner rather than later. It is probably necessary to believe steadfastly in that eventuality, and there is no shortage of evidence of decay. But, ridden by the impossibility of these people, I've become so mistrustful of our time that I find myself in gloomy moments believing that the impossible in it is possible.

Warm regards! T.


*December 17, 1934*
*11, rue du Congrès*
*Nice (A.M.)*

Dear Tommy,

I would have written you this very day even if your kind letter had not come. I've wanted news from you for a long time now and didn't want to wait any longer with mine. The *N[eue] Zür[cher] Z[eitung]* with your article was shown to me and I had also heard about your appearance in Basel. Thank you for the materials you sent; reading it all will be a pleasure. I overestimated the incident with the National Front; more accurately: it was overestimated. Your correction was reassuring. Hopefully you can also deny what I heard mentioned in Prague: that your health has not always been good of late? In any case, I may assume that you are feeling better since you are planning a trip for January.

My life is being made difficult by how easily fatigued I am and how oversensitive I've become, both familiar conditions; and the longer they last the more intimate the acquaintance—also in the sense that I have learned patience and resignation. Much experience dividing my energies has made it possible for me to work more in the two years of so-called exile than I have since days long past. The novel has grown to its full proportions; *Young Henry* has possibly amounted to too much paper for a single volume. I'll finish the second-to-last of the major sections after New Year's. If all goes well, the book will appear in the spring. I like working on it. It's an opportunity to find a place for what I know—the more so later on, in the other part, "Sieg und Auflösung." It's also an opportunity to use favorite images and scenes I've been gathering over the years. That produces a connection to my earliest works, a very interesting case. The editor from Mondadori in Milan—I had no idea she'd received the proofs—wrote something to Stefan Zweig about the youthfulness of the story: encouraging in my situation. This much is certain, that in contrast, the novels of the Republic, which I had to write before this one, seem oldish. It was asking too much to extol that life, when everything was headed toward nothing but decline. But when will things be different there? They are now giving up the final pretexts of their so-called popular uprising and are becoming the unqualified exploiter and slave state that their financial supporters always had in mind. Only in regard to culture is national socialism being allowed to continue ravaging what's left, in the moment, music. To return there? If it were permitted, I would have my books published there—why not exercise whatever countereffect one can? Personally, however, I would probably in that case as well maintain a well-calculated distance. The people there have pushed things too far in their misunderstanding of nature. Their compensatory reeducation toward the normal will have to be accomplished in laborious detail. Nothing would be achieved by a mere revolution; but not even that can be attempted. On the other hand, it seems impossible over the long run for an—unsuccessful—dictatorship to maintain itself, when right next door democracy is in the course of renewal and ascent. I get this impression, ever more clearly, of France, at least of the forces active within it. Resistance to the bad example Germany offers has become vital here again: it awakens certain moral forces. The question is which one overcomes the other, the bad example there or the striving for moral renewal here.

Tell me how things are going with your third volume—and please send me the essay collection. My regards to my child and her mother in Prague. The earnings from my trip allowed me to rent them an apartment. We enjoyed some very nice days together; my wishes for the same for you with Erika. All the best in the new year, to you, Katja, and your children!

Most warmly, H.

*Küsnacht-Zurich*
*Schiedhaldenstraße 33*
*January 3, 1935*

Dear Heinrich,

Many thanks. I received everything in proper order, and my apologies for failing to confirm the arrival of your letter before the last. Things have been in tumult here; the children all came for Christmas (and now they are gradually dispersing), and we also had other overnight guests, so that the house was filled to overflowing and life was amusing and boisterous. Then I was indisposed for a few days: the usual stomach complaints, with depressed nerves and low blood pressure. I'm still recovering and not quite thinking straight.

The proclamation to Moscow has meanwhile been superseded by events, i.e., numerous executions. It is a desperately sad situation, when the only thing humanity has left to hope for, and which one would like to believe in, proves itself, by resorting to the same mendacious and bloody methods, to be as compromised as what we find so hateful.

Landshoff was only here for two days. It is annoying that he had just left when your letter arrived. How is it possible that there are still so many errors in the proofs of your book! Was it typeset by non-Germans or something? In any case, some sort of remedy must be found. Incidentally, Mazzucchetti, who read the proofs, wrote enthusiastically to me about the youthful freshness of your work.

I would like to convey your condolences to Mrs. Fischer. But what keeps you from writing yourself? Only letters being sent from Germany are likely to be opened, and hardly those being sent in. Not a single person to whom I've written, frankly, has yet to complain to me.

I wonder if we will be getting any more good news from home. My attorney seems now to have lost all hope in the possibility of retrieving all my possessions; in regard to the other things as well, I can scarcely believe that I'll gain any moral satisfaction, or that there will be any genuine settlement at all. It's not impossible that Germany will be forced to join a French peace arrangement. But the regime will remain, although its inane uselessness will then be as clear as day.

We often discuss plans to come to your coast for a couple of weeks in February or March. If only I'm not too tired after the trip east, which is coming up soon enough.

Warm regards for a good new year! T.

*Küsnacht*
*March 10, 1935*

Dear Heinrich,

I read your article with pleasure and wicked amusement. In general, I think that the characterization and discussion of that wretched sinkhole is beyond the powers of language. You at least find a tone in which to speak about it, a cold manner with the requisite eeriness, which is a powerful trick.

France remains the most fertile soil for such suggestions. Things look worse in England, as evidenced by the effect achieved by the scoundrel with his cancellation coup. English political idealism, the intellectuals there, feel that the Versailles Treaty represents a moral defeat for England; in full accord with the truth, they oppose the government, holding the German frame of mind responsible for European armament. This is the idealism of English socialism, which obviously is not sharing the fate of its German comrades, and the pig is attempting to mobilize it for his own purposes, and to use for his "game." It is a pitiful spectacle. And it's not even possible to hold it against the English advocates of respectable behavior and peace, if their internal affairs are more important than external ones, if their shirts are nearer their skin than their coats, and a foreign morality less immediate than their own.

I can be brief with news, because we're coming soon. The meetings of the *Comité permanent des Lettres et des Arts* will take place in Nice at the beginning of April; that means a free trip and a per diem, and thus offers the best chance for a visit to your coast. We are very much looking forward to seeing you again, although, unfortunately, for me the trip involves formulating a silly academic address about *La formation de l'homme moderne*, which is giving me headaches. A nice formation. I'll simply complain.

We were in Prague, Vienna, Budapest, and briefly in Brünn, a pleasant trip offering encouraging impressions. In Vienna I had two very full evenings of events the likes of which have apparently not been seen since Bruno Walter conducted there the first time after he was expelled from Germany. And to think, assuming it were possible, that it would not have been otherwise in Germany today, indeed would have been even more amazing. Incidentally, my old friend Seitz, the former mayor, was present, and we shook hands *coram publico*.

In Prague we enjoyed a friendly lunch at Mimi and Goschi's, who are pleased with their nice new apartment. It is true that Mimi, or Maria Mánnowa, as she's called now, was melancholy on the topic of her health.

A rest stop at St. Moritz–Chantarella was spoiled by bad weather. But instead we're enjoying a sunny frost of 39 degrees, which has never happened before.

I'm making progress on my third volume, but there remains much to do.

So, we'll see you very soon. T.

*Küsnacht*
*March 26, 1935*

Dear Heinrich,

We arrive from Marseille the morning of the 30th at 8:45, and have made reservations at the Hotel d'Angleterre. Don't put yourself to any trouble at such an early hour. We'll get in touch immediately, and since the meetings do not start on the 1st, we'll have two entire days beforehand to be together.

Till soon! We're very much looking forward to it. T.


*Küsnacht*
*March 28, 1935*

Dear Heinrich,

I have to give you the sad news that our reunion plans will come to nothing at the moment. My health fluctuates wildly, the insanity of public affairs mounts daily, and with it, my grief over the shameful state of Germany. The memoir I wrote for the *Comité des Lettres et des Arts* has turned into such a direct, painful expression of this state that it, between us, is likely to prove distressingly inappropriate, and might cause difficulties even for the League. I've therefore informed Geneva that I must decline to participate in the meetings right now, and I have also expressed my wish that my contribution not be aired beyond the narrow circle of the *Comité*. Our travel plans, which had been so firm, are thus no longer valid for the moment. But we do intend most definitely to make the trip privately before the end of spring, roughly in May—which is some consolation for the immediate failure of my hopes to see you again and speak with you.

Accept my regards until then, and forgive the surely bewildering back and forth! The fault lies with the abnormality of the times, which is as ill-suited and trying to my nature as can be.

Warmly, T.


*March 30, 1935*
*11, rue du Congrès*
*Nice (A.M.)*

Dear Tommy,

Today I thought I saw you and heard you talking: at least I want to say these words to you. What deeply distresses me is not the delay of your trip; that will hopefully be minor. But you are suffering, and that also affects me. I fear that you are having physical pains and that through them the psychological ones are coming to expression. How good your theoretical piece must have become in that state! I wish I could read it. But it would be your preference not to have to do such good things, which cost you so much. More than you, I tend to discharge my emotional disturbances through writing; but I've also had enough of that by now and would be much relieved if the catastrophe simply came. It needn't be war; better that they should collapse economically and be required to deal with their chaos themselves, instead of dragging the world into it with them. There has to be an end to that someday, and fate must bring the case of Germany to a close through judgment. Negotiations drag on forever.

These are my reflections; it will be possible perhaps to consider them for years to come. What truly concerns me is the question of your condition. I want to believe that nothing has really changed in the state of your health, and that not even the sadness and disgust could really affect it? I would like you to reassure me about this and would also like to know how you are thinking of celebrating your sixtieth birthday: above all, where. You probably have a circle of people in Zurich with a justified claim on doing the honors, and the border is also close enough that guests could come. But it is not all right for me. Whenever I see visitors from the Third Reich sitting at a table here it makes me sick. Places where they appear in greater numbers wouldn't be healthy for me. In a technical sense they are even life-threatening. For you less so, no doubt incomparably less; but do you really not notice one thing with certainty, that the nearness of the border affects your condition? We are vulnerable enough intellectually to the catastrophe: physical proximity is yet spared us! Here I can—sometimes, far from always—read the newspapers like fairy tales, and return to my novel as if to truth and life. Your nature demands that just as much and more. Think it over with Katja, to whom I send my warm regards, whether a longer stay here on the coast isn't called for. It would do you good; I would be happy. On your birthday I could reciprocate all the fraternal attention you gave me four years ago. There wouldn't be a lot of festivities; what remains today are commemoration and knowledge. Demonstrate something? We watch others demonstrating something now, and that's enough for us.

These are wishes, comforts, unfortunately even excuses. You do what you find best, and hopes for getting together soon remain in any case.

Warmly, H.


*Küsnacht-Zurich*
*Schiedhaldenstraße 33*
*April 3, 1935*

Dear Heinrich,

My warmest thanks for your words. I'm sending you the "memorandum," since you expressed interest in it. The League of Nations objected to two passages, the "swastika" and something else. That served to make it clear to me that my presence there on the spot would cause confusion and perhaps embarrassment. Nor was I fond of the idea of having what I want to say heard in a flattened French translation. To that was added, somewhat tardily, for I hadn't "given it a thought," the consideration that I would have had to inform Bermann (as well as my Munich attorney) in advance of taking any such step. The consequence would likely have been my expulsion, the banning of my books, and the exposure of the S. Fischer Verlag. I hadn't wanted to do it like that, in a way that would hardly have been satisfying to me, half by accident, the other half clumsily, and since, characteristically, I had also wrecked my nerves writing the little piece, I let the matter drop.

There's nothing further concerning my health. My heart, with justice, is no longer quite the old one, and my head meanwhile shows signs of fatigue and agitation. How could it be otherwise. Through Annette Kolb I have a good doctor in Basel, Prof. Gigon, and I have him check me periodically; he prescribed a mild heart medicine supplemented with iron. Otherwise, physically and morally, I'm just about worn out. If Hitler would only meet the end he deserves, everything would return to normal—thirst, my appetite, sleep.

It could be that this, my weaker side, is more directly vulnerable to the aggressive onslaught here than it would be in Nice. I'm also finding my anxious desire to remain within the sphere of German culture and language less pressing than it was at the beginning. It is true that the eastern Swiss have the great advantage for me of representing a bit of old Germany, while at the same time belonging to western Europe. But we've always regarded our stay here as provisional, and Nice remains in reserve. You know that the immediate issue now is the children's education; we didn't want to transplant them yet again, this time into a foreign language. Once they're all on their own feet, we would hardly remain here, but move close to you. Conditions that would cause us, or merely make it possible, to return to Germany are scarcely conceivable.

Katja's parents are coming after Easter, as they do twice a year, for a visit of ten to fourteen days. In May we definitely want to make our private trip to your coast, to see you and some close or otherwise related friends. We'll spend my birthday here, appropriately quietly. The children will come. Right afterwards, we have to hop back over to America. Harvard University in Cambridge, Mass. wants to make me an honorary doctor of letters on its commencement day, and as casually as I was inclined to treat it at first, I've since been made aware, understandably, that Harvard is very noble, the finest of the fine and most prestigious, and that I must by all means make the trip. What weighs most heavily for me: Harvard is the university that so coolly refused Hanfstängls's impudent offer, which greatly annoyed the German dictators. In this case, the annoyance will be even greater.

The Swiss-German conflict is very absorbing. It can be taken as a touchstone for the extent to which the idea of law retains its validity in Europe. Germany is convinced that it is no longer valid; it is in this sense the "most progressive." The others haven't learned this lesson yet the way the Germans have. Still, things are beginning to appear the same to them as well, in a somewhat pale and weak and flatter form, and the interesting question is just how much *élan* they're in fact still able to muster for it. It is remarkable that we have as yet failed to consider what is ultimately the most wretched possibility, worse than war, and what seems perhaps to be happening: peace as the product of demoralization, a peace in which anyone with sufficient audacity can do whatever he wants.

What I'm most sorry about is that the Jacob case will have eliminated whatever remained of your desire to visit Zurich. I would so have liked to show you our landscape, the house, my beautiful study (which I like better than the one in Munich), and in the evenings we would have played Tchaikovsky for you on our excellent phonograph. Certainly there would be no real danger for you, and I don't even believe that you're the type the executioners are after. But I can understand your fear.

So, we'll see you in a few weeks. You can return the manuscript to me then.

Warmly, T.

*April 8, 1935*
*11, rue du Congrès*
*Nice (A.M.)*

Dear Tommy,

Your letter relieves me as to my main concern, and presumably with justice. Who has ever escaped finding his heart and head getting fatigued on occasion by events? You need to recuperate and will do so sufficiently, so I hope, if you spend May here and June on your overseas voyage. I didn't mean that you should move here permanently: I merely recommended an extended vacation, and naturally expected something from it for myself as well. Where to in midsummer? We'll be able to talk about that.

I have to thank you for your book, which is dear to me. It contains as a whole the truth that is also mine, and that truth is presented in a good and singular way. To mention one example: I would have chosen the same poem from Platen, have always known it myself by heart, and with Storm, too, I would have focused on that verse. In my copy, which I first read when I was twenty, there is—if it still exists anywhere—a small bit of paper from the hand of our sister Carla, a pink flowerpot with blue violets, and underneath: "I always draw these and then I paint them." She was ten years old.—Very frequently and ever again I shall refer to your understanding of Goethe, and to his own understandings, as you have summarized them.

The lecture conveys some profound remarks around page eight and is very powerful. I'll leave it in my drawer; soon we'll want to discuss everything. Until we meet.

Warmly, H.

*Küsnacht*
*May 12, 1935*

Dear Heinrich,

We're leaving the day after tomorrow by car for Geneva, where we'll board a train in the evening, hoping, therefore, to be in Nice on the morning of the 15th. We'll get in touch immediately from the Hotel d'Angleterre. Till then! Visitors caused us to delay the trip, but now we'll keep to our word.

Warmly, T.


*Küsnacht*
*May 22, 1935*

Dear Heinrich,

Here's to let you know that we arrived home safely, and that our thoughts return to you in gratitude. After a wonderful supper, we spent a somewhat fitful night, tossed by the frequent switching of the sleeping car. But yesterday's trip by car through a summery Switzerland, via Lausanne, Bern, and Baden, was once again a pleasure, and we were already home by half past six. Passport matters we were also able to arrange satisfactorily in Bern. Now there are the many items of business we left lying. All in all, it was nice to be together again, and Nice, because you are there, remains in our feelings a home in reserve. Our regards to Frau Kröger!

Warmly, T.


*May 24, 1935*
*11, rue du Congrès*
*Nice (A.M.)*

Dear Tommy,

With great pleasure I received notice of your safe arrival. We had calculated correctly to the hour. They were nice days—happiness enjoyed amid a certain agitation, because time was pressing. Only afterward did I begin to consider properly how and when our reunion in Zurich could be arranged. You want to remain there over the summer. Perhaps the second half of August, say, I could visit you with my daughter? This is a very provisional plan and proposal; you will let me know sometime whether it wouldn't be too much with the two of us, whether the timing is right and you're not having other guests. Then, whatever we decide, I would have to get busy here applying for exit and reentry visas. That was a lengthy process the last time. So much seems certain: we would have more from being together then than from the hectic time of celebrations that's now approaching; and I'm not seeing anyone. Already I would ask you not to speak at all of the possibility of my visit.

I promptly transposed the doctor who denounced his professor to Paris in 1589: back then and there it happened in exactly the same way.

Today we went to Mont Boron and thought of the previous Saturday, when we took the same path with the two of you. Frau Kröger preserves a comforting memory of Katja and her friendliness; she, along with me, returns your regards.

Warmly, H.

May I ask once more that you speak with Oprecht concerning Frey?


*Küsnacht*
*May 27, 1935*

Dear Heinrich,

Your plan is wonderful. Katja and I are enchanted with it and discuss it eagerly. To you and Goschi we both extend our warm welcome, though you would do well to begin with the formalities, because they take time. You certainly should be able to do what is necessary without specifying the timing of your trip exactly. For August, only the 19th to the 27th are impossible, because those dates are the ones for which I've agreed to deliver some lectures in Salzburg. I regret that now. But Katja is also not entirely sure in the moment whether and when the children are coming in the summer. We're moving quickly now to clarify our plans, and will soon know whether to propose that you and Goschi visit in the first half of August or around the first of September (usually a very pleasant time of the year here). The trip must come off in any case, and I also much prefer that your visit be a good thing in its own right, and not coincide with all the birthday fuss.

Yesterday's celebration in the theater was truly a fine success, and I'm enclosing the program for you.

Warmly, T.

I'll be seeing Oprecht in the next few days.


*June 3, 1935*
*11, rue du Congrès*
*Nice (A.M.)*

Dear Tommy,

Instead of conveying my birthday wishes, I'm tempted to quote what Henri says before the first of his decisive battles:

"We must conquer for our honor's sake, or at least win eternal life. The way lies before us. Forward, in the name of God, for whom we fight."

To the astonishment of the enemy, his army knelt down and prayed in the words of Psalm 118: "O give thanks unto the Lord, for He is gracious; and His mercy endureth for ever."

This battle was called "the joyful day," and so may you also designate your battles. One's sixtieth birthday, as far as I know, is equally a memorial to the last and a preliminary celebration of the next. I am with you in my most profound best wishes.

I am grateful for your letter and shall further consider the plan. After your return from America you'll let me know what time would be best.

Frau Kröger sends her congratulations.

I discussed my projected work schedule and budgetary requirements for the next two years with Landshoff. It's actually all fantasy. But I really do hope to complete my first Henri IV this week.

Most warmly, H.

*Küsnacht*

*June 3, 1935*

Dear Heinrich, I was deeply moved just now as I sat here rereading your fine, brotherly congratulations, and it gave me the urge to thank you once again from the heart. Your words, their intonation, their loftiness and goodness, will touch many, and rarely has a piece of prose given me such a strong feeling for the purifying, ennobling, and shaming effects it is capable of—who knows how broadly.—I'm enjoying a great deal of kind attention. The big Swiss papers have all published supplements, including some very good essays, and it's been raining letters of congratulations for days—some even from Germany.—I'll give you more precise information on the *date* very soon.

Warmly, T.

*Steamship* Lafayette

*June 17, 1935*

Dear Heinrich, Warm regards from our travels, two days away from the destination. And thanks for your loving wishes. It was a terrible fuss, and K. and I have had to work hard on the ship preparing thank-you notes. Germans wrote, and how, with return addresses! We often speak of your visit.

Till soon,

T.

*On Board*
*Cunard White Star*
Berengaria
*July 7, 1935*

Dear Heinrich,

Just as last year, my regards from underway, this time on the return trip. America, with its heat and adventures, is already two days behind me, and in four more this gigantic ship (actually German soil; it is the former *Imperator*) will have delivered us to Cherbourg, from where we will continue on directly to Zurich to meet Katja's parents, who are coming to celebrate her mother's eightieth birthday.

Have I written to you of the hundreds of letters I received from Germany for my sixtieth? And what letters they were, in part—with return addresses, from work camps, even from young people. Certainly the love of freedom and respectability remains there in abundant reserves.

Altogether I've been experiencing a great deal of affection. Bermann brought over a lovely carton of well-wishes from international literary figures, and the major Swiss papers had their own birthday supplements, including some very good articles. The children were all together, and at six in the evening we had a small party, leaving me with the single wish that I had the peace and quiet to let it all sink in. Instead, we had to get busy right away packing for this trip, which I didn't regard as necessary, but which has passed happily and left me rich with impressions.

At Harvard I was awarded my degree along with Albert Einstein, and the applause from the 6,000 people present went on in each case for minutes. The entire thing was carefully planned by the president of the university, Prof. Conant, a respected chemist, just forty years old, and with whom we stayed, and coordinated with President Roosevelt, a former Harvard student. The President invited us to Washington, and, after spending a few days in the country, in Riverside, at the home of a Dutch-American writer, Hendrik van Loon, we flew an hour and twenty minutes from New York to Washington, a surprisingly pretty and very presentable city, where we then enjoyed a very lovely and also interesting family dinner with the Roosevelts—very private, of course, with no sign of the ambassador. I have to tell you about it in person. My impression was quite sympathetic—on the basis of a favorable predisposition. For I would not have gone but for my sincere admiration for the handicapped man, who is hated by many, namely, the rich, but also by abstract enthusiasts of freedom and the "constitution," of which we had a sample in Congress. With him I had more the sense of a certain disdain for parliamentarianism and a tendency for one-man rule, but I'm convinced that he means well for democracy, and that his entire experiment is directed toward the end of saving it.

The summer heat in Washington is simply tropical, a genuine ordeal. New York, although also on roughly the same latitude as Naples, seemed to us almost fresh in comparison. We spent a few busy days there at the end, and have now resumed our accustomed, but always remarkable hotel life on the open seas: the sense of rushing ceaselessly forward, which is noticeable, however, if at all, only in a faint pulsing of the deck, for the gigantic ship moves with utter calm. It's odd to think that our cabin, like a hotel room with ten-foot ceilings, is the same place we sat in the sultry New York air drinking whiskey and soda with the Knopfs on the evening of our departure. It is the same room, but in a completely different place with a completely different climate, for we've gotten beyond the Gulf Stream and it has become quite cool, as indeed it must be in Europe, with the hot days probably over.

We speak often of your visit, and look forward with pleasure to seeing you and Goschi. Since our trip to Salzburg is also planned for August, it would be best to schedule yours for early September. Of the children, only Golo will still be there then, and that is also when the weather is likely to be best. It will be nice to show you where we live in Switzerland, to take a few trips in the car, and listen to music in the evenings.

So we'll see you then. Write soon to Küsnacht, letting me know if that is a good time for you!

Your, T.


*Briançon (Hautes Alpes)*
*Hotel du Cours*
*July 16, 1935*

Dear Tommy,

You must have been home for a few days by now and you have brought pleasing impressions with you. In Paris I saw Klaus and Golo, in particular the latter in the capacity of an ardent visitor to the Congress. The Congress, before an audience of thousands, went off quite as impressively as any event can that is organized by an opposition. The writers did it exactly as the French leftist parties do; precisely this unqualified union of nonfascists is what was missing earlier. Whenever a German took the podium the audience rose and people began singing the "Internationale." But the singers were shouted down: Discipline, comrades!—and then they would stop. The speeches by the Russians—Ehrenburg, Alexis Tolstoi, Koltsov—were wholly in the spirit of the defense of culture. One can't ask for more. Incidentally, I'm enclosing the telegram from which you will see that you were elected to the board of the newly founded League. It doesn't look purely Communist. I was also elected *in absentia;* I had already departed before the final day. I say to myself meanwhile that western Europe would be lost without the Russian support. That is the only choice we have. According to an American report, you are supposed to have said something similar, and *Die Weltbühne* asked you on July 11th whether it was true.

Now I would like to ask when my visit would suit the two of you. For me, it's like this: I'm in the French Alps, near Grenoble, and from here Switzerland would not be far. It would save me much traveling around and also money if I were to leave here as early as the end of July for Zurich. Otherwise, I would return to Nice and then have to hope that in September there would be another chance. You are perhaps especially desirous, right after the trip, of being alone and working a lot: in that case I'm completely agreed to postpone the visit. I don't want this question to disturb the arrangements you have made, but simply to let you know that I would be ready. Perhaps you can telegraph a word to me here as to whether I would be welcome for eight days at the end of July; then I would make appropriate plans. Otherwise, a letter will do, and I will be very pleased to read your news. The greetings from your American friends I receive with sincere gratitude.

My warm regards to both of you. Frau Kröger thanks you for the greeting and returns it.

H.


*July 27, 1935*
*Bandol (Var)*
*Bd V.-Hugo, chez Gagna*

Dear Tommy,

Your telegram has gone unanswered until now because I wanted to consider the circumstances precisely. I did not yet have a visa for the trip to Switzerland, and someone would have had to travel back to Nice to get one. I would have been without papers for a few days. But what was decisive was my impression that a visit in September would be preferable to the two of you after all. I hope that I'll be able to arrange one then. Meanwhile, we have come to familiar Bandol, and have found a nice, quiet apartment above the sea and the beach, up the street to the right from the harbor. The bookseller Aboab helped us; I'm still in touch with him concerning the copies of my French articles. In the moment, the latter provide me with an interesting opportunity to talk about "Wackeln." I also read a letter from Berlin, not addressed to me:

If "Aunt Minna" continues in her present ways, she will end up in an asylum! This as a voice from the broader public.

The past three weeks have included one of the most beautiful summer journeys. Before I drove over these Alps in a motor bus, I hadn't known they existed. Day before yesterday from Briançon to Grenoble was without doubt a high point of terrestrial life, with snow-capped mountains, fantastic shapes in naked stone, and the windy heights, where the bus stopped in the emptiness. Quite remarkable; travel by road, as far as I'm concerned, has now been discovered. There is also a direct connection to Geneva, perhaps with a one-night stopover.

First the motor bus, and then a pleasant surprise from Russia on top of it. I was afraid that they wouldn't have much understanding of a novel about a king. Instead, a letter from the publisher of "International Literature" (from the state press)—I had never before received such a thing. For an author without his own country, this is the kind of success that is possible. There's nothing more to be done, at least not until "Aunt Minna" has been committed.

Holidays are nice after one has been busy for years. I take the hardships in stride and say to myself: Why not? Nothing is demanded of me. I hope that you're finding things completely to your satisfaction and that you're having a happy summer.

Many regards to you and Katja. My thanks again for such a warm telegram.

H.


*Küsnacht*

*July 29, 1935*

Dear Heinrich,

Thanks for the news. The only thing for us that would have spoken against your coming now would have been the absence of our youngest ones, in whom you after all have a share, and who couldn't have performed for you. They're off on a holiday bicycle tour to Salzburg.—Now we're actually a bit disappointed. But hopefully the beauties of traveling by car (which was also recommended to us, and had we not already had tickets for the sleeping car, there's no doubt that's how we would have gone from Nice to Geneva) offer you a new incentive to make the trip in September.

I'm glad that you are enjoying your vacation so much, and especially glad to hear about your Russian successes. It simply is a better world there, class domination or not. Now they want to join the bourgeois democracies standing against fascism. In a presentiment of that development, I spoke in similar terms in America about communism, that *La Humanité* has its friends. Russian admiration for your book shows that I was right. It has always been impossible for me not to regard the Germans' incredible hatred toward you, also, incidentally, toward Erika and Klaus, as a particularly telling sign of their miserable stupidity.

All the visitors from Germany report on how unbearably thick the air has become there. That the new wave of madness and lunatic enthusiasm was a sign of strength and security is scarcely plausible. Of course emigration is increasing, not only among the Jews, but among others as well. People with minor nervous tics or an epileptic great-uncle are crossing the border out of fear of being sterilized. You have to laugh, but it is horrible, and most horrible of all is that no one is interfering, instead doing everything possible to continue as if it were a state like any other.

Warmly, T.

*Küsnacht*
*September 1, 1935*

Dear Heinrich,

We're back from Salzburg, where the festival this year in particular was an extraordinary success—which is pleasant news from several perspectives. There was beauty to see and hear in abundance, the high point probably *Fidelio* conducted by Toscanini—a work of gripping contemporary relevance. We all agreed that it was as if it had been specifically created for the occasion of a festival performance.—Back home, I found an advance copy of your *Henry* already here . . . And what about your visit? I know that it is no small decision from more than one point of view. But the plan was made, and it was a good one. Do tell me what you're thinking about it now! Everything would be ready for you here.

Warmly, T.


*September 2, 1935*
*11, rue du Congrès*
*Nice (A.M.)*

Dear Tommy,

How are you, and how have the two of you spent the summer? Entirely in Küsnacht, it seems, and you have probably continued with your work. Mine was finished at the beginning of June. The book is in publication; I made urgent requests for you to receive the first copy. It might have been simply a stapled-together advance copy. I myself find that preferable to the heavy volumes; and, to be frank, I very much like reading in the big picture-book, which is probably something else again. But viewed externally there are 103 scenes. I assume that you will find some better than others, can also guess which ones. I would like most to hear your judgment in general from your own lips and talk it over with you.

I'm still very tired, I sleep hardly at all, which in practical terms means that the vacation was of little value and the effects of my exertions with Henri IV by no means overcome. But fall for me, especially following serious work, is usually like this; I'm not spoiled and wait patiently for my capabilities to increase again. In the moment, I'm even shrinking from the trip, as happy as I would be to see you again and as firmly planned as it was. But I want to confess that it's not only tiredness holding me back. The general situation has become much more tense in the meantime; one finds oneself preparing for the collapse of the Third Reich—an emotional, rather mysterious process, how one prepares oneself. It is not, however, confined entirely to personal concerns; a few steps are being taken otherwise as well; on the condition that those involved will keep silent for now, as agreed.—Berlin is full not only of mysterious presentiments, but spies. If nothing much works otherwise, the spies do, and unfortunately they almost work best in the country I had been planning to visit.

Enough; I may not go into any further detail here. But what about this: F in Sanary maintained that you were intending to come here in the fall? If that were true! I would be infinitely pleased; seriously, it would be the nicest surprise I could yet wish for this year. Do come, and before the days get too short. We would make excursions, I would be always at your disposal, and your stay should be somewhat more extended than the last time. Tell me if we may think about it and look forward to it before September comes to an end. I hope that Katja is in the best of health. For you, especially following a summer filled with work, the change of air would be good. First you would have the pretty road trip, then the comfortable journey here. Incidentally, there are motor buses from Geneva to Nice, in case the weather stays warm. There's a warning out against a coach labeled "Grimma Travel Agency, Saxony." With this feeble joke but full of hope, I close and send my regards to both of you. Frau K sends hers as well.

Warmly, H.


*Küsnacht*
*September 5, 1935*

Dear Heinrich,

It's both a pity and painful, but I understand the reasons. We do have cause to hope that certain things, if they were to come about, would make it much easier for us to get together again. But even if they don't, we will do what is necessary to achieve the result, though perhaps not right away. The America trip and more recently the Salzburg festival have put me behind in my work.—For days now I've been reading nothing but your novel, neglecting even the newspapers. All of us in emigration can be proud of this work; Germany, incidentally, too—France, too. I'll write more when I've finished it.

Warmly, T.


*October 3, 1935*
*11, rue du Congrès*
*Nice (A.M.)*

Dear Tommy,

Your letter is so beautiful I would have most liked to have answered it right away on the same day. But I had just come from Paris and had to write an article every day, in addition to my preliminary work on the further life of King Henri IV. Really, I had hoped you would have those impressions, even your special mention of the chapter "Death and the Nursemaid" I was able to foresee. But what makes me happier yet is your unreserved warmth for the book, your friendship for the object and the hand that made it. That is what we now need—together with the confirmation that we haven't let up in these last years, but have become more. Imperative as never before, certainly, is that we summon our strength and hold our ground.

Of course you noticed the quotation. I think that the determining factor was a mere feeling: in this extreme case it was necessary to put in whatever had played a very great role in my life, the entire *humanoria*, including, certainly, Faust. It's the same epoch stretching from Montaigne to Goethe: that has now been decided, since its glow has nearly faded completely. And it was also only through the inspiration of the feeling that I added the *moralités*, in the style of the great moralists, to which our friend Bertaux, unbidden but movingly, bore witness. I wanted this one time for the French and the German to be interwoven. I always hoped for the best for the world from that. At least I will have had a book from it myself.

You think that I should also have something more from it, like the rosette. But neither the times nor our contemporaries are right for that, and whoever is suspect to the powers in his own country is suspect to every power. The individual with no country behind him counts for so little in the order of things that I even wonder what sort of exception is being made of you and ultimately of myself as well. It's probably obvious that there is a difference in regard to you, but you are still regarded as an émigré. For a short time I've been on the executive board of the World Committee Against War and Fascism; Barbusse had arranged it—Rolland, Langevin, several other French and perhaps an English member, but otherwise I'm the only one from outside. The Committee is powerful enough that I could probably become French through its auspices, especially if the *Front populaire* were to come to power next year. There are reasons for waiting. There is also the reason that my daughter in Prague can get a work permit only if my passport is Czech.

How are you? That's what I've really wanted to ask the whole time, instead of what I've written. Please let me know that you have recovered and are in good spirits for your work. It is so important and so beautiful. How remarkable if the third volume of your great work ends up getting published in Zurich and London after all. The inexorability of things. Do you count on Bermann having to give up the German market? Even if he's allowed to keep it, the added guarantee abroad is only good. Inside, whether the Third Reich stands or falls, it can only get worse—for books and people. Among other stolen wares, that society also invokes occasionally the word "work plan." Whereby its only work is to prepare the great campaign of plunder, and they'll only get started on that once they begin dying. How it has disintegrated!

You've traveled a great deal recently and don't like to think of boarding a train. Nor do I, incidentally; but if we could see each other again we would perhaps think over whether we shouldn't make the great, apparently necessary informational trip to the Soviet Union together. You no doubt also receive frequent invitations. They are more like exhortations, and one sees oneself already indebted to the Bolsheviks. Without them—where at all would there remain anything real for the left to rely on? I would like to tell you about a discussion of the German left. There's no one anymore who wouldn't regard radical socialist measures as self-evidently necessary if the ultimate should transpire. Among the most remarkable present was a young Catholic, who told me that he gets to see you now and again.

Concerning the Russian trip, one apparently has to travel to Constantinople independently. From there on the organizers take care of everything. Feuchtwanger is urging me to join in the trip next May. So far I've been searching for ways to protect myself from overexertion.—Write to me, stay healthy, greetings to Katja, accept my thanks and warm regards.

H.

*Küsnacht*
*October 10, 1935*

Dear Heinrich,

The Bolsheviks have really become very friendly, even though they disapproved of me earlier as bourgeois. Recently, I read in a Prague paper the altogether unexpected news that *The Magic Mountain* has just come out as the fifth volume of the Soviet edition of my works. Klaus had brought me all kinds of lovely things from Moscow, purchased with my royalties being held there. But in response to my request, they've even sent me money, quite a lot. That no doubt signals some degree of special attention; and in Salzburg there was a young conductor working in Moscow whose urgent and enticing invitation to pay a visit there very soon seemed rather as if it were authorized. My desire to heed the call then becomes very real as well. That the two of us, and me in particular, can be sure that we would be waited on hand and foot there (and we can) shows how much things have shifted of late and how much Russia, intellectually and politically, is approaching democracy and the West, for the purpose of joining together to stand up to Nazism, the most shameful thing on earth. The visit by Soviet writers to Prague, which went off so harmoniously, paints the same picture.

It is at bottom a splendid idea for the two of us to go there together, and it would no doubt occasion quite a sensation. But for the spring I've already agreed to a Spanish trip with a French *conférence*, to Barcelona, Madrid, Valencia, and Bilbao, which will be well paid—and then nothing on that scale would be conceivable until next spring. If anything causes me pause, it is the prevailing fear of Russian communism, also in bourgeois

Switzerland, which could subject a visitor like myself to certain administrative disadvantages. A Russian stamp in one's passport remains very serious and alarming here. In any case, I would have to ask Motta first, and apply for an exemption, which would probably be granted. But, as I said, since such a trip could only be considered for the spring, it would have to wait until next year. Should we agree on spring 1937? My impression is that you wouldn't mind a bit more time yourself. I admit, it's bold of me to want to plan for everyone so far in advance, and if you want to go ahead with Feuchtwanger—someone in your situation is no doubt less patient.

My professor, as usual, has found everything of an organic nature to be in good order. He did, however, prescribe a small dose of arsenic, together with a sedative. For the fatigue, it would simply be good to go to bed earlier. But when I've listened to music in the evening, I still like to read a bit, so I'm often up past midnight. On the whole, because one does after all remain the same person, there is a tendency to continue living like a forty-year-old. But one is not the same.

Your address to the fellows in Berlin is highly amusing, irrefutable, and refreshing. You ought to send such refreshments more often! They do us all good.

Warmly, T.


*Küsnacht*

*October 24, 1935*

Dear Heinrich,

I recently sent the enclosed letter to Oslo. Perhaps you'll be happy to read it. Do you think it will make any impression? Unfortunately, from impression to effect is still a long step.

Please send the carbon back to me, for any further use that might arise.

The November darkness and winter cold has set in early here. In Tessin it's also been raining without letup for weeks. It's really sad.

What's going on between London and Rome? Will they make peace? It was just looking as if the English had resolved to put an end to fascism, which would have been a good start. Meanwhile, Hitler and Göbbels get the feeling that no one is watching them anymore and "are doing it," as did Putt-Höneken, "much too crudely." Göbbels has now prohibited having Jewish names on the memorials for the war dead. They have to be eradicated. As a Reichswehr officer who was here put it, that's the last straw. Apparently, Göbbels has delivered some very strange speeches indeed.

Warm regards! T.

*October 26, 1935*
*11, rue du Congrès*
*Nice (A.M.)*

Dear Tommy,

The letter to Oslo might well be the most beautiful and powerful of your public
statements. I return the carbon to you moved and very gratified.

Who knows if your letter won't work a miracle. It seems unbelievable, but we want
to believe.

England will come to an agreement with the gentleman in Rome, since it doesn't
even reproach the gentleman in Berlin on any matter of principle. It wouldn't have gone
so easily without the zeal of the fascist Laval. The right man always appears at the right
time whenever there's an opportunity to impede the good, which, quite by accident, did
have a chance to prevail.

The maniacs back there with their Jews. What will they do when they finally have
no more of them. In the meantime they are preparing no other future for themselves
than their Jews. Today it is no longer fantastic to think that an utterly destitute, disintegrated Germany will be taken under foreign control and itself become a colony—instead
of the Ukraine. For everything is subject to reversals; and the world is now learning from
German military science what it means to draw ultimate conclusions from a victory.—
Otherwise, everything fine.

Warm regards. H.


*Küsnacht*
*November 15, 1935*

Dear Heinrich,

Many thanks for the clipping. It is altogether useful and commendable to say these
things, and to make it clear to the bourgeois world that fascism is simply a Western form
of bolshevism, and that it has nothing to offer the "old world." Much would be gained
from the broad dissemination of this insight, but still more from an English recognition
that they must refrain from helping the dictatorships gain prestige, and, if they want
peace, topple them instead. Thanks to Mussolini's clumsiness, a beginning has been
made. Churchill and the article in the *Times* on the German persecution of Jews were
very good, and so, once more, there's not much left of German-English friendship. The
same is true of German-Polish friendship; and so long as France doesn't—which it appears it won't—seek a way out of its admittedly precarious situation via Berlin, then there
is reason to be reassured as concerns the foreign policy prospects of the Third Reich.

Internal affairs are a disaster in any case, according to all the news I've heard. What
I'm anticipating less pleasantly than anything so far, including the Saar referendum, is
the Olympiade, which threatens to turn into a gigantic advertisement for Nazi Germany.

If only there had been, on the part of a couple of the better nations, sufficient resolve to refuse to take part! It could have been justified in thoroughly nonaggressive and natural terms—and it might have meant the end of the regime. Do they *want* to preserve it? The games will be set up in the most humanitarian style, including denials of anti-Semitism; to the whole world they will be friendly and peaceful, with Schiller's ode to joy and all that goes with that, and enormously advantageous. Add to that the order, the perfect organization, the gigantic modern structures—a catastrophic propaganda yield. If only it were possible to thwart such shameless plans!

Dr. Hans Bauer, editor of the *Baseler Nationalzeitung*, asked me for your address, and so I want to put in a good word for him and pass along what he urgently wants from you. He is the main organizer of the Swiss Europa-Union against the war and has the burning desire that you come and speak in one, or many, meetings of that sort. Won't you do it? I ask with little confidence. But it would be nice.

Warmly, T.


*November 20, 1935*
*11, rue du Congrès*
*Nice (A.M.)*

Dear Tommy,

Your news about the arrangements being made for the Olympiade was new to me, and I am taking the liberty of using it for my next French article. Tomorrow I shall travel to Paris and ask Koenen, the former member of parliament from the KPD,[13] what sort of damage his counterpropaganda on the Olympiade has been able to do so far.

There will be much to discuss in many *comités*, and I'm also supposed to speak— hopefully not to a large public: when one does that a summons to the commissariat tends to arrive the next day and there are threats of expulsion. But in my case the event is French and the gentlemen in charge should be sufficiently influential.

On November 26 I'm supposed to go with other delegates to Geneva; we shall be received on the 28th by the League of Nations. Following the death of the High Commissioner, émigrés were given authorization to represent themselves. Now it is happening. I'll probably be in Geneva the 27th and 28th, but I could stay over the 29th—if you were to take the time and trouble to meet me there. I know that it's not usually possible to simply get free. I would be extraordinarily pleased.

You can reach me by letter or telegram until the 25th in Paris (7e) Hôtel Lutetia, Bd Raspail. You can find out my Geneva address then.—Gatherings in Switzerland—not yet, please.

Most warmly, H.

13. Kommunistische Partei Deutschlands: the Communist Party of Germany.

*Küsnacht-Zurich*
*Schiedhaldenstraße 33*
*December 23, 1935*

Dear Heinrich, On the eve of festivities, a quick word of greeting and thanks for your lines. The ten-volume edition has turned out to be quite incomplete; much is missing. Fontane, which will meanwhile have gotten to you, is also incomplete. I was disappointed: Fischer is no longer putting out the big edition with letters and everything. Stupidly, I never bought it.—Klaus is very happy about your letter. I read it today after dinner. Everything is here, the house overflowing, and Katja exhausted from shopping. We have freezing temperatures and deep snow, so everything is by the book. May both of you enjoy the lobsters!

T.

*Küsnacht-Zurich*
*Schiedhaldenstraße 33*
*January 7, 1936*

Dear Heinrich, Klaus will soon be traveling to London, via Paris, and will therefore probably be able to take part in the meeting. I cannot, if only because we are going to Arosa toward the end of the month, nor can I sign. On the other hand, I have agreed to have my letter to Oslo picked up in the circular. That is certainly possible at all events, even if I have to count on it getting immediately to the propaganda ministry. I do what I can, for example, the Wassermann foreword as well, also the article in the *St. Galler Tagblatt*, but I must keep to certain limits for now. On the 10th I have another reading in Basel to benefit émigré aid in Geneva. On the 13th we're traveling to Arosa, the Neues Waldhotel.

Warmly, T.

*February 6, 1936*
*11, rue du Congrès*
*Nice (A.M.)*

Dear Tommy,

You can imagine that I am extremely moved by the events, to the extent that they affected you. Your package, for which I thank you, would no longer have been necessary. I was away for a week and taxed to the point of exhaustion in Paris by our new endeavors: otherwise I would have gotten in touch with you sooner. In the Swiss *Nation* you've said good things about my novel and, as if that weren't enough, you have personally enlightened Mr. Korrodi concerning the errors he committed in regard to me. He's lagging behind; clever people no longer compromise themselves with the Third Reich—and against us.

But that is the least of things. I've been told that Bermann's foreign activities have been put into question, while, from the other side, he is being cut from the list of German publishers. You seem yourself to have burned your bridges with your "Letter," or called for them to be burned. You know that it has always been my opinion that your books, for as long as it is in any way possible, must be sold "inside." Should your step, and the results of the situation, cause that now to cease, then my belief is: the interruption won't be a long one. So much for my statement; now I would very much like to have yours.

The proofs of *Es kommt ein Tag: Deutsches Lesebuch* have just arrived. Tell Katja that I send my friendly regards.

Most warmly, H.


*Küsnacht-Zurich*
*Schiedhaldenstraße 33*
*February 11, 1936*

Dear Heinrich,

Korrodi's nasty string of comments about emigration first appeared in the context of a statement of ours against Schwarzschild in favor of the emigrating Bermann, and so I had the feeling that it was necessary, finally, to announce without qualification my personal allegiance to those who have fled or were expelled from the Third Reich. This step has also become necessary to counter what had appeared in the world at large as some confusion about my relation to Hitler's Reich. Above all, however, it became a psychological necessity for me to express my opinion, if in measured words, to the scoundrels in power, and to let them know that I do not fear their vengeance. I believe I've not done badly in choosing the moment, and feel better since I did it. If they do expel me and ban my books, then I'll be able to say to myself that either there will be a war in a year and a half or two—or conditions will have to have changed in the same period, such that my books can be circulated again. Incidentally, I'm not at all so certain that they will strike back. It is altogether possible that they will swallow this step, as they have previous ones, and content themselves with continuing to withhold my possessions and passport. The Olympiade and foreign policy considerations both speak for that.

Bermann is having difficulties in Zurich. The guild is against him out of jealousy. Failure is not yet certain; if it does turn out that way, then Vienna and Prague will remain. Bermann has joined together with Heinemann, London; it will become an international firm of Fischer-Heinemann with American and English capital, and considerable political independence, in that it will manage the German department B on its own. That makes it a good, thoroughly promising affair. Schwarzschild's attack went completely wrong. Landshoff himself writes to me that he has never seen any danger in the founding of additional presses abroad, but, on the contrary, an easing of the burden. In his view, a monopoly position by too few publishers is detrimental over the long run.— The main question remains, under what conditions, in any case with something like a black eye, Bermann gets away from Berlin.

As I have said, my thinking is that I shall keep to my previous position. Contribution to a Moscow periodical is not in my line. I owe my host country Switzerland a certain consideration, and I would very much like to be naturalized here before the legal time limit runs out. Whatever my sympathies, I would not at all like to be too explicitly identified as having Communist leanings.

Warmly, T.


*Küsnacht-Zurich*
*Schiedhaldenstraße 33*
*February 26, 1936*

Dear Heinrich,

The appeal is so good that I had to take a couple of days to think it over. But it would contradict my established resolve to join in here, and my "host country" is not fond of overly vigorous political activity on the part of its guests. In addition: do you have even a glimmer of hope that this manifesto will compel the official scoundrels in Germany to release political prisoners? And then: "Amnesty." Are authorities who hold people captive without courts and legal sentences in any position to "amnesty"? Does this demand not already cede too much honor to them? It is an isolated political gesture that does not address the whole. At the right moment, I often think, an appeal, signed with thousands of names from all over the world, composed in sincere, good, and grand tones, must be directed to the German people. It would give them the sense that they can topple the infamous dictatorship and return to law, reason, and human respectability, to the benefit of themselves and everyone else. It would have to be signed by representatives, organized and unorganized, of the American and European cultural world—not by a dozen leftists—and it would have to appear in the world press to ensure that those to whom it is addressed actually see it. Even my open letter reaches them in myriad ways. Germans who have managed to get out take it back with them and read it to others.

I spoke again today with a man, an aristocratic lawyer, from Berlin. I asked him how much longer it could last. He feared it could be very long, he said. So, how long? In *two* years at the latest, he replied, there would be absolutely no way to avoid economic collapse, and then the conflict will be carried into "the streets," and that's where it will be decided. He called that long!—The question then will be whether the Reichswehr opens fire on "the streets," or rather, when it does open fire, whether also on the SS.

Warm regards! T.

*March 1, 1936*
*11, rue du Congrès*
*Nice (A.M.)*

Dear Katja,

Accept my deeply felt thanks and please tell the serious young scholar that I and my *Lesebuch* are much indebted to him. The quotations certainly could still be included; the question is whether Landshoff will approve the delay and added costs it would involve. I would be disappointed if these excellent materials were to be left out.

The madness of the times becomes so conspicuous in fact that it must therefore be logical and intended. And why not? It has never happened yet that a human undertaking has been stopped as a result of timely reflection. Rather, each one has carried on to its more or less bloody end. Thus the nationalistic anarchy of the moment, an obvious process of disintegration.

I'm in agreement with Tommy's answer and his decision not to sign. When I'm called upon to present him with such temptations in the future, I shall hold most of them back.

Perhaps it would interest you and Tommy to read the enclosed article. Warm regards, to Golo, too, whose address I would like to have. I must send him the book, with or without the quotations.

Your brother-in-law, Heinrich

*March 29, 1936*
*11, rue du Congrès*
*Nice (A.M.)*

Dear Tommy,

Your congratulations brought me pleasure, I thank you all. In the birthday article you considered my life lovingly and deeply; I delight in your fraternal solicitude and in the happy conclusions to which you come. Yes, finally all will be returned to order, and by now order nearly means usual and normal. Until somewhat beyond the first half of life, I experienced myself as a difficult exception, but have noted since then with astonishment, if not actually shame, that in very fundamental terms all has proceeded as it presumably does for others as well. For that reason I am now intent upon simplicity above all else and am learning to write for the readership of the *AIZ* or *Pravda*.

Your Golo wrote me a good and beautiful letter. If you happen to have the chance, please extend him my preliminary thanks. I will respond to him soon.

Katja, many thanks for your efforts with Mr. Oprecht. May they be successful!

We had guests yesterday, Mrs. Landshoff, Dr. Oscar Levy, whose birthday also occurs in these days, and his daughter. We celebrated with lobster, chicken, and Veuve Clicquot—quite good enough. For Easter and in May we are expecting visitors from abroad. And you—on your way to Spain? It would be nice for us to see each other again soon. My warm regards to all of you, Frau Kröger's particularly to Katja.

Your H.


*Küsnacht-Zurich*
*Schiedhaldenstraße 33*
*April 1, 1936*

Dear Heinrich,

You no doubt have much writing to do just now, and so I thank you especially for your lines. In my printed birthday greetings there are a few bothersome typographical errors. For my peace of mind, please correct them in your copy! Of course it has to be: "of King Henry," and a couple of lines farther: "*to cause* no damage," rather than "caused."—Klaus wrote: "How cocky of Father, to write in *Die Weltbühne!*"

Our travel plans have changed. Spain is out for the moment. On May 6th, at the invitation of the Akademische Gesellschaft für medizinische Psychologie, I'm supposed to deliver the keynote address for Freud's eightieth birthday. Then, at the beginning of June, I have to take part in the meetings of the League of Nations *comité* on the arts and sciences, which is being held this time in Budapest, after which I shall go once more to Vienna for a reading from *Joseph*, as part of the festival there. I'm still in the dark myself as to whether I'm going to keep my word and go with Katja in late summer to the PEN Club congress in Buenos Aires. It depends on conditions, or on my own state. I can't actually think beyond finishing my third volume, which, this time for the sake of the Freud address, I'm going to have to interrupt yet again right at the finish line. Despite its 700 pages and more, it still doesn't reach the end, but stops with the catastrophe of Potiphar's wife, and what remains after that will have to await a fourth volume. Those who know it consider the third the best one. The love story has turned into something quite remarkable, and the character of Mut-em-enet (Potiphar's wife) amounts to a genuine vindication. The book, which is already being printed (and translated), is to appear in midsummer—the only question is where. Bermann, who has indeed merged with

W. Heinemann-Fischer to establish the English-German firm Heinemann-Fischer, has not received authorization to set up an office here, and is trying his luck in Vienna, where, however, Zsolnay will probably fight it however he can. If he fails there as well, he will go to London, in which case that would be where my books appear. Strange.

Enough about me. Political events of recent weeks were nerve-wracking, and England's behavior exasperating. But Laval has had his revenge. People have no idea of the hatred prevailing here for Hitler's Germany. It is essentially fear and trembling. 235 million Franconians in favor of national defense!—If you have written anything about the most recent events, will you send it to me?—Emil Ludwig has just called in desperation from Ascona: He listened in on the memorandum read out by the German broadcaster and found it so captivating that he feels we've lost a major battle. My opinion is that the real losers were the poor Germans living in the Reich.

Warmly, T.


*April 3, 1936*
*11, rue du Congrès*
*Nice (A.M.)*

Dear Tommy,

Yes, I noticed quite clearly that you have made your first contribution to an émigré publication. Meanwhile, after your statements in the Swiss press, it no longer seemed to me to pose an additional risk: they will simply be obliged to accept it. For everyone gets what he merits, and Hauptmann is always having to send admiring telegrams just to get performed in Bomst. (Does Bomst still belong to Germany?)

Imagine this, just today I also began seriously considering Buenos Aires. I say to myself: I'm by the sea the whole year. Two summer months here in the Alps would be preferable, climatically and in terms of rest. A congress doesn't offer any real recuperation, still less if there are lectures to be given. Crémieux, in the foreign ministry, wanted to arrange lecture evenings for me—where? In Rio. My whole life I have been intending to see this homeland of mine before my birth. Now I'm perhaps too tired for it—although not always. I'll also let it depend upon circumstances and my condition. If we do make the trip, is it to be assumed that we will travel on the same ship as the French, of whom there are supposed to be a large number?

The third volume will offer me fine reading for the summer; I'm very much looking forward to it, and especially to the love story. These things only take on their truly remarkable qualities when they are viewed in retrospect and from the perspective of the background. (Very soon I'll be dealing with the relations between Henri and Gabrielle d'Estrée; which have also always been taken much too lightly.)

May Bermann establish himself in Vienna and do what damage he can to that scoundrel Zsolnay, before the government of the German Popular Front puts an end to him—and to the other traitors of his ilk. If I'm around, there will be a law passed that bans German distribution for every foreign press that was of service to the Third Reich and confiscates the German rights. But there are certainly greater things to be done.

I don't like it that one hears talk of "lost battles," even of major ones, before there are any grounds for judgment. Hitler's "peace plan" offers nothing new and there is absolutely nothing that could restore credibility to these people. He is virtually done for and only survives de facto. But that is the least of it, one must only be able to wait. Here in France the latest maneuver was immediately understood perfectly, down to the syllables. As far as England is concerned—would that the memorandum had been yet less dexterous in its cunning. Let it go—England is in the process of maneuvering itself out of Europe. After Hitler is gone the continent will pull together to a man, and pan-Europe— with three main parts, the U.S.S.R., the German Republics, and France—will come into existence before you can turn around. Before Hitler—no thought of it. Today self-evident. One must only be able to wait; and there must by all means be no war.

I had a "preparatory" article in *Dépêche* and sent it to you. *Weltbühne*, no. 12: "Der Vertragsbruch"; next Thursday: "Ein schwerer Anfall" (the elections). You no doubt get it there, otherwise I'll arrange for them to be sent.

If only Oprecht agrees! Kind regards to Katja.

Warmly, H.


*April 26, 1936*
*11, rue du Congrès*
*Nice (A.M.)*

Dear Tommy,

Enclosed another one of those things. It wasn't me. You agreed with the Prague people to lend your name to the assistance fund. You advised them above all to write an appeal; you wanted to sign it. Thus Burschell's report to me. But to whom does he turn to write the appeal? To me. If they didn't want to do it in Prague, then the simplest thing would have been to ask you. I don't imagine that I can write your appeal better than you can. Please do with it what you want. I'll let them know in Prague that I've done my duty.

I hope that the two of you are having a nice spring and hope to hear good news from you soon.

Warmly, H.

*Enclosure to the Letter of April 26, 1936*

THOMAS MANN ASSISTANCE FUND

The German writers in exile have formed an emergency association. The Emergency Association of Exiled German Writers requests contributions to its assistance fund, the name of which is: the Thomas Mann Assistance Fund.

In this fashion I want to say that my comrades in exile appear to me deserving of assistance. I want to emphasize that it is not compassion that causes me to lend my name to the organization that is to help them: it is much more accurate to say that I do it out of admiration. They have left their country in order to be free. They have assumed the burden of exile in order to remain honest.

They are not beggars; it is precisely beggars that they are not. Each one of them would be able to support himself with his work on German territory and was able to do so before a hateful power cut that ground from beneath his feet. The Third Reich is begrudgingly maintaining the shadow of a literature. The vital part of German literature is composed of the writers in exile.

I appeal to all who feel an obligation to the culture of our country or who merely find value in facilitating the material livelihood of a few of the good contributors to this culture. I ask you to contribute to the assistance fund.


*Küsnacht-Zurich*
*May 4, 1936*
*Schiedhaldenstraße 33*

Dear Heinrich, Belated thanks for your lines of April 19. Congratulations on Oprecht's decision! We were very happy about it. Meanwhile I have arranged to receive all of your *Weltbühne* essays and caught up on the ones I didn't know. Making perhaps the most powerful impression on me was the one on the destruction of the Reich. Many Germans live with similar ideas. Now I want to announce myself "on the road." We travel day after tomorrow to Vienna, where I shall deliver a nice mytho-psychological address on Freud's eightieth birthday and, incidentally, shall also visit Schuschnigg. And then we shall also visit Prague (tenth and eleventh) and therefore see Mimi and Goschi.

Warmly, T.

*Küsnacht-Zurich*
*May 19, 1936*
*Schiedhaldenstraße 33*

Dear Heinrich,

Most important: we found Goschi and her mother in a very comfortable state, in their pretty apartment filled with splendid furnishings that inspired in me the envy of the "have not": Mimi better than the last time, relatively healthy, complaining about her fat, to be sure, but now apparently quite free of her premonitions of death, and Goschi cheerful and gentle. Draped in beautiful garments, she performed for us a very soft and joyful dance, and proved quite confident that a diet would allow her to shed some of her plumpness, which might stand in the way of her dancing career outside Czechoslovakia: only outside, for local tastes are thoroughly attuned to her present condition, judging from the practically glorious success, in Mimi's words, that she recently had from her appearance in Prague. It was a very good and agreeable lunch we had there. Another time we made up a lunch party of four on the mountain with the Beneshes—it was an inexcusably lengthy visit, from 1:15 to 3:35, and the congenial, sharp-eyed, and lively president spoke with comforting trust about the political situation, including English politics, the civility and phlegmatic nature of which he fundamentally regards as superior and wise. We knew that he had just spoken with Chamberlain.

I also met with Schuschnigg, but it was not a very productive audience, and one I had to petition for, because he had already indicated his support for our immediate naturalization if we were to move to Vienna. But can one do that? The city remains charming, it is true, and my lecture, "Freud and the Future," met with an unexpectedly nice and solid success, despite a somewhat overmythologized passage about the life of Jesus, which I'd already had my doubts about . . .

Argentina—it's funny how even here while writing I'm trying yet again to avoid the topic, to put off talking about it. To be honest, I have no desire for it and would prefer to spend the two or two-and-a-half months it would cost in a more peaceful manner. I've given my agreement, have exchanged several letters with the eager Mr. Aita, and am in possession of the finest of assurances, namely, that it would cost me nothing at all. But the closer we come to the date, the more dubious it seems to me. The thought of arriving in August in burning Marseille and then being together on the ship with all the delegates for three weeks before the congress starts, and then spending fourteen days in Buenos Aires, which is notoriously uninteresting—the thought becomes increasingly oppressive. I'm not even sure that I'll be able to coordinate it with the conclusion of my third volume and its printing, for in just less than three weeks it will be time for a new trip to Vienna and Budapest (League of Nations *comité*). In short, if you ask me, the possibility of *our* going has become nearly unlikely and I think we'd be better off meeting somewhere this summer on the French coast—how about Bretagne?

Warmly, T.

*Küsnacht*

*July 2, 1936*

Dear Heinrich,

Thanks for your card. It must be lovely up there, and I hope you are thoroughly enjoying your hard-earned rest. I myself have unfortunately taken too much time off, not for rest but for distraction. Our last trip to Budapest and Vienna was great fun, especially the stay in Budapest, with the sessions of the *Comité*, the Freud lecture, a second lecture in the Innerstädt[isches] Theater, and much gala opera and banqueting. The Hungarian government took pains to display itself as civilized, but we refused the invitations from government ministers which arrived in spite of our staying with Hatvany. The nicest touch was that the German ambassador telephoned the minister of the interior to ask that the press pay less attention to me. For I had delivered an address at the *Comité* on "militant humanism" which was much talked about. Everyone ignored his request. But isn't it delightful to think of the German ambassador protesting against publicity given to the only German participant in a meeting of European intellectuals?—Festivities went on much the same for a while in Vienna. After my reading we went to hear *Tristan* conducted by Walter, arriving in time for the third act and entering a vile-smelling house. The Nazis had thrown stink bombs, but the performance was continued—ultimately with just the orchestra, for the Isolde, who had vomited throughout the intermission, merely made a lovely gesture of incapacity and did not rise from Tristan's corpse. Incidentally, the same thing had been done punctually to the minute in the Burgtheater and three cinemas—a prank aimed against the summer festival. That, too, is an experience worth having; now at least I know exactly what Nazism smells like: sweaty feet raised to a high power.

Now I must pay for the holiday by taking up my neglected affairs. *Joseph in Egypt*, which is to be published in Vienna in October and is already being printed, is not yet finished, and I am very much afraid of getting into a jam with it. Just a few final important chapters must be done, and given how tired I am, I doubt whether I can manage them this month. But I simply have to. Afterwards I shall badly need a rest and have been considering Majorca, which our eldest children visited not long ago and strongly recommend. What do you think about it? Toward fall might well be nicest.

For France one can feel only love and admiration. The response of the international bourgeois press, for example, the *N[eue] Z[ürcher] Z[eitung]*, is unspeakably base. As for the German press, it of course revels in hopes of general collapse.

Warmly, T.

*July 18, 1936*
*Briançon (H. Alpes)*
*Hôtel du Cours*

Dear Tommy,

I would like to have a look at the address on militant humanism as soon as it's convenient. The trips must have been nice for you. Austria, however, is now nearing the end. Are you going to settle there? The detour would lead to Hitler. I commend my Czechoslovakia instead, Russia's mother-airport. The good Fleischmann is courting you—it would be his crowning achievement. You should have seen the consul in Marseille. They are very touching people, but not only that, capable as well. One doesn't "fool around with them."

The trip in the summer or fall: it depends on what it's supposed to be. In midsummer it's best to go to the ocean, and later I no longer see the necessity for a long trip. A nice beach resort on the Mediterranean—Sainte-Maxime has the nicest bay—would surely have the same climate as the Balearic Islands, requires only half the trip and is free of certain insects: see enclosure.

I don't think I'll leave France as long as I'm tolerated here. Otherwise I have to go to Prague in the fall; it's been too long since my daughter and I saw each other. Many projects and essays make the trip difficult for me. But I would like to have Goschi come here to the sea and would be very happy if we could all be together, you with your two little ones and hopefully Golo as well. That would be festive. As for Goschi, I started by asking her whether she can come in September and still wants to; for she is diligent in her work. If yes, she would travel on from Zurich with you, if that's all right. I hope this plan isn't being discussed in vain, as did happen once. Please tell me seriously what you have in mind.

Oprecht will have sent you my book. And I'm also sending to you a copy for that helpful young scholar. My articles will continue even through the vacation, but not the novel. I extend my best wishes for your work on yours and await news.

Warm regards to you and Katja, and as well to the children you have with you.

H.


*Küsnacht-Zurich*
*July 20, 1936*
*Schiedhaldenstraße 33*

Dear Heinrich,

The most important thing: your *Lesebuch* has arrived, a blistering text. I read in it for two days without interruption and after I had absorbed all the selections I hadn't seen before, I repeated those I already knew. It is a great pleasure and a great satisfaction. I'm convinced that this manifesto will one day in the future play an extremely honorable historical role—an honor-saving role for Germany, along with those few others, for example, the statement to Hitler by Niemöller and his people, which the wretched subject passed on to his "Minister of Churches." The reader is especially grateful for the humor you unleash. I often had to laugh aloud, and later on that will be more freely possible, with less torment and more of one's heart in it.

Your travel proposals were illuminating. There's no reason it has to be Mallorca. Since it will certainly be the end of August before I'm really finished, Sainte-Maxime will surely be the right choice. Let's just settle on that. Our plans are to go at least as far as Geneva in the car, but perhaps to go ahead and drive all the way in two or three days so we'll have the car when we get there. We'll hear soon what Goschi has decided. If we don't have the children, she could easily come with us on the drive.

I'm sending you my latest "digression," in which, incidentally, I stuck pretty much to the point. Bermann did a lovely job designing the booklet. It is his debut. It's not coming out for four weeks.

Warmly, T.

Of course now I'm no longer considering Vienna, but nor can I really make up my mind otherwise. If we stay here—and it looks as though we will—then in about three years we could become Swiss. That would seem the most correct solution to me. But soon Fleischmann will be here for a visit.

*August 2, 1936*
*Briançon (H. Alpes)*
*Hôtel du Cours*

Dear Tommy,

'tis war, 'tis war, Oh preserve us Holy Angel—. Which he did already when he kept us from going to Mallorca, upon which island the bombs are now raining down. To the two powers now openly waging war against the Spanish people belong both the Lido and Heringsdorf. I would truly like to see those places again and am, like you, connected to Venice through memory and work. However, we have to "realize" that, for better or worse, the world is becoming smaller. Two years ago I traveled right across the country of the other ally, but now I regard it as closed—and it's impossible to know what might happen, so it's better if you don't go there either. We could still meet here this year. France "won't let itself be provoked," as the German social democrats didn't let the Nazis provoke them back then. The result of that is a respite, for us as well: this year yet, as I said.

I told my Goschi that she should also come. Confidentially to her mother, however,

I recommended all possible precautions for the trip through Austria. Following the annexation, Austria immediately chose my book as the first one to ban; that's an unmistakable warning—only for me and my daughter of course. There is no reason for you to fear Austria yourself, perhaps not even Italy. I don't want to exaggerate out of self-interest and deter you from taking an enjoyable trip. If it is to be Venice this time, then I painfully regret that we'll not be meeting; but I would still prefer that to your being disappointed here or missing that beautiful city too much.

I would be very grateful to find out soon about your plans. Are you coming? And when? And could you bring Goschi along in your car? If your little ones will squeeze together a bit, they will have the company of a third young person. Otherwise, I'll have her come a bit earlier and drive a ways from here to meet her. In any case, I'll look for the beach hotel you wanted before you arrive. Driving by, as I was paying a visit in a villa, I saw some very attractive hotels; they were situated similarly to the Grand Hôtel Bandol, but both they and the bay looked more festive.

Hopefully you will make it possible very soon for me to adjust my plans to your decisions. Meanwhile, warm regards to you and Katia.

Yours H.


*Küsnacht-Zurich*
*August 4, 1936*
*Schiedhaldenstraße 33*

Dear Heinrich,

You are right, let's drop the idea. It's not that I believe anything would happen to any of us in Venice, but since my recent visit to Triebschen, where, in a beautiful natural setting, by the way, Wagner spent six years of exile (it was the height of his friendship with Nietzsche, whose traces we then followed in Sils Maria), I have been drawn back to Vienna. I thought: what is right for one is cheap for the other. It was an anachronism, and, incidentally, one that has become more so since I sent the letter. Nor do I have any desire to be the guest of the accomplices of those patriots who declare that "Marxism" must be rooted out in Spain, even if half the people die in the process.—If the Spanish Republic wins under present circumstances, it will be a heroic deed without parallel. The zeal with which the capitalist press, including, for example, our *N[eue] Z[ürcher] Z[eitung]*, keeps its eye on French neutrality, while Italian and German neutrality don't trouble it in the least, is an unfathomable infamy. Those who rejoice in the *naïve*, I mean, the shameless priority of interest over all intellectual decency—the present time was made for them.

Your bitter words, that France "won't let itself be provoked," summarizes the disaster as a whole. The thought that Germany could become *very* big and Hitler could depart this life a supremely esteemed figure, often robs me of sleep.

So we'll stick to your coast. Our visit, the end of this or the beginning of next month, is certain and settled. But I can't say the precise date, because that depends on my concluding chapter getting finished; I mustn't force that, and I'll not be able to say how many days' work it's going to require until I'm approaching the last word. Goschi's travel, therefore, should not be tied to the uncertain hour of our departure. I mean you should have her come and we'll join you later. Perhaps then we can bring her back with us in the car.

I sent you a printed text, a booklet. I almost have the impression that it *and* a letter, the last one before the one with the Venice proposal, got lost. Should it have reached you after all, I wanted to ask you to be discreet about it for the moment. It's coming out only toward the end of the month and Bermann actually did forbid me to send it around any earlier.

Warmly, T.


*August 7, 1936*
*Briançon (H. Alpes)*
*Hôtel du Cours*

Dear Tommy,

With rapt attention I read your address. I understand that it represents no digression at all; it lies on your path. I admire especially the way you maintain respect for Freud, while you nonetheless let the respected old man know that philosophical thought is superior to his or at least takes precedence over it. The same must always be said anew to those whose thought is subject to mere economic determination, if with caution on account of the necessity of unity, and, besides, they don't understand it.

Hitler, or "the subject," as you designated him appropriately, will, however, probably not depart this life a supremely esteemed figure. In that case he couldn't be the mere instrument of a condemned cast. Napoleon III, not to mention the first, went personally into real battles, which he fought for an idea that was still on the rise. We see the subject not fighting. He wants to rise by means of the battles fought by others; and we may hope that this will already work to his disadvantage in the case of Spain. That would be his first palpable defeat. Our destiny, too, is being decided there.

I'm happy that you've decided to come here. For my part, I'll have Goschi travel earlier; hopefully they aren't having reservations there—she doesn't write. May she spend the night with you if the best route takes her through Zurich?

Warmly, H.

*Küsnacht-Zurich*
*August 24, 1936*
*Schiedhaldenstraße 33*

Dear Heinrich,

The Brussels Congress is a great thing and we understand your decision to attend it, even if it necessarily encroaches on the time we'll have together. It is too bad, for it's primarily on your account that we're coming to the French Riviera—otherwise we would have been at least as happy to simply return over the Julier to Sils Baselgia, which we've learned to value as a place to restore one's strength. I wound up my volume yesterday; the closing passage has yet to be copied, but that will have been done by tomorrow. Then, however, every day I spend here will be a pity. As Katja probably wrote to you, we've set Thursday, the 27th, as the day of our departure. We're traveling by car, at a comfortable pace, stopping for the night in Geneva, then somewhere in France, and planning on arriving in St-Cyr-s/mer on the third day, where the Schickeles (who are still there) will likely have arranged lodging for us in a hotel. The coast is gradually emptying, with French holidays either at or nearing their end, and there will be room in September. Sanary is already advertising in the *N[eue] Z[ürcher] [Zeitung]*.—In view of the new situation, we've decided to remain in St-Cyr until you come to Ste-Maxime, and to meet up with you there. We're indeed deserving of taking three weeks' time for a vacation, so there will still be a few days for us to be together. To put off the trip, even aside from my need for relaxation, is no longer possible in consideration of the household, the girls' vacations, and the like. We have to be back around September 20th, because then we're expecting houseguests.

Naturally it would be excellent if Dr. Levy would arrange lodging for us in Ste-Maxime for the same date he's doing it for you. We need two rooms with single beds, facing the sea if possible, and if possible with bathrooms, and hopefully at postseason prices. We can receive news at St-Cyr, *poste restante.*

Now I wish you a safe trip on Sunday and good, not overly stressful days in Brussels.

Do you have a rendezvous with Goschi in Paris? Or is she traveling with you to the south? In the latter case, she could stop over in Zurich on the return trip.

Warmly, T.


*September 21, 1936*

Dear Heinrich, we've gotten as far as Valence today, which is already a considerable stretch in the world, and we will arrive on time tomorrow in Geneva. Our thanks for a good visit, despite everything, the high point of which was the *Henri* reading—which would better not have been followed by another. Warm wishes for your stay! T.

Warmest regards to you and Goschi,

from your Katia

*Küsnacht*

*September 27, 1936*

Dear Heinrich, we had, especially from Geneva on, such a lovely trip, but scarcely had I unpacked my things here than, my teeth chattering, I had to take to bed with erysipelas, and I'm still far from getting up. What makes it remarkable is that we were just speaking of that illness and also the problem of whether attacks are linked with angina or just accompany it by chance. It's precipitated by something completely different, but the left-sidedness is obvious. It is a moderate case, with no high fever, and the doctor is satisfied, although the swelling continues to wander. I'm being treated with injections and compresses.—Dr. Fiedler emerged from the house like a ghost to meet us upon our arrival. He escaped from the Würzburg jail, over two walls—not knowing himself how he did it—and was rowed by a valiant fellow across Lake Constance. "For God's sake, ferryman, your boat!" Now he's being sheltered and cared for.

Warm regards! T.


*October 23, 1936*

*18, rue Rossini*

*Nice*

Dear Tommy,

With joy and in great admiration I received your powerful book. There is no doubt that such depth and persistency are the hallmarks of the most honorable possible approach one can adopt toward the times. What I do myself, I demand otherwise of no one, especially not of you, and it is often a burden to have to demand it of myself.

This winter I want wherever possible to put limits on everything that is not my novel. Aside from work, what remains to me as a lasting pleasure is your writing. Accept my thanks for the book, and for the dedication.

I'm hoping for the information from Katja that I asked her for.

My warm regards, H.


Dr. Thomas Mann Küsnacht-Zurich

*Schiedhaldenstraße 33*

*November 15, 1936*

Dear Heinrich,

The appeal is good, but to sign would be too direct for me. Instead I've decided to allow the address I prepared a while ago for Nice, which I've rounded out into an article, to be distributed through the Presse-Coopération in Paris; it is also not bitter.

I like to think of you reading *Joseph* III. There are a few things in the second half that worked out well. All I know of *Mephisto* is the little that Klaus read to us. But I know that your characterization is correct.

More or less recovered from my various physical afflictions (only the rheumatism lingers, which is making me consider the sulfur-baths in Baden), I'm going back to a story I've long had planned, in which I finally do put Goethe, sixty-seven years old, on his feet. After I avoided it at forty (which was the origin of *Death in Venice*), I want to indulge myself at sixty, if only in the form of comedy. I'm truly pleasantly excited.

Warmly, T.

*Küsnacht-Zurich*
*December 12, 1936*
*Schiedhaldenstraße 33*

Dear Heinrich,

Many thanks for your fine statement concerning recent German measures. You have once again offered us one of those little moral gems, which are only indirectly concerned with "politics," and will, I do believe, be regarded one day very highly by the world of the future, Germany not excepted. The environment in which they are now appearing is not the most agreeable, as it must seem at least to me—but what is one to do? If Hiller's apologetic patronage was already hardly pleasant, then I find the impudent condescension of Ernst Bloch completely unbearable. Already in Germany that caustic fellow had treated me disgracefully; today his language seems to me even less appropriate to the facts. As just one of 65 million he was useful and necessary. Now, outside in pure culture, he's behaving worse than one would like to concede in public.

The Czech government is attempting to intervene on behalf of my Munich possessions. I'm doubtful of success. The scoundrels can put whatever date they please on my "expulsion." Anyway, I've gotten used to not having those things and most of them have also been damaged or dispersed long since.

These days were somewhat stressful after all. It has been a little bit like after the Nobel Prize or on decennial birthdays, and, on the other hand, the news continues to exercise a certain irrational shock effect. Irrational, for how long will all this nonsense remain in force? It's less possible today than ever to believe that this regime will make it even as long as the poor Weimar Republic. It can be assumed that this disbelief, even should one not live to see the end of the regime, will bring with it the consolation of increasing confirmation.

Merry Christmas in this spirit! T.

*December 16, 1936*
*18, rue Rossini*
*Nice*

Dear Tommy,

The exciting days just past have also brought you further signs that people inside Germany don't believe in the regime: otherwise they would be demoralized and wouldn't treat your expatriation like a birthday party. I'm also finding out over and over that people inside are sooner to expect changes than we are. It's simply that no one has a plan, and those wholly out of touch are relying on the general staff. I just received a letter saying that in Spain several Reichswehr soldiers have already deserted. A novelty, scarcely conceivable in the last war it would seem, but perhaps now it will make that wretched general staff think. This once aristocratic institution has acquiesced to an ordinary adventure. And that's how the wars should go from now on: every fascist uprising in every country confronted by the International Brigade, with the numbers of the latter increased by deserting formations.

If we should see Germany again, it will also be time to liquidate merely intellectual journalism. It's actually a holdover from the prewar period, when writers bore no responsibility, which is something they didn't learn to do during the republic. I didn't read what Hiller had to say about you; but the capable, well-meaning Budzislawski was quite shocked by the matter. He committed himself a long time ago to publish it, and then it came at the worst possible moment. He is sorry. Hiller is no longer associated with him.

May the government of our republic successfully press its demands against that thieving mob. If not, there always remains the house and property: one day that will come back to you without problems.

Merry Christmas to you all. I still have to be in Paris three days beforehand. The third of the five parts of my novel will soon be finished. Every evening I read in yours, want to continue it over Christmas, and I'm always filled with astonishment. Most recently it was the presentation of the truly intimate conversation of the husband and wife about Joseph, a very visual passage. "Wie det arbeet!"[14] said Liebermann, referring to a dramatic plot. Very personal is the simple passing of Mont-kaw, and quite extraordinary the structure of Joseph's success—actually just a few steps or parts, but clear and convincing, like the role of the dwarfs. Beyond this, it is all music for the soul, just as it should be in certain periods of life. I tried something of the sort for Henri, in a chapter called "Meditation."

And: Merry Christmas. H.

14. "How it works!" in dialect.

*January 19, 1937*
*18, rue Rossini*
*Nice*

Dear Tommy,

I read your *Exchange of Letters* with great satisfaction. You say everything at once with extreme effectiveness. I, in my many articles, have to start up again at a different point every time and never get to the end. You have truly neglected nothing previously; what you say now is simply definitive.

Now I'm also reading the last pages of *Joseph*. You were completely justified in saying that there were "some successes" in the second half. In the first half just as much. But as it moves toward the conclusion the depiction becomes light, it takes on an internal cheerfulness, more palpably than in the entire book to that point. Not only "The Ladies' Party," which we already know, but other things here also have that effect, funny—and uncanny—like fairy tales. The scene with the dwarf and the eunuchs, one forgets the deeper meaning and reads and reads. On the other hand, the deeper meaning, in the chapter on Joseph's chastity, is treated like a game, so exactly and weightlessly. It is a very beautiful, a unique book also among your works—I haven't forgotten: based on the chastity of the hero. It makes him the figure that he is and the book the exception.

A newspaper came from Prague with a picture of my library, and you with Katia in front of it. It touched and pleased me. I hope that you two visit Goschi again. I can see her only seldom—and my books not at all.

Warm regards to you and Katia. H.


*Küsnacht-Zurich*
*Shiedhaldenstraße 33*
*February 24, 1937*

Dear Heinrich,

Things are supposed to get serious now with the new journal—*Maß und Wert*, it's supposed to be called. The financier, a rich Mrs. Mayrisch (the name is supposed to be kept secret), was recently here with her French representative, Jean Schlumberger, and there were conferences with Oprecht, me (I'm to function as the publisher), and Ferdinand Lion, who will oversee the editorial duties. We reached a decision, and Lion, in contact with me, has begun planning and gathering material. The first issue is to appear at the beginning of June.

I have to say that I'm pleased with the decision and eager to see what might come of it. The journal is intended to make the most positive possible impression, be productive, simultaneously protective of the past and open to the future, and endeavor to gain trust, indeed, authority, as a recognized forum of free German intellectual life. Something like that.

Of course, we are all counting very much on you. Lion will [write] you himself, probably with some more precise requests. With these lines, I want only to pave the way for him. In any case, I've been thinking especially of a piece from the second volume of *Henri*. But perhaps it will be possible to agree on other things as well.

We were in Arosa for three weeks, and it did us good. I'm working on my Goethe novella with genuine excitement, and enjoying the powerful effect the *Exchange* is having; the German version is now up to 15,000 in circulation, and there are already many translations. The French version is appearing in *Marianne*.

Your essay about Hitler's "Speech" was very funny and a great pleasure.

Warmly, T.

*June 4, 1937*
*18, rue Rossini*
*Nice (France)*

Dear Tommy,

Your birthday is here again and here I am with my congratulations.

May your fourth volume be finished and be as great as the third. May you find the same pleasure as always in the other aspect of your activity. I hear that your American trip was successful and that your influence there lingers.

Landshoff was here and told me that you brought home a case of neuralgia or sciatica. Those are the less happy results—scarcely avoidable with so many demands upon your person. I hope that you don't let the illness get you down and that you overcome it quickly.

Your letter to the dean in Bonn is also circulating as a highly suggestive rumor in places where it is not to be found and read. That was how a local professor spoke of it to me.

The people in Berlin are having yet more defeats inflicted upon them; the blows are falling more frequently and it's scarcely to be understood how they expect to last much longer. Their only chance is equivocal England. For war, if that's the way out they seek, is truly not to be termed a chance. Yet I admit that I've trembled for days now as I've opened the newspapers; and the danger will cease only with the regime. Those who don't want to acknowledge that will have the lesson forced upon them.

May you in your next year see the end of the regime.

Most warmly, H.

*July 23, 1937*
*Briançon (Hautes Alpes)*
*Grand Hôtel*

Dear Tommy,

In Paris I had the pleasure of seeing Erika and Klaus. Erika is now a quite "successful artist" and very brave. She will make her steady way there.

I discussed with her and with Klaus the matter of the Klub der Sauberen,[15] that embarrassing venture less on the part of Schwarzschild than of one Konrad Heiden. I ask you urgently: refuse to take part. Klaus is leaving it, so he says, and Schwarzschild himself has had enough of it, so he believes. A personal hatred that is indulged leads far and then farther; one thing it must not be allowed to lead to is the collaborators of a magazine joining together as the only untainted ones.

You are working again, I know it from your children. The treatment has helped to that extent, and that is a lot. I sent a letter inquiring about your health when I thought you were still in Ragaz. For myself, I have to watch out how I come here from a particularly strenuous trip to Paris to recuperate and nevertheless finish my novel.

My warmest regards. Greetings to Katja.

Your H.


*July 30, 1937*
*Briançon (Hautes Alpes)*
*Grand Hôtel*

Dear Tommy,

I found your news pleasing in various respects: Club der Sauberen, Jules Romain—especially Golo. It's wonderful how thorough and reliable he is. With just a word from me he put himself and his learning to work so that I could substantiate my opinions. Go ahead and let him edit your journal. Why have another, when the best one is already there? Golo has everything, the knowledge that is indispensable for such a journal to flourish, and the psychological receptivity. I have not forgotten how he wrote me that the verses in my first *Henri* were suitable for recitation aloud on strolls.

And you know how highly I estimated Klaus at his expressive best, in Tchaikovsky. I find it the more painful then that he is personally inaccessible—this due not so much to severity as forgetfulness. In Paris we had arranged for a second meeting, which I thought would be more substantive than the brief get-together late in the evening. It didn't happen because of a misunderstanding, which also might ultimately have been evasion. But that certain Heiden Klaus found immediately; he listened willingly to him and remained

---

15. Club of the Untainted.

in the Club der Sauberen, although he doesn't feel right about it, as he told me. He forgot to say where the bad feeling comes from: it probably has to do with the fact that we nonmembers are supposed to be defamed by it. It has no other purpose. Bernhard was to be destroyed first of all, then the Popular Front, in which he has a seat and a vote. It was in his honor, a bourgeois democrat, that the *Tagebuch* developed its anti-Bolshevism and began printing Gide. The latter opposes Stalin because Stalin is supposed not to be a genuine Bolshevik anymore. It seems a particularly untainted practice to use Gide for anti-Bolshevik purposes.

In a letter I fundamentally regret, I pointed out to Klaus that once the Popular Front was successfully destroyed, there would be nothing left but Strasser, who is a thwarted Hitler, and the party directorate in Prague. The latter would once again rehearse the Weimar Republic and all its consequences. The league of the untainted would be an insignificant appendage. Schwarzschild says: it must be all right to be a liberal, which is what it is absolutely not all right to be in view of the German situation. He at least has his personal reasons. But Klaus? I regret that I had to write him an earnest first letter. Later perhaps he will understand it. My impulse was less impatience than concern. The young recipient will be inclined to suspect infringement and dismiss it. If you take the opportunity of discussing the matter with him, assure him in any case of my good opinion and intentions.

Warmly, H.


*August 15, 1937*
*18, rue Rossini*
*Nice (France)*

Dear Tommy,

The journal came yesterday; I read nothing but your novel, but that right away—and with such feeling as I can scarcely explain myself. Perhaps the incomprehensible change that has taken place among the Germans? It is just this comparison that makes *The Beloved Returns* very timely. I'm looking forward to the continuation and I thank you.

The enclosed material concerning the founder of the Club der Sauberen comes from the *Deutsche Volkszeitung Prag*, which is Communist and has its reason to reject it. As a witness to events and conversations, however, I can confirm that Sch. remained in the Popular Front (together with Communists) only as long as he hoped to be able to win over capitalists and capital to it. When that failed, his hatred for Bernhard gave him a second reason to quit. This affair (S.-B.) simply provided the pretext. If, however, I had granted Sch's motion to remove B. from the P.F. directorate, what would have become of S? He would still be sitting with the Communists as the victor over B.—He and his concerns are dubious, and just barely that. Klaus, who was in America, doesn't know the context. He could have gotten himself informed—not by Heiden, who is a famous nobody, but preferably by me. But he didn't even respond.

The Club der Sauberen is of course not going to be calmly tolerated. It's to be predicted that this or that irreproachable name is soon going to disappear from its lists. Klaus runs the danger of ending up in an association with predominantly undesirable members. But he has his and our name to protect. If we want to assume that everything will be forgotten anyway, then by all means. If, however, we take democracy seriously, why has our Klaus joined up with the worst reactionaries (who, be it noted, customarily begin like Radek and his comrades: in complete ignorance of what ought to become of them).

The Popular Front has consisted until now of a largish number of organizations and relatively few prominent individuals. That should change. I hope to be able to report to you on this soon, if possible in person. You would certainly not find it overly burdensome. I'm happiest myself, incidentally, when I'm busy with the Edict of Nantes.

Warmly, H.


*October 2, 1937*
*18, rue Rossini*
*Nice (France)*

Dear Tommy,

I hardly have to explain the enclosed circular. You'll see what it requests of you. I don't know whether the anonymous figures from the Freedom Party sought your authorization before they distributed your *Exchange of Letters*. I, in any case, must do so.

The publication of the *Exchange* in Germany has been of great benefit. The essay with which you introduced *Maß und Wert* should be put to use much more broadly and effectively.

The members of the association that now wants to act are intellectuals; I'll name them for you: Professors Marck—Dijon (philosopher), Gumbel—Lyon (statistician), Lips—Washington (anthropologist), Fritz Lieb—Basel (Prot. theology), Paul L. Landsberg—Paris (Catholic philosopher), Georg Bernhard—Paris (political economist), Aron Gurwitsch—Paris, Rudolf Olden—Oxford (lecturer). Further, Dr. Maximilian Beck—Prague (philosopher), Dr. Feblowicz (physician), Lion Feuchtwanger.

I would like to take this opportunity to excuse myself to Golo for not being able to be in Paris on September 20. I was there later and returned home immediately.

Warmly, H.

*Küsnacht-Zurich*
*November 4, 1937*
*Schiedhaldenstraße 33*

Dear Heinrich, Querido has done his duty. Hopefully Oprecht did not neglect his and has sent you the second issue of *Maß und Wert*. The third is supposed to include a longer review of the first Henri novel. Meanwhile I've had a chance to see the continuation of the second one in *Intern. Literatur*. It will be a quite extraordinary book, one that boldly distinguishes itself from all other German works.

I'd no more gotten rid of the sciatica than I plunged into the most depressing tooth crisis (terminal stage). I'm not well otherwise either, but have to prepare lectures for America: by the beginning of next year I will have completed a great journey, to points deep in the West.

Warmly, T.


*Thomas Mann's letter of January 2, 1938, was partially torn off vertically. There is consequently no continuous text.*

*Küsnacht-Zurich*
*January 2, 1938*
*[date on the postmark]*

Dear Heinrich,

To you and Frau Kröger [ . . . ]
and all the best for the new year.
It is a splendid occasion [ . . . ]
pleasure to hear of the extraordin[ . . . ]
*Henri* in America. It is an hon[ . . . ]
country. No book there is in the slight [ . . . ]
*and* "Leipzig" or "Vienna *and* Zurich" [ . . . ]
Incidentally, your triumph there is [ . . . ]
bank will no doubt continue, which [ . . . ]
Nobel Prize definitely freer. To the [ . . . ]
ist public opinion, one is [ . . . ]
cessible.
All in all, we ca[ . . . ]
rd Reich. Of pessimi[ . . . ]
out of the Reich, it is they in reference [ . . . ]
"That takes forever," they say. "The [ . . . ]
a political form suitable to them [ . . . ]

"Aryan" who come out say [ . . . ]
It won't last another year." They a[ . . . ]

*Page 2*

[ . . . ] was in great danger. He had high fe-
[ . . . ], and after several uncertain days was
[ . . . ] as a mercifully light case of infantile par-
[ . . . ], which, after the meningeal inflammation,
[ . . . ] of the right eye was attacked and initially
[ . . . ] displayed symptoms that disturbed the doctors.
[ . . . ] recovery went with record speed, and
[ . . . ], who was still confined to bed on Christmas eve
[ . . . ] private tree), is already returning in
[ . . . ]nd. He has grown a bit and looks pale
[ . . . ] in.
[ . . . ] pleases me that you found the Wagner lecture in-
[ . . . ] about Schopenhauer in Arosa
[ . . . ] the same American collection, that you also
[ . . . ] have.

Warmly, T.


*Cunard White Star*
*RMS* Queen Mary
*February 20, 1938*

Dear Heinrich,

Greetings from our fourth voyage to America, and hopes for your well-being while we're underway. You will have been devastated as well by the new political outrages. Who would have thought that Austria would have fallen so suddenly and with so little resistance! Public opinion, the Swiss press included, was completely disoriented at first; they represented the whole thing as a setback for Ribbentrop. We only learned how things really are from the Paris newspapers. Poor betrayed and forsaken Schuschnigg! Now he's imploring his Nazis "not to abuse their new rights." In Graz they already had "order patrols."—We are getting very sparse information for these few days (until tomorrow), and it's hard to get an overview of the situation. For me, Vienna is a big loss. I got a moving reception there as recently as last winter. The question is whether Prague will remain open. Our territory is shrinking more and more. At the journal, we also failed to foresee losing Austria so quickly. The timing is bad, since there's no one to discuss it with at the moment.

I imagined the winter crossing would be worse. We've had a very calm trip; the gigantic ship, nearly unassailable, it seems, rolled *laterally* just one day, and that doesn't make one seasick. This time things will get serious in America: a lecture tour through fourteen cities, all the way to Los Angeles, on the topic, "the coming victory of democracy"[16]—nothing but courage. It begins on the first of March in Chicago for some four thousand people; it's sold out. The prelude is at Yale University in New Haven, where I also have to speak at the opening of the Th. M. Collection, a kind of archive, with manuscripts, translations, etc.

It will be strenuous, and on top of it all, the uncertainty of the situation oppresses me. I emigrated very reluctantly. And yet, probably the cleverest thing would be to go ahead and establish residence now in America.

If you want to write, use my manager's address: Harold R. Prat, 2 West 45th Street, N.Y.

Warmly, T.


*Beverly Hills*
*April 21, 1938*
*California*

Dear Heinrich,

Thanks for your letter, which I received on the lecture tour. We're resting a bit here, but soon we must move on to fresh deeds in the Midwest and then set out for New York. We will probably spend the summer in a little house on Long Island, which someone there made available for us. America as a whole makes itself wonderfully available, in a way that's unknown in Europe. We have decided not to return there for the time being. Erika is going to Zurich at the beginning of May to break up the household there and see to the shipment of our possessions. All the children, except Moni who will probably return to Florence, are supposed to come over. The best prospects for all of them are here, the only prospects at all. It appears that I will receive an honorary professorship at an American university, which will assure me a basic living. It's up to me to decide in favor of the East, with its European familiarity, or the land of the future, cheap and climatically magnificent California. By autumn it will be arranged.

It is a repugnantly soothing thought that there will probably not be a war. For you that means the calm you need to finish your great work. My warmest wishes. For a *visit* we shall certainly come sometime soon.

Your T.


16. In English in original.

*June 10, 1938*
*18, rue Rossini*
*Nice (France)*

Dear Tommy,

You will have received my letter for the sixth of June; it was addressed to Peat New York, and your letter of May 29th pleased me very much. Written correspondence is tedious, and always makes me think of mail coaches. By the time a letter gets from Weimar to Rome, Weimar doesn't exist anymore.

You've probably acted wisely, establishing yourself there. But in the summer you have reason enough to come here for a visit; for my part, I want to facilitate our meeting however I can. Please let me know when you will arrive in Switzerland. I'll gladly come there, especially to a resort. Hopefully yours isn't higher than 800 meters; I mustn't subject myself to any great climactic strains—I'm strained enough as it is and the book is not finished. I have to deliver the last part by August. A moderate elevation in the mountains would perhaps help me.

It's very nice that you thought of our getting together, I had wanted it very much. I await news from you, assured that you will meanwhile have a pleasant time.

Warm greetings to you and Katja.

Till we meet. Your H.


TRANSLATION, WINSTONS

*Küsnacht-Zurich*
*August 6, 1938*
*Schiedhaldenstraße 33*

Dear Heinrich,

I hear your great work is finished. If so, that would be glorious—and the time is particularly favorable for a visit. The thing is that, realizing that we would otherwise not finish up here and would be pressed in making final arrangements, we have decided to give up the idea of a longish vacation. Actually we are rather pleased, for we are fully enjoying our way of life here and need nothing better. At most we want to spend a week in the Engadine, at Sils Maria or Sils Baselgia, where Erika already is. That will be too high for you (1,800 meters); but Leuk in the Valais would not really suit you either. We are starting our "homeward" journey to Princeton on September 15. Would you be our house guest here in Küsnacht toward the end of the month and into September? The woods and lake shore, an easy drive, are so beautiful, and you would be coming to a country whose attitude toward *l'infâme* has turned into the most gratifying resoluteness since Austria. I have never felt endangered here for as much as a moment, and no one need even know that you are here. What do you think? Around August 26 would be the right time, from the point of view of our own convenience. I am counting on your being free when I offer this date. At the moment we have Moni, Medi, and Golo, who has developed wonderfully and is writing excellent things for *Maß und Wert*. Have you sent off your Nietzsche introduction? I have written not twenty but sixty pages on Schopenhauer. Why was I ever set on that track? Now the foreword has had to be carved out of the surplus again.—Golo has already attended to that, too.

You have time to think over your visit, for which I hope you'll have cooler weather. We were pleased when it turned hot at last, but the pleasure is already proving a calamity.

Warmly, T.

*September 9, 1938*
*18, rue Rossini*
*Nice (France)*

Dear Katja,

Those were lovely days in Küsnacht, and I wanted to thank you warmly once again immediately upon my return. The high point was by no means, as Tommy said as we took our leave, my poorly read fragments; the best part was much more that I was able to be with my brother and his family before you all go far away. Incidentally, it is only in our thoughts that it is far, and I may hope that you all will repeat your visit as early as next May or June. Best of luck in the meantime.

Yesterday it did not look like war. For today and tomorrow we know nothing. If the aggressor lets the right moment pass, then, instead, the hour of the German opposition will have come. In Paris the unqualified renunciation of all internal conflict would be desirable. May I ask Erika to inform me of the outcome?—I was just reading that the decision is supposed to be made in Nürnberg on the twelfth. The world anticipates it with every conceivable feeling—save only the most warranted one: shame.

I preserve the best thoughts of all of you. Your friendly regards, dear Katja, are returned by Frau Kröger.

Your H.M.

*November 22, 1938*
*2 rue Alphonse Karr*
*Nice (France)*

Dear Tommy,

Many thanks. I'm glad that you found yourself in agreement with my "Nietzsche." Despite manifold differences, disdain did not tempt me even once, and I hope that my understanding, as far as it goes, is not only "charitable" but respectful. Something like "charitable" is what Golo felt when he got the piece to read. He wrote me about it very cordially, with one objection in reference to the words concerning the future of the workers—that they can't simply be accepted without qualification, subject as they are to all of Nietzsche's hostility toward socialism. That's correct, to the extent that it's a question of socialism. The words about the future of the workers as the ruling class are not socialist. Nor does it concern me in the slightest that Ley and his cohorts, for their deceitful purposes, say something similar. But I see that this is the spot that would have to be expanded for a book. For now it can stay as is. Much more at issue are cuts, and those you suggested don't seem to me to threaten the meaning. I'm grateful for the pains you took. Your time and energy are understandably much in demand.

Mine too in the moment. First, I have to finish hurriedly compiling articles from the last two years for a book. Second, I'm sitting in an incompletely furnished apartment at an "early" Empire table, from the time of the Egyptian adventure; the matching cabinet likewise displays sphinx heads and famous geniuses in bronze, and the whole thing was cheaper than a modern *bureau.* My third concern is the news I received from Bertaux that my daughter Goschi is supposedly engaged to an American. I know no more than this and ask only what kind of Americans it could be who get themselves engaged at present in Prague, and to my daughter. She has no desire to go to the only country that would be glad to take her in; and there where she's living she's certainly in danger. An engagement that occurs under such circumstances—"desired—and there he comes"— is not enough to reassure me. I sent a telegram, but the prepaid reply never came, like all replies since the state has been under lock and key. Goschi wanted me to meet her in Zurich; I asked her to come by plane to Cannes. Bertaux will have to repeat the request in his own name. Such is our life.

By the time this letter reaches you some good fortune will probably have occurred or, who knows, deliverance. I would be infinitely grateful for a little peace. Things are such now that I can hardly predict what I shall have to say or do in the future. This much is certain, that we are meant to have courage; we're not being asked to withstand these great shocks for nothing.

My regards to your family.

Warmly, H.

I anxiously await your manifesto—I think that it is one—every day. Perhaps you will remind the publisher about it, in case you haven't sent it to me yourself.

*December 29, 1938*
*2 rue Alphonse Karr*
*Nice (France)*

Dear Tommy,

Your two texts with the brotherly dedications did me good. In "This Peace," masterfully expressed, is everything there was to be said concerning the provisionally final chapter of the pessimistic novel *Europa*. Your commentary on it will continue. My desire is nearly exhausted, and permission can also be retracted. Should the outcome you foresee really transpire—general fascist transformation with limitations and variations according to the respective histories of the peoples—then "You can see to your muck yourselves," as spoken by a wise if drunken king. Be the expression ever so genteel, there would be nothing else to do. Nor must there be, say the people in Fontane. It always works that way too, you say.

Have you meanwhile received my novel? It has been out since last month, but my copies only arrived yesterday, and I had no chance to write the dedication in yours. It would go roughly: "To the only person close to me."

My daughter really did marry her Dr. Aschermann and is sunk in marital bliss, until she deserts me for America. The industrial concern managed by the father of the young man is being removed overseas, as is now customary. Although one should consider a chairman well-off, I had to play my proper role as a paying father—flattering for a, let's say, man of independent means. I saw my child briefly in Geneva; I don't know if for the last time. For once she's over there, she's vanished for good.

Much more do I hope that you find your way back—to what kind of Europe? We shall see. To raise once more the immediate specter of war, and then save us from it again—that won't be easy. The wonder of Berchtesgaden will naturally have to venture something, why would it be a two-headed calf? Therese von Konnersreuth was also a great sensation and wanted not to be forgotten. Speaking seriously, it appears that in the case of Tunis fascism will confront its first resistance. All that's missing is another battle lost in Spain, so that—. But our hopes are now nearing six years old. No one but the local astrologers are still dating the fall of the one in 1940, the other in 1941.

For 1939, I wish you complete personal happiness, that is the surest thing. May all go well for your family. May we see each other again.

Warmly, H.

*January 25, 1939*
*2 rue Alphonse Karr*
*Nice (France)*

Dear Tommy,

Did you get my novel the *King of France?* Querido has again been instructed to see to it. Perhaps your confirmation will arrive before the book makes the long trip a second time.

"Europe Beware!" is a document for the ages and meanwhile for our great satisfaction. I thank you very much.

My daughter got married in Zurich, to Dr. Aschermann, who works in a chemical enterprise under his father as chairman. The business is being transferred from Vienna to New York. The young man must soon go there himself. Goschi, however, is required to deposit a rather considerable sum in her own bank account in America, and I was able to give her only a very minor portion. Earlier a businessman would easily have come up with a few thousand dollars. That seems to have changed. Given sufficiently influential connections, would authorities perhaps be content if the young woman deposited only $3,000? This inquiry is not meant to obligate you in the slightest, but comes from concern for the child who would be truly unhappy to be left behind here.

I hope that you are working and contented. My next project is slowly being invented. With my best regards to your family.

Warmly, H.

TRANSLATION, WINSTONS

*Princeton, N.J.*
*March 2, 1939*
*65 Stockton Street*

Dear Heinrich,

Your novel arrived at last a few days ago. And I can truly say that I am reading it day and night, by day in every free half hour, and at night in the quiet before I switch off the lamp—which, thanks to you, happens late. As I read I am never without the sense of an exciting uniqueness, the sense of having to do with the best, the proudest, the highest this age has to offer. Certainly people will wonder someday how our debased times could bring forth anything of the sort—and will realize that all the blatant idiocy and crimes are not so very important after all and that the human spirit, fundamentally undisturbed, meanwhile goes its way and creates its works. The book is great in love, in art, boldness, freedom, wisdom, kindness, exceedingly rich in intelligence, wit, imagination, and feeling—a great and beautiful thing, synthesis and résumé of your life and your personality.

It must be said that such growth—such transformation of the static into the dynamic, such perseverance, and such a harvesting—is particularly European. Here in America the writers are short-lived; they write one good book, follow it with two poor ones, and then are finished. "Life" in the Goethean sense is our tradition alone; it is less a matter of vitality than of intelligence and will. Kesten, in the essay we were fortunate enough to be able to publish in the last issue of *Maß und Wert*, took many of the words right out of my mouth; in this case, one must admit, enthusiasm helped him surpass himself. I imagine you too were affected by it; it is virtually a model of a favorable review, and since he sees the whole, it also forms a kind of homage to a life. I can imagine that the German exiles as a group feel proud of this monument! And ultimately, for don't we know how such things go, Germany too will take pride in it. "For he was ours." Well, yes, in a manner of speaking.

There's another matter I want to mention, not the most pleasant: the affair with your son-in-law, my nephew, Dr. A. He was here, paid a short visit to his uncle, as he is wont to call me, then departed for a long stay in the West (he said "South" but meant California). What he had to say about the transfer of the business (a chemical factory is, after all, not transportable, and I doubt that there is anything at all to be transferred) and about the guaranty sum for Goschi (a man who has entered this country as an immigrant and is settled here can bring his wife over without more ado, as I have already told you), was all rather vague and indefinite. Nor was it clear what he intended to do in California. A few days later an American, Morton W. Lieberman of South Orange, New Jersey, came to see us to warn us. He said that there is an indictment pending against Dr. A. for embezzlement of objects of value, jewels and the like, which a Jewish lady had given him to spirit out of Germany. The Jewish lady had succeeded in getting out herself, and so she was able to institute proceedings against him, while many other Jewish people of substance, for whom he had also taken out valuables, can do nothing because they are still in Germany or Austria. Mr. Lieberman impressed me as being sensible and well-meaning; and we had previously heard from people in Prague that they wished Mimi and Goschi the best of everything, but that someone seemed to have been acting too precipitately. In view of all this, we have begun to worry about what you have done about your furniture, which I suppose A. also brought out and which, he made haste to say, might be delayed for months. And indeed, we wonder what you have done about this whole connection. God knows whether the young man is being unjustly suspected. People may be maligning him to us. But I can't really see why they should bother, and sorry as I am to trouble you, I thought you had better know about it. Golo thinks so too and has written to Mimi, though not so bluntly as I am doing here. These rumors and charges are going the rounds; the suspicion that A.'s marriage to Goschi might be a dishonest person's exploitation of your name and mine cannot be rejected out of hand; and for good or ill you should both govern your attitude accordingly, not send Goschi here prematurely, and in general be somewhat on your guard. I hope it all turns out to be sheer nonsense.

Another week and my lecture tour starts in Boston, then leads to the Middle West and West—five weeks of it. There will be three of us; Erika will come along as secretary and assistant. It will be strenuous, but I know how it goes now, and the American sleeping-car beds in private compartments are excellent.

With warm congratulations, T.


*Princeton, N.J.*
*May 14, 1939*
*65 Stockton Street*

Dear Heinrich,

Yesterday we had a visit from Landshoff, who saw you in Nice, and from him we heard about your wife's suffering and the worries and problems that naturally result from it, in addition to all the rest, for you. The news touched us deeply, and I immediately decided to write you, which I would have done long since, incidentally, if it hadn't been for the nearly six-week lecture trip I've just put behind me and the string of political, literary, and social obligations waiting for me here upon my return. This country, in its tremendously naive eagerness, eats one up. If, however, I had known how difficult things are for you now, I would nevertheless have written to extend our sympathetic and understanding thoughts. A certain psychic and physical reaction to the completion of your enormous work, the pressure of which you had withstood so long, was likely not to be avoided anyway, and so these further circumstances, your concern for your wife's suffering and all the aggravations that go with it, have come at the worst moment.

I was amazed, or should say was filled with admiration, at how you could write a few of your best political essays right after the greatest effort of your life. The one about the Nazi Reich as the deformation and disintegration of Germany (which, however, is the cunning of history: it is meant as accumulation for war but functions as disintegration) was just as brilliant as the address to the German soldiers. Erika sent the first one to *The Nation;* it would be extremely gratifying if it were to appear in this country. Hopefully the various forms of illegal ingenuity will take care of the dissemination of the latter in the German barracks.

That brings me to the object of this letter, which I'll go ahead and enclose with these lines. Making contact with the people of Germany, even if it is won only by cunning and smuggling, is a matter of supreme importance, and the organization of such contact should not be put off until after war breaks out. Receptivity is no doubt tremendous, and yet greater, I believe, is the simple thirst for literature created in freedom that brings with it the air of freedom, the indirect effect of which is perhaps stronger precisely among the Germans than any directly propagandistic work. The letter gives you the details. Upon Erika's urging, I'm now trying to get together a *comité* of prominent German names to appear on the letterhead and whose help here would easily allow us to collect a considerable sum of money for the sole purpose of getting texts produced especially for this purpose into Germany in a suitable form. We are requesting your name and your support.

I cannot tell you how fervently I wish for a quick improvement in your wife's health, and for your circumstances therefore also to become easier and more cheerful.

Warmly, T.


*Princeton, N.J.*
*May 14, 1939*
*65 Stockton Street*

Dear Heinrich,

In the midst of turmoil and uncertainty, of threats of war and fresh danger of appeasement, one thing is becoming increasingly clear: the decision must and will be made in Germany. Until the German people have liberated themselves from this "leadership" there will not be lasting world peace. We have long known that, and the world is beginning to grasp it. We also know that the Germans basically hate their regime and that the only thing they fear more than Hitler is war. The suspicion and frightened disgust that the Germans feel toward the Nazi government is not primarily "political" in character. What horrifies the better Germans is the moral abyss into which they are sinking—the abominable depravity in morals and culture. We know that within the past six months a considerable number of Germans who could not be considered "tainted" either "politically" or "racially" have left their country. They left simply because the November pogroms and the propaganda campaign against Czechoslovakia have been too much for them. They speak of the avidity with which they snatched at statements from outside, from the world of freedom. Dangerous though it was, nothing could quench their thirst for truth, for decency, above all for dignity, for quiet recollection. They describe their longing for the voices of intelligence and civilization. And while the books of the prize-winning government writers no longer find any readers in Germany, however much they are trumpeted, translations are what "sell." Works of the few "permitted" foreign authors are devoured. But our friends in Germany are yearning intensely, urgently, to hear from us. In the course of the campaign against the intelligentsia, the *Schwarze Corps* [17] denounced booksellers only a few weeks ago, declaring that if it were up to them nothing but exile literature would be sold. On this point we have every reason to believe the *Schwarze Corps.*

It is imperative for the Germans inside the country, and for us, the representatives of intellectual Germany on the outside, to make contact with one another. There must

17. *Das Schwarze Korps,* the weekly newspaper of Hitler's SS.

be an end to the unnatural situation in which we who might teach the Germans to re-member their better selves are cut off from them. For if we speak insistently enough, our voices will be heard at home. This is my plan:

In the course of a year some twenty-four pamphlets, written *for the Germans* by rep-resentatives of the German intelligentsia, will be sent into the country. The series will not be narrowly political. It is meant to appeal to the better instincts of our fellow coun-trymen, whereas Hitler can arouse only their most dangerous impulses. A committee of American friends (under the chairmanship of Dr. Frank Kingdon, president of Newark University) will undertake the financing of the project. In the next few months I shall ap-proach some twenty-four German writers, scholars, theologians, and artists with definite proposals. For the moment I am asking you for nothing more than your agreement in principle. I should like permission to add your name, which carries weight and persua-siveness in Germany and the world, to the roster of my German committee. If you con-sent, you will soon hear more details.

I am writing similar letters to the following friends and colleagues: Wilhelm Die-terle, Dr. Bruno Frank, Professor James Franck, Leonhard Frank, Lotte Lehmann, Dr. Hermann Rauschning, Professor Max Reinhardt, Ludwig Renn, René Schickele, Professor Erwin Schrödinger, Professor Paul Tillich, Fritz von Unruh, Stefan Zweig.

In the next few weeks I myself will begin one of the articles.

As for methods of distribution, these are numerous—they might even be sent through the mails. We are counting on printing at least 5,000 copies per pamphlet, and every copy will be read many times over. The articles are to be paid for, modestly, at about the rate offered by American magazines such as *The Nation* or *The New Republic*.

May I sum up, dear Heinrich? Together with our own proper and personal tasks, to-gether with the "demands of the hour" and beyond them, we are duty-bound to use our influence on the Germans. War can be averted only if the Germans make an end of Hit-ler. If it is not averted, any hope for a peace that will not once again contain the seeds of a new war depends upon the Germans repudiating the regime *before the defeat*. The Ger-mans must be brought to their senses; and who will do it if we remain silent?

Let me hear from you soon. With my best regards,

Your T.

PS. This letter is to serve to inform you about my plan and request your formal con-currence. Since your works have been banned bestsellers in Germany for years, I know, of course, that we are agreed in principle.

*May 25, 1939*
*2, rue Alphonse Karr*
*Nice (France)*

Dear Tommy,

Your birthday is approaching, and that my congratulations might arrive on time I'm thinking of the event well in advance. I received the *Life* magazine with the old recollections and the new pictures. May your circumstances remain ever friendly and blessed with fruitful work.

Your plan concerning getting propaganda into the country has my agreement and cooperation. The *Weltbühne* articles, for example, are at your disposal. The appeal to the German soldiers has already been distributed a number of times, an appeal to the workers has also been broadcast a few times. In these matters there can never be too much done. I made a phonograph record of my response to "The Birthday Address of an Inferior." I no longer keep track of how many India-paper manifestos I've produced. My goal in all of this is yours: the German revolt must come before the war.

The Germans are preparing themselves internally; they will understand us earlier than others. The shameful part is that it remains the case that no one anywhere is counting on a German uprising. On June 9, I'm supposed to speak to the most influential journalists at the home of a member of the 200 families. I'm preparing an address, the sense of which is to make them ponder the country's more recent moral condition. They should be confronting the question of whether it's the German opposition that is ultimately to be taken seriously, and no longer the regime.

I might then go to London for the same purpose. The invitation is at hand and some have expressed the desire to support our propaganda. Unfortunately, we are familiar with the process. Our prospects, in any case, are better, because the dubious unanimity of the opposition as a whole is simply unnecessary. The action committee consists of a small number of persons and they operate undisturbed by contradiction. English help might be afforded us under the single condition that we are successful. That, incidentally, is also my condition if I am to devote all of 1939 to this activity. By the end of the year Hitler must have been defeated; otherwise what will follow would be unforeseeable, at least for me.

It was a difficult winter: work, the success of which is uncertain, Frau Kröger ill, and an unhappy child. My personal discomforts are well enough explained by age. I can help Frau Kröger regain her health, if I marry her. After ten years, not all of which were easy, she has come to richly deserve it. I had hesitated primarily until my daughter was married. Now it seems that her marriage was an unhappy one, but that must not be allowed to affect Frau Kröger. Accept my special thanks for your interest in her affairs; it was a real consolation.

If Katia will allow it, I'll include here my acknowledgment of her lines to me.

I hadn't known that even the address of the thieving mother-in-law was false. The most inexcusable part: she traveled with Goschi through Germany. The arrest of the child would probably have suited her purposes. From the foolish Mimi she took an expensive piece of jewelry, exactly the fraud for which her son is being pursued in America. I had refused to pay him the dowry before the marriage was final. Afterward, I transferred three-quarters of the amount to Goschi herself. In vain; she handed it all over to him. Since then he has disappeared. Could you inquire as to whether it's possible for me to join in the action pending there? I have tried repeatedly to get a bit of money to Prague, so far without success. Letters from the two reached me via Sweden. They should try to escape there, and then on to Moscow, where I have money for them. Might Katia remind them of this single way out?

Warmly, H.


TRANSLATION, WINSTONS

*Grand Hotel & Kurhaus*
*"Huis Ter Duin"*
*Noordwijk aan Zee*
*(Holland)*
*June 19, 1939*

Dear Heinrich,

You must be back home by now, and we have installed ourselves here, together with Erika, for the first stage of our European summer. Let me say once again how happily Paris fitted in, and how exhilarated all three of us were by this first meeting with you. We feel that from now on we must meet fate halfway in arranging such happy accidents, and if it's at all possible we hope to pay you a visit in Nice before our holidays are over, so that we can see your new home and continue our Paris conversation in a domestic atmosphere. For there's no saying when we shall see each other again. Much, to be sure, depends on how much longer it will take before the old ones in Munich receive their passports so we don't have to avoid Switzerland.

It seems we have done well after all to choose this place. The hotel is excellent, the beach glorious, and the air has something like the effect of the Engadine. So we hope to strengthen ourselves after a winter in which I, at least, have asked a little too much of myself. Incidentally, in spite of our American background it was not at all easy for us to enter the country on our Czech passports. But a visit to the Dutch ambassador and a letter of recommendation from him have worked miracles, and secured for us not only the Belgian transit visa, but also special respect and expedited treatment at the border. Nevertheless, Europe with its military customs officials and passport scrutinizers seems to us narrow, overcrowded, and ill-tempered. At least, it did during the journey.

Here one still has a sense of emptiness and space—except for Sundays, when the place fills up with people whom Idachen Springer in Travemünde used to call "day-flies." There are Germans among them too; one looks at them as one glances at a German newspaper. Rhineland industrialists sat behind us on the grand terrace of the hotel, and I gathered from their conversation that they often cannot make deliveries for weeks because of the shortage of raw materials. From time to time they dropped into whispers. It was fascinating.

This is also meant as thanks for your birthday letter, which has not yet reached me here. It will be the first batch of mail from Princeton, which is being forwarded by Dr. Meisel, my secretary.

Keep well! And let's hope to see each other once more this summer.

Warmly, T.


*Noordwijk aan Zee*
*(Holland)*
*June 28, 1939*
Dear Heinrich,

In the mail today from Princeton, just a few days after your letter, was *Mut*, your lovely birthday present. The jacket note is quite definitely not saying too much when it speaks of an historical document. All of this will remain to bear witness and inspire admiration after the plague is long gone. Moreover, one really should not lose courage.[18] Precisely when everything has assumed such vile form, an international sphere of freedom and the intellect will take shape, a private circle of betters who will always assure us a vital setting for our thoughts and works.

Warmly, T.


*Grand Hotel "Huis Ter Duin"*
*Noordwijk aan Zee—Holland*
*July 5, 1939*
Dear Heinrich, please let Mr. Grund know that I immediately applied myself to his cause in New York and shall see to it that he is not robbed of the honor.

Katja is still awaiting a reply from Melantrich.

Warmly, T.


18. Courage: *Mut*, the title of the book mentioned a few lines previously.

*Grand Hotel & Kurhaus*
*"Huis Ter Duin"*
*Noordwijk aan Zee*
*(Holland)*
*July 17, 1939*

Dear Heinrich, of course I understand that you can't make the trip to Sweden, and Olden must understand it too. For me, Stockholm was on my summer program anyway, assuming that all goes "well"; that is, that we have a nice, lazy *appeasement*.[19] If things start looking too much otherwise, then we, of course, will have to rush head over heels back to Princeton. I've also got a lecture and everything scheduled for Stockholm.

Melantrich, poor man, has announced that he's not to have anything more to do with me and can't make payments either inside or outside the country. Unfortunately, there's nothing to be done about that.

Warmly, T.


*Grand Hotel & Kurhaus*
*"Huis Ter Duin"*
*Noordwijk aan Zee*
*(Holland)*
*July 20, 1939*

Dear Heinrich,

I received the enclosed from Bruno Frank. There's probably nothing that argues against signing it. Please do so yourself and be kind enough to pass the paper on to Feuchtwanger.

May the baths at Digne have been good for you and continue to be. I'm fully absorbed in work here, for it would be a great gain if I could get the novel out by this autumn.

Do read the book by Klaus, *Der Vulkan!* It would do him good to hear a positive word from his famous uncle. He's been left quite isolated with it; I think three hundred copies have sold. And it is a very talented and, all lightness aside, a serious book, which moved me more and more in the reading.

Warmly, T.


19. In English in original.

*Princeton*
*November 26, 1939*

Dear Heinrich,

You know how we lost contact with you. After our happy meeting in Paris, the refreshing seven weeks in Holland, and trips to Switzerland and London, we went to Sweden for the PEN Club Congress—which didn't take place, as it turned out. The war began, and our intention of returning to Switzerland and from there arranging to see you again came to nothing. In the interest of our safety, people tried to persuade us "to spend the war period in Sweden." Thank God we did not, although the return voyage did have its problems. Precisely for reasons of safety, we could not use a Swedish ship. We had to fly to England in order to obtain an American ship that was bringing citizens home, and the flight from Malmö to Amsterdam, passing not far over Helgoland, was precarious. But everything turned out well, and from Southampton the American liner *Washington* brought us here—amid the throng of 2,000 persons who spent the nights on improvised cots in public rooms transformed into concentration camps.

We were happy—as happy as one can be nowadays—to have regained our base. But correspondence with Europe is hampered and complicated to the point of discouragement. Let's leave politics aside. I am writing you chiefly to congratulate the two of you, in Katia's name as well as mine, on your marriage. We are both delighted. It is a good and fine, a reassuring act. It seals a well-tested relationship, which no longer stands in such urgent need of blessings as that of our little Medi with the man who has now become her husband, G. A. Borgese. Yes, we too have had a wedding: Medi has married her antifascist professor, who at the age of fifty-seven probably no longer expected to win so much youth. But the child wanted it and brought it off. He is a brilliant, charming, and excellently preserved man, that must be granted, and the bitterest hater of his Duce, whom out of pure nationalism he regards as the worst of the worst. He castigates this nationalism of his with remarks such as "Germany is an organ and Italy a mere violin." But the "merely" means nothing. Once he went so far as to say: "Europe—that is, Germany with fringes."[20] Which might very well please Hitler. But at the same time he is an enthusiastic American, and although Medi knows Italian and he German, they speak only English to one another.

They will live in Chicago, where Borgese teaches. Thus we are left all alone in the big house, with a delightful black French poodle for company, a present from a patroness. Katia is reassured to know that her very old parents have at last actually reached Switzerland. It was finally managed with the help of the House Wahnfried, and for the

20. Second quote in English in original.

time left to them the old couple, onetime millionaires, have enough to live on. But will they ever see their daughter again? That depends on what everything depends on.

I am well—that is to say, I am not sick, and at our age I suppose one must be content with that. The stay in Noordwijk happily gave the Goethe novel such a vigorous push that I was able to finish it here within the first few weeks after our return. The final manuscript reached Stockholm successfully (by way of Portugal, in Swiss diplomatic mail), and thus the German edition can be "published" before Christmas. I am curious to see how it will strike the tiny band of Swiss, Dutch, and Scandinavians who will make up its audience. And to hear how you like it!

It will be a good while before you receive this letter. I had better send you New Year's greetings right off. Let us hear from you, if you can manage it. I have done all in my power for the interned German and Austrian writers. Giraudoux has been very kind and has written to me in great detail, and Jules Romains has also done his best. A large sum of money has been sent from here for the people involved.

Warm regards and best wishes, T.


*Nice*
*2, rue Alphonse Karr*
*Nice (A.M.), France*
*December 9, 1939*

Dear Tommy,

First, my warmest wishes to you for the new year. May things continue to go well for you and yours. We are not allowed any concerns beyond our private ones; I no longer assume the right to them. Things are tangled and very far-reaching; they exceed the span of the life we are allotted. The first of these events was with me in the crib; the second came in the powerful middle of life, when one still knows and wants everything. Now I'm a silent onlooker, with no five-year-plan, so to speak. The major actors don't have one either, by the way, aside from England, where courage and wisdom prevail. Just three months ago, I wouldn't have said that, and I'll let it rest there.

This is my first German letter in a long while. Whenever it suffices, I send a card in French. This deviation is justified by the abundance of happy events in the family. I don't know why, but the marriage of your Medi has something gratifying about it. May I ask you to extend to her my particular congratulations, and my respectful regards to her husband. Further, there was great satisfaction in finding out, for Katja's sake, that her parents are safe. Your successful return voyage, what a happy circumstance! And how fine that you have completed your novel! I just read the seventh chapter, carefully, absorbed. It is an extraordinary composition, and an inner image of old age, true, a pleasure for connoisseurs.

My wife is happy; with her Czech papers she feels properly situated and responsible. The consul in Marseille visits us from time to time, and she knits for his soldiers. We also have mobilized French friends, whom we see on their vacations. Strange expression. The "last time" I had a nightmare. A crowd was pushing me slowly forward between picket fences, with a passport control at the end, and I had none, or had a false one. Then I probably had Italy in mind. My great desire now would be to go there once more. I regret the cities I missed; I tune the radio to Bari, where I never was, but also to Florence, and listen to opera. "Abbiamo trasmesso dal Teatro Communale di Bologna—"

The dark spot is the fate of my daughter. If I'd only prevented the unhappy marriage! But it was done so quickly. After I'd given all I had, the child stayed in Prague. They are living with the grandmother, from what I've heard through third parties. The Red Cross has so far given me no assistance. I can only hope that the worst experiences don't repeat themselves. One way or the other, the state will be reconstituted, probably inside a Donau federation—which Beneš also supports now. A few "concentrated writers" are of the, probably unfounded, opinion, that I helped them get out. I managed to achieve nothing for the publisher of the *Weltbühne*. A member of the Czech *Conseil national*, Ripka, is vouching for him. Do you want to try to get Giraudoux and J. Romains interested?

Once again, in conclusion, my new year's wishes to you.

Warmly, H.

*January 17, 1940*
*2, rue Alphonse Karr*
*Nice (A.M.) France*

Dear Tommy,

Yesterday morning, at twenty minutes to one, I read the conclusion of *The Beloved Returns*. The conclusion is the most moving part, as you will know. When the book reached me a few days ago, I began there where *Maß und Wert* left off; soon I came to Goethe. He makes his first appearance just lying there, the whole proceeding in silence and secrecy, without us being aware right off of his presence. Madame Privy Chancellor Kestner (née Buff) is also unaware at first, noting only a bit later, in the carriage, who sits next to her. The effect both times is tender and strong—there's something ghostly about the second, with the first dreamlike.

The 7th chapter offers a successive interweaving of interior life and external circumstances; it produces in a measured space both the character and the overall impression he makes, drawn from greatness, doubtfulness, from the futile efforts of the others to get close to him, and from those other more successful attempts to use him. It wouldn't do to leave out "Herr John" the copyist. Nor the move on the part of August, who allows his father to determine the day on which the invitations will be made, while having quite correctly decided it himself. It's not enough that the colossus is fundamentally hated; the others also make fun, the only way to love him nevertheless. But how he himself hates and loves—always returning to Schiller. That is what touches me most.

The reader has already had the true Goethe when the spectacle begins in chapter 8. 7 is the precise preparation; 8 wouldn't otherwise have the same meaning. In 8 the house and the collection of extras take part in the drama. I see an opera decor, the movements are "regulated"—and that coincides with the specific "regulation" for Charlotte, so that she keeps her distance. This act, as I say instinctively, benefits from an extraordinary direction. But I would be very sorrowfully parted from the first reading if the dark farewell in chapter 9 were not yet to come. I had sensed it before, even though I am then somewhat more shocked over the man in the coat than the reasonable woman who discovered him.

These are impressions. I hope they also convey what I feel for your book, a very personal affection. I think it is the most beautiful from your present stage of life. I do not say the best; better than *Joseph* it probably cannot be. It also seems to me "the most beautiful" only because it touched me very deeply. The prolonged pursuit of the beautiful makes people lachrymose, a notion I believe myself to have read in *The Beloved Returns*. Especially at this time. Ultimately one compares oneself with the waiter, Mager, whom you bring into an allegorical relationship with the author on the last page.

I thank you from my heart. H.

Now I want to read *Werther* again, in French as I have it here with me, with the article by Sainte-Beuve, which is deeply felt.

TRANSLATION, WINSTONS

*Princeton*
*March 3, 1940*

Dear Heinrich,

I received your good letter of January 17 somewhere deep in the state of Texas, on the lecture tour that I may have told you was impending. Before the trip back to New York, a matter of forty hours, we had a few days' rest in San Antonio, near the Gulf of Mexico, where it was already very summery. The population there has a strong Mexican admixture, a frequently most attractive type and a relief after the eternal Yankeedom. The city also has beautiful Spanish missions from the seventeenth century, the most picturesque things I have seen in America.

It touched me very much that you once again dealt so lovingly with my novel, and I am glad that it could hold you and move you. I don't know whether it is my most beautiful, but it is dearest to me, because it contains the most about love and erotic union, in spite of all the mocking and ironically veristic aspects in which this love is clothed. Hence I see its weaknesses and pedantries with particular clarity. It would not be a novel at all, but something like a monograph in dialogue, were it not for an element of excitement in the initial conception that seems to have been retained in the execution. Of course it is connected with the realization of myth, in which *Joseph* has given me practice. The reader has the illusion of learning exactly what *he* [Goethe] was really like, as though he himself had been on the scene. That is something of an exploit, with the result that a critic in one Swiss journal wrote that he devoured the book as he had done the Indian tales of his boyhood.

What you say about the last chapter shows me that it was a happy invention, even more so than I knew. In reality no second meeting took place, and so I helped myself out by having Lotte, overwhelmed by the verse play as she is, bring about the meeting. It is the only really fictitious scene, although the conversations throughout are also imaginary enough.

After the summery days in San Antonio we are again back in the snow. I have much to do, must prepare lectures for the *boys* on the *art of the novel,*[21] my major effort consisting in not doing the thing too well. I often wonder what you are doing and writing now. I cannot really believe you are content to be merely an onlooker, as you hint, because I myself must admit to being far from that, and often feel torn apart by hatred and a craving to see justice done. In the course of this tour I once again propagandized to the very limits permitted by "neutrality" and also wrote a counterpart to *This Peace: This War,* which is shortly to be published in London and, I hear, is also to be broadcast to Germany.

Keep well. Golo is doing his job splendidly in Zurich. Can you give him a contribution sometime?

T.


*May 5, 1940*
*2, rue Alphonse Karr*
*Nice/H.M./*

Dear Tommy,

Your letter of March 3rd arrived on the 26th, one day before my sixty-ninth birthday. If you did not intend it, the coincidence is the more remarkable; it gave me great pleasure. Now it is your turn to become sixty-five, which you termed a new stage when I reached it. May it not be a terribly obvious one for you. May everything succeed and continue as before, the activity and the satisfaction. One doesn't see the shadows from a distance, so it could be even more upsetting to experience events from there. We have become hard-boiled veterans of our experience. In September 1938, sixty thousand people suddenly left this place; threw their shoes and loose coat hangers in the car,

21. In English in original.

and raced off to the interior, if not directly across the channel. A little later, attracting little attention, they were back. That sort of thing doesn't seem to happen much anymore, although it would be more justified now than then.

For my part, I'm rather resigned to world events, even when they get close to home, without that meaning that I can boast of having particularly steady nerves. I'm putting my trust in Great Britain. All my life, my interest for England has been weak; I haven't even learned the language. My recent experience, then, moves me all the more deeply. Reason, foresight, and resolve are there. They are really fighting; they act and negotiate without prejudice, free of the usual superstitions. They begin with an image of a viable Europe, and want to realize it. It will be difficult; all the same, they have learned. Their religious education seems to encourage what is best, the power of conviction and an uprightness, which, in comparison to the rank opportunism of the enemy, becomes a great virtue. They have forgiven you *This Peace* and want to broadcast *This War* to Germany. I listen to the radio every evening, hoping to happen upon the broadcast.

You asked what I'm doing. This. As befits my circumstances, however, relatively quietly. I would welcome disappearing into the silent mass. I'm uneasy because of the lengthy nature of the process, as is generally assumed, also by our Czechs, who, incidentally, are my consolation whenever I see them. A horrible surgical intervention will resolve matters, and I don't know whether I wish to be around for that. What I won't see, I still believe I know. Everything depends on the British plan, supported by a few eastern developments, which would come of themselves. I'm well acquainted with the various opposed tendencies, which would keep the villain around in a moderately tamed state. By now it is no longer worth considering the most extreme failure of instincts, or the possibility of its triumph; in that case it is preferable not to think at all. My mistake is to jump the gun. I don't even bother myself with that anymore; what I find worthy of effort is Europe, in England's sense.

I've also given some thought to what I might be able to offer our excellent Golo. Something current is out of the question. There are some novellas that have not appeared in any of my books. They must have come out sometime in a Germany that has long since ceased to exist; I've forgotten when and where. I've proposed to him that we have one of these products searched out. He hasn't responded yet; he probably still has the earlier notions of published and unpublished. And they remain valid only with qualifications.

Here, as my birthday greetings, I've given you my impressions, hopefully only the reliable ones, and I would like to know yours. Of course it's not the same when four weeks go by before we can read each other's letters. I've framed a colored picture of you from an American magazine and hung it on the wall; it peers with a confident smile into my dining room. But what will be the look on our faces today and tomorrow? *Ars lunga, vita breve* [sic]—that is as fitting as ever.

My warm thoughts, H.

*July 23, 1940*
*2, rue Alphonse Karr*
*Nice*

Dear Tommy,

A question from Oprecht allows me to surmise that you have made inquiries. Perhaps you have also written me directly, since March 26, when the latest news from you arrived. I've received none since that time, just as you have probably not gotten my letter intended for June 6 and, afterward, my two cablegrams. The first I sent before German control took effect here. The second was a repetition of the first. I asked you to do whatever you could to help my wife and me receive entry visas. It would have been necessary to instruct the local consulate appropriately. In that case, we would now be over there or on the way. However, I was too late in making the arrangements.

Now I have to undertake an alternative plan, without entirely giving up thinking about America. Staying here would not exactly be healthy. The threat comes from two sides: a) the demand that we be extradited; b) the understandable inclination to make us pay. On the other hand, people in a position to know think that authorities would perhaps not refuse to extradite us, but would impede its being carried out. The goodwill to see us to safety appears to persist here and there. It should soon become clear whether we could disappear to north Africa—and be "safe" there. That means above all: free; and means: being able to get to Portugal and onto a ship.

Morocco is not a province, only a protectorate, and a tourist visa is good for six months. It would be a good enough place to wait and see if England stands firm and the Führer of Europe "falls off his pedestal," which is, after all, what's destined to happen to him sooner or later. If yes, then I have no reason to depart the Old World any sooner than the world itself. For the less favorable case, an American entry visa is always desirable. It would be issued, on order of the government, by the consulate in Marseille. In addition I will approach my close acquaintance the Czech consul Vochoč, 57 rue de la République in Marseille. He will certainly try to persuade the American consulate to have this letter delivered through diplomatic channels; otherwise you would not receive it either. Perhaps Vochoč can even manage to get the other consul to recommend me to his superiors. Your personal intervention would, however, certainly be the most important.

Once outside the continental borders, my connection with Marseille will be extremely uncertain. (Not to mention Nice. The local consulate is out of the question.) Yet another difficulty is that I probably have enough money to await events for a considerable time; but not enough for the crossing. My credit at Knopf could be used; but the transfer of money appears not to be permitted; and if they would permit you there to buy two tickets for the ship, then I don't know if they would find their way to me. You could send them to the American consulate in Marseille, assuming that he is amenable. But the letter in which I would have to inform the consulate of my address could be intercepted. Let's first see if you receive this letter and I get your answer, which can likewise go through the consulate—by courier.

The details I've given you are somewhat tangled. You'll probably have to read them twice. I've marshaled my energies to be able to act accordingly. Goethe took exception to people taking to their heels before their final rest. And why indeed? I could just as well be in Berlin next year, not extradited but summoned there professionally. To know nothing is the best thing for us. Aside from that, I'm suffering less so far than I ever would have thought given premature knowledge of these circumstances. "It's always possible to do it differently," you write. The one who is suffering more, to the point of it being intolerable, is my poor wife, along with many others. Particularly for her sake, I must endeavor to get away into a milder climate. Since my connections were all broken, I've been pursuing our common interests with Marcu, whom you know, and a Czech, who had recruited the volunteers. Neither of them are particularly "on top of things."

Since the letter from Zurich did not come from him, I presume Golo is with you and I'm glad of that. In the broadcast from London I recently heard your name mentioned. I hope that you are working. I too am productively occupied; without much prospect that the thing will ever see the light, at most that it will fall into the wrong hands. But for myself, the efforts are beneficial.

May things always go well for you and your family.

Warmly, H.


I was just brought greetings from Golo in Nîmes. I hope that you already know and are not learning the painful news from me first. Nîmes (Provence) has a big assembly camp for foreigners—now probably only foreigners that no other country is accepting. He is by no means in German captivity; nor would he be extradited any more easily than I. But why couldn't he have stayed in Zurich, and why does Oprecht, with his brother's help, not demand that he be returned there? I was more shocked by the news than most others. My wife immediately lost her head; she left with the woman who brought the news, who should, on the contrary, have waited for me; then I might know more. In other times, not yet long ago, I could help this and that person get out of the camp. Today I have to take care to evade the worst myself. If I find out anything more precise about Golo before this letter is to be taken to Marseille, I'll enclose it. You should get the American government interested in the fate of your son. Perhaps he came to fight for France and this is the thanks he got. He would probably have written me, but nothing gets here. This continent is disintegrating completely, only England's white cliffs are still standing.

—According to my latest inquiries Golo was on his way to a French port. Even an Italian one would have been preferable, but what does one know. He was picked up on the streets of Nîmes when he was on "vacation." Gradually they are all supposed to be released.

**Testament**

En cas de décès, naturel ou non, je laisse à mon épouse, Madame Emmy (Nelly) Mann, toutes les valeurs en ma possession au moment de ma mort: agent comptant, livres, manuscrits, meubles, et le reste.

Pour les revenus ultérieurs qui se produiraient par la vente de mes romans, pièces de théâtre, films et autres travaux, je désire que ces revenus soient partagés à parts égaux entre mon épouse et ma fille Léonie, domicilée à Prague, Tchécoslovaquie.

*Nice*

*28 août*

*1940*

Henri Mann

*Los Angeles, Brentwood*
*September 22, 1940* •

Dear Heinrich,

Finally, our fervent wishes have been fulfilled, and you have unhappy France behind you! To get the rest of the way here to us is now the smaller step. If you've already embarked upon it, and this letter comes too late, all the better. In any case, I must tell you what worries were lifted by your telegram (telegrams came from all sides: from the Rescue Committee, from the Unitarians, from Washington, etc.), and how eagerly we are anticipating our suddenly impending reunion. Soon we shall be able to follow developments together in relative peace. There are no doubt many more horrible things to come, but they will necessarily eventuate in a humane new order, which is to say, one not determined by the great gangster of our time.

You understood why I didn't write, and were always secure, as good Golo was too, in the knowledge that we were working on your rescue, and not only on yours, with the aid of the positive forces in this country. Erika was the most active of all, but that wasn't enough. She couldn't stand it here and has flown to England—with a guilty conscience on our account and with assurances that "she would be beside herself should anything happen to her." But she had to be there on the spot, helping out in her own way, and it would not have been right for us to have interfered. Unfortunately, that means that she will not be here to welcome you. She doesn't want to return until November.

Golo's appointment to the New School in New York pleases me; it might be the start of an academic career. Waiting for you here is a film contract, which is no fiction, and offers you a basic livelihood for a start. That, in any case, is pleasant.

I'm wondering whether you will arrive before us in N.Y. That could happen if you are traveling on the Clipper or have located a ship quickly. We're leaving here on October 6, will stay one day with Medi in Chicago, and are obliged then, to give our negro driver time to drive back with the car, to spend a couple of days with friends in the country, so that we'll probably be back in Princeton around the 15th. In the worst case, Klaus will be there to receive you. Then there will be room for all three of you at Stockton Street. We'll keep the house until March. Then we want to come back here, where it is prettiest, and where a few days ago we took possession of a property with seven palms and many citrus trees. I'm thinking that we will stay here and build, and here is where the two of you will like it best as well.

Have a good trip, and accept my embrace in advance!

T.


*Windermere Hotel*
*Chicago*
*November 14, 1940*

Dear Heinrich,

It was a pleasure and a relief to receive your telegram. So the journey began well and your first impressions of Beverly and Hollywood were encouraging. That is what we hoped for and desired, indeed, expected. The secretary who has been assigned to you has also written that your prospects are good, and that it is very possible that one of your books will soon be made into a film. That would be great, and would stand you in good stead for a time.

We arrived here this afternoon, finding Medi not yet through her ordeal. Since we have nearly a week to stay, we'll probably be present for the event.

You will have learned the results of the *election* [22] underway. It was at all events a suspenseful night. Success was as good as assured by midnight, and I went to sleep at 1:00, but got up again at 5:00 to reassure myself. The first really joyful and satisfying turn in seven years or longer. Nothing but setbacks up till then. So I had scant belief in it, feeling that, as an event, it would fall outside the frame of our epoch. Now we learn that the frame is broader after all than was thought. Good instincts guided the American populace: a fortunate backwardness, if you will. Victory is accordingly only a matter of time, if a very long time. A fourth term will probably be necessary.

May the two of you settle in well and feel comfortable there. Enjoy the sun—here it is freezing cold and snowing. As soon as we're back in Princeton, we want to get down to business with the house question, before the prices rise.

Warmly, T.


22. In English in original.

1. Heinrich and Thomas Mann, 1900. All photographs courtesy of Thomas Mann Archive, Zurich.

2. Katja Mann with her children—(*left to right*) Golo, Michael, Katja, Klaus, Elisabeth, and Erika, in Munich, 1919.

3. Heinrich and Thomas, in Berlin, 1930.

4. Heinrich with his wife, Nelly Mann-Kröger, 1938.

5. Thomas, Michael, Katja, Golo, Erika, Klaus, Elisabeth, in Princeton, about 1940.

6. Thomas and Heinrich, 1940.

9. Thomas with grandchildren Frido and Tonio, in Pacific Palisades, September 1948.

7. Thomas and Katja, in Pacific Palisades, 1940.

8. Heinrich (?), about 1945.

10. Thomas (?), about 1948.

11. Thomas with Katja and Erika, in Pacific Palisades, about 1950.

*November 16, 1940*
*Hollywood*
*Canterbury House*
*North Cherokee*

Dear Tommy,

Many thanks for your greetings, they got here before mine reached you. Since my dear wife had written first to our traveling companion, Golo, I went ahead and added something there that you should also read. Now I hope to reach you with it in Chicago.

My wishes to Medi and her parents that the event might have come off happily in the meantime. Assure the child, who now should have one of her own, that my heartfelt thoughts are with her. A somewhat distant uncle, and I've not yet had the privilege of seeing her husband; but sympathetic interest sometimes comes from far away; our readers surprise us by drawing unanticipated connections. (Charell, of the theater, raved about Henri here, and precisely about the second volume, which is the more important, less well known part.)

My condition here yields to conventional expectations. People vacillate between veneration or indulgence and the need to put me properly to work. So far I've been working on the "novella," as the abridged novel is called, at home. I may have to move to an office in the "studio" as early as tomorrow in order to waste the time between 10 and 1 in consultations and chatter. Of course everyone who has a film running wants me to see it. I see them and talk. Certainly, however, I could talk without having seen.

Social demands are moderate and by pleading work commitments I can moderate them still further. Only in regard to the touching Frau Lisl Frank do I fulfill genuine obligations. Care for the house and the car fall to my wife; everything is doubtful when it's meant for an uncertain period of time.

On the night of the election the train personnel was intensely astir; it seemed they wanted to call us to the radio, but soon dismissed us as idiots. I was dead tired and let destiny take its course. "It worked out well once again." But when I think about a fourth term! It must not be that the pseudo-victor Hitler will be allowed to snatch up the antes for that long. It gets to be too much—and becomes legal. It's said that the duchess of Windsor is abominably active here, not to mention other dangers.

Hopefully you will be able to conclude things in Princeton quickly and favorably. May we get together here very soon! My grateful regards to Katja, and Nelly's no less friendly ones.

Warmly, H.

In my letters to Golo and Klaus there was a request for a recommendation from you to the Rescue Committee for the two Rottenbergs, who are waiting anxiously in Lisbon and quite deserving of being saved. They've been battered enough and it's about time they got a visa. When one knows people personally, as I know these two, it is painful to think of the son they lost, their unjust impoverishment, and the mortal danger they are in. The Committee already has my surety—along with the particulars.

*December 6, 1940*
*264 Doheny Drive*
*Beverly Hills, Calif.*

Dear Tommy,

I learned yesterday from Golo of the happy event. It was truly a relief; you and your worries had been very much in my thoughts. Now please convey my congratulations to your Medi and her husband. I am pleased along with you and Katia.

All the better if the other news proves true and the two of you are thinking seriously of coming here.

Warmly, H.

My dear and much admired Katja,

I too share your pleasure in the recent addition to the family, and wish Mädi all the best. That you really are coming soon is excellent. We're not quite settled in and accustomed to our new surroundings, but have a very nice house. All the rest will come in time. We think often and fondly of the pleasant time in Princeton.

Warm regards, Your Nelly

Thomas Mann

*65 Stockton Street*
*Princeton, N.J.*
*December 8, 1940*

Dear Heinrich,

Golo told me that he has informed you of the birth of Medi's baby, little Angelica Borgese. I'm sorry I didn't pass on the news to you immediately, but the whole thing went so curiously. Since we were right there, we stayed on, waiting a full two weeks for the event, which could have come any day. Finally, since we really had no more time— and I was also getting tired of hearing Borgese complain about the Holy See, which he considers the real evil in the world, while I would certainly be able to come to some arrangement—we departed. Perhaps we were well in doing so, for barely a day and a half after we arrived back here labor started, which, with the guidance and mitigation of a good doctor, proceeded very smoothly in just a few hours, so that there is no doubt that Elizabeth will recover quickly. She's already writing very chipper letters from her childbed, just as the whole time she was patient and cheerful with her pregnancy. But

I had the clear feeling that it was just our presence that put off the delivery, whether from the distraction or some sort of embarrassment, so that it was probably simply the right thing to do for us to discreetly turn our backs.

I still wanted to tell you that.

The English are no doubt bearing heavy sacrifices, but it's not as bad for them as what is being done here—which is intentional. I also heard directly from Washington that F.D.R. is indeed thinking of nothing but Hitler's *downfall*.[23] Even social issues take a back seat to that; properly, for what could be gained in that area without his downfall?

Warmly, T.

*December 23, 1940*
*264 Doheny Drive*
*Beverly Hills, Calif.*

Dear Tommy,

My best wishes. May 1941 bring us joy. Some bitterness will be mixed in—that's in the nature of the wishes that should be fulfilled. May 1941 bring contentment to you, Katja, and your children. For my part, I'll be happy if I manage to look like the enclosed picture, taken by the talented Mr. Knopf.

When are you coming here?

Warmly, H.

All my best wishes for the New Year—hopefully you are coming soon!?

Warm regards, Nelly

*February 3, 1941*
*264 So[uth] Doheny Drive*
*Beverly Hills, Calif.*

Dear Tommy,

That was a surprise, this new book and quick intermezzo! A "minor" entertainment it was not, although entertaining and even light—if one takes as the opposite of light, not significant, but therefore heavy. The book transposes meanings, like heads. What is painful frequently turns into laughter, within the pleasure and value of life is encompassed the allure of death, and annihilation gains much from a gallant game. The senses are disdained and celebrated all at once. One dies after very brief reflection, but before the little ones who follow us lies the most unmistakable existence. It delights—1. the gift of those

23. In English in original.

involved to make the best of everything; 2. the universality of life processes, with no single one preferred to the others; 3. the cheerfulness, the gallant disregard of everything dangerous or offensive. Love or slaughter floats lightly by, in a lofty indifference to experience, as recently in Voltaire when I reread his likewise oriental and meaningful novels.—That doesn't come along often. It could be that this small book is the equal of the less conditional works; of such there are few.

I am very pleased and grateful.—Concerning myself the only thing to say is that I really am supposed to turn seventy next month. It astonishes me in a casual way, like the head that cut itself off, which, however, also represented only an accomplished, therefore credible fact.

Accept with Katja the best regards from me and from Nelly, who is proud of the dedication.

Warmly yours, H.

Bermann-Fischer announces: *Adel des Geistes, Das Problem der Freiheit,*[24] *Die schönsten Erzählungen.* My library abandoned in Nice did not include these books. Incidentally, it seems to be stuck in Spain; it would be the third library I have lost. I would like to begin a fourth with the three books mentioned, as a souvenir of my birthday.


*Princeton*
*February 4, 1941*

Dear Heinrich,

I've not yet thanked you for your last letter, nor for the excellent photograph from Knopf which was enclosed—the best one I've seen, I believe. Knopf has meanwhile given me a few others taken at the same time. They're all quite lively, but you have chosen the best one.

It's strange: a number of weeks ago, before our last trip to Washington and to the South, I mailed off two copies of a book called *Die vertauschten Köpfe,* one to you and one to Frank, and neither from him nor from you have I received confirmation that they arrived. That is really odd. We know the American post is not especially *reliable,*[25] but to suppose that both items have gotten lost is improbable, though there's scarcely an alternative explanation. It would all amount to nothing but a small irritation, but I'm sorry about the two copies, for only a few have made it over here by now.

We are eager to hear how things are suiting the two of you over the long run there. The date of our reunion draws nearer; we are in avid correspondence with Davidson, our architect, and have reached a basic agreement on the plans, so work on the house

24. *Das Problem der Freiheit* contains passages from the earlier address in English, "The Problem of Freedom," but is not identical with it.
25. In English in original.

can begin soon. By your birthday, we hope to have made our move and be near you. What remains for now is finding a suitable rental in Brentwood, Beverly, or Santa Monica, where we can live until our own house is finished. I'm sure the Franks will offer their assistance once again.

The most interesting episode on the trip I mentioned was a two-day stay at the White House—the three of us, including Erika. The president is decidedly a fascinating man, sunny in the face of his handicap, spoiled, cheerful, and clever, also something of an actor. Nevertheless, he is a man of profound and unshakable convictions, the born counterpart to the European miscreant, whom he hates as much as we do. He suffered more than a little over not being able to make his views public sooner. To have done so would have put his reelection at risk, which, with complete justice, was his first consideration.

I shudder at breaking up our household here, the packing, the exertions Katja will have to endure, and the transitional state until a new order gets established. But that too will pass.

Warmly, T.


*February 23, 1941*

Dear Tommy,

Soon I shall have to travel to Mexico in order to immigrate from there. No minor matter in view of the cost and my nonexistent papers. But a helpful attorney wants to accompany us. Only the affidavit is indispensable, and I am supposed to request it from you and no one else. I don't like to do this, since I don't know if it's merely a formality or if it entails serious obligations on your part. In any case, I will try to avoid its having any consequences. I'm also writing to Knopf to have him confirm that I have earned money there in the past and can do so again. You will perhaps know how such a document—*of the port*,[26] I believe it's called—is supposed to be drafted. If it seems harmless to you, please send it to me right away. Otherwise you are excused. Accept my warmest thanks for the effort.

You had already gotten my letter about your book when I received your kind letter. I'd rather you didn't speak about my birthday. The number, meanwhile, is too high to be mentioned, especially for a *writer* for whose *job* the younger natives are waiting.

My regards, also to Golo whom I thank for his news. I'll soon be sending him a few notes that illumine Voltaire and his critic de Maistre.

Warmly, H.

Of course the affidavit must apply to Mrs. Nelly Mann too.


26. In English in original.

*Princeton*
*February 25, 1941*

Dear Heinrich,

Things can't move so quickly with the affidavit. It's a rather cumbersome affair and will take a few days. That I'm doing it for you goes without saying, even though I fear overdrawing my credit somewhat; besides the three children, we've already vouched for several other émigrés. Your case is special and natural. But I have to draw the line there; the affidavit cannot apply to Nelly. That has to be separate. Nelly has relatives in America; they are closest to her, and will not refuse.

We'll get on the matter right away.

Have you two had the pleasure of our abomination's latest *speech?*[27] It was one of his more modest swaggers. No more talk of victory this year and mounting invasions, just about the U-boat war; the numbers of ships allegedly sunk is obvious nonsense. Still, England could be finished in six months. If not, may it win in six years. But how things will look then *all over* the world—I wonder if we're to live to see it?

Warmly, T.

*February 28, 1941*
*264 Doheny Drive*
*Beverly Hills, Calif.*

Dear Tommy,

My warmest thanks for the trouble you are taking on my account. My Nelly has meanwhile decided that her relatives would certainly be the persons closest to her. They are business people who have been settled here for a long time and are, so to speak, secure, aside from the unknown factor of their bank accounts. But what all is unknown. If I weren't being pressured, I'd probably simply remain a *visitor*;[28] on the assumption that all of us will end up in camps anyway following the outbreak of local nationalism; exceptions only to those with the best protection. I've already received an anonymous phone call: I was to leave the country immediately. The telephone and house are now under police surveillance. In seven and a half years in France such a thing never happened. But then Los Angeles, with its weapons factories, is overflowing with Nazi spies. One was fired from the film industry: the war industry hired him. The world wants to be what it is; to its small weaknesses it utters a slovenly yes. Nor can the results in six years interrupt eternity.

At just the right moment the musician Friedrich Holländer has written a novel, in English even, and asks me to recommend him to you. His dream is to have a preface by

27. In English in original.
28. In English in original.

you. I answered him: "Simply send it. There won't be large numbers of manuscripts submitted now, who can afford to write novels." Moreover, who knows, perhaps he's had an idea. I didn't manage right away to warn him against sending it, and would that have satisfied him anyway?

Enough for this morning. Now I'll get back to work on my film-novel; that is temporarily a permissible, indeed, mandatory, genre.

Warmly, H.

Thomas Mann

*65 Stockton Street*
*Princeton, N.J.*
*February 29, 1941*

Dear Heinrich,

I was deeply touched that you set down so pleasantly and precisely your impressions of the Indian story. I was ashamed of having asked about it. Frank was ailing and incommunicado. So I was unable to ward off the impression that the packages had gotten lost in the mail.

Today I just wanted to let you know about the books you mentioned. *Adel des Geistes* was a planned anthology of essays, which Bermann was supposed to have published in Stockholm in connection with the new collected edition. Nothing came of it, and the Stockholm edition came to a halt after *The Magic Mountain*. *Das Problem der Freiheit* is an address that did in fact appear in a Bermann series. But there are no copies in this country, and I can't give you the book. The only thing I have available is the *Schönsten Erzählungen*, published by the Forum Bücherei. I'm sending them to you—hopefully not to begin your library anew, but to expand it. It certainly could still come.

Till we meet—we'll arrive in the West exactly on your birthday. I hear that there's a small celebration being prepared. The winter here is long and hard. I've frequently had colds, and am longing for your sunshine.

Warmly, T.

*Telegram*

*Chicago, Ill 20*
*March 21, 1941*

Dear Heinrich

An awful dilemma Berkeley offered to welcome me with the Dr. juris in conjunction with their Academic Day exactly on the 27th Stop I declined but they insisted so that it is hard and questionable even to me to insult them with a stubborn refusal Stop What is one to do under these circumstances about the birthday dinner Stop I hear it is to take place in a private house for a rather intimate circle and also hear that it is not exactly of great importance to you Stop If we put it off it must be for 10 to 14 days because I have further obligations in northern California Stop Would painfully regret having to miss it but would also fully understand if you stick by the actual birthday will see each other in any case on the 26th Address Colorado Springs Colorado Broad Moore Hotel

Warmest Tommy


*[New Orleans, October 19, 1941]*

Dear Heinrich, to you and Nelly our warm regards from one of the stations of our calvary, unfortunately only the second. It is distinguished by high humidity and heat. Onward, onward, however. Till we meet! T.


*Pacific Palisades, California*
*740 Amalfi Drive*
*December 30, 1941*

Dear Heinrich,

We haven't seen each other for a long time. It seems that you haven't been well or have wanted to avoid potential harm by staying home in the inclement weather. As soon as you're in the mood to get together, let us know!

For the New Year we wish you health and whatever one can otherwise wish and hope for in any reasonable way right now. That is: may things go fairly well. Before we're allowed to hope that things simply go well, we'll probably have to celebrate another New Year or two.

An extraordinarily interesting book has come out about Russia: *Mission to Moscow*, by the U.S. ambassador I. E. Davies. It's made up of confidential reports to the secretary of state and the president, as well as diary entries, from the period of the trials, the executions in the Red Army, etc. I recommend it highly to you.

Over the holidays our house was full to overflowing: aside from Golo and the vivacious Erika, there was my brother-in-law from Berkeley, and also our little grandson whom we brought with us for a few weeks from San Francisco, an enchanting child. His presence takes us back to younger days.

I made another broadcast to Germany today and found myself becoming unusually aggressive toward Schicklgruber. It does one good.

Accept, along with Nelly, regards from all of us!

Warmly, T.

Dear Tommy,

We return your good wishes from the heart; we already sent you a telegram, but well wishes can't be conveyed often enough: it happens so rarely.

I am working on things one after the other, and even at the same time, depending on whether they promise earnings. Not one has yet come through. In the extreme case, I'll have to wait out the war and its immediate results. I was paid for my earliest books fifteen years after they were published. What takes you back is your little grandchild; for me it's loneliness and ingratitude: I've been through all of this once already, when I had nothing behind me as yet. These realizations offer some psychological peace: the illusion of being young again, however, is beyond their reach. What I owe you and thank you for, my heirs will have to settle, assuming it turns out that I didn't have the opportunity to do so myself. It could come in a few months, right away, or not at all; it's out of my hands and therefore a matter of chance.

My cold was over quickly, but I know that your house is full.

As soon as it's convenient for you, we'd like to come. Regards and thanks to Katja.

Warmly, H.

*April 4, 1942*
*301 S. Swall Drive*
*Los Angeles*

Dear Katja,

I am filled with gratitude for the checks we received and worried about the last one sent, which has not arrived. From Monday to today it would have been underway for five days: there's not much hope left for it. In the best of cases it would have gone back to you. That is not likely for we have inquired about delivery only too often at the post offices in Beverly Hills and Los Angeles.

Other letters, unfortunately not the ones we're searching for, we've picked up off the street either in front of our former apartment or in a stranger's yard at 301 Swall Drive in Beverly Hills. There are supposed to be four streets named Swall; the two remaining ones we've not yet found.

It's no longer possible to avoid the suspicion that someone has opened the letter and taken the check. Perhaps you would consider it wise to block payment at your bank. Anyone else could certainly cash it just as well as we. Meanwhile we owe the rent and only open the door when there's no creditor behind it. Thus were things destined, and without your kindness it would be still worse.—My warm regards to Tommy.

Yours, H.

*April 15, 1942*
*301 S. Swall Drive*
*Los Angeles*

Dear Tommy,

I was very touched. It's comforting knowing someone else, who could only be you, is so seriously concerned about my situation. Our natural connection forbids me to be ashamed, and also my—I'd rather say surrender than resignation to God's will. Since conditions are always changing, one might become resigned at the wrong moment. Russia, that land of destiny, shows me that I too am not suddenly superfluous: they also accept what I've done into their great cause. When, moreover, they give me money, it is truly more a mark of distinction than compensation, and counts for many times as much if one considers that country's own terribly strained circumstances.

Now the insipid question of how far the sum can last. To New York and somewhat beyond, I hope, and consider, incidentally, as reasons for resettling the same ones you name. It is true that several necessary payments will have to be subtracted from the 750 dollars, as soon as it arrives, especially the dentist, who's suddenly become a vitally important figure. I went to him with an unusually advanced cyst; getting rid of it supposedly would not have been enough, and he removed all trace of my own teeth. My naked jawbones are now awaiting new ones; the whole procedure is estimated to cost at least $250, a heavy blow. The debt would be transferred to a bank if I chose to pay it in installments, which increases the cost over the long term and, as I know since purchasing the car, causes anxiety. For the car itself there's still $300 to pay, and before that's settled I'm not allowed to transfer title. Deducting the two sums brings the expected 750 immediately down to 225, but after the trip, which would cost least by automobile, it would be possible to sell the car there and have enough for a few months.

I'm not justified in demanding more than a few secure months; nevertheless the disappointed expectations that I have behind me in this country make me nervous about the ones that therefore might lie in the future. I would like to share your assumption; to be present on the spot is always something; it's only that I'm not just now in the best state for it, physically and in regard to that sense of natural ease with which one best presents oneself and proves one's value. Meanwhile there's nothing unusual about that; now even young people are familiar with the like. More tangibly, I'm made reluctant by the fact that I have three unfinished works and I shall be forced to postpone working on them, though hopefully not much longer. If it were to happen that someone was awaiting them and offered an advance, my state could improve sooner. So I want to make the trip and let things depend on whether some luck comes my way.

If, however, luck leaves me waiting, then the question immediately arises as to whether I may once again impose on you. It's already asking too much of you here, and in New York it would be even worse. I am quite conscious of your obligations toward yourself and your family; the house, too, is justified—over the long run there will be nothing lost there. But to have to give lectures and then to be expected to maintain your brother—that really does exceed allowable limits. I shall have to see to it that I make it on my own and that your monthly support becomes unnecessary once Litvinov has transferred the money. I shall thank Mr. Litvinov as soon as I receive it.

In New York, if I make it there, I'll be able to see you even less often; it was already too seldom here, although I would always have had time. You are busy; certainly with other people as well: me they leave alone, which is just fine. It's only that, in regard to you, something is lost that cannot be made up; otherwise this would be a complaint ill-suited to the times. It may be that ultimately one's personal present retreats behind memories. With no prior intention and scarcely knowing why, I've suddenly begun reading *Buddenbrooks*.

Warmly, H.


*Pacific Palisades, California*
*May 19, 1942*
Dear Heinrich,

It's good anyway that the money's there. The ruble was unpredictable. But you are right: morally it is a positive experience, and it does offer some relief. If you think it's all right for me to withdraw for the present, for June, then I shall do so gratefully. Give me a wink as soon as my help is desirable once again.

And you are also right that your move to New York should be put off until the efforts of your friends there have turned up definite possibilities. The idea as such has been becoming more and more peculiar and unpleasant to me as the summer draws near. To think of you there in a small apartment in the muggy heat, and on my advice at that, is impossible. Golo recently had a clever idea. If a move is to be made, he thought, why not then to Mexico? It offers high-altitude air, Spanish instead of *Yankee-Doodles*,[29] and a congenial political atmosphere. Not dumb. But I would understand it only too well if you would most prefer to stay where you are. Perhaps the war will be over by autumn. I'm afraid, however, that it will drag on. The Russians can't do it on their own, and I don't believe in any victory that's not brought about by the outbreak of revolutions in

29. In English in original.

Europe, which would sweep away the reactionary leaders, who fear victory more than they desire it, and turn the war into an honorable war for the freedom of all peoples.

Warmly, T.

*1550 San Remo Drive*
*Pacific Palisades, California*
*July 31, 1942*

Dear Heinrich,

You will see that the monthly check has been issued this time by the European Film Fund. That should not be a cause of confusion. The simple facts of the matter are that we've combined forces to set up a fund for the benefit of outstanding German and Austrian writers who are being hindered in the practice of their craft by present circumstances. It is administered by the European Film Fund. We are among the contributors responsible for deciding how the money is to be used. It is no more than self-evident that you are one of the first to be considered. Since my contribution to the fund is less than what I've previously made available to you and, moreover, is tax-deductible, this modus represents considerable relief to me and no disadvantage at all to you.

We're in the midst of a domestic emergency; our coloreds are leaving us and new ones are either unaffordable or intolerable. But we'll get it straightened out soon and hope then to have you and Nelly over for an evening. With warm regards from both of us and the children,

Your T.

*October 25, 1942*
*301 So. Swall Drive*
*Los Angeles, Calif.*

Dear Tommy,

Your book *Order of the Day* is a wonderful present; it so happens that I have the leisure to enjoy it. So I read first the four essays you designated and found everything not only confirmed—as to what we are capable of ourselves—but actually fulfilled. The foreword is the justified summary of your intellectual achievements, which advanced age is even obligated to set down clearly: only scoundrels are modest.

"Europe Beware!"[30] puts in definitive form all the observations that have been ventured for a long time. I did what I could to deal just with France, for six years of constant

30. In English in original.

repetition and naturally in vain.—To me it was also as if your words about Niemöller were already familiar; in the meantime they've become the more impressive the more time has passed: understood in this way, they'll not be forgotten.—I approached the characterization of the *fellow* as *a brother* somewhat hesitantly; in my memory the chap was accorded too much honor in the Zurich lecture. Then came the happy surprise that all is in order; toward such genius one can only wish that it had gotten stuck in mid-development or, still better, that it had never been born. A former guest of the Café Stephanie recently supplied a bit of evidence for your idea of a dark craving. Every day at noon Hitler appeared and went into a telephone booth, which wasn't at all private—he could have blathered his utterly treasonous secrets elsewhere with less notice. But he was drawn to a place frequented by literary artists, inasmuch as they were luxuriating in future fame and eating eggs in a glass.

His last revelation, more accurately the last one we heard of—it's supposed to have occurred nine days before the war started—was a comparison of his genius with that of Genghis Khan. How instructive that even in such a case as his, self-knowledge taps at the door. Of course it's turned into praise. "I too am subject to regret,"—was just one of the things said by poor Wilhelm, who therefore dispatched his adjutant von Möller to his counterpart in order to dissuade him from war.

My thanks and my warm regards. H.


*Pacif. Palis.*
*April 6, 1943*
Dear Heinrich,

I received this letter from Brazil to pass on to you.

I conveyed my congratulations and also held out the prospect that I too might speak there some time. Perhaps "after the war" we'll travel down there together.

I'm still tired from a severe cold, cough, and sore throat. The two of you are coming soon, Katja says. It would be especially nice if you would bring something along to read to us.

Warmly, T.

*Telegram*[31]

*September 11, 1943*
*Heinrich Mann*
*301 Swall Dr Hollywood Calif.*

On behalf of U.S. Treasury Department may we enlist your aid in promoting third war loan drive by contributing an original published manuscript of your work to be auctioned at war bond rally. Treasury Department intends to give nationwide intensive publicity to gifts by you and other distinguished immigrant authors. Artists, scientists, others, as your special contribution to success to third war bond drive. Your promptest response appreciated. Please advise what you will contribute by collect wire to Julian Street, Jr., third war loan drive. Room 3005. RKO Building. 1270 sixth avenue New York City. Ship your contribution by registered airmail or collect air express to Mr Street—

Elizabeth Bergner    Albert Einstein
Lotte Lehmann    Emil Ludwig    Thomas Mann
Franz Werfel


*1550 San Remo Drive*
*Pacific Palisades, California*
*December 21, 1943*

Dear Heinrich,

We were expecting the two of you one afternoon recently. It had been planned by Nelly and Katja. But now I hear that Nelly was taken ill and even in the hospital. Hopefully it was nothing serious and she has completely recovered.

Among other things, I would have liked to have talked to you about that letter of Bruckner's and asked your opinion. I can't formulate one at all, because it truly doesn't interest me. Did you answer? How? I received the letter weeks ago in New York, but didn't want to say anything without knowing what you were going to do.

I hear that the agent Fles, in whom I believed I shouldn't set much store, proved himself able in your case. All the better and warm congratulations!

T.

31. English original.

*Hotel Windermere, Chicago*
*March 24, 1944*

Dear Heinrich,

The 27th is approaching and it is, if not high time, nevertheless getting to be time for both of us, Katja and I, to send you our warm wishes on the occasion of that festive day that is so significant to many people far and wide. Satisfaction was great all around concerning the *New York Tribune's* obviously brilliantly done anticipation of the event. In your statement, which I read in an émigré paper, you spoke of the phoenix-like rise of your works after the last war. That applied at the time primarily to Germany. This time, if indications prove true, the same will be repeated on a world scale. Just yesterday an American writer, Louis Bromfield, expressed to me the conviction that we would inevitably see the united Soviet Republics of Europe after the war. Well, that would indeed be a whole different setting for your phoenix to spread its wings than the poor German republic.

Our Medi has very quickly and happily brought a second little daughter into the world, but she still looks pale and sickly and definitely became active again too soon. We hope that she'll recover while she's with us in Pacific Palisades, for in the beginning of September we'll take in the little family there once again for three months. Erika will turn up there by April, before she, probably, returns to Europe. Golo, who's underway to England, will remain here a few days yet giving lectures. We've gotten sparse news from Klaus in Italy, but it sounds as though he's doing well and his work is satisfying—personally; for in general it doesn't look very satisfying in that war zone. News from the year 1925: "The Russians enter Toulon. Fierce fighting continues near Cassino"[32] (popular American joke).

Well, we wish you a wonderful and happy day, good health for both of you and smooth progress in all your undertakings.

T.


*1550 San Remo Drive*
*Pacific Palisades, California*
*July 29, 1944*

Dear Heinrich,

I'm sending you right away, since I read your letter to Katja, my author's copy of *Joseph, The Provider,* so as not to have to wait for the copies I ordered from Bermann.

You will see that it is a thoroughly humorous and popular book, and that nothing

---

32. Quoted passage in English in original.

is more false than the description most American critics have been giving of it, namely, that it is crammed full of pretentious wisdom.

This German edition, like so much today, has to it an emergency character, and swarms with silly little printing mistakes—always "hatte" instead of "hätte" and "dann" instead of "denn." Che vuole di questa gente!

What a pity I wasn't able to hear the pages about the old and new times! I'm very much looking forward to them. The old times are being brought back to me again too, since I've moved my musician hero, who, like Nietzsche, suffers from a slowly progressing and highly stimulating paralysis, for a time to our Bernardini's in Palestrina. A daring enterprise, since the definitive depiction of this little place is *The Little Town!* But for me it's only a temporary setting.

May you recover your health quickly and completely! Bibi and Gret are very preoccupied with the idea of visiting you up there.

Your T.

*September 2, 1944*
*c/o Ananda Ashrama*
*Box 577*
*La Crescenta, Calif.*

Dear Tommy,

Your book has kept me busy for weeks on end and I need only to think about it to revive strong impressions. The overall impression is continually gratifying, like every example of accomplished, relatively accomplished, perfection. Above all, the characters: the most moving is the pharaoh, the most solid, Joseph himself. The juxtaposition of the two leads to heights at which much is experienced all at once, the whole encounter between two people of rare rank, how they discover each other, how it becomes history, and becomes this story.

The minor characters! "But then there's Widow Pittelkow!" says Fontane, after he's declared the others "so-so." There is in your book, in four pages of Mut-em-enet, the unquestionable conclusion of a life that, once interesting, now resolves itself, sober, but proud. The skepticism with which it is observed, a perspective transposed from your bourgeois themes onto seductively uncontrollable ones, results in complete human credibility. The modest representative of the chosen style seems to me to be the "calm" man: he is prepared for anything, which makes the unnatural impossible.

Just now I was reading an old newspaper in which the *Juif errant* (by Eugène Sue) was printed. Questions of art aside, what I find nearly intolerable is the principled exaggeration, experienced as romantic, as several European generations really did experience it. Such temptations were not yours. Your concern, cultivated personally as well over a long period, was to refer ancient enormity back onto a human scale, to bring the mythical near to us.

The realistic disclosure of a world believed to be impossibly distant allows it nevertheless to remain sacred: first makes it properly sacred. The whole reason is that they themselves, both the initiated and the masses, each in his own way, respect the spiritual, have more respect for the incomprehensible than for the "waters and the winds," as it's put in one of the chapter titles. The "droll" Egyptian proves himself, with the father "in heaven," no less holy—holy amid difficulties—than Israel. This was my final impression.

Intellectuality (for holiness) comes to secular expression in the social legislation of a Judeo-Egyptian. That, however, is a process like our own, in view of Roosevelt and Churchill (the draft legislation of his Beveridge, who terms need a scandal), and as the first contemporaries of the Soviet Union. My own book is meant to salvage the honor of this epoch: it is not merely dreadful; it displays the rare phenomenon of intellectuals in power.

I find that again in your book, and my related interest makes the last volume of your great work so worthy to me of love and gratitude.

Warmly, H.


*Thomas Mann*
*1550 San Remo Drive*
*Pacific Palisades, California*
*September 7, 1944*

Dear Heinrich,

Your letter, a small masterpiece, shamed me in more than one connection. I failed to write to you in such a way about *Lidiçe*—a wild frolic, too wild and too great for the good Czechs—which certainly offered material enough for a better sort of letter. Sometimes now I have to let things *go*. The main reason is that I have once again gotten started, perhaps too late, on a big novel, one rich in implications, which indeed keeps me constantly engaged and interested, but for which my powers are no longer quite a match. So I have to limit myself elsewhere.

I don't need to say that your brotherly and constructive critique of *Joseph* warmed me and did me good. Aside from you, only the reviewer from the *New Leader*, a social-democratic paper, took any note of the Roosevelt-Beveridge element. In the American press, the book has always been forbiddingly represented as a monster, hard to read, overstuffed with a taxing form of wisdom. For myself, I consider it an essentially humorous and thoroughly popular work—which coincides with distribution figures (naturally, because of its selection by the Book Club) exceeding 200,000. Among so many people, of course there must be any number who are bored.

You let few words drop about your book on our epoch, but they were enough to rekindle my enormous curiosity about it. It will be finished at exactly the right moment, so it can appear in German and French, in Russian on top of that, and not only in English for the dumb Americans. Even here, however, it could become a sensation. What generosity—the apologia for an age, which, not least toward yourself, has conducted itself most indecently! None of the three, the powers of our time, is an intellectual in the narrow sense. Joe Stalin surely understands little of books and art; Churchill is indeed capable of good prose, but, as he admits himself, he is a naive autodidact, with the limited education of an aristocratic lieutenant. Roosevelt *never* reads anything aside from mystery stories when he goes to bed. And yet you are right to honor them with that title, if one understands by intellectuality simply political service to the right-minded cause. Roosevelt, the only one of them I experienced at close range, has felt himself to be Hitler's born counterpart from the start; the crafty politician of the good, he knows every trick in the book. To see this type triumph over criminal stupidity, which we Germans had the misfortune of supplying, is indeed worth something; the measure of inconveniences demanded of us by the epoch may be gladly accepted in exchange.

You've had a flu in the meantime, which we heard with concern. But your letter, a good witness to your present state, was a pleasant reassurance on that score.

Till we meet! T.


*[Pacific Palisades*
*September 24, 1944]*

Dear Heinrich:

Martin Gumpert's address is 728 Park Avenue, New York.

We enjoyed the lovely hours recently spent outdoors with the two of you, and were happy to find your health so obviously improved. Hopefully, we'll be able to come again sometime soon with Medi.

The books will be sent with this same post.

Warm regards, to Nelly, too, Your Katia.

Didn't you find F.D.R.'s election speech truly refreshing?


*May 19, 1945*
*301 So. Swall Drive*
*Los Angeles 36, Calif.*

Dear Tommy,

Reading your lecture surprised me. Although I expected a lot, it is yet more. I want to express myself as strongly as I mean it. The sentence, "Wicked Germany is merely good Germany gone astray, good Germany in misfortune, in guilt, and ruin"—this fundamental thought, to have discovered and formulated it with such unforgettable precision, would be enough to justify the entire life of any author. The author, however, is you alone. That was not known to anyone before.

You will stand before your listeners in the attitude of a confessor. "I have it in me too." It is an attitude that will move the people emotionally, even if they are reluctant in their understanding. A good reception seems assured; there's no need to wish you luck in advance.

Bermann-Fischer has a collection of congratulations ready for June 6; mine is among them. For now, have a good trip. Till we meet again! H.


*June 3, 1945*
*301 So. Swall Drive*
*Los Angeles 36, Calif.*

Dear Tommy,

On this festive day I wish you happiness, in the sense that you might happily accept the happiness that is there. Of which I don't doubt. We are at bottom gifted with cheerfulness.

I read the article about you by the columnist Marquis Childs. How many Americans have the same said about them? None, probably. My remarks in the *Neue Rundschau* must have been more than hunches; they are proving themselves true.

Happily enjoy what is your lot,
Gladly forsake what you've not got. [33]
          (Album verse)

With warm thoughts, H.


TRANSLATION, WINSTONS/RENEAU

*The St. Regis*
*New York*
*June 9, 1945*

Dear Heinrich,

I could not restrain my tears as I read your letter and also your magnificent essay in the *Rundschau*. Let me thank you as well as I can, amid the unsought but still not exactly avoided brouhaha of these days, for all your love and loyalty, which would not move me so deeply if I did not have the same strong feelings toward you.

---

33. "Geniesse froh was dir bescheiden, / Entbehre gern was du nicht hast!"

For the rest, it is not so easy, what with all the accolades from kind people, to assume the right bearing, both outward and inward. There is something comic about having a lump in one's throat. I have had to look at it all as a kind of test of nerves, and play the part in spite of thorough skepticism, in fact melancholic knowledge, that it isn't really justified. Joseph knows very well that his life was "play and playing [at] salvation," "not quite seriously a calling or a gift." On the other hand there's Judas, who says to himself: "Who would have thought it. For the oil is trickling down my head, God have mercy on me, for I am the one!" An aspect of experience is expressed by each.

Your contribution is of course the greatest piece in Bermann's issue. It is charming on the personal matters, especially moving in its memories of Papa (whom I too have thought of so often in the course of this life), and a wonderful document where it describes our fraternally dissimilar relationship to Germanness. The prose is unique. I have the feeling, not for the first time, that this condensed and intellectually pliant plainness is the language of the future, the idiom of the new world.

I'm looking forward to seeing you as soon as we are back!

T.


*Handwritten draft of a telegram*[34]

*[Spring 1946]*
*Mrs Katia Mann*
*c/o Professor Antonio Borgese*
*Chicago*

Doctor Rosenthal gave me exakt report stop I fight to have confidence and I ask Tommy to retain his admirable courage stop my beloved brother you must have the strength to live and you will stop you are indispensable to your great purposes and to all persons who love you stop there is one who would feel vain to continue without you stop this is the moment for confessing you my absolute attachment stop may my ardent wishes help you to support the danger and to recover health stop

Faithfully yours Heinrich

Sender: H. M.

34. English original.

*Savoy Hotel, London*
*May 22, 1947*

Dear Heinrich,

A greeting from this venerable capital before we leave it again—as a sign of remembrance in the turmoil of the world. God knows why one plunges into it instead of sensibly staying "at home." It was probably the feeling that at last I had to exert myself in some other way, after the long exertion at the desk. Certainly plenty is happening. The ten days in New York alone were grotesquely lively after the customary uniformity. The crossing on the giant ship was somewhat marred by a continuous rolling because the ship is so tall—not restful at all. The arrival in Southampton with two thousand people and their masses of baggage was confused to the point of being catastrophic. The first days here I had to fight a gastric and intestinal affliction, in spite of which I went through everything: *interviews, press conferences, receptions, broadcasts,* and, to a great throng, the *lecture*[35] in London University. The Nietzsche lecture, simplistic as it is, went over well here, as it did in Washington and New York. Listeners will be more critical in Zurich, and notice that it was done for ignorant Anglo-Saxons.

We are flying to Zurich on Saturday morning. I hope a warmer spring awaits us there. Here it has been dark and cold the whole while. London seems quite downcast, and in spite of diligent repairs, traces of the ordeal the city has been through are visible everywhere. The nervous strain caused by the bombs and the V-missiles must at times have been scarcely endurable, and one wonders whether any other nation would have endured it without screaming for peace at any price. Everybody believes in the necessity of preserving the Labour government except for fascistic soapbox orators, one of whom I listened to. I saw only indifferent or disgusted faces in the audience. Even conservatives like Harold Nicolson are joining the party.

I hope you are faring well. Warm greetings from Katia and Erika. T.

*[dedication]*

Dear Tommy,

An old memory.

You: "How's it going with your new book?"

Me: "Professor Unrat? My usual two thousand."

You: "Well, it's still a new release."

That was 1904. Now it's a new release once again, having gone through a lot in the meantime, including a different title.

1948                                                                                                          H.

---

35. In English in original.

*Stockholm*

*May 24, 1949*

Dear Heinrich:

We didn't cable you, since we could have added nothing to the news you had already read in the newspaper or gotten from Feuchtwanger. It reached us completely unexpected, as we happily returned home from an evening out. I mean, unexpected at that moment, because in fact in his case, it was necessary to be prepared for it constantly, and I was. But at the time there was no acute cause at all for worry. We had received another letter from him, written the same evening he then went on to take the overdose, which obviously did not anticipate his taking that step. What happened to him then, we'll never know; nor did he leave any lines behind explaining. His longing for death was evidently insurmountable. It was going to be fulfilled sometime. It is very hard for both of us, but worst of all for poor Erika.

Actually, immediately upon hearing the news, we wanted to break off our trip and return home. But then it seemed more right after all for Tommy to complete the lecture tour; then we may stop for a bit to recuperate in Switzerland, which would put us back home sometime in July. We're skipping Frankfurt in any case, in these circumstances. Thank you for your warning, which was not the only one we received.

We heard with great regret that you suffered another asthma attack. Such things can certainly recur now and again, and in spite of them the overall condition continues to improve. But for you to undertake the adventure of moving back I could never recommend wholeheartedly. We are obviously of the opinion that you should keep the *nurse*.[36] I'm enclosing a check for $200 for another four weeks, and if encouraging signs and options fail to eventuate by then, I'll send another one.

So much for today.

Warm regards from all three of us.

Your Katia.


*Grand Hôtel*

*Stockholm*

*May 26, 1949*

Dear Heinrich, these are sad days. Katja sighs heavily, and it pains me so to see Erika always in tears. She is abandoned, has lost her companion, whom she always tried to keep clutched to her side. It is hard to understand how he could do this to her. How deranged he must have been in that moment! But it had long been probably his deepest longing, and his face in death is supposed to have worn the expression of a child having its wish fulfilled.

36. In English in original.

At first we wanted to throw everything over and go home. But it would not have been good. Anything social we've canceled, but I want to honor my obligations, here and in Switzerland. And Germany, of course, but that would likely exceed my powers.

Everything was so cheerfully strenuous at the beginning, as I love it to be from time to time. Now it proceeds earnestly and in a dampened spirit. The audience in the Academy rose silently from their seats as we made our entrance. The newspapers here have published sympathetic articles about Klaus and his work. He was extraordinarily loved in Stockholm, for his impromptu English addresses, which were a great success. His case is so very strange and painful, such skill, charm, cosmopolitanism, and in his heart a death wish.

I'm sending you a small stage set from Oxford. The hall was so very beautiful in the fourteenth century.

Warmly,
Your T.


*Basel*
*June 24, 1949*
Dear Heinrich,

Another letter is long since due, so I'm taking advantage of a quiet hour in Basel to send word from us. We have just arrived for the *final* reading in Switzerland, which this time is a blessing. There's scarcely anything special to report. A shadow has fallen over the trip, and although Tommy is just as enchanted as ever by Switzerland, it's simply not the right mood for it. Under these conditions things are more strenuous for him than otherwise, and I am glad that today is the last time. Then we want to travel for three weeks to *Schuls-Tarasp, Hotel Schweizerhof Unter-Engadin,** where it is pretty and full of trees and there are also supposed to be therapeutic baths. I'd of course have preferred Gastein, but Tommy doesn't want to separate from Switzerland. On *July 25th,** then, we're supposed to arrive in *Frankfurt** after all. By no means did we want to wait until Goethe's birthday on August 28th, but since everyone agreed to the earlier dates, Tommy didn't want to refuse. A pure joy it definitely will not be. For *August 5th** we've reserved seats on the *Dutch steamer New Amsterdam**—the voyage by sea is more peaceful than flying—and just past the *middle** of the month, we should probably be in California.

Golo joined us a few days ago, and passed on the information that you're doing gratifyingly well. May things remain so! Once again, I'm enclosing a check for Mrs. Weyl.

For a couple of days we had Viko's Nelly with us for a visit. She made a quite sympathetic and worthy impression, deeply sad, but very composed. Just in this last year, Viko has been doing so much better than when we were in Switzerland, and as she left him in the hospital that evening, he was obviously not worrying at all about his condition.

He seems then to have gone to sleep and not reawakened.—Materially, Nelly seems to be more or less secure, on account of a modest pension.

Now you have our address for the next three weeks. Otherwise, we can certainly always be reached through Oprecht, Rämistraße 5 in Zürich.

*Der Atem* is out, but we unfortunately don't have a copy yet. Landshoff seems more overworked and less accessible than ever, and of Bermann we hear only the most unfavorable things in every country we visit.

All the best, looking forward to our now not distant reunion.

Your Katia.

Warmest regards. Thanks for your thoughts on my birthday, and till our reunion in mid-August.

T.


*Vulpera, Engadin*
*July 14, 1949*

Dear Heinrich,

The various stresses and irritations (childish ones, about examples of German vulgarity, a planned visit in Weimar, etc.) of all of these weeks, together with the low barometric pressure here, have produced another couple of vigorous nosebleeds (burst vein), the last of which the resort physician was barely able to stanch in an hour and a half. I have, however, rather too much blood than too little, so the whole thing is to be understood as a not undesirable but only very inconvenient and messy blood-letting. But I haven't felt really well for a long time now (since "the absence of my son") and it cost me tremendous effort to bring off an address here in Frankfurt. That's why I haven't written for so long, although I've wanted to, and, moreover, am saving stories about how the trip went for a report in person.

A man by the name of Großhut in Sweden sent me a very favorable review of *Der Atem*, which had appeared in *Expressen*. He asked me to get it to you. We've had the book here for a few days and Katja and I trade off reading it. There's no need to say that it represents something unique and incomparable in modern literature, or better, in modern literatures, which it, no longer national, rises above, with the result that the reader discovers the existence, above languages, of language. It presents us with a venerable avant-gardism, as the extreme point in a personal development. There are other examples in specific great cases (Parsifal, Goethe, also Falstaff), but here and as it is, your book has the effect of a wholly new event. Moreover, avant-gardists these days tend to be reactionaries, and you are the exception (Lukács would perhaps say that it's similar to the way I am an exception as a traditionalist). Besides, it's not as if there's no tradition in your work: from Balzac you have the grandiose excess and ingenious exaggeration of political intrigues, the extravagance of which is thoroughly *realistic* and appropriate to the time. Very malicious and exciting. I've been thinking the whole time about "synarchism," and about everything else in this style that might be yet to come. We wanted to ask whether you had invented the word or whether the conspiracy was and is really called that. Against the latter possibility, I maintained that *managerial revolutionaries*[37] and the national traitors of capitalism love anonymity.—It's fantastic how the hard, indeed, cutting, clear and yet cunning, cool and overconcentrated essayism of the piece achieves a lyrical transfiguration and how the effect of the sensational can be moving.

These are just a few half-formulated notes, probably also beside the point. Take care!—We will still be in Zurich from the 19th to the 22nd and then travel with Swiss friends by car through Basel to Frankfurt. Great kindness, to my surprise, from the *Military Permit Office. Military facilities!*[38] And on the other hand, the Russians are picking me up in a car *in Frankfurt* to take me to Weimar. Unbelievable. We've reserved places on the *New Amsterdam* for August 5, and thus hope to be at home by the middle of the month.

Once again, take care!

Warmly, T

37. In English in original.
38. In English in original.

# DOCUMENTS

—⁓—

## HEINRICH MANN, "PRETENTIOUSNESS"

*In* Die Zukunft, *March 31, 1906, 500–502*

*Florence*

Dear Herr Harden!

In the *Berliner Tageblatt*, more precisely, in *Zeitgeist*, Richard Schaukal declared *Fiorenza*, by Thomas Mann, an example of "literature" and pretentiousness. That made me think. Not about the authenticity or falseness of my brother's drama, for familial circumstances, after all, make it possible for me to see somewhat deeper into his work than his critics. Rather, I thought about pretentiousness as such, and about its current popularity as a reproach.

It is supposed to happen (I do not understand how) that an author can have nothing to write, that he discovers nothing compelling in himself, no destiny that stirs his passion. Why, then, did he become a writer? He must know. Enough: a bit apprehensive, he goes seeking stimulation. He need not wait long; when people hear that someone is a writer, they like to tell the story of their lives. He comes across a sufficiently amusing problem and takes it up, treats it. Sometimes someone else has already done it. But he communicates: when necessary at face value.

Or, on the other hand: perhaps our writer had enough in himself to write, but the world he sees at the moment is occupied with things that he has not experienced, so he quickly tries to conform, betraying himself in the process by submitting to the yoke of impersonal fashion. Why? Here as well, I fail to understand. Stage plays, which is to say, good business, are one thing. But the novel, in nearly all cases, offers nothing to those who cultivate it, neither money nor fame: only the satisfaction, which is broad and full, of dispatching one's own life in torrents, and being allowed to make out the larger rhythms in the flood. If the writer renounces this, what does he have left? What? The externalities of plot, description, character, which are meaningful to me only as the symbol of what I have experienced—am I to make these ends in themselves? Spend long years of grim determination constructing out of them a cardboard world that is of no concern to me and for which I will not even be paid? Does anyone believe in so much self-sacrifice? Herr Schaukal, the capable expert of the soul, expects it of every second person, myself as well as my brother, Jakob Wassermann as well as myself. He strictly forbade me the setting of my *Göttinnen*. For him, a writer's rights extend only as far as his heritage and the territory in which he has lived his daily life. "Wassermann should stick with his Jews, as Keller does with his Swiss."

This childish aesthetic, as everyone can see, emerged within the notion of *Heimatkunst* [native art], without which it would never have occurred to anyone in so undisguised and naive a form. It would surely not have occurred to Herr Schaukal, for the good things he has (long ago) accomplished are descriptions of Velazquez portraits, seicento figures, rococo moods—enticing delicacies, which do not appear native to Austrian provincial life. In the meantime, out of the desire of his simple heart, which is incapable of beating to a rhythm of its own, he has unknowingly conformed. That is the source of a book like his *Großmutter*, which has as its sole object the wooing of favor. It woos with all its might, with whatever you like: with the melancholy of the letters that never reached him; with the dreaminess of Jörn Uhl; with the eternal riddles that are once again in demand. All of it is weak, but all of it is there. And, since this perspective is still new to him, Herr Schaukal feels the need to be constantly examining it, vowing ever anew that only things found on the street belong to life, that only local sensibilities are genuine. A writer creates characters he has never seen with his own eyes? Pretentiousness. Someone asserts that a foreigner's melody is his own? That he has a part in others' adventurous doings? That they live in him as dreams? Literature, pretentiousness.

Herr Richard Schaukal stands for many; that is why he leads the discussion and can regard himself as a critic. In reality, such an unfree spirit, one so vulnerable to passing seductions, is naturally the one least suited to the critic. What people may also have believed at one time or another, is that the first requirement of a great critic is that he be a strong personality. In those whom he represents, he lends form to and asserts himself: no different from the writer. Given a small shift in his circumstances or inner destiny, he would have become a writer. And it is out of the question that the great critic, yielding to the creative drive of a dilettante, should produce a weak novel. *Volupté* is on a technical par with *Lundis*; and Taine made countries and peoples, as well as intellectual systems, palpable to his readers. Whatever Herr Schaukal might have to say about others, however, will never exceed the personalistic value of his *Großmutter*: it is too meager, to put it concisely, for him to be measured on the model of Thomas Mann.

But nothing is more perplexing than a bad review. What? This thing, of which not a thread remains intact, was once the object of admiration? No one likes to feel duped by pretentiousness. In other respects, there is nothing to be gained by defending oneself against someone who is, after all, an expert. It is a relief to give up one's reverence, to no longer be obliged to recognize any superior authority. So easily, with so little ado, is the balance line drawn with a writer, even one before whom, at the time of *Buddenbrooks*, people were bowing in the hundreds of thousands. None of his "friends" and "admirers" are disturbed that he is supposed to have forsaken his honesty, to have become a creator of "pretentiousness" and "literature." No one responds publicly to senseless diatribes and no one disputes them in private.

Do people really believe that the writer of *Buddenbrooks* has suddenly begun working in willful frivolity, as if engaged in some kind of wager? That he has failed to maintain ties with his previous work? They should at least see the most obvious ones. In *Buddenbrooks* a bourgeois family declines; and a bourgeois in decline is Lorenzo Medici. They were bourgeois, these dukes, and degenerated as bourgeois: not as knights tend to degenerate, with atavistic relapses into murderous lust, the hunt their greatest passion, until they go senile. Bourgeois decline runs to moral and sensual overrefinements, aestheticism, a weakened sense of self, the result of insight having become overly complex. Really: the bourgeois son who has become the writer is at home in the chamber where

Lorenzo died. He knows about the struggle that culminates there, between the man who worships beauty and the saint. He has fought the same struggle, as early as his novella "Tristan." Lorenzo's is his own decline, that which also drags him down; the prior is his will to become strong, to achieve the courage of his convictions, to be a holy, rather than frivolous, artist. "I speak the truth I have suffered." "I hate this corrupt tolerance of contradictions." Reliance on the self and a challenge to the self. In a moment in which enemies understand each other with marvelous ease, the one in the words of the other, each registering the melody of his own life, their dialogue about life and death harmonizes and reveals itself as self-contained within the writer. Here it becomes apparent that the two are one person, and that nothing can be more lyrical, nothing can be less pretentious, than this work.

Its failings lie in its lyricism. Artists, the representatives of "art of the eye and appearance," are seen from the spiteful view of the intellect. As soon as these clowns appear, the times, of which they are also the lasting expression, become too small. One of them reintroduces Cellini's lies, another a novella by Boccaccio; and it would have been easy to have invented something else in the same sense to put in their mouths. But the lyricist, who is at work here, disdains exploring things that are not his own. The part of the stone into which he cannot hammer his own soul, he prefers leaving unsculpted. The Renaissance overpowers him just as little as any other epoch does. An automobile manufacturer can perhaps swoon about modernity, or a junk dealer about the past. A writer (as this one experiences writing) uses people of distant times and famous names in order the more solemnly to bear witness to his own, always only his own, destiny.

Dear Herr Mann,

I am just barely acquainted with the accomplishments of the gentleman who, for you, "stands for many." But I do know somewhat the feeling of one who expects that a response will come, must come, from somewhere, to the most senseless diatribes; and waits in vain. For the power of the written word remains such that only a few dare to inveigh against it. If only the man in the street had been waylaid! But so. And in the end he makes nothing of it; perhaps takes it to be a good advertisement. In any case, caution counsels first waiting a bit, to see how the business goes. It is possible that what was celebrated yesterday will be at the bottom of the heap tomorrow—and then one wants to be standing by the *victrix causa*. Such an experience does not encourage one to admire people. But your brother can bear it. He wrote "Tristan" and *Buddenbrooks*.

## HEINRICH MANN, "DER TOD IN VENEDIG: NOVELLE VON THOMAS MANN"

*In v. 7, n. 13, März 1913, 478–79*

Which is prior, reality or literature? Do things not turn out the way that literary art demands they must? When Zola had only just composed his great social novel of the Second Empire, the land of adventurers and orgies of greed, festivals of speculation, a never equaled, unfettered saturnalia of bourgeois culture, outfitting it with a precipitous decline through the mire of gold, sex, disgrace, and blood to collapse, to the collapse of the regime, as willed by the artist's mind and dictated by the logic of the book—then it collapsed in reality. Who would have suspected it? Just yesterday it was still ruling over Paris and the world.

In the same way, the course taken by the fate of a certain Gustav Aschenbach would not have been possible had not an entire city been rendered pliable to his needs. This is not a matter of the influence of milieu. Rather, a soul has embarked upon its adventure, and somewhere the adventure erupts also in the exterior world, as if called upon to do so by the individual's fate, and the one enfolds itself into the other. The city of Venice, stricken by a terrible plague, and a rare man entering the final, most dangerous turn of his destiny—they call to each other. As long as he was moving securely, ever the great worker, mentally rigorous and a shaper of knowledge, the courtesan of cities could have meant for him nothing beyond the indifferent enjoyment of his rest. A man between forty and fifty, away in a crude mountain dwelling, secluded in the discipline of the mind and the obligations of fame, writes his mature works. *Friedrich of Prussia* made Gustav Aschenbach the nation's writer; *Misery* pointed the way for a new generation, beyond debilitating knowledge, to a new naturalness and reborn moral effectiveness. The books went out into the world, conquered, worked their effects; and what came back into the room of the isolated writer were the daily indications of human trust, requests for a guiding word, all bearing witness to serious public credibility, and, finally, signs of state recognition, since they indeed are the last thing on which the intellectuals of this country may count. Gustav von Aschenbach is officially ennobled only after, having outgrown his gypsy infatuations and the amorality of his curiosity to know, he becomes noble himself through the nobility of mind . . . What mistaken path is conceivable between here and the abyss, to such private shame that he would no longer resist sinking into self-forgetfulness? Only one—the one in which beauty takes the lead! But beauty always precedes the artist, on good paths and bad. Only by way of beauty can the sensual rise to the level of the mind and its nobility. In a moment of exhaustion, of lapsed self-protection, and, perhaps, of the mortal fear of the aging man, beauty is capable of destroying all restraint; the cult of forms bursts into the flames of delirium and desire, sentiment once heavy with thought turns into wild, wanton emotion. For precisely that reason, he has "already given in to death." To death in Venice. The day will come when this master, this protector of noble form, a model for youth and spokesman of the nation, sits, destroyed, there on the edge of an overgrown fountain in the middle of a decayed square in Venice, awash in the carbolic haze of the diseased city, lipstick on his lips, directing depraved, beautiful words at the youth he desires.

This man has tossed away what had seemed to him most desirable: a productive old age, the artistry of life's final phase, wisdom, completion. He will no longer write; he will not accede to the watchtower of venerability, in which a body of work and a life first become truly encompassing—and in which it is cold. His years will be shortened, the hours of his exit deranged and bewitched by unruly emotional impulse. And in this way they will become human, will, without his hoping for it, redeem him once more from his lofty loneliness through love, a wordless, unrealizable love, and the last beats of his heart will swell his breast, as if they were his first. Should he have regrets? He does not even ask. All around him the city is sick, and, like the courtesan that it is, it keeps it secret in the name of greed. It is beauty that seduces and murders. From far in the distance, with dreamy faces and mysterious messengers in ill-defined masks of death, it has drawn into its spell a man who was ready to die on its breast. Its sweet, suspicious, sultry air, the blessed colors of its decay, its voluptuous corruption: this is a parable, a brother's fate. A soul mixes its experience, wild and final, into the world around it, and in the interplay of both lust and fear come events of great profundity and meaning, of breath being held, yet filled with voices, the voices of the seabirds, of plague, of the sweet figure of a man, and the voices of majesty and downfall. They resound through a city and a soul: resound and fade away in death, death in Venice.

## THOMAS MANN ON HEINRICH MANN'S NOVEL *DER KOPF* (1925) GERMAN LETTER IV

*From* The Dial *(Camden, N.J.) 79, no. 4 (October 1925): 333–38*

I regret having given the *Dial* reason to complain about the negligence of one of its German contributors. More months have passed than were absolutely necessary, in the interest of discretion and a dignified reserve, since I last had the privilege of reporting about some of our loftier endeavors. I ask you to excuse me: there was too much work at home, added to which, your correspondent undertook more travels than are ideal for producing well-composed articles—in part for purposes of pleasure and to gather information, but in part as a representative in the good, important cause of general European contact and exchange, for example, in Florence, in Vienna . . .

Of Florence, I say only that a Week of International Culture was held there, mainly in the form of an exhibition of beautiful books on display in national pavilions, essentially from Italy, England, France, and Germany. A noble competition, dedicated to the glorification, through the publishing crafts, of exalted intellectual works of fiction or reflection! I am pleased to be able to report that my country held its own. All of the major publishers of the Reich went to great lengths to show off the best and most exquisite of their wares, to dazzle with deluxe printings and fine collected editions. Truly, our display offered so many examples of sterling taste—which, though less conservative than the French or English, still stops far short of eccentricity—that other nations seemed inclined to cede the honors to German publishing. Exhibits also included lectures, which captured not only the attention of the various national colonies, but happily that of the Italian public as well. Your correspondent had the honor of entering into a respectful competition with a scientific celebrity of the highest order, and most merciful speaker, the famous classical philologist and translator of antique tragedies, his excellency Wilamowitz-Moellendorff.

To move on to Vienna, I was a guest of the PEN Club there, as I was a year ago in London. Have you heard of this club? It is an English creation, sprung from the most reasonable intentions, for it brings together men and women who take seriously our poor, old, romantic, unreasonable part of the world, and are intent, at least in the intellectual sphere, on maintaining comradely international ties. Its members are *publishers, editors, and novelists,* three words, the first letters of which, oddly enough, spell the word *pen*.[39] The club now has organizations, aside from London, in Paris, Brussels, Vienna, and Berlin, and, in my opinion, ought to establish a branch in America. It could be a means of our getting to know one another better, quite possibly by way of personal exchange, for we in Germany in fact do not know all that much about contemporary American intellectual life, and, were it not for the *Dial,* we would know even less. Head of the club in London is John Galsworthy; in Vienna, the president is Arthur Schnitzler, a name so well known on your side of the ocean. I had the pleasure of dining with this kind man and extraordinary artist, while, at the same moment, my brother Heinrich was representing the German element at the international PEN congress in Paris . . .

There is more to report on this. In the heart of the Berlin organization, there had been doubts as to whether national considerations would allow us to send delegates to Paris. Opposition had arisen, to the overcoming of which your correspondent may boast to have contributed as he was able. The outcome was the best imaginable. Not only that the address by Heinrich Mann, which this student of Stendhal and Zola possessed sufficient *courtoisie* to deliver in French, was received with rousing applause, but also that *Berlin* was selected by a large majority as the site of the next congress, even though the Belgians pleaded for Brussels. It is an amiable settlement, and it can only be expected that the French speaker take pains in our capital city to deliver his address in German.

Arthur Schnitzler and Heinrich Mann, each with significant new works, are once again in the forefront, as regards literary interests. I would like to assume that the English-American translation of *Fräulein Else* is already underway. If not, it should be begun posthaste; there is no doubt that the story will prove as entertaining and moving over there as it has here. This man of the [18]60s makes gripping use of concision, shaming an entire generation of affected efforts in that direction. His new work is a kind of monodrama, amounting to little more than a hundred pages. It is a virtuoso performance, which makes do without essentially all narrative devices, conveying nothing but the interior experiences of a young woman, who, trapped in a conflict between her own purity and unprincipled lust in her environment, falls into spiritual crisis. She suffers a severe psychological shock, and kills herself with Veronal. The external setting is a fash-

39. In English in original.

ionable mountain resort, and everything objective, which amounts to an entire social portrait, is reflected only in the on-going interior monologue of the heroine, with which Schnitzler proves that he is more dramatic as a novelist than are many others when they take up the drama. *Fräulein Else* is one of the biggest literary successes of recent years.

The new novel by Heinrich Mann, titled *Der Kopf,* traces a broad historical-political horizon, in contrast to the moral intimacy of Schnitzler's talent. The novel is the work of many years, a book rich in characters and their destinies. Yet it comprises only the third part, if a thoroughly rounded and independent part, of an epic trilogy, under the general title *Das Kaiserreich: Die Romane der deutschen Gesellschaft im Zeitalter Wilhelms II.* The other parts are the world-famous *Der Untertan* (a novel of the bourgeoisie) and *Die Armen* (a novel of the proletariat). This is now the novel of the *leader,* and I judge perfectly objectively when I say that it is not only the towering pinnacle of this series of social criticism, not only signifies within that larger work a powerful artistic intensification, but also belongs among the absolutely finest and mightiest achievements of this brilliant, in the best sense, sensational writer; it ranks for me with his masterpieces, *Die kleine Stadt* and *Professor Unrat.*

Of all the German writers, Heinrich Mann is the most social. His social political impulse, not unusual in the western and more recently the Latin parts of Europe, is unheard of in our country, even as the stern lessons it has been our national destiny to learn make it very contemporary. What makes us care about others are their metaphysical, moral, pedagogical, in short, interpersonal motives and interests. The novel of education and development, the confessional novel, has always been the specifically German variety of this artistic genre. In the case of this author alone, and only in his case with such artistic brilliance, the moral element has been infused from the beginning, not by "innerworldly asceticism," to borrow a theological term, but by a social and critical and political extension. Even as times were good, he suffered most deeply from the intellectual stagnation of our urban life and dragged our leaders before the forum of the intellect with his literary manifestos, the fulminating excesses of which were justified by superior right. And at the end of his novel of the German *Untertan,* a work mad with caricatures, he prophesied the collapse of imperial Germany. And now, he is telling, in free artistic form, the story of that downfall, telling it in a prose style that represents neither more nor less than the German counterpart to *La débacle.*

It is the book of a fifty-four-year-old, mature and moderate, which, far from the racing satire of its predecessors, is fairer to all sides and thoroughly human and warm. How could it be otherwise from a literary talent, the particularity of which is to find what is poetic and humane in the social, in such a way that society elevates and gives meaning to poetry and poetry lends soul and humanity to society. It is great, the way an individual fate becomes entwined in the tragedy of the time, and the way the artistic instrumentation of the novel, its pathos, intensifies as it unfolds, moving from provincial intimacy to life on the general European plane. I regret that there is no space for a real analysis and description of this extraordinary book, but it would be truly desirable if those engaged in such an endeavor were not restricted to the country of its origin. The most beautiful aspect of the novel, from a literary point of view, is the story of the friendship of two men, their crisscrossing fates suffused by the melancholy experience of the conflict between the pure idea and human inadequacy. Wilhelm II himself gets a couple of brilliant scenes, in which the hysteria and dangerous half-genius of this pompous and pitiable representative are perfectly characterized. They take place in the house of Prince Lanas, a character with liberal borrowings from Prince von Bülow. Due to a freely admitted submissive streak, which leaves him finally unable to truly confront evil, but also thanks to his cleverness and his thoughtful nature, Lanas grows to become the most important character in the book.

The novel, to turn now to a consideration in principle of aesthetic rank, is the literary art form in which the plastic and the critical, the poetic and the literary, the "naive" and the "sentimental" elements most easily and happily intermingle. No wonder, in this tumultuous and intellectually needy time, that the prose epopee has come to be the truly modern, the prevailing literary form. This is true even in Germany, where, for theoretical reasons and thanks to the practical propaganda made for the drama by Schiller and Wagner, a pair of triumphant dramatic geniuses, drama until recently has been regarded as the crown of the literary arts. The social, moral, and general intellectual shocks to which we have been subjected, have had the effect in Germany that novelists can take positions in the public interest, in a manner that, until recently, was reserved for dramatists. When, before the war, in *Death in Venice*, I anticipated the coming to national greatness of a prose stylist, it was called implausible; never in Germany could a novelist, "the half-brother of the poet," as Schiller says, partake of such prestige as was attributed to Gustav von Aschenbach. Today this possibility is a complete reality, as the concomitant of a de facto, if unwanted and unrecognized, democracy. The novel dominates—especially so, since what is being produced in this area quite simply exceeds in significance that in drama. A novel like *Der Kopf*—and I dare say, technically, its fraternal counterpart, *The Magic Mountain* (or, more distantly, the great books of Alfred Döblin, and I reproach myself for not having discussed them in these pages)—is not to be compared, in terms of its conception and effect, to any contemporary theatrical product.

Publishers are far from failing to recognize the situation. They reach back into the past in order to attend to the needs of our time, completing the triumph of the epos. The collected works of Balzac, in several translations, appear in one edition after the other. Now a book series is about to come out, which I wanted to discuss specifically: titled *Epikon, A Collection of Classical Novels*, consisting of thirty works of world literature, thus a true epic pantheon, whereby the publisher, Paul List in Leipzig, "wants to bring together everything of greatness and permanence created by the novel out of the experience of humanity in the last century." The selection, made by a young Austrian writer by the name of E. A. Rheinhardt, is excellent. Of German authors, Immermann, Jean Paul, Goethe, Keller, and Stifter are represented; among the English, Meredith, Dickens, Thackeray, Fielding, Defoe; the French, Stendhal, Balzac, Flaubert, and Hugo; the Russians, Turgenev, Tolstoy, Gogol, Goncharov; the Italians, Manzoni and Fogazzaro; and, on top of this, neither *Don Quixote* nor *Nils Lyhne* nor, for another example, the immortal *Ulenspiegel* by de Coster is missing. The translators were carefully chosen, and their achievement is extraordinary. Writers of the rank of a Gerhart Hauptmann, Hermann Hesse, Hugo von Hofmannsthal, Rudolf Kaßner, of a Hermann Keyserling, Heinrich Mann, Rudolf Borchardt, and Jakob Wassermann have lent their services, in the form of prefaces or afterwords to the individual works. Your correspondent himself was given the anxious but glorious task of introducing Goethe's *Elective Affinities*, and, if personal pleasure motivates the report, that does not mean a more general warrant is lacking. This collection is worthy of being praised abroad. It is a monument of cosmopolitan literary sensibility after Goethe's heart. The design is simple and noble, arrived at by means of a special competition. The set consists of soft clothbound individual books, in a nice Antiqua type on thin non-blotting paper, which makes it possible to put together works of a thousand or more pages in a handy volume.

Very briefly, I want to conclude by mentioning a publication, as curious as it is impressive, which might be something for Americans. For a few days now I have been in the possession of a treasure: it is a true and authentic handwritten version of the orchestral score of Wagner's *Tristan und Isolde!* It was given me for my birthday, and every day I perform my devotions in front of it. I do not want to say that it is the actual and only original score of this highly sophisticated opera—that is in Bayreuth. But, in a splendid single volume, made possible by the most advanced technology, it is such a perfect facsimile of Wagner's painstakingly colossal manuscript that it requires no imagination to let uniqueness and originality go without a thought, and feel oneself in the bewildering possession of something sacred. These vast masses of tidy runes signify and designate a final and highest instance, a love unsurpassed, from which Nietzsche took eternal leave for all of us in a final parting to the point of death: to a world we Germans today are forbidden by our conscience from loving all too much. It is the peak and the fulfillment of romanticism, its extreme artistic expansion, the imperialism of a world-conquering celebration of death—not wholesome for the European soul. It requires a good bit of work to save life and reason from its attractions, a matter of the kind of self-overcoming of which Nietzsche provided such a heroic example. Never has the split between aesthetic splendor and ethical responsibility, at least for those born early enough still to love that world (for youth know scarcely anything about it anymore), yawned as deeply as it does today. Let us recognize it as the origin of irony! Our love of life defends itself ironically against the fascination of death; but artistic method remains for us a matter of dispute, whether or not ironic, when it turns against life and virtue, knowing the appeal of forbidden love, which is a deeper, indeed religious appeal. In this sense it happens that we make solemn use of the simulated original score of *Tristan* to cultivate in our study an ironic cult of melancholy.

The specialists at Drei-Masken Verlag in Munich are responsible for these astounding editions. A facsimile of the *Meistersinger* manuscript preceded *Tristan*, and *Parsifal*, currently in preparation, will follow.

## THOMAS MANN, NOTE ON *DIE GROßE SACHE*

*From* Die Literarische Welt *6, no. 50 (December 1930): 1f.*

We live from stimuli, and among the forces that vitalize and intensify life, art is the most powerful because it stimulates both the intellect and the senses; it affects and stirs life systematically as a whole. "Stimulus" is a biological concept of the first order and mysteriously ambiguous in reference to life; its primary function is probably not simply to evoke and activate responses, but simultaneously to call into being, to produce new capacities, to inspire creativity. It is ambiguous, too, in its reference to desire and aversion, toward which it is first of all indifferent, with the fluid boundary between the two determined in individual instances as a response to the duration and degree of the stimulus. Here there is no distinction to be drawn between an artistic stimulus and some other, psychological, one. The former is sometimes of an enduring and thus extremely painful intensity, so removed in its effect from all manner of comfort that—assuming we are speaking of the epic—a kind of contradiction arises between the effect and the essence of the art form; for we are accustomed to associating with the idea of the epic a certain agreeableness and goodness, not to say a certain good-naturedness.

The new novel by Heinrich Mann, *Die große Sache*—though it has always been so in the case of this great artist—is loaded and overloaded with stimuli to such a degree that the pleasure it offers is always on the verge of turning into pain; the reading hurts—and hurts worse, therefore, in that it is also irresistible. Really, when one returns from this new novel to any other of those manifestly modern narratives (which had perhaps been put aside in honor of the former) to Hemingway, Hamsun, or even Döblin, one senses the relative absence of that stimulating suspense, of the bated breath, the laughter, pain, and admiration, which has been one's lot for the while. The other stories proceed more moderately, however audacious they might be; they proceed more contemplatively, more epically, in the calmly expansive, cozily narrational sense of the word. Even Döblin, who, after all, is regarded as a very radical writer, even his *Berlin Alexanderplatz*, of which the jargon in *Die große Sache* occasionally reminds us, exercises from this vantage a comparatively good-natured effect—whereby there can of course be no question here of any superiority on the part of one or the other in his humane or intellectual, in his, so to speak, personal goodness. What superior and knowing paternal goodness there is in the character of that remarkable old magician and mystifier of a chief engineer by the name of Birk, who in every respect is the soul and driving force of the book, and behind whose mask is—thinly—concealed the countenance of the sixty-year-old author. What a vibrato of goodness there is in the words that he, already dying, "musing back upon joy," directs imploringly at the young: "Learn to be joyful. The big deal [*die große Sache*] does not exist, it must be invented. What is real is your hearts—which are yet healthy!" We have here a spirit that is already biblical and Christmassy. "And again I say to you: Be joyful!" That is, incidentally, asking a lot—on page 404 of a painfully truthful witches' sabbath of murderous commercial frenzy, ice-cold existential *angst*, and head-over-heels rascality. But the intellectual goodness that makes itself available here—and not only here—to the twenty-year-olds, to their *angst* and saucy audacity, is something other than that which one would call epic goodness.

That is lacking. The tempo of the novel alone is merciless and breathless; abandoning the reading is inconceivable. Stimulated and spellbound by a style unequaled in its noble verve, a blend of sloppiness and brilliance, of current slang and high intellectual tension, the reader is ripped from one whirlwind to the next, to land benumbed from the topsy-turvy of vehemently farcical adventures and crass travesties, exhausted from laughing about their grand improbability and moved to tears by the goodness of mind they all imply.

That, too, this goodness has a suspenseful brilliance about it; it is the source of the most exacting stimulus. I love it like a brother. But perhaps even more suitable for awakening in me fraternal memories and feelings are those stimuli wrought of supreme hilarity and highly parodic jests scattered with a dangerous crackle throughout the work. There is, for example, Murderer Mulle—he calls himself by that name. "I'm Murderer Mulle, he introduced himself proudly to the people."—When we were young our sisters painted a silly picture book with captions like this: "The murder of public official Hagemann by the robber Georg Schandpfahl. The perpetrator enters the bedroom of the sleeping victim." There is much of that in Murderer Mulle, and not only in him . . . Bodies age and one matures in one's earnestness toward one or another big deal. And such a lesson as "Be joyful!" can be delivered only by age, with youth left standing there somewhat at a loss. Murderer Mulle, however, teaches that we have remained at bottom who we were: destined to jest about the most solemn of things—for what could be more solemn in the original sense of the word than murder?

"That's my victim," says Mulle, pointing at the reclined figure of Schattich, an unbelievable chairman-of-the-board and former chancellor of the Reich. "Then it's Olle's turn. I'll be certifiably the youngest double murderer," he states in advance of the event. "I'll break the record. Are the gentlemen from the press here?" Murder, records the press. This is the pass to which that primal solemnity, murder, has come under the disintegrating influence of civilization, that the murderer's first thought is of the press. How do you like the sarcasm, you conservatives? Would you have expected it from this corner? It is in any case inseparable from the ridicule of even that primal phenomenon, in the person of Murderer Mulle, whose offensive excess admittedly leaves his youthful forerunners from the picture book far behind. "Why make all the fuss?" he is asked. He answers: "And my heritage means nothing? I am his son. He dispossessed my mother and disinherited me. That's a stab in the back of the existing social order." The journalistic phrase belongs to Murderer Mulle's thieves' Latin, and he enlists it in the service of his veneration of the existing social order—on which, however, such partisanship as his casts a dubious light. How is upright conservatism supposed to understand itself in the context of such a presentation?

There is confusion otherwise as well. The novel, the unruly "plot" of which pays homage to the genre of that name in an almost atavistic fashion, betrays a hint of magic and the occult that gives one to thinking. That chief engineer Birk, ailing as a result of an accident—though one never quite knows how, how seriously, or even whether—manages to get out of himself, leaving his body in the hospital, and, as a ghost, carefully interfere in events right where they are proceeding most turbulently. His daughter—one of them, for there are two, both very lovingly modeled female characters—is connected, via a technological-parapsychological process, clairvoyantly to the big sports stadium, where at just that moment important personages are among those present at a sensational box-ing match—a mass scene of grotesque power and comedy, incidentally, probably the most vital in the book—with Margo, that is, participating eyes and ears, as if she were not somewhere else entirely. How do such miracles conform to the rational humanitarian reputation of the author? Must he not fear that by admitting the extrarational he will open wide the door to evil, as he understands it? Is it a case of creeping old-age mysti-cism? Of connivance against our currently fashionable hatred for everything signified by *ratio*—a hatred, as he must certainly be aware, that has its political side? We have to iden-tify negligence here, authorial negligence in matters pertaining to *humanitas*, a skeptical recklessness, which is completely unknown to the pure antihumanist opposition—and that is its strength. Does freedom deserve the name of a principle? Not by a long shot, absolutely not. And only quite ultimately, suddenly: yes.

What is "The Big Deal"? The title is taken from business jargon; the big deal is a matter of millions, which all are trying to arrange for themselves—a mystification, in-cidentally, Birk's "invention." Occasionally it is love, ultimately, death. But altogether ultimately and outside the book, it is freedom, unending critique, the intellect itself, disguised as art and wrapped in an adventure that cares nothing about its own implausi-bility. The author's relation to the world, which these desperate and irresponsible jests set aspin, is a question worth considering. This social visionary, who is at the same time a social prophet, has seen the times accommodate themselves to the thorough-going so-cial and political orientation of his talent. Naturally he hates the war; but he must be grateful to it for what it has made of Germany, grateful that it, contrary to all expecta-tions, has released the nation from the grip of authoritarian paralysis, has set it in mo-tion, republicanized it, effected a democratic affliction, introduced popular participation into the destiny of the state. Crisis, social upheaval and adventure, politicization to the marrow—there is no lack of life here, and the social novelist is in his element. He, who saw all this and wanted it while the rest of us, at best, saw it and did not dare to want it, no longer wants it so unconditionally, simply because it has come to pass. To the young people, who were born into all of this, he says: "All that is real is your hearts—which are yet healthy." The statement is worthy of being accompanied by a political "Hear, hear!" It is the statement of leadership, and signifies a resumption, a turn. The heart, "joy"— that is none other than the individual. Who would have thought it? The big deal—the heart. How dependent is truth on its moment!

As concerns republican society, there is no mortal enemy of freedom who could pour more scorn over it and depict it in a more slapstick fashion than what takes place in this novel. And what should be more capable of that than freedom itself? The opposition lacks the talent. But let no one be mistaken: the self-criticism of freedom supplies no grist to the enemy's mill. Its skeptical recklessness goes to extremes—in order at the last moment to declare: all this must be, the corruption, the anguished slapstick must be; they are much better, much more humane and also more moral, than dead order.

The excitement continues! I already said roughly how. Wolfish rapacity, the dreadful primitivism of the instincts, the cultural failing that answers to the name of objectivity, the gruesomely pathetic reduction of a humanity that has lost and forgotten everything—it, as is well enough known in reality, is lent the exaggerated intensity of a farce by means of an aestheticism that reproaches the ordinary only with not being ordinary enough, thus lifting it into a surrealistic realm. This intellectual heightening and de-concretization prevails everywhere and renders everything, including the dialogue, imaginary and abstract, so that one vacillates wondering whether it is all taking place in reality or only in the mind. Actually conciliatory and cozy, in contrast, is the existential *angst* mentioned above; the whole world has sweaty palms on account of it, not only Boxer Brüstung, but also Chairman Schattich and probably even "Charles the Great," the unfathomable divinity atop the "concern," under whose jurisdiction the whole takes place. A brighter ray is love . . .

Social spirit is an erotic spirit; its relationship to nature is its relationship to sex. Spirit with sex, phallic spirit, the spirit as artist. One senses here no narrowness of sensibility. At a wild business conference concerning an invention worth forty million, the young Emanuel also offers up his "youthful charms" to the elder of his two partners— "he smiled provocatively into his eyes." That is what I call endowing a business meeting with life. And the elder partner proves not at all inaccessible: "it surprised him himself. His daughter was grown, his business was facing the end; he found it necessary to give his emotional life a new turn; here was its yet vague anticipation." Excellent. But truly brilliant is the character Nora Schattich, a character as if from Toulouse-Lautrec, dazzling, dangerous, a "lady" from before the Flood, with erotic traditions, superior, antiprimitive, and bad, very colorfully and humorously drawn.

Once again, this is all strictly disciplined, also in its jests and in its goodness, strict and painful, lonely in its sociability, knowing and unwitting, fascinating and hard to endure, moving and insulting—like what? Like genius.

## THOMAS MANN, "ON THE PROFESSION OF THE GERMAN WRITER IN OUR TIME: ADDRESS IN HONOR OF A BROTHER"

*Delivered on March 27, 1931, at the celebration of Heinrich Mann's sixtieth birthday, Prussian Academy of the Arts, Berlin*

Dear Heinrich—following the state minister and the great painter whom you admire so deeply for such good personal reasons, your brother now takes the floor. His need to speak is the most fraternal, I think, in that he wishes to lend expression to his and doubtlessly also to your feeling for the profound singularity of this moment, convinced that reality cannot have so hardened you, that you cannot have grown so habituated to the world or to fame to have become alienated from this childlike feeling. Being brothers—it means being youngsters together in a respectable provincial nook of the fatherland and making fun of that respectable provincial nook; it means sharing the freedom, irreality, essential purity, the absolute Bohemia of youth. And then, individually, but always in the context of an organic bond and in mutual intellectual reference, it means growing older, maturing into a life approached with the same radical irony as before, maturing, above all, through work, which, though meant as the product of absolute Bohemia, turns out to have been inspired by life, to have been performed in its service, and thus to represent a moral force. Being brothers, the way we are brothers, however, also means remaining profoundly faithful to that irrealistic lightheartedness of old; it means combining with the irony of early times that bashful excitation inspired in us by the vastness of the real world, which is partly intellectual but partly still the response of the provincial child; and, in especially stirring moments of things come true, things unbelievable from the childhood perspective, it means each of us finding our way out of our individual existences, finding our way back together and smiling, saying to each other, if not with our voices, then the more so with our eyes, saying, "Who would have thought it?"

So were you by my side when my fiftieth birthday was celebrated in Munich's town hall: you stood up at the table, you spoke in oddly and cheerfully stirring accents of birthdays in our parental home as children, and were the great success of the evening. It was you who, when Sweden, out of sympathy for my Nordically flavored novel of the bourgeoisie, had bestowed upon me its great prize, who informed the German world of this event with a brother's excited and festive words on the radio. With me, you no doubt thought of our youth as you were speaking, of our room with the stone walls in Rome where we first exchanged views on my unruly plan, thinking little more than that a couple of easily amused people would find something to laugh at in it. You, by the way, had already written a family novel at the time: it was even called *In einer Familie;* it was dedicated to Paul Bourget, for the studied and delicate psychology of the conservative Frenchman was then your model, just as your conservative period lay altogether in your youth. The genuine fraternal counterpart to *Buddenbrooks*, however, which as its counterpart allowed readers to recognize the vast range of variability in what remains fundamentally fraternal, came only with that great work of which you at that time had not yet thought or were only beginning to think: the simultaneously baroque and strictly disciplined novel trilogy, *Die Göttinnen*, that work aglow with art, effervescing with characters, ecstatic and colorful—that explosion of talent, which offered many a young reader of the time a new, exciting experience of prose, and established your fame.

The serious big moments of our lives are not set in public halls. They are unpretentious in their productivity; we ourselves scarcely notice their passing and we are necessarily alone with them. But life supplies us with what I would like to term the childlike big moments, times of celebration and honors, times of practical realization and "who would have thought it"; and in those life has bestowed upon you, I have until now been all too seldom at your side. I had to be far away, for example, when a crowd of fifty thousand, at the Victor Hugo ceremony in Paris's Trocadero, welcomed in you the representative of intellectual Germany with a long, generous round of passionate applause. What might you, the admirer and pupil of the Gallic genius from the time of your youth on, have felt in this hour of love's fulfillment? I would have liked to read it in your face. But I have let nothing prevent me from being here today to see you, sixty years old—after a prolific life full of artistic discipline, purity, the courage of truth, leadership—a premier figure of European intellectual society, receive the homage of cultural Berlin, the honor of the new state, the congratulations of the Prussian Academy of the Arts. And from whose mouth did you receive these congratulations? From the mouth of a German-European painter of genius, who among all your contemporaries is the closest to you in heart and mind, of the friend and peer of the great Parisian impressionists, from the mouth of the esteemed Max Liebermann. Times of celebration and honors, times of practical realization, of love's fulfillment—this is one such time; and for you it will be similar to another, when you were yet young, as you showed the admiring Steinlen, for the cover of your *Göttinnen*, that beautiful picture of a woman you had drawn, in which you recognized with deep emotion the finished portrait of your heroine Violante.

This old Lübeck, dear brother, in which we were little boys, is a peculiar nest. It is, with its picturesque silhouette, just a middling city like any other, modern after a fashion, with a Social Democratic mayor and Communist fraction in the local parliament—a wild state of affairs, regarded through the eyes of our fathers, but now completely normal. I do not want to sow doubts about this modern normalcy and by no means cast suspicion on the civic health of our origins. I am glad that I have been forgiven there for *Buddenbrooks* and trust that one day you will be forgiven as well for *The Blue Angel*. In any case, I have no desire to give offense. And nevertheless, when I do have a look at them, at these origins—and due to a certain aristocratic interest I often have had a look—then it seems to me that there is something strangely suspect about its civic health, something not altogether canny, not altogether uninteresting. There squats in its gothic nooks and slinks through its gabled alleys something spooklike and all too old, something burdensome from the past—something hysterical from the Middle Ages, a superannuated nervous eccentricity, something like a religious disorder of the psyche. One would not be too surprised if, the Marxist mayor notwithstanding, if yet today there suddenly broke out a Saint Vitus' dance or children's crusade—it would not violate the style of the city. Our artistry, that it is and also how it is—I have never been able to resist seeking its connection with this secretly coursing, not altogether canny city spook. And not only with it: there remains the romantic admixture of blood, which surely made among other contributors its contribution, but which would scarcely have had the effect it did had it not run up against that archaism in the city's psyche.

Lübeck gothic and a touch of Latin—it would be an error to try to find exclusively the one or the other in each of us: the Old German in me, because I wrote *Buddenbrooks*, the romantic in you, because you wrote *Die Göttinnen*, *The Little Town*, and a few Italian stories. In the novel that I already named and that has now won, alongside its literary fame, a democratic popularity in the form of a film, in *The Blue Angel* there is so much of the local gothic spook that one can say that the whole of it is in there; and one needs only to look more carefully to find particular aspects of it elsewhere about you. Certain, however, is that in your case, in terms of overall outlook, earliest educational inclinations, and artistic temperament, the romantic has critically and decisively prevailed. You are, at a later stage, a classical representative of the Germanic-Mediterranean artistic genius, of an intellectual life form that nationalist pressures have caused nearly to be forgotten today, in this time of a widespread renunciation of the universal and humane, of a renunciation, that is, of a Germanness that simply was more encompassing, richer, and fuller than that often favored and demanded today. In such circumstances, this life form can be called alien, un-German, even anti-German, although it is something full of tradition and thoroughly familiar to us, lacking though it may be in those warmed-over commonplaces that a certain nationalist tendency requires as a reminder of the homeland before it will speak of German mastery.

German mastery! We want to love and value it—from its basis in a common bond that no one should underestimate. Mastery—that word opens for us the world of Dürer with everything that Goethe termed its "masculinity and constancy," with its gallantry of death and the devil, with its bent for passion, its affinity for suffering and that hint of the tomb, its Faustian melancholy, its mortifying pettiness, the latter with one eye fixed on eternity. Here the graphic dominates over color. Probity, fidelity, authenticity, art, and maturity come together here in that simultaneously ethical and intellectual leadership which is the essence of the concept. Audacity informs respectability. Diligence becomes profundity, precision—greatness. Forbearance and heroism, majesty and doubt, the cultivation of tradition and the challenge of the not-yet-known—all this comes together, all this becomes one. Oh, and what all there is of an ancient inheritance, of a national and profoundly natural inadequacy, of contorted awkwardness in this overexact, day-dreaming, infantile-aged, comic-demonic, eternity-stricken world of German art, shameful and nonetheless frankly manifest: philistinism and pedantry, brooding laboriousness, self-torment, calculating anxiety—together again and flowing into a single current with that absoluteness, that stubborn exactingness, that extreme neediness that matures a taste for the arduous: this spare-not-yourself, this searching out of the ultimate difficulty, this better-spoil-a-work-and-ruin-its-chances-in-the-world than not take it in every way to the extreme . . .

Yes, all this is German mastery. But inseparable from it, precisely in its great and greatest cases, inseparable actually from the concept, is something broader and definitive: the dissatisfaction with the self, the need for completion and deliverance through the wholly other, the South—the brightness, clarity, and facility, the *gift* of the beautiful. Goethe complained, referring to Dürer, about "dreary form and excessive imagination"—giving voice to his Mediterranean mind, to his principled aversion to the "distorted visage," the North. But the half-Hungarian Nürnberger and he were after all brothers in an unself-satisfied, expansive, and transcendent Germanness; these two, these supreme Germans who could not but "freeze and shiver after the sun." We know the roles that Mantegna and Venice played in Dürer's life; and it remains symbolic that, for Goethe, there stands a classical variant alongside the romantic Walpurgisnacht. There is Schiller, whose immensely popular work incarnated the symbiosis between Königsberg philosophy and the French *grand siècle*. There is Wagner, who, filled with an actor's blood as he was, donned one of Dürer's caps and impersonated for his gullible people the "German master" of pure exclusivist culture—he whose first admirers and heralds, and for good reason, had been European artists and decadents like Baudelaire . . . Oh, yes, the German master! I know one, a musician of considerable rank, a captivating artistic personality, certainly, and full of character, emphatically German, most typically German, German in a political, a polemical way, as you know—a man turned in stubborn melancholy back upon his Germanness. He has created motifs—just between us—that could have come from Puccini. But there his political, polemical followers turn a blind eye. The following little story is told about him. A somewhat prejudiced celebration—it will have been his fiftieth birthday—was held in his honor in Munich. Whatever can be found on the banks of the Isar in the way of faithful German and antirepublican sentiment was represented there, Dr. von Kahr in the lead, and for three hours Pfitzner was acclaimed emphatically as a German master. It was late, he took his leave and stepped with his wife out into the night air. Outside in front of the door, he stopped and sighed deeply. "Do you know," he asked, "what I would like now? I would like to see a Jew!"— That is the German master, overheard in a moment when he could endure it no longer.

It is to his honor that he could not endure it. He is the greater the less he can endure it. *Only* German, that is petty-German, is not world-German; it is Germanness of a mean and stunted sort. No antiuniversalist movement, no matter how popular it may be for a decade or two, can change anything of that, and there is greater justice in reversing the charge of un-Germanness, in directing against the most militant representatives of such a narrow point of view. If he ever did exist, the German master without the world, without Europe in his blood—today he cannot possibly exist; in a world that sees the walls of aristocratic naïveté and self-satisfaction everywhere in the process of demolition, in a Europe that is growing together intellectually and, in all likelihood in the near future, economically and politically as well, a mastery devoted to narrowness, to obduracy and the provincial nest would be a sorrowful phenomenon. For Germany it was Nietzsche who Europeanized and psychologized German prose, who effected changes in the intellectual atmosphere such that a conservatively German orientation of the spirit succumbed in its own stifling air and forfeited all claim to higher validity. It was he, really, who took up the old opposition between North and South, between romantic and classic, the transcendence of which had been the aim of great German minds, and broadened and sharpened it into a distinction between the national and the European. A yearning interest in the Mediterranean created German classicism; Nietzsche's neoclassical synthesis yields: the good European.

One could say, dear brother, that your nature clings to the older German synthesis of North and South, could term you conservative in that sense. Not for nothing did I call you a classical representative of the Germanic-Mediterranean artistic genius; the Slavic, which was so powerful in Nietzsche, the Scandinavian, or perhaps the Anglo-Saxon, has touched you scantly or only fleetingly. "As soon as I could," you say in an early autobiography, "I went home to Italy." "Home"—what all there is of interiority and challenge in that syllable. In the land of German classicism's longing for the South you spent critical years of your youth; the happiest of your masterpieces are set there. And yet the source of your intellectual education and guidance was, to a much greater degree than the southern land of the Apennines, that other part of the romance world, the one produced of a Celtic modification: France, the France of Voltaire, Michelet, Stendhal, and Anatole France, which is your homeland, such as it is possible for man, thrall to nature, to have a homeland outside the one he was born to. Un-German? Oh yes, un-German is your loving submission to this Gallic influence, which colors your literary timbre, determines the cadence, the bearing of your prose—un-German in the sense of that resignation to the exclusion once and for all from the concept of the German identity of certain qualities—brightness, brio, style and polish, critique, color, a sensuous intellectuality, psychological instinct, artistic delicacy; un-German to the extent of a resigned assertion that such qualities as these will never be a German's due. And when once they are? When it happens that they are practiced in Germany such that no Frenchman could do it better, what then? Should it not, as an expansion of the nation's potential, be an object of satisfaction and an occasion for pointing out: "See, we have that too"? Instead of, along with Schnabel, sniping at it, declaring it treason to the nation? Truly, what is German, what all can be German and what place your work will take in the history of German forms—it will not be those who today presume authority over the by no means simple concept of the German who will finally have to consider that.

One can say that in the European-German-Latin synthesis, which you embody, the psychic aspect is German and only the intellectual is French. The expressive radicalism of your aesthetic was what destined the pre- and postwar generation of German expressionists, with its gothic allegiances, to see in you its father and leader. Assimilated Frenchness, in contrast, is the paradoxical and therefore classically Voltairean blend of pessimism and high-mindedness, of disdain for humanity and revolutionary élan; it is literature's pride and concept of honor, the aesthetic disdain of the base, the critique of reality by an intellect committed to beauty. But who wants to continue calling it French, after it has become German? Significant minds have always altered the image by which the world identifies national character. If in today's Germany, too, the inseparable organic connection between art and critique has prevailed over the literature of the psyche, with its formal weaknesses and its confinement to pure interiority, if it has relegated that genre to the provinces, to second rank, to semi-validity; if the type of the *grand écrivain*, the European moralist, is now at home in Germany and no longer a stranger—you were certainly neither alone nor the ultimate founder of this development, but your work belongs among that which has promoted it most powerfully.

When we were young, during that preliminary period in Rome, you sat down at the table daily for weeks on end and worked with your pen and ink on an endless series of pictures, which we called "The Life Work" and the actual title of which was "The Social Order." And these pages, which we glued together into a long, thickly rolled frieze, really did depict human society in all its types and groupings, from the kaiser and the pope to the lumpenproletariat and beggars—there was nothing left out in this *trionfo* social pyramid; we had time and amused ourselves as we could. But there was a twofold intimation of things to come, both playful and preliminary, in this diverting exercise in youthful presumption and stamina. In the form of the sense for the great undertaking, the monument, the standard work, the gigantic composition, the grand test of endurance—this sense that belongs to our century, the nineteenth, the century of the *Ring of the Niebelungs* and *Rougon-Macquart*, this sense that your novel trilogy confirms. And second, in theme, the social spirit of the romance countries, which, Germanized, defines your essence, your social-critical and political passion and sensitivity. Excruciating though they were, these qualities sharpened your eye for German abuses, which did not seem to a purely culturally oriented, musical-metaphysical Germany as urgent as they did to you, and in your case inspired that work full of loyal bitterness and clarity of vision, the novel of the German patrioteer.

This social spirit of yours, leaving aside the matter of artistic genius, is critically responsible for the position you occupy today in German life. It, too, is an artistic spirit, for it represents a will to form. The official and public recognition, inclusion, and prominence of literature brought about by the new republican state—how fully this corresponds to your intentions, and how fortunate and right it was, thanks to your move to Berlin, that the Prussian Academy of the Arts could name you as its head! The Academy salutes you today as its leader and, through me, dear Heinrich, in collegial admiration and respect, conveys to you its most heartfelt congratulations on your sixtieth birthday.

## HEINRICH MANN, "THE SIXTY-YEAR-OLD"

*In* Die Sammlung *(Amsterdam), June 1935*

It has already been a lengthy path, and it should have yet a ways to go. We set off upon it in the same house; still earlier it was the same room. We have covered great stretches together, while for others we were apart. Recently we have been met by our most kindred destiny: we would of course have prepared it ourselves, each on his own in secret unanimity. Recent events have given us to understand that we never had reason to take our differences altogether seriously. We departed from the same homeland, having learned in its regard that flight beyond the German borders is the most decent, therefore the mildest, of what could have happened, and it happened to us as brothers.

We have both lived our lives in reason, that great word, if we dare pronounce it in the sense of its eternal meaning: as a human law, not as a partisan motto. The fathers, to be sure, say rationalism, until it happens that their sons, or yet they themselves, cross over into the irrational. Reason, in contrast, is not replaceable by a contrary, and it is not subject to the dominion of any new generation clearing away the old. They must not clear away the word. The word: that is the precise word. It is the strictness of language. It is the self-discipline we exercise when, to the best of our abilities, we honor truth, and ourselves approximate its consummate expression.

The man of the word believes that it is also reason and that outside the word there really is none. Human things first attain reality through self-identifying expression. Only through expression do they come to partake of reason, while a life lived without the supervision of the word seldom behaves other than head over heels and with shameful imprecision. The word is what lends body to reality, yes, the word invests it with a certain duration: otherwise it would amount to no more than passing shadows—no one knowing why they are flying by. What doubtless partakes the most of reason and what disappoints relatively little is to work on the word. Moreover, it is something solid, actual, while reality never gets beyond "jest and allusion."

In *Joseph*, by Thomas Mann, these two words refer to a process that the uninitiated would mistake for authentic and immediate: young Joseph being thrown by his brothers into a pit. The story is called "merely a beginning and an attempt at fulfillment, which is not to be taken altogether seriously, but is only a jest and an allusion." The pit, as well as the brother being thrown into it and the whole story itself, should by no means have already been, but should be very much in the process of becoming. That is said there by a character who is justifiably suspected of being an angel and of having come from the realm of the spirit. For him what really happens is only "jest and allusion." Allusion to what? To something behind the events, to pasts, ancient depths, in which everything human constantly repeats itself and is finally lost in unfathomable depths. Abraham as well as the servant Eliezer, they are not actually who they seem to be, are at least simultaneously others, much older; they do not regard themselves as unequivocal or bound to this single phenomenal appearance. Even the Tower of Babel is that particular one, and nonetheless one much older. These are mysteries—because the word, when it lends precise expression to things human, confronts mysteries. The mysteries of reason: they are those that are allowed in honor of the intellect. Intended in *Joseph* is a humanization of myth. Achieved is just as much a mysticism of reason. In that way too is *Joseph* such a new book. One must always be attempting something new, in the opinion of its author, whether he really knows or not what he has already done.

The writer of *Joseph* has done much. Life is long and has time for the popular simplicity of a novel of bourgeois family life and also for the representation in recognizable human form of the saints, of the earliest ancients. Nevertheless, it is possible that the novel of the bourgeois family had already had in mind more venerable things than it appears to have narrated. One might consider only the deaths, the death of Senator Buddenbrook, of the consul's old wife, and finally of the boy, who is the final member of the family. So too do people die in timeless legends: it has the same inner solemnity, and the same ironic uncertainty, expressed much later by the angel, asking whether it is not "jest and allusion" that have taken charge here. It was on account of its "decline" that the family became the object of the novel in the first place; it was to become, to die, to rise again in the word—as Joseph, in observance of an endlessly repeated rite, sinks into the grave in order thereafter to rise up.

The Buddenbrooks and Joseph—I endeavor to retrace the invisible bridges between them, since a life and the work of that life are necessarily one. "One must be something in order to do anything." It is only that one does it differently at sixty than at twenty-five. In his youth, this writer acknowledged himself a realist, much later even regarded this novel of his youth as the only entirely realistic work among German novels of its time. In the meantime he has revealed an all too ironic relationship to reality, and more anxious notice of death, than would permit of a temperament rooted solidly in life and joyousness. The secure and able author of *Goetz*, at about the same age, wrote the scarcely self-possessed *Werther.* That likewise befell this young novelist, and, indeed, in one and the same book. It no longer bears witness to the nihilism of the unsettled adolescent, but perhaps to the memory of it.

When a sixty-year-old terms the processes of reality "jest and allusion" or simply has a suspect character term them such, then it is obviously something different, something that begins to be called wisdom. No matter—the magical word sets forth its search for the unfathomable depths. There is scarcely a contradiction if, around the fortieth year, the most naive age in the life of a man, he acts as if he were standing on solid ground: everything is now to have its proper order and just here, nowhere else, are right and triumph to dwell. And so did this forty-year-old behave in regard to the world and its struggle at that time, which was precisely the early period of war. He endeavored grandly and movingly in Germany's favor: he sought to save it intellectually, to lend it honest expression and to cleanse it to the point of the sublime. The *Reflections of a Nonpolitical Man* were also gratefully received by a particular side, because distress just then was great. To be sure, at that time there still was a German society deserving of intellectual exertion. It had persisted through the collapse of everything because it said: this is the country of Luther, of Goethe, of Nietzsche; it cannot be condemned, cannot perish. It has given the world too much and is too closely bound to the world.

The process is to be understood as follows: a mind that was never confined within the national frame seeks a deep connection to the Germany of its day, in the early period by way of Nietzsche and Wagner, in more mature years through a truly personal identification with Goethe. As a result, the man no longer distinguishes greatly between what is his and what is German. He regards himself as comprehended within a powerful tradition: he wants it thus. That makes him worthy of his achievement and worthy of Germany. At first it was met with gratitude.

When in 1933, for the fiftieth anniversary of Wagner's death, he undertook once more to do the same, he found no gratitude but inspired great anger. This is a time very ill-suited to praise of the Germans' connection to the world. Your breeding, the education of your feelings, your intellectuality—you share all this with the world, you exchange it with the world; the most German of you belong as well to the so-called foreigners, sometimes more to them than to yourselves: look at Wagner. This is a manner of celebrating the German that is little appropriate to the times. What is German is understood at this moment just the other way around: no natural tie to all the rest, but a vehement separation from it, a violent willfulness. Thus is a separation achieved not only from the external world beyond the borders, but just as completely from the universality of intellect. Universality, however, is what characterizes the German intellect in particular, to the extent that it is lofty and refined, is what characterizes all who exceed the merely provincial and who once had Germany or still have or could have it.

It is evident today that the heroic may not be analyzed and understood. It must be crudely enlarged, exaggerated, must be opportunistically disfigured. Such methods captivate the stupid and one becomes stupid oneself, ventures, like humans at the beginning of time, into a terrifying world of giant scaly monsters. The mission of the writer is therefore the first thing to be nullified. "But he was a liberator as is every poet and man of letters: he liberates by arousing the emotions and extending by analysis our knowledge of man," thus does Thomas Mann explain to himself his Goethe. Liberators have meanwhile fallen from favor and been cast aside. "It is necessary to keep pace with the progress of life," thus Goethe's command. That is now being roundly rejected. He, incidentally, stated himself: "The human mob fears nothing so much as it fears understanding; it is stupidity they should be afraid of, if they grasped what is fearful: but the former is uncomfortable and must be put out of sight; the latter is only pernicious, and that can be endured." It diminishes the status and importance of a writer in Germany to have quoted this statement as late as 1932 and to repeat it in 1935 in "Leiden und Größe der Meister." To have renounced his reason, however, would have diminished him more: it would have diminished his soul. There is something on the doctrine and the novel of the soul in the prelude, "Descent into Hell," which introduces the "Tales of Jacob" and is, in itself, a most remarkable piece of prose: primitive humanity or the soul is presented as having been God's chosen warrior in the struggle against the evil that had infiltrated creation at the very beginning. Thus it is. The struggle against evil, it has also brought both of us, in every sense, to where we are.

Dear brother, despite everything, and as you yourself know best, it was worth it. It is true that their classical figures soar over the heads of the Germans like cranes, which someone already noted in better days. Precisely for that reason the position and worth of the classics, as well as your own, are completely secure: the range of both surpasses national boundaries. On the other hand, for such as we it is the most genuine form of national community: to take part in the transmission of tradition, to be joined with those minds that have come before, assured of their recognition. The balance of earthly events transpires incidentally and only very provisionally; neither you nor I overestimate a temporary catastrophe, in regard to its effect on us personally. My own sixtieth birthday was the occasion for several of the last celebratory events that German society, already face to face with disintegration, yet allowed itself. In a festive hall before an approving audience we embraced each other then, after you, as a writer and a brother, had delivered an address in my honor. We embrace again on your sixtieth, and can continue doing so beyond the confines of celebrations and borders as long as we live, since we are brothers; yes, can still do so afterward, since we are writers.

## THOMAS MANN, "TO THE SIXTY-FIVE-YEAR-OLD"

*In* Die Neue Weltbühne, *March 26, 1936*

*Küsnacht am Zürichsee, March 13, 1936*

To pay loving homage to my brother Heinrich on his birthday, in public as well as privately, is a matter close to my heart and I am grateful to your magazine for offering me the space to do so.

The sixty-five-year-old is truly deserving of congratulations. In this year of his life, a rather late one after all, he has triumphantly completed—in addition to a host of smaller contributions to the contemporary battle of ideas, each one of which we read almost cheerfully on account of its moral clarity and certainty—a great novel of the youth of King Henri. A work of the first order in which goodness and audacity are blended together in such a way as could, if translated from the intellectual realm into reality, offer deliverance to a continent; a poem of history and humanity whose mournful irony and fierce knowledge of infernal evil does no injury to its faith in reason and the good; a synthesis of all the talents of this great artist, in which the already politically invigorated aestheticism of his youth merges admirably with the utterly unique militant sensitivity of his later years. This life displays a clear unity; since it is moreover a life on a large scale, it affords us that still incomparable pleasure of catching sight of a personality. And if it is true, as Goethe says, that "he is happiest who can forge a connection between the end of his life and its beginning," then your form-giving life, dear brother, despite whatever bitterness inviolable laws dictate it contains, is to be termed the happiest.

What should be my wish for you on this day? Well, the most natural, the greatest, the one that comprehends all others: That in five years, when you turn seventy, our people and our country might once again have need of us.

## HEINRICH MANN, "WELCOMING THE EXILE"

*In* Die Neue Weltbühne, *December 10, 1936*

But is it even necessary to welcome him among the other exiles? The most famous of German writers regards no one as a member of the Third Reich. The world outside of Germany anticipated the event; it has long been of the opinion that he belongs to it, and not to the *Kleindeutschland* of Hitler. The empire of German intellectuals has forever stretched more broadly than the country's borders. Even expanded borders would never catch up with them. If you think I was in Weimar, then I'm already in Jena: Goethe said something to this effect, but he had continents in mind and could see a century ahead.

Let us be modest. Thomas Mann, as of very recently, no longer a "German," has this much, at least this much, in common with Goethe: he makes the necessary effort; he bears the burden. Where is the one who made the effort, and bears the burden, whom we have carried? This statement of Goethe's is not given here word for word, but translated back into German. In the manifesto to the Europeans, composed as a warning to them by Thomas Mann, the statement was there to be read in all its dialects. A German, on the verge of being expelled, joins forces with another German, Goethe, who would not himself be in Weimar, who would also have had his house and possessions taken from him; he shares the exile with all of us. He would write French as easily as German; already in his lifetime Napoleon had called him to Paris. Accordingly, a hundred years later, a German issues his appeal to the Europeans in all of their languages.

Perhaps this appeal provided the final impetus to expel him. He says to European youth precisely what the Third Reich does not want them to hear: the personality is an individual's highest good. For it seeks development. Europe is declining, because the new

Europeans no longer want to undertake their essential work. They know nothing, which would be bad enough; but they arrogate their ignorance to themselves as a preference. Work on their own improvement, personal responsibility and effort, all of this gets short shrift when they are allowed to seek it by joining together in groups to follow "leaders." That is the comfortable way, and it yields the cheapest variety of psychological intoxication: instead of Dionysian, collective. There is no need to improve oneself; one needs neither knowledge nor responsibility, both of which in exalted emotional moments attain to an intellectual intoxication. That path requires long, honest labors, until one finally reaches the summit, where all living things are one with oneself. No, instead they pursue their egotistical enjoyments, intoxicate themselves with subordination, march in step, singing all the while the headlines from the propaganda ministry.

It is remarkable enough that the Third Reich and its propaganda ministry would tolerate such language in a German as long as they did. Their motives were naturally of the most vulgar sort; exclusively those bearing on external appearances—and the foreign office. They would not have it become public knowledge that, now, the final writer of world repute has left their jurisdiction. They had wanted to profit dishonestly from his name. Until they had robbed other people of their countries, and swollen their honor with the breadth of their territory, the only honor they understand, until then, they wanted to present the Nobel laureate as one of their own. That gained them nothing; the Nobel laureate saw to it himself that it would fail. Meanwhile, the world has been richly informed about a Reich, the chief concern of which is that it not be talked about. Nowhere were people ignorant of what was going on in German bookstores, that the works of the Nobel laureate, carried by every bookseller in Europe, could be sold only under the counter in his native land. What does expelling him change?

It demonstrates openly that Hitler's Germany is repudiated and rejected by the European mind. The reverse interpretation is pretense and sham. Hitler did not expel Thomas Mann; rather, Europe expelled Hitler. This contemporary of ours overestimates his power in every respect, militarily, ideologically, but especially in regard to the personalities who did not "seize power," but have worked to merit and to win the right to themselves, and thus to their Germany, their Europe, to the future and the Reich, through the whole of their serious lives.


THOMAS MANN, "ADDRESS ON HEINRICH MANN'S SEVENTIETH BIRTHDAY"

*Delivered on May 2, 1941, during a gathering at Frau Salka Viertel's*

Well, then, this festive gathering is taking place after all—the occasion for it—such a moving and distinguished occasion!—by now so far in the past that it is almost necessary to recall it to mind. It is your seventieth birthday, dear brother, which is actually March 27th, and that we were not able to get together earlier to celebrate it is my fault, or at least the fault of circumstances that affected me. You, for your part, have made the day on which you are honored into a day of honor for this country: you are completing the formalities of your immigration. And since it is the moment for congratulations, we want to congratulate you on that as well—congratulate you, above all, on the fact that you are among us, that you are safe, that in the last second we succeeded in opening the way for you to join us just before poor, broken France, a nation estranged from itself, was forced by those vile torturers, those defilers of humanity now ruling Europe, to fulfill its monstrous obligations.

I well know, and we all know, that you were forced to leave a country that you love, a country whose culture helped to form your own, whose language you have made your own to the point of artistic mastery, and that here in this young land you necessarily feel yourself to be foreign. But, ultimately, what today is the meaning of foreign, the meaning of homeland? Lübeck on the Trave we left, in any case, long ago. When the homeland becomes foreign, the foreign becomes the homeland. Most profoundly foreign to us today is Germany, that savage, reckless, and disintegrated country of our heritage and language, and, compared to its fatal foreignness, every foreign place seems familiar. The world has become small and intimate; it is everywhere the same stage for one and the same battle: the worldwide civil war in which we are living, in which we must stand our ground, has nothing to do with nations and national cultures; it is at once cause and consequence, it is simply the expression of the unification of the world. And if people were still saying a generation ago that Europe will become one; so do they say today, emphatically and unmistakably, the world will become one.

Unity, unification, is the key word of the times. Goethe knew this already: "National literature has little to say today; world literature is on the agenda." He would know and say today: "Nation states and national cultures do not mean anything anymore; world unity and world culture is the order of the day."—One hears a lot today about the total or totalitarian state. That it is nothing other than total war we always knew, and it has proved so. The reason is that, in this misconception of the new, the idea of unity is mixed with the old, national idea, from which there is no more good to be had. The result is a sordid abomination and historical blunder, which is nothing more than a bloody froth of words. What we oppose to the misdeeds of the total state is the total individual.

The times are long past in which one could regard the humane as divided up among various spheres, of which one was the political: a special sphere that one could leave to its own devices. The question of the individual, the problem of humanity has long since appeared to our eyes as an indivisible whole and as a whole it weighs upon our intellectual conscience. The problem of humanity, however, includes the political question; the latter is not the whole, but a part, a segment, a side of the whole. Indeed, one can say that the question of the individual today presents itself in essentially political form, that it, more perhaps than in any earlier epoch, has taken on a political complexion. The problem of humanity as a unity, the political comprehended within the question of the individual—

it was that of which the bourgeois intellect in Germany was ignorant. It was the fateful error of this educated German middle class that it drew a sharp distinction between mind and life, thought and reality, and looked down in contempt on the sphere of the social and the political from the heights of absolute culture. It is this that was responsible for the present degradation of the bourgeois intellect in Germany. The reason for the helplessness and impotence of democracy in Germany lies here: in the perhaps fundamental lack of the sort of pragmatism that amounts to nothing other than a feeling of benevolence toward life, a commitment to life, a sense of the intellect's responsibility for life and for the results of thought in reality, in the social and political life of the individual.

I recently read an essay by an English author, his reflections on culture and freedom, and he does not shrink from a critique of the nature and fate of the German intellect. "I feel," says the writer, "for German culture a sympathy which is deep and genuine. But at the same time this feeling of sympathy has always been accompanied by a feeling of despair. It is as though every road taken by German poets and philosophers led to the edge of an abyss—an abyss from which they could not withdraw, but must fall into headlong—an abyss of intellect no longer controlled by any awareness of the sensuous realities of life."—That is excellent; and it is not necessary to say that the despair, the pain, which foreign admirers of German culture feel when looking at it, is only too familiar to those of us who are native to German culture, those of us who stand in its tradition. There exists something among us Germans, something I believe does not exist among other peoples: the torment we experience in our great men.

Consider, if you will, Nietzsche, the creator of what is probably the most fascinating and colorful philosophical or lyrical-critical work of our epoch. Where other than in Nietzsche would one find clearer expression of that sense of doom that rules over the pathways of the German intellect, that weakness for the intellectual abyss, on the edge of which all feeling of responsibility for the consequences of thought in the realm of the real and the human is extinguished? Personally, he was of a sensitive, complicated artistic nature, was profoundly capable of suffering, foreign to all brutality and primitive healthiness—a Christian nature, if not in the religious sense, then distinctly in the constitutional meaning of the word. But in heroic contradiction to himself, he elaborated an exhilaratingly antihumanist doctrine, the favored concepts of which were power, instinct, dynamism, the rule of the superman, naive cruelty, the "blond beast," the amorally triumphal life force. Occasionally, in his letters, there appeared a completely different Nietzsche from the one of his books. When Kaiser Friedrich III, the anglophile liberal, had died of cancer, the man who had glorified Cesare Borgia wrote to a friend that the death was a great, critical misfortune for Germany, that the last *hope for German freedom* had gone with him to the grave.—That is the simple, natural, and constrained statement of an intellectual man, who, as such, loves freedom and relies on it. It is Nietzsche's deliberate and, in comparison to the frantic risk-taking of his philosophy, even banal expression of his relationship to the reality of life, to *his* reality, in contrast to the romantic poem that was his work. Who doubts that he would turn over in his grave if he found out down there what has been made of his philosophy of power? And were he still alive—his personal fate would correspond to the simple and intellectually natural passage I quoted from the letter; with his doctrine it had nothing to do. He, who already under the Kaiserreich lived as an émigré—where would he be today? He would be with us, in America.

Since his provocative critique of morals, time has sharpened our conscience for the obligation of thought toward life and reality, an obligation that was very poorly fulfilled by the hara-kari committed by intellect in honor of life. There are spectacles in thinking and writing that strike us, not the way they did earlier, as impressive, but rather as wanton and lacking in instinct. The intellect today is unmistakably entering into a *moral* epoch, an epoch in which a new religious and moral distinction is being drawn between good and evil. That signifies a certain simplification and rejuvenation of intellect, in opposition to all manner of tired and skeptical sophistication—it is *its* way to "rebarbarize" itself. We have caught sight of evil in such an extremely vile and forbidding form that Nietzsche's distinction between evil and *bad* has nothing more to say to us: the bad is the evil, it is the most evil of all, and evil is the worst that can be—thus have we experienced it, and in an entirely unironic way that just a short time ago would not have been regarded as worthy of intellect, we have decided for the good. Freedom, truth, right, humanity—intellect dares, dares once again, to pronounce these words; it is no longer ashamed, as it believed it had to be so long as they appeared self-evident. Because they are in extreme danger, intellect has become conscious that they are its daily bread, its life's breath, its life itself, and it understands that it must fight for them or itself perish.

You, dear Heinrich, perceived and understood this new situation confronting the intellect earlier than probably any of us; you pronounced the word "democracy" when the rest of us scarcely knew what to make of it, and in your works, which combine the most distinguished art with prophesy, you proclaimed the totality of the humane, as a sphere that encompasses politics. Do we not take note today of books like *The Patrioteer, The Blue Angel*, and *The Little Town* as fulfilled prophecy? If genius is anticipation, foresight, the passionate figuration of things to come, then your work bears the stamp of genius, and beyond its ventures in the aesthetic realm, it is a moral phenomenon. I spoke of a simplification and rejuvenation of mind—your militant writings against the absolute infamy that is now pouring forth its bloody froth of words, these writings, in their blend of literary brilliance and—I would almost say: a fairy-tale simplicity, a popularity on the scale of humanity, are the greatest examples of it. School readers of the future, I believe, will offer them to a generation of younger people who will no longer have a feel for the suffering, the sublime hatred from which they came, but whose hearts will nevertheless beat faster as they read.

This future, these young people, will come, we want to remain assured of that. Our Germans believe too strongly in crude success, in force, in war. They believe that all they had to do was create iron facts, before which humanity would surely bow down. It will not bow down before them, because it cannot. Be one's thoughts of humanity ever so bitter and dubious—there is, with all the wretchedness, a divine spark in it, the spark of the intellect and the good. It cannot accept the final triumph of evil, of lies and force—it simply cannot live with it. The world, the one resulting from the victory of Hitler, would indeed be not only a world of universal slavery, but also a world of absolute cynicism, a world that flew in the face of every belief in the good, in the higher qualities within human beings, a world that belonged utterly to evil, a world submissive to evil. There is no such world; that would not be tolerated. The revolt of humanity against a Hitlerian world of the complete negation of what is best in human beings—this revolt is the most certain of certainties; it will be an elemental revolt, before which "iron facts" will splinter like tinder.

A generation ago, dear brother, you gave us the myth of Professor Unrat.[40] Hitler is no professor—far from it. But *Unrat* [garbage] he is, nothing but *Unrat*, and soon he will be the rubbish of history. If you, as I trust you do, have the physical patience to endure, then your old eyes will see what you in your bold youth described: the end of a tyrant.

## HEINRICH MANN, "AFTERDINNER REMARKS AT FRAU VIERTEL'S"

*Delivered May 2, 1941*

Dear Brother,

Thank you for your words, which we all, but especially I, have taken to heart. Although I really mustn't accept your unqualified estimation of my work and my person, I'm doing it today anyway. For, first of all, it is a special day, and I am allowed more than on other days, in other years. So, you mean what you say. Your sincerity, the masterly penetration of the truths you speak, is what has always won hearts—mine as well, believe me, even during that time when our thinking diverged. Divergence—that suggests the entirety of a life. Our life and our thinking have always remained fraternal, and it is not only my birth, but my heart and knowledge, that justify the pride I take in your greatness, your fame—"as if it were a piece of myself." If I were to need consolation for myself and my condition, then I am consoled. For us it is as the song puts it: "He walked by my side." And the bullets that come flying are aimed at both of us.

To the others of you at the table—or should I say, at the party? My gratitude for your presence obliges me to speak; simple modesty counsels against it. Certainly, it is due to your particular goodness that you celebrate my birthday—in consideration of my age, which once was the occasion for special recognition. Today, you think about that basically as I do. Even ninety years would scarcely suffice to justify someone standing here and saying, here I am; that was I.

---

40. The English translation of *Professor Unrat* is *The Blue Angel*.

Too many will never again be thanked for their existence, because they had to die before living the life span I have lived, which they could have lived. Conditions and events, the state of affairs we all have in common, in actuality demand that we fall silent and remain alone. Consistency—but who behaves consistently—justifies nothing more than mourning and anxious anticipation.

By the time we know our destiny and see the results of decisions long-since enacted, our world already lying behind us, some have reservations about appearing in public, even if only for a demonstration of their current abilities. Accomplishments already known from the past are better left sleeping. On the other hand, life is short, and art is no respecter of time. What do you think would happen should Shakespeare, his very self, return to earth, initially, of course, to the English-speaking countries. For my part, I'm tempted to believe that the war would stop. It would sink altogether, with all its tanks and horrific instruments, into the ground or *to the bottom*.[41]

The enemy would have to die of shame. He already more or less annexed the greatest Briton, before it occurred to him to conquer his island as well. The last, or by now not even the last, Shakespeare drama that played in Berlin was, appropriately enough, *Richard II*, with its brazen hymn to England. You know it:

"This royal throne of kings, this sceptre'd isle";

and further:

"This fortress built by Nature for herself
Against infection and the hand of war—"

It is quite possible that these lines, and the many that followed, each intensifying the last, were finally simply cut from the German performance. How would they have been spoken? Emphatically, to mislead the enemy? Or with irony—but against whom, if it is impossible to do without the author of the lines? Perhaps in a conversational tone, so that the words get lost in the shuffle. Nevertheless, the play was performed, and what was accomplished by that does not die. More likely is the end of the untimely war, which was provoked against the aims of the historical process by an ape. The word and the talent to use it never end.

This, dear table companions and fellow celebrants, by no means lacks reference to ourselves and to the modest occasion of our sumptuous meal. When Goethe refused to compare himself to Tieck, he added that he did not compare himself to Shakespeare either. Every intellectual talent, without comparison to others, is justified in concluding from ancient experience: as long as the forces of destruction are active, so long do we persist in our efforts. We have often survived the late aftereffects of the destructive and the ignorant.

People of our sort achieve a mastery of contemporary passions and fears. They could

41. In English in original.

not be understood later, but for the form we lend them, our day of judgment. We must preserve the hope of growing older than virulent hatred and sensation, which is the source of its own ghostly mischief. And, not to forget a wholesome measure of doubt: "When the world drags itself out of one mud hole, it falls into another; moral centuries follow centuries of barbarism. Barbarism is soon swept away; soon it comes again: a continual succession of day and night." This was said in a century of morality—by Voltaire, and the age was moral only with him.

We congratulate no one individually, and therefore the more so all of us. I raise my glass; *je lève mon verre*, said the tipsy *maire* of Monaco, inviting me to a banquet in Monte Carlo. I rendered honor where it was due, and offer it today to our dear hostess. My thanks to all of you. This glass is for Frau Salka Viertel.

## HEINRICH MANN, "MY BROTHER"

*Preprint from* Ein Zeitalter wird besichtigt *(published in* Die neue Rundschau *[June 1945]: 3–12)*

After my brother had immigrated to the United States, he declared simply and rightly: "Where I am, there is German culture." Only here do we fully understand the words: "What you have inherited from your forefathers, inherit it that you might possess it!" We are speaking of our birthright in substantive ideas and opinions, images and views. In the whole of life they do not change essentially, although they are enriched and deepened. Finally, they are no longer bound to any one nation.

Our culture—and every culture—has the nation of one's birth as its origin and reason for being. Without a place of birth, there is no world citizenship. There can be no fathoming of other languages, even literatures, in the absence of the experience, to the point of desperation, to the point of bliss, of the idiom, both oral and written, into which we are born. At the beginning of his twenties my brother gave himself to the Russian masters, the half of my existence was composed of French sentences. Both of us learned to write German—only for that reason properly, in my belief.

I see him by my side, both of us young, usually on trips, together or alone: with no ties—one would have said, not knowing how much pitiless obligation one destined to produce literature his whole life long bears with him as a young man wherever he goes. It was harder than the memory of it I can conjure today. Later on, the state of anticipation would have been unbearable. We needed all the hardiness of our youth to withstand it.

I do not want to press too far ahead; the examination of my own pains I put off to better times, in fear of giving them permanent anchor. The good times never come, but learning to live with the pains, of which, incidentally, there is an ample and shifting selection, is actually the lesson of how one is to live. My brother understood this earlier than I.

We were walking, after the heat of one summer day had subsided, from our little

Roman mountain city—ten years later the setting of my novel *The Little Town*—up a country road. Before us, all around us, we had a sky colored massively in gold. I said, "Byzantine pictures are based in gold. This is no likeness that we're seeing; it is an optical fact. It lacks only the slender head of the Virgin, with her far too heavy crown, looking impassively down from her sculpted zenith!" My brother took exception to the sentimentality. "That is the external aspect," he said.

He would never leave his little dog at home. "Should we really go alone?" he asked whenever Titino was not around. We had found it by a haystack. Its behavior in all situations, the expressions of its little instincts, like ours, only less affected—these brought him consolation and taught him lessons. Titino, the realist, was a cheerful corrective whenever the young spirits of its master were inclined to melancholy.

The best antidote was called *Buddenbrooks: Decline of a Family*. In our cool stone hall, halfway up a stairwell, the novice began, unknown to himself, a work—soon many would hear of it, decades later it belonged to the whole world. In the draft he undertook at that time, it was simply our story, the life of our parents, ancestors, back to the generations from which we received our tradition, indirectly or from them themselves.

The old ones counted their days more deliberately than we; they kept books. The births in the family house, first school years, illnesses, and what they called the establishment of their children; joining the firm, getting married, everything was preserved in writing, the kitchen recipes in particular precision, and the astonishing low prices of foodstuffs—though a great-grandmother complained of inflation. These things, as we were recalling them to each other, lay a hundred years in the past, those we lived through, however, scarcely ten.

If I may allow myself the honor, I had my share in that famous book; simply as a son in the same household, who could also contribute something to the existing material. Yet had there been standing behind us a gentleman in old-fashioned dress, with powdered hair, long since deceased, he would have had more to say than I. The young writer heard him: knowledge of the details of the individual lives was indispensable. Each demanded a choreography of its own. The essence, their harmony, the direction in which the totality of the persons moved—the idea itself—belonged to the author alone.

Only he grasped at that time the fact of decline; learned precisely through his own fearful rise how it is when one declines, when a large family becomes a small one and the loss of the last remaining capable man is never overcome. The tender youth who is left dies, and everything for all eternity has been said. In reality, as it then became apparent, there remained much to add, if not for eternity then for the few decades that are under our control. The "decayed" family, so characterized overhastily by the pastor, was yet to be conspicuously productive.

This was the energetic manner of a new beginning, to liberate himself from the temptations of his not yet settled disposition. Once his novel, along with its success, was there, I never again saw his life cause him to suffer. Or he was now strong enough to come to terms with himself. The last able man of the family was by no means gone. In my brother was thoroughly manifest the steadfastness of our father, and also the ambition, which was a virtue. Ambition ennobles egotism, if it does not distract from it.

After sixty years I again hear my father, his response to a remark from a fellow citizen that his name was being mentioned again. "Yes, I'm always around wherever there's no money to be made." The businessman valued unpaid works that served the general good. The tax obligations of his city-state cost him more effort and time than a member of the governing senate received in exchange. Although for twenty-five years he directed the firm, I do not believe he increased its fortune.

His business was to buy grain, store it, and ship it. He took me along as a boy to the villages. At the time he still hoped that I could succeed him. He let me christen a ship, he introduced me to his people. That all died away as I read too many books and I could not recite the names of the houses on the street. We traveled across the country in a rented automobile. No one, scarcely even millionaires, kept at that time their own, which now even unpropertied persons have. Amid the stomping of hooves the peasant appeared before his cottage and the purchase was concluded without further inspection; on both sides there was trust. It was just to keep valued friendship fresh that my father traveled.

His popularity, which was considerable and sincere—sincerely sought and bestowed—appears to me as the model when I consider the extraordinary renown of my brother. He began on this course earlier than he himself was aware of it. He is renowned beyond comparison, in the manner of a patrician who embodies his tradition. Prejudices that attach to tradition are not brought to bear on the descendant. They are also accompanied by skepticism. An unmastered aversion to novelties, because they represent a threat, is to be found, socially speaking, among the nouveaux riches and, intellectually, among those who have not yet gotten their bearings.

Our father worked with the same conscientiousness for his family as he did for the public good. Neither the one nor the other would he have left casually to chance. Those who maintain and build have nothing to fear quite so much as chance. But to first lend form to something that will last, one must be punctual and precise. There is no genius outside business hours. The most solemn among the great in past times have laughed and chattered nonsense with their friends. One keeps one's hours. Genius is not, incidentally, in our power: only its consummation, assuming our strength and reliability.

If I see things right, even more than genius, others impute to my brother the practice of finishing what he begins. The attainment of complete consummation would be beyond human capabilities. To approximate it tirelessly already defines the maximum allowable achievement. Unselfish ambition, which is egoless because it seeks only the work even without acknowledgment—it alarms and dismays both people and peoples. For both, as concerns their self-regard, are rather more careless. As long as it remains possible, they make things easy for themselves.

This would offer us an incomplete explanation for why many Americans, his new public, are agreed in naming Thomas Mann the premier writer in the world. If we think back, most Germans were of the same opinion and were only reluctant for various reasons to express it. For an individual to win this kind of unquestioned prestige, he has to represent more than just himself: A country and its tradition, and yet more, an overall moral orientation, a supranational consciousness of humanity. The one like the other has borne, up to the present day, the name of Europe. It was Europe itself.

The Americans are convinced, likely with justice, of their future destiny as a contributor in the formation of world culture. Uncertainty as to whether this would be easy to accomplish is evident in their unconditional recognition of the man who writes in German, who is German. And even if he wanted it otherwise, he would be helpless against his heritage and life-long education. Now, on a daily basis and before audiences as well, he speaks English. But I have heard him name German his "sacred" language.

Erasmus of Rotterdam, whose picture was already hanging next to my brother's desk long ago, wrote in Latin. German is—for how long?—dead. We must be translated if we are to be read. Leibniz, though he was thoroughly in command of the scholarly language, preferred to express himself in French, directly to laymen. Who acted in accord with the higher ambition, Leibniz or Erasmus? It is astounding how many émigré authors, needing a brief pause, now express their thoughts in English—an approximate English and approximate thoughts. The most respected of all writers remains German and is becoming sacred.

As old age approaches, in the aftermath of many trials and toward the end of a life of meaningful representation, such is to be permitted. To represent, he says, was the aim of his nature. Not to disavow. He previously supported Germany, as it was, against the world's fury and against his own reservations. His conscience traveled a difficult course before it resolved against his country. All the more lavishly was his resolve requited, here with love, there with hate. He is an uncommon witness. And he is not lukewarm.

The princess of Oranien, Madame d'Orange, as her century called her, made, through my mediation, her confession. "I go through events always the same: that is a great failing. We are supposed to be burdened by crimes, so that we might heal them through knowledge and will. I had no burden whatever to lay down, neither arrogance nor ambition nor selfishness." At the end the princess repeats: "And it all cost me nothing. I didn't struggle, was guided by a cheerful obstinacy, which one mistakenly calls virtuous."

The Christian princess clearly sought atonement through hardness toward herself; she says, "Never to err, by our Lord in heaven, that is to be lukewarm."

Now, she fails to recognize in this an idealization of her own human frailty. As she understands herself, she was never lukewarm. Indifference to this extent toward the universal passions is unknown. Moreover, there are degrees of emotional engagement or lukewarm remove. Today the person engaged is my brother. Germany disappointed him, more than most others. What it has since then made of itself—or how it allowed itself to be taken for such—the enemy of reason, of thought, of humanity: an anathema—that struck him personally, the more so the later it struck. He felt himself betrayed.

When we had as yet published little, he once made reference to another's words that I no longer remember precisely: behind me breathes a people—that was the sense. Already back then, solitary before a sheet of paper, he wished for a nation to stand behind him looking over his shoulder and agreeing. His need was to be new and profound, but to be so for the entirety of his contemporaries. How much greater were his wishes when the nation really did offer him to the world as a master! When there is no nation to offer us, the foreigners learn of us late or not at all.

Things have turned out such that a few foreign countries have been allowed to become acquainted with him, no longer all of them, and his own country only last. He has always intended his words precisely for his own nation; they reached the others thanks to his superiority within German words. It is true that the summits of European literature stand near to each other above nations. The foundation and inception of such works become hidden from view. It truly no longer concerns a single country when the hand of an author makes of the Joseph legends a likeness of old, in essence immutable humanity. That lives for all. It lives in all of us.

But *Joseph*, like the earlier *Magic Mountain*, is a novel of personal development: since *Wilhelm Meister* the German form of the novel as such—aside from Voltaire's *L'Ingénu*, with its concluding chapter that is a magical fairy tale of morality and simplicity itself.

In *The Magic Mountain*, too, all that is learned is life. To teach how to live is the intention of literature, theology, and medicine. All three, and yet a few other disciplines as well, had to be absorbed through sober study from one book to the next, so that the gift of his imagination would be capable, so to speak, of invention. "I haven't actually invented anything at all," said this author, so persuaded is he by his stories.

Writing, one educates oneself, encompasses more of life with each book, attains by way of successive expansions of knowledge to wisdom, which is the goal. What has Germany to do with that? It gives nothing to the work and can take nothing from it. Yes, but there it stands, even with its houses in rubble. But the house out of which he came is upright in his memory, and so too the country as it was, as he wanted it to be. The pain caused by moral collapse, however, is stronger than when cities are destroyed. He had believed Germany to be morally secure. From that comes a wrath that yields no ground.

One's relation to one's own country sometimes takes a different form. A person can come into conflict with it prematurely, not knowing why. Perhaps by virtue of his youthful identification with other areas, or for reasons that reach back before his birth. I doubted my contemporary Germany early, to the justified vexation of my brother. But what can one do against one's own vital impressions?

In 1906 in a café on Unter den Linden I was observing the dense crowd of its bourgeois clients. I found them loud and lacking in dignity; their challenging manner betrayed to me their secret cowardice. They thronged heavily against the broad window-panes when, outside, the kaiser rode by. He had the bearing of an indolent conqueror. When he was greeted, he smiled—less sternly than in frivolous disregard.

A worker was expelled from the café. He had had the remarkable idea that he, for the same low price as those who were dressed differently, might enjoy his coffee there. Under a ceiling from which hung life-sized plaster figures! Between the badly painted military parades on both sidewalls! Although the man put up no resistance, the manager and the waiters were far from satisfied until the world had been rid of the embarrassing incident.

I required six years of ever intensifying experiences, then I was ripe for *The Patrio-teer*, my novel of the bourgeoisie in the age of Wilhelm II. The novel of the proletariat, called *The Poor*, was written in 1916 during the war. I took on the leading figures of the Kaiserreich only in the summer of 1918, a few months before its collapse—the timing of which was uncertain until the end. For the first draft of my novel *Der Kopf*, I yet found it advisable to set the story in a country with a fictitious name.

My revolt did not occur early; my inspiration had nothing of prophecy in it. But certainly I did begin as the facts were yet dawning. And they did not exactly rise like suns. Did I suffer from my perceptions, which could have been noted by anyone at the same time? Was I a fighter? I gave form to what I saw and sought also to make what I knew persuasive and, at most, also practicable.

It was not put into practice. After the Kaiserreich I observed the republic and re-spected it rather precisely as much as it was worthy. The condition that succeeded it, the utterly dreadful sum of conditions prevailing previously, this Hitler Germany, had to dis-gust me as it did every other individual of taste, self-respect, and compassion. I have suf-fered, thanks to Hitler, his rule, and his war, fears, pains, and the deepest humiliation of my existence.

Not, actually, wrath. Wrath takes us unawares. We have to have considered people who incensed us incapable of their infamy. Only the charitable do they cause truly to lose their composure. We must not have noted the omens, the preliminary stages too clearly if we, one rueful day, are to make the acquaintance of wrath. My brother knows it now.

That means he was benevolent. He necessarily believed in the Germans—for the sake, certainly, of his work; it needed the moral German soil that has brought forth much honest work. But he also trusted the Germans out of friendliness. How otherwise could he have helped them, how might he have borne their good name—not only his—abroad? The acute psychologist that he is does not found his wisdom on any problematic totality. Individual Germans—Goethe distinguishes them from the nation—were often virtuous.

One taken unawares by his wrath has to move cautiously to avoid condemning the nation along with a few scoundrels or a wicked generation just then alive. When we now discuss what this epoch is about, the whole fine mess it displays—we do so seldom and concisely: but more likely I am the one who fails to see in the unhappy country of our origin a singularly monstrous case.

Let it be well understood that I, too, am aware of what this country is guilty or what it certainly did bring about. I have examples enough, which affected me or others, of its sorry debasement.

It is only that I take into account that this is not the first attempt at world conquest and will not be the last. The realist Stalin says: "There will always be wars." But what are wars in a world in which distance is more easily mastered? They can only be the subjugation of humanity by one or two powers. That must repeat itself—if Napoleon, who should have been enough for everyone, could nonetheless be repeated. This time historical destiny chose Germany. The next is perhaps not distant. "The feet of those who will take you away are at the door."

Oh! the conquerors are dissimilar to each other in their ways of thinking and feeling. The France that followed its emperor brought peoples the best, human rights, freedom—secured by imperial fortresses. One prospered wonderfully from it, breathed in admiration for years on end, and a genuine superiority emanated from the friend of the peoples.

How differently things have turned out for the hated Germans. More precisely, their arrogated role has not waited for the last act to become detestable. It was that way right from the beginning. In their lightning charge through the world they had nothing, absolutely nothing inspiring for themselves and for others to take with them. Their breath was lies and annihilation their first word. Dreadful, is it not? But aside from the fact that they thirsted after vengeance and had brooded over a degenerate pride, they might have become noble, assuming their unanimous reception as the longed-for unifiers and protectors of the continent.

Which is probably inconceivable, and they knew that. That is why they were abominable and became ever more abominable. The next conqueror will once again be filled with the purest of intentions. We may rely on that! The motives alternate, after this German version its opposites are called for. Unfortunately, they can change nothing of the results. One calculates thirty million direct victims of the current war, fifty million if it continues;—the immediate results. The next war will sacrifice the larger part of living humanity to an unrelentingly advanced technology.

Not a word of all this is do I really know. I have simply seen in the course of the epoch that coincides with my life that all things have proceeded to the point of their uttermost extremity: as long as they were pernicious things. That proves nothing; my skepticism is unjustified. The irrationalism that drove me out of my country and yet farther has run its course. Next is to be reason—not to be all-powerful, but to be embraced as an experiment, which has the charm of novelty and more besides to recommend it.

My brother is not one to express such doubts, as to the absolute and unqualified guilt of the Germans, as to whether the lessons learned by the planet will endure. I, too, should keep my doubts quiet and to myself. It is only to confess my lukewarmness. I have done what others call struggle—without being conscious of a struggle. I did not hate blindly enough for that and was not taken unawares by wrath. I have loved urgently, that is true. But my love? What happened to it, where are its traces?

As we were yet in the first half of our working lives my brother and I told to each other the same secret thought. We wanted to write a book together. I spoke first, but he was already prepared for it. We never got back to it. Perhaps it would have become the most remarkable work of all. People do not have their earliest companions, those born with them, for no reason. Our father would have recognized his house in our collective labor. Gradually I forget that he has been gone for more than fifty years.

## THOMAS MANN, "REPORT ON MY BROTHER, ON THE OCCASION OF THE 75TH BIRTHDAY OF HEINRICH MANN, MARCH 27, 1946"

*In* Freies Deutschland *(Mexico) 5, no. 3–4 (March–April 1946): 3f.*

My dear Sirs of *Freies Deutschland,*

As my brother's seventy-fifth birthday approaches, you have asked me about his welfare. He is doing quite well, thank you. The loss of his companion, almost a year and a half ago, of the woman who accompanied him, that twenty-first of February, 1933, to the streetcar in Berlin, then to the train to Frankfurt (first stop, Frankfurt), bravely fighting back her tears, he has overcome with the characteristic force and composure of his mind, the equal of destiny. His solitude, a fundamentally natural element for people like him, and familiar from his years of youth and early manhood, is enlivened and discreetly tended by admiring friends, by the deferential love of those closest to him.

The distances here are inconvenient, but the separation in our case could be worse: it is a half-hour trip by car, if you are lucky with the lights. We live nearer to the ocean, into the hills of Santa Monica, while his apartment is in a more urban area, landward, not exactly *down-town,*[42] but in Los Angeles. He is happy to have us pick him up, at least once a week, and take him out of the city, where he spends with us the hours from lunch until it gets dark. For a change, we sometimes visit him for a kind of picnic dinner, which tends always to be warm and pleasant. Afterwards he might read from something remarkable he has written, or ask to hear something I have done.

We chat, talk about the past, about the days in Italy, the odd course our life has taken, of which we find ourselves approving, or about recent events. His way of expressing himself about these latter, you could call jovial, since it is not far distant from what critical observers called Goethe's "ungentle tolerance." No, gentle he is not, but patient from top to bottom, and quite pessimistic. He has ceded fascism yet a large future—of

42. In English in original.

course, since the war against it was never pursued with serious and unbroken will, it has not been defeated and is, consciously, half-consciously, or, by preference, unconsciously, abetted now as much as in the time of *appeasement*.[43] Fear of its abominations, which are finally abominations of order, are far outweighed by fear of the alternative, socialism, and so people's minds remain open to it. American soldiers learn fascism in Europe—they could learn it just as well at home, if they even need to learn it to begin with. The epoch itself is fascist—a finding arrived at calmly, but one that bears the mark of resignation.

We have no difference of opinion about these things. On his way home with his niece Erika, my oldest daughter, he once said, "Politically, I really do get along quite well with your father now. He is just a little more radical than I." It sounded terribly funny, but what he meant was our relationship to Germany, still cherished, toward which he was less angry than I, for the simple reason that he knew the score earlier and suffered no disillusionment. Today he refuses to see in German conduct a wholly and completely "singularly monstrous case," a case of "absolute and unqualified guilt"—I am using his words. Everything is contingent and explicable, if not excusable, and Germans are only people too: I believe that to claim they were so utterly exceptionally bad appears to him as a form of nationalism. He was forced to endure as much torment and sacrifice by the German madness as I—even more, since he was actually in danger for his life as he fled from France. But he manages not to hold it against the people there so much as I do, after a fashion, keeping them accountable for the loss of friends, who were the joy of my life (Karel Capek, who died of a broken heart; Menno ter Braak, who shot himself in Holland). The critical fact is that he, although physically more delicate than I, has always been much more balanced psychologically, and, in that, a political presence much earlier.

Had a saving revolution broken out in Germany when it should have, he would necessarily have been called to be president of a second republic, he and no other. And even now—how ridiculous that all this silly noise is being made about me, whether I will return, whether perhaps I wouldn't—while no one seemed to be asking about him. In which of the two of us has our Latin political heritage been active from the start? Who was the socially critical prophet and organizer? Who wrote *Der Untertan*, and who declared for democracy in Germany, when others were succumbing to the melancholy defense of Protestant, romantic, antipolitical German bourgeois intellectuality? I bit my lip, when finally, in a gentle tone, he asked: "Why is it that people are leaving me entirely alone?" And it was a genuine relief to me when, finally, the call came from Germany, naturally from the Russian zone: Becher wrote to him, saying that everything was there and waiting for him. Now, it was time. He will hardly go; he is, God knows, excused. Still, he was asked for.

43. In English in original.

"The way things are today," he said recently, "it's best to stay at home." That, too, came out with touching humor, for it is, to say the least, a somewhat accidental home that he is naming—somewhere in the area where Los Angeles gives over into Beverly Hills. But he likes his comfortable little ground-floor apartment on South Swall Street, from which he can do his shopping on foot and in which the breath of the dead still stirs. The *living room*,[44] facing the street, well furnished, with an elegant desk—which he never uses, since he withdraws to the bedroom to work—has an excellent radio, and in the evenings he often listens to music. In California, of all places, he has significantly broadened and deepened his knowledge of the world's symphonies. At certain hours of the day he reads in French, German, and English—aloud, if the prose is worthy of it. Mornings, after having his cup of strong coffee, from seven generally until noon, he writes, continues producing imperturbably with his old boldness and self-confidence, borne by his belief in the mission of literature, which he has so often acknowledged in words of proud beauty; he carries on with his current work, still dipping his steel-nib in the inkwell, covering page after page with his utterly clear and distinctly formed Latin script—certainly not without effort, for the good is difficult, but nonetheless with the trained facility of a great worker.

Here, then, is where the new works originate, marked not by fatigue but by the stamp of his unmistakable spirit, and which will be heard of soon enough: The scenes of epic drama, shining with that special enamel radiance of historical coloration, narrating dialogically the life of the Prussian Friedrich—a surprising choice of subject; the novel *Empfang bei der Welt*, a ghostly social satire set everywhere and nowhere at all; and yet another novel, about what I do not know. And above all (I think, above all) the fascinating memoir *Ein Zeitalter wird besichtigt*, of which lengthy excerpts have been made available in Moscow's *Internationale Literatur* and an English translation is already planned. It is an autobiography conceived as a critique of the epoch experienced by its author; a work of an indescribably rigorous and cheerful brilliance, of naive wisdom and moral dignity, written in a prose style of such supple intellectual simplicity that it sometimes strikes me as the language of the future. Indeed, I am convinced that German school texts of the twenty-first century will use samples from this book as models. It is being printed in Stockholm now, and, for my part, I can hardly wait for it to be available to our German readers at home. Of course, they will be insulted—when have they ever not been? They have a need, constantly and at all costs, to feel insulted and misunderstood, and if they are understood only too well, then they are the more insulted. But that is childishness. The objective fact, that this seventy-five-year-old was a German writer of genius, will prove stronger than their momentary mood, and sooner or later it will overcome resistance and seize a place in their consciousness.

44. In English in original.

# THOMAS MANN, "LETTER ON THE DEATH OF MY BROTHER HEINRICH"

*In* The Germanic Review *(New York) 25, no. 4 (December 1950): 243ff.*

It was a pleasure to hear from you, and I was touched by indications in your letter that you have plans to take note of my seventy-fifth birthday with one or another kind consideration of my life's work. I was still more gratified to hear that you want to combine this notice of my own work with an homage to the genius of my late brother, toward whom this country, as you say, in fact has certain amends to make. He lived here quite unrecognized, quite isolated, and if I, as long as it was not obviously too late, encouraged him to accept the earnest invitation of the popular democratic German government to come to Berlin, it was because I knew that there the evening of his life would have been full of honor. That was my wish for him, and I saw it coming and therefore supported the desire of German officials, although his move at that time would probably have meant that I would never have seen him again and also although it was becoming increasingly clear that he wanted nothing more than to be left in peace.

He had become very old toward the end, afflicted by a variety of ailments. He no longer worked, wrote a few letters in which he spoke of making preparations for his departure; he read a little, listened to music. Productivity is a peculiar thing: when one finally grows too weary for it, then it is not missed. I never heard him complain about his flagging ability to work; it apparently left him entirely indifferent. He probably also knew that his work—a powerful body of work!—was accomplished, even if his last major undertaking—the dialogic narration of the life of the Prussian Friedrich (a surprising choice of subject matter!) in scenes of epic drama, shining with that special enamel radiance of historical coloration—was left unfinished. How much could be made of the fact that these fragments remained fragments! His life as an artist came to a consummate end with the last two novels, *Empfang bei der Welt*, a visionary social satire, set everywhere and nowhere, and *Atem*, this last fulfillment of his art, the product of an elderly avant-gardism, extremely sharp, as ever, in that it fades and passes.

In precisely this same way, the great essayist concluded his life with the fascinating memoir *Ein Zeitalter wird besichtigt*—an autobiography conceived as a critique of the author's era, a work of an indescribably rigorous and cheerful brilliance, of naive wisdom and moral dignity, written in a prose style of such supple intellectual simplicity that it sometimes strikes me as the language of the future. Indeed, I am convinced that German school texts of the twenty-first century will use samples from this book as models. For the fact that my late brother was one of the greatest German writers will sooner or later overcome resistance and seize a place in Germans' consciousness.

His last evening, he stayed up unusually late, enjoying listening to music until nearly midnight, and only with difficulty was his attendant able to persuade him to go to bed. Then, we do not know precisely the time, the cerebral hemorrhage, without a sound and without stirring. In the morning it was simply not possible to awaken him. His heart continued working into the following night, with no measurable blood pressure and through what was decidedly an irretrievable loss of consciousness. It was, at bottom, the most merciful outcome.

It was a dignified funeral. Feuchtwanger and the Rev. Stephen Fritschman of the Unitarian Church spoke, and the Temianka quartet played a beautiful long passage from Debussy. He would have approved. Then I accompanied the coffin across the warm lawn of the cemetery in Santa Monica.

He rests in peace following an active life, the traces of which, in my opinion, could disappear only with the decline of culture itself and the self-respect of humanity.

# NOTES

OCTOBER 24, 1900

**success:** Heinrich Mann, *Im Schlaraffenland: Ein Roman unter feinen Leuten.* The book was published in 1900 by the Verlag Albert Langen (Munich) in an edition of 2,000 copies. The same publisher issued a second edition of 2,000 copies in 1901. The novel was begun in January 1898 in Rome and finished in March 1900 in Riva. "I was overtaken by my talent on the Via Argentina in Rome in 1898, and I didn't know what I was doing. I thought I was writing a pencil draft, but produced the nearly finished novel" (Heinrich Mann to Karl Lemke, January 1, 1947). First English edition: *Berlin: The Land of Cockaigne.*

**Piepsam:** main character in Thomas Mann's story "Der Weg zum Friedhof," *Simplicissimus,* September 20, 1900, 238–39 (in English: "The Way to the Churchyard," in *Stories of Three Decades*).

**Dr. von Staat:** in *Reflections of a Nonpolitical Man,* 178 (*Gesammelte Werke,* 12:247; hereafter, references to this German edition will be to \**GW,* with volume and pages. For it, as for other works identified in notes at their first mention by an asterisk, see the parallel abbreviated title in the bibliography after the work's full entry, to link it to the short title here—DR), Thomas Mann wrote: "As a boy I liked to personify the state to myself in my imagination; I though of it as a stern, stiff figure in a dress coat, with a full black beard, with a star on its breast, and decked out with a mixture of military-academic titles that appropriately symbolized its power and legality: as *General Doktor von Staat.*"

**barracks:** on October 1, 1900, Thomas Mann was called up as a one-year volunteer in the Königlich-Bayerischen Infanterie-Leibregiment. He was discharged in December as unfit for duty. "After only a quarter year, yet before Christmas, I was dismissed unceremoniously since my feet did not want to accustom themselves to that ideal and manly gait called the parade march" (*GW* 11:331). See his letter of April 27, 1912.

**Otto Grautoff** (1876–1937): schoolmate and closest boyhood friend of Thomas Mann, copublisher of the school periodical *Der Frühlingssturm* (1893). The school chapter of *Buddenbrooks* is dedicated to him. Wrote *Exzentrische Liebes- und Künstlergeschichten* (Leipzig, 1907), with the printed dedication: "To Thomas Mann, the man and the writer, for many years of loyal friendship." The hero of his first story, Hans Pahlen, resembles Thomas Mann in certain respects.

Grautoff became an art historian, studied in Munich, Paris, and Switzerland; Ph.D., lecturer at the Lessing-Hochschule and the Handelhochschule in Berlin. Founded the Deutsch-Französische Gesellschaft in 1925 in Berlin. Died in 1937 in Paris. Among his works: *Moritz von Schwind* (1904); *Auguste Rodin* (1908); "Lübeck," *Stätten der Kultur,* vol. 9 (Leipzig, 1908), with a printed dedication to Mrs. Julia Löhr (née Mann); *Die neue Kunst* (1920); *Zur Psychologie Frankreichs* (1922); *Das gegenwärtige Frankreich* (1926); *Französen sehen Deutschland: Begegnungen, Gespräche, Bekenntnisse* (1931).

See Peter de Mendelssohn, ed., *Thomas Mann, Briefe an Otto Grautoff 1894–1901* (Frankfurt, 1975).

**Savonarola:** Thomas Mann was occupied at the time with the preliminary studies for *Fiorenza* (in *Stories of Three Decades*).

**Riva:** see the letter of December 29, 1900.

**research trip to Florence:** Thomas Mann's trip to Florence did not take place until May 1901.

**Arthur Holitscher** (1869–1941): writer. By this time had published the following works: *Leidende Menschen*, stories (1893); *Weisse Liebe*, novel (1896); *An die Schönheit*, dramatic tragedy (1896); *Der vergiftete Brunnen*, novel (1900). In the early years a close acquaintance of Thomas Mann. In his *Lebensgeschichte eines Rebellen* (1924), he made reference to Thomas Mann's apartment at that time: "An upright piano stood in the study; to be seen on the desk was a portrait of Tolstoy, the frame embellished by a narrow wreath; large manuscript sheets, covered with precise, slanting script, lay stacked to a considerable height in front of the picture. It was the nearly finished manuscript of *Buddenbrooks*. Mann was an excellent violinist and I accompanied him as best I could." Holitscher was offended when he recognized himself in Detlev Spinell, the writer in "Tristan," in *Stories of Three Decades*.

**Buddenbrooks:** Thomas Mann had sent the novel in manuscript to Samuel Fischer and was now waiting for a report from the publisher.

NOVEMBER 2, 1900

**Dr. von Staat:** s.v., letter of October 24, 1900.

**card from Ferrara:** reference not found.

**Samuel Fischer** (1859–1934): Thomas Mann's publisher in Berlin. See Thomas Mann, "S. Fischer zum siebzigsten Geburtstag" (*GW* 10:458) and "In memoriam S. Fischer" (*GW* 10:472).

Thomas Mann is alluding to Samuel Fischer's letter of October 26, 1900.

**Piepsam:** main character in Thomas Mann's story "The Way to the Churchyard," in *Stories of Three Decades*.

**Reinhold Geheeb** (1872–1932): as of March 1900, the responsible editor of *Simplicissimus*. Brother of the country school pedagogue Paul Geheeb. See Thomas Mann, "Glückwunsch an den *Simplicissimus*" (*GW* 10:850); further, Thomas Mann, *A Sketch of My Life*, 16 (*GW* 11:105f.).

NOVEMBER 25, 1900

**Herzogstraße:** the apartment of Thomas Mann's mother at that time was on Herzogstraße 3 in Munich (see Viktor Mann, *Wir waren fünf*, 79–92).

**Hofrath [Richard] May** (1863–1936): Munich doctor. Appointed to University of Munich in 1886, tenured in 1894; extraordinary professor in 1901; professor of internal medicine and the history of medicine from 1911. Caricatured in *Confessions of Felix Krull, Confidence Man* as Düsing, the health board official. See letter of April 27, 1912, s.v. military.

**Cockaigne:** s.v., letter of October 24, 1900.

**Grautoff:** s.v., letter of October 24, 1900.

**Sternberg:** presumably August Sternberg, a banker in Berlin who was implicated in corruption trials. See letter of December 17, 1900.

**Richard Schaukal** (1874–1942): had already published several volumes of poetry at the time, in addition to the play *Rückkehr* (1894). He reviewed *Buddenbrooks* for the *Wiener Abendpost* on January 24, 1902. Thomas Mann became personally acquainted with him in September 1902 and dedicated the story "Little Lizzy" to him (originally published in the *Tristan* volume; English version in *Stories of Three Decades*), which Schaukal reviewed in the *Wiener Abendpost*, July 25, 1903. The break occurred following Schaukal's negative review of *Fiorenza* in *Zeitgeist*, the supplement to the *Berliner Tageblatt* of March 5, 1906 (see Thomas Mann's letter of March 13, 1906, s.v. Schaukal). In the notes for *Geist und Kunst*, Thomas Mann made repeated critical references to Schaukal, in particular in regard to his popular work, *Leben und Meinungen des Herrn Andreas von Balthesser* (1907).

**Lobgott Piepsam:** s.v., letter of October 24, 1900.

**Der König von Florenz:** title originally planned for *Fiorenza*.

**The Civilization of the Renaissance:** Jacob Burckhardt's major work first published in 1860, one of the sources for *Fiorenza*. The edition in Thomas Mann's possession was the seventh German edition of 1899 (see letter of December 17, 1900). English edition: *The Civilization of the Renaissance in Italy*, trans. S. G. C. Middlemore (New York: Harper, 1958).

**Duchess:** the duchess d'Assy, in Heinrich Mann, *Die Göttinnen oder die drei Romane der Herzogin von Assy* (Munich: Verlag Albert Langen, 1903). Conceived in Riva, 1899–1900. *Diana:* began writing in Florence, November 1900; *Minerva/Venus:* Munich, Ulental, and elsewhere, 1901–1902. Finished: November–December 1902.

DECEMBER 17, 1900

**trip to Florence:** s.v., letter of October 24, 1900.

**Sternberg:** s.v., letter of November 25, 1900.

**Ludwig Ewers** (1870–1946): writer, journalist, critic. Schoolmate of Heinrich Mann in Lübeck; had friendly ties to both brothers. Editor of the *Bonner Zeitung*, as of 1902 of the *Leipziger Allgemeine Zeitung*; later the *Königsberger Allgemeine Zeitung*; as of 1913 of the *Hamburger Nachrichten*. Among his works: *Kinderaugen*, sketches (1896); *Frau Ingeborgs Liebesgarten*, novel (1906); *Geschichten aus der Krone*, stories (1913); *Die Großvaterstadt*, novel (1926). Ewers's article "Ein neuer sozialer Roman" appeared in the *Bonner Zeitung* of October 28, 1900.

**Eduard Engels** (1869–1958): Munich journalist. The Christmas book list appeared under the title "Briefe an eine Münchener Dame" in the *Münchener Zeitung* of December 15, 1900. Along with Heinrich's *Cockaigne*, d'Annunzio's *Il fuoco* was also named.

**bruciamento delle vanità:** "bonfire of the vanities" on Florentine carnival days in 1497 and 1498. See also "Gladius Dei," in *Stories of Three Decades* (*GW* 8:212ff.).

**brochure about Sternberg:** reference not found.

DECEMBER 29, 1900

**Hartungens:** Dr. Christoph Hartung von Hartungen (1849–1917) was the director of a convalescent home in Riva for persons afflicted with nervous disorders and diabetes. The brothers Mann stayed there repeatedly. Heinrich portrayed him as Dr. von Männigen in *Göttinnen*.

**the Löhrs:** in 1900 Julia Mann (1877–1927), the sister of Heinrich and Thomas, married Dr. Josef Löhr, director of the Bayerische Handelsbank, Munich.

**Dr. von Staat:** s.v., letter of October 24, 1900.

*Savonarola:* along with *Der König von Florenz,* one of the titles intended for *Fiorenza.*

**story of a bitter-melancholic character:** "Tonio Kröger," in *Stories of Three Decades.*

**Copieen exhibition:** the following information comes from the exhibition catalogue, *Secession,* published by the Verein bildender Künstler Münchens: Jacopo della Quercia (1374–1438); Andrea Pisan (1273–1349); Giovanni Pisano (1240–ca. 1321); Niccolò Pisano (1206–1278); Andrea della Robbia (1435–1525); Luca della Robbia (1399–1482); Mino da Fiesole (1431–1484).

**Krafft Tesdorpf** (1842–1902): Lübeck businessman, legal guardian of Thomas Mann.

JANUARY 8, 1901

**between two candles:** allusion to the "two candles" by the light of which Consul Buddenbrook drew up the balance of his fortune "with a cold sharp gaze," *Buddenbrooks,* 37 *(GW* 1:48, 50).

**Vicco:** Viktor Mann (1890–1949), youngest brother of Heinrich and Thomas Mann. Author of *Wir waren fünf: Bildnis der Familie Mann,* first edition, Constance, 1949.

**"You ask—o please don't ask me, why":** From Platen's *Liedern und Romanzen:*

| | |
|---|---|
| Ich schleich' umher | I steal about |
| Betrübt und stumm, | downcast and shy |
| Du fragst, o frage | You ask, o please |
| Mich nicht, warum? | don't ask me, why? |

**What I am writing now:** "Tonio Kröger" (see letter of December 29, 1900).

**Richard Strauss** (1864–1949): as of 1894, chief conductor of the Hofoper. Went to Berlin in 1898 as court conductor. Occasional guest conductor in Munich.

**Ludwig Wüllner** (1858–1938): actor, singer, recitationist. Appeared repeatedly in the Munich Hoftheater; especially celebrated as Shylock and Hamlet.

**programs of the Literary Society:** the Literarische Gesellschaft was founded on December 19, 1897, by Ernst von Wolzogen and Ludwig Ganghofer.

**stories:** soon after Thomas Mann interrupted work on "Tonio Kröger" to write "Tristan" (see letter of December 13, 1901). Probably near the end of 1899, in the third *Notizbuch,* Thomas Mann had also made a note to himself regarding "Gladius Dei": "The Christian youngster in the gallery. (Psychol. study to Savonarola)." The exact dating of the story is not known. It was published in the July 12–19, 1902, issue of the Vienna weekly *Die Zeit.*

**Burckhardt:** s.v., Thomas Mann's letter of November 25, 1900.

**Pasquale Villari** (1827–1917): *Die Geschichte Girolama Savonarolas und seiner Zeit,* nach neuen Quellen dargestellt, unter Mitwirkung des Verfassers aus dem Italienischen übersetzt von Moritz Berduschek, 2 vols (Leipzig, 1868). This German translation of *La storia di Girolamo Savonarola e de' suoi tempi,* narrata da Pasquale Villari con l'aiuto di nuovi documenti, 2 vols. (Florence: Felice le Monnier, 1859–1861), is one of the main sources for *Fiorenza* (among the holdings in the library of the Thomas Mann estate).

**Leo Greiner** (1876–1928): writer, member of the Munich cabaret Die elf Scharfrichter; later director of the drama department of the S. Fischer Verlag.

The review in question was Leo Greiner, "Neue Romane" (Arthur Holitscher, *Der vergiftete Brunnen;* Heinrich Mann, *Berlin: The Land of Cockaigne;* Kurt Aram, *Unter Wolken*), *Münchener Zeitung,* December 12, 1900.

**Holitscher:** s.v., letter of October 24, 1900.

Albert Langen (1869–1909): prominent Munich publisher. Publisher of *Simplicissimus*. Thomas Mann worked for him as a reader and proofreader from 1898 to 1900. Langen published a few of the early novels of Heinrich Mann: *Die Göttinnen* (1903); *Die Jagd nach Liebe* (1903); *Professor Unrat* [*The Blue Angel*] (1905).

Ferdinand Grautoff (1871–1935): writer, Ph.D., political editor of the *Leipziger neueste Nachrichten;* brother of Thomas Mann's boyhood friend Otto Grautoff.

Samuel Fischer (1859–1934): s.v., letter of November 2, 1900.

changeling: *Buddenbrooks*.

JANUARY 21, 1901

The raving praises: the *Münchner neueste Nachrichten* carried the following review on January 19, 1901: "At the meeting of the Akademisch-dramatischer Verein on Thursday [January 17, 1901], Messrs Kurt Martens and Thomas Mann read from various works. [ . . . ] Thomas Mann concluded the evening with his splendid story, 'The Way to the Churchyard.' This creation, through its blend of sublime symbolism and farcical comedy conveyed in an individual, spirited style, strikes quite a new tone in contemporary German literature. With biting finesse, Mann knows how to lead the way with humor to moving seriousness, illuminating for us the background of life. Both authors—Mann in particular—earned hearty applause." The article is unsigned but was obviously written by Otto Grautoff.

J. Georg Stollberg (1853–1926): director. Began as an extra in the Vienna Theater in der Josefstadt. Student of Otto Brahm in Berlin; involved in the famous production of *The Weavers* in the Deutsche Theater. In 1891–1892, directed ten modern plays at the Belle-Alliance-Theater in Berlin for the Berliner Freie Volksbühne. Also introduced a modern program at the Tivoli Theater in Weimar. Moved in 1895 to the Deutsches Theater in Munich. Together with Schmederer founded the Schauspielhaus on Munich's Neuturmstraße. The performance of Wedekind's *Erdgeist* led to a scandal. From 1901 to 1919, director of the Schauspielhaus on Maximilianstraße. (Opening on April 4, 1901, with a performance of Sudermann's *Johannes;* Stollberg ended his career on March 2, 1919, with the two-hundred-fiftieth performance of Max Halbe's *Jugend.*)

Korfiz Holm (1872–1942): schoolmate of Thomas Mann and his "squad leader" at the Lübeck Katharineum. Contributed to the school paper *Der Frühlingssturm* under the pseudonym "Anthropos." Editor of *Simplicissimus* in Munich. Director and, as of 1918, partner in the Albert Langen Verlag. Author of novels, stories, and the memoir *ich—kleingeschrieben, Heitere Erlebnisse eines Verlegers* (1932). Published a translation of Dostoevsky's novel *Podrostok* (English: *A Raw Youth*) as *Ein Werdender* in 1905, which is included in the library of Thomas Mann's estate. See *A Sketch of My Life*, 16 (*GW* 11:105).

Alfred Capus (1858–1922): French writer and journalist. His novel *Qui perd gagne* (*Wer zuletzt lacht . . .*) was published by Langen in 1901 in a translation by Heinrich Mann.

JANUARY 25, 1901

Rieger: bookstore in Munich: the Rieger'sche Münchener Universitätsbuchhandlung, Odeonsplatz 2.

The Yriarte books: Charles Yriarte, *Un condottiere au XVe siècle: Rimini, études sur les lettres et les arts à la cour des Malatesta* (Paris, 1882). In the library of the Heinrich Mann estate (Heinrich-Mann-Archiv, Berlin).

Kurt Martens (1870–1945): writer, J. D. Feuilleton editor for the *Münchner neueste*

*Nachrichten.* Thomas Mann's closest friend from about 1900 to 1905. Dedicated a volume of stories, *Katastrophen,* to Thomas Mann in 1904. On March 24, 1906, published the essay "Die Gebrüder Mann" in the *Leipziger Tageblatt* (see Thomas Mann's letter of March 28, 1906, in E. Mann, ed., *Briefe* [hereafter, simply *Briefe*] 1:61; English version in *Letters of Thomas Mann 1889–1955*). Commented on Heinrich Mann's novel *Berlin: The Land of Cockaigne* in his book *Literatur in Deutschland* (Berlin, 1910, 129–30). The first volume of his *Schonungslosen Lebenschronik* appeared in 1921 (see Thomas Mann's review "Ein Schriftstellerleben," *GW* X, 613). Martens later settled in Dresden. Among his works: *Roman aus der Décadence* (1898); *Die Vollendung,* novel (1902); *Kaspar Hauser,* play (1903); *Kreislauf der Liebe,* novel (1906); *Die alten Ideale* [*Deutschland marschiert—Pia—Hier und drüben*], novel trilogy (1915); *Schonungslosen Lebenschronik,* autobiography (1921–1924); *Die deutsche Literatur unserer Zeit* (1921); *Abenteuer der Seele,* novellas (1923); *Gabriele Bach,* novel (1935); *Die junge Cosima,* novel (1937); *Verzicht und Vollendung,* novel (1941).

**the book on English art:** unknown.

FEBRUARY 13, 1901

**Giorgio Vasari** (1511–1574): Italian painter, builder, and writer. Author of *Vite de' più eccelenti pittori, scultori ed architetti italiani,* 1550; expanded edition 1568. Thomas Mann may have used Giorgio Vasari, *Sammlung ausgewählter Biographien,* Zum Gebrauche bei Vorlesungen, 4 vols., ed. Carl Frey (Berlin, 1885–1887). See Heinrich Mann, *Die Göttinnen,* afterword by Alfred Kantorowicz, 172.

**turbulent winter:** the difficult friendship with the painter Paul Ehrenberg (1878–1949). Ehrenberg was a student of Zügel. A member of the Luitpoldgruppe and the Künstlergenossenschaft, he was represented in all the big Munich exhibits with portraits, landscapes, still lifes, and animal paintings. His painting *Die Hetzjagd* hung for a time in Thomas Mann's room. Ehrenberg later married the painter Lilly Teufel. He was an excellent violinist and vacillated originally between music and painting. Hans Hansen in "Tonio Kröger," the painter in the story "The Hungry," in *Stories of Three Decades,* and Rudi Schwerdtfeger in *Doctor Faustus* bear resemblances to Paul Ehrenberg. See also Thomas Mann's letter of November 17, 1950, to Richard Braungart: "Among Zügel's students was also the recently deceased friend of my youth Paul Ehrenberg, brother of Professor Carl E., who was active at the Musik-Akademie in Munich. Back then, fifty years ago, Paul painted a portrait of me. We always called the picture *Writer in the Sun.*"

**letter from S. Fischer:** the letter of February 4, 1901, is reproduced in Paul Scherrer, "Bruchstücke der Buddenbrooks-Urhandschrift und Zeugnisse zu ihrer Enstehung 1897–1901," *Die neue Rundschau* 69, no. 2 (1958): 278f.

**volume of my stories:** *Tristan,* Thomas Mann's second story volume, published in the spring of 1903 by S. Fischer. It included: "Der Weg zum Friedhof," "Tristan," "Der Kleiderschrank," "Luischen," "Gladius Dei," "Tonio Kröger" (English versions: "The Way to the Churchyard," "Tristan," "The Wardrobe," "Little Lizzy," "Gladius Dei," "Tonio Kröger," in *Stories of Three Decades*).

**"Literature":** "Tonio Kröger." (The story was conceived in the autumn of 1899; in September Thomas Mann traveled to Denmark and before Christmas he had entered his first thoughts on the story in his third *Notizbuch.* Writing perhaps began immediately following the conclusion of *Buddenbrooks.* Following various interruptions and new beginnings, he finished the manuscript in late autumn 1902. See Hans Wysling, "Dokumente zur Entstehung des 'Tonio Kröger,'" in *Thomas-Mann-Studien* 1 [Bern and Munich, 1967], 48–69.)

**translation of** *Cockaigne:* *Au pays de Cocagne* (Paris, 1903).
**typhoid fever:** see *Buddenbrooks,* 598–99 (*GW* 1:751).

MARCH 7, 1901

**"nobility":** *Buddenbrooks,* 498 (*GW* 1:618).
**typhoid:** allusion to the death of Hanno Buddenbrook, *Buddenbrooks,* 598ff. (*GW* 1:751ff.).
**"Wunderreich der Nacht":** phrase from *Tristan und Isolde,* act 2, love duet.
**friendship:** s.v., Thomas Mann's letter of February 13, 1901.
**book of fairy tales:** reference not found.

MARCH 25–27, 1901

**Happy birthday:** Heinrich Mann's thirtieth birthday was on March 27, 1901.
**tickle of spring:** ironic allusion to "Tonio Kröger" (*Stories of Three Decades,* 102; *GW* 8:294).
*Läben* [life]: allusion to the *Bilderbuch für artige Kinder,* which Thomas and Heinrich Mann drew and wrote in the winter of 1897 in Rome (see Viktor Mann, *Wir waren fünf,* 46–61. Thomas Mann's drawing *Das Läben* is reproduced there opposite 56).
**picture:** Paul Ehrenberg's portrait of Thomas Mann has not been preserved. See letter of April 1, 1901.
**Platen:** the (inaccurately) quoted lines are from the poem "Antwort," which belongs to the *Lieder und Romanzen.* The correct lines are:

| | |
|---|---|
| Dem frohen Tage folgt ein trüber | A cheerless day succeeds a glad one, |
| Doch alles wiegt zuletzt sich auf. | And, finally, all is balanced out. |

Thomas Mann also quoted Platen in his letter of January 8, 1901 (see *Briefe* 3:444). For a while he intended to quote a verse from Platen's *Romanzen und Jugendliedern* at the beginning of *Buddenbrooks:*

| | |
|---|---|
| So ward ich ruhiger und kalt zuletzt, | Then I became quieter and finally cold, |
| Und gerne möcht' ich jetzt | And truly I would now like |
| Die Welt, wie außer ihr, von ferne schau'n: | To see the world from afar, as if outside it: |
| Erlitten hat das bange Herz | My uneasy heart has suffered |
| Begier und Furcht und Grau'n, | Longing and fear and dread. |
| Erlitten hat es seinen Theil von Schmerz, | It has suffered its share of pain, |
| Und in das Leben setzt es kein Vertrau'n; | And places no trust in life; |
| Ihm werde die gewaltige Natur | Let powerful nature for it |
| Zum Mittel nur, | Only become a means |
| Aus eigner Kraft sich eine Welt zu bau'n. | To build itself a world with its own strength. |

The verse was written in pencil on the first page of the *Buddenbrooks* manuscript but was not printed. Thomas Mann quoted it in the *Reflections of a Nonpolitical Man,* 137 (*GW* 12:191). In his third *Notizbuch,* 7, Thomas Mann recorded his intention of reading *Platen's Tagebücher* around New Year 1899. (The diaries were published from 1896 to 1900 by Cotta.) His library contains Platen's works in two volumes, ed. C. A. Wolff and V. Schweizer (Leipzig: Meyers Klassiker-Ausgaben, 1895). In 1926 Thomas Mann received the Cotta edition of Platen's works in five volumes, a gift from Ernst Bertram.

Heinrich Mann also turned his attention to Platen toward the end of the 1890s; in the Heinrich-Mann-Archiv is an unprinted text, "Platen in Italien," dated March 22, 1899. In a letter of November 18, 1900, to Richard Schaukal, Heinrich wrote: "Platen and the Emaux et Camées are still sitting on my desk" (see André Banuls, *Heinrich Mann* [Paris, 1966], 52, 123).

**letter from Fischer and his editor:** S. Fischer's letter of March 23, 1901, is reproduced in Paul Scherrer, "Bruchstücke der Buddenbrooks-Urhandschrift und Zeugnisse zu ihrer Enstehung 1897–1901," *Die neue Rundschau* 69, no. 2 (1958): 282f.

**Dr. Moritz Heimann** (1868–1925): essayist, writer, dramatist. Reader for S. Fischer Verlag. A selection of his essays have been made available again in *Die Wahrheit liegt nicht in der Mitte* (Frankfurt, 1966).

**waggery [*Gipprigkeit*]:** in the letter of February 18, 1905, Thomas Mann mentions a "Gipper-novel," which he and his brother conceived together in Palestrina. (The verb *gippern* also appears in early letters. It is not to be found in available German dictionaries but is probably synonomous with *verulken:* to make fun of or tease.)

### APRIL 1, 1901

**new story:** probably "Tonio Kröger." In the seventh *Notizbuch*, 41, the following appears regarding the beginning of the story (see *GW* 8:271): "A kind of soft hail was falling, not ice, not snow." This note is probably to be dated before the trip to Italy (May–June). See Thomas Mann's letter of February 13, 1901.

**the good fellow:** Paul Ehrenberg.

**a section of *Buddenbrooks:*** in the first edition, Thomas Mann dedicated part nine as follows: "To Paul Ehrenberg, the bold painter, in memory of our musical-literary evenings in Munich."

**book of Schaukal's:** presumably *Intérieurs aus dem Leben der Zwanzigjährigen*, vol. 19 (Leipzig: Bibliothek Tiefenbach, 1901).

### MAY 7, 1901

**publisher:** context unknown.

**Papyria:** reference not found.

**Miss Edith and Miss Mary [Smith]:** in *A Sketch of My Life*, 33 (*GW* 11:117), Thomas Mann writes concerning himself and Mary: "There followed a tender relationship and talk of marriage." The dedication of the story "Gladius Dei" reads (in English): "To M.S. in remembrance of our days in Florence."

### SEPTEMBER 15, 1903

***Hedda Gabler:*** Eleonora Duse was performing with her troupe in the Gärtnertheater. The premieres in the Schauspielhaus mentioned in the letter could not be confirmed with certainty: on October 10, 1902, Eduard von Keyserling's *Peter Hawel* was performed for the first time; on October 31, 1903, followed Max Halbe's *Strom*.

**article:** Richard Schaukal, "Thomas Mann," *Rheinisch-Westfälische Zeitung*, August 8, 1903.

### DECEMBER 5, 1903

**"a King as well":** reference from Thomas Mann's copy of the *Kinder- und Hausmärchen* of the brothers Grimm (complete edition, Halle: Otto Hendel, n.d. [1894]), "Des Teufels rußiger

Bruder." An unemployed soldier hires himself out to the devil in exchange for some gold. "'I only need you for seven years, then you shall be free,' says the devil. 'But one thing you must know. You are not to wash, comb or trim your hair, or cut your nails, or wipe the water from your eyes.'" His drudgery in hell finally over, the soldier explains his unkempt appearance as instructed by the devil, saying that he is "the devil's sooty brother, and a King as well." Later he really does become king (in English: "The Devil's Sooty Brother," *The Wedding of Mrs. Fox and Other Stories from the Brothers Grimm*, retold by Vera Gissing [London: Bedford Press, 1986], 110–14). In the context of Thomas Mann's letter, hell corresponds to the "distress and affliction of work on a deadline."

**work on a deadline:** Thomas Mann, "Ein Glück," *Die neue Rundschau* 15, no. 1 (January 1904): 85–93; in English: "A Gleam," in *Stories of Three Decades*.

**Oscar Bie** (1864–1938): writer on art and music. Editor of *Die neue Rundschau* from 1894. Thomas Mann had sent him the manuscript of "Der Kleine Herr Friedemann" in December 1896 (in English: "Little Herr Friedemann," in *Stories of Three Decades*). In response, Bie requested that he be sent everything Mann had written. He also supported the publication of *Buddenbrooks*. Thomas Mann visited him in Berlin in December 1904. Along with Emil Faktor and Herbert Ihering, Bie was a critic on the staff of the *Berliner Börsen-Courier*. Bie was a lecturer, later professor, of art history, at the Technische Universität in Berlin. Among his works: *Der Tanz* (1906); *Die Oper* (1913); *Franz Schubert* (1925).

**Berlin:** Thomas Mann spent the week of October 20–27, 1903, in Königsberg and Berlin (his first meeting with Gerhart Hauptmann in the home of the publisher Samuel Fischer).

**gotten completely away from me:** see Thomas Mann's letter to Carl Ehrenberg of November 20, 1903 (*Br.* 3:447): "Yesterday I sent my manuscript off, happy to be rid of it, but disgusted and disappointed. As a result of the bad weather and an utter lack of good spirits, it got entirely away from me, and it would probably be for the best if it never saw the light of day. It is not intended, by the way, to do anything new, and is indeed marked clearly enough as an occasional piece done on commission."

**reading:** Thomas Mann read from "Tonio Kröger" for the Literarische Gesellschaft in Königsberg.

**Ida Springer:** governess in Senator Mann's household.

**Grandmama:** Elizabeth Mann, née Marty (1811–1890).

**Ludwig Ewers** (1870–1946): s.v., letter of December 17, 1900. Heinrich Mann, *Briefe an Ludwig Ewers 1889–1913*, ed. Ulrich Dietzel and Rosemarie Eggert (1980).

**Leipzig:** Ewers had been editor of the *Leipziger Allgemeine Zeitung* in 1902.

**Ferdinand Grautoff** (1871–1935): s.v., letter of January 8, 1901.

**"fantastic novel":** probably a reference to *Frau Ingeborgs Liebesgarten* (1906).

**poems:** unknown. "Zweimaliger Abschied" could be meant, in any case, by the poem on the sea (*GW* 8:1102). The walnut tree is to be found repeatedly in the early stories, e.g., "Tonio Kröger," *Stories of Three Decades*, 87 (*GW* 8:274).

**Hauptmann:** the meeting with Hauptmann took place at the end of October in Berlin.

**Üz:** reference not found.

*Rose Bernd:* Gerhart Hauptmann, *Rose Bernd, Schauspiel in fünf Akten* (Berlin: S. Fischer, 1903).

**Cockaigne-comedy:** in his novel *Berlin: Land of Cockaigne*, Heinrich Mann had caricatured the literary scene in Berlin.

**Otto Brahm** (1856–1912): critic and stage manager. Cofounder of the Freie Bühne in Berlin. From 1894 to 1904, director of the Deutsches Theater. From 1904 to 1912, director of the Lessing-Theater.

**novel:** Heinrich Mann, *Die Jagd nach Liebe* (Munich: Langen, 1903). The novel was conceived in January 1903, on the Gardasee. Writing began in Florence in February 1903; concluded in Polling, summer 1903.

**Claude's meditation:** *Die Jagd nach Liebe*, 437.

**plebeian:** in the *Freistatt* review (s.v., above), the following words were aimed at Heinrich Mann's *Göttinnen:* "What I wanted to say is this: We poor plebeians and tschandalas, we who suffer the derisory smiles of the Renaissance men for revering a feminine cultural and artistic ideal, we who believe as artists in pain, in experience, in profound depths and the suffering of love and who confront beautiful superficiality a touch ironically: it must most likely be from among us that the most remarkable and interesting work is to be expected from woman *as artist*, indeed, that she someday will rise among us to leadership and mastery. [ . . . ] There is nothing in that, what stiff, cold pagans call 'the beautiful.'" In the paragraph preceding were the words: "For those who know love also know pain. (But those who do not know love, at most they know 'the beautiful.')"

**attacks on the reader's interest:** in the review referred to above, Thomas Mann emphasizes the "gently elevated" language of Schwabe over the importunity of certain modern novels: "Nothing of raging and desperate attacks on the reader's interest. An enlivened word that surprises, pleases, bears listening to. A vital detail that suddenly flashes and entices one on. And with every line, the certainty grows that this is something. Indeed, that this is art. Exquisite art."

**"bellows":** in the same review, Thomas Mann had written: "A tender forcefulness of effect is achieved, which, to describe it more precisely, is roughly the opposite of the bellows-poetry that has been arriving here for some years from the beautiful land of Italy. There are occasional places in Storm where, without the slightest linguistic extravagance, the mood suddenly thickens, where one closes the eyes and feels how the melancholy tightens the throat." Bellows-poetry: a reference directed against the ardour in Heinrich Mann's style enkindled by d'Annunzio and Balzac (see *GW* 6:181). The critique in *Freistatt* was originally aimed at Heinrich Mann's *Göttinnen*. Thomas Mann raises the same objection to *Die Jagd nach Liebe* in his letter of December 5, 1903. On December 30, 1903, he wrote to Kurt Martens that he had "conducted a very serious and fundamental correspondence" with his brother over the latter's most recent book, *Die Jagd nach Liebe:* "Do you know it? What do you you think? I am quite at a loss."

**Ernst Ritter von Possart** (1841–1921): actor, director. From 1895 to 1905 in charge of the Königlich Bayerische Hofbühnen. See Thomas Mann's "Erinnerungen ans Münchner Residenz-Theater" (*GW* 11:517). Because of the air of "drastic virtuosity" (*GW* 13:284) with which he graced his private as well as professional appearances, Possart became the continual subject of anecdotes.

**Salome/Cavalleria:** Oscar Wilde, *Salome*, a one-act tragedy. First appeared in 1891 in French. English version by Lord Alfred Douglas (1904). German translation by Hedwig Lachmann (1903) (the basis for the opera by Richard Strauss, which premiered on December 9, 1905). Pietro Mascagni, *Cavalleria rusticana* (1890).

**Royal Highness:** Thomas Mann's plans for *Royal Highness* go back to 1903.

**"Wunderbare":** Heinrich Mann, story "Das Wunderbare," *Pan* 2, no. 3 (November 1896): 193–204.

**Otto Grautoff** (1876–1937): s.v., letter of November 25, 1900.

**Grautoff's impossible sham:** *Die Jagd nach Liebe*, 32–34.

**Riva:** refers most likely to the brothers' stay together in Riva in December 1901. It is possible that Heinrich Mann had also visited his brother there in October 1902, on his way to Florence.

**"The Loved Ones" [*Die Geliebten*]:** since the winter of 1901–1902, Thomas Mann had planned a story with the title "Die Geliebten." The plan later became part of the "Maja project," a social novel set in Munich. See Hans Wysling, "Zu Thomas Manns Maja-Projekt," *Thomas-Mann-Studien* 1 (1967): 23–47.

*Göttinnen:* Heinrich Mann, *Die Göttinnen oder Die drei Romane der Herzogin von Assy* (Munich: Langen, 1903). In "Die Geliebten" (The beloved) Thomas Mann is taken to have offered a veiled portrayal of his love for the painter Paul Ehrenberg. In Heinrich Mann's *Göttinnen*, Nino belongs among the beloved, Siebelind to the unbeloved. Siebelind bears resemblances to Thomas Mann (see *Die Göttinnen*, 434).

**Alexander von Fielitz** (1860–1930): composer and conductor. Chief conductor of the Lübecker Stadttheater in Thomas Mann's youth. See Thomas Mann, "Erinnerungen ans Lübecker Stadttheater" (*GW* 11:417).

**Richard Schaukal** (1874–1942): s.v., letter of November 25, 1900.

**deathbed:** *Die Jagd nach Liebe*, 48ff.

**Frà Girolamo:** in Thomas Mann's *Fiorenza* the ascetic counterpart to Lorenzo de' Medici.

**saying of Börne's:** "Uprightness is the source of all genius, and the people would be more ingenious if they were more moral." The statement is from Börne's essay "Die Kunst, in drei Tagen ein Original-Schriftsteller zu werden" (1823), in Ludwig Börne, *Gesammelte Schriften*, (Hamburg, 1862), 2:245.

**Matteo Maria Boiardo** (ca. 1440–1494): writer and translator. Thomas Mann is probably alluding here to the epic *Orlando innamorato* (1495). Luigi Pulci (1432–1484): writer born in Florence, initially the friend of Lorenzo de' Medici. *Il morgante*, a tragicomic chivalric epic in twenty-eight songs (1483), likewise encompasses the fate of Charlemagne and his Paladines.

**"tears":** from Goethe's *Prometheus*.

DECEMBER 23, 1903

**review in *Freistatt*:** see letter of December 5, 1903.

**studies:** "Das Wunderkind," *Neue Freie Presse*, December 25, 1903 (in English: "The Infant Prodigy," in *Stories of Three Decades*). "Ein Glück," *Die neue Rundschau* (January 1904): 85–93 (in English: "A Gleam," in *Stories of Three Decades*).

JANUARY 8, 1904

*The italicized lines were marked in the margin in blue pencil by Heinrich Mann.*

**lines I recently sent:** letter of December 23, 1903.

**indifference:** the letter has not been preserved. In her letter to Heinrich of November 20, 1904, Julia Mann alluded to *Die Jagd nach Liebe* (printed in André Banuls, *Heinrich Mann* [Paris, 1966], 593ff.):

Now my dear Heinrich, to another topic, about which you were generous enough to write to me candidly (by the way, I once again admired your splendid style in the letter, the more so since you surrender yourself entirely to your state of mind). But, Heinrich, I am distressed by just this state of mind, which certainly must be having an effect on your spirits. If that had been the extent of it, that T. and L[öhr]s, like a large part of the reading public, sharply condemned your latest novel—but that you have turned away from your siblings, makes me feel *very sorry* for you. Hold with them, my dear Heinrich, send them a few friendly lines or reviews now and again, and don't let them see that you don't feel yourself to be as highly regarded by the literary world as T. is in the moment—or *if so*, then not in such a way that the feeling puts you out of sorts. You wanted to hold a mirror up to the world and have, in part, gained a harvest of ingratitude and indignation (admittedly: because it hit too close to home)—but, at the same time, have now expressed yourself adequately in this vein (in *my* opinion) and are moving in a new direction, isn't that right? Yet I feel, dear Heinrich, that it's presumptuous of me to want to lay down guidelines for you in your art, but I simply want to be open with you. To come back to the previous point: I find that as long as *personal* feelings among siblings and friends, mother and children are not disturbed, the tie holds; I've had such experiences and at those times done everything a mother can do to prevent the tie from breaking, and it has proved true. Please, please, dear Heinrich, follow my advice and don't withdraw from T. and the L.s; keep your personal charm about you, and from now on demonstrate once again that you are capable of satisfying the more sensitive class of readers. One mustn't be too much an idealist, for then one would indeed be understood by only the smallest share of one's fellows. And Tommy knows, too, that he doesn't receive the praise of absolutely everyone and that not all of what he writes pleases his followers. By the way, when I told him that you had sent me good reviews, his response was approximately: just be proud that H. sends them to you; I and the L.s don't get anything of the sort from him anymore— H. must know himself how highly *I* regard him, despite my finding much in his last novels I can't goûtire—Now that's not unfair, is it?—That you were too daring in *Die Jagd nach Liebe*, in the way you drew well-known Munich figures into it, is somewhat unpleasant for *Löhr* in his position; [ . . . ] but what all doesn't get written and how challenges are issued and wars fought also with the *pen;* you aren't the only one in this position. But, once again, my dear Heinrich, that *other* thing that you're going to write after the translation is also supposed to expose less extreme indecencies, isn't it? I wish *with all my heart* that you would also get your share of public recognition, because, unfortunately, a writer can't do without it, and to *me,* personally, as your mother, unfavorable reviews of one of you cuts every time to the quick; just as approving reviews, like the ones you sent me, and verbal praise and the pecuniary gains of all of you please me very much every time. With the translations you are also doing quite well, no? and that is also something that not everyone can do. You are *both* divinely favored people, dear Heinrich—don't let your personal relationship with T. and the L.s be disturbed; how could a year and a half change it so drastically just because your last work didn't find general acclaim. But that has *nothing to do* with your family relationships! I shall say nothing to them of your letter to me, for you can get things back on track *yourself*—that is, only if you ask me to let T. know *why you* stayed away the whole winter, or to tell the Löhrs that you feel psychologically estranged from T.—then perhaps I would do it; but to me it seems that that would still not be openness toward them from your side, and therefore what I advised above is better.

**Uncle Friedel:** Friedrich Wilhelm Lebrecht Mann (1847–1926), physical model for Christian Buddenbrook. On October 28, 1913, Uncle Friedl leveled the same reproach in a notice in the Lübeck advertisements (s.v., letter of November 11, 1913). In the margin Heinrich Mann wrote in pencil: "Ida Springer."

**Hans Müller,** pseud. Müller-Einigen (1882–1950): J.D., dramatist, writer, theatrical producer. Last residence Einigen am Thunersee. Among his works: *Dämmer,* poems (1900); *Das stärkere Leben,* one-act cycle (1900); *Die lockende Geige,* poems (1904); *Der Garten des Lebens: Eine biblische Dichtung* (1904); *Buch der Abenteuer,* stories (1905); the story "Die Rosen des heiligen Antonius" is included in the latter collection. The beginning of the quote is indicated in the margin with a blue mark. Schaukal's letter has not been preserved, nor the enclosure mentioned.

Gerhard Ouckama Knoop (1861–1913): writer. Among his works: *Die Dekadenten*, novel (1898); *Das Element*, novel (1901); *Outsider*, stories (1901); *Die Grenzen*, novel in two volumes (1903–1905).

**Renate:** Jakob Wassermann, *Die Geschichte der jungen Renate Fuchs* (1900).

**"won't-let-it-count":** quotation from Heinrich Mann's answer to the letter of December 23, 1903.

**Lucifer and a clown:** the formulation "a blend of Lucifer and a clown" recurs in *Geist und Kunst*, note 59 (*Thomas-Mann-Studien*, 1:182), in "Der alter Fontane" (*GW* 9:18), and in Thomas Mann's letter of June 13, 1910, to Samuel Lublinski.

**"Ein Gang vors Thor":** Heinrich Mann, "Ein Gang vors Tor," *Die Insel* 3, no. 1 (October–December 1901): 137–49.

**Löhrs:** Joseph Löhr, Thomas Mann's brother-in-law, and Julia Löhr-Mann, Thomas Mann's sister.

***the character Pico:*** the lines "reaction . . . but must have" are marked in the left margin in pencil, and the words "the character Pico" underlined in addition. The character Pico della Mirandola in *Fiorenza* bears traits of Paul Ehrenberg.

**Heine's book:** Heinrich Heine, *Ludwig Börne*, 22.

**book about Börne:** in *Ludwig Börne*, Heine distinguishes between Nazarenes (Jews and Christians) and "Hellenes" (*Sämtliche Werke* [1876], 12:21): "all people are either Jews or Hellenes, individuals with drives of an ascetic, anti-figural, and relentlessly spiritualizing nature, or individuals obsessed in a more realistic vein with life's cheerfulness and their pride in development. [ . . . ] Börne was wholly Nazarene, his antipathy for Goethe proceeded directly from his Nazarene disposition."

**occasional pieces:** Thomas Mann, "Das Wunderkind," *Neue Freie Presse*, December 25, 1903 (in English: "The Infant Prodigy," in *Stories of Three Decades*). Thomas Mann, "Ein Glück," *Die neue Rundschau* (January 1904): 85–93 (in English: "A Gleam," in *Stories of Three Decades*).

**Gabr. Reuter's new novel:** Thomas Mann, "Gabriele Reuter," *Der Tag* (Berlin), February 14 and 17, 1904. Specifically, a review of her novel *Liselotte von Reckling*.

FEBRUARY 27, 1904

**story:** "Fulvia." The date of the story's composition cannot be determined with certainty. It first appeared in Heinrich Mann, *Flöten und Dolche* (Munich: Langen, 1905).

**Die Jagd nach Liebe:** Heinrich Mann, *Die Jagd nach Liebe* (Munich: Langen, 1903).

**essay:** Thomas Mann, "Gabriele Reuter," *Der Tag* (Berlin), February 14 and 17, 1904.

**dialogue:** "*Fiorenza*, drei Akte von Thomas Mann," *Die neue Rundschau* (July and August 1905): 785ff., 944ff.

**"The Infant Prodigy":** Thomas Mann, "Das Wunderkind," *Neue Freie Presse*, December 25, 1903 (in English: "The Infant Prodigy," in *Stories of Three Decades*).

**new Verein:** on November 11, 1903, the university senate issued a prohibition against the Akademisch-Dramatischer Verein. There followed on December 11, 1903, the founding of the Neuer [new] Verein, an independent literary and artistic society no longer subject to the academic authorities. Chair and executive committee: Josef Ruederer, Dr. Wilhelm Rosenthal, Otto Falckenberg, and Dr. Philipp Witkop.

**Bernsteins:** Max Bernstein (1854–1925), attorney, writer. From 1881 in Munich. Long-time theater critic for the *Münchner neueste Nachrichten*. Wrote comedies in particular.

Elsa Bernstein, née Porges, pseud. Ernst Rosmer (1866–1949), writer. Wife of Max Bernstein. Her dramatic fairy tale *Königskinder* (1895) premiered in 1897 in the Hoftheater (scored later by Humperdinck); it might possibly have influenced *Royal Highness*. Among her other works: *Dämmerung*, play (1893), in English: *Twilight* (1912); *Themistokles*, tragedy (1897); *Nausikaa*, tragedy (1906); *Maria Arndt*, play (1908); *Achill*, tragedy (1910).

In *A Sketch of My Life*, 31 (*GW* 11:116), Thomas Mann writes: "Still, I did begin to frequent a few Munich drawing-rooms, where there was an artistic and literary atmosphere: in particular that of the poetess Ernst Rosmer, the wife of the well-known lawyer Max Bernstein. And thence to the Pringsheim home in Arcisstraße."

**Pringsheims:** Alfred Pringsheim (1850–1941), professor of mathematics at the University of Munich. Passionate Wagnerian, art collector. His house on Arcisstraße was one of the cultural centers of Munich.

Hedwig Pringsheim-Dohm (1855–1942), daughter of Ernst Dohm, the founder and publisher of the Berlin humor magazine *Kladderadatsch*, and Hedwig Dohm, writer and women's rights activist (see *A Sketch of My Life*, 31f. [*GW* 11:116f.], and "Little Grandma," [*GW* 11:467]).

**Franz von Lenbach** (1836–1904): Munich portrait painter (painted, among others, Ludwig I, Liszt, Pope Leo XIII, Eleonora Duse, Paul Heyse, Bismarck, Moltke, Kaiser Wilhelm I).

*giallo antico:* yellow marble. In the story "Beim Propheten" (*GW* 7:366) ("At the Prophet's," *Stories of Three Decades*, 286), Thomas Mann writes of the "rich lady" (Hedwig Pringsheim): "She came from the city in her satin-lined coupé, from her splendid house with the tapestries on the walls and the giallo-antico door-jambs."

**Hans Thoma** (1839–1924): painter. Lived in Munich from 1870 to 1876, where he was close to Leibl, Steinhausen, and Böcklin. Academy professor in Karlsruhe from 1899 to 1919. The wall frieze mentioned here is reproduced in Henry Thode, ed., *Thoma, Des Meisters Gemälde in 874 Abbildungen* (Stuttgart and Leipzig, 1909).

**princely talent for making an impression:** Thomas Mann's plans for *Royal Highness* go back to 1903; on December 5, 1903, he wrote to Walter Opitz: "One leads, I wish to say, a symbolic existence, one devoted to impression, similarly to a prince—and look! In this pathos lies the seed of a quite singular phenomenon, which I'm thinking of writing about some time, a prince novel, counterpart to 'Tonio Kröger,' which is to have the title, *Royal Highness*."

**Klaus Pringsheim** (1883–1972): twin brother of Katja Pringsheim. Conductor. Student of Gustav Mahler, occasionally musical director for Max Reinhardt. Worked for decades in Tokyo.

**Humpty Dumpty:** in Andersen's fairy tale "The Fir Tree." The "short, thick man" tells the story of "Humpty Dumpty, who fell downstairs, and yet came to the throne and won the princess."


MARCH 27, 1904

**the great issue of my life:** in the seventh *Notizbuch* there appears the entry: "Saturday, the 9th of April: Big disc[ussion] with K[atja] P[ringsheim]." On page 132 follows the entry: "Monday, the 16th of May: Second big discussion with K.P. On Thursday the 19th of May began the period of waiting." Major events in the waiting period were those letters to Katja that Thomas Mann later copied in part for use in *Royal Highness* (*Br.* 1:42–57).

**Riva:** Thomas Mann spent from April 16 to May 6, 1904, at the Villa Cristoforo on Lago di Garda, the sanatorium of Christoph Hartung von Hartungen, M.D.

**refer simply to "Katja":** see "Beim Propheten" (*GW* 8:370), "At the Prophet's," *Stories of Three Decades*, 289: "He looked anxiously into her face to see how she would take his speaking simply of Sonia and not of 'Fräulein Sonia' or 'your daughter.'"

**engagement:** it took place on October 3, 1904.

**Berlin:** on November 28, 1904, Thomas Mann traveled with Mrs. Pringsheim and Katja to Berlin and was introduced there to his fiancée's grandmother, the writer Hedwig Dohm. On November 29, 1904, at the Verein für Kunst, he read from "Tonio Kröger," "The Infant Prodigy," and "A Gleam" (all in *Stories of Three Decades*).

**Lübeck:** on December 2, 1904, at the Literarische Gesellschaft, Lübecker Leseabend von 1890, Thomas Mann read from *Fiorenza* and "The Infant Prodigy" (in *Stories of Three Decades*). On the return trip via Berlin, he met with Oscar Bie, the editor of *Die neue Rundschau*.

**titlark:** Julia Löhr-Mann compares Katja with the lark from the fairy tale "The Singing, Soaring Lark," from *Grimm's Fairy Tales* (New York: Pantheon Books, 1944).

**Carla:** sister of Thomas Mann (1881–1910), actress. Heinrich Mann, who was closest to her among all the siblings, took her as the model for the main female character in the novel *Die Jagd nach Liebe* (1903) and the heroine of *Die Schauspielerin* (1906). Carla committed suicide on July 30, 1910, in her mother's apartment in Polling. Heinrich Mann wrote the play *Die Schauspielerin* (1911) in her memory; Thomas Mann portrayed her fate in *A Sketch of My Life*, 35ff. (*GW* 11:119ff.) and in chapter 35 of *Doctor Faustus*, 380ff. (*GW* 6:503ff.).

**my wife:** Thomas Mann's marriage to Katja Pringsheim took place on February 11, 1905, in Munich. They had their honeymoon in Switzerland. On February 23, 1905, the newlyweds returned to Munich.

**Tiergartenstraße:** the family house of Hermann Rosenberg-Pringsheim (Rosenberg, director of the Berliner Handelsgesellschaft, was married to Else Pringsheim, Katja Mann's aunt) was located on Berlin's Tiergartenstraße. "It was splendid," recalls Erika Mann, who stayed repeatedly at the house as a child. "Hedwig Dohm had her modest quarters on the top floor, for which reason the house was also outfitted with a noiseless elevator. There had indeed been automobiles for a long time, but the refined Rosenbergs drove exclusively in their two-horse equipage.—The gift from Tiergartenstraße was by no means ostentatious; to be precise it was simply our silver tea service, just the one which we are still using today. But Thomas Mann, ashamed somehow toward Heinrich because he had married a prosperous girl, was fond of disparaging the gifts from these quarters."

**Gipper-novel:** s.v., letter of March 27, 1901.

**Palestrina:** the brothers spent a few summer weeks in the Casa Bernardini in 1895 and 1897. There Thomas Mann began preliminary work on *Buddenbrooks*. Leverkühn's conversation with the Devil (*Doctor Faustus*, 211ff., 221ff. [*GW* 6:281ff., 294ff.]) is set in Palestrina.

**Guido Biermann** (1846–?): insurance salesman, husband of Alice Haag, a cousin of the brothers. In *Buddenbrooks* he appears as Hugo Weinschenk. See *Buddenbrooks*, 363, 426f, 447, 515 (*GW* 1:438, 524, 553, 640).

**Lübeck:** see Thomas Mann's letter of December 23, 1904.

**Baur au Lac:** it is apparent from a later note to the confidence man novel that Thomas Mann thought of having Felix Krull appear as a waiter in Baur au Lac, Zurich.

**Solneß-crash:** allusion to Ibsen's tragedy *The Master Builder*, which was then being performed again in the Münchner Schauspielhaus.

**Bie:** s.v., letter of December 5, 1903.

**Hermann Bahr** (1863–1934): Viennese writer and critic. Studied political economy as well as law and classical philology, in Vienna, Berlin, and other places. Was acquainted with Arno Holz during his Berlin period (1884–1887). Managed, with Otto Brahm, the Freie Bühne. As of 1894, critic in Vienna; for a time one of the major figures of Junger Wien. Copublisher of the liberal magazine *Die Zeit.* In 1906–1907 producer for Max Reinhardt in Berlin. Residence as of 1912 in Salzburg; chief producer of the Vienna Burgtheater in 1918–1919. From 1922 in Munich. Among his early works: *Die neuen Menschen,* play (1887); *Die Mutter,* play (1891); *Neben der Liebe,* novel (1891); *Theater,* novel (1897); *Der Meister,* comedy (1904; in English: *The Master,* 1918). The young Thomas Mann was impressed by Bahr's "nervous romanticism" and dedicated the prose sketch "Vision" (*Der Frühlingssturm* [1893], *GW* 8:9) to him. Bahr's *Kritik der Moderne* (1890) and *Die Überwindung des Naturalismus* (1891) also influenced him. When it became apparent that Bahr's theatrical nature left him open to all tendencies, Thomas Mann turned away from him (see letter to Kurt Martens of January 11, 1910, *Br.* 1:79; in English: *Letters of Thomas Mann 1889–1955,* 55–56). The quotation comes from Hermann Bahr, "Dialog vom Marsyas," *Die neue Rundschau* (1904): 1187.

**"Schauspielerin":** story by Heinrich Mann (Leipzig, 1906); s.v., Thomas Mann's letter of January 17, 1906.

**Hermione von Preuschen,** actually Hermine von Zitelmann (1857–1918): painter and writer. Heinrich Mann is supposedly portrayed in the story "Monte Brè," which appeared in 1901 in the collection *Lebenssphinx.*

OCTOBER 15–17, 1905

**Rudolf Johannes Schmied** (1878–1935): writer. Brother of Ines Schmied, the girlfriend of Heinrich Mann at the time. Schmied was born in Buenos Aires. Little is known of his life. In Berlin he frequented the Café Größenwahn (Romanisches Café) and Café des Westens, where he was admired in the circle of Paul Schneebart, Ludwig Rubiner, van Hoddis, and Else Lasker-Schüler as a great teller of anecdotes. He spent the last decades of his life in South America. He died on May 2, 1935, in Trinidad, Paraguay. On October 12, 1905, Schmied read at the Neuer Verein in Munich from his book *Carlos und Nicolas, Kinderjahre in Agentinien,* which was published in 1906 by Piper. (Heinrich Mann reviewed the work under the title "Doppelte Heimat," in *Mnais und Ginerva* [Munich: Piper, 1906], 77–80.) The second part, *Carlos und Nicolas auf dem Meere,* appeared in 1909.

**Riva:** Dr. von Hartungen's sanatorium in Riva on Lago di Garda.

**Hans von Gumppenberg** (1866–1928): writer, theater critic of the *Münchner neueste Nachrichten.* Member of the cabaret Die elf Scharfrichter. Gumppenberg's report concerning Schmied's evening of readings appeared in the *Münchner neueste Nachrichten* of October 13, 1905.

**Felix Salten,** actually Siegmund Salzmann (1869–1947): writer. Became the Burgtheater critic for the *Wiener Allgemeine Zeitung,* later feuilleton editor for *Die Zeit,* and in 1906 for *Die Berliner Morgenpost.* Finally, theater reporter for the *Neue Freie Presse* in Vienna. Emigrated to the United States in 1933. Among his works: "Die kleine Veronika," story (1903); "Der Schrei der Liebe," story (1904); *Wiener Adel,* essays (1905); *Das Buch der Königen,* caricatures (1905); later: *Bambi* (1923; English version, 1928). Salten's essay "Gottes Segen bei Bong" (about Edward Stilgebauer, *Götz Krafft, Die Geschichte einer Jugend* [Berlin, 1904–1905]) appeared in *Die Zeit,* October 1, 1905.

**Georg [Freiherr] von Ompteda** (1863–1931): writer. Published novels (at first under the pseudonym Georg Egerstoff) that were very popular at the time. Translated Maupassant. His *Erinnerungen* appeared in 1927–1928 in *Velhagen & Klasings Monatsheften.*

**Schaukal:** the letter to Schaukal has not been preserved. Schaukal had sent Thomas Mann a "fat manuscript" for him to arrange to have published by Fischer (see Thomas Mann's letter of March 13, 1906).

**engagement announcement:** Paul Ehrenberg had become engaged to the painter Lilly Teufel (see "The Hungry," in *Stories of Three Decades; GW* 8:263).

*Fiorenza:* published in book form by S. Fischer, Berlin, 1906.

**Julie Wassermann-Speyer** (1876–1963): first wife of Jakob Wassermann. Wrote *Jakob Wassermann und sein Werk* (1923) and *Das lebendige Herz, Roman einer Ehe* (1928). Essay not identified.

*Zukunft* **contribution:** Heinrich Mann, "Jungfrauen," story, in *Die Zukunft*, October 7, 1905, 31–37. Reprinted in *Stürmische Morgen* (Munich: Langen, 1906). The little girls Ada and Claire are possibly drawn on the models of Julia and Carla Mann.

**Tiergarten story:** the story "Wälsungsblut" (in English: "The Blood of the Walsungs," in *Stories of Three Decades*) is set, like Heinrich Mann's *Cockaigne*, in the Tiergarten district in Berlin. In the letter of February 27, 1904, Thomas Mann described the Pringsheim house on Arcisstraße as "Tiergarten with genuine culture" (s.v., letter of February 18, 1905).

**"temptations":** Gustave Flaubert, *Die Versuchung des heiligen Antonius*, trans. F. Paul Greve (Minden: Bruns, 1905); French original: *La tentation de saint Antoine* (Paris: Carpentier, 1874).

**birth of the child:** Erika Mann, born November 9, 1905, died August 27, 1969; see Thomas Mann's letter of November 20, 1905.

**art trip:** Thomas Mann traveled to Dresden and Breslau in December 1905 to give readings.


OCTOBER 22, 1905

**this work:** *Fiorenza.*

**feuilleton:** Editha du Rieux, "Renaissance," *Fremden-Blatt* (Vienna), October 15, 1905. *Fiorenza* was characterized here as an "extremely interesting work of the cleverly pondering, reasonable north German."


NOVEMBER 20, 1905

**part of** *Buddenbrooks:* Thomas Mann had dedicated part eight of the novel to his brother: "To my brother Heinrich, in honor of the person and the writer." It begins with the Weinschenk episode that the two brothers had once planned together as the "Gipper-novel" (see Thomas Mann's letter of February 18, 1905). Heinrich Mann refers to this collective plan in his reminiscences, *Ein Zeitalter wird besichtigt* (Stockholm: Neuer Verlag, 1945), 243.

**story:** "Abdankung," *Simplicissimus*, January 22, 1906, 508f. and 511. Dedication: "To my brother Thomas." See Thomas Mann's letter of January 22, 1906.

**a girl:** Erika Mann was born on November 9, 1905.

**"The Blood of the Walsungs":** on the original conclusion of this story, s.v., Thomas Mann's letter of December 5, 1905.

**Gustav Frenssen** (1863–1945): writer. Studied theology. From 1890 to 1902, pastor in Hennstedt and Hemme (Dithmarschen). In *Jörn Uhl* (1901; English version, 1905) he depicted the Low German people and established his fame as an author of novels of the homeland; see Thomas Mann's letter to Kurt Martens of October 16, 1902 (*Br.* 1:36), and *A Sketch of My Life*, 28; (*GW* 11:114). From 1902 a freelance writer in Meldorf; 1906–1912 in Blanksee; after 1916 in Barlt. The novel mentioned here might have been *Hilligenlei* (1905). Among his other works: *Der Pastor von Poggsee*, novel (1921; in English: *The Pastor of Poggsee*, 1931); *Lebens-bericht* (1940).

DECEMBER 5, 1905

**trip:** Thomas Mann gave readings in Prague, Dresden, and Breslau (see letter of January 17, 1906).

**"The Blood of the Walsungs":** the story was supposed to appear in the January issue of *Die neue Rundschau* but was withdrawn by Thomas Mann in accord with the wishes of his father-in-law. The book edition was first published by Phantasus-Verlag, Munich, in 1921, with lithographs by Th. Th. Heine. The conclusion printed there corresponds to the variant under consideration here, which is also known now from the *Gesammelte Werke* in twelve volumes (Frankfurt, 1960) (*GW* 8:410), and the English version in *Stories of Three Decades*, 319. The conclusion objected to by Bie is appended as a "textual variant" in the *Gesammelte Werke*: "Oh," he said—and for a second the marks of his race stood out strong upon his face—"what about him? *Beganeft* him, we have—the goy!" (The Yiddish expression *beganeft* means roughly "deceive, cheat." *Goy* [people] in Biblical language signifies all peoples, including the Jewish; in later times it serves primarily to designate foreign, non-Jewish peoples and is frequently used in a derogatory sense.)

The translation changed on Bie's wishes had already been printed at the end of 1905. The proofs were ultimately used as packing material, and by accident the bookseller's apprentice Rudolf Brettschneider noticed that it contained a text by Thomas Mann. He later wrote a report about his discovery (*Die Bücherstube* [Munich, 1920], 110–20):

> One day I unpacked another big shipment, thereby gathering a whole bunch of such waste sheets with Tiemann's initials on them. At noon I took them home with me and, as I was eating my soup, I began casually reading the printed sheets lying there before me on the table. I read one page and a second. "A devilishly good style!" I'm thinking. "From whom might it be?" I read on, attentive and anxious. By dessert I feel quite sure of myself: that was Thomas Mann. I searched through all the sheets. No title to be found, no beginning, far and wide no author identified. Well, then! The main thing is that I've enriched my Tiemann alphabet by twelve letters. I lit a cigarette and returned to my bookshop.
>
> The next Sunday I was invited to Dr. F.B.'s for tea. A small circle of artists and literary sorts met there regularly and nothing, such things being as they are, was discussed but art and literature. Criticism, projects, wicked anecdotes, gossip from Schwabing, funny and sometimes quite sarcastic exchanges. Suddenly the name Thomas Mann comes up. Someone is telling of a new story by the master, a story that was supposed to have appeared in *Die neue Rundschau*, but which had been withdrawn from publication for reasons of a private nature. Fischer is supposed to have assumed the burden of having the issue scrapped and pulped. For quite some time the conversation turned on this interesting topic. One of those present even knew the title of the story: "The Blood of the Walsungs" it was supposed to be called.—I sat silently in my armchair and attended with open ears to every word. My scrap sheets came back to mind. Heavens! that would be such a find! To possess an unpublished story by Thomas Mann. A copy, an unique example, of this pulped first edition! And there was no doubt. The crumpled sheets that I had put away in my desk contained a fragment of the curious story; the name Thomas Mann had occurred to me spontaneously during my hurried reading. And that which I had read, that could quite well go with the title "The Blood of the Walsungs." Presumably, however, I had only a small piece of the text in my hands. And perhaps the story was to have appeared in several installments?—I quickly took my leave, for I could scarcely wait to get home and arrange my scrap sheets to check for their completeness. As far as I could tell, all that was missing was the first page. [ . . . ]

The next day was Monday and another book shipment from Leipzig was scheduled to arrive. To hope that it once again included scrap sheets of Thomas Mann's story, and, moreover, that they would be precisely the ones I was missing, was almost absurd, clear insanity, an absolute impossibility.—But just this absurd, insane impossibility is what happened. The shipment included two packages from the S. Fischer Verlag, and one of them was packed in the sheets I was missing. My joy knew no bounds; entranced I looked at that crumpled but so valuable sheet of paper. "The Blood of the Walsungs. Story by Thomas Mann" was the heading of the first page, nicely printed and adorned with a large Tiemann initial. Now my unique example was complete. At home I put the sheets carefully together, moistened and pressed them, and fastened them together in a cover of pretty colored paper.

"The Blood of the Walsungs" was for a time without doubt the most valuable holding in my then still quite modest library.

See Thomas Mann's letter of February 6, 1906, to Samuel Fischer. And further, the detailed report by Klaus Pringsheim, "Ein Nachtrag zu 'Wälsungsblut,'" *Neue Zürcher Zeitung*, December 17, 1961.

**new novel:** Heinrich Mann, *Zwischen den Rassen* (Leipzig: Langen, 1907). Begun in 1905 in Rossholzen bei Brannenburg; finished 1907. The mother's memoirs appeared later as a book: Julia Mann, *Aus Dodo's Kindheit* (Constance, 1958).

**article for Die M. Neueste Nachrichten:** "Bilse und ich," *Münchner neueste Nachrichten*, February 15–16, 1906 (*GW* 10:9–22).

**reply in Die Lübecker Anzeigen:** Thomas Mann, "Ein Nachwort," *Lübecker Generalanzeiger*, November 7, 1905. The writer Richard Dohse from Lübeck wrote a novel in which the character portrayals were all too similar to people from Tondern. An attorney by the name of Ritter brought suit against the writer. The plaintiff was represented by the Lübeck attorney Enrico von Brocken. The latter brought up *Buddenbrooks* to support the suit against Dohse, calling it a "novel à la Bilse." Fritz Oswald Bilse (Fritz von der Kyrburg) was the author of a novel *Aus einer kleinen Garnison, Ein militärische Zeitbild* (Braunschweig, 1903). Thomas Mann did not relish being compared to Bilse and protested with the article "Ein Nachwort" (*GW* 11:546–49). Shortly thereafter he followed up with the essay "Bilse und ich" (s.v., above).

**Maximilian Harden,** originally Maximilian Felix Ernst Witkowski (1861–1927): Berlin essayist and journalist. Founded in 1892 the leading weekly *Die Zukunft*, in which he sharply opposed the policies of Wilhelm II. His unceasing support for democratic ideas won him many enemies in the ranks of the radical nationalists and anti-Semites. In 1923 he gave up his journalistic activity and withdrew to Switzerland. Among his early works: *Literatur und Theater* (1896); *Kampfgenosse Sudermann* (1903; in English: *Word Portraits*, 1911); *Köpfe*, essays, 4 vols. (1905–1915).

**Frank Wedekind** (1864–1918): dramatist and actor. Youth in Schloß Lenzburg/Aargau. Studied law and journalism. From 1886, advertising manager for the firm Maggi in Kemptthal bei Zürich. From 1888, secretary of the Herzog circus. Then freelance writer in Zurich and Paris; after 1890, mostly in Munich. From 1896, contributor to *Simplicissimus* (imprisoned 1899–1900 for *lèse-majesté*). 1901–1902 director, reciter, and singer for the cabaret Die elf Scharfrichter. Married to the actress Mathilde (Tilly) Newes. In 1906 member of the Deutsches Theater in Berlin; then back to Munich. Had written by then, among other works: *Frühlingserwachen*, play (1891; in English: *Spring's Awakening*, 1952); *Der Erdgeist*, tragedy (1895, 1903 under the title *Lulu*; in English: *Earth-Spirit*, 1952); *Der Marquis von Keith*, play (1901; English version, 1990); *Die Büchse Pandora*, tragedy (1904; in English: *Pandora's Box*, 1972); *Hidalla*, play (1904). The Mann brothers, especially Heinrich, were friends of his. Along with other writers, they voiced their opposition to the harassment of Wedekind's work by police and censorship authorities. Both contributed to the protest volume *Für Frank Wedekind*, in honor of his fiftieth birthday on July 24, 1914. Heinrich Mann wrote several essays about Wedekind, among them: "Über Wedekind, Wie ich ihn kennenlernte," *Das Forum* 1, no. 4 (July 1914): 246–47; "Zu Ehren Wedekinds," *Berliner Tageblatt,* March 22, 1918 (eulogy); "Erinnerung an Frank Wedekind," *Neuer Zürcher Zeitung,* June 20–21, 1923; "Wedekind und sein Publikum," *Frankfurter Zeitung,* March 13, 1928 (memorial address on the tenth anniversary of Wedekind's death, delivered March 13, 1928, in the Münchner Schauspielhaus). In *Ein Zeitalter wird besichtigt,* he counted Wedekind among his "companions"; in the comedy *Das Strumpfband* (written in 1902), he had Wedekind appear in the character of the bohemian Killich. In 1914, Thomas Mann wrote the essay "Über eine Szene von Wedekind" (*GW* 10:70).

**Carlyle's *Frederick the Great:*** Thomas Mann probably used the abridged edition in one volume, prepared and introduced by Karl Linnebach (Berlin, 1905) (see *GW* 10:568). A roughly contemporary full-length English original is Thomas Carlyle, *History of Friedrich the Second, Called Frederick the Great,* 7 vols. (New York: Collier, 1921).

**malice:** Thomas Mann learned about the "malice of understanding" above all in Nietzsche's critique of Wagner. In his ninth *Notizbuch,* 58f. (1908) he remarked: "Nothing is of more burning interest than the critique of modernity: I felt that already at nineteen, when I read Nietzsche's critique of Wagner for the first time. [ . . . ] Germany is lacking in psychology, understanding, sensitiveness, the *malice* of understanding, it lacks critical passion." He used the passage in his polemic against Theodor Lessing (see *GW* 11:723).

**the prince of Prussia, who was in love with Voss:** August Wilhelm, prince of Prussia (1722–1758); Sophie Marie, countess von Voss (1729–1814), lady in waiting at the court of the Prussian king.

**event in Munich:** Bahr's Munich plans were never realized; Hans Wagner's *Münchner Theaterchronik* (Munich, 1958) reported on March 14, 1906: "The disagreeable case of Hermann Bahr has been brought to an end. The engagement of the writer as theatrical producer has been irrevocably canceled. Bahr is withdrawing, having collected a settlement of 24,000 marks."


JANUARY 17, 1906

**Christmas present:** Heinrich Mann, *Schauspielerin,* story (Vienna: Wiener Verlag, 1906; Bibliothek moderner deutscher Autoren, vol. 12). In this story Heinrich Mann refers to his relationship with his sister Carla.

**newspaper installments:** a previous printing of *Schauspielerin* has not been identified. See Thomas Mann's letter of February 18, 1905.

**Bahr:** see letter of December 5, 1905.

**Basel:** at the end of January and beginning of February 1906, Thomas Mann gave two readings in Basel (from *Fiorenza,* "The Infant Prodigy," and "A Weary Hour"). The readings were organized by the Allgemeine Lesegesellschaft. See the report on the first evening by E. J., in the *Basler Nachrichten,* February 2, 1906, 1.

**Aunt Elisabeth:** Maria Elisabeth Hippolythe Haag, née Mann (1838–1917). Sister of Senator Mann. Model for Tony Buddenbrook. See Viktor Mann, *Wir waren fünf,* 39f.

**popularity:** Thomas Mann returned to this topic later in "Versuch über das Theater," and then again in the notes for *Geist und Kunst.*

**dignity:** in the left margin Heinrich noted in pencil: "And the 'great men' are supposed to be equal to the dignity of their object, their people, their ideas?"

**big-city novel:** Thomas Mann was then gathering material for a social novel set in Munich, which was probably conceived as the counterpart to Heinrich's *Cockaigne.* The work was supposed to have the Schopenhauerian title *Maja;* the illusionary aspect of life and the world was to have been its theme. Thomas Mann later surrendered the projected novel to Gustav von Aschenbach. But he eventually made use of the collected material himself, in the Munich chapter of *Doctor Faustus.*

**"Schiller":** Thomas Mann, "Schwere Stunde," *Simplicissimus,* May 9, 1905 (in English: "A Weary Hour," in *Stories of Three Decades).*

**skepticism:** marginal comment by Heinrich Mann: "So there is such a thing then as the enthusiastic skeptic."

**Schiller's letters to Goethe:** on December 29, 1797, Schiller wrote:

> If the drama is really being patronized by the bad tendency of the age, as I have no doubt it is, one would need to begin the reform with the drama, and obtain air and light by suppressing the common imitation of nature in art. And this, it seems to me, could among other things be most successfully accomplished by the introduction of symbolical expedients, which should take the place of the subject in all that which does not belong to the true artistic world of the poet, and which therefore should not be represented, only indicated. I have not yet quite succeeded in unravelling this idea of the symbolical in poetry, but it seems to me that a great deal is contained in it. If its use were defined, the natural consequence would be that poetry would become purified, its sphere narrower and more significant, and be the more effective within this limit.
>
> I always had a certain faith in the Opera, that, out of it as out of the Choruses of the ancient festival of Bacchus, tragedy would develop into a nobler form. In the opera one really does drop those servile imitations of nature, and—even though it were only under the name of indulgence—the ideal might in this manner steal its way on to the stage. The opera, by means of the power of music and a freer fascination of the senses by harmony, places the mind in a finer state of susceptibility; here we actually have a freer play even in the pathos itself, inasmuch as it is accompanied by music, and the element of marvel which is here tolerated, necessarily makes one more indifferent to the subject-matter. (*Correspondence Between Schiller and Goethe, from 1794 to 1805,* trans. L. Dora Schmitz [London: George Bell and Sons, 1877], 1:458–59)

**friendship and family:** Heinrich Mann was associating at the time with Ines (Nena) Schmied and her brother Rudolf Schmied.

**article:** "Bilse und ich," *Münchner neueste Nachrichten,* February 15–16, 1906.

JANUARY 22, 1906

**story:** Heinrich Mann, "Abdankung," *Simplicissimus,* January 22, 1906, 508ff.

**Klösterlein:** Erika Mann has written to us in this regard: "The person meant is a certain Mr. Achim von Klösterlein, who was a writer and made himself immortal among us through a reading of a story of his own authorship. The first sentence of this story—delivered very significantly—was: 'The Jordan stinks.' Whether Klösterlein ever published anything we don't know. And otherwise as well we know absolutely nothing about him."

MARCH 13, 1906

**Schaukal:** in *Zeitgeist* (supplement to the *Berliner Tageblatt,* March 5, 1906) Schaukal published a devastating review of *Fiorenza* under the title "Thomas Mann und die Renaissance." The second paragraph reads as follows:

> Yet it cannot but seem to me as if the relationship of the brilliant novelist to this theme, which he so ardently loves—"worldly she-devils versus Mind"—is to be compared to the

most fervid and unrequited passion: in both cases, the story and the "drama," the theme maintains a cool distance from the tireless suitor. "Gladius Dei" leaves the reader with an equivocal impression one might describe by the casual formula "neither warm nor cold." *Fiorenza* achieves no effect whatever: a frosty coldness emanates from the work. Only the author—doubly and trebly loquacious in the presence of these oppositions—has leave to speak; but the beloved Fiorenza declines to yield to the verbosity. What is the cause of this utter failure? Why could Thomas Mann, the creator, the form-giver, the unsurpassable master of his creations, not in this case cross over the invisible boundary that distinguishes in the realm of art the living character from the caricature? Is it simply a matter of the material? But in that case at least the contours of Mann the artist would have to remain distinctly intact, the reader would have to be able to recover from the obvious failure of the Savonarola-writer by way of a sympathy that finds satisfaction in the winning visage of his earlier triumphant self. But that is not at all the way it is. Mann also loses, and not only in terms of the position that he, defeated and humiliated, comes to occupy. The writer of "Tonio Kröger" is scarcely to be recognized in the pale flashes of a few characteristic moments. This time he behaves (astonishingly, as his admirer acknowledges) like one of those new epigones ill-famed in good society: literary to the marrow. Might this be an essential trait, one previously hidden, of the otherwise so measured and tactful author? "Gladius Dei" supplies the answer: Mann is not *à son aise*, he feels embarrassed and conceals his embarrassment behind verbal convolutions. It's a matter of the relationship, which proves itself unfruitful. One thing becomes clear: Mann is not a writer who will go on surprising us, is no Proteus; he lacks versatility. Where he cannot charmingly and comfortably be entirely himself he will inevitably disappoint. Uhland, Giebel, Saar, as dramatists, Grillparzer, Kleist as poets, Hebbel as novelist: there simply are limits. This is not to be understood in the sense that Mann would be incapable of writing another excellent play for us; it is not a failure in the sphere of the drama that must regrettably be identified here, but rather a complete failure, determined by the violence of the undertaking, in the larger sphere of the literary. That *Fiorenza* presents us with no "drama" is of little import. Kleist's wonderful Penthesilea, Grabbe's Napoleon, the renaissance scenes of Count Gobineau are equally inadequate if judged from the angle of their suitability for the stage. In *Fiorenza*—the reader (dumbfounded) becomes increasingly conscious of this with continued, dull reading—Mann's helplessness is that of a writer; and—this must be emphasized—the effect is not "dilettantish," which would remain warm-blooded, but thin, poor, lifeless, that is, "literary." In the manner of d'Annunzio and his imitators, the stretches between the conversations are crowded with scenic word painting. Long-winded emotional outpourings, autobiographies, as if gliding out on heraldic bends through automated lips, replace characterization, the unfolding of the self from within. First the more or less indifferent historical name; at the end an annulated string of carefully appended "gems," proof of diligent research, but in themselves soulless talk, mere material, and—not even inadequate. And the whole is assembled of disconnected, stylized ornaments, delivered in that tortured language of modernity such as adolescent snobs cultivate everywhere nowadays. Not even does it lack those stylistic remisses, the crude infractions of the rules of grammar, which accompany the wilful ornamentation with the scoffing titter of the "object."

In his letter of March 28, 1906, to Kurt Martens, Thomas Mann makes reference to this review (*Br.* 1:64; English version in *Letters of Thomas Mann*, 51). Although Heinrich Mann could not yet have forgotten his brother's attacks on *Die Göttinnen* and *Die Jagd nach Liebe*, he offered his assistance by stating his opposition to Schaukal in an open letter to Maximilian Harden: "Mache," *Die Zukunft*, March 31, 1906, 500–502. A further installment followed in *Die Zukunft* of April 4, 1906: an open letter from Richard Schaukal (74–76) and Heinrich Mann's response (76).

**that letter from me:** see Thomas Mann's letter of October 15, 1905, s.v. Schaukal.

**Dresden:** in May 1906 Thomas Mann entered the sanatorium Weißer Hirsch, where his publisher Samuel Fischer put him up in the Villa Thalblick. The resort was directed by Dr. Heinrich Lahmann and was very popular in the 1920s. Nevertheless, Thomas Mann wrote to Fischer on July 15, 1906 (*Brw. Fischer, 406): "In terms of my health, Lahmann has been of no use whatsoever, not in the slightest. Afterwards I was even more tired and gloomy than before." In order to fully recuperate, Thomas Mann had already written to Fischer on May 25, 1906, "one would have to keep at the business for six months, even a year—which is not to be endured." See the introduction of the story "Railway Accident," in *Stories of Three Decades*, 320 (*GW* 8:416). On the trip he took with him the notes and beginning of the manuscript of the "Fürsten-Novelle."

**Venice:** the trip seems not to have taken place. During his summer stay in Oberammergau Thomas Mann worked on *Royal Highness*, which he had meanwhile reconceived as a novel (see letter of July 15, 1906, to Samuel Fischer, Brw. Fischer, 406f.).

MARCH 21, 1906

**article:** Heinrich Mann, "Mache," *Die Zukunft*, March 31, 1906, 500–502. See Thomas Mann's letter of March 13, 1906, to Heinrich and of March 20, 1906, to Maximilian Harden (unpublished, Thomas-Mann-Archiv, Zurich).

**Samuel Lublinski** (1868–1910): dramatist and critic. At the time he was regarded, alongside Paul Ernst and Wilhelm von Scholz, as the most renowned representative of neoclassical drama. After naturalistic early works, he wrote historical tragedies that follow in the footsteps of Hebbel: *Der Imperator* (1900); *Hannibal* (1902); *Elizabeth und Essex* (1903); *Peter von Rußland* (1906); *Gunther und Brunhild* (1908); *Kaiser und Kanzler* (1910). In a review in the *Berliner Tageblatt* in 1901, Lublinski was one of the first to praise *Buddenbrooks*. In his *Bilanz der Moderne* (1904) he named Thomas Mann the most significant novelist of the time without reservation. His critical commentary on the times, *Ausgang der Moderne* (1909), confirmed his reputation as one of the shrewdest critics of naturalism and neoromanticism. Beginning in 1904, Thomas Mann carried on a correspondence with him. When Lublinski was attacked by Theodor Lessing in 1910, Thomas Mann came to his defense in several polemical essays (see "Der Doktor Lessing," *GW* 11:719ff., and *Thomas-Mann-Studien*, *GW* 1:108ff).

JUNE 7–8, 1906

**Stürmische Morgen:** volume of stories by Heinrich Mann (Munich: Langen, 1906); including: "Heldin," "Der Unbekannte," "Jungfrauen," "Abdankung."

**the one dedicated to me:** "Abdankung."

**Björnson:** Maximilian Harden, in an essay entitled "Ibsen" (*Die Zukunft*, June 2, 1906), quoted from an essay that Björnstjerne Björnson had published years previously in the same journal (311f.): "The dramatist's intellectual force probably achieves its strongest expression in his psychology; and in Ibsen's work the latter is not always possessed of a solid basis. The structure is always exemplary; thus, for example, in *Nora*; but the foundation on which it rests leaves much to be desired; that is, Nora (who lies—and who is more worldly-wise than those who are able to lie?) is not supposed to know what a forgery is. The precondition for the plot of *The Wild Duck* is that the fourteen-year-old martyr believes her father, although that babbler is scarcely capable of uttering a true word. Now, we all know that no one can discern more quickly than a child whether the words of those on whom one depends may be trusted. Hedwig had certainly known what the situation was since she was four years old; if anyone doubts this, just consider the mother! How it could happen that the good professor in *Hedda Gabler*, who had been raised by women, would bring Hedda home with him as his wife—that is certainly just as incomprehensible as the circumstance that this dynamite-charged lady could endure for approximately thirty years before ever even the smallest explosion occurred, and without those around knowing how things stood with her. In addition, there is the daring application of studies of suggestion, hypnotism, and heredity. The still little understood power of heredity Ibsen takes as greater than upbringing, which he fails to consider in the slightest."

**Lothar Brieger-Wasservogel,** actually Brieger (1879–1949): Berlin bookseller and art critic. Among his works: *Max Klinger* (1902); *Auguste Rodin* (1902); *Deutsche Maler* (1903); *Plato und Aristoteles* (1905); *Der Fall Liebermann. Über das Virtuosentum in der bildenden Kunst* (1906); *Die Darstellung der Frau in der modernen Kunst* (1906). Possibly the reference here is to the series "Aus der Gedankenwelt grosser Meister," which Brieger-Wasservogel had edited since 1906.

**Georg Hirschfeld** (1873–1942): dramatist and story writer. Promoted by Brahm, Hauptmann, and Fontane. Had already written, among other works, at the time: *Dämon Kleist*, story (1895); *Zu Hause*, play (1896); *Die Mutter*, play (1896; in English: *The Mothers*, 1916); *Agnes Jordan*, play (1897); *Der Weg zum Licht*, fairy-tale play (1902); *Nebeneinander*, play (1904).

**Hugo Salus** (1866–1929): poet and story writer. As of 1895, gynecologist in Prague. Had written to this date, among other works: *Gedichte*, poems (1898); *Susanna im Bade*, play (1901); *Ernte*, poems (1903); *Novellen des Lyrikers*, stories (1904).

**Toni Schwabe** (1877–1951): writer. Lived until 1950 in Bad Blankenburg, finally in Weimar. Among her early works: *Ein Liebeslied* (1900); *Die Hochzeit der Esther Franzenius*, novel (first edition 1902, second edition 1905); *Die Stadt mit lichten Türmen*, novel (1903). See Thomas Mann's letter of December 5, 1903.

JUNE 11, 1906

**your fiancée:** Ines Schmied, singer, born in Buenos Aires in 1883, sister of Rudolf Schmied; companion of Heinrich Mann from ca. 1905 to 1910, regarded as his fiancée. Julia Mann, the mother, wrote on April 20, 1908, to Ludwig Ewers: "Heinrich, inimitable as usual, got himself engaged in Florence a year and a half ago without letting us know. About three weeks ago in Munich he suddenly introduced his fiancée to me, Ines Schmied, from Buenos Aires, medium-sized, elegant, golden blond, goldish-brown eyes, complexion like milk and blood, amiable, like a good fairy. They've recently gone to the Hotel-Pension Windsor in Meran. Before long they will marry just as noiselessly as they found each other!" Viktor Mann, in *Wir waren fünf*, reports (291f.): "When Heinrich came to Munich in those years, which did not happen very often, he stayed in a pension on Türkenstraße, and we usually met only at Mama's. Once, however, I met him in the foyer of a varieté and was introduced to a woman of such beauty that the effect was almost shocking. I had to think immediately of Señora da Silva and Lola in *Zwischen den Rassen*. And in fact I learned that the woman came originally from South America. Unfortunately, I never met her again." The marriage never took place. Ines Schmied is taken to be the model for the young Branzilla and Lola (*Zwischen den Rassen*) and Flora Garlinda (*Die kleine Stadt* [Leipzig: Insel-Verlag, 1909]; in English, *The Little Town*).

**Zieblandstraße:** information as to when Heinrich Mann lived on Munich's Zieblandstraße has not been discovered.

**Eckerthal:** Heinrich Mann was staying at the time in the Harz mountains.

*Maja:* see Thomas Mann's letter of January 17, 1906, s.v. big city novel.

**stories:** among the stories planned at the time was "Bekenntnisse des Hochstaplers Felix Krull" (in English: "Felix Krull," in *Stories of Three Decades*).

**Otto Erich Hartleben** (1864–1905): writer. Contributor to the art and literary journal *Pan*. As of 1901 mostly in Munich. Among his works: *Angele*, comedy (1891); *Die Geschichte vom abgerissene Knopfe*, stories (1893); *Vom gastfreien Pastor*, stories (1895); *Die sittliche Forderung*, comedy (1897); *Der römische Maler*, stories (1898); *Rosenmontag*, tragedy (1900; in English: *Love's Carnival*, 1904); *Meine Verse*, poems (1902); *Liebe kleine Mama*, stories (1904); *Diogenes*, scenes of a comedy in verse (1905); *Tagebuch*, diary (1906).


MAY 27, 1907

**Grand Hôtel:** probably refers to Thomas Mann's trip to Venice (May 1907), where he seems to have met Heinrich Mann.

**Fiorenza:** the premiere took place on May 11, 1907, in the Frankfurt Schauspielhaus. Thomas and Katja Mann attended a performance on May 23, 1907.

**Zwischen den Rassen:** novel by Heinrich Mann (Munich: Langen, 1907).

**Carl Busse** (1872–1918): writer, critic. As of 1893 mostly in Berlin. In the *Zwanzigsten Jahrhundert* 6, no. 1 (October 1895): 468–72, an article appeared in which the author—presumably Heinrich Mann—made fun of "form-lyricist Busse's pretty talent." In November 1906 Busse wrote in *Velhagen & Klasings Monatsheften* 21, no. 3: 383: "Whipped up fantasy with an inner coldness . . . And the writings that result from it, no matter if they are called *Die Göttinnen* or *Die Jagd nach Liebe*, *Flöten und Dolche* or *Professor Unrat* [*The Blue Angel*], *Stürmische Morgen* or whatever they are called, and no matter how much 'art' they might contain individually, they belong to that category of works which I will fight to my dying breath." (Heinrich Mann still recalls the review in his letter of July 20, 1947, to Karl Lemke.)

**Hesse:** the review to which Thomas Mann is referring here could not be identified. Hesse had reviewed *Tristan*, a collection of stories, in *Die neue Zürcher Zeitung* of December 5, 1903.


JUNE 7, 1907

**you've finished something else:** "Die Branzilla" or "Die Tyrann," stories published in Heinrich Mann, *Die Bösen* (Leipzig: Insel-Verlag, 1908). "Die Branzilla" had presumably already appeared around the end of 1906 in the Vienna weekly *Die Zeit*.

**with your last one:** *Zwischen den Rassen*.

**breaking up our household:** Thomas Mann and his family spent the summer in Seeshaupt on the Starnberger See, where Heinrich Mann visited him in August.

**Ryl. Highness:** s.v., Thomas Mann's letter of March 25, 1909.

**Polling:** village near Weilheim (called Pfeiffering in *Doctor Faustus*). Mrs. Julia Mann had rented an apartment there.


JUNE 19, 1907

**Lula:** Julia Löhr-Mann (1877–1927): married the Munich bank director Josef Löhr in 1900. Thomas Mann dedicated the third part of *Buddenbrooks* to her: "This part dedicated warmly to my sister Julia in memory of our bay on the North Sea." Julia Mann committed suicide in 1927.

**Paul Busching:** political editor of *Die Münchner neueste Nachrichten.*
**Emil Grimm:** feuilleton editor of *Die Münchner neueste Nachrichten.*
**"Versuch über das Theater":** first appeared in *Nord und Süd* 32, nos. 370–71 (January–February 1908). In his "Mitteilung an die literar-historische Gesellschaft in Bonn" (*GW* 11: 713), Thomas Mann writes: "Some time ago the journal *Nord und Süd* conducted a survey about the theater. [ . . . ] And thus did the issue of the theater become a barb in my flesh: in an excited, agitated, dialectical state I paced back and forth, reasoned, disputed, composed, tossed a few points down on paper from my fevered brain . . . in short, I decided to put aside the novel on which I was working 'for a few days' and to give the journal the best answer of all it would receive. What resulted was a manuscript of one hundred and thirty large quarto sheets, entitled 'Versuch über das Theater.' I was engaged in struggle with it, not a few days, but weeks. More than once I became desperately fed up with the thing; more than once, in view of the contradictions that necessarily arise in the treatment of an artistic person's relationship to the theater, I wanted to drop it, but I had engaged myself and honored my categorical imperative 'persevere!'"
**Harden:** Thomas Mann is referring here to two articles on the Eulenburg affair: Maximilian Harden, "Nur ein Paar Worte," *Die Zukunft,* June 15, 1907, 367–74; "Die Freunde," *Die Zukunft,* June 22, 1907, 405–25.

**Flaubert for Müller:** the edition was evidently not produced. In 1907–1909, however, J. C. C. Bruns in Munich published the "first German complete edition authorized by the estate of Flaubert," in ten volumes, ed. E. W. Fischer. Heinrich Mann was not involved in it.

**Otto Eisenschitz,** actually Eisenschütz (1863–ca. 1943, Theresienstadt concentration camp): Viennese theater producer, journalist, writer. For many years feuilleton correspondent for *Die Frankfurter Zeitung.* Producer at the Josefstädter Theater and later the Parisiana-Theater in Vienna.
*Fiorenza:* the Munich performance took place on December 17, 1907, in the Residenztheater. It was not directed by Otto Falckenburg, but, with Otto Hierl-Deronko as artistic adviser, by the actor Albert Heine, who also, rather than Matthieu Lützenkirchen, performed the role of Lorenzo. Savonarola was played by Emil Höfer, Fiore by Josefine Rottmann.
**Otto Falckenburg** (1873–1947): dramatist and director. He came to Munich in 1896, where he directed many productions of the Akademisch-Dramatischer Verein; cofounder in 1901 of Die elf Scharfrichter; and finally, from 1916 to 1944, manager of the Münchner Kammerspiele.

**Gabriele d'Annunzio** (1863–1938): Heinrich Mann was influenced by d'Annunzio's Renaissance cult: *Minerva,* the second part of *Die Göttinnen,* was set in the Venice of d'Annunzio, whose novel *Il Fuoco* was published in German translation in 1900 by Langen/Müller in Munich (in English: *The Flame of Life,* 1909) and thus could serve as a model for Heinrich Mann.

Thomas Mann speaks in *Geist und Kunst* (*Notiz* 12) and in *Reflections* about "d'Annunzio's insufferable pontification about beauty" (*Reflections*, 74; *GW* 12:106), calling him there the "aper of Wagner" (*Reflections*, 426; *GW* 12:570). He had already opposed Heinrich's "hysterical renaissance" (*Reflections*, 399; *GW* 12:540) in "Tonio Kröger" and *Fiorenza;* he caricatured "Renaissance men" in the characters Axel Martini and Helmut Institoris (see letter of December 5, 1903, s.v. plebeian). The circumstance to which Thomas Mann alludes in this letter is not clear. D'Annunzio went voluntarily into exile in France in 1908.

**trial:** Phillip, prince of Eulenburg and Hertefeld (1847–1921), Wilhelm II's confidant, was accused in the press, above all in Harden's *Die Zukunft*, of exercising a pernicious influence on the kaiser. Harden accused him further of homosexual acts. Before this charge had been investigated, the kaiser made it clearly known that Eulenburg had fallen into disfavor. The criminal trial of Eulenburg was never carried through to its conclusion because the defendant became severely ill. Present-day historians represent the opinion that Eulenburg was innocent. They regard the reproach that he exercised a pernicious influence on Wilhelm II as certainly unjustified, for Eulenburg reportedly took pains on frequent occasions to restrain the kaiser from ill-considered steps. Nevertheless, the Eulenburg trial inspired the impression among the public of the time that for years the kaiser had allowed himself to be influenced in his political decisions by a person of doubtful morality (according to Bruno Gebhart, *Handbuch der deutschen Geschichte*, 8th ed. [Stuttgart, 1960], 302). Thomas Mann published a statement on December 13, 1907, in the Berlin newspaper *Morgen*, "Über Maximilian Harden." He also referred to the Eulenburg trial in *Geist und Kunst*.

FEBRUARY 6, 1908

**Dräge:** not identified. Perhaps the brothers named an unknown person in Rome in 1897 after their Munich drawing teacher Georg Heinrich Wilhelm Drege (1841–1919).

**Genzano:** restaurant in Rome which the brothers frequented in 1897–1898; see Thomas Mann, *A Sketch of My Life*, 13 (*GW* 11:103).

**"Little Lizzy":** story by Thomas Mann (in *Stories of Three Decades*). First published as "Luischen" in *Die Gesellschaft* (Leipzig) 16, no. 1 (1900). "Villa B." probably refers to the Villa Borghese. See *Buddenbrooks*, 21 (*GW* 1:32): Jean Jacques Hoffstede told "of the Villa Borghese, where Goethe had written part of his *Faust;* he waxed enthusiastic over the beautiful Renaissance fountains that wafted coolness upon the warm Italian air, and the formal gardens through the avenues of which it was so enchanting to stroll."

**details of the trial:** Eulenburg trial (s.v., Thomas Mann's letter of January 15, 1908). Count Kuno von Moltke had meanwhile filed a civil action against Harden; it led to Harden being called before the court in Munich on a charge of libel. State Counsel Bernstein took over Harden's defense. See Harden's depiction in *Die Zukunft*, "Der zweite Prozeß," February 15, 1908; "Der zweite Prozeß II," February 29, 1908; "Der zweite Prozeß III," March 21, 1908 (in this article Harden reported on Lily von Elbe, former countess of Moltke).

**Magnus Hirschfeld** (1868–1935): physician. Founder of the Institut für Sexualwissenschaft in Berlin; frequently called as an expert witness in trials involving sexual matters.

**Siegfried Jacobsohn** (1881–1926): Berlin critic. From 1905, publisher of *Die Schaubühne*. Wrote a monograph about Reinhardt. Antipode to Alfred Kerr. See Günther Rühle, *Theater für die Republik* (Frankfurt, 1967), 1169ff.

**Hermann Georg Stilke** (1870–1928): publisher. In 1904 took over management of the publishing house founded by his father, Georg Stilke, in 1872 (*Gegenwart* from 1872; *Nord und*

*Süd* from 1877; also *Die Preußische Jahrbücher* from 1896, which Harden's *Die Zukunft* followed later; established the first train station bookstore at the metropolitan railway in Berlin in 1882).

**Werdandi-Bund**: named after one of the three goddesses of fate, with the goal "of increasing the direct influence of those artists whose art rests on the foundation of a healthy German disposition" (*Kürschners Deutscher Literatur-Kalendar* of 1909). The organ of the league was the *Werdandi-Zeitschrift*. Among the members of the honorary advisory committee were Henry Thode, Hans Thoma, Ernst von Wildenbruch, and Siegfried Wagner. Thomas Mann also polemicized against the Werdandi-Bund in *Geist und Kunst*, note 18.

**Uncle Friedl:** Friedrich Wilhelm Lebrecht Mann (1847–1926) was the model for Christian Buddenbrook. The latter told his sister of a "girl" who is supposed to have occasionally sung the song, "That's Maria." "Maria is the most scandalous of the lot" (*Buddenbrooks*, 217; *GW* 1:263).

**Henry Thode** (1857–1920): art historian. Wrote *Wie ist R. Wagner vom deutschen Volk zu feiern?* (1903). See *Geist und Kunst*, note 19.

**Richard Nordhausen,** pseudonym Caliban (1868–?): Berlin writer. Close to the Werdandi-Bund. Among his works: *Vestigia Leonis*, epic poem (1893); *Die rote Tinktur*, novel (1895); *Deutsche Lieder* (1896); *Was war es?*, novel (1898); *Zwischen vierzehn und achtzehn* (1910, first volume in the *Werdandi-Bücherei*); *Die versunkene Stadt*, novel (1911). Reference here is to Nordhausen's "Berliner Brief," *Münchner neueste Nachrichten*, January 23, 1908.

**in the *Neue Revue*:** Walter Behrend, "Heinrich Mann, ein Künstlerproblem," *Neue Revue* (Halbmonatsschrift für das öffentliche Leben, edited by Josef Ad. Bondy and Fritz Wolff) 1 (January 1908): 448–54. George-Schüler's first sentence is as follows: "The creator of the fiery stories of the duchess of Assy was born in Lübeck, that northern city with the gothic festival of spires rising in the heavy sea air and, as befit the command of the shrewd and proud spirit of generations of valiant merchants, reaching defiantly and dreamily in dawning majesty for the heavenly azure."

**extensive review:** "Thomas Mann," *Nuova antologia di lettere, scienze et arti*, January 16, 1908, 346–48 (the author is not named).

**Aram's critique:** Kurt Aram, actually Hans Fischer (1869–1934), dramatist and story writer. Lived from 1904 in Munich-Schwabing. Editor of the biweekly *März*. Editor of *Das Berliner Tageblatt* from 1908. Among his works: *Wetterleuchten*, play (1898); *Unter Wolken*, novel (1900); *Pastorengeschichte*, stories (1906); *Jugendsünden*, novel (1908). Referred to here is Kurt Aram, "Literarische Monats-Bericht," *Nord und Süd* 124, no. 370 (January 1908): 176–82 (on *Mnais und Ginerva*, 181).

**essay:** Heinrich Mann, "Flaubert und die Kritik," *Nord und Süd* 124, no. 370 (January 1908): 142–48.

**beginning of my piece:** the first installment of Thomas Mann, "Versuch über das Theater," appeared in the January issue of *Nord und Süd* (116–19); parts 2 through 6 followed in the February issue (259–90).

APRIL 29, 1908

**Ines:** Ines Schmied.

**Hugo Isenbiel:** attorney general (see Maximilian Harden, "Der zweite Prozeß," *Die Zukunft*, February 15, 1908, 218).

**the *bon juge* Meyer:** Court of Appeals Justice Wilhelm Meyer.

**Insel-Verlag:** *Die Bösen* by Heinrich Mann was published in 1908 by the Insel-Verlag in Leipzig (contents: "Die Branzilla," "Der Tyrann").

**your novel:** Heinrich Mann, *Die kleine Stadt* (Leipzig: Insel-Verlag, 1909) (in English, *The Little Town*). (The novel did not appear in *Die neue Rundschau*; see letter of December 7, 1908.)

**Antony and Cleopatra:** Shakespeare's play was then being performed in the Hoftheater.

**Wiese:** Theresienwiese, where the Munich Oktoberfest took place annually.

NOVEMBER 10, 1908

**your manuscript:** *The Little Town.*

**discussion in the Reichstag:** the "Daily Telegraph Affair" was discussed on November 10–11, 1908, in the Reichstag. (In an interview, Wilhelm II had declared that he had impeded the formation of a Continental League against England during the Boer War; he claimed that he was a friend of England but found support for this position only from a minority of the German people. The interview unleashed a storm of indignation in Germany. Under the shock effect of general criticism, Wilhelm was forced to acknowledge a week later to the chancellor, von Bülow, that in the future he would endeavor to respect constitutional responsibilities in the nation's politics.) Heinrich Mann alluded to this affair in his novel *Der Kopf* (1925).

**Bernhard von Bülow** (1849–1929): foreign minister in 1879. Chancellor from 1900 to 1909. Was on a friendly footing with Kaiser Wilhelm II, until the *Daily Telegraph* affair destabilized his position. He was dismissed on July 14, 1909, following the failure of financial reform plans for the Reich. His posthumous *Denkwürdigkeiten* (1930–1931; in English: *Memoirs*, 4 vols., 1931–32) unleashed a passionate polemic on account of its misrepresentations.

DECEMBER 7, 1908

**N[eue] Fr[eie] Pr[esse]:** Thomas Mann, "Das Eisenbahnunglück," *Neue Freie Presse*, January 6, 1909 (in English: "Railway Accident," in *Stories of Three Decades*).

**Vienna excursion:** Thomas Mann was in Vienna from the end of November to the beginning of December. He met with Schnitzler, Wassermann, and Hofmannsthal.

**at the edge of exhaustion:** the formulation found its way into *Death in Venice*, 11 (*GW* 8:453).

**novel:** Heinrich Mann began *The Litte Town* in Florence in 1907 and finished it in Meran in 1908.

**Wilhelm Herzog** (1884–1960): writer and journalist. Lifelong pacifist socialist. For decades Heinrich Mann's closest friend. Reader for Paul Cassirer; published various of Heinrich Mann's works in *Pan*. Became an editor for the Munich weekly *März* in 1912; published the montly *Das Forum* in 1914–1915 (it was banned for its antiwar attitude); in 1916 cofounded, with Walter Hirth, the monthly *Die Weltliteratur*. After the revolution, the socialist daily newspaper *Die Republik* was formed under his direction. Travels in the Soviet Union and to South America. From 1929 in Sanary-sur-Mer. From 1933 to 1939 contributor to *Die Nation* and the Zurich *National-Zeitung*. From 1941 to 1945, on the island of Trinidad; 1945–1947 in the United States. Returned later to Munich, where he founded the cultural and political society Forum 52. Herzog reported extensively on his relations with the brothers Mann in *Menschen, denen ich begegnete*. Editor of Lichtenberg's writings (1907), of Kleist's works and letters (1908–1911); among his works: *Im Zwischendeck nach Südamerika* (1924); *Die Affaire Dreyfus*, play (1929); *Panama*, play (1931); from 1950 on, Herzog worked on his *Kritische Enzyklopädie*.

**poems:** in the library of Thomas Mann's estate, there is to be found only a dedication copy of the 1911 edition.

*R[oyal] H[ighness]:* *Royal Highness* was finished on February 13, 1909.

**new edition:** Thomas Mann, *Der kleine Herr Friedemann und andere Novellen* (Berlin: Fischer, 1909).

**"The Hungry":** story by Thomas Mann, in *Stories of Three Decades* (see letter of October 22, 1902, to Paul and Carl Ehrenberg, Thomas-Mann-Archiv, Zurich). The study first appeared on January 21, 1903, in Harden's *Die Zukunft.*

**"Railway Accident":** see Thomas Mann's letter of December 7, 1908.

**essay:** *Geist und Kunst.* The essay was never written; only Thomas Mann's notes for it have been preserved (they appear in edited form in *Thomas-Mann-Studien,* 1:152–223).

**story:** "Felix Krull," in *Stories of Three Decades.*

**"eighteenth century":** reference to Thomas Mann's preliminary work on the "Friedrich" novel.

**expect Katja to deliver:** Angelus Gottfried Thomas (Golo) Mann was born on March 27, 1909, and died on April 7, 1994.

**The seventeen hours with Katja:** Golo Mann's birth; see letter of March 25, 1909.

**the Ines-Lula problem:** Julia Löhr-Mann, the strictly bourgeois but at the same time very unstable sister of Thomas and Heinrich, got along very poorly with Ines Schmied. On the back of the letter of April 1, 1909, the outline of a response:

Ines is guiltless, knew nothing.
Your parents-in-law—but Lula and her sister-in-law!
Cordiality: I'm the one who seeks it.
Why am I the one reproached. The bad
treatment is wholly one-sided.
It is not a *social* matter, a sister.

*R[oyal] H[ighness]:* *Royal Highness* first appeared at that time in installments in *Die neue Rundschau.* Albrecht, the older brother of Klaus Heinrich, is a portrait by Thomas Mann of his brother Heinrich; Ditlind bears resemblances to Julia Mann.

**Beckergrube No. 52:** in 1881 Senator Mann acquired the property at Beckergrube 52 and had a house built there. Thomas Mann wrote about the house in *A Sketch of My Life,* 7 (*GW* 11:98): "My childhood was sheltered and happy. We five brothers and sisters, three boys and two girls, grew up in a spacious and dignified house, built by my father for him and his; though we rejoiced in a second home in the old family dwelling beside Saint Mary's, where my maternal grandmother lived alone, and which is shown to the curious as 'the Buddenbrook house.'"

**the Zeppelin:** later, in the notes for *Geist und Kunst,* Thomas Mann scoffed at the fact that Count Zeppelin was proclaimed a German national hero.

**Max Osborn** (1870–1946): critic. From 1900 to 1909 along with Karl Frenzel for *Die National-Zeitung;* editor of *Nord und Süd* for a short time; made art critic of the *BZ am Mittag* in 1910 and in 1914 of the *Vossische Zeitung.* Later theater reporter for *Die Berliner Morgenpost.*

Emigrated to France and then the United States. Died in New York. See Thomas Mann's letter on the occasion of his seventy-fifth birthday (*Br.* 2:394), which served as a foreword to Osborn's memoirs, *Der bunte Spiegel* (1945).

**Mucki:** nickname for Erika Mann in her first years.

APRIL 5, 1909

**Taine:** Samuel Sänger, "Der Kampf um Taine," *Die Zukunft,* April 3, 1909, 3–13.

**Gogol:** Dimitrij Mereschkowskij, "Gogol," *Die Zukunft,* April 3, 1909, 29–33.

**article:** Karl Scheffler, [review of Georg Hirth's] "Wege zur Heimat," *Die neue Rundschau* (1909): 617f.

**Felix Mottl** (1856–1911): director. From 1903 general music director of the Munich Hofoper, from 1907 its director.

**Friedrich August von Kaulbach** (1850–1920): painter. From 1886 to 1891 director of the Akademie der bildenden Künste in Munich. The Pringsheim children are depicted in his painting *Kinderkarneval* (reproduced in Katia Mann, *Meine ungeschriebene Memoiren,* ed. Elisabeth Plessen and Michael Mann [Frankfurt, 1974]; in English: Katia Mann, *Unwritten Memories,* trans. Hunter and Hildegard Hannum [New York: Alfred A. Knopf, 1975]).

**Thomas Knorr** (1851–1911): publisher and journalist. With his brother-in-law, Dr. Georg Hirth, took over the Verlag Knorr und Hirth after the death of his father, Julius Knorr (died 1881). Publisher of the *Münchner neueste Nachrichten* and the magazine *Jugend.* His house at Briennerstraße 18 was a center of Munich cultural life (Richard Wagner lived in the house as a guest in 1864–1865).

**Hugo von Maffei** (1836–1921): Munich industrialist.

**Albert Frh. von Speidel** (1858–1912): general director of the Munich Hoftheater. A note for "Krull" makes reference to this company (*Thomas-Mann-Studien* 5 [1982]: 414).

MAY 10, 1909

**Bircher-Brenner:** private clinic of Dr. Maximilian Oskar Bircher-Brenner in Zurich. Treatment with raw vegetarian fare, exposure to light and air, cold and warm water applications, therapeutic gymnastics. In the notes to a chapter about Krull's life in a penitentiary, Bircher-Brenner is once again called the "hygienic penitentiary": "He can, with the approval of the doctor, be assigned *work in the garden* (Bircher)."

JUNE 3, 1909

**Martini scene:** Thomas Mann wrote, in his letter of July 25, 1909, to Hugo von Hofmannsthal (*Br.* 1:76f.; *Letters of Thomas Mann 1889–1955,* 54): "During the writing, I referred back to the dialogue in *The Pretenders* between Skule and the skald—perhaps wrongly so."

**"The gift of sorrow":** in *The Pretenders,* act 4, the skald Jatgejr says to King Skule: "I received the gift of sorrow, and found myself a singer."

**Weber:** vital counterpart to Martini (*Royal Highness,* 165ff; *GW* 2:179ff.).

**work:** at the time, Thomas Mann was working on his "Literatur-Essay"; he was also occupied with the preliminary work on *Friedrich* and *Felix Krull.*

SEPTEMBER 30, 1909

**reading:** on an evening of readings organized by the Allgemeine Vereinigung deutscher Buchhandlungsgehilfen, Heinrich Mann read a chapter from *Die Jagd nach Liebe* and the introductory chapter of *The Litte Town.*

**work:** notes to *Geist und Kunst*. On August 26, 1909, Thomas Mann wrote to Walter Opitz (*Br.* 1:77): "I've let myself in for something there, something critical, a treatise, and every morning I wear down my nerves on it so much that in the afternoons I'm closer to imbecility than epistolography. Yes, Schiller was right when he said that it was harder to write a letter of Julius's than to create the best scene!"

**mass in the cathedral:** here Thomas Mann is discussing scenes from Heinrich Mann's new novel, *The Small Town*.

OCTOBER 23, 1909

**picture book:** perhaps *Der Kinder Wundergarten* (see Thomas Mann's letter of September 18, 1910).

DECEMBER 12, 1909

*Fiorenza:* the play was not performed in Berlin until January 3, 1913 (see letter of January 16, 1913).

**two clippings:** two reviews of *Royal Highness:* Franz Servaes, "*Königliche Hoheit*," *Literarisches Echo*, December 1, 1909, 356–58; Carl Busse, "Neues vom Büchertisch," *Velhagen & Klasings Monatshefte* 24, no. 4 (December 1909): 612–16.

**Bahr:** reference is to Hermann Bahr's review of *Royal Highness* (*Die neue Rundschau* [1909]: 1803–1808). See Thomas Mann's letter of January 11, 1910, to Kurt Martens (*Thomas Mann Jahrbuch* [Frankfurt, 1991], 4:187–88; *Letters of Thomas Mann 1889–1955*, 55–56).

**Wassermann:** reference is to Jakob Wassermann's essay *Der Literat oder Mythos und Persönlichkeit* (Leipzig, 1910) (a portion of the essay appeared in *Die neue Rundschau* [1910]: 1236–46, under the title "Der Literat als Psycholog"). In his essay Wassermann treated themes similar to those Thomas Mann was to have discussed in *Geist und Kunst*.

**Ewers:** Heinrich Mann's childhood friend reviewed the brothers' just published novels under the title "Die Gebrüder Mann" (*Bonner Zeitung*, December 12, 1909; *Königsberger Blätter für Literatur und Kunst*, supplement to the *Königsberger Allgemeine Zeitung*, December 10, 1909).

DECEMBER 18, 1909

**an Italian article:** G. Caprin, "Altezza Reale," *Marzocco* 14 (1909).

DECEMBER 30, 1909

*Pester Lloyd:* "*Die kleine Stadt*," *Pester Lloyd* (Budapest, December 12, 1909), signed by M. J. E-r.

*B.Z. am Mittag:* Karl Georg Wendriner, "*Die kleine Stadt*, Ein Satyrspiel von Kunst und Liebe," *BZ am Mittag* (December 21, 1909).

**Alfred Walter Heymel** (1878–1914): poet, publisher. Along with Otto Julius Bierbaum and Rudolf Alexander Schröder, founded the journal *Die Insel*. From 1909 in Munich. Among his works: *Ritter Ungestüm*, story (1900); *Der Tod des Narcissus*, play (1901); *Spiegel, Freundschaft, Spiele*, studies (1908); *Gesammelte Gedichte 1895–1914*, poetry (1914). O. J. Biermann had Heymel appear in *Prinz Kuckuck* (1907), and Jakob Wassermann in *Christian Wahnschaffe* (1919); but Claude Marehn in *Die Jagd nach Liebe* also bears resemblances to Heymel. See R. A. Schröder, "Zum Gedächtnis Alfred Walter Heymels," *Das Inselschiff* 7 (1925): 5.

**lead article in the *Frankfurter*:** in an unsigned article in the *Frankfurter Zeitung* of January 8, 1910, *Royal Highness* was compared with Prof. Wilhelm Münch's book about the education of a prince: "Nothing is more natural," the article states, "than for a writer to write a novel and a professor a textbook. But sometimes the unnatural occurs, and then the novel is the textbook and the textbook, if certainly not a novel, then nonetheless a kind of belles-lettres. The book by Münch will not be able to hold its own as an instructional text against *Royal Highness* by Mann."

**the Schickele plan:** reference not found.

**Heinrich Jaffé** (1862–1922): Munich bookseller. See Thomas Mann's "Brief an Herrn Jaffé," in *1903–1913, Katalog der Buchhandlung Jaffé* (Munich, 1912) (*GW* 10:843).

**the confidence man:** *Confessions of Felix Krull, Confidence Man.*

**Alfred Kerr,** actually Alfred Kempner (1867–1948): critic. On October 10, 1909, Kerr had published a derogatory review of *Royal Highness* in *Der Tag* (Berlin); see the reprint in Alfred Kerr, *Gesammelte Schriften* (Berlin, 1917), 4:266. The sentence quoted here comes from his essay "Shaws Anfang und Ende," *Die neue Rundschau* (1910): 115–25.

**Hermann Sudermann** (1857–1928): studied philosophy in Königsberg and Berlin. Lived as a freelance writer in Königsberg and Dresden, and as of 1896 in Berlin or at his country home Blankensee bei Trebbin. Became known through his autobiographical novel *Frau Sorge* (1887; in English: *Dame Care*, 1891). His social play *Die Ehre* (1889; in English: *Honor*, 1915) was performed shortly after Hauptmann's *Vor Sonnenaufgang* by the revolutionary Freie Bühne. Among his early works: *Der Katzensteg*, novel (1890; in English: *The Cat Walk*, 1987); *Sodoms Ende*, tragedy (1891); *Die Heimat*, play (1893; English version, 1899); *Morituri*, three one-act plays (1896; English version, 1910); *Johannisfeuer*, play (1900; in English: *Fires of St. John*, 1904); *Es lebe das Leben!*, play (1902; in English: *The Joy of Living*, 1928); *Das Blumenboot*, play (1905); *Das Hohe Lied*, novel (1908; in English: *The Song of Songs*, 1909); *Strandkinder*, play (1909). Kerr had first attacked Sudermann in the pamphlet *Herr Sudermann, der D . . . Di . . . Dichter: Ein kritisches Vademecum* (Berlin, 1903).

**Monty Jacobs** (1875–1945): journalist and theater critic. From 1905 to 1910 for the *Berliner Tageblatt;* from 1914 to 1918 as the successor to Arthur Eloesser at the *Vossische Zeitung;* from 1921 to 1933 as feuilleton editor. The article mentioned here, "Heinrich Manns Kleinstadtroman," appeared on January 19, 1910, in the *Berliner Tageblatt.*

**Hedda Sauer** (1875–1953): Prague poet. Carried on correspondence with F. v. Saar, M. Ebner-Eschenbach, R. M. Rilke, M. Mell, and others. Author of several volumes of poetry. The essay mentioned was not identified. See Hedda Sauer, "Heinrich Mann," *Literarisches Echo*, October 1, 1908, cols. 16–21.

**Lucia Dora Frost** (1882–?): critic, women's rights activist. Published a review of *The Little Town* in *Die Zukunft* on January 22, 1910. Heinrich Mann responded in the same journal of February 19, 1910. See Thomas Mann's letter of February 20, 1910.

**Max Reinhardt** (1873–1943): Thomas Mann also remarked on the famous director and theater manager in the notes to *Geist und Kunst;* see especially *Notiz* 102. Thomas Mann delivered his "Gedenkrede auf Max Reinhardt" at the Max-Reinhardt memorial on December 15, 1943 (*GW* 10:490).

**the "austere happiness":** this concluding phrase from *Royal Highness* had already appeared in Heinrich Mann's *Jagd nach Liebe* (*Gesammelte Romane und Novellen* [Leipzig, 1917], 5:328).

**review by the Literarhistorische Gesellschaft in Bonn:** by Ernst Bertram, "Thomas Mann, Zum Roman, *Königliche Hoheit,*" *Mitteilungen der Literarhistorischen Gesellschaft Bonn* 4, no. 8 (November 1909). Later, Thomas Mann enjoyed a friendship of many years with Ernst Bertram (1884–1957); see Inge Jens, ed., *Thomas Mann an Ernst Bertram* (Pfullingen, 1960).

**a bit popularly skewed:** Thomas Mann wrote in similar terms to Ernst Bertram on January 28, 1910.

***Friedrich:*** see Thomas Mann's letter of December 5, 1905.

FEBRUARY 17, 1910

**the psychological material:** for *Confessions of Felix Krull, Confidence Man*, which was initially planned as a story.

**Goethe-Voltaire chapter:** Heinrich Mann, "Französischer Geist" (later under the title "Voltaire-Goethe"), *Der Sozialist* 2, no. 11 (June 1910). See "Voltaire-Goethe," in Heinrich Mann, *Macht und Mensch* (Munich: Wolff, 1919), 10–16.

FEBRUARY 20, 1910

**letter in *Die Zukunft:*** Heinrich Mann, "Die kleine Stadt, Brief an Fräulein Lucia Dora Frost," *Die Zukunft*, February 19, 1910.

**essay:** presumably Heinrich Mann, "Geist und Tat," *Pan* 1, no.5 (January 1911): 137–43 (see *Essays*, 7–14).

MARCH 16, 1910

**trophies:** reviews of Heinrich Mann's play *Der Tyrann*. The one-act play was performed on March 2, 1910, in the Neues Deutsches Theater zu Berlin.

**Theodor Lessing** (1872–1933): philosopher, writer, columnist. Friendship with Ludwig Klages at the Lyceum Hannover. Began medical education, alongside philosophical studies, in 1892 in Freiburg, continued in 1893–1894 in Bonn and Munich. In Munich once again with Ludwig Klages (break in 1899). Member of Munich literary circles. Ph.D. in 1899 in Erlangen. Teacher in the Haubinda country boarding school in 1902. Break with the school in 1903. Back in Munich in 1904. Divorce from Maria von Stach. Lectures in Dresden (Schopenhauer, Wagner, Nietzsche). *Habilitation* rejected in Dresden. Lecturer in 1907, later professor, in Hannover. Conscripted as physician in 1914. Discharged from his teaching position in 1926 for criticizing Hindenberg. Emigrated to Czechoslovakia in 1933 (Lessing was of Jewish heritage). Murdered on August 31, 1933, in Marienbad by National Socialist agitators. (For a biography, see Ekkehard Hieronimus, *Theodor Lessing, Otto Meyerdorff, Leonard Nelson, Bedeutende Juden in Niedersachsen* [Hannover, 1964], 5–57.) Among his works: *Comödie*, novel in two volumes (1893); *Laute und leise Lieder* (1896); *Die Nation*, play (1896); *Weiber! 301 Stosseufzer über das "schöne" Geschlecht* (1897); *Das Recht des Lebens*, play (1898); *Einsame Gesänge* (1899); *Schopenhauer, Wagner, Nietzsche, Einführung in die moderne Philosophie* (1906); *Theater-Seele, Studie über Bühnenästhetik und Schauspielkunst* (1907); *Studien zur Wertaxiomatic, Untersuchungen über reine Ethik und reines Recht* (1908); *Weib, Frau, Dame*, essay (1910); *Der fröhliche Eselsquell: Gedanken über Theater, Schauspieler, Drama* (1912); *Philosophie als Tat* (1914); *Europa und Asien* (1914); *Geschichte als Sinngebung des Sinnlosen* (1919); *Nietzsche* (1925); *Der jüdische Selbsthass*

(1936); *Einmal und nie wieder,* autobiography (1935). Theodor Lessing had publically attacked the critic Samuel Lublinski. Thomas Mann took a stand in favor of Lublinski in *Das literarische Echo,* March and April 1910. On this controversy, see Hans Wysling, "'Ein Elender,' Zu einem Novellenplan Thomas Manns," in *Thomas-Mann-Studien,* 1:106–22.

**Ines's brother:** Rudolf Schmied. As early as January 6, 1909, Ines Schmied had written to Heinrich Mann as follows (Heinrich-Mann-Archiv, Berlin): "I can still see your brother's face, how cold, indifferent, and yet somehow discontented his gaze is. And on top of that this sober, utterly unpoetic region [Tölz]. A dab of mountains, a dab of meadow, a dab of woods, of everything a little. Nothing big, nothing beautiful, in a word, sober, bourgeois, cold . . . That your relatives can't stand me is no wonder, but that I can't stand them is not one either."

MARCH 20, 1910

**a poor simpleton:** Theodor Lessing.
**a silly babbler:** Rudolf Schmied (see letter of March 16, 1910).
**The Reinhardt matter:** as far as can be determined, Reinhardt's plan to stage a performance of scenes from *Fiorenza* together with Heinrich Mann's one-act play *Der Tyrann* did not materialize. *Fiorenza* was first performed in Berlin on January 3, 1913.
**your story:** Heinrich Mann, "Das Herz," *Neue Freie Presse,* March 27, 1910.

JUNE 16, 1910

**happy outcome:** Heinrich Mann had signed a contract on June 14, 1910, with the Berlin publisher Paul Cassirer. It provided for a royalty of 25 percent of the cover price and a guaranteed annual income of 6,000 marks, payable in monthly instalments of 500 marks.

AUGUST 4, 1910

**photographs of Carla's body:** Carla Mann had committed suicide on July 30, 1910, in Polling (see Viktor Mann, *Wir waren fünf,* 305–15). Of all the siblings, she was the closest to Heinrich Mann: "The being toward whom I was aware of being closest was my sister. She was an actress, beautiful and elegant, a child of life, her heart eager and open to it, and yet in her deepest recesses she took it seriously only as a game that she had mastered; and since she eventually lost sight of this and wanted to be completely 'serious,' she had to die" (*Autobiographische Abriß,* Florence, February 21–22, 1911). Ute in *Die Jagd nach Liebe* (novel, 1906) and Leonie in *Schauspielerin* (play, 1911) are modeled on her (letter of October 26, 1948, to Karl Lemke): "The long story 'Schauspielerin' and the play of the same title are both my sister herself, in different renditions of her fate. The book appeared in 1911 in Vienna and was quite successful, but this is a case in which the theater asserts its worldly preeminence over literature. Strangers don't speak to an author on the street because he has written something, but only when it has been performed publicly. A great woman, Tilla Durieux, played the lead role in a splendid series of guest performances; the character appeared not only to the eyes of a writer, but a brother saw his dead sister conjured back from there where she still lives—that is, in his heart. Her own was still beating when she read *Die Jagd nach Liebe.* 'I recognize everything in it, even Nathanael's skull on my dresser.' The theater break permitted them a period of togetherness; he picked her up from her engagement and they stayed on a wild mountain in south Tyrolia; in Venice on the Lido with Thomas and his wife; for a long time over the Piazza Signoria. It was precisely Florence that held for him in reserve a later discovery: on a suburban street, behind the glass door of a pitiful stationery shop hung her postcards—everywhere this figure, colored and surrounded by flowers."

**cousin:** Käte Rosenberg (1883–1960), translator from the Russian.

**Aunt E[lisabeth]:** s.v., Thomas Mann's letter of January 17, 1906.

**Lula:** Heinrich Mann had had a falling out with his sister Julia Löhr-Mann when he saw that Ines Schmied would not be accepted by her. His use of Josef Löhr's acquaintances as models for his Munich social satire *Die Jagd nach Liebe* may have added to the tensions.

AUGUST 7, 1910

**a long letter:** the draft was not preserved. On the family quarrels, see Thomas Mann's letters of March 16, 1910, and August 4, 1910.

SEPTEMBER 18, 1910

**Kerr:** in his article "Gedanken und Erinnerungen Wedekinds," *Die neue Rundschau* (1910): 1300–1302, Alfred Kerr writes: "He is in favor of critics being well paid. But he thinks in terms of the provinces. He does not know that today a critic sometimes earns as much as a theatrical star, can staunch every mood, lead a gallant life in all quarters of the globe, and look upon artworks as a connoisseur, moving at will. (And that is how it must be.)"

**Ida ihr Pinger:** The way the little Julia Mann pronounced the name Ida Springer.

***Der Kinder Wundergarten:*** Fairy tales from all over the world, with eighty woodcuts by C. v. Binzer, Oscar Pletsch, Ludwig Richter, et al., published by Friedrich Hoffmann (Leipzig, 1904; 36th edition in popular format; first Collector's Edition published in 1874). Erika Mann wrote: "Of course we possessed *Der Kinder Wundergarten*. It was very beautiful, but it got lost *anno* 33."

**comedy:** presumably Heinrich Mann, *Variété* (Berlin: Cassirer, 1910). First appeared in *Pan* 1, nos. 1–2 (November 1910): 16–30, 51–59.

**Mahler symphony:** the premiere performance of Gustav Mahler's Eighth Symphony took place on September 12, 1910. Following the concert, Thomas Mann met with Mahler and Reinhardt. The first name and facial features of Gustav von Aschenbach, the hero of *Death in Venice*, are taken from Mahler.

***Weltspiegel:*** in *Weltspiegel*, the illustrated semi-weekly chronicle of *Das Berliner Tageblatt*, there appeared on August 25, 1910, a notice of Thomas Mann's father-in-law's sixtieth birthday with a portrait of the professor.

OCTOBER 5, 1910

**Fontane:** The remark refers perhaps to Wilhelm Wolters [Wilhelm Wolfsohn], ed., *Theodor Fontanes Briefwechsel mit Wilhelm Wolfson* (Berlin, 1910). Thomas Mann wrote the essay "Der alte Fontane" in July (published on October 1, 1910, in *Die Zukunft*).

**proofs:** presumably the reprint of Heinrich Mann's story "Contessina," in Hermann Beuttenmüller, ed., *Deutsches Novellenbuch* (Leipzig and Berlin: Moeser, 1910).

**moving:** the move to the new apartment on Mauerkircherstraße 13 took place on October 1, 1910.

**christening:** Monika Mann, born June 7, 1910.

**Georg Martin Richter** (1875–1941): art historian, writer. He was living at the time in Munich-Schwabing and in Feldafing, later in Florence. Emigrated in 1933 to London, 1939 to the United States. Godfather of Michael Mann, Thomas Mann's youngest son.

**Weimar:** reading tour in November 1910.

**two newspaper pieces:** "Peter Schlemihl," *Berliner Tageblatt*, December 12, 1910 (reprinted in *Blätter der Thomas-Mann-Gesellschaft*, no. 5 [1965]: 17–21). The second piece is probably "Wie Jappe und Do Escobar sich prügelten," which Thomas Mann read in the presence of the family on December 11, 1910, and published in February 1911, in the *Süddeutschen Monatshefte* (in English: "The Fight Between Jappe and Do Escobar," in *Stories of Three Decades*).

**the three:** see Thomas Mann's letter of November 24, 1910.

**in the Vitzthum household:** Thomas Mann was the guest in Weimar of a former schoolmate, Count Vitzthum von Eckstädt, who had been one of the contributors to the school periodical *Der Frühlingssturm*.

NOVEMBER 24, 1910

**what happened in Berlin:** The premiere of Heinrich Mann's one-act plays *Variété, Die Unschuldigen*, and *Der Tyrann* took place on November 21, 1910, in Berlin's Kleines Theater. Kerr's review appeared on November 24, 1910, in *Der Tag*. In December 1910 *Pan* printed excerpts from the reviews of the most important Berlin dailies; appearing in the same issue (*Pan* 1, no. 3) was Lucia Dora Frost's article, "Heinrich Manns Einakter," 83–86.

DECEMBER 23, 1910

**list:** context not determined.
**Vicco:** Viktor Mann.

JANUARY 26, 1911

**excerpt from "Geist und That":** Heinrich Mann, "Geist und Tat," *Pan* 1, no. 5 (January 1911): 137–43.

*D[eutsche] Tageszeitung:* article not identified.

**Uncle Friedel's Maria:** s.v., Thomas Mann's letter of February 6, 1908.

**trip:** reading tour to the Ruhr district and Westphalia. In Mülheim a. d. Ruhr, Thomas Mann presumably visited Adeline Stinnes-Coupienne (1844–1925), wife of the industrialist and shipowner Hugo Stinnes (1842–1887). In the satirical fairy tale "Kobes" (Berlin: Propyläen-Verlag, 1925, with ten lithographs by George Grosz), Heinrich Mann refers to her second son, the prominent industrialist Hugo Stinnes (1870–1924); see Raphael Gaston, *Hugo Stinnes, der Mensch, sein Werk, sein Wirken* (Berlin, 1925).

**Melchior Lechter** (1865–1937): painter and book designer from the George circle.

**Lublinski:** s.v., Thomas Mann's letter of March 21, 1906. Lublinski died on December 26, 1910. Theodor Lessing's eulogy appeared in *Die Schaubühne* 7, no. 1 (1911): 41–46.

MARCH 24, 1911

**"Die Rückkehr vom Hades":** story by Heinrich Mann; first appeared in *Pan* 1, nos. 9–10 (March 1911): 292–301, 333–46. Then in: *Die Rückkehr vom Hades, Novellen* (Leipzig: Insel-Verlag, 1911).

**three-act play:** Heinrich Mann, *Schauspielerin*, Drama in 3 Akten (Berlin: Cassirer, 1911).

***Pan*-Jagow affair:** the Berlin police chief von Jagow had issue no. 6 of *Pan* confiscated because it printed "obscene" excerpts from Flaubert's diaries; no. 7 was censored for the same reason. Kerr then attacked him for infringement of freedom of the press: "Jagow, Flaubert, *Pan*," *Pan* 1, no. 7 (February 1911): 217–23. In his "Vorletzten Brief an Jagow," *Pan* 1, no. 9 (March 1911): 287–90, Kerr made much of the police chief's "affair" with the actress Tilla Durieux, the wife of the publisher (and copublisher of *Pan*) Paul Cassirer. In two clarifications, Cassirer distanced himself from Kerr but assured him of the right to discuss "the public and legal aspect of the case." Kerr concluded this first stage of his polemic in no. 10 (March 15, 1911, 321–26) with an article entitled "Nachlese." Wilhelm Herzog reported on the trial initiated by Kerr in no. 18 ([August 1911]: 587–90); Kerr had his "Prozeß-Ballade" published with the report. The case included a few subsequent developments that do not merit description here. At the end of 1911 Kerr left the *Pan* editorial board.

**Dalmatian trip:** reference to Hermann Bahr's "Dalmatinische Reise," which appeared in 1909 in *Die neue Rundschau*. The trip took Thomas Mann to Brioni and Venice (conception of *Death in Venice*).

OCTOBER 3, 1911

**your play:** Heinrich Mann, *Der Schauspielerin* (Berlin: Cassirer, 1911). The play was based on the fate of his sister Carla.

FEBRUARY 17, 1912

**father-in-law:** Prof. Alfred Pringsheim.

APRIL 2, 1912

**injection treatment:** Katja Mann spent from March 10 to September 25, 1912, at the mountain sanatorium in Davos (under the direction of Dr. Friedrich Jessen). Thomas Mann visited her there from May 15 to June 12, 1912 (*A Sketch of My Life*, 43; *GW* 11:125), using the occasion to gather his first impressions for *The Magic Mountain*.

***Death in Venice:*** the novella appeared in the summer of 1912 in an edition of one hundred from Hans von Weber's Hyperion Verlag in Munich.

**your play:** Heinrich Mann, *Die große Liebe*, Drama in 4 Akten (Berlin: Cassirer, 1912).

**Bernhard von Jakobi** (1880–1914): actor for the Königlich Bayerische Hofbühnen.

APRIL 27, 1912

**completion of the play:** *Die große Liebe*.
**novella:** *Death in Venice*.
**The military:** see Thomas Mann's letters of November 25, 1900, and December 17, 1900. Thomas Mann made use of the impressions left from his time in the military in *Confessions of Felix Krull, Confidence Man*, 84–105 (*GW* 7:349–72). Heinrich Mann relied on his brother's report for passages in *The Patrioteer*.

JUNE 8, 1912

**success of your play:** *Die große Liebe*, Berlin, 1912.
**Ewers:** Thomas Mann's mother made futile attempts to secure Ewers, who was working in Königsberg, an editorial position in Munich. In 1913, Ewers became an editor of the *Hamburger Nachrichten*. See Thomas Mann's letter of June 14, 1912.

**Eugenie Schäuffelen:** close friend of the Pringsheims; godmother of Katja Mann.

**your play:** *Die große Liebe*.

**Bruno Frank** (1887–1945): writer. Close friend of Thomas Mann. In Munich until 1933; later in Austria, Switzerland, France, and England; from 1938 in California. A neighbor there of Thomas Mann, as he once was in Munich's Herzogpark (see *GW* 10:484, 497, 566). Among Bruno Frank's publications as of 1912: *Aus der goldenen Schale*, poems (1905); *Die Nachtwache*, novel (1909).

**novella:** Thomas Mann, *Tod in Venedig* [*Death in Venice*], *Die neue Rundschau* (1912): 1368ff., 1499ff.

**Alexander Moissi** (1880–1935): actor for the Deutsches Theater in Berlin. Moissi performed Hamlet under Reinhardt in Munich in 1909 and appeared as a guest performer in the role of Oswald in 1911 at the Volkstheater.

**Berlin adventure:** the premiere of *Fiorenza* took place on January 3, 1913, in Berlin. Eduard von Winterstein (1871–1961) directed; Paul Wegener (1874–1948) played Lorenzo. Kerr's review appeared on January 5, 1913, in the Berlin paper *Der Tag*. Thomas Mann requested that the review be returned so that he would be able to use it as material for the planned psychological study "Ein Elender" [The abject]. See the letters of January 9, 1913, to Hugo von Hofmannsthal (*Br.* 1:100) and of January 30, 1913, to Ernst Bertram: "and if the *Geist und Kunst* essay will probably remain the work of my deceased friend G. v. Aschenbach, I'm fairly certain that the story of the 'The Abject' will one day get written. What studies I have made!! It could become a really good 'character' story."

**Herzog:** s.v., Thomas Mann's letter of December 7, 1908.

**your *première:*** *Die große Liebe* was premiered in Berlin's Lessing Theater with Tilla Durieux in the lead role (the date of the premiere could not be determined).

**the *Patrioteer:*** Heinrich Mann's novel *The Patrioteer* was finished in July 1914. Excerpts had already appeared in *Licht und Schatten* (1912), *Simplicissimus* (1911–1912), *März* (1913), and *Zeit und Bild* (1914). The publisher Kurt Wolff issued a private printing of ten copies in 1916. The first mass printing was in 1918. The Russian translation by Adele Polotsky had already been available since 1914. Concerning the writing of the novel, Heinrich Mann wrote to Alfred Kantorowicz on March 3, 1943: "my first notes for *The Patrioteer* were made in 1906. It was written from 1912 to 1914 (appeared before the war in a periodical, as a book only in December 1918; achieved a printing of 100,000 copies in six weeks)." On the writing of the novel, see also *Weimarer Beiträge* (1960), 112–31.

**Eißi:** Klaus Mann (1906–1949), Thomas Mann's oldest son. Writer. Editor of the periodicals *Die Sammlung* (1933–1935) and *Decision* (1941–1942). Served in the American army during the war. Committed suicide in 1949 in Cannes. Autobiographies: *Kind dieser Zeit* (1932); *The Turning Point* (1942); *Der Wendepunkt* (1952, expanded version of *The Turning Point*). Other works: *Der fromme Tanz*, novel (1926; in English: *The Pious Dance*, 1987); *Alexander*, novel (1929); *Symphonie pathétique*, novel (1935; in English: *Pathetic Symphony: A Novel about Tchaikovsky*, 1970); *Mephisto*, novel (1936; English version, 1977); *Der Vulkan*, novel (1939); *André Gide and the Crisis of Modern Thought* (1943). See Thomas Mann's letter concerning the novel *Der Vulkan* (*GW* 10:766); "Vorwort zu einem Gedächtnisbuch für Klaus Mann" (*GW* 11:510).

**the property:** on February 25, 1913, Thomas and Katja Mann purchased the property at Poschingerstraße 1 in Munich.

**energy and desire to work:** in July 1913 Thomas Mann had once again put the *Confidence Man* novel aside and begun the preliminary work on *The Magic Mountain*.

NOVEMBER 11, 1913

**Uncle Friedl's excess:** Friedrich Mann took out the following notice in the *Lübekkischen Anzeigen* of October 28, 1913:

> Over the twelve years since the publication of *Buddenbrooks*, written by my nephew, *Mr. Thomas Mann of Munich*, I have been subjected to a tremendous number of nuisances, which have been of the most wretched consequences to myself and to which is now added the publication of the book by Alberts, *Thomas Mann und sein Pflicht*.
> *I therefore see myself compelled to turn to the reading public of Lübeck and to request of the same that it assess the above-mentioned book accordingly.*
> If the author of *Buddenbrooks* chooses to caricature his closest relations and drag them through the filth, to subject their destinies to sheer exposé, then every right-thinking person will regard that as reprehensible. It is a sad bird that fouls its own nest.
> Friedrich Mann, Hamburg

The notice was published and commented upon in many German newspapers. The book by Alberts is: Wilhelm Alberts, *Thomas Mann und sein Beruf* (1913).

**I'm a Jew now:** in *Deutsche Dichtung der Gegenwart* (Leipzig, 1910, 307ff.), Adolf Bartels had written: "The Mann brothers, Heinrich and Thomas, of whom the latter enjoyed a great success with the novel *Buddenbrooks*, are not, according to Thomas's testimony, Jews, but their art also appears to be essentially Jewish." On December 8, 1912, the Berlin *Staatsbürgerzeitung* published a letter by Thomas Mann dated December 5, 1912, in which he refuted the assertion that he belonged to the group of Jewish authors of the Fischer Verlag. On December 15, 1913, under the title, "Das Rassenbekenntnis Thomas Manns," a further letter of Thomas Mann's appeared, dated December 12, 1912; it contained his response to an attack by Adolf Bartels that had been published in *Deutsche Stimme*.

**doctor's direst orders:** Katja Mann departed on November 15, 1913, for treatment in Meran.

JANUARY 7, 1914

**storm of "practical affairs":** see *Death in Venice*, 29 (*GW* 8:457).
**moved into the house with the children:** Poschingerstr. 1. See letter of January 6, 1914,

to Ernst Bertram: "It is very distressing that my wife was not able to move in with me. She has been in Arosa since yesterday: she is being required to return to the mountains for a six-month stay. It is hard."

**your play:** Heinrich Mann, *Madame Legros* (Berlin: Cassirer, 1913).

**Oppenheimer's picture:** the etching by Max Oppenheimer (December 1913) is reproduced in Theo Piana, *Heinrich Mann* (Leipzig, 1964), 31. The picture exhibited by Thannhauser could not be identified. Max Oppenheimer's portrait of Thomas Mann is reproduced in Heinz Saueressig, *Die Entstehung des Romans Der Zauberberg* (Biberach an der Riß, 1965), opposite 20. Max Oppenheimer, who was called Mopp (1885–1954), belonged to the circle of Heinrich Mann's friends (see Viktor Mann, *Wir waren fünf*, 427). On January 1, 1926, Thomas Mann published an essay about him in the *Berliner Tageblatt:* "Symphonie" (*GW* 10:877). Heinrich Thannhauser's modern gallery was located at Theatinerstraße 7.

**married:** on August 12, 1914, Heinrich Mann married the Jewish actress Maria (Mimi) Kanova (1886–1946) from Prague, whom he had met during the rehearsals of his play *Die große Liebe*. In 1916, a daughter, Carla Maria Henriette Leonie, was born, and Leonie is also the name of the Carla Mann character in the story "Schauspielerin." After their divorce (around 1930), Maria Kanova returned to Czechoslovakia. During the occupation, she spent five years in the Theresienstadt concentration camp. She died shortly after the camp was liberated.

**story:** *The Magic Mountain.*

JULY 30, 1914

**completion of your big work:** *The Patrioteer;* s.v., Thomas Mann's letter of November 8, 1913.

**August 12:** marriage of Heinrich Mann and Maria Kanova.

**Vicco:** the wartime marriage of Viktor Mann to Magdalena (Nelly) Kilian of Munich took place on August 1, 1914. Vicco then joined his regiment in the field as a sergeant-major in the artillery.

AUGUST 7, 1914

**Katja's brother:** Heinz Pringsheim (1882–1974), originally archeologist, then music critic in Munich. Enlisted as a lieutenant in the cavalry.

**Maximilian Brantl** (1881–1959): Munich attorney. Friend of Heinrich and Thomas Mann. Also active as a writer.

**wedding:** Thomas Mann did not take part in his older brother's wedding. The newlyweds lived at Leopoldstraße 59 in Munich.

**What a visitation:** the outbreak of World War I on August 1, 1914. The same formulation is to be found in the letter of August 12, 1914, to Kurt Martens (*Thomas Mann Jahrbuch*, 4:206).

**that you have just finished:** see the letter of July 30, 1914. The first edition of *The Patrioteer* includes the publisher's remark: "Completed the beginning of July 1914."

**my task:** reference, presumably, is to work on *The Magic Mountain.* Thus it was in August 1914 that Thomas Mann began writing the article "Gedanken im Kriege," which appeared in November 1914, in *Die neue Rundschau.* In September there followed the writing of the essay "Friedrich und die große Koalition, Ein Abriß für den Tag und die Stunde" (*Der neue Merkur* [January–February 1915]; in English: "Frederick the Great and the Grand Coalition," in *Three Essays*).

**so involved financially:** due to the construction of the house at Poschingerstraße 1 in Munich.

**Emma Gramman:** related to the Mann family through the Crolls and Martys.

*Handwritten draft*

**article in the *B[erliner] T[ageblatt]:*** Thomas Mann, "Weltfrieden?" *Berliner Tageblatt,* December 27, 1917. The complete text is reproduced below:

World peace . . . Humanity should not presume all too much morality. If we do manage to achieve world peace, to achieve a world peace—it will not be because we have traveled the path of morality to get there. Schneidemann said recently that democracy will be able to make great strides on account of the general exhaustion. That is not very honorable for democracy—nor for humanity. For the morality of exhaustion is not such a moral morality.

Moreover, however—and I know precisely what counts as right and proper—but, moreover, it could be doubted that the conceptual compound "democratic world peace" represents an especially indissoluble compound. That the rule of the people is the rule of reason or even of the intellect, that it implies a secure peace has not been verified—not as far as I can see. The peoples of Europe want peace, and they want it unconditionally, as they do once a war has lasted a long time and been very difficult. Prior to attaining that condition, the status of their virtue is so-so. Rousseau's doctrine of the "good people," as well as revolutionary optimism altogether, that is: faith in politics, in the anthill, socialism and the *république démocratique, sociale et universelle*—I know exactly what counts today as proper, but according to my nature and education I cannot adhere to this doctrine and cannot share this faith. The Russian and the German mind, Dostoevsky and Schiller, are agreed in their insistence that the problem of humanity is absolutely beyond the reach of a political solution, that it can be solved only on the plane of the morality and the soul: through religion, through the Christian self-improvement *of the individual*—thus the one; through art, through the "aesthetic education" and liberation *of the individual*—thus the other. In Richard Dehmel's remarkable new play, it is said by a character with some understanding of affairs of the conscience, "Even the grandest feeling becomes small when it decks itself out in grand concepts; a little goodness from man to man is better than all love for humanity." So it is, just believe it! Rhetorical-political love for humanity is a quite peripheral type of love and is usually proclaimed most sweetly when something has gone wrong closer to home. Become better yourself, less hard, less dogmatically conceited, less aggressively self-righteous, before you play the philanthropist . . . The effect on the public of someone who knows how to say very beautifully, "I love God!" can be significant. But when he, at the same time, "hates his brother," then, according to the Gospel of St. John, his love of God is nothing other than belles lettres and sacrificial smoke that does not rise.

World peace . . . Not for a day, nor even amid the profoundest national animosity, have I been incapable of the thought that the hatred and enmity among the nations of Europe is finally an illusion, an error—that the sides flaying each other are not basically factions, but are working together under God's will, in brotherly pain, for the renewal of the world and the soul. Yes, one may dream of a placated and reconciled Europe—even if goodness and higher harmony will owe their existence only to exhaustion and to that sensitivity and refinement that is created by great suffering. For the refinement from suffering is higher and more humane than that from happiness and the life of luxury; I believe in this, and in a hopeful sense I also believe in that future Europe, a Europe that, dedicated to religious humanity and to tolerant intellectuality, will remember only with shame and scorn today's bitter ideological quarrel: May this Europe be undoctrinaire, undogmatic, and without belief in slogans and antitheses, free, cheerful, and gentle, and only shrug off "aristocracy" and "democracy." Goethe remarked about an ephemeral play that the whole idea was concerned only with aristocracy and democracy, and that this had no general human interest. Thus spoke an antipolitical artist; and will it not be antipolitical and artistic, this postwar Europe? Will it not, in defiance of those who cry for the complete dominance of politics, for "political atmosphere," have humanity and culture as guiding stars? But it should certainly show respect for the *one* aristocratic principle: its own. May it learn to *set great store* in matters of culture and taste, as it did not know how to do before, may it renounce lascivious aestheticism and exoticism, the self-betraying tendency to barbarism it pandered to in an unbridled way, taboo crazes in clothes styles and foolish infantilisms in its art, and adopt an attitude of noble rejection of anthropophagic sculpture and South American harbor-saloon dances. Such as these bring nothing good. As long as Europe is inclined to such nonsense it will continue to be liable to war, that is certain. By the way, will it not be *poor* for a while, our Europe, will not the sacrifices it has made have taught it to find the simple and the natural precious, and to enjoy gratefully a meal of eggs, ham, and milk rather than some kind of vomitorium-gluttony of the past? Yes, let us imagine it to be filled with disgust for its former negrolike craving for pleasure and the ostentatiousness of civilization, let us think of it as simple and graceful in manners and dedicated to an art that would be the pure expression of its condition: tender, unadorned, kind, intellectual, of the highest humane noblesse, full of form, restrained and powerful through the intensity of its humanity.

I am afraid the "European intellectual" will dispute my right to such dreams. It is true that I discovered myself to be more national than I had known I was; but a Nationalist, an "artist of the homeland," I never was. I found it impossible to let the war "mean nothing" to me—for example, because war has nothing to do with culture, which is a very risky assertion. Shaken, stirred up, sharply challenged, I threw myself into the fray and defended what was mine. But God knows I will feel better when my soul will again be permitted to view life and humanity purified of politics; my nature will be better able to stand the test when the nations live alongside one another behind peaceful borders in dignity and honor, and exchange their finest goods: the beautiful Englishman, the polished Frenchman, the humane Russian, and the knowing German.

See *Reflections,* chapter 9, "Some Comments on Humanity" (352, 359–60; *GW* 12:478, 487). In the spring of 1916, Thomas Mann had noted (*Notizbuch* 10, 42): 1 John 4:20–21: "If any one says, 'I love God,' and hates his brother, he is a liar; for he who does not love his brother whom he has seen, cannot love God whom he has not seen."

**"Goodness of man to man":** in his copy of Dehmel's play *Die Menschenfreunde* (Berlin, 1917), Thomas Mann underlined the sentence from which the quote is taken (77): "Even the grandest feeling becomes small when it decks itself out in grand concepts; a little goodness from man to man is better than all love for humanity." On Richard Dehmel, see Thomas Mann's letter of January 3, 1918.

*Freistatt:* Thomas Mann, "Das Ewig-Weibliche," *Freistatt,* March 21, 1903. See Thomas Mann's letter of December 23, 1903.

**your most recent book:** probably Thomas Mann, *Betrachtungen eines Unpolitischen* (Berlin: Fischer, 1918); excerpts from the work had already been published: "Der Taugenichts," *Die neue Rundschau* (November 1916) (in the English version, *Reflections of a Nonpolitical Man,* from chap. 8); "Kunst und Politik," *Münchner neueste Nachrichten,* February 16, 1917; "Einkehr," *Die neue Rundschau* (March 1917) (from chap. 4); "Palestrina," *Die neue Rundschau* (October 1917) (from chap. 8); "Das unliterarische Land," *Berliner Tageblatt,* September 26, 1918 (from chap. 2).

**"Zola":** Heinrich Mann, "Zola," *Die weiße Blätter* 2, no. 11 (November 1915). It includes the sentence, right at the start: "Those who are destined to dry up early step out deliberately when they have scarcely entered their twenties, a match for the world." Thomas Mann, who, on November 8, 1913, in a moment of discouragement, had expressed similar fears to Heinrich—"My time is up, I think, and I probably should never have been allowed to become a writer"—reacted extremely sharply to this sentence. When he returned the November issue of *Die weiße Blätter* to Maximilian Brantl on June 18, 1916, he added the note: "I'm finally returning *Die weiße Blätter*, with a thousand apologies for the pencil marks. I began to erase them, but feared only making matters worse. Besides, this article practically requires pencil marks; it seems that the choicest double entendres are not noticed by the majority of readers." The erasure marks next to the second sentence of the essay are still clearly visible today in the copy preserved among Brantl's papers. Thomas Mann quoted the sentence in a passage directed against his brother in *Reflections*, 136–37 (*GW* 12:190); in his letter of January 3, 1918, he termed it "monstrously excessive." Heinrich Mann omitted "for later printings of the Zola essay certain sentences of a personal nature" (see Thomas Mann's letter of July 1, 1954, to Alfred Kantorowicz).

**birth of our child:** Carla Maria Henriette Leonie Mann was born on September 10, 1916.

**your most recent indictment:** the article mentioned at the beginning of the letter, "Weltfrieden?"

Instead of this last sentence, Heinrich Mann had first written: "If there are other reasons for it, I must resign myself and can only ask that, instead of misunderstanding this letter, you simply consider it as unwritten. In regard to me, I believe it would be gratifying or promising for you to begin listening to me again. I only wanted to say that you needn't think of me as an enemy."

JANUARY 3, 1918

**trip:** reading tour to Hamburg and Lübeck.

**compare:** perhaps an allusion to the second epigraph of *Reflections:* "Compare yourself with others! Know what you are! (Goethe, *Tasso*)."

**galley-slave's work:** allusion to the first epigraph of *Reflections:* "Que diable allait-il faire dans cette galère? (Molière, *Les Fourberies de Scapin*)."

**parasite:** allusion to Heinrich Mann's Zola essay. The expression is quoted in *Reflections*, 140, 143 (*GW* 12:194, 199).

**Stifter:** the sentence occurs in Stifter's letter of February 22, 1850, to Joseph Türck. Thomas Mann first quoted it in a letter of December 25, 1917, to Ernst Bertram: "Yesterday, in a review of Stifter's letters, I found the following passage, which you did not point out to me and which would absolutely have to appear in my book, if it weren't already expressed there in other words: 'My books are not poetic creations alone; as moral revelations, as *human dignity preserved* with austere seriousness, they have a value which will last longer than their poetry.' Good. Good. One could substitute for the 'frivolous literature' of that time our expressionism, which leads to sloppiness and spoils prose." He then reintroduces the quote in a tirade directed against Heinrich in *Reflections*, 159 (*GW* 12:220). Bertram, for his part, then cites an abridgement of the statement in his lecture *Adalbert Stifter* (Bonn, 1919), 66f.

***contrat social:*** allusion to *Reflections*, 158 (*GW* 12:220): "I did not stand there, one hand on my heart and the other in the air, and recite the *contrat social*" (Heinrich Mann had indicated his respect for Rousseau in "Geist und Tat").

**Richard Dehmel** (1863–1920): from 1895, freelance writer in Berlin. Strongly influenced by Nietzsche, he pushed the naturalistic revolution against the Heyse school further than his close ally Detlev von Liliencron. Settled in Blankenese in 1901. Among his works: *Erlösungen*, poems (1891); *Aber die Liebe*, poems (1893); *Weib und Welt*, poems (1896); *Zwei Menschen*, novel in ballads (1903); *Gesammelte Werke*, 10 volumes (1906–1909); *Die Verwandlungen der Venus*, poems (1907); *Michel Michael*, comedy (1911); *Die Menschenfreunde*, play (1917); *Mein Leben* (1922). Dehmel had favorably assessed Thomas Mann's first story, "Gefallen"; Thomas Mann then submitted the manuscripts of "Der kleine Professor" and "Walter Weiler" for evaluation (see letters to Dehmel of 1894–1895, *Letters of Thomas Mann*, 5–6; *Br.* 1:5f.). Dehmel volunteered for service in the First World War; he sent Thomas Mann his "Gruß aus dem Felde" (see Thomas Mann's response of December 14, 1914, *Letters of Thomas Mann*, 71–72; *Brw. Autoren, 150f.).

**my first war article:** Thomas Mann, "Gedanken im Kriege," *Die neue Rundschau* 25, no. 11 (November 1914).

JANUARY 5, 1918

*Handwritten notes and draft of an answer*

**not sent:** not even their mother believed herself able at that time to arrange a reconciliation between the brothers. On January 7, 1918, she wrote the following letter to Heinrich:

> Dear Heinrich!
>
> How sadly disappointed I am! Your letter was the last anchor for my hopes.
>
> And I ask you please to have Mimi cease inquiring about how things are between you and your brothers and sisters; discussions of the matter have generally been prompted by her questions.
>
> Now I no longer even believe that all of you would be brought back together even by *my death*, since Carla's death wasn't able to do it. Now you, just as I, have to accept the fact that what recently happened on your initiative was the final, clearly *well-intentioned* act.\* Now I ask you from my heart to let it all rest, *including things in print*, and not betray even a *trace* of criticism to the eyes of those who should not be involved, who want only to make a sensation of a quarrel between two great brothers. It was with *you* that I last spoke about this matter, which is so sad for me, with T. *no longer*, as dear as he is to me. But I *did* expect that, by way of mutual forgiveness, he would have welcomed reconciliation.\*\*
>
> So, dear Heinrich, I remain to you what I was, what I have never ceased being, and hope to see you soon.
>
> With warm regards!
>
> Your Mama

\*But it was *good* that you did it!

\*\*I heard a long time ago, and did read something of it myself, which shocked me, that you expressed yourself in public very unpleasantly regarding T.—it probably happened impetuously as a first reaction to some event—but it appears that T. cannot overcome *that*, and doesn't regard it as possible to resume lasting relations alongside or with each other as brothers, although *I* thought it was possible, as long as the desire was there to make amends for mistakes committed on both sides.

> Have the spices from Lübeck arrived yet? If no whole cinnamon came, I can give you some.

The brothers apparently saw each other only twice in these years, once in 1917 at a lecture by Karl Kraus (see "Über Karl Kraus," *GW* 10:847) and in March 1918, when Heinrich delivered a eulogy for Wedekind (see *Reflections*, 394; *GW* 12:535).

As late as April 6, 1921, Thomas Mann was still expressing such sentiments as these to Ludwig Ewers:

> Dear Ludwig Ewers:
>
> Your fine article for Heinrich's fiftieth birthday touched and pleased me greatly, as I am certain was true of its object as well. Heinrich is now being compensated by disproportionate honors for everything he missed—more bitterly than I ever dreamed—in earlier years. That, no doubt, was the psychological origin of the poison that threatened to destroy his writing. If the previous neglect could have such a decisive influence on him, then he will be no less subject today to the praise. I think that he has become more content as a person, reconciled to the world and even to the fatherland, and that, in the bottom of his heart, he will perhaps once again prefer your friendship to that of his Jewish radical errand-boys and heralds. You know yourself how things stand between us as brothers. The war could not but have made our differences more acute. As for me, you are well enough acquainted with my nature to believe that I would gladly have maintained the relationship, whatever the cost. Years ago, however, Heinrich took his solemn leave of me, expressing it in a highly literary fashion in his Zola essay, and could scarcely have esteemed me highly if I had responded easily and good-naturedly to the considered attempt at reconciliation he undertook a while ago, just as his boldest hopes in regard to Germany were being fulfilled. In the end, a quarrel like ours should be respected, and one should not try to deprive it of its deadly earnest accent. Perhaps we are *more* each other's brother separated than we would be sitting down together at a banquet feast.
>
> Yours, Thomas Mann

**via Argentina trenta quattro:** during their stay in Rome in 1897–1898, the brothers had lived at Via Torre Argentina 34.

**play:** Heinrich Mann, *Madame Legros* (Berlin: Cassirer, 1913) was performed simultaneously by the Münchner Kammerspiele and the Lübecker Stadttheater. On August 27, 1917, Thomas Mann wrote to Paul Amann: "My brother's play (a Berlin humor sheet called it *Mme Engros* because of the length of the run) is unquestionably a powerful throw of the dice. [ . . . ] The relationship between my brother and myself, delicate for years, was no longer tenable after the outbreak of the war. I would gladly have kept it going a while longer, come what may and cost what it might; but my brother's political passion is stronger than his human feelings; he despises Germany, or at any rate the Germany of this war, too intensely to have forborne branding my attitude as a crime against justice and truth and making the break. A painful and shameful affair. I gladly do him the honor of believing that he too suffers on its account" (*Letters to Paul Amann, 1915–1952*, 96–97). In a letter of February 21, 1917, to Philipp Witkop (unprinted, Thomas-Mann-Archiv, Zurich), he wrote: "The latest cultural event is the brilliant theatrical success of my brother Heinrich with his play *Madame Legros* in the local Kammerspiele. It is not immediately concerned with the war, but actually it is; for my brother, of course, was thoroughly *entente* even before the war and the play is thoroughly anti-German, an apotheosis of French revolutionary idealism, which, however, no one noticed or at least to which no one took the slightest offense—one of those basic German facts about which one neither knows nor ever will know whether to rejoice or despair. Something comparable would be the performance of a piece on Luther or Bismarck in Paris, now in wartime. The reception would be a little mixed, I tend to think. Here, as I said, it wasn't at all: the greatest theatrical success of recent years, I believe, the main reason for which, in my judgment, was not the play's literary felicities but its revolutionary ethic in the context of the specific mindset of the audience at a Kammerspiele premiere. There is much to be said concerning such tendencies. But I did believe I should tell you briefly about the event."

**difficult days:** on February 2, 1922, Thomas Mann wrote to Ernst Bertram (*Letters of Thomas Mann 1889–1955*, 116–18):

> My brother [ . . . ] became severely ill several days ago: grippe, appendicitis, and peritonitis; he underwent an operation while suffering from a bronchial catarrh which made the doctors fear lung complications. His heart, too, worried us, and for three or four days the situation was about as grave as it could be. You can imagine how wrought-up we were. My wife visited his wife. He was told of my concern, my daily inquiries, and I was told of his delight. This delight, it seemed, reached its climax when I sent flowers and a few lines as soon as there was no more risk that such a gesture might do harm. I said we had passed through difficult days but now we were over the hill and would go better—together, if he felt as I did. He sent back his thanks, and said that from now on—whatever our opinions—"let us never lose each other again."
>
> Joyful, in fact wildly shaken with emotion though I am, I have no illusions about the fragility and difficulty of the revived relationship. A decently human *modus vivendi* will be all that it can come to. Real friendship is scarcely conceivable. The monuments of our dispute still stand—incidentally, people tell me that he has never read my *Reflections*. That is good, and then again it is not; for it means that he has no idea what I have gone through. It wrenches my heart when I hear that after reading a few sentences in the *Berliner Tageblatt* in which I refer to those who proclaim the love of God and hate their brother, he sat down and wept. But my long struggle for everything I value, waged moreover for years in a state of physical undernourishment, left me no time for tears. He knows nothing of that, nothing of how time has forged me into a man, how I have grown in the process and even become the support and leader of others. Perhaps he will feel it somehow when we actually meet. As yet he is not allowed to see anyone.
>
> He is said to have become softer, kindlier in these past years. It is impossible that his views have not undergone some rectification. Perhaps we may after all speak of a certain evolution toward one another: I feel this may have happened when I realize that the thought which truly dominates my mind these days is of a new, personal fulfillment of the idea of humanity.

Thomas Mann attempted to identify more precisely the fruit of this development in his address "Von deutscher Republik" (*GW* 11:809); in English: "The German Republic," in *Order of the Day*.

**Resort Hotel:** Heinrich Mann recuperated in Überlingen from the operation he had to undergo at the end of January in Munich. Afterward he went to Berlin on business and spent a few days with Thomas Mann on the Baltic Sea.

**Berlin adventure:** on October 15, 1922, Thomas Mann delivered his address "The German Republic" in the Beethovensaal zu Berlin. He had begun writing it in July 1922. On October 6, 1922, he read it to his brother and a few friends—Kurt Martens, Emil Preetorius, and Björn Björnson—for the first time. He then delivered the address in various cities in Germany and abroad. In a letter of March 1, 1923, to Félix Bertaux (*Letters of Thomas Mann 1889–1955*, 124), Thomas Mann called the *Reflections* a "wartime project that contains a good many peripheral matters which today seem untenable even to me. But only a crude misunderstanding can convert the book's apolitical humanism into political reaction. A certain antiliberal tendency in its profession of beliefs can be explained by my relationship to Goethe and Nietzsche, whom I view as my supreme masters—if it is not impertinent to call oneself the disciple of such higher beings. I have tried to convey my idea of humanity in the essay 'The German Republic,' which has been denounced as apostasy from Germanism and as contradicting the *Reflections*, whereas inwardly it constitutes the linear continuation of that work."

**campaign speaker for Ebert:** Friedrich Ebert (1871–1925), leader of the majority Socialists during the war; elected interim president by the National Assembly in Weimar on February 11, 1919, a position he retained after the Weimar constitution went into effect. To avoid an electoral campaign at a critical juncture, the Reichstag passed a constitutional amendment on October 27, 1922, extending his term to June 30, 1925, without requiring a popular vote.

FEBRUARY 17, 1923

**lecture tours:** in Dresden Thomas Mann had read from *The Magic Mountain*, which was now once again his "main occupation." He had had talks in Berlin concerning a film version of *Buddenbrooks*. In Augsburg on February 27, 1923, he read from the essay "An Experience in the Occult," in *Three Essays* (in December and January he had taken part in three spiritualist sessions in the home of Freiherr von Schrenck-Notzing).

**news about the Ruhr:** the French and Belgian occupation of the Ruhr district in January 1923.

APRIL 1, 1923

**departure:** on his eastern lecture tour to Vienna, Budapest, and Prague, Thomas Mann once again read his essay "An Experience in the Occult" (*Die neue Rundschau* [March 1923]).

**Arthur Schnitzler** (1862–1931): Austrian writer, physician. With Hermann Bahr, Peter Altenberg, Richard Beer-Hofmann, and Hugo von Hofmannsthal, active in the Wiener Moderne. His plays dealt primarily in psychological and social-critical issues. The most well-known works: *Liebelei*, play (1896; in English: *Flirtations*, 1982); *Lieutenant Gustl*, novella (1901; English version, 1982); *Reigen*, play (1903; in English: *Hands Around*, 1920); *Der Weg ins Freie*, novel (1908; in English: *The Road into the Open*, 1992); *Casanova's Heimfahrt*, novella (1918; in English: *Casanova's Homecoming*, 1982); *Komödie der Verführung* (1924; in English: *Seduction Comedy*, 1992). See Thomas Mann's homages to Schnitzler on his fiftieth and sixtieth birthdays (*GW* 10:406, 428).

**Raoul Auernheimer** (1876–1948): Burgtheater critic, feuilletonist. Editor of *Die Neue Freie Presse*. Emigrated in 1939 to the United States. Wrote novels and comedies.

**Mimi:** Maria Mann-Kanova.

**Hofmannsthal:** see Thomas Mann, "Hofmannsthals Lesebuch" (*GW* 10:636); "In memoriam Hugo von Hofmannsthal" (*GW* 10:453); Thomas Mann, *Briefwechsel mit Hugo von Hofmannsthal* (in Brw. Autoren, 193–225, 627–37).

OCTOBER 17, 1923

**Hauptmann:** Thomas Mann conceived the character Mynnheer Peeperkorn at that time: "I was seeking a character vital to my novel and long since provided for in its scheme, but whom I did not see, did not hear, did not hold. Uneasy, anxious, and perplexed, I came to Bozen—and there, over wine, was unwittingly offered what I should never, never have allowed myself to accept, speaking in human and personal terms, but which in a state of lowered human responsibility I did accept, imagined I had the right to accept. I did so blinded by the passionate conviction, foreknowledge, certainty, that in my transmutation (for, of course, it was not a question of a portrait but of a transmutation and stylization into a totally foreign element, in which even the externals were barely akin to reality) I should be able to create the most remarkable character of a book which, I no longer doubt, is itself remarkable" (letter to Hauptmann of April 11, 1925; *GW* 11:597ff.; *Thomas Mann Jahrbuch*, 6:260f.).

**those bad, unbridled children:** Erika and Klaus Mann.

MAY 6, 1924

**Amsterdam:** as the guest of the Letterkundige Kring, Thomas Mann delivered an after-dinner address entitled "Demokratie und Leben" (*Vossische Zeitung* [Berlin], May 23, 1924). In London Thomas Mann was the honored guest of the PEN Club. Galsworthy, president of the club at the time, delivered the welcoming speech.

**John Galsworthy** (1867–1933): novelist and dramatist. His best-known work is the novel trilogy *The Forsyte Saga* (1906–1921).

**Herbert George Wells** (1866–1946): novelist and essayist. Became president of the PEN Club following Galsworthy. Famous for his first novels, science fiction fantasies in the style of Jules Verne, e.g., *The Time Machine* (1895).

**George Bernard Shaw** (1856–1950): writer, dramatist, critic. Joined the socialist Fabian Society in 1884. As social critic, in the immediate tradition of Ibsen; at the time had just written *Saint Joan* (1923).

**Katia:** postscript by Katja Mann.

NOVEMBER 16, 1924

*Abrechnungen:* anthology with new stories by Heinrich Mann (Berlin: Propyläen-Verlag, [1924]). Contains: "Der Gläubiger," "Szene," "Der Bruder," "Die Verjagten," "Liebesspiele," "Ehrenhandel," "Die Tote."

DECEMBER 11, 1924

**your book:** Thomas Mann, *The Magic Mountain* (Berlin: Fischer, 1924).

**my own:** Heinrich Mann, *Der Kopf* (Berlin, Leipzig: Zsolnay, 1925). See Thomas Mann's review in *The Dial* (*GW* 13:309–12), reprinted in Documents above.

MARCH 18, 1925

**Greece:** from March 2 to 25 Thomas Mann undertook a Mediterranean voyage on the MS *General San Martin* at the invitation of the Stinnes Line; it also took him to Egypt, the setting for his next major work. On February 4, 1925, he had written to Ernst Bertram: "I will be underway in this fashion for about four weeks [ . . . ], whereby for me, without wanting to do any injustice to the humanistic aspects, the main point is Egypt. I shall have a look at the desert, the pyramids, and the Sphinx, which is the reason I accepted the invitation, for it could turn out to be useful in regard to certain plans, if still somewhat shadowy ones, which I'm cultivating in secret." See "Unterwegs" (*GW* 11:355).

APRIL 22, 1925

*Thomas Mann mistakenly dated the letter May*

**your novel:** *Der Kopf.*

**Florence:** in connection with the Internationale Kulturwoche (May 9–16, 1925), Thomas Mann read the address "Goethe und Tolstoi" (in English: "Goethe and Tolstoy," in *Essays of Three Decades*).

**Vienna:** during his stay in Vienna (June 8–11, 1925), Thomas Mann read the address "Natur und Nation" to the PEN Club. At the banquet held in his honor, he delivered the address "Zum Problem des Österreichtums," *Neue Freie Presse*, June 11, 1925.

AUGUST 24, 1925

**Salzburg:** from August 20 to 30, 1925, Thomas Mann was present at the Salzburg Festival.

**essay:** Heinrich Mann, "Victor Hugo und '1793,'" *Der neue Merkur* 8, no. 10 (August 1925): 861–70.

MAY 17, 1926

**Arosa:** Thomas Mann was in Arosa from May 6 to 28, 1926. There he worked on the address for the 700th anniversary celebration of his hometown: "Lübeck als geistige Lebensform" (Lübeck: Quitzow, 1926). On August 1, 1926, he wrote to Félix Bertaux: "I'm deeply immersed in the preliminary work on a small, difficult, but altogether exciting novel: *Joseph in Egypt*. It is the Biblical story itself, which I want to retell in a realistic and humorous fashion."

MARCH 15–16, 1927

**Warszawa:** the trip to Warsaw followed the invitation of the Polish PEN Club. Thomas Mann delivered the address "Freiheit und Vornehmheit."

**censorship protest:** before a session of the Literary Section of the Prussian Academy of the Arts at the beginning of March Thomas Mann read Heinrich Mann's protest against the censorship law being prepared at the time in the Reichstag. The Literary Section was founded on October 27, 1926; see Thomas Mann's address "Rede zur Gründung der Sektion für Dichtkunst der Preußischen Akademie der Künste" (*GW* 10:211). In 1928 Heinrich Mann established his residence in Berlin, and he became president of the section in 1931.

**Danzig:** Thomas Mann delivered the lecture "Freiheit und Vornehmheit" at the Kunstverein (published as "Goethe and Tolstoy" in *Essays of Three Decades*).

AUGUST 19, 1927

**Sylt:** the Thomas Mann family vacationed here from August 10 to September 11, 1927.

AUGUST 23, 1927

**Ponten:** Ponten's letter to Heinrich Mann has not been found.

*Comoedia:* Milano 1919–1934. The precise reference has not been identified.

**the current president:** on November 18, 1926, the newly constituted section for the literary arts, by a vote of the Berlin members, had elected Wilhelm von Scholz as chair and Ludwig Fulda as vice-chair.

**program:** see Heinrich's letter of August [September] 6, 1927, s.v. draft program.

**secretary:** Alexander Amersdorffer.

**Herr Ponten:** see Thomas Mann's letter to Josef Ponten of August 30, 1927 (reproduced in notes of Thomas Mann's letter to Heinrich of August 29, 1930).

AUGUST 29, 1927

**Wilhelm Schäfer** (1868–1952): from 1898 freelance writer in Berlin; friend of Dehmel. In Vallendar in 1900, publisher of the periodical *Die Rheinlande*. From 1918 in Ludwigshafen am Bodensee, later in Überlingen. Works by Schäfer that had appeared at that time: *Winckelmanns Ende*, novella (1925); *Hölderlins Einkehr*, novella (1925); *Huldreich Zwingli*, novel (1926); *Neue Anekdoten* (1926).

**Joseph Ponten** (1883–1940): story- and travel-writer. From 1920 in Munich. Thomas Mann had praised his novel *Der Babylonische Turm* (1918); see letters to Ponten of January 1 and June 6, 1919. In an "Offener Brief an Thomas Mann" (*Deutsche Rundschau* 51, no. 1 [October 1924]), Ponten criticized Thomas Mann because of the latter's protest (in his essay "Zum sechzigsten Geburtstag Ricarda Huch") against the "hostile fools" (*GW* 10:432) who, "with their heads in the sand" persist "in repeating the dreary rot about the German poet [*Dichter*] and unGerman man of letters [*Schriftsteller*]." "Is it necessary," he had asked, "to repeat that hopelessly insipid antithesis between the poetic arts [*Dichtung*] and writing [*Schriftstellertum*] [ . . . ]? It should not be necessary." See Thomas Mann's letters to Ponten of January 21 (*Letters of Thomas Mann*, 133–36) and April 22, 1925 (*Letters of Thomas Mann*, 142–43).

**this move:** on August 21, 1927, Thomas Mann wrote as follows to Ponten: "As I said, I'm not altogether at ease with the situation. It could appear as if the step I did endorse was part of the conscious preparation of this other one. Also, the idea of a nonresident section president needed perhaps to have been made somewhat more plausible to those concerned." Following Heinrich's intervention of August 23, 1927, he sent Ponten the following letter of August 30, 1927:

> Dear Ponten,
>
> I must write to you again immediately because a letter I got from my brother, who, as you know, was among the recipients of your questionnaire, has raised precise and sound objections to my candidacy and in fact persuaded me against it. He will, of course, support your proposal in public, in order to avoid tedious misunderstandings, but privately he is against it. He considers it necessary to have a resident president, or, more precisely, a director, who can devote the majority of his energy to the work of the Academy for years to come. He opposes turning the post into an honorary position for individuals. Much more than prestigious representation, the Academy needs a director or general secretary who works for the Academy and is paid for it. You, in fact, want the same thing; it is just that you also want the prestige. The lack of a comprehensive treatment of the issue in your circular, which I was quick to point out to you, immediately took its toll, at least in the case of my brother. In this, however, he is unquestionably correct, that prestige is a second-order concern and that the essential point is to find a man, whether a present member of the Academy or not, who is resolved *to do* something. Little of a material nature would be gained from my selection, and when I consider that it might be assumed that the step I endorsed sought nothing more than that, it makes me nervous. Moreover, I would find it highly disagreeable to force my brother to go along in public with what he privately opposes. So there remains no option but to inform the recipients of your questionnaire that there is no longer any point to it, since, upon further

consideration, I have declined the offer. *I ask you to do this immediately.* A statement "to all concerned" will suffice.

Yours, Thomas Mann

**Ludwig Fulda** (1862–1939): writer. Studied Germanistik. From 1884 to 1888, freelance writer in Munich, later in Berlin. Cofounder of the Freie Bühne, which helped establish the success of Sudermann and Hauptmann. Also supported Arno Holz and Arthur Schnitzler. Translator of Molière, Rostand, Beaumarchais, Petöfi. Among his works: *Das Recht der Frau,* comedy (1884); *Das verlorene Paradies,* play (1892); numerous social satires: *Des Esels Schatten* (1921); *Die Gegenkandidaten* (1924); *Filmromantik* (1928); *Die verzauberte Prinzessin* (1930); and others.

AUGUST [PROBABLY SEPTEMBER] 6, 1927

**the current president:** Wilhelm von Scholz.

**draft program:** see Inge Jens, *Dichter zwischen rechts und links.* Die Geschichte der Sektion für Dichtkunst der Preußischen Akademie der Künste dargestellt nach Dokumenten (Munich: Piper Verlag, 1971). Printed in its appendix 3 are Thomas and Heinrich Mann's replies (December 3 and 6, 1926) to the questionnaire concerning the goals and tasks of a section within the academy devoted to the literary arts (244–48).

**Schickele:** s.v., letter of May 14, 1939.

**Wilhelm von Scholz** (1874–1969): writer. Gymnasium education in Berlin. From 1890 in Constance. Ph.D. (1897) in Munich. From 1916 to 1922 producer and stage manager at the Hoftheater in Stuttgart. Dr.h.c. (1944) from the University of Heidelberg. In 1949 president of Der Verband deutscher Bühnenschriftsteller. Last residence on Gut Seeheim bei Konstanz. Among his numerous works: *Frühlingsfahrt* (1896); *Hohenklingen,* poems (1898); *Der Jude von Konstanz* (1900); *Der Bodensee* (1907); *Die Unwirklichen,* stories (1916); *Zwischenreich,* stories (1922). On his life, see his own depictions, *Lebensjahre* (1939) and *Lebenslandschaft* (1943).

APRIL 18, 1931

**draft statutes:** new statutes of the Prussian Academy of the Arts, Literary Section.

**Paul F. Hübner:** ministerial director, Ministry of Science, Art, and Education.

**celebration at the Academy:** Heinrich Mann's sixtieth birthday was celebrated at the Prussian Academy of the Arts on March 27, 1931 (addresses by the minister of culture, Adolf Grimme and Gottfried Benn, Lion Feuchtwanger, and Thomas Mann). See *Heinrich Mann, Fünf Reden und eine Entgegnung zum sechzigsten Geburtstag* (Berlin: Kiepenhauer, 1931). Thomas Mann's "Vom Beruf des deutschen Schriftstellers in unserer Zeit" ["On the Profession of the German Writer in Our Time"] also appeared in *Die neue Rundschau* (May 1931); see Documents above.

**Pelzer's:** wine restaurant on Tauentzienstraße 12b, Berlin.

**Max Liebermann:** Impressionist painter (1847–1935). Founded the Berliner Sezession in 1898. From 1920 to 1923 president of the Prussian Academy of Arts. On commission from S. Fischer, drew a portrait study of Thomas Mann for the ten-volume edition of his works published on the author's fiftieth birthday (1925). See Thomas Mann, "Max Liebermann zum achtzigsten Geburtstag" (*GW* 10:442), s.v., letter of August (probably September) 6, 1927.

**Carl Heinrich Becker** (1876–1933): Prussian minister of science, art, and education.

**Adolf Grimme** (1889–1963): Becker's successor as Prussian minister of culture.

**Erwin Guido Kolbenheyer** (1878–1962): from 1919 freelance writer, first in Tübingen, then from 1932 in Munich; became member of the Prussian Academy of the Arts in 1926; co-founder of the fascist Kampfbund für deutsche Kultur in 1928. Prohibited from publishing after the Second World War. Known above all for his *Paraclesus* trilogy (1917, 1922, 1926).

**Hesse's [resignation]:** Hesse resigned from the Academy—although for different reasons—at the same time as Kolbenheyer and Schäfer; in his letter of November 27, 1931, Thomas Mann attempted to persuade him to rejoin (see *The Hesse-Mann Letters*, 21–23).

**Max Halbe** (1865–1944): began as naturalistic dramatist, later wrote psychological novels. From 1888 freelance writer in Berlin; from 1895 resident of Munich. Friend of Wedekind, Hartleben, Eduard Graf Keyserling, and Thoma. Among his works: *Jugend*, play (1893; in English: *Youth*, 1916); *Jahrhundertwende, Geschichte meines Lebens 1893–1914*, autobiography (1935).

**Alfred Döblin** (1878–1957): Berlin writer and physician. Son of a Jewish merchant from Stettin. In 1910 cofounder and contributor to the expressionist periodical *Der Sturm*. Military doctor at the end of 1914. Developed a libertarian humanistic socialism. Became famous with his novel of urban life *Berlin Alexanderplatz* (1929; English version, 1931). Fled through Zurich to Paris in 1933; in 1940 through Spain and Portugal to New York and Los Angeles. Converted to Catholicism while fleeing. Head of the literary office of the Direction de l'éducation publique in Baden-Baden in 1945, later in Mainz. From 1946 to 1951 publisher of the literary periodical *Das goldene Tor*. Found himself isolated and forgotten as a writer in Germany. Returned in 1951 to Paris. In sanatoriums near Freiburg i. Br. from March 1956 to his death. Among his works: *Die Ermordung einer Butterblume*, stories (1913); *Die drei Sprünge des Wanglun*, novel (1915; in English: *The Three Leaps of Wang Lun*, 1991); *Wadzeks Kampf mit der Dampfturbine*, novel (1918); *Wallenstein*, novel (1920); *Berge, Meere, Giganten*, novel (1924); *Manos*, epic (1927); *Babylonische Wandrung*, novel (1934); *Pardon wird nicht gegeben*, novel (1935; in English: *Man without Mercy*, 1937); *Das Land ohne Tod*, novel trilogy (1937–1948); *November 1918*, novel trilogy (1948–1950; English version, 1983); *Schicksalsreise, Bericht und Bekenntnis* (1949; in English: *Destiny's Journey*, 1992); *Hamlet*, novel (1956; in English: *Tales of a Long Night*, 1984); *Die Zeitlupe*, posthumous occasional prose (1962). See Thomas Mann, "An Alfred Döblin" (*GW* 10:489f.); Heinrich Mann, "Der Dichter Alfred Döblin," *Freies Deutschland* (Mexico) 2, no. 12 (November 1943).

**the literary senate:** the separate senate for the literary arts was formed on October 8, 1931. The original members were Heinrich Mann, Thomas Mann, Ricarda Huch, Walter von Molo, Alfred Döblin, and Ludwig Fulda.

**Oskar Loerke** (1884–1941): lyricist, writer. From 1917 to his death, editor at S. Fischer Verlag in Berlin, contributor to *Die neue Rundschau*. In 1927 senator and third permanent secretary of the Literary Section of the Prussian Academy of the Arts. Among his works: *Wanderschaft*, poems (1911); *Gedichte*, poems (1916; new edition under the title *Panmusik*, 1929); *Der Oger*, novel (1921); *Der längste Tag*, poems (1926); *Atem der Erde*, poems (1930); *Tagebücher 1903–1939*, ed. Hermann Kasack (1955); *Reden und kleinere Aufsätze*, ed. Hermann Kasack (1957); *Gedichte und Prosa*, ed. Peter Suhrkamp (1958); *Der Bücherkarren, Besprechungen im Berliner Börsen-Courier 1920 bis 1928*, ed. Hermann Kasack (1964); *Literarische Aufsätze aus der "Neuen Rundschau,"* ed. Reinhard Tgahrt (1967).

**Julius Petersen** (1878–1941): literary historian. Lecturer in Munich in 1909; professor in Basel in 1913; 1915 in Frankfurt a. M.; as of 1920 in Berlin.

**theatrical director:** Ernst Legal was chosen as the literary senate's liaison to the Prussian Staatstheater in Berlin.

**Alexander Amersdorffer** (1875–1946): from 1910 to 1946 first permanent secretary of the Royal and later Prussian Academy of the Arts in Berlin.

**lawyer:** Paul F. Hübner.

**Ricarda Huch** (1864–1947): writer. Early education in Braunschweig. Ph.D. in Zurich in 1892. From 1891 to 1898 employed at the Zentralbibliothek in Zurich. In Triest in 1906, later primarily in Munich, Berlin, Heidelberg, Freiburg, Jena, Schönberg (Taunus). Resigned in protest from the Prussian Academy of the Arts in 1933. Before her death began a book about the German resistance movement, *Der lautlose Aufstand*. Among her works: *Erinnerung von Ludolf Urslen dem Jüngeren*, novel (1893); *Aus der Triumphgasse*, novel (1902); *Seifenblasen*, stories (1905); *Der große Krieg in Deutschland* (1912–1914). Other literary works: *Die Blütezeit der Romantik* (1899); *Gottfried Keller* (1904); *Die Romantik* (1908).

JUNE 15, 1931

**address:** Thomas Mann, "Vom Beruf des deutschen Schriftstellers in unserer Zeit" (see "On the Profession of the German Writer in our Time," 215–29). In Heinrich Mann, *Fünf Reden und eine Entgegnung zum sechzigsten Geburtstag* (Berlin: Kiepenhauer, 1931).

**Attersee:** on July 29, 1896, Thomas Mann wrote a postcard to Otto Grautoff from Unterach am Attersee, Salzkammergut, Hotel "Zur Post." (The vacation plans proposed by Heinrich did not materialize; from the middle of July to the beginning of September in 1931, Thomas Mann stayed at his summer home near Nidden.)

**plenary session of the section:** Heinrich Mann was elected to the chair of the Literary Section of the Prussian Academy of the Arts at the beginning of 1931.

**Federation:** the Writers' International met from May 26 to 28, 1931, at the Hôtel de Massa in Paris. See Heinrich Mann's report in the collection *Das öffentliche Leben* (Berlin, 1932).

**conversation with Briand:** Heinrich Mann was received by Aristide Briand on June 3, 1931, in Paris. He reported on the meeting in the periodical *Europe* 29 (1931): 34–39. See "Gespräch mit Briand" in *Das öffentliche Leben* (Berlin, 1932).

MAY 31, 1932

**book:** Heinrich Mann, *Das öffentliche Leben* (Berlin: Zsolnay, 1932).

**barbarism:** see Heinrich Mann's article "Die Entscheidung," *Berliner Tageblatt*, March 27, 1932, and "Autoritäre Demokratie," *Vossische Zeitung*, April 21, 1932.

**Heinrich Brüning** (1885–1970): from 1924 to 1933 member of the Reichstag from the Zentrum. German Reichskanzler from March 28, 1930, to the end of May 1932. In December 1931, he also took over the foreign ministry. Resolved in April 1932, with the agreement of the Reichspräsident, on taking decisive steps against National Socialism (prohibition of the SA). Took over leadership of the Zentrum in May 1933 but found himself compelled to dissolve the party in July 1933. Escaped arrest by emigrating to the United States. Professor at Harvard University. German citizenship revoked in 1938. Returned to Germany in 1952; professor at the University of Cologne.

**president:** Max von Schillings (1868–1933). Composer and conductor. Replaced Max Liebermann in office on October 1, 1932. It was under his direction on February 2, 1933, that the meeting took place at which it was suggested to Heinrich Mann and Käthe Kollwitz that they resign from the Academy (see Inge Jens, *Dichter zwischen rechts und links*, 181ff.). On March 22, 1933, Max von Schillings wrote to Thomas Mann, who had announced his resignation from the Academy five days earlier, as follows:

Esteemed Professor Mann,

I am confirming the reception of your registered letter of the 17th of this month from Lenzerheide. I am obliged to conclude from it that you are no longer disposed to continue your membership in the Academy. Given the firmness of your resolve to resign your membership, it is not for me to express an opinion on the matter. I would not, however, like to complete the formalities of your departure without expressing my thanks to you for your membership in the Academy and for your activity as a senator.

With my greatest respect,

Your very devoted Max v. Schillings

(The original of the letter is in the Thomas-Mann-Archiv der ETH in Zurich.)


JUNE 2, 1932

**Alfons Paquet** (1881–1944): writer. Traveled in Siberia, the United States, Syria, and Asia Minor; his travel reports were somewhat influenced by Whitman. Lived in Dresden-Hellerau; finally as a freelance writer in Frankfurt, where he died of a heart attack during an air raid. Social problems and world political tendencies occupy the foreground of his narrative and dramatic works. The play *Fahnen* was produced by Erwin Piscator for the Berliner Volksbühne in 1924. Among his works: *Lieder und Gesänge* (1902); *Held Namelos*, poems (1911); *Kamerad Fleming*, novel (1911–1926); *Prophezeiungen*, stories (1922; in English: *Prophecies*, 1983); *Fahnen*, play (1923); *Sturmflut*, play (1926). Paquet withdrew from the Prussian Academy of the Arts in protest in 1933. See the biographical introduction to his *Gesammelte Werke* (1971) and Inge Jens, *Dichter zwischen rechts und links*, 212.


NOVEMBER 1, 1932

**Dr. Fiedler:** s.v., letter of September 27, 1936, and *Blätter der Thomas-Mann-Gesellschaft*, nos. 11–12 (1971–1972).

**my final word on nationalism:** Heinrich Mann, "Das Bekenntnis zum Übernationalen," *Die neue Rundschau* 43, no. 12 (December 1932): 721–46. See Thomas Mann's letter of December 7, 1932, to Wilhelm Herzog: "Have you seen the magnificent essay by my brother in *Die neue Rundschau?* It is an event, as remarkable as it may be that the expression of all of these obvious truths can be experienced as an event. There is rage and satisfaction in the fact that both will be ample in Germany."

**Hans Heinrich Lammers** (1879–1962): attorney, politician. From 1921 to 1933 in the Ministry of the Interior; from 1933 to 1945 head of the Reichskanzlei; from 1939 to 1945 he was simultaneously member and managing officer of the ministerial council on national defense. In the Wilhelmstraße Trial in Nuremberg in 1949 he was sentenced to twenty years' imprisonment; released in 1952.

**novel:** Heinrich Mann, *Ein ernstes Leben* (Berlin: Zsolnay, 1932); conceived in Nizza in 1931, finished in Berlin in 1932.


NOVEMBER 26, 1932

**Your letter:** not in the holdings of the Thomas-Mann-Archiv in Zurich.

**novel:** *Ein ernstes Leben.*

**Bäuerlein:** Attorney Bäuerlein, character in Heinrich Mann's new novel.

**the week devoted to honoring him:** Thomas Mann delivered his address "An Gerhart Hauptmann" (*Vossische Zeitung*, Berlin, December 15, 1932; *GW* 10:331) on November 11, 1932, at the Munich Nationaltheater at the celebration of Gerhart Hauptmann's seventieth birthday (November 15, 1932). Hauptmann's birthday was also energetically celebrated in Berlin.

**your world-historical novel:** *Joseph and His Brothers.*

**essay:** Heinrich Mann, "Das Bekenntnis zum Übernationalen," *Die neue Rundschau* 43, no. 12 (December 1932): 721–46.

**Treaty of Verdun:** in the year 843.

**Heinrich Sahm** (1877–1939): politician. From 1931 to 1935 mayor of Berlin; from 1936 to 1939 envoy in Oslo.

**Joseph-Arthur Gobineau** (1816–1882): diplomat, writer. His work *La Renaissance: Savonarola, César Borgia, Jules II, Léon X, Michel-Ange, scènes historiques* (1887) was among the sources of Heinrich Mann's *Göttinnen* and Thomas Mann's *Fiorenza*. His essay *The Inequality of the Races* (1853–1855) influenced Nietzsche, Wagner, Chamberlain, and Barrès. In the novel *Les Pléiades* (1874) he advanced his thesis of the superiority of the master race.

JANUARY 29, 1933

*whom we select ourselves:* italic text underlined or marked in the margin by Thomas Mann.

**Paul Fechter** (1880–1958): writer, journalist. Studied in Berlin and Erlangen. From 1911 to 1915 feuilleton editor of *Die Vossische Zeitung;* from 1918 to 1933 editor at *Die Deutsche Allgemeine Zeitung.* Afterward theater critic and art reporter for the periodical *Deutsche Zukunft.* Among his works: *Der Expressionismus* (1914); *Frank Wedekind* (1920); *Die Tragödie der Architektur* (1921); *Gerhart Hauptmann* (1922); stories and plays. See letter of February 9, 1933, s.v. manifesto.

FEBRUARY 9, 1933

**manifesto:** on December 6, 1932, Franz Werfel had moved that the Literary Section issue a public warning against Paul Fechter's literary history, which the Deutsche Buchgemeinschaft was just then distributing in a mass edition. In the section meeting of February 6, 1933—the last chaired by Heinrich Mann—the decision was made against a manifesto against Fechter. His literary history gained even broader circulation under the Nazis (see Inge Jens, *Dichter zwischen rechts und links,* 176–80).

**Rudolf Olden** (1885–1940): writer and journalist. Until 1933 political editor of *Das Berliner Tageblatt.* Emigrated in 1933 to Prague, 1934 to Paris, and from there to England. Drowned when the English evacuation ship *City of Benares* was sunk on the crossing to Canada. Among his later works: *Hitler. Der Agent der Macht* (1935); *The History of Liberty* (1939); *Is Germany a Hopeless Case?* (1940).

APRIL 15, 1933

**where you are staying:** Thomas Mann was in Lugano from March 24 to April 29, 1933.

**Madame Bertaux:** Céline Bertaux-Piquet, wife of Félix Bertaux.

**professor:** Alfred Pringsheim (1850–1941), Thomas Mann's father-in-law.

*La Croix:* Quotidien catholique d'information, Paris (the article mentioned has not been identified).

**scene with Göring:** see Heinrich Mann, "Goering zittert und schwitzt," in *Der Haß* (1933): 115–23.

**James Louis Garvin** (1868–1947): English journalist. Wrote primarily for *The Daily Telegraph;* later (1908–42) for the *Observer.* From 1926 to 1929 publisher of the *Encyclopedia Britan-*

*nica*, 14th edition. Among his works: *The Life of Joseph Chamberlain*, 3 vols (1932–1934). The article mentioned has not been identified.

**essay:** Thomas Mann's essay "Leiden und Grösse Richard Wagner," translated by Félix Bertaux under the title "Souffrances et grandeur de Richard Wagner," in *Europe* 31 (1933): 305–38 (in English: "Sufferings and Greatness of Richard Wagner," *Essays of Three Decades*).

**Karl Häusser** (1842–1907): actor.

**Ernst Ritter von Possart** (1841–1921): s.v., letter of December 5, 1903.

**summer:** in spring 1933 Thomas Mann was considering whether he should settle in Bolzano, in the south of France, or Basel.

**Bandol:** from May 10 to June 11, 1933, Thomas Mann took up temporary residence in Bandol (Var) on the French Riviera. Heinrich Mann arrived in Bandol on May 16. The time from June 12 to September 22, 1933, Thomas Mann then spent in Sanary-sur-Mer.

**Hans Frank** (1900–1946): member of the National Socialist [Nazi] Party in 1927. Member of Reichstag in 1930. Bavarian minister of justice and National Socialist national director for legal affairs in 1933. Governor-general of the occupied Polish territories in 1939; regime of terror, mass annihilation, deportations. Condemned to death by hanging by the international military court in Nuremberg in 1946.

**Leipzig trial:** trial of the alleged perpetrators of the Reichstag fire. It lasted from September 21 to December 23, 1933. The court condemned the (mentally handicapped) van der Lubbe to death but acquitted his codefendants. Göring boasted later that he knew best who had started the fire, because he had done it himself.

**attorney:** reference is probably to Valentin Heins (1894–1971), Thomas Mann's Munich attorney.

**Heinrich Hauser** (1901–1955): writer. In Hamburg as naval cadet and seaman. Wrote mainly travel reports and stories of sea voyages. Friend of the Irish writer Liam O'Flaherty. Hauser translated his *Return of the Brute* and *The House of Gold*. Embraced the Nazis in 1933 but later turned away from Hitler. In the United States from 1938 to 1948. Then chief editor of the weekly magazine *Stern*. Among his works: *Brackwasser* (1928; in English: *Bitter Water*, 1930); *Donner überm Meer* (1929; in English: *Thunder above the Sea*, 1931); *Noch nicht* (1932); *Männer am Bord* (1936); *Notre Dame von den Wogen* (1937); *Gigant Hirn* (1958); reports: *Schwarzes Revier*, reportage from the Ruhr district (1929); *Die letzten Segelschiffe* (1930); *Feldwege nach Chicago* (1931); *Kampf*, autobiography (1934; in English: *Once Your Enemy*, 1936). Books about the Balkans, Canada, Australia. On Heinrich Mann's comments, see Peter de Mendelssohn, *S. Fischer und sein Verlag* (Frankfurt, 1970), 1279f.:

> Only one author created a seriously intolerable situation for the press. In January 1933 Heinrich Hauser delivered the manuscript of his new book, *Ein Mann lernt Fliegen*, which went directly to press and was scheduled to appear in May. In April, however, he suddenly demanded that the book be preceded by a dedication to the former combat pilot and then National Socialist prime minister, Hermann Göring. A rejection of the demand, as Bermann

Fischer justifiably feared, could have led to the closing or expropriation of the press and measures against the Fischer family and their employees; acceding to it would have seemed like a deplorable "genuflexion," which would have cost the press the sympathy of all opponents of the regime both inside and outside Germany. Bermann Fischer tried to find a way out. He demanded of Hauser that he produce Göring's express approval of the dedication, convinced that Göring would naturally refuse to give it to a "Jewish" press. But Göring was flattered and accepted it; the book had to appear with a dedication to "our archenemy and persecutor." As if that were not enough, Hauser published, in the same May 1933 issue of *Die neue Rundschau* in which Suhrkamp's essay "März 33" appeared, a glorifying depiction of the National Socialist May rally at Tempelhof: "The hands of the millions were lifted slowly above their heads and remained there like the foam on the crest of an approaching wave. The batteries of selzer bottles arranged on the perimeter of the encampment glinted in the sun. Ten thousand banners made their inexorable approach blowing like a forest in a storm. The blowing flags shined like flowing blood . . . A strange rapture and exaltation spread over the sea. The feeling of one's own mass and endlessness exalted every atom . . . No one present there will ever forget that day." The press broke relations with Hauser; Eugen Diederichs took over the contract for three books which Hauser had not yet delivered but for which he had already received a substantial advance payment."

See Gottfried Bermann Fischer, *Bedroht—Bewahrt: Weg eines Verlegers* (Frankfurt, 1967), 293f.
   **my book:** Heinrich Mann, *Der Haß: Deutsche Zeitgeschichte* (Amsterdam: Querido, 1933).
   **your first volume:** Thomas Mann, *Die Geschichte Jaakobs* (Berlin: S. Fischer, 1933; in English: *The Tales of Jacob*). The first volume of the Joseph novel appeared on October 10, 1933.
   **Erika:** in September 1933 Erika Mann was seeking permission from the Swiss authorities to continue performances in Zurich of her literary-political cabaret Die Pfeffermühle, which had been banned in Munich at the end of February. When it reopened at the Hirsch Hotel on Hirschenplatz in Zurich on September 30, 1933, it was a rousing success. See Thomas Mann's entries in his *Tagebuch* of September 30 to October 5, 1933.

OCTOBER 17, 1933

**Your book:** *The Tales of Jacob.*
**dedication:**

To Heinrich
In memory of the exchange
of a summer they couldn't deny us.
Zurich-Küsnacht, October 12, 1933

(See Heinz Saueressig, "Die gegenseitigen Buchwidmungen von Heinrich und Thomas Mann, Eine Dokumentation," in Georg Wenzel, ed., *Betrachtungen und Überblicke: Zum Werk Thomas Manns* [Berlin and Weimar, 1966], 485.)
   **withdrawal of "Germany":** Germany withdrew from the League of Nations on October 19, 1933.

NOVEMBER 3–4, 1933

**success:** there were two more printings of *The Tales of Jacob* in 1933 (copies 11,000 to 15,000 and 16,000 to 20,000).
   *Der Haß:* Heinrich Mann, *Der Haß: Deutsche Zeitgeschichte* (Amsterdam: Querido, 1933; French translation: *La Haine: histoire contemporaine d'Allemagne* [Paris: Gallimard, 1933]).
   **Lion Feuchtwanger** (1884–1958): s.v., letter of October 3, 1935.

**Ernst Torgler** (1893–1963): at the time chairman of the KPD faction in the Reichstag; arrested after the Reichstag fire (February 27, 1933) as one of the arsonists but released later for lack of evidence. Immediately following his release, however, the Nazis took him into "protective custody" and then sent him to a concentration camp. See Thomas Mann, "Leiden an Deutschland: Tagebuchblätter aus den Jahren 1933–1934" (*GW* 12:688, 724).

**Oswald Spengler** (1880–1936): philosopher of history. From 1908 to 1911 gymnasium teacher in Hamburg, then freelance writer. His most important work, *The Decline of the West*, appeared in its original German edition over the years 1918 to 1922. Among his other works: *Preußentum und Sozialismus* (1920; in *Selected Essays*, 1967); *Neubau des deutschen Reiches* (1924); *Politische Pflichten der deutschen Jugend* (1924); *Der Mensch und die Technik* (1931; in English: *Man and Technics*, 1932); *Politische Schriften* (1932); *Jahre der Entscheidung* (1933; in English: *The Hour of Decision*, 1934); *Reden und Aufsätze* (1937).

**Franz von Papen** (1879–1969): politician. Elected successor to Brüning as Reichskanzler on June 1, 1932. His dispute with the minister of defense von Schleicher led to his resignation from office on December 3, 1932. Schleicher took over as Reichskanzler at the beginning of December. Von Papen had a meeting with Hitler on January 4, 1933, in Cologne and was largely responsible in the following weeks for toppling Schleicher. He was made Vizekanzler under Hitler on January 30, 1933. Attempted vainly to oppose the total seizure of power by the National Socialists. Personally in danger after the Röhm putsch of June 30, 1934, he resigned from Hitler's cabinet. Made Hitler's envoy to Vienna at the end of July 1934. Later ambassador to Turkey. Acquitted in the Nuremberg trials in 1946 but sentenced by the denazification court to eight years in a labor camp. Released in 1949. Among his works: *Appell an das deutsche Gewissen*, addresses (1933); *Der Wahrheit eine Gasse*, memoirs (1952).

**Kurt von Schleicher** (1882–1934): professional soldier and politician; from an old Prussian military family. From 1913 on the general staff; 1918–1919 political advisor on Groener's staff, then in the General Army Offices as a close associate of Seeckt. In 1926 department head in the ministry of defense; 1929 head of the newly created ministerial office under Groener. Critically involved in the formation of Brüning's cabinet. Made minister of defense in June 1932. As Reichskanzler (December 1932 to January 1933) attempted vainly to counter the danger of a National Socialist government by splitting the National Socialists and forming an alliance between the army and the unions. Murdered by the SS in 1934.

**88 "writers":** at the end of October, beginning of November there appeared in various German and Swiss newspapers the following "Proclamation of Loyalty of German Writers" (reproduced here as printed with partially garbled names):

"88 German writers have appended their signatures to the following vow of loyalty to Reichskanzler Adolf *Hitler:* 'Peace, work, honor, and freedom are the most sacred goods of every nation and the precondition of an upright coexistence of peoples among each other. The consciousness of our power and recovered unity, our upright will to serve unreservedly the cause of peace within and without the nation, our profound conviction of our tasks in the rebuilding of the Reich, and our resolve to do nothing that is not compatible with the honor of ourselves and our fatherland have caused us in this grave hour to solemnly submit to you, Herr Reichskanzler, this avowal of our most faithful obedience.'

Friedrich Ahrenhövel, Gottfried Benn, Werner Beumelburg, Rudolf G. Binding, Walter Bloem, Max Karl Böttcher, Hans Fr. Blunck, Hermann Claudius, Hans Martin Cremer, Marie Dies, Peter Dörfler, Max Dreyer, Franz Dülberg, Ferdinand Eckardt, Richard Euringer, Ludwig Finkh, Hans Franck, Otto Flake, Heinrich von Gleichen, von Gleichen-Rußwurm, Gustav Frenssen, Friedrich Griese, Max Grube, Johannes Günther, Max Halbe, Isle Hamel, Agnes Harder, Carl Haensel, Hans Ludwig Held, Karl Heinl, Friedrich W. Herzog, Rudolf Herzog,

Hans von Hülsen, Paul Oskar Höcker, Rudolf Huch, Bruno W. Jahn, Hanns Johst, Max Jungnickel, Hans Knudsen, Ruth Köhler-Irrgang, Gustav Kohne, Karl Lange, Joh. von Leers, Heinrich Lilienfein, Heinrich Lersch, Oskar Loerke, Herybert Menzel, Gerhard Menzel, Alfred Richard Meyer, Agnes Miegel, Walter von Molo, Börries Frhr. von Naso, Helene von Nostiz-Wallwitz, Josef Ponten, Rudolf Presber, Hofrat Rehbein, Ilse Reicke, Hans Richter, Heinz Schauwecker, Johannes Schlaf, Anton Schnack, Friedrich Schnack, Rich. Schneider-Edenkoben, Wilhelm von Scholz, Lothar Schreyer, Gustav Schröer, Schussen (Wilhelm), Ina Seidel, Prof. Heinrich Sohnrey, Dr. Willy Seidel, Diedrich Speckmann, Heinz Steguweit, Lulu v. Strauß u. Torney, Eduard Stucken, Will Vesper, Magnus Wehner, Leo Weißmantel, Bruno Werner, Heinrich Zerkaulen, Hans Caspar von Zobeltitz."

Rebecca Christine **Caroline Claudius** (1819–1900) and Emilie **Rebecca Claudius** (1828–1900): Two granddaughters of the Hamburg writer Matthias Claudius who lived for a few years around 1890 at Beckergrube 48, that is, two doors away from Beckergrube 52. Models for Lea Gerhardt and her sister in *Buddenbrooks*. Thomas Mann probably gave them the name of Paul Gerhardt because he was aware of the sisters' literary heritage (according to Hans Bürgin's friendly suggestion).

*has authorized such* . . . : italic text underlined and/or marked in the margin in pencil by Thomas Mann.

**Beermann:** the publisher Gottfried Bermann Fischer.

**Paul Zsolnay** (1895–1961): publisher. Founded the Paul-Zsolnay-Verlag (Berlin and Vienna) in 1923. Among his authors were Werfel, Meier-Graefe, Däubler, Schnitzler, and Salten. He was Heinrich Mann's publisher from 1925 to 1933. (Previously Mann had had his works published primarily by Langen, Cassirer, and Wolff; in the years of exile Querido took over publishing his works.)

NOVEMBER 18, 1933

**Nice:** Heinrich Mann and Käthe Kollwitz were expelled from the Prussian Academy of the Arts on February 15, 1933, because they, along with Albert Einstein, had signed a call for the unification of the leftist parties and thus for resistance to the fascist threat. Heinrich Mann took the expulsion as a warning and fled on February 21, 1933, to France; Nelly Kröger soon followed him to Nice. In August 1933 his German citizenship was revoked. See Thomas Mann's letter of February 26, 1933, to Alfred Döblin.

**"Prelude":** "Descent into Hell," introduction to the *Joseph* tetralogy, the first volume of which, *Die Geschichten Jaakobs* (*The Tales of Jacob*) was published on October 10, 1933, by S. Fischer.

**Anatole France,** actually Jacques-Anatole Thibault (1844–1924): Heinrich Mann is probably referring here to the novel *La révolte des anges* (1914). He had translated France's *Histoire comique* (1903) into German (*Komödiantengeschichte*, Munich: Langen, 1904).

**Robert Aron** (1898–1975): French writer. From 1922 to 1939 collaborator on the *Editions de la Nouvelle Revue Française*. Among his works: *La révolution nécessaire*, with Arnaud Dandieu (1934); *Victoire à Waterloo* (1937); *Le piège où nous a pris l'histoire* (1950); *Histoire de Vichy* (1954); *Histoire de la libération de la France* (1959); *De Gaulle* (1964).

**André Gide** (1869–1951): had joined the Communists in the early 1930s but distanced himself from them following a trip to the Soviet Union (1935).

**Swiss tour:** January 28–February 9, 1934. Thomas Mann generally read his lecture on Wagner or "The Coat of Many Colors" from *Joseph*.

**my two books:** presumably Heinrich Mann, *Das Bekenntnis zum Übernationalen* (Berlin: Zsolnay, 1933); *Der Haß: Deutsche Zeitgeschichte* (Amsterdam: Querido, 1933).

**Nelly Kröger** (1898–1944): later the wife of Heinrich Mann (marriage on September 9, 1939; see Thomas Mann's letter of November 26, 1939). See Joachim Seyppel, "Wer war Nelly Mann? Biographische Notizen zur zweiten Ehefrau Heinrich Manns," in *Heinrich-Mann-Jahrbuch* (Lübeck, 1986), 4:39–55.

NOVEMBER 18, 1933

**in both versions:** Heinrich Mann, *Der Haß: Deutsche Zeitgeschichte. Essays* (Amsterdam: Querido, 1933). The French edition was published under the title *La haine*. See Thomas Mann's November 15, 1933 entry in his *Tagebuch:* "Read this evening in the French edition of Heinrich's book about the German Revolution." On November 17, 1933, he wrote: "Now the German edition of Heinrich's *Der Haß* has come. I read in it after dinner, deeply affected by his pathos, despite his weaknesses, mistakes, and real errors. Still the best piece in it is the great introductory essay, which I read much to my benefit. [ . . . ] Read this evening for a long time still in Heinrich's book, which frequently provides intense satisfaction, but more often has the effect of pure fantasy than an analysis of the real, and is diverted or deflected into the unreal."

**document in the *Petit Parisien*:** *Le Petit Parisien* was the Third Republic's largest daily newspaper, published, from October 15, 1876, to August 24, 1944, primarily in Paris, and thus was one of the few papers that could continue to appear during the Second World War. On November 16 and 17, 1933, it published two articles under the title "Le vrai visage des maîtres du IIIe Reich." At issue were directives sent from the Propaganda Ministry in Berlin to overseas diplomats, especially to those in North and South America. The classified document communicated the foreign policy aims of National Socialism and described propaganda activities (still in the process of being organized) in those countries. It was published in French, along with an extremely critical commentary by Albert Jullien. It prompted a German denial, which was judged false from the beginning and worked primarily to confirm the document's authenticity. On November 18, 1933, there followed the publication of a renewed denial, along with skeptical opinions from the press in France and elsewhere. Then Goebbels himself became involved, eventually leading to a protest lodged with the French government by the German ambassador. On November 22, 1933, *Le Petit Parisien* then published the third part of the document, not without reference to rights of free speech as established in France. Statements from all over the world supported the outrage expressed by *Le Petit Parisien;* but publication, as history was to demonstrate, did not lead to the necessary hearing of the issues.

On November 18, 1933, Thomas Mann noted in his *Tagebuch:* "The publication of the documents by *Petit Parisien* spoils a little, if not sufficiently, Hitler's concept of peace, which is at least as counterfeit as the document." And on November 25, 1933: "Constantly outraged by the intellectual shamelessness of the German powers that be. According to *Le Temps*, the *Völkerischer Beobachter* countered revelations from *Le Petit Parisien* by accusing that paper of whipping up war fever on behalf of the 'armament industry.' It was the armament manufacturers who for the sake of their filthy profits wanted to see the soil of Europe drenched with the blood of its young men. Anyone who made such statements in the past was branded as anti-German, called a peace-mongering hyena, a pacifist and traitor, a downright Republican, and is now forced to chant while sitting in a concentration camp, 'I was a Communist pig.' The impudence with which they appropriate suppressed ideas is nothing new, but it never ceases to astound. Evidently they enjoy doing this. No one dares to point out their idiotic lack of principle" (Thomas Mann, *Diaries*, 182).

**your recent question:** see Heinrich Mann's letter of November 3 and 4, 1933, to Thomas Mann.

**Rascher:** the Zurich publisher Rascher & Cie. sought to publish a volume of essays by

Thomas Mann in the autumn of 1933. Rascher welcomed the plan, but Gottfried Bermann Fischer was not prepared to give up the rights. See Thomas Mann's letter of July 19 [July 9], 1933, to Gottfried Bermann Fischer.

**Since Sanary:** Thomas Mann and his family resided from June 12 to September 22, 1933, in Sanary-sur-Mer, which at the time was a gathering point for émigré writers.

DECEMBER 25, 1933

**a few pages of your book:** *The Tales of Jacob.*

**In the summer:** Thomas Mann had settled in Bandol on the Côte d'Azur in May 1933. In June he moved to Sanary-sur-Mer, which had become at the time a gathering point for émigré writers. In October 1933, he took up residence in Küsnacht near Zurich.

**Ferdinand Bruckner,** actually Theodor Tagger (1891–1958): dramatist and theatrical producer. Publisher in 1917 of the monthly *Marsyas.* In 1923 chief producer of the Renaissance theater in Berlin. Emigrated in 1933 to France, in 1939 to New York. Among his works: *Die Vollendung eines Herzens,* novella (1917); *1920 oder Die Komödie vom Untergang der Welt* (1920); *Krankheit der Jugend,* play (1928); *Die Verbrecher,* play (1929); *Die Kreatur,* play (1930); *Elisabeth von England,* play (1930); *Timon,* tragedy (1932); *Die Marquise von O.,* play (1933); *Napoleon I,* play (1936); *Die Befreiten,* play (1945); *Simon Bolivar,* play (1945); *Fährten,* play (1948). Reference here is presumably to the play *Die Rassen* (1933).

**Golo Mann** (1909–1994): Thomas Mann's second son. Historian. From 1933 to 1936 teacher of German literature and history at the Ecole Normale Supérieure, St-Cloud. From 1937 to 1940 lecturer at the University of Rennes. Coeditor of the periodical *Maß und Wert,* published by Thomas Mann and Konrad Falke, in Zurich. Went to France as a war volunteer in May 1940; fled in late fall to the United States. Professor at Olivet College in Michigan and the Claremont Colleges in California. Guest professor in Münster in 1958–1959. From 1960 to 1964 professor of political science at the Technische Hochschule in Stuttgart. Until death private scholar and journalist in Kilchberg am Zürichsee. Among his works: *Friedrich von Gentz, Geschichte eines europäischen Staatsmannes* (1947; in English: *Secretary of Europe,* 1946); *Vom Geist Amerikas, Eine Einführung in amerikanisches Denken und Handeln im 20. Jahrhundert* (1954); *Deutsche Geschichte des 19. und 20. Jahrhunderts* (1958; in English: *The History of Germany since 1789,* 1968); *Geschichte und Geschichten,* essays (1961); *Wallenstein* (1971). Editor of the Propyläen-Weltgeschichte. From 1963 to 1980 copublisher of *Die neue Rundschau.*

JANUARY 25, 1934

**Paul Graetz** (1890–1937): cabaret artist, actor. Appeared in the 1920s in the cabaret Schall und Rauch (Friedrich Holländer/Kurt Tucholsky). Around 1930 member of the Kabaretts der Komiker (with Curt Bois, Paul Morgan, Siegfried Arno). Appeared in 1927 in the Ufa silent film *Monna Vanna* (director, Richard Eichberg), in 1927 in the sports comedy *Der große Sprung* (with Luis Trenker). Emigrated in 1933 to England, where he appeared in the English film of the Feuchtwanger novel *Jud Süß* (director, Lothar Mendes); Veit Harlen later produced the infamous Nazi version of the same material. Around 1935 Graetz went to Hollywood, where he had a role in *Mr. Cohn Takes a Walk* (director, Irving Asher). Ernst Lubitsch clearly had him in mind for a part in the Garbo film *Ninotschka* (1938–1939), but he died immediately prior to shooting.

**press agent of the Circus Busch:** Karl Lemke (1895–1969), journalist and writer (wrote under the pseudonyms Fr. Massan, Charles Scott, Role). In 1918 editor for the Königsberg

*Ostpreußische Zeitung.* From 1924 freelance writer, in 1930 in Freiburg im Breisgau, 1936 in Breisach am Rhein, from where he maintained contact with several émigré writers through the post offices in Colmar and Basel. Moved to Munich in 1939. From 1949 editor for the *Jüdische Nachrichten.* Lemke became acquainted with Heinrich Mann in the late 1920s in Berlin. In 1933, after Heinrich's flight, he intervened for his friend with a pamphlet, *Damit Heinrich Mann gelesen wird.* In 1946 his essay "Heinrich Mann" appeared; see Heinrich Mann, *Briefe an Karl Lemke und Klaus Pinkus,* ed. Deutschen Akademie der Künste, Berlin (Hamburg: Claassen, 1964). Among his works: *Samo und Sämlinde,* novella (1917); *Claus, der Seeman,* novel (1938); *Ambra,* novel (1940); *Die Reise ins Glück,* novel (1940); *Zug der Zeit,* poems (1943); *Meister des Wortes,* essays (1946); *Erlebnis in Paris,* travel report (1961).

**Balder Olden** (1882–1949): writer. Brother of Rudolf Olden. Emigrated in 1933 through Czechoslovakia, France, and Argentina to Uruguay. Member of the honorary presidium of the Latin American committee Freies Deutschland, to which Heinrich Mann also belonged. Died in Montevideo. Numerous novels of experience and love: *Kilimandscharo* (1922; in English: *On Virgin Soil,* 1930); *Ich bin Ich* (1927); *Das Herz mit einem Traum genährt* (1929). At issue here is the novel *Dawn of Darkness* (London, 1933; in German: *Anbruch der Finsternis: Roman eines Nazi* [Berlin, 1981]). Depicting Germany from December 1932 to May 1933, the work prompted the National Socialists to expatriate Olden and burn his books.

**Golo's piece:** probably Golo Mann, "Ernst Jünger," in *Die Sammlung* (Literarische Monatsschrift unter dem Patronat von André Gide, Aldous Huxley, Heinrich Mann, ed. Klaus Mann) 1, no. 5 (January 1934): 249–59. It could, however, be the essay "Wallenstein und die deutsche Politik," which appeared in the periodical's issue no. 10, 509–17 (reprint of *Die Sammlung* by Kraus Reprint, Nendeln/Lichtenstein, 1970).

**Wassermann:** Jakob Wassermann (born 1873) died in the early morning hours of January 1, 1934, in Altaussee. Although already severely ill, he had recently completed a lecture tour in Holland. During the final years of his life Wassermann had been involved in endless trials and legal disputes begun by his first wife, Julie Wassermann-Speyer. Wassermann depicts these conflicts in his autobiographical roman à clef *Joseph Kerkhovens dritte Existenz,* the third volume in the Etzel-Andergast trilogy. Julie, who is unmistakably portrayed in the novel, attempted to block publication of the book by threatening S. Fischer Verlag and other presses with damage suits. The novel was published in 1934 only after Wassermann's death, by the Querido Verlag in Amsterdam. See Wassermann's letter of December 27, 1933, to Gottfried Bermann Fischer.

**Your book:** Thomas Mann, *The Tales of Jacob.* There was a printing of 25,000 copies in 1934.

**my great king:** Heinrich Mann, *Die Jugend des Königs Henri Quatre* (Amsterdam: Querido, 1935; in English: *Young Henry of Navarre*).

**intellectual freedom:** see Heinrich Mann, "Denken nach Vorschrift," *Die Neue Weltbühne,* March 8, 1934. The American periodical could not be identified.

**change in systems:** Heinrich Mann, "Changement de régime," *La Dépêche,* March 7, 1934.

MARCH 5, 1934

**January 30th:** the letter has not been preserved.

**My novel:** *Henri Quatre.*

**"something that lasts":** not identified. Heinrich Mann also quoted the sentence in "Nietzsche," *Maß und Wert* 2, no. 3 (January–February 1939): 302.

**a first volume of the novel:** Heinrich Mann, *Die Jugend des Königs Henri Quatre* (Amsterdam, 1935).

**The third volume:** Thomas Mann, *Joseph in Ägypten* (Vienna: Bermann-Fischer, 1936; in English: *Joseph in Egypt*).

**essay volume:** Thomas Mann, *Leiden und Größe der Meister* (Berlin: S. Fischer, 1935).

**the *Ligue:*** the anti-Huguenot Holy League was founded in 1576 by the duke of Guise.

**Georges Boulanger** (1837–1891): French general and politician. Retired from the army in 1888. With the support of the Boulganists and the monarchists, demanded a revision of the constitution, but was indicted in 1889 for his plans and fled to Brussels.

**Heinz Liepmann** (1905–1966): writer and journalist. Went to Holland in 1934, where he was arrested in response to the antifascist book he published there, *Das Vaterland*, and sentenced to one-month imprisonment for the "wilful affront of a state allied with Holland." Deported to Belgium after his release. In 1935 to France, 1936 to England. Contributor to *Die Neue Weltbühne*. From 1937 to 1947 in the United States. Contributor to various American periodicals. Later in Hamburg. Among his works: *Das Vaterland*, novel (1933); . . . *wird mit dem Tode bestraft*, novel (1935); *Death from the Skies* (1938).

**naturalization:** on November 16, 1935, René Schickele wrote to Thomas Mann: "Your brother would have been naturalized long since had not this Stavisky gotten in the way. Sarraut simply couldn't manage it. . . . Now the *three-year* stay in France must be 'an accomplished fact'" (*Brw. Schickele, 89). Alexandre Stavisky, a Romanian confidence man implicated in a corruption scandal, had shot himself in February 1934. As a result of the scandal, several ministers in Daladier's cabinet were compromised and forced to resign, as was Daladier himself. The French authorities took the Stavisky affair as the occasion for enforcing immigration laws more strictly. Thus Heinrich Mann, despite his personal ties to the brothers Maurice and Albert Sarraut (politician and publisher of *La Dépêche* in Toulouse), had to fulfill the legal obligations for French citizenship like all other immigrants.

**Florence:** spurred by reports from his Munich friend Alfred Neumann and his wife, who had emigrated in 1933 to Florence, Thomas and Katja Mann considered in January/February 1934 whether they should move there themselves. See Thomas Mann's letter of February 2, 1934, to René Schickele and of February 4, 1934, to Alexander Moritz Frey.

**Schickele:** René Schickele and his wife, Anna, moved from Sanary-sur-Mer to Nice-Fabron in March 1934, renting there the villa La Florida, chemin de la Lanterne. The move was made for health reasons: both Schickele and his son Hans suffered from severe asthma. See Schickele's diary entry for January 11, 1934.

**young Hans:** Hans Schickele, the second son of René Schickele. At the time he was studying architecture at the Ecole des Beaux-Arts in Nice; he and his family now live in Berkeley, California.

**this summer:** Thomas Mann returned to the south of France only in August/September 1936.

**Klaus Pinkus:** known for his correspondence with Robert Musil and Heinrich Mann (see Heinrich Mann, *Briefe an Karl Lemke und Klaus Pinkus* [Hamburg, 1964]). Today lives in Worpswede.

**Hjalmar Schacht** (1877–1970): banker and politician. From 1924 to 1929 president of the Reichsbank. Later supported the formation of Hitler's government. From 1933 to 1939 again president of the Reichsbank; from 1934 to 1937 minister of economics, then minister without portfolio. In a concentration camp in 1944–1945. Acquitted in the Nuremberg trials in 1946. Arrested in 1948 by German authorities. In 1953 co-owner of a private bank in Düsseldorf. Among his works: *Abrechnung mit Hitler* (1948; in English: *Account Settled*, 1949); *76 Jahre meines Lebens* (1953; in English: *My First Seventy-Six Years*, 1955).

**"Dr. Paul Aron":** further details not available. It is possible that Robert Aron is meant, who, with Arnaud Dandieu, published the periodical *L'ordre nouveau* from 1933 to 1938.

APRIL 19, 1934

*Enclosed with this letter was a newspaper article, "Révolutions vraies et fausses," by Guglielmo Ferrero; according to a handwritten note by Heinrich Mann, the article is from* La Dépêche de Toulouse, *April 15, 1934.*

**Theodor Tagger:** Ferdinand Bruckner (s.v., Heinrich Mann's letter of December 25, 1933).

**Gustav Hartung** (1887–1946): director. Worked as head producer or theatrical director, among other activities, in Cologne and Darmstadt. Founder of the Heidelberg Festspiele (in 1926, with R. K. Goldschmit). From 1927 to 1933 manager of the Berlin Renaissance theater. Emigrated via Zurich to Basel, where he was active as a director for the Stadttheater. Heinrich Mann had been invited by Gustav Hartung, at the time director of the Zurich Schauspielhaus, to give a lecture. Thomas Mann stepped in for him, delivering the talk "Goethe als Repräsentant des bürgerlichen Zeitalters." See *Tagebuch* entry of April 23, 1934.

**of my novel:** *Young Henry of Navarre.*

**Sanary:** the vacation together did not take place. In May Thomas Mann traveled to the United States for the first time. In July he took part in the International Art Congress in Venice.

MAY 13, 1934

**America:** Thomas Mann made his first trip to the United States in May 1934. He was invited by the publisher Alfred A. Knopf on the occasion of the American publication of *The Tales of Jacob*, translated by H. T. Lowe-Porter.

**in your letter:** not preserved.

**Oscar Ludwig Levy** (1867–1946): Nietzsche scholar; publisher of *The Complete Works of Friedrich Nietzsche*, 18 vols. (Edinburgh and London, 1909–1913). Friend of Heinrich Mann and also well acquainted with Thomas Mann.

**business with Schickele:** on January 25, 1934, René Schickele wrote to Thomas Mann: "The essay by H.M. in the latest Sammlung has left me outraged. I do not envy him the placidity with which he foresees war. That such a horrible prospect is supposed to be an attempt by the National Socialists to intimidate others is likely to be lost on precisely those nations, France and Russia, that are most desirous of peace. It is in the nature of the emigration that its political spokesmen are pushed irresistibly to the most extreme wings, to the nationalists or the communists. But woe to the nationalist who dared to say in the French assembly what H.M. expresses so calmly in his essay! He would be 'swept away by the storm of indignation.' I don't at all like the idea of writing him about this, and will have to wait until I can talk to him. Unfortunately, we understand each other less and less" (Brw. Schickele, 54).

**Arnold Zweig** (1887–1968): writer. Studied German literature in Munich. Awarded the Kleist Prize in 1914. Settled after the war as a freelance writer on the Starnberger See. From 1923 to 1933 in Berlin. Emigrated in 1933 to Haifa. Returned in 1948 to East Berlin, where he became president of the German Academy of the Arts. Among his works: *Novellen um Claudia*

(1912; English version, 1930); *Abigail und Nabal,* tragedy (1913); cycle of novels analyzing the period of the First World War: *Der Streit um den Sergeanten Grischa* (1927; in English: *The Case of Sergeant Grischa,* 1954); *Junge Frau von 1914* (1931; in English: *Young Woman of 1914,* 1932); *Erziehung vor Verdun* (1935; in English: *Education Before Verdun,* 1936); *Einsetzung eines Königs* (1937; in English: *The Crowning of a King,* 1936).

JUNE 27, 1934

*New York Herald:* Dorothy Thompson, "The most eminent living man of letters, Thomas Mann, gives an old tale new beauty and significance: Joseph and his Brothers," *New York Herald Tribune* (June 10, 1934).

**Carl von Ossietzky** (1889–1938): journalist. Secretary of the Deutsche Friedensgesellschaft. In 1927 succeeded Siegfried Jacobsohn as chief editor of *Die Weltbühne.* Criticized German armament from a pacifist position. Sentenced to prison for treason in 1931; amnestied in 1932. From 1933 in concentration camps. Awarded the Nobel Peace Prize in 1936, whereupon the National Socialist government prohibited German nationals from accepting the Nobel Prize. Heinrich and Thomas Mann wrote a series of articles about Ossietzky (see letter of October 26, 1935, s.v., letter to Oslo). On Ossietzky, see Kurt R. Grossmann, *Ossietzky, Ein deutscher Patriot* (Munich, 1963).

JULY 2, 1934

**Max Pallenberg** (1877–1934): actor. Active in comic roles in Vienna, Munich, and Berlin. Married to Fritzi Massary from 1918. Died in an airplane crash in Karlsbad.

**abominations in Berlin:** Ernst Röhm, chief of staff of the SA, was shot along with other SA-men on the orders of Hitler. That he had planned a putsch is not subject to documentation. See Thomas Mann's *Tagebuch,* June 30–July 12, 1934.

**Fritzi Massary,** actually Masareck (1882–1969): operetta singer and actress. Born in Vienna, married to Max Pallenberg. Famous for her appearances in Berlin (until 1933) and Vienna. Lead roles in operettas by Lehár, Kálmán, Fall, Oscar Straus, Offenbach. Later in Beverly Hills, California.

JULY 5, 1934

**Prof. Böök:** the Swedish specialist in German literature, Martin Fredrik Böök (1882–1961) was importantly involved in the decision to award Thomas Mann the Nobel Prize for Literature in 1929. On Thomas Mann's personal relationship to Böök, see Georg C. Schoolfield, "Thomas Mann und Fredrik Böök," in *Deutsche Weltliteratur—Festgabe für J. Alan Pfeffer* (Tübingen, 1972), 158–88.

**Hermann Stehr** (1864–1940): writer. Member of the Prussian Dichterakademie from 1926. Became famous after World War I for his novel *Der Heiligenhof* (1918), but, as one of S. Fischer Verlag's authors, remained in the shadow of Gerhart Hauptmann. Among Stehr's works: *Die Schindelmacher,* novellas (1899); *Leonore Griebel,* novel (1900); *Der begrabene Gott,* novel (1905); *Drei Nächte,* novel (1909); *Peter Brindeisener,* novel (1924); *Das Geschlecht der Maechler,* novel trilogy (1929, 1933, 1944); *Mein Leben,* autobiography (1934).

**Hermann Hesse:** see the letter of February 4, 1934, from Thomas Mann to Martin Fredrik Böök, in which he expresses the desire to see the 1934 Nobel Prize go to Hermann

Hesse: "By selecting him, you would honor Switzerland along with the older, true, pure, sacred, and eternal Germany." In a letter of July 18, 1934, to Martin Fredrik Böök, Thomas Mann once again drew attention to Hermann Hesse as a possible candidate for the Nobel Prize. "It would have the effect of honoring and crowning something truly and undoubtedly German, without courting the misunderstanding that the intention was *also* to honor and crown something else."

**the Franks in Sanary:** the writer Bruno Frank and his wife, Elisabeth [Liesl], lived temporarily in Sanary-sur-Mer after they had left Germany on the day following the Reichstag fire (February 27, 1933). Pallenberg's widow, the famous opera diva Fritzi Massary, was the mother of Liesl Frank. See Thomas Mann's entry in his *Tagebuch* of June 27, 1934: "Newspaper report of the death of Max Pallenberg in a plane accident. The end of a grotesque, complex genius, a brilliant phenomenon; we shall miss him. Telegraphed the Franks in Sanary."

**bloody obscenities:** the murder of Ernst Röhm on June 30, 1934.

**express my thanks:** Thomas Mann, "American Address, At the Testimonial Dinner in New York on his 59th Birthday on June 6, 1934," *Saturday Review of Literature*, June 16, 1934, 749, 754.

**La Guardia:** Fiorello La Guardia (1882–1947), from 1933 to 1945 mayor of New York.

**George Groß:** the painter and graphic artist George Grosz (actually Georg Ehrenfried [1893–1959]) went to the United States in 1932, lived in New York, and was involved in the Dada movement, taking up important themes from futurism. His earlier attitude of class struggle he gave up in the United States in favor of an undemanding realism. Among his works: *Ecce homo* (1922; English version, 1965); *Das Gesicht der herrschenden Klasse* (1923; in English: *The Face of the Ruling Class*, 1984); *Die Gezeichneten* (1930; English version in *Love Above All and Other Drawings*, 1971); also portraits of Max Herrmann-Neisse (1925), Max Schmeling (1926).

**essay on democracy:** Heinrich Mann, "Revolutionäre Demokratie," *Europäische Hefte* 1, no. 8 (1934): 208ff.

**king novel:** Heinrich Mann, *Young Henry of Navarre*.


SEPTEMBER 6, 1934

**engrossed in your third volume:** *Joseph in Egypt*.
**into my first [volume]:** *Young Henry of Navarre*.
**Joseph film:** on August 11, 1934, Thomas Mann wrote to Stephan Zweig, "A London film firm, London Film Production, for which an acquaintance of mine, the Hungarian writer Ludwig Biro, works as a dramaturg, has approached me about a film version of my biblical novel." An option deal incorporating the terms desired by Thomas Mann was arranged, but the film itself was never made.

**King Vidor** (1896–1982): film director. Had made the following films by 1935: *Turn in the Road* (1920); *The Sky Pilot* (1921); *Three Wise Fools* (1923); *The Big Parade* (1925); *La Bohème* (1926); *The Crowd* (1928); *Hallelujah* (1929); *Billy the Kid* (1930); *The Champ* (1931); *Bird of Paradise* (1932); *Our Daily Bread* (1935).


SEPTEMBER 11, 1934

*Die Sammlung:* Heinrich Mann, "Sammlung der Kräfte," *Die Sammlung* 2, no. 1 (September 1934): 1–9 (written from July 25 to August 2, 1934, in Bagnères de Bigorre).

**visitors from the Reich:** among Thomas Mann's visitors in these days were Alfred Neumann, Peter Pringsheim, Prof. Perron (Munich), Dr. Erich Knoche (dentist from Munich), Emil Preetorius, Annette Kolb, Wilhelm Kiefer, Carl Zuckmayer, and Gottfried Bermann Fischer.

**student body:** see Thomas Mann's entry in his *Tagebuch* on August 7, 1934: "*Der Sturmer* has been banned for fourteen days. [ . . . ] The purported reason is an insult to Masaryk, in reality, a student's letter that bluntly betrayed the oppositional mood at the Munich University. (See the demand for a course about me.)"

***Der Stürmer:*** *Der Stürmer, Deutsches Wochenblatt zum Kampfe um die Wahrheit*, published by Julius Streicher (1885–1946), the National Socialist gauleiter in Franconia.

**Thomas Garrigue Masaryk** (1850–1937): president of the Czech republic. Founder of the CSR, and president without interruption from 1917. Resigned at age 85 on December 14, 1935.

**Romanov:** the Russian royal dynasty; ruled from 1613 to 1730; in the Romanov-Holstein-Gattorp branch to 1917.

**Goethe said simply:** see Wilhelm von Humboldt's letter of November 17–18, 1808, to his wife: "He [Goethe] offered assurances on the point that he would no longer concern himself with others, but wanted only to go his own way, and he pushed it so far as to suggest that the best possible advice would be for the Germans, like the Jews, to disperse throughout the world; only away from home were they tolerable." See *The Return of the Beloved (GW* 2:665).

**the "dismissive one":** "but firmer than all of them, the dismissive one." The sentence refers to Goethe. In Heinrich Mann, "Sammlung der Kräfte," *Die Sammlung* 2, no. 1 (September 1934): 8.

**Alexander Viller:** *Briefe eines Unbekannten.* Selection from the correspondence of Alexander Heinrich von Villers (1812–1880). Thomas Mann possessed the two-volume edition, newly published by Karl Graf Lanckoronski & Wilhelm Weigand (Leipzig: Insel-Verlag, 1910).

**Old-Testament spectacle:** the reference is to the film *The Eternal Road*, directed by Max Reinhardt, written by Franz Werfel (*Der Weg der Verheißung, Ein Bibelspiel in vier Teilen*, in Franz Werfel, *Die Dramen*, v. 2 [Frankfurt: S. Fischer, 1959]); music by Kurt Weill. The film was first shown from January 7 to May 17, 1937, at the Manhattan Opera House in New York. See Thomas Mann's entry in his *Tagebuch* on August 25, 1934: "More mail, from, among others, Zweig, who advised me to take advantage of things going on in London film production, since a monster Jewish-patriarchal film by Werfel-Reinhardt is underway." See also Edda Fuhrich-Leisler and Gisela Prossnitz, *Max Reinhardt in Amerika*, Publikation der Max Reinhardt-Forschungsstätte V (Salzburg: Otto Müller Verlag, 1976), 135–79.

**polemic:** in April 1934 Thomas Mann repeated his plan "to write a book about Germany" (see *Dichter über Dichtungen, Thomas Mann, Teil II* [Munich, 1979], 431–35). On August 10, 1934, he wrote to René Schickele (*Briefe* 1:371): "Daily events, developments in Germany are having such a pointed effect on my moral and critical conscience that work on my third volume has come to a complete standstill and I'm on the verge of giving it up and turning to a political polemic, in which I would recklessly relieve my heart, take revenge for all the intellectual indecencies I've suffered over the last year and a half, and perhaps strike a noticeable blow against the regime. Of course I'm painfully sorry on account of the novel, which has already dragged on anyway, and I'm quite aware of how much speaks against such an investment of time and energy." See *Tagebuch* entry from July 31, 1934: "The idea of writing about Germany—to save my soul with a profoundly reasoned open letter to the *Times*, in which I implore the world, and reluctant England in particular, to put an end to the abominable regime in

Berlin—gives me no peace, occupies me deeply. Perhaps it is truly the right time for it; perhaps it is precisely I who can help Germany make a new turn, and rejoin the community of moral nations?"

**feuilleton:** Thomas Mann, "Meerfahrt mit Don Quixote," first published in *Die neue Zürcher Zeitung*, November 5–15, 1934, and later as the concluding piece in his essay volume *Leiden und Größe der Meister* (in English: "Voyage with Don Quixote," in *Essays of Three Decades*).

**volume of essays:** Thomas Mann, *Leiden und Größe der Meister.*

**your novel:** *Young Henry of Navarre.*

**proofs:** Klaus Mann, *Flucht in den Norden*, novel (Amsterdam: Querido, 1934). English: *Journey into Freedom*, trans. Rita Reil (New York: Alfred A. Knopf, 1963). Thomas Mann began reading the proofs on September 5, 1934. See his *Tagebuch* entry: "Began reading Klaus's *Flucht in den Norden*. Charming."

SEPTEMBER 20, 1934

**article:** perhaps: "Une nation tragique," *La Dépêche*, October 7, 1934, or "Verfall einer geistigen Welt," *Die Neue Weltbühne*, December 6, 1934.

**Victor-Henri de Rochefort** (1830–1913): Republican politician. Following the revolution of September 4, 1871, member of the government of national defense; took part in the uprising of the Commune. From 1880 opposed the policies of Gambetta and Ferry in his periodical *L'Intransigeant.* Joined Boulanger in 1887. Source of citation not identified.

**through a French newspaper:** presumably Heinrich Mann, "Liberté et nation," *La Dépêche*, October 30, 1934.

**Prague:** Heinrich Mann spent October 1934 in Prague, where he delivered the lecture "Nation und Freiheit" on October 19, 1934, and was the guest of honor at a banquet put on by the Czechoslovakian PEN Club.

DECEMBER 13, 1934

**feuilleton:** see September 11, 1934, s.v. feuilleton.

***Baseler Nationalzeitung:*** on November 11, 1934, Thomas Mann took part in the "Tag der Völkerverstandigung," an event sponsored by the Europa-Union, and also gave a speech. See Hans Wysling, "Thomas Manns Rede vor der 'Europa-Union' in Basel," *Blätter der Thomas-Mann-Gesellschaft*, no. 20 (1983–1984): 5–13. Thomas Mann's address is also printed here, as well as the report by the *Baseler Nationalzeitung* of November 12, 1934.

**Goschi:** Heinrich Mann's daughter, Carla Maria Henriette Leonie, from his first marriage with the actress Maria Kanova.

**an address:** whether this address to the students in Basel took place could not be determined.

***Madame Legros:*** Heinrich Mann, *Madame Legros*, play in three acts (Berlin: Cassirer, 1913).

**Die Pfeffermühle:** on October 1, 1933, Erika Mann had once again begun performing her cabaret Die Pfeffermühle in the Zurich club Zum Hirschen. Performances in November 1934 at the Kursaal in Zurich were disrupted by members of the National Front (see *Neue Zürcher Zeitung*, from November 19 to 25, 1934).

**in January:** Thomas Mann was on a lecture tour from January 19 to 31, 1935, which took him to Prague, Brünn, Vienna, and Budapest. He read the essay "Leiden und Größe Richard

Wagners" (in English: "Sufferings and Greatness of Richard Wagner," in *Essays of Three Decades*).

**novel:** Heinrich Mann, *Die Jugend des Königs Henri Quatre* (Amsterdam, 1935).

**"Sieg und Auflösung":** the second volume of the Henri novel was published in 1938 under the title *Die Vollendung des Königs Henri Quatre* (in English: *Henry, King of France*). The manuscript was completed on August 16, 1938, in Nice. An excerpt had already appeared in *Internationale Literatur*, Moscow (see Thomas Mann's letter of November 4, 1937, s.v. continuation).

**Arnoldo Mondadori:** publisher in Milano. Published Thomas Mann's works in Italian translation.

**my child:** Carla Maria Henriette Leonie (Goschi) Mann, later Aškenazi-Mann, was born on September 10, 1916. Lived as of 1933 with her mother in Prague, then for a time in Paris. In 1968 lived briefly with her family in Munich, then in Bolzano. Died on October 25, 1986, in Berlin. See Klaus Schröter, "Leonie Mann zu Gedenken," in *Heinrich-Mann-Jahrbuch* (Lübeck, 1986), 4:1f.

**mother:** Maria (Mimi) Mann-Kanova (1886–1946), actress. Married to Heinrich Mann from 1914 to 1930. She left the Munich apartment in 1933 and moved to her parents' house in Prague. With Masaryk's help, Heinrich Mann's library and a number of manuscripts were removed to Prague. Following the occupation of Czechoslovakia, Maria Kanova-Mann was imprisoned for five years in the Theresienstadt concentration camp. She died in 1946 from the effects of her incarceration.

**overnight guests:** Hans Reisiger, one of Thomas Mann's closest friends, stayed with the Manns from December 27, 1934. Further overnight guests included the actress Therese Giehse (from December 29, 1934) and Fritz H. Landshoff, director of the German division of the Querido Verlag in Amsterdam (from December 31, 1934).

**proclamation to Moscow:** unknown.

**executions:** the reference is probably to the purges beginning with the murder of S. M. Kirov (December 1, 1934). By the end of 1934, some one hundred people had fallen victim to execution.

**Fritz H. Landshoff** (1901–1988): publisher. Until 1933, director of the Gustav Kiepenhauer Verlag in Berlin and, in 1933, founder of the German division of the Querido Verlag in Amsterdam. A major share of the exile literature by well-known German authors appeared between 1933 and 1940 under his auspices at the Querido Verlag. Together with Landshoff, Gottfried Bermann Fischer founded the L. B. Fischer Corp. in New York following their emigration to the United States.

**your book:** *Young Henry of Navarre*.

**Lavinia Mazzucchetti** (1889–1963): Italian Germanist and translator. Published important studies of Thomas Mann after the First World War and translated a few of his works after 1945. The letter from Lavinia Mazzucchetti has not been preserved.

**your condolences:** just before his 75th birthday, on October 15, 1934, the publisher Samuel Fischer died in Berlin.

**my attorney:** Valentin Heins (1894–1971), attorney in Munich. Thomas Mann had entrusted Heins with looking after his interests in relation to the German authorities. Heins spent years, finally without success, attempting to secure the reversal of measures undertaken against Thomas Mann (seizure of property, confiscation of the house on Poschingerstraße, refusal of a passport).

**trip east:** lecture tour to Prague, Brünn, Vienna, and Budapest, from January 20–30, 1935.

MARCH 10, 1935

**article:** perhaps Heinrich Mann, "Das Trampeltier," *Pariser Tageblatt*, January 22, 1935.

**cancellation coup:** England and France had been seeking since the beginning of February to conclude a nonaggression and arms limitation agreement with Germany; on March 7, 1935, the English foreign minister Hoare was to meet with Hitler in Berlin for discussions concerning a so-called air convention. The Germans appeared to be interested in talks at first but then obviously changed their mind: at the beginning of March, they requested on short notice that the English foreign minister postpone his visit. The claim was that Hitler had contracted a light cold and was very hoarse.

**Nice:** on February 6, 1935, Thomas Mann received an invitation from the Société des Nations (League of Nations) to attend the meetings of the Comité permanent des Lettres et des Arts from April 1 to 3, 1935, in Nice. From March 8 to 14, with this session in mind, he wrote the address "La formation de l'homme moderne" ("Achtung, Europa!" in German; "Europe, Beware!" in English), which he was to deliver on April 2, 1935. At the urging of Gottfried Bermann Fischer, who was concerned about receiving authorization for his press to emigrate, Thomas Mann withdrew his agreement to participate (see *Tagebuch* entry from March 27, 1935). Thomas Mann also requested that the Comité not allow his text to circulate beyond those present at the meeting. At the session, the address was read in French. It was published in an anthology put out by the Institut international de coopération intellectuelle in Paris (and in the German version in *Das neue Wiener Tagblatt*, February 15–22, 1936, and in a volume of selected essays under the same title by the Bermann-Fischer Verlag, Stockholm, 1938). Thomas Mann then visited his brother and René Schickele the following May.

**Seitz:** the Social Democratic politician Karl Seitz (1869–1950); he was mayor of Vienna from 1923 to 1934.

**Mimi and Goschi's:** Heinrich Mann's first wife, Maria Kanova (Mimi), and daughter, Carla Maria Henriette Leonie (Goschi).

**rest stop:** Thomas Mann stayed from February 8 to 21 in St. Moritz at the Hotel Chantarella, where he frequently got together with Bruno Walter and his wife.

**third volume:** *Joseph in Egypt.*

MARCH 26, 1935

**meetings:** see Thomas Mann's letter of March 10, 1935, to Heinrich Mann, s.v. Nice.

MARCH 28, 1935

**memoir:** Thomas Mann, "La formation de l'homme moderne," in *La formation de l'homme moderne*, ed. Société des Nations (Paris: Institut international de coopération intellectuelle, 1935; later in German as "Achtung, Europa!"; in English: "Europe, Beware!" in *Order of the Day*).

**Geneva:** see Thomas Mann's letter of March 30, 1935, to Massimo Pilotty (undersecretary for intellectual cooperation, League of Nations, Geneva): "Your concern for my present circumstances and your urgent desire that I undertake the trip to Nice after all touched me deeply, and would not fail to have their influence on me were it not impossible for me to change my decision now. What I said in my letter about how the experiences of recent years and especially, the last few weeks, have undermined my health was no phrase, but meant seriously. In addition, the light censure of my exposé that even the League of Nations felt obligated to make has made me realize for the first time how much this mémoire is a product of a very specifically German distress, which is not what is either expected or desired of me at this moment. Presented in this venue, it would necessarily have an off-putting effect."

MARCH 30, 1935

**birthday:** on June 6, 1935, Thomas Mann celebrated his sixtieth birthday in the company of his family, Hans Reisiger, Therese Giehse, Gottfried Bermann Fischer, and about twenty other friends (see *Tagebuch*, June 6, 1935). As a present from the S. Fischer Verlag, Thomas Mann received a carton with handwritten congratulations from nearly all the Fischer authors and numerous other friends. Heinrich Mann published a birthday article ("Der Sechzigjährige," *Die Sammlung* 2, no. 10 [June 1935]: 505–9); see "The Sixty-Year-Old" in the Documents above.

**attention:** Thomas Mann, "On the Profession of the German Writer in Our Time," address in honor of his brother given on March 27, 1931, at the Prussian Academy of the Arts in Berlin (see Documents above).

APRIL 3, 1935

**Gottfried Bermann Fischer** (born 1897): physician, publisher. Son-in-law of Samuel Fischer. Following the death of the latter in 1934 took over direction of the S. Fischer Verlag. Established the press in emigration, Bermann-Fischer, in Vienna in 1936 and, with the help of the Bonnier publishing house, in Stockholm in 1938. With the Querido editor Fritz H. Landshoff, founded the L. B. Fischer Verlag in New York in 1941. In 1947, he set up the Bermann-Fischer Verlag in Vienna and combined his Stockholm firm with the Querido Verlag to make the Bermann-Fischer/Querido Verlag in Amsterdam. In 1950, the S. Fischer Verlag was reestablished in its previous form in Frankfurt and Berlin. See Gottfried Bermann Fischer, *Bedroht—Bewahrt* (Frankfurt, 1967).

**Annette Kolb** (1870–1967): novelist and essayist. She was a friend of Katja Mann's from their youth and associated with the Mann household for decades. She left Germany in March 1933, emigrating to Switzerland and from there to Paris; spent the war years in the United States. Among her works: *Das Exemplar*, novel (1913); *Dreizehn Briefe einer Deutsch-Französin*, correspondence (1921); *Daphne Herbst*, novel (1928); *Beschwedebuch*, essays (1932); *Die Schaukel*, novel (1934); *Mozart*, biography (1937; English version, 1939); *Franz Schubert*, biography (1941); *Memento*, memoirs (1960).

**Alfred Gigon** (1883–1975): physician in Basel; Thomas Mann consulted him regularly.

**Katja's parents:** Alfred Pringsheim and his wife, Hedwig Pringsheim-Dohm, visited in Küsnacht from the end of April to the middle of May.

**private trip:** on May 14, 1935, Thomas and Katja Mann traveled by car to Geneva and by train from there to Nice, where they stayed in the Hôtel d'Angleterre until May 20, 1935. They visited there with Klaus Mann, Heinrich Mann, and René Schickele.

**America:** Thomas Mann made his second trip to the United States from June 10 to July 13, 1935, at the invitation of Harvard University, which planned to award him, along with Albert Einstein, an honorary doctorate of letters on June 20, the anniversary of the founding of the university.

**Ernst ("Putzi") Hanfstängl** (1887–1975): foreign press secretary of the Hitler regime. Harvard University had rejected a fellowship offered by Hanfstängl, whereupon the German government distanced itself from any official representation at the Harvard anniversary celebration. Ernst Hanfstängl was an old confidant of Hitler's; he broke with him in 1937, however, and fled to England and then to Canada. His sister, Erna Hanfstängl, was a neighbor of Thomas Mann in Munich's Herzogpark, and both were known to the Mann family.

**conflict:** the reference is to the Swiss-German conflict in connection with the kidnapping of Berthold Jacob (1898–1944), journalist and specialist on military policy for the *Weltbühne*. His revelations had focused considerable attention on the so-called Schwarze Reichswehr and inspired the hatred of the National Socialists. He emigrated to Strasbourg in 1932, was then enticed to Switzerland in 1935 by the Nazi agent Wesemann, and taken from there by the Gestapo to Germany. Upon the persistent intervention of the Swiss government, Jacob was released and returned to Switzerland, whereupon his German citizenship was revoked.

APRIL 8, 1935

**overseas voyage:** second trip to the United States, June 9 to July 13, 1935.

**your book:** Thomas Mann, *Leiden und Größe der Meister* (Berlin: S. Fischer, 1935; English versions in *Essays of Three Decades:* "Goethe as Representative of the Bourgeois Age"; "Goethe's Career as a Man of Letters"; "Sufferings and Greatness of Richard Wagner"; "Platen"; "Theodor Storm"; "Voyage with Don Quixote").

**the same poem:** August von Platen, "Tristan."

**lecture:** probably "La Formation de l'homme moderne," Thomas Mann's address for the meeting of the Comité permanent des Lettres et des Arts from April 1 to 3, 1935, in Nice, which he did not attend (later published in German under the title "Achtung, Europa!" and in English as "Europe, Beware!").

MAY 12, 1935

**Visitors:** the Pringsheims, Thomas Mann's elderly parents-in-law, spent from the end of April to the middle of May visiting in Küsnacht.

MAY 24, 1935

**doctor:** context unclear.

**Emil Oprecht** (1895–1952): Zurich publisher and book dealer. Founded the Dr. Oprecht book firm in 1924 and the Europa Verlag in 1933. Published *Maß und Wert* and Thomas Mann's *Briefwechsel* with the dean of the University of Bonn. President of the Neuer Schauspiel AG (Zürcher Schauspielhaus). Active for years as a Social Democrat. Gave generous assistance to refugees from Germany. Along with his wife, Emmie (née Fehlmann), belonged to Thomas Mann's closest circle of friends in Zurich.

**Alexander Moritz Frey** (1881–1956): writer. Emigrated in 1933 from Munich to Austria, in 1938 to Basel. Extensive correspondence with Thomas Mann. Among his works: *Dunkle Gänge*, stories (1913); *Solneman [Namenlos] der Unsichtbare*, novel (1918); *Kastan und die Dirnen*, novel (1918); farcical and comical stories: *Spuk des Alltags* (1920); *Sprünge* (1922); *Der unheimliche Abend* (1923); *Phantastische Orgie* (1924); *Phantome* (1925); *Robinsonade zu zwölft*, novel (1925); *Das abenteuerliche Dasein*, novel (1930); *Hölle und Himmel*, novel (1945); *Kleine Menagerie*, introduction by Thomas Mann (1955); *Verteufeltes Theater*, novel (1957).

MAY 27, 1935

**Salzburg:** Thomas Mann spent from August 18 to 29, 1935, in Bad Gastein and Salzburg. On the 20th he read from the *Joseph* novel in Bad Gastein; on the 21st he delivered a Wagner lecture in Salzburg; and on the 27th of August he read the "Report of Mont-kaw's Modest Death" from *Joseph* in the Mozarteum. He also listened to Beethoven's *Fidelio*, conducted by Arturo Toscanini, and Mozart's *Don Giovanni*, conducted by Bruno Walter.

**in the theater:** the reference is to the official celebration of Thomas Mann's sixtieth birthday on May 26, 1935, in Zurich's Corso Theater, organized by the Hottingen readers' circle. The program was as follows:

    I.   Overture: Concerto grosso in d-minor by Antonio Vivaldi, played by the Corso Orchestra, with reinforcements
         Musical Direction: Robert Blum
   II.  Speech: Prof. Robert Faesi
 III.  Gift Presentation by the city of Zurich, presented by Vice-President Gschwend of the City Council
 IV.  Address by Dr. Thomas Mann
  V.  Performance: *Fiorenza*, Act III, play by Thomas Mann
        Director: F. Falkenhausen

JUNE 3, 1935

**quote:** *Young Henry of Navarre*, 528.

JUNE 3, 1935

**congratulations:** Heinrich Mann, "Der Sechzigjährige," *Die Sammlung* 2, no. 10 (June 1935): 505–9; printed as "The Sixty-Year-Old," in the Documents above.

**Germany:** on June 7, 1935, Thomas Mann wrote to René Schickele: "Here the waves are surging, and I don't deny that the hundreds of letters from Germany, yes, yes, from Germany, some even from work camps, are doing my heart good."

JULY 7, 1935

**carton:** Gottfried Bermann Fischer, owner of the S. Fischer Verlag, presented Thomas Mann, for his sixtieth birthday, a carton filled with handwritten congratulations from nearly all of the Fischer authors and other close friends, including Albert Einstein, Bernard Shaw, Alfred Kubin, Knut Hamsun, and Karl Kerényi.

**Harvard:** on June 20, 1935, Thomas Mann was awarded an honorary doctorate from Harvard University.

**James B. Conant** (1893–1978): became a professor of chemistry at Harvard University in 1929 and was rector of the university from 1933 to 1953. From 1953 to 1955, he served as the American high commissioner in Germany, and became in 1957 the first American ambassador to the Federal Republic of Germany. From 1963 to 1965 he was active as an advisor on educational matters for the Ford Foundation in Berlin.

**Hendrik van Loon** (1882–1944): Dutch writer living in America and writing in English; successful popularizer of science and comic graphic artist. He took up the cause of German writers in exile, offering them assistance and great hospitality.

**Washington:** Thomas and Katja Mann were received by President and Mrs. Roosevelt for a private dinner in the White House on June 29, 1935.

JULY 16, 1935

**Congress:** Heinrich Mann delivered the keynote address, entitled "Probleme des Schaffens und Würde des Denkens," at the International Writers' Congress on the Defense of Culture, which took place from June 21 to 25, 1935, in the Mutualité in Paris. Henri Barbusse, Romain Rolland, André Gide, and André Malraux were among the other participants. See Heinrich Mann's report on the Congress: "Wir sind da," *Pariser Tageblatt*, June 30, 1935. Further: "Ein denkwürdiger Sommer" [A memorable summer], *Internationale Literatur* 6, no. 1 (1936): 21–22. The text of this essay is reprinted in *Der Bienenstock* (Blätter des Aufbau-Verlags), no. 91 (spring 1971):

> The summer of the year 1935 will remain memorable to me because of the International Writers' Congress, which was held at the end of June in Paris. It was something completely new: so many working intellectuals from many countries and several continents, but all from the same front, all resolved on the "defense of culture." The subjugation of the intellect has triumphed in one part of the world. That had to happen for us all to find our way together and for Marxists as well as bourgeois writers to discover their profound kinship. Both wanted a thinking society rather than a stupefied one.
>
> The subjugated countries believe that it is possible to save society by doing away with thought. Everyone in Paris was convinced of the contrary, that when a society forfeits thought, it loses all right to further existence. There is no reason whatever for people to continue feeling personally tied to a society once it forcibly suppresses knowledge and the material realization of the fruits of knowledge. The interest people have in any society is defined precisely by the extent to which it realizes knowledge. The fruits of true knowledge always correspond in a remarkable way to an improvement of the human condition.
>
> An honest democrat, given the turn things have now taken, is obliged to acknowledge that Marxism alone creates the preconditions for real democracy. And those with serious religious convictions see in socialism the realization of their faith. At the same time, victorious socialism, which is now in secure possession of a major portion of the earth, must become conscious of its humane mission. Democracy, the political equality of all, is possible for strong peoples. As long as there are still persons around who can rise to a position of economic, and therefore political, dominance, democracy will be delayed. Humanism, too, may justifiably be claimed only by those who have behind them a people secure in their rights. Nobility of a properly humane and healthy sort can be achieved only on the basis of changes in real life which have rendered the latter just and true.
>
> Thus did it happen at the Congress that the participants from the Soviet Union and those from the capitalist countries were very well able to speak the same or a kindred language. The former had learned it from the attempt of their country to become better. The others, in particular the Germans, were taught it by the disgraceful burden that has reduced their country to ever greater degrees of degradation. The thousands of listeners understood the one as well as the other and esteemed in both their respective struggles, regardless of how different they were in the one place and the other. That, however, is the critical point: to be understandable by many, actually by all people, indeed, to set them an example. The

Congress of Writers, as the first one held so publicly, lent courage to an extraordinary number of people. All of these people were able to see and to hear resolute champions of their cause.

Humanists will amount to something when, instead of merely thinking, they also begin to strike. Henri Barbusse, who, as the last of his earthly deeds, conceived and brought about the Paris Congress of June 1935, was disputatious, and so should we be as well. He had a sense for the real as the instrument of intellectual aims, and a sense for power that is tangible. I myself had published at the end of this summer of 1935 my novel *Young Henry of Navarre*. In it the humanists of the sixteenth century also know how to ride and how to strike. In France they had a prince—he was the prince of the poor and oppressed, just as he was the prince of the thinking people. Young Henry, though, experienced life like an average person.

From his adventures, deeds, and suffering I composed a long series of images and scenes, which are colorful in the reading and regarding. Taken altogether, it means that what is evil and dreadful can be overcome by fighters whom misfortune has taught to think, as well as by thinkers who have learned to ride and to strike. They even emerge strengthened from the Massacre of St. Bartholomew's Eve. And only after having learned from hard experience was I able to write my book about the most humane, because the most tested, of kings. It appeared in the summer of 1935 and that will help in keeping it memorable to me.

**Ilya Ehrenburg** (1891–1967): Russian writer and journalist. Arrested in 1908 for revolutionary agitation; flight to Paris. Returned to Russia in 1917. Following disputes with the Bolsheviks in 1921, correspondent in Paris, then in Belgium. In the Soviet Union from time to time from 1923 on, more regularly from about 1930 on; many trips abroad. War correspondent in Spain in 1936. Wrote for *Pravda* and *Krasnaia Zvezda* from 1940. From 1959 member of the presidium of the Writers' Union. Author of numerous novels, stories, and essays. Among his works: *The Extraordinary Adventures of Julio Jurenito* (1923); *Moskva slezam ne verit* (1933); *The Fall of Paris* (1943); *The Storm* (1949).

**Alexei N. Tolstoi** (1883–1945): Russian writer. From old noble family. Studied until 1908 at the Technological Institute in St. Petersburg. First literary efforts in 1905; often describes the decline of the rural nobility in his works. War correspondent during the First World War. Emigrated in 1918 to Paris. Returned to Moscow in 1923; initially wrote fantastic and utopian science fiction in the manner of his friend H. G. Wells, also satirical novels about the émigré community. In 1941 completed his novel trilogy *Ordeal*, a depiction of the Russian intelligentsia in the prewar, war, and revolutionary period, which leads to a recognition of bolshevism. Among his works: *Nikita's Childhood*, novel (1921); *Ordeal*, novel trilogy (1921–1941); *The Garin Death Ray*, novel (1937); *Peter the First*, novel (1929–1945).

**Mikhail Yefimovich Koltsov** (1898–1942): chairman of the Soviet Writers' Union, 1922–1938. Feuilleton editor of *Pravda*.

**telegram** (Paris, June 28, 1935):

> CONGRES INTERNATIONAL ECRIVAINS POUR DEFENSE CULTURE VOUS A NOMME PAR ACCLAMATIONS UNANIMITE MEMBRE PRESIDIUM ASSOCIATION INTERNATIONALE ECRIVAINS FONDEE FIN CONGRES AUX COTES GIDE BARBUSSE ROLLAND HEINRICH MANN GORKI FORSTER HUXLEY SHAW SINCLAIR LEWIS LAGERIOFF [*sic*] VALLE INCLAN.

**According to an American report:** on June 30, 1935, Thomas Mann gave an interview to the *Washington Post*. It was published on July 1, 1935, and the *Pariser Tageblatt* quoted from the interview in its July 6, 1935, issue: "I am not a Communist, you know. But I must confess that communism is the only idea, the only thing one can oppose to fascism. In comparison, I prefer communism." Thomas Mann denied having made the statement. A letter to the S. Fischer Verlag of September 5, 1935, which, in exoneration of Thomas Mann, the press passed on to the interior ministry, runs as follows: "The conversation conducted in Washington was of course [ . . . ] not reproduced altogether accurately [ . . . ] It was a conversation of the sort one has all over the world with educated people about the form to be assumed by the postliberal state. I stated that I wasn't a Communist and would not be happy under communism; but this much could be admitted: that communism, if freedom really is dead, is the only positive idea with which one could oppose fascism." See further the detailed description of the context in Paul Egon Hübinger, *Thomas Mann, die Universität Bonn und die Zeitgeschichte*, 470ff.

*Die Weltbühne: Die Neue Weltbühne* of July 11, 1935. There appeared in this issue, under the title "Die Verteidigung der Kultur," an excerpt from Heinrich Mann's address at the International Writers' Congress.

### JULY 27, 1935

**"Wackeln":** Heinrich Mann, "Wackeln," *Pariser Tageblatt*, August 2, 1935.
**"Aunt Minna":** context unknown. Presumably encoded information about conditions in Nazi Germany.

### JULY 29, 1935

**Russian successes:** the reference is presumably to the Russian editions of Heinrich Mann's novels, *Young Henry of Navarre* and *Henry, King of France*, both published by the State Publisher of the National Minorities, Kiev, 1938.
**La Humanité:** Paris newspaper, organ of the Communist Party of France. The reference is to the interview conducted by the *Washington Post* on July 1, 1935, concerning the significance of communism. See letter of July 16, 1935, s.v. an American report.

### SEPTEMBER 1, 1935

**Salzburg:** s.v., letter of May 27, 1935.
**advance copy of your *Henry*:** Heinrich Mann, *Young Henry of Navarre*.

### SEPTEMBER 2, 1935

**The book:** *Young Henry of Navarre*. Finished on June 8, 1935.
**Sanary:** Sanary had become a meeting place for German émigrés. Present there aside from Lion Feuchtwanger were Bertolt Brecht, Wilhelm Herzog, Hermann Kesten, Ludwig Marcuse, Fritzi Massary, Balder Olden, Erwin Piscator, Ernst Toller, Franz Werfel, and Arnold Zweig. Heinrich Mann and René Schickele settled in Nice, Julius Meier-Graefe in Saint-Cyr.

### SEPTEMBER 5, 1935

**your novel:** Heinrich Mann, *Young Henry of Navarre*.

### OCTOBER 3, 1935

**Your letter:** Thomas Mann's letter of September 26, 1935, has not been preserved. See Thomas Mann's letter to René Schickele of October 31, 1935:

> I have the highest admiration for Heinrich's novel. Unquestionably it's great literature, and I do not think Europe has anything better to offer today, to say nothing of the towering heights

to which mediocrity has risen in Germany. Writing to Heinrich, I too have remarked that his frequent pointing up of contemporary parallels to historical situations verges on journalism. But after all, why not? One feels rather pitiable and at any rate too "German" when one acts as a preserver of Pure Literature. Besides, there is no lack of the literary element in his novel; I am thinking not only of the chapter "Death and the Nursemaid," but also of the pervasive wisdom, irony, moral beauty, and straightforwardness of the book. It moves me as the synthesis of all the gifts of the author, as a magnificent personal summation of the epoch from Montaigne to Goethe (see the little *Faust* quotations scattered throughout). The conjunction of the German and the French spirit is nothing less than the Faustian spirit of Germany and Greece; in essence these two spirits are perhaps the same. And the *moralités*, which Bertaux declares are written in classical French, could be amply justified as homage to that beloved realm to which he owes the greater part of his education, and which should show him a certain gratitude, too. By rights he should long ago have received the Legion of Honor, not just the ribbon, the rosette, instead of having to do battle like an ordinary exile with the Nice government offices—to which, just to make things more difficult, he unfortunately also sends his mistress. (Brw. Schickele, 88; *Letters of Thomas Mann*, 239–40)

**article:** enclosed in this letter was a newspaper clipping of an article by Heinrich Mann: "Kastendeutschland," *Pariser Tageblatt*, October 3, 1935. Handwritten remark by Heinrich Mann: "Something like this appears every 8 days."

**"Death and the Nursemaid":** chapter in book five, "The School of Misery," *Young Henry of Navarre*.

*moralités:* Heinrich Mann appended *moralités* to individual chapters of his novel, short moralizing reflections in French that summarized and assessed what had just happened. He conceived them in homage to Montaigne, whose *Essais* had had an influence on the novel and who—in an episode invented by Heinrich Mann—personally appears in it.

**Félix Bertaux** (1881–1948): French scholar of German literature and translator. Friend of Heinrich and Thomas Mann. Translated *Death in Venice* in 1925 and "Sufferings and Greatness of Richard Wagner" in 1933. See Heinrich Mann, *Ein Zeitalter wird besichtigt* (Berlin: Aufbau-Verlag, 1947), 237ff.

**rosette:** the red buttonhole rosette of the Cross of the Legion of Honor. See Thomas Mann's letter of October 31, 1935, to René Schickele.

**executive board of the World Committee Against War and Fascism:** Henri Barbusse (1873–1935), Romain Rolland (1866–1944), Paul Langevin (1872–1946).

**the third volume:** Thomas Mann, *Joseph in Egypt* (Vienna: Bermann-Fischer, 1936). The volume was finished on August 23, 1936, and appeared on October 15, 1936.

**informational trip to the Soviet Union:** the trip to Russia planned—together with Lion Feuchtwanger—for May 1936 did not take place; neither Heinrich nor Thomas Mann ever visited the Soviet Union.

**Lion Feuchtwanger** (1884–1958): writer. Emigrated in 1933 to the south of France, in 1940 to the United States. Friend of Bertolt Brecht and Thomas Mann. See Thomas Mann's essay "Freund Feuchtwanger" (*GW* 10:533). Among his works: *Die häßliche Herzogin*, novel (1923; in English, *The Ugly Duchess: A Historical Romance*, 1927); *Jud Süss*, novel (1925; in English, *Power*, 1926); *Erfolg*, novel (1930; in English, *Success*, 1930).

OCTOBER 10, 1935

**Soviet edition:** the reference is to the Russian edition of the collected works: V. A. Sorgenfrei, ed., *Sobranie sochinenii*, 6 vols. (Leningrad: Gospolizdat, 1934–1938).

vol. 1:  *Buddenbroki*, novel, I (1935)
vol. 2:  *Buddenbroki*, novel, II (1936)
vol. 3:  *Novelly* (1936)
vol. 4:  *Volsebnaya gora* (The magic mountain), novel, I (1934)
vol. 5:  *Volsebnaya gora*, novel, II (1935)
vol. 6:  *Fiorenza* (1938)

**visit by Soviet writers to Prague:** the visit took place in the context of Soviet-Czech cultural exchange efforts of the time. A delegation of Czech journalists, at the invitation of the Soviet Union of Journalists (under the direction of M. I. Kolzov), was in the Soviet Union at the end of 1934, beginning of 1935, where they were shown Soviet cultural, economic, and technological accomplishments, in the expectation that seeing conditions firsthand would result in more "objective" reporting in the bourgeois press in Czechoslovakia. In the summer of 1935, there followed the corresponding invitation by Czech journalists. The Soviet delegation was made up of journalists and political officials, as well as the writers listed below; they arrived in Prague on October 5, 1935, and remained in Czechoslovakia on an official visitors' tour (including a meeting with Eduard Beneš, the foreign minister) until October 21, 1935. Alexei Tolstoi and Mikhail I. Kolzov reported extensively on the visit in *Pravda*; Sergei Mikhailovich Tretiakov published his travel memoirs in book form.

**Spanish trip:** the trip did not take place. See Thomas Mann's letter of April 1, 1936, to Heinrich Mann: "Our travel plans have changed. Spain is out for the moment."

**Giuseppe Motta** (1871–1940): Swiss statesman; member of the Swiss Federal Council from 1912; in 1920, director of the political department of the foreign ministry. He was president of the federation a total of five times, finally in 1932 and 1937.

**My professor:** Prof. Alfred Gigon (1883–1975); physician in Basel.

**Your address:** the reference is probably to Heinrich Mann's article "Kastendeutschland," in the *Pariser Tageblatt*, October 3, 1935; reprinted in *Es kommt der Tag* (Zurich: Europa-Verlag, 1936), 175–78. The opening sentence reads: "Herr Hitler, Do you not also have the feeling that it is all coming to an end?"

OCTOBER 24, 1935

**sent the enclosed letter to Oslo:** Thomas Mann, "Nobelpriset och Carl von Ossietzky," *Göteborgs Handels- och Sjöfarts-Tidning*, July 11, 1936. German: "An das Nobel-Friedenspreis Comité, Oslo," in Felix Burger and Kurt Singer, *Carl von Ossietzky* (Zurich: Europa-Verlag, 1937), 117–21.

**make peace:** refers to the Italian-Abyssinian war. Disregarding worldwide diplomatic efforts, the Italian head-of-state, Benito Mussolini, ordered his armed forces to invade Abyssinia on October 3, 1935. On October 7, 1935, the council of the League of Nations condemned Italy as the aggressor, and on October 19, 1935, concluded a conference of the league with recommendations that sanctions be levied against the warring parties. Economic sanctions were begun on November 18 (weapons and credit embargo, import and export embargo against Italy), without the participation of Germany, Austria, Switzerland, Hungary, and Albania. Beginning on December 9, 1935, a conference was held in Paris, which worked out a peace plan—the so-called Hoare-Laval Plan—for the peaceful resolution of the Abyssinian conflict. Since the plan included significant concesssions to Italy, opposition parties in England and France declared it a betrayal of the League of Nations, and it was subsequently dropped. See in this context: Heinrich Mann, "Rede vor dem Völkerbund," *Die Neue Weltbühne*, December 19, 1935, 1599–1601. See also Thomas Mann's letter of October 31, 1935, to René Schickele.

**Putt-Höneken:** *Putthöhneken,* a term of affection for a chicken, nestling (Klaus Groth, *Gesammelte Werke* [Kiel, 1904], 2:213). From the mating call, *Putt, putt, putt!* (Otto Mensing, ed., *Schleswig-Holsteinisches Wörterbuch* [Neumünster, 1925–1935], vol. 3, col. 1158).

**Reichswehr officer:** unknown.

OCTOBER 26, 1935

**Pierre Laval** (1883–1945): Socialist politician. French prime minister in 1931–1932, then foreign minister. Prime minister again from June 1935 to January 1936. Once again prime minister under Pétain. Executed in 1945 for collaboration with Germany.

**Jews:** see Heinrich Mann, "Die Deutschen und ihre Juden," *Die Neue Weltbühne,* December 5, 1935, 1532–36.

NOVEMBER 15, 1935

**clipping:** unknown.

**Mussolini's clumsiness:** presumably refers to Italy's protest on November 11, 1935, to the council members of the League of Nations against their recommendation of sanctions.

**Saar referendum:** following the ceasefire on November 11, 1918, the Saarland was removed from the German Reich. The goal of the French policy was to weaken German military potential as long as possible, to avoid a repetition of the catastrophe. Attempts on the part of Germany to regain the Saarland, such as those undertaken by Foreign Minister Stresemann in 1926, foundered on both domestic and foreign opposition. The first referendum on the question did not take place until January 13, 1935; 8.8 percent of the votes were for the status quo; 0.4 percent for France; 90.8 percent favored the reentry of the Saarland into Germany. That was the course taken, on March 1, 1935, with Germany paying 900 million French francs to buy back the mines in the region. Thomas Mann followed the preparations for the vote attentively, and with aversion, since he saw it as an advertisement for the Hitler regime (see his letter of January 1, 1935, to René Schickele; and diary entries of December 15, 1934, January 4–12, 1935). The election results he characterized as "a fact from which I turn away as calmly as possible" (*Tagebuch* entry, January 15, 1935; see also the entries of January 19 and March 5, 1935).

**Hans Bauer** (born 1901): president of the Europa-Union, which Thomas Mann addressed on November 11, 1934, in the Great Hall of the Mustermesse in Basel (see *Blätter der Thomas-Mann-Gesellschaft,* no. 20 [1983–1984]: 5ff. Bauer was editor of the *Baseler Zeitung* from September 1, 1926, to February 1, 1952).

NOVEMBER 20, 1935

**French article:** Heinrich Mann, "L'Olympiade" (later, "Hochglanz," in *Es kommt der Tag*), *La Dépêche,* January 14, 1936.

**Wilhelm Koenen** (1886–1963): politician and writer. Member of the Prussian council of state from 1926 to 1932. After 1935, member of the central committee of the Socialist Unity Party in the German Democratic Republic.

**League of Nations:** see Heinrich Mann, "Rede vor dem Völkerbund," *Die Neue Weltbühne,* December 19, 1935, 1599–1601.

DECEMBER 23, 1935

**edition:** Thomas Mann, *Gesammelte Werke* (Berlin: S. Fischer, 1925).

**Fontane:** Theodor Fontane, *Gesamtausgabe der erzählenden Schriften,* 9 vols. (Berlin: S. Fischer, 1925).

**your letter:** Heinrich Mann's letter of December 18, 1935, to Klaus Mann, in Klaus Mann, *Briefe und Antworten* (Munich: Ellermann-Verlag, 1975), 1:239.

JANUARY 7, 1936

**meeting:** Heinrich Mann led a series of discussions aimed at the creation of a German popular front. The participants (Communists and Social Democrats, but also Catholics and bourgeois oppositionists) formed the so-called Lutetia circle, after the name of the hotel where Heinrich Mann usually stayed.

**Arosa:** Thomas Mann stayed in Arosa, at the Waldhotel, from January 13 to 27, 1936.

**my letter to Oslo:** Thomas Mann, "Nobelpriset och Carl von Ossietzky."

**Wassermann foreword:** Thomas Mann, "Zum Geleit," in Martha Karlweis, *Jakob Wassermann: Bild, Kampf und Werk* (Amsterdam: Querido, 1935), 5–11.

**St. Galler Tagblatt:** Thomas Mann, "Hoffnungen und Befürchtungen für 1936," *St. Galler Tagblatt*, December 30, 1935, n. 610 (*GW* 10:917f.).

**émigré aid:** on January 10, 1936, Thomas Mann gave a reading in Basel, as a benefit for the Hilfwerk für die Flüchtlinge aus geistigen Berufen.

FEBRUARY 6, 1936

**Nation:** Thomas Mann, "Das beste Buch des Jahres," *Die Nation*, November 28, 1935. In the article, Thomas Mann reviewed two books in addition to *Young Henry of Navarre: Der Erkenntnistrieb als Lebens- und Todesprinzip*, by Jakob Klatzkin, and *Briefe Napoleons*, a new edition from S. Fischer. See *Tagebuch*, November 4, 1935.

**Korrodi:** in an open letter to Eduard Korrodi, dated February 2, 1936, Thomas Mann protested against his article "Deutsche Literatur in Emigrantenspiegel." This public declaration of solidarity in regard to emigration signified an irrevocable break with the National Socialist regime (*Br.* 1:409–13; *Letters of Thomas Mann*, 244–48).

**Bermann's foreign activities:** Gottfried Bermann Fischer had tried repeatedly to persuade Samuel Fischer to move the press out of Germany, but the latter consistently refused. Following his death on October 15, 1934, his widow, then the press's sole proprietor, finally agreed to a move, although she personally had no intention of leaving Germany. In spring 1935 Bermann Fischer successfully negotiated an agreement with the propaganda ministry, according to which the rights to undesirable or banned authors, as well as their previously published works and certain other assets, would be released for emigration on the condition that what remained of the publishing house would be offered for sale and transferred into "reliable hands." Peter Suhrkamp brought a group of investors together to make the purchase, allowing the press to continue under his direction. Bermann Fischer agreed to a merger with the large London publishing house William Heinemann, Ltd., with the aim of establishing the press in Switzerland. This plan foundered, however, on the objections of Swiss publishers, whereupon Bermann Fischer turned to Vienna. But Austria seemed too risky for the British partners, who withdrew from the merger agreement. Bermann Fischer then proceeded on his own to Vienna, founding the Bermann-Fischer Verlag, which was henceforth the publisher of Thomas Mann's works. *Leiden und Größe der Meister* was thus the last of Thomas Mann's books to be published by the old S. Fischer Verlag in Berlin. Bermann Fischer had originally hoped that Hermann Hesse would also follow him abroad, but Hesse remained with the S. Fischer Verlag in Berlin.

**proofs:** Heinrich Mann, *Es kommt der Tag, Deutsches Lesebuch* (Zurich: Europa-Verlag, 1936).

**string of comments:** the exile weekly, *Das Neue Tage-Buch*, published in Paris by Leopold Schwarzschild (1891–1950), published on January 11, 1936, a sharp attack on Gottfried Bermann Fischer, the director of the S. Fischer Verlag. Bermann Fischer was accused of seeking, with Goebbels's understanding, and Thomas Mann as a major literary asset, to found a "camouflaged exile press" in Vienna (the full text of the article is in Klaus Schröter, *Thomas Mann im Urteil seiner Zeit* [Hamburg: Wegner, 1969], 259–60). Bermann Fischer, telephoning from London, where he was involved in negotiations with the Heinemann Verlag, asked Thomas Mann to make a public protest. It appeared, signed by Thomas Mann, Hermann Hesse, and Annette Kolb, under the title "Ein Protest," in the *Neue Zürcher Zeitung* on January 18, 1936 (see also *GW* 11:787). Leopold Schwarzschild answered the protest with a "Response to Thomas Mann" in *Das Neue Tage-Buch* of January 25, 1936, in which he called on Thomas Mann to distance himself from Bermann Fischer's plans (the full text is in Klaus Schröter, *Thomas Mann im Urteil seiner Zeit*, 260–66). But the *Neue Zürcher Zeitung* also responded to Thomas Mann's protest: Eduard Korrodi, a Swiss journalist and literary historian, from 1914 the feuilleton editor of the *Neue Zürcher Zeitung*, polemicized against Schwarzschild's "Response to Thomas Mann" in his essay "Deutsche Literatur im Emigrantenspiegel" (*Neue Zürcher Zeitung*, January 26, 1936). Thomas Mann again responded to Korrodi's "nasty string of comments" in an "Offener Brief an Korrodi" (*Neue Zürcher Zeitung*, February 3, 1936; see also *GW* 11:788–93). This essay represents Thomas Mann's first public renunciation of Nazi Germany; he openly proclaims his solidarity with the Germans in exile. See Hans Wysling, "Die ersten Jahre des Exils: Briefe von Schriftstellern an Thomas Mann," part three: 1936–1939, *Blätter der Thomas-Mann-Gesellschaft*, no. 15 (1975), 5ff.

**some confusion:** see Thomas Mann's letter to René Schickele of February 19, 1936: "Sooner or later I had to speak out, and I chose a moment when someone was insidiously attempting to draw a line between me and the exiles, and with the feeling moreover that unpleasant and half-and-half notions of my relations to the Third Reich prevail in some parts of the world. But in addition, simply from inner, psychic reasons. It was in good part a temperamental act, a natural reaction to all the insults and outrages that daily come raining down upon us all. It was also the real and deep conviction that this mischief will mean the doom of the whole continent if it continues, and that I must oppose it here and now, so far as my feeble strength permits, as I have already opposed it at home" (*Letters of Thomas Mann*, 250).

**If they do expel me:** on December 2, 1936, Thomas Mann's German citizenship was revoked, on the basis of the Law on the Revocation of Naturalization and the Deprivation of German Citizenship of July 14, 1933. Mrs. Katja Mann and the four younger children were made part of this disposition.

**Olympiade:** on August 1, Hitler opened the XI Summer Olympic Games.

**guild:** on the basis of economic considerations, the Gutenberg book guild in Zurich resisted Bermann Fischer's establishment of his exile press in Zurich. A January 1, 1936, meeting of the directorates of the Swiss booksellers' association and the publishers' association, which was still independent at that time, led to the issuance of a report, claiming that the establishment of a major foreign press in Zurich would severely jeopardize the overall interests of the Swiss publishing industry. This report seems then to have been followed as well by the cantonal immigration authorities. They not only refused to allow the stocks of German books released by the Nazi regime into Switzerland but also refused Bermann Fischer's attempt to establish a press in Zurich.

**Vienna and Prague:** the Bermann-Fischer Verlag began production in the summer of 1936 in Vienna; offices were located at Esteplatz 5, Vienna III.

**Heinemann:** attempts to establish a collaborative publishing venture between Heinemann and Fischer did not come to fruition; see letter of February 6, 1936, s.v. Korrodi.

**Moscow periodical:** presumably *Internationale Literatur*, in which Heinrich Mann had published a report on the International Writers' Congress on the Defense of Culture, held in Paris in the summer of 1935: "Ein denkwürdiger Sommer," *Internationale Literatur* 6, no. 1 (1936): 21–22. Thomas Mann is referring here to Fritz Landshoff's letter of February 5, 1936 (Thomas-Mann-Archiv, Zurich).

FEBRUARY 26, 1936

**appeal:** presumably Heinrich Mann, "Einheit! Einheit! Einheit! Gegen Faschismus und Krieg," *Die Volks-Illustrierte* 1, no. 12 (1936): 179. The reference may also be to Heinrich Mann, "Seid einig!," *Arbeiter-Illustrierte-Zeitung*, March 29, 1936, 220. See Thomas Mann's *Tagebuch* entry of February 26, 1936: "Handwritten note to Heinrich in the afternoon: idea of a call to the German people signed by cultural luminaries of Europe and America."

**open letter:** Thomas Mann, "Open Letter to Korrodi," *Neue Zürcher Zeitung*, February 3, 1936.

**lawyer:** in his *Tagebuch*, Thomas Mann noted on February 26, 1936: "To a conference in Baur au Lac with attorney v. Brandenstein from Berlin. Sat in the same corner of the hall as with Wassermann, fourteen days before he died. [Discussed] with B. German situation and prospects. Wants to acknowledge real events like the inner reality of the 'Arbeitsfront.' Adds, however, that it 'would not be possible' to live in Germany with the negativism of the émigrés. Anticipates, incidentally, economic collapse in one and a half to two years, and the 'street' taking action. Schacht can't do it anymore, and doesn't want to. Cheerful. Good to wait two years, if what comes then is fundamental and instructive. B. appears half-Jewish."

MARCH 1, 1936

**the serious young scholar:** Golo Mann had contributed a few texts to Heinrich Mann's *Lesebuch*.

**Lesebuch:** Heinrich Mann, *Es kommt der Tag, Deutsches Lesebuch* (Zurich: Europa-Verlag, 1936).

MARCH 29, 1936

**birthday article:** "Dem Fünfundsechzigjährige," *Die Neue Weltbühne*, March 26, 1936; "To the Sixty-Five-Year-Old"; see Documents above.

**AIZ:** in the *Arbeiter-Illustrierte-Zeitung*, Prague, Heinrich Mann published the article "Der Welt-Friedenskongress" on July 15, 1936. Further articles followed.

**Spain:** see Thomas Mann's letter of October 10, 1935, s.v., Spanish trip.

APRIL 1, 1936

**for Freud's eightieth birthday:** Thomas Mann was on a lecture tour from May 6 to 14, 1936 in Vienna, Brünn, and Prague. In connection with the eightieth birthday of Sigmund Freud (May 6, 1936), Thomas Mann delivered his address "Freud and the Future" to the Akademischer Verein für medizinische Psychologie on May 8.

**Budapest:** from June 5 to 18, 1936, Thomas Mann was present at a meeting of the Comité international de la coopération intellectuelle in Budapest. On June 7 he read from *Joseph* at the Innerstädtisches Theater; from June 8 to 12 he took part in a meeting of the committee and, on June 9, delivered the address "Humanoria und Humanism." On June 12 he repeated the lecture "Freud and the Future" (Innerstädtisches Theater). He then returned to Vienna, where he read from *Joseph in Egypt.*

**reading from *Joseph*:** see previous note.

**Buenos Aires:** the trip to Buenos Aires did not take place; instead, Thomas Mann visited his brother Heinrich on the Côte d'Azur in the late summer.

**my third volume:** *Joseph in Egypt.* On August 23, Thomas Mann concluded this volume. It appeared on October 15, 1936.

**Zsolnay:** the Austrian publisher Paul Zsolnay (1895–1961); in 1923, he founded the Zsolnay-Verlag, a major publisher of belles-lettres; emigrated to England in 1938, and returned in 1946 to Vienna.

**England's behavior:** the outstanding political event of "recent weeks" was the nullification of the 1925 Locarno Pact by Adolf Hitler on March 7, 1936, and the resulting invasion by German forces of the demilitarized zone of the Rhineland. On March 19, 1936, the special ambassador Joachim von Ribbentrop presented the German position to the council of the League of Nations. The council then declared Germany guilty of violating the treaty of Versailles. The declaration, however, was merely noted by a few member states, Great Britain among them; there was no talk of taking appropriate measures.

**Emil Ludwig** (1881–1948): writer and journalist.

**memorandum:** in his *Tagebuch* entry of April 1, 1936, Thomas Mann noted: "While we were eating: agitated, desperate phone call from Emil Ludwig in Ascona, who had listened in on the memorandum read out by the German broadcaster and found it so captivating that he had the feeling we'd lost a major battle. Heard a short excerpt from Bern, and the report that the Engl. press characterized the counterproposal as conciliatory. Is the man going to succeed, with the help of his peace lies, to fortify his Reich, and to get the League of Nations referring, not to the Versailles Treaty, but the Reichstag fire?" On March 7, 1936, there followed the German invasion of the Rhineland, which had been designated a demilitarized zone by the Locarno Pact of 1925. Hitler, declaring the pact nullified, proclaimed the restitution of full German sovereignty. The occupation prompted a burst of diplomatic activity. France and Belgium insisted on the security guarantees of the Locarno Pact; England took an intermediate position. On March 9, 1936, the council of the League of Nations condemned German behavior as a violation of the Versailles treaty of 1919. On the same day, however, the Locarno powers indicated their readiness to negotiate with Germany concerning a revision of the status of the Rhineland and on questions of armaments and security, under the condition that Germany maintain its military presence in the Rhineland at current levels. There was no demand for a withdrawal of troops. On March 24, 1936, Germany issued a preliminary response to the proposal, and on April 1, Ribbentrop arrived in London with a German "peace plan." This memorandum spoke of the desire for discussions and reconciliation and offered assurances that Germany had no intention of ever attacking France or Belgium. At the same time, it pressed Germany's rights to self-defense within its own boundaries (including unrestricted military presence in the Rhineland). No concrete promises (e.g., stabilizing troop strength) were made. (Keesing's Archiv der Gegenwart, March–April 1936, esp. 2455D, 2476F, 2498E; *Völkischer Beobachter*, Süddeutsche Ausgabe, Munich, April 2, 1936.)

APRIL 3, 1936

**émigré publication:** Thomas Mann's article for Heinrich's sixty-fifth birthday appeared on March 26, 1936, in *Die Neue Weltbühne* (*GW* 10:483).

**Bomst:** former county-seat in the border area of Posnania-West Prussia. Polish since 1945 (Babimost).

**congress:** international PEN Congress, from September 5 to 16, 1936, in Buenos Aires.

Probably **Benjamin Crémieux** (1888–1944): French critic. Head for a long time of the *Nouvelle Revue Française;* translated Pirandello. Died in a German concentration camp.

**love story:** Mut-em-enet's passion for Joseph, depicted in *Joseph in Egypt.*

**Henri and Gabrielle d'Estrée:** *Henry, King of France,* book two, "Vicissitudes of Love."

**article:** Heinrich Mann, "Fin de régime?" *La Dépêche,* March 31, 1936. German (abridged): "Hitler bedeutet Krieg!" *Pariser Tageblatt,* April 5, 1936.

**"Der Vertragsbruch":** Heinrich Mann, "Der Vertragsbruch," *Die Neue Weltbühne,* March 19, 1936, 364–67.

**"Ein schwerer Anfall":** Heinrich Mann, "Ein schwerer Anfall," *Die Neue Weltbühne,* April 9, 1936, 452–57.


APRIL 26, 1936

**Friedrich Burschell** (1889–1970): writer, biographer. Worked for *Die Frankfurter Zeitung, Die neue Rundschau,* and *Die weiße Blätter.* Emigrated in 1933 to France, then to Spain, then Czechoslovakia; in 1938 to England. Lived from 1954 in Munich. Among his works: *Jean Paul* (1925); *Heine und Boerne in Exile* (1943); *Schiller* (1958). At the time Burschell was secretary of the Thomas-Mann-Gesellschaft, which had been founded in Prague.


MAY 4, 1936

**Oprecht's decision:** Oprecht had decided to publish Heinrich Mann's anthology *Es kommt der Tag* (see Thomas Mann's letter of July 20, 1936).

***Weltbühne* essays:** a list of the numerous essays Heinrich Mann published in these years in *Die Neue Weltbühne* has now been compiled in Edith Zenker's *Heinrich-Mann-Bibliographie.* Reference for "destruction of the Reich" is perhaps "Verfall einer geistigen Welt," *Die Neue Weltbühne,* December 6, 1934.

**Freud's eightieth birthday:** on May 8, 1936, in Vienna, Thomas Mann delivered the address "Freud und die Zukunft" (*GW* 9:478; "Freud and the Future," in *Essays of Three Decades*). Since Freud was too ill to attend the official celebration at the Akademischer Verein für medizinische Psychologie, Thomas Mann read the address again the next day to the family and a few friends at the Freud residence.

**Kurt von Schuschnigg** (1897–1977): from 1934 to 1938 chancellor of Austria. From 1938 to 1945 detained in various prisons and concentration camps; freed by the Americans. From 1948 professor at St. Louis University in the United States. Returned to Austria in 1967 (Mutters bei Innsbruck).


MAY 19, 1936

**the Benesches:** Eduard Beneš (1884–1948), from 1935 to 1938 president of Czechoslovakia. With his help Heinrich and Thomas Mann were granted Czechoslovakian citizenship.

**Arthur Neville Chamberlain** (1869–1940): British prime minister from 1937 to 1940. Signed the Munich Agreement in 1938.

**naturalization:** see Bruno Walter's letter of December 6, 1912, to Thomas Mann and Thomas Mann's letter of December 10, 1936, to Bruno Walter.

**passage about the life of Jesus:** Thomas Mann, "Freud und die Zukunft" (*GW* 9:496f.; "Freud and the Future," *Essays of Three Decades*, 425).

**Antonio Aita:** secretary of the PEN Club in Buenos Aires, Argentina.

**conclusion of my third volume:** Thomas Mann was working at the time on the final chapters of *Joseph in Egypt*.

**trip:** s.v., Thomas Mann's letter of July 2, 1936.

**summer:** on his trip to the south of France from August 27 to September 23, 1936, Thomas Mann visited René Schickele in St-Cyr-sur-Mer and then stayed with Heinrich and his daughter, Leonie (Goschi), in Aiguebelle-Le Lavandou on the Côte d'Azur.

### JULY 2, 1936

**up there:** Heinrich Mann lived at the time in Briançon (Hautes Alpes), Hôtel du Cours.

**Lajos Hatvany** (1880–1961): Hungarian writer. Leading member of the Radical Party after the First World War. Fled from the Horthy regime; arrested on his return. Exile in Oxford. Later returned to Budapest. See Thomas Mann, "Brief an den Verteidiger L. Hatvanys" (*GW* 11:773).

**address:** Thomas Mann, "Der Humanismus und Europa," *Pester Lloyd* (June 11, 1936). From the address delivered on June 9, 1936, at the meeting of the Comité international de coopération intellectuelle in Budapest (*GW* 13:633). See Thomas Mann, "Humaniora und Humanismus" (*GW* 10:339).

**Vienna:** on June 13, 1936, Thomas Mann read from *Joseph in Egypt* in the Konzerthaus.

**Bruno Walter** (1876–1962): conductor. General music director in Munich from 1913 to 1922 and a close friend of Thomas Mann's since that time. Emigrated to Austria in 1933. From 1934 to 1936 director of the Staatsoper in Vienna. To the United States in 1940. His autobiography, *Thema und Variationen* was published in 1947 by the Bermann-Fischer Verlag in Stockholm; English edition: *Theme and Variations: An Autobiography*, trans. James A. Galston (New York: Alfred A. Knopf, 1947). See Thomas Mann, "Musik in München" (*GW* 11:339); "Für Bruno Walter" [for his sixtieth birthday] (*GW* 10:479); "An Bruno Walter zum siebzigsten Geburtstag" (*GW* 10:507).

*Joseph in Egypt:* concluded on August 23, 1936. The volume was published in mid-October by Bermann-Fischer in Vienna. The copy for Heinrich bears the dedication: "This was my way, dear Heinrich, of putting up a bold front for the last three years. May it not have been entirely in vain! Küsnacht, October 18, 1936. Your brother, T."

**France:** Hitler had occupied the demilitarized zone stipulated in the Versailles treaty. France undertook preparations to resist but relented to the fait accompli as it saw that the other signatories were not going to offer support.

### JULY 18, 1936

**Rudolf Fleischmann:** thanks to the assistance of the businessman Rudolf Fleischmann, Heinrich and Thomas Mann received civic rights in the Czech municipality of Proseč, which was the precondition for naturalization in Czechoslovakia. Heinrich on April 24, 1936, and Thomas on November 19, 1936, were granted Czech citizenship. See Gertrude Albrecht, "Thomas Mann—Staatsbürger der Tschechoslovakei," in *Vollendung und Größe Thomas Manns* (Halle/Saale, 1962), 118–29.

**my book:** *Es kommt der Tag.*

**that helpful young scholar:** Golo Mann.

*Lesebuch: Es kommt der Tag, Deutsches Lesebuch.* See *Tagebuch*, July 11, 1936: "Before dinner and through the evening continued reading of H.'s book. Moved by these often naive, but self-confident and brilliant moral manifestos, which I believe will be held in high honor in the future."

**statement . . . by Niemöller:** the Protestant theologian Martin Niemöller (1892–1984) was the most prominent representative of the Confessional Church. He resisted the intervention of the fascist state in church affairs. From 1937 to 1945 in the concentration camps Dachau and Buchenwald. See Thomas Mann, "Niemöller," 1941 (*GW* 12:910–18).

**"digression":** *Freud und die Zukunft* (Vienna: Bermann-Fischer, 1936; in English: "Freud and the Future," in *Essays of Three Decades*).

**Fleischmann:** see *Tagebuch* entry of August 6, 1936: "Herr Fleischmann from Proseč, Č.S.R., at dinner. Stirring man, who with a sense of sacred duty and 'historical' solemnity is seeking honorary citizenship for myself and the family. Prof. Frankl then happened to appear, for coffee. Vigorous discussions, a remarkable, perhaps memorable day. I signed the immigration application for the Czech municipality. In consideration of the prospect of getting back my possessions and the publication of the third Joseph, the matter will be handled discreetly for the moment. But am secured with regard to the Reich by my repeated warnings that I would be forced to accept citizenship elsewhere."

**'tis war:** Matthias Claudius, "Kriegslied." See Heinrich Mann, "Kriegslied," *Pariser Tageszeitung*, October 28, 1936.

**against the Spanish people:** on July 7, 1936, the military revolt led by Franco, which grew into the Spanish civil war, took place in Spanish Morocco. The International Brigade fought on the side of the government. Beginning in July 1936, Franco received the support of Italian volunteers and the German Legion Condor.

**Goschi:** Heinrich Mann's daughter, Leonie (Goschi) Mann.

**mother:** Maria (Mimi) Mann-Kanova (1886–1946), actress. Married to Heinrich Mann from 1914 to 1930. In 1933 she moved to Prague. The mediation of Masaryk allowed Heinrich Mann's library and a number of manuscripts to be transported to Prague.

**Triebschen:** see *Tagebuch*, July 17, 1936.
**Sils Maria:** Thomas Mann had spent a few days in Sils (Engadine) at the end of July.
**coast:** see Heinrich Mann's letter of August 7, 1936, s.v. "to come here."
**booklet:** *Freud and the Future.*

**address:** "Freud and the Future."

**Brussels Congress:** World Congress of the World Peace Movement, from September 3 to 6, 1936.

**my volume:** *Joseph in Egypt.*
**Oskar Ludwig Levy** (1867–1946): Nietzsche scholar.


SEPTEMBER 21, 1936

**a good visit, despite everything:** Thomas Mann was suffering from angina.
*Henri* **reading:** see *Tagebuch*, September 19, 1936: "Down to dinner. Afterwards, H. read in the living room from chapter 3 of the second volume of his Henri. Nice things: Renaissance, Doré, springtime of modernity."


SEPTEMBER 27, 1936

**Kuno Fiedler** (1895–1973): Protestant pastor. Acquainted with Thomas Mann since the First World War; christened Thomas Mann's youngest daughter, Elisabeth. Arrested for his resistance to the "coordination" [*Gleichschaltung*] of the Protestant church; escaped from the Würzburg city jail and found his first shelter in Thomas Mann's house in Küsnacht. Later pastor in St. Antönien/Graubünden. Then lived in Purasca/Tessin. Among his works: *Der Anbruch des Nihilismus* (1923); *Die Stufen der Erkenntnis* (1929); *Glaube, Gnade und Erlösung nach dem Jesus der Synoptiker* (1939; see Thomas Mann's review in *Maß und Wert* 3, no. 4 [1940]); *Bekennen und Bekenntnis* (1943). See Hans Wysling, ed., "Aus dem Briefwechsel Thomas Mann—Kuno Fiedler," *Blätter der Thomas-Mann-Gesellschaft*, nos. 11–12 (1971–1972).


OCTOBER 23, 1936

**powerful book:** Thomas Mann, *Joseph in Egypt.* Heinrich's copy bore the inscription: "This was my way, dear Heinrich, of putting up a bold front for the last three years. May it not have entirely been in vain! Küsnacht, October 18, 1936. Your brother, T."
**my novel:** Heinrich Mann, *Henry, King of France.*
**information from Katja:** unknown.


NOVEMBER 15, 1936

**appeal:** the reference is perhaps to "Spanien-Aufruf der deutschen Opposition. Hitler führt Krieg," *Pariser Tageszeitung*, December 25, 1936. The appeal was signed by Heinrich Mann, Georg Bernhard, Otto Klepper, Rudolf Breitscheid, Max Braun, Georg Denicke, Franz Dahlem, Kurt Frank, Willi Münzenberg.
**article:** Thomas Mann had written a paper, "La formation de l'homme moderne," for the meeting of the League of Nations commission for intellectual cooperation in Nice, from April 1 to 3, 1935. The paper, which was not presented, appeared in German under the title "Achtung, Europa!" in *Das Neue Wiener Journal*, February 15–22, 1936, and later in the volume of collected essays by the same title (Stockholm: Bermann-Fischer Verlag, 1938; in English: "Europe, Beware!"). The edited version was distributed to a large number of European newspapers under the title "Offene Worte." See Thomas Mann's *Tagebuch* entries from November 1–7, 1936; November 11, 1936; November 17, 1936.
*Mephisto:* Klaus Mann, *Mephisto: Roman einer Karriere* (Amsterdam: Querido, 1936). See Thomas Mann's letter of December 12, 1936, to Klaus Mann: "I don't know whether you had the feeling of being a moralist here, but in the book as a whole, that is what you are, and what is new and remarkable in it, what gives the novel its specific character in the history of ideas and

that for which it will one day be recognized. [ . . . ] The best and most significant moments in your novel are perhaps those in which the idea of evil is conveyed and shown, how the comic hero discovers his sympathy for evil and then devotes himself to it" (Klaus Mann, *Briefe und Antworten, 1922–1949* [Munich, 1987], 274).

**Baden:** see Thomas Mann's *Tagebuch* for November 13, 1936, and November 16, 1936. He did not end up taking the cure: "Hope that the rheumatism goes away on its own."

**story:** Thomas Mann, *Lotte in Weimar* (English: *The Return of the Beloved*). Before writing his Venice novella, Thomas Mann had planned another with the title "Goethe in Marienbad." See *Notizbuch 9*, 67, and Thomas Mann's letters of September 6, 1915, to Elisabeth Zimmer; of September 10, 1915, to Paul Amann; and of July 4, 1920, to Carl Maria Weber. The larger context is presented in *Thomas-Mann-Studien*, 1:119.

### DECEMBER 12, 1936

**your fine statement:** Thomas Mann and his family had their citizenship revoked on December 12, 1936. Heinrich Mann published an article about it, "Begrüssung des Ausgebürgerten," *Die Neue Weltbühne*, December 10, 1936.

**Kurt Hiller** (1885–1972): journalist, writer. Studied law in Berlin and Freiburg im Breisgau. Contributor to *Die Weltbühne, Der Sturm,* and *Die Aktion;* from 1915 publisher of the *Ziel* annuals. In 1918 chairman of the Politischer Rat Geistiger Arbeiter. Joined the Deutsche Friedensgesellschaft in 1920. In 1926 founder and until 1933 president of a group of revolutionary pacifists. In 1933–1934 in a concentration camp. Fled to Prague in September 1934. In Paris collaborator on the Internationales Sozialistisches Kampfbund and the *Editions Nouvelles Internationales.* Moved in December 1938, to London; from 1938 to 1946 chairman of the group of independent German authors there. Returned to Germany in 1955. Among his works: *Die Weisheit der Langeweile* (1913); *Geist, werde Herr* (1920); *Aufbruch zum Paradies* (1922); *Verwirklichung des Geistes im Staat* (1931); *Profile, Prosa aus einem Jahrzehnt* (1937); *Köpfe und Tröpfe* (1950); *Rote Ritter* (1951); *Ratioaktiv*, addresses (1966); *Leben gegen die Zeit* (1969). See Kurt Hiller, "Für Thomas Mann," *Die Neue Weltbühne* (1936), 1540–43.

**Ernst Bloch** (1885–1977): philosopher and writer. Graduate degree in Würzburg in 1908 with a work about the neo-Kantian Heinrich Rickert. Lived as freelance writer in Berlin, Heidelberg, and Munich. Emigrated in 1915 to Bern, supported the pacifist endeavors of Zweig, Rolland, and Hesse. Back in Berlin after the First World War; regular contributor to *Die Frankfurter Zeitung* and *Die Vossische Zeitung.* Did not return to Germany from a stay in Switzerland in 1933. Exile in Czechoslovakia in 1936; contributor to *Die Neue Weltbühne.* Went to Paris in 1938, then to New York; cofounder of the Aurora-Verlag. Accepted a call from the Leipziger Universität in 1949; made emeritus professor for "championing revisionists strivings." Returned to West Germany in 1957. From 1961 professor of philosophy at the University of Tübingen. Among his works: *Geist der Utopie* (1918; exp. ed. 1923); *Erbschaft dieser Zeit* (1935; in English: *Heritage of Our Times*, 1991); *Das Prinzip Hoffnung* (1954–1958; in English: *The Principle of Hope*, 1995); *Gesamtausgabe*, 15 vols. (since 1962). Thomas Mann is referring here to an article Bloch had published in *Die Neue Weltbühne* of December 10, 1936: "Nobelpreis und Ausbürgerung" (Ossietzky und Thomas Mann). He later (1939–1940) corresponded with Bloch about reworking myths and had obviously read Bloch's *Geist der Utopie* and *Erbschaft dieser Zeit*, as well as parts of an early version of *Das Prinzip Hoffnung* in manuscript. Bloch contributed the essay "Über das noch nicht bewußte Wissen" to *Maß und Wert* 3, nos. 5–6 (1940).

**The exciting days:** Thomas Mann's citizenship was revoked on December 12, 1936.

**Hiller:** see Kurt Hiller, "Für Thomas Mann," *Die Neue Weltbühne* (1936), 1540–43.

**Hermann Budzislawski** (1901–1978): journalist, Ph.D. Emigrated through Prague and Paris to the United States (1940–1948). Returned to Europe; professor in Leipzig. From March 1934 to 1939 publisher of *Die Neue Weltbühne*. On Heinrich Mann's contributions to *Die Neue Weltbühne*, see Hans-Albert Walter, "Heinrich Mann im französischen Exil," in *Text und Kritik*, special issue on Heinrich Mann (1971): 140.

**my novel:** probably "The Death Leap." In its final version, *Henry, King of France* had eight parts.

**in yours:** *Joseph in Egypt.*

**"Meditation":** *Henry, King of France*, 165ff.

**Exchange of Letters:** Thomas Mann, *An Exchange of Letters* (letter of December 19, 1936, from the dean of the philosophical faculty of the University of Bonn and Thomas Mann's response to the dean from the turn of the year 1936–1937), *Neue Zürcher Zeitung*, January 24, 1937.

**Joseph:** *Joseph in Egypt.*

**newspaper:** not identified.

**Maß und Wert:** bimonthly devoted to independent German culture, published by Thomas Mann and Konrad Falke; ed. Ferdinand Lion (vol. 3, ed. Golo Mann and Emil Oprecht). Published volumes 1, nos. 1–6 (September–October 1937 to July–August 1938); 2, nos. 1–6 (September–October 1938 to July–August 1939); 3, nos. 1–6 (November–December 1939 to September–November 1940).

**Aline Mayrisch de Saint-Hubert:** widow of the Luxemburg steel magnate Emile Mayrisch; assisted, without publicity, many exiled German writers—among them, Annette Kolb—and, beginning in 1937, was a major financial contributor to Thomas Mann's *Maß und Wert*.

**Jean Schlumberger** (1877–1968): French essayist, journalist, and novelist. With André Gide and Jacques Rivière, founded the *Nouvelle Revue Française* and, beginning in 1938, wrote regularly about French-German issues for the Parisian daily *Figaro*. Among his works: *L'inquiète paternité*, novel (1913); *Un homme heureux*, novel (1920); *La mort de Sparte*, play (1921); *Les yeux de dix-huit ans*, novel (1928); *Saint-Saturnin*, novel (1931; English version, 1932); *Plaisir à Corneille*, essays (1936); *Stéphane le glorieux*, novel (1940; in English: *Stephan the Proud*, 1946); *Jalons*, essays (1941); *Nouveaux jalons*, essays (1943); *Madeleine et André Gide*, biography (1956; English version, 1980).

**Emil Oprecht** (1895–1952): Zurich publisher and bookseller. He published the periodical *Maß und Wert*.

**Ferdinand Lion** (1883–1965): Alsacian literary and culture critic and essayist. (Thomas Mann knew him from his time in Munich.) Author of the monograph (1947; exp. ed. 1955) *Thomas Mann. Leben und Werk*, and was editor of *Maß und Wert* from 1937 to 1938.

**Arosa:** Thomas and Katja Mann, with Lajos Baron Hatvany and his wife, spent from January 20 to February 9 in Arosa.

**Goethe novella:** Thomas Mann, *Lotte im Weimar* (Stockholm: Bermann-Fischer, 1939); English: *The Beloved Returns.*

**Exchange:** Thomas Mann, *Ein Briefwechsel* (Zurich: Oprecht, 1937). English: *An Exchange of Letters.*

**Marianne:** Parisian weekly magazine. The French translation of *Ein Briefwechsel* appeared under the title *Avertissement à l'Europe*, trans. Rainer Biemel (Paris: Gallimard, 1937) [contents: André Gide, "Préface à quelque écrits récents de Thomas Mann"; Thomas Mann, "Ein Briefwechsel"; "Achtung, Europa!"; "Spanien"; "Christentum und Sozialismus"].

**Hitler's "Speech":** Heinrich Mann, "Die Rede [II]," *Die Neue Weltbühne*, February 4, 1937, 196–201.


JUNE 4, 1937

**your fourth volume:** *Joseph, der Ernährer* (*Joseph the Provider*).

**American trip:** Thomas Mann undertook his third trip to the United States from April 6 to May 1, 1937, at the invitation of the New School for Social Research in New York. April 15, keynote address, "The Living Spirit," at a banquet held at the school in celebration of the fourth anniversary of the founding of the Graduate Faculty of Political and Social Sciences. April 19, Wagner address, at the New School. Around April 20, address "On the Establishment of the American Guild for German Cultural Freedom and the German Akademie." On this trip Thomas Mann met the publisher of the *Washington Post*, Eugene Meyer, and his wife, Agnes E. Meyer, as well as the psychoanalyst Caroline Newton, a great admirer of his and collector of his works.


JULY 23, 1937

**Klub der Sauberen:** in this club Leopold Schwarzschild and Konrad Heiden sought to gather around themselves non- and anti-Communist émigrés. Involved primarily were contributors to *Das Neue Tagebuch*. See letter of July 30, 1937.

**Leopold Schwarzschild** (1891–1950): journalist. Took a stand in the *Europäische Staats- und Wirtschaftszeitung* against militarism and nationalism during the First World War. Founded, with Stefan Grossmann, *Montag-Morgen* in Berlin in 1923. Founded the *Magazin der Wirtschaft* in 1925. From 1927 publisher of the weekly *Das Tagebuch*, founded by Stefan Grossmann. Emigrated in 1933 to Paris. Editor of *Das Neue Tagebuch*. Temporarily involved in the Popular Front. Emigrated to the United States in 1940. Returned to Europe in 1950. Died in Santa Margherita. Among his works: *Das Ende der Illusion* (1934; in English: *End to Illusion*, 1934); *World in Trance* (1942); *Hamilton* (1943); *The Red Prussian: The Life and Legend of Karl Marx* (1947); *Von Krieg zu Krieg* (1947).

**Konrad Heiden** (1901–1966): journalist and writer. From 1919 to 1923 studied jurisprudence and economics in Munich. Began study of the Hitler movement in 1920. Met personally with Hitler and other leaders of the National Socialist Party. From 1923 to 1930 contributor to *Die Frankfurter Zeitung*, then freelance writer. Emigrated in 1933 to the Saar district. From 1935 to 1940 in Paris. In 1940 through Portugal to the United States. Died in New York. Among his works: *Adolf Hitler, eine Biographie* (1936–1937; in English, 1938); *Europäisches Schicksal* (1937); *The New Inquisition* (1939); *Les Vêpres hitlériennes* (1939); *Der Führer. Hitler's Rise to Power* (1943). See Thomas Mann, *Deutsche Hörer!*, February 28, 1944 (*GW* 11:1094; in English: *Listen Germany!* Only twenty-five of the fifty-five broadcasts appeared in English translation).

**verses:** in the first volume of *Henry, King of France*, Agrippa d'Aubigné declaims the following verse: "Not so far away is death, and then at last / life without death, a life that cannot cheat / For life is saved, death brought unto defeat, / who would not long to see his perils past? / Now the glad voyager in harbour lies, / And journey's end shall purge his weary eyes."

**Tchaikovsky:** Klaus Mann, *Symphonique pathétique, Ein Tschaikowsky-Roman* (Amsterdam: Querido, 1935).

**Georg Bernhard** (1875–1944): journalist. Bank official, bookkeeper, and broker from 1892 to 1898. In 1898, in the commercial section of *Die Berliner Zeitung*. From 1901 to 1903, regular contributor to Maximilian Harden's *Die Zukunft*. Own periodical in 1904 under the title *Plutus*. From 1909 on editorial board of *Die Vossische Zeitung*. In 1914, head editor and business manager of the Ullstein press agency. From 1916, professor at the Berlin Handelshochschule für Bank-, Börsen-, und Geldwesen. In 1928 member of parliament from the German Democratic Party; chairman of the Reichsverband der deutschen Presse until 1930; involved in the founding of the extreme pacifist Radical Democratic Party. Emigrated to Paris in 1933; founded *Das Pariser Tageblatt* in 1933 and *Die Pariser Tageszeitung* in 1936; worked on the Paris committee of the Popular Front; detained near Bordeaux in 1940. Emigrated to the United States in 1941. Died in New York. Among his works: *Die deutsche Tragödie. Der Selbstmord einer Republik* (1933); *Meister und Dilettanten am Kapitalismus im Reich der Hohenzollern* (1936).

**use Gide for anti-Bolshevik purposes:** see letter of November 18, 1933, s.v. Rascher.

**Otto Strasser** (1897–1974): journalist and politician. Took part in the First World War as volunteer. Member of the Social Democratic Party until 1920. Studied jurisprudence. Friend of Moeller van den Bruck. Member of the National Socialist Party from 1925 to 1930. Founded the Kampfverlag; publisher of *Die Berliner Arbeiterzeitung*. Emphasized, in contrast to Hitler, the socialist ideas in the party program. Confrontation with Hitler in 1926 concerning the expropriation of royalty. Left the party in 1930. Emigrated through Vienna, Prague, and Paris to Canada in 1940. Returned to Germany in 1955. Founded the Deutsche Soziale Union in 1956. Since 1957 publisher of *Vorschau*. Works: *Exil*, autobiography (1958); *Deutschland und der 3. Weltkrieg* (1961); *Der Faschismus, Geschichte und Gefahr* (1965).

**an earnest first letter:** Heinrich's letters of July 27 and August 21, 1937, to Klaus Mann are printed in *Brw. T.—H. Mann*, 468ff. On August 24, 1937, Klaus Mann wrote as follows to his uncle:

> *K.M. Küsnacht/Zurich*
> *August 24, 1937*
> Dear Uncle Heinrich—
>
> In response to your letter I've given the whole situation—as, incidentally, I've done frequently in the last weeks and days—another thorough going-over in my mind. No, it quite likely won't do: I don't belong in this "group" and it would be shallow and weak of me to remain in it out of deference to external considerations.
>
> I'm therefore writing by the same post to Schwarzschild, Heiden, and the secretary of the association that I am resigning. My name may no longer be used in listings of the members.
>
> The final consideration I'm insisting upon is that my decision not be publicized. Those whose opinions in this matter mean most to me I will notify myself. Since I am and remain a sworn enemy of all *éclats* within the émigré community, it seems to me most proper that I resign in silence. To those who have an interest in these matters it will become apparent

in time anyway, since my name will no longer figure in the Schwarzschild group. And we'll simply have to see whether I continue to play a role in regard to *Das Neue Tage-Buch*.

My thanks to you for your nice and urgent words. From now on I will be more careful, and think it over seven times seventy times before I "join" anything.

Faithful as always, your Klaus

The letter is also printed in Klaus Mann, *Briefe und Antworten* (Munich, 1975), 1:312f. On Schwarzschild and Bernhard, see Hermann Hesse to Klaus Mann, late January 1936; to an unknown recipient, roughly February 1936 (*Die neue Rundschau* 83, no. 2 [1972]: 224ff.).

AUGUST 15, 1937

**novel:** Thomas Mann, *Lotte in Weimar*, first chapter in *Maß und Wert* 1, no. 1 (September–October 1937): 17–34 (in English: *The Beloved Returns*).
*Deutsche Volkszeitung Prag:* not identified.
**Sch.:** Schwarzschild.
**P.F.:** Popular Front.
**Karl Radek,** actually Karl Sobelssohn (1885–1939?): Russian journalist and politician. From 1918 active in Berlin on the organization of the KPD (Communist Party of Germany); expelled in 1919. From 1919 to 1924 member of the central committee of the Communist Party of the Soviet Union and the executive committee of the Comintern. As its representative in 1923, attempted to coordinate the policies of the German and Soviet Communist parties. From 1927 to 1929 and again from 1937 to 1939 imprisoned as alleged Trotskyist and conspirator against the U.S.S.R. Then disappeared. See *Ein Zeitalter wird besichtigt* (Stockholm, 1945), 120.
**Edict of Nantes:** see *Young Henry of Navarre*, 570–71.

OCTOBER 2, 1937

**enclosed circular:** text of the typewritten carbon copy enclosed in the letter:

October 2, 1937

*18, rue Rossini*
*Nice (A.M.)*

Dear Sir,

The new social-liberal grouping of the Popular Front, of which you are a member, is seeking for the first time to initiate steps in public. It is of great significance that German intellectuals in particular, but also persons in other countries, learn of the existence of this select group of intellectuals belonging to the Popular Front. It has recently become conceivable that the major democracies, at least those which are of the greatest importance for Germany, are prepared to recognize a German liberation movement. The condition is precisely the appearance of a leadership able to inspire trust. All parties, insofar as they embrace democracy, are welcome. In practical terms, the expectation is that prominent figures will be working toward the dissolution of the existing regime.

Propaganda for the *Liberal Socialist Alliance* is to be initiated by the dissemination both inside and outside Germany, on India paper and in a reduced format, of the essay with which Thomas Mann inaugurated his journal, *Maß und Wert*. A better formulation of the fundamental view of the true, humane Germany of the future would be difficult to find. The express consent of the author for the planned distribution of his text will be secured.

While this is being done, I am asking you to approve the following steps:

1) that the distribution of the essay be undertaken in the name of the *Liberal Socialist Alliance*, and that

2) the names of the members, including your own, be listed on the inside title page.

The considerable funds necessary for this first propagandistic action have already been made available. In order for it to get underway, your authorization is required, and I ask you to inform me of it as quickly as circumstances allow.

**essay:** Thomas Mann, "Mass und Wert," foreword to *Maß und Wert* 1, no. 1 (September–October 1937): 1–16.

NOVEMBER 4, 1937

**Querido:** Emanuel Querido (1871–1943), Dutch publisher. Added a German division to his press in 1933, which became a significant center of the exile literature. Querido Verlag published Heinrich Mann's *Henri Quatre* (1935–1938) and later the novel *Der Atem* (1949). Querido also published Klaus Mann's journal *Die Sammlung*. Following the occupation of Holland (1940), Querido was deported to a camp, where he died. Querido had obviously sent Heinrich Mann the expanded edition of *Bekenntnisse des Hochstaplers Felix Krull* (Amsterdam, 1937).

*Maß und Wert:* bimonthly dedicated to free German culture. The periodical was published by Thomas Mann and Konrad Falke through the Verlag Oprecht in Zurich. It appeared from September 1937 to November 1940. Editors, Ferdinand Lion (1937–1939) and Golo Mann (1939–1940). The second issue (November–December 1937) contained "Lottes Gespräch mit Riemer," chapter three of *The Beloved Returns*, which is untitled in the English edition.

**review:** Hermann Kesten, "Heinrich Mann und sein Henri Quatre," *Maß und Wert* 2, no. 4 (March–April 1939).

**continuation:** *Die Vollendung des Königs Henri Quatre* (in English: *Henry, King of France*), *Internationale Literatur* 7, nos. 1–9; 8, nos. 1–7, 11–12; 9, nos. 1–4 (1937–1939).

**America:** between February and July 1938, Thomas Mann delivered his address "The Coming Victory of Democracy" in fifteen American cities. The German version of the address was published the same year by Oprecht in Zurich: *Vom zukünftigen Sieg der Demokratie* (see *GW* 11:910).

FEBRUARY 20, 1938

**voyage to America:** fourth trip to the United States. Following the annexation of Austria on March 13, 1938, Thomas Mann decided to remain in the U.S. On June 29 he made the passage to Europe once again, to spend the following two months dissolving the Swiss household. On September 14 he traveled back to the United States.

**Austria's fall:** on the Obersalzberg bei Berechtesgaden, on February 12, 1938, Hitler demanded of Chancellor Kurt Schuschnigg that Austria fulfill unconditionally all of the points of the treaty concluded on July 11, 1936, in particular an amnesty for all National Socialists incarcerated in Austria. On February 16, 1938, Schuschnigg reorganized the government, naming Arthur Seyss-Inquart, a proponent of the "greater Germany" solution, as interior minister. On

March 11, 1938, Schuschnigg, under German pressure, announced his resignation. German forces immediately invaded Austria, on March 12, and on March 13 the law reuniting Austria with the German Reich was enacted.

**Joachim von Ribbentrop** (1893–1946): originally a businessman, Hitler's chief advisor on foreign policy. As a special ambassador, he concluded the British-German naval treaty in June 1935, became the ambassador in London in August 1936, and was then, from 1938 to 1945, German foreign minister. In 1946 he was condemned to death for war crimes in Nuremberg and executed.

**Kurt von Schuschnigg** (1897–1977): Austrian chancellor.

**lecture tour:** February 10 to July 11, 1938. Fourth trip to the United States. See Thomas Mann's letter of November 4, 1937, s.v. America.

**Long Island:** in May and June 1938 Thomas Mann spent a few weeks in the country home of Miss Caroline Newton in Jamestown, Rhode Island. There he finished the Schopenhauer essay ("Presenting Schopenhauer," commissioned by The Living Thoughts Library and published in 1939 in a translation by H. T. Lowe-Porter) and resumed work on *The Beloved Returns*. And there he reluctantly resolved to return to Europe, despite the insecure political situation, to break up the household in Küsnacht and make arrangements for the publication of *Maß und Wert*. See *Tagebuch*, entries of May 27, May 31, and June 7, 1938.

**Moni:** Monika Mann-Lányi (1910–): writer. Married to the art historian Jenö Lányi, who drowned in 1940 in the sinking of the *City of Benares*. Autobiography: *Vergangenes und Gegenwärtiges* (1956; in English: *Past and Present*, 1960).

**honorary professorship:** in May 1938 during his fourth trip to the United States, Thomas Mann was offered an honorary professorship by Princeton University. It obligated him to four lectures during the course of a year, for which he would receive $6,000 in exchange. In a letter of May 27, 1938, to Harold Willis Dodds, the president of Princeton University, Thomas Mann accepted the honorary position.

**letter for the sixth of June:** Thomas Mann's sixty-third birthday.

**summer:** Thomas Mann spent from July 7 to September 14, 1938, in Küsnacht. During this time he continued work on *The Beloved Returns*.

**book:** *Die Vollendung des Königs Henri Quatre* (Amsterdam: Querido, 1938; Kiev: State Publishing House of the National Minorities of the U.S.S.R., 1938).

**your great work:** *Henry, King of France.*

**Engadine:** From August 13 to 21, 1938, Thomas Mann was in Sils Baselgia.

*l'infâme:* Hitler marched into Austria on March 12, 1938.

**Nietzsche introduction:** Heinrich Mann, "Nietzsche," *Maß und Wert* 2, no. 3 (January–February 1939) (introduction to *The Living Thoughts of Nietzsche: Presented by Heinrich Mann* [New York: Longmans, Green, 1939]).

**Schopenhauer:** Thomas Mann, *Schopenhauer* (Stockholm: Bermann-Fischer, 1938).

**Küsnacht:** Heinrich Mann was in Küsnacht for a visit from August 26 to September 6, 1938.

**fragments:** Heinrich Mann had read from *Henry, King of France* in Küsnacht.

**decision:** on September 12, 1939, Hitler delivered a speech at the national party congress in which he attacked the Czechoslovakian state and President Beneš, and assumed as his own the cause of the German population in the Sudetenland.

**"Nietszche":** s.v., Thomas Mann's letter of August 6, 1938.

**Robert Ley** (1890–1945): from 1933 national head of the Deutsche Arbeitsfront.

**compiling articles . . . for a book:** Heinrich Mann, *Mut* (Paris: Association internationale des Ecrivains, éd. du 10 mai 1939).

**time of the Egyptian adventure:** Napoleon's expedition to Egypt, 1798–1799.

**an American:** Ludvik Aškenazi [Aschermann] (died 1986), son-in-law of Heinrich Mann. See letters of December 29, 1938, January 25, March 2, and May 25, 1939.

**"desired—and there he comes":** in Lessing's *Philotas*, King Aridäus cries at the end of scene 7: "Wished for! And there he comes!"

**manifesto:** Thomas Mann, "Dieser Friede" (Stockholm: Bermann-Fischer, 1938; in English: *This Peace*).

**texts:** *Dieser Friede.* Dedication: "To Heinrich 'allied securely with the best.' Princeton, N.J. Christmas, 1938. T." (in English: *This Peace*). Thomas Mann, "Achtung, Europa!" Dedication: "To Heinrich with fraternal affection. Princeton, Christmas, 1938. T." (in English: "Europe Beware!" in *Order of the Day*).

***Europa:*** see Thomas Mann's letter of December 31, 1938, to René Schickele: "I've had my full share of the depression—one cannot call it anything else—the better part of humanity has suffered on account of the Munich peace. I poured my sorrow into the foreword of the pamphlet "Europe Beware!," which I wrote from the heart the first days back, still in the midst of settling in. You have perhaps already seen it by now, but I want anyway to include it here with these lines. These nihilistic vermin will not organize Europe and will not take over the world" (Brw. Schickele, 131).

**"You can see to your muck yourselves":** statement of King Friedrich August III of Saxony when his abdication was called for in 1918.

**my novel:** *Henry, King of France.*

**Dr. Aschermann:** son-in-law of Heinrich Mann [Aškenazi]. S.v., letter of November 22, 1938.

**Therese von Konnersreuth,** actually Therese Neumann (1898–1962): stigmatized since Lent 1926.

**"Europe Beware!":** see Heinrich Mann's letter of December 29, 1938, s.v. texts.

**my next project:** presumably *Empfang bei der Welt.* See Heinrich Mann's letter of April 15, 1942, s.v. three unfinished works.

**Your novel:** *Henry, King of France.*

**Hermann Kesten** (1900–): writer. Editor, then head of the literature division at Kiepenheuer-Verlag, Berlin, from 1927 to 1933. Emigrated in 1933 to Paris, Brussels, Nice, London, Amsterdam; from 1933 to 1940 head of the division in charge of émigré literature at the A. de Lange-Verlag in Amsterdam. From May 1940 in New York, where, together with Thomas Mann and others, he supported the Emergency Rescue Committee. Returned to Europe in 1949, where he established himself as a freelance writer in Rome. Known for numerous novels, among them: *Die Zwillinge von Nürnberg* (1947); *Die fremden Götter* (1949); and other works: *Dichter im Café* (1959); *Lauter Literaten* (1963). The reference is to Kesten's essay "Heinrich Mann und sein Henri Quatre," *Maß und Wert* 2, no. 4 (March–April 1939).

**the affair with your son-in-law:** see Heinrich Mann's letter of November 22, 1938, s.v. an American.

**lecture tour:** from March 8 to mid-April 1939, Thomas Mann read the lecture "The Problem of Freedom," as well as others, in Boston, New York, Detroit, Chicago, and Baltimore (parts of "The Problem of Freedom" were taken over in the later German version, "Das Problem der Freiheit").

**obligations:** after returning from his tour, Thomas Mann lectured on Goethe's *Faust* in Princeton (around April 20). On May 8, 1939, in New York, he delivered an "Ansprache auf dem Weltkongreß der Schriftsteller" (excerpt in *Literaturnaia Gazeta* [Moscow], June 10, 1939). On May 10, 1939, he read his "Einführung in den *Zauberberg*" in Princeton. The lecture was printed as an introduction to the one-volume edition of *The Magic Mountain* (New York: A. A. Knopf, 1962).

**essays:** Heinrich Mann, "Verfall eines Staates," *Die Neue Weltbühne*, March 2, 1939; "Die deutschen Soldaten," ibid., April 13, 1939.

***The Nation:*** left-liberal political-literary weekly, published by Freda Kirchwey; Thomas Mann read it regularly and published a number of pieces in it.

**object of this letter:** see the following letter from Thomas Mann, likewise of May 14, 1939.

**November pogroms:** *Kristallnacht*, November 9, 1938.

**the *Schwarze Corps*:** *Das schwarze Korps*, weekly newspaper of the SS.

**Frank Kingdon** (1894–1972): university professor and radio commentator. From 1936 to 1940 president of the University of Newark. Chairman of the International Rescue and Relief Committee; New York chairman of the Committee to Defend America by Aiding the Allies; chairman of the Fight for Freedom Committee and the Committee for Care of European Children. Also cofounder of the Emergency Rescue Committee. Was in close contact with Thomas Mann. Among his works: *The Man in the White House: You and Your President*, biography of Roosevelt (1944); *An Uncommon Man: Henry Wallace and 60 Million Jobs* (1945); *Architects of the Republic* (1947).

**Wilhelm (William) Dieterle** (1893–1972): actor and director. Began work in the theater in 1910 (Heilbronn, Mainz, Zurich, Munich, Berlin). From 1932 in Hollywood. Back in Germany in 1958; from 1962 director of the Hersfelder Festspiele. Afterward in Triesen,

Liechtenstein. Among his films: *Die Heilige und ihr Narr; A Midsummer Night's Dream; The Life of Emile Zola; Dr. Ehrlich's Magic Bullet; Portrait of Jennie.*

**James Franck** (1882–1964): physicist. Until 1935 at the Kaiser Wilhelm-Institut, Berlin. Emigrated to the United States; first taught at Johns Hopkins University; from 1938 professor of physical chemistry at the University of Chicago. Nobel Prize in 1925.

**Leonhard Frank** (1882–1961): writer. Originally wanted to be a painter and went for that purpose to Munich in 1904. From 1910 in Berlin. Emigrated in 1914 to Switzerland. Back in Munich in 1918 and from 1920 to 1933 freelance writer in Berlin. Fled to Zurich in 1933, to Paris in 1937; detained repeatedly in France. Fled to Lisbon and to the United States in 1940 (first to Hollywood, then from 1945 in New York). Returned to Munich in 1950. Among his works: *Die Räuberbande,* novel (1914; in English: *The Robber Band,* 1928); *Der Mensch ist gut,* stories (1918); *Das Ochsenfurter Männerquartett,* novel (1927; in English: *The Singers,* 1932); *Karl und Anna,* story (1927; as play, 1929; English version, 1930); *Bruder und Schwester,* novel (1929; in English: *Brother and Sister,* 1941); *Links, wo das Herz ist,* memoirs (1952, 1967; in English: *Heart on the Left,* 1954).

**Lotte Lehmann** (1888–1976): singer. In 1910 at the Staatstheater in Hamburg, from 1914 to 1938 at the Vienna Staatsoper, and from 1934 also at the Metropolitan Opera in New York. Taught in Santa Barbara, California. First performed the role of Christine in Richard Strauss's *Intermezzo;* turned more to the singing of songs in her later years. Also wrote a novel, *Orplid, mein Land* (1937). Autobiographies: *Anfang und Aufstieg* (1937); *My Many Lives* (1948). Introduction to the interpretation of song: *More than Singing* (1945); *Five Operas and Richard Strauss* (1963).

**Hermann Rauschning** (1887–1982): journalist and diplomat. Until 1936 president of the senate of the free city of Danzig; first regarded as confidant of Hitler but fled in 1936 to Switzerland; to France in 1938, to England in 1940, and in 1941 to the United States. Lived from 1948 as a farmer in Portland, Oregon. *Revolution des Nihilisms* (1938; in English: *Germany's Revolution of Destruction,* 1939); *Gespräche mit Hitler* (1939; in English: *Hitler Speaks,* 1940); *Die Zeit des Deliriums* (1944; in English: *Time of Delirium,* 1946). Contributor to *Maß und Wert.*

**Ludwig Renn,** actually Arnold Friedrich Vieth von Golssenau (1887–1979): writer. Author of the well-known novel *Krieg* (1928; in English: *War,* 1929). Joined the Communist Party in 1928. Sentenced to two-and-a-half years' imprisonment for treason following the Reichstag fire. Fled upon his release in 1936 to Switzerland. Took part in the Spanish civil war. Emigrated in 1939 through France, England, and the United States to Mexico. Professor of modern European history at the University of Morelia in 1940. President of the Freies Deutschland movement. From 1947 professor of anthropology at the Technische Hochschule in Dresden. Further works: *Vor großen Wandlungen,* novel (1936); *Adel im Untergang,* novel (1944). See Heinrich Mann, "Zu Ludwig Renns 50. Geburtstag," *Internationale Literatur* 9, no. 5 (1939): 135.

**René Schickele** (1883–1940): writer. Childhood in Alsace, student in Strasbourg. Founded the periodical *Der Stürmer* with Otto Flake and Ernst Stadler. Worked as a journalist in Munich, Paris, and Berlin. Publisher of the periodical *Das neue Magazin für Literatur.* Travels in Europe, North Africa, and India. Published *Die weiße Blätter* from 1915 to 1919 in Zurich. In Badenweier from 1920 to 1932. Emigrated in 1932 to Sanary-sur-Mer. Among his works: *Die Fremde,* novel (1909); *Das Erbe am Rhein,* novel trilogy (1925–1931); *Die Flaschenpost,* novel (1937); *Die Heimkehr,* story (1939).

**Erwin Schrödinger** (1887–1961): physicist. Taught in Stuttgart, Breslau, and Zurich;

Planck's successor in Berlin in 1927. Nobel Prize in 1933. Emigrated in 1933 to Oxford. In Graz in 1936, Dublin in 1940, then the United States; from 1956 in Vienna.

**Paul Tillich** (1886–1965): theologian. Lecturer in 1919 in Berlin. Taught in Marbach, Dresden, and Frankfurt. Proponent of "religious socialism." Emigrated in 1933 to the United States; professor at the Union Theological Seminary in New York. From 1955 at Harvard Divinity School. During the preparatory work on *Doctor Faustus*, Thomas Mann asked him for a description of theological training. Tillich's response of May 25, 1943, is printed in the *Blätter der Thomas-Mann-Gesellschaft*, no. 5 (1965): 48–51. Among his works: *Kairos* (1926–1929); *Die sozialistische Entscheidung* (1933); *The Protestant Era* (1948); *Systematic Theology* (1951–1957); *The New Being* (1955); *Auf der Grenze*, essays (1963).

**Fritz von Unruh** (1885–1970): writer. From an old officer family, became a pacifist from his experience of the First World War. Lived in Diez/Lahn and in Switzerland; emigrated in 1932 to Italy and France. Detained there in 1940. Fled to New York. From 1948 alternately in Germany and the United States. Settled again in Diez in 1952. Returned to New York in 1955, then to Atlantic City. From 1962 in Frankfurt am Main. Among his works: *Offiziere*, play (1911); *Louis Ferdinand, Prinz von Preußen*, play (1913); *Opfergang*, novel (1916; in English, *War of Sacrifice*, 1928); *Ein Geschlecht*, tragedy (1918); *The End Is Not Yet* (1947); *Die Heilige*, novel (1952; in English, *The Saint*, 1950); *Der Sohn des Generals*, autobiographical novel (1957).

**one of the articles:** possibly a reference to the essay "Kultur und Politik" (*GW* 12:853).

MAY 25, 1939

*Life* **magazine:** Marquis Childs, "Thomas Mann, Germany's foremost literary exile speaks now for freedom and democracy in America," *Life*, April 17, 1939, 56–59, 74–76.

**India-paper manifestos:** see Edith Zenker, *Heinrich-Mann-Bibliographie*, Essays, Reden, Aufrufe.

**address:** details unclear. Possibly connected with Heinrich Mann's article "Das andere Deutschland," *Deutsche Volkszeitung* (Paris), August 17, 1939.

**I can help Frau Kröger:** Heinrich Mann's marriage to Nelly Kröger took place on September 9, 1939, in Nice.

**my daughter:** Leonie (Goschi) Mann.

**Mimi:** Maria Kanova, Heinrich Mann's first wife.

**her son:** Dr. Aschermann.

JUNE 19, 1939

**first stage of our European summer:** European trip from June 6 to mid-September 1939. The brothers were together in Paris from June 14 to 17, 1939. Thomas Mann then spent a few weeks on vacation in Nordwijk aan Zee; on August 7, 1939, he traveled to Zurich (work on chapter eight of *The Beloved Returns*). After a stay in London (August 21–24, 1939), Thomas Mann flew to Stockholm, where he was supposed to address the PEN Congress on "The Problem of Freedom." Because of the invasion of Poland by German troops, he returned earlier than planned to Princeton.

**the old ones:** Prof. Alfred Pringsheim and his wife emigrated to Switzerland in November 1939.

**Idachen Springer:** governess in the household of Senator Mann.

**Hans Meisel** (1900–): writer. Left Germany in 1934, went to the United States in 1938.

From 1938 to 1940 Thomas Mann's secretary. Later professor of political science at the University of Michigan. Among his works: *The Myth of the Ruling Class* (1958).

JUNE 28, 1939

**Mut:** see Heinrich Mann's letter of November 22, 1938, s.v. compiling articles.

JULY 5, 1939

**Peter Grund,** pseudonym for Otto Mainzer (1903–): constitutional lawyer and legal philosopher. In 1929 published the book *Gleichheit vor dem Gesetz, Gerechtigkeit und Recht.* Emigrated prior to receiving a permanent professorship in 1933 to Paris, then to the United States. In exile began publishing fiction. His story *Prometheus, das Werk ohne Ende* was distinguished as particularly worthy of publication by the prize judges, among them, Thomas Mann, of the American Guild for German Cultural Freedom. As the decision was challenged in the guild, Otto Mainzer asked Heinrich Mann to intervene. Among his works: *Der zärtliche Vorstoß*, poems (1939); *Die sexuelle Zwangswirtschaft—Ein erotisches Manifest* (1981, written in the 1930s); unpublished: *Prometheus-Trilogie*, novel; *Astarte*; *Die olympische Krankheit*; *Hochzeit*, plays; *Die Eroberung des Geschlechts*, essay.

**Melantrich:** publishing house in Prague, which had brought out Thomas Mann's works in Czech since roughly 1930.

JULY 17, 1939

**Rudolf Olden** (1885–1940): s.v., Heinrich Mann's letter of February 9, 1933.

**lecture . . . for Stockholm:** Thomas Mann, *Das Problem der Freiheit* (Stockholm: Bermann-Fischer, 1939). See Thomas Mann's letter of June 19, 1939, s.v. first stage.

**nothing to be done:** at Heinrich's request, Thomas Mann had attempted to transfer money to Leonie Mann, who was living in Prague.

JULY 20, 1939

**enclosed:** "Botschaft aus Deutschland," submitted by Bruno Frank.

**novel:** Thomas Mann, *Lotte in Weimar* (Stockholm: Bermann-Fischer, [November] 1939; in English: *The Beloved Returns*).

**Der Vulkan:** Klaus Mann, *Der Vulkan* (Amsterdam, 1939).

> But the time is long overdue for me to report to you on your novel. Mielein for her part has already done so in detail, after holding on to our copy for a long while. But since I have had it, I have written various people to call their attention to the book seriously and to ask them to do something for it because it is really a first-rate thing which is only too naturally being neglected by a world caught up in stupidity and malice. I've written Alfred Neumann, Uncle Heinrich, Fränkchen, and others. I am convinced that everyone who gives it a chance, even in a skeptical frame of mind, will read to the end, fascinated, entertained, touched, and moved. That's what I did; and in saying this I confess that I had the secret intention of taking only a look at it, though a closer one than the ordinary reader. But nothing came of that intention. The book held, amused, and stirred me so that for several days I read until long after Mielein had put out her lamp—read it through word by word. [ . . . ] Well, then: I read it through all the way, with emotion and gaiety, enjoyment and satisfaction, and more than once a deep sympathy. For a long time people did not take you seriously, regarded you as a

spoiled brat and a humbug; there was nothing I could do about that. But by now it cannot be denied that you are capable of more than most—this is the reason for my satisfaction as I read; and my other feelings had their good reasons also. Before I was finished I was completely reassured that the book as an enterprise, as an exile novel, is totally without a rival because of its personal qualities, and that you needn't fear any other book of its kind, not even by Werfel. (*Letters of Thomas Mann*, 308–10)

## NOVEMBER 26, 1939

**flight from Malmö to Amsterdam:** see Erika Mann's report in *The Last Year of Thomas Mann: A Revealing Memoir by His Daughter, Erika Mann*, trans. Richard Graves (Farrar, Straus and Cudahy, 1958), 62ff.

**marriage:** Heinrich Mann married his companion of many years, Nelly Kröger, on September 9, 1939.

**wedding:** on November 23, 1939, Elisabeth Mann married the historian and writer Giuseppe Antonio Borgese (1882–1952), professor of German literature at the universities of Rome and Milano. He was guest professor of Italian literature at the University of California, Berkeley, in 1931, at Smith College from 1932 to 1936, and afterward, until 1947, at the University of Chicago, where he also taught political science. From 1946 to 1951 he was general secretary of the Committee to Frame a World Constitution and publisher of the periodical *Common Cause*. In 1951 he returned to Italy, where he was guest professor at the University of Milano. Lived finally in Florence. Among his works: *Gabriele d'Annunzio* (1909); *La vita e il libro*, essays, 3 vols. (1910–1913); *Rubè*, novel (1921); *I vivi e i morti*, novel (1923); *Goliath, the March of Fascism* (1937); *Common Cause* (1943); *Foundation of the World Republic* (1953). Translated Goethe's *Wahlverwandtschaften* (Elective affinities) into Italian.

**patroness:** Miss Caroline Newton gave Thomas Mann the poodle Nico.

**with the help of the House Wahnfried:** on this Erika Mann supplied the following information: "The House Wahnfried was not at all involved in the departure of the Pringsheim couple. Professor Haushofer, however, was helpful, an old college friend from the university."

**I am well—that is to say, I am not sick:** *Tasso*, act 3, scene 1, the princess to Leonore.

**Goethe novel:** *The Beloved Returns* was finished in October 1939.

**Jean Giraudoux** (1882–1944): French diplomat and writer. Among his plays: *Amphitryon 38* (1929; English version, 1938); *La guerre de Troie n'aura pas lieu* (1935; in English: *The Trojan War Will Not Take Place*, 1953); *Ondine* (1939; English version, 1956); *La folle de Chaillot* (1945; in English, *The Madwoman of Chaillot*, 1960). See Jean Giraudoux's letter to Thomas Mann of October 11, 1939, and Klaus Mann's letter to Katja Mann of the same date: "I don't know if the Clipper-letter to Giraudoux has already been sent, and whether—if it has already gone—it would be possible to rush off another one, this in regard to *le pauvre* Kesten. Perhaps, if Giraudoux doesn't mind the bother a second time, something could be arranged with Geneviève or with little Bertaux or with Monsieur Lazareff of *Paris Soir*. Kesten, in any case—like Speyer, Neumann, etc.—likely belongs among those for whom one wants to make a special effort, aside from more general efforts" (Klaus Mann, *Briefe und Antworten, 1922–1949* [Munich, 1987], 398).

**Jules Romains,** actually Louis Farigoule (1885–1972): French writer. Active in these years on behalf of German émigrés. Among his works: *La vie unanime* (1908); *Mort de quelqu'un*, novel (1911; in English: *Death of a Nobody*, 1975); *Knock, ou le triomphe de la médicine* (1923; in English: *Dr. Knock*, 1925); *Les hommes de bonne volonté*, novel cycle of 28 volumes (1932–1956; in English: *Men of Good Will*, 1933–1946).

**events:** reference is to the Franco-Prussian War of 1870–1871.

**middle of life:** reference to World War I, 1914–1918.

**Medi:** Elisabeth Mann married Giuseppe Antonio Borgese in November 1939.

**her parents:** in November 1939 the parents of Katja Mann, Alfred Pringsheim and his wife, Hedwig, emigrated to Switzerland.

**your novel:** Thomas Mann, *Lotte im Weimar* (Stockholm: Bermann-Fischer, 1939); English: *The Beloved Returns.*

**My wife:** in September 1939 Heinrich Mann married Nelly Kröger, his companion of many years' standing.

**marriage:** Heinrich Mann's daughter, Leonie, had married Dr. Aschermann (actually Ludvik Aškenazi) in Zurich.

**Beneš:** the Czechoslovakian statesman Eduard Beneš (1884–1948); he was T. G. Masaryk's closest associate in the founding of the Czech republic. Foreign minister, 1918–1935, also prime minister, 1921–1922; became president of the Czech republic upon the resignation of Masaryk, 1935. After the treaty of Munich and the forced separation of the Sudetenland, he resigned on October 5, 1938, and was president of the Czechoslovakian government in exile in London from 1940 to 1945. On May 16, 1945, he returned to Prague, became president once again, and left office in February 1948, after the Communist coup d'état.

**publisher of the *Weltbühne*:** Hermann Budzislawski (1901–1978); lived in Czechoslovakia from 1934, and was publisher of *Die Neue Weltbühne* from 1934 to 1939 in Prague and Paris.

**Hubert Ripka** (1895–1958): Czech journalist and politician. Editor of *Narodní osvobozeni* from 1925 to 1930; editor of *Lidové noviny* from 1930 to 1938. Emigrated to France in 1939, and to England in 1940. Minister in the Czechoslovakian exile government in London, then return to Czechoslovakia as minister of foreign trade, 1945–1948. Emigration, 1948.

**The Beloved Returns:** chapters 1–3, 5–7 had appeared in *Maß und Wert* from 1937 to 1939. Obviously Heinrich Mann had not yet read the November–December issue, in which a part of chapter 7 was published.

**Charles-Augustin Sainte-Beuve** (1804–1869): the reference is presumably to Sainte-Beuve's preface for Goethe, *Werther; Hermann et Dorothée* (Paris, 1880).

**lecture tour:** in February 1940 Thomas Mann delivered his lecture "The Problem of Freedom" in a few American cities; on February 19 in Dallas, on February 21 in Houston. From February 22 on he stayed in San Antonio but gave his lecture again on the 26th in Denton, Texas.

**my novel:** *The Beloved Returns.*

**lectures:** Thomas Mann lectured in March on "Goethe's Werther," on April 10, 1940, on "The Art of the Novel" (both printed for the first time in *Altes und Neues* [Frankfurt: Fischer, 1953]); on May 2, 3, and 5, 1940, he delivered the lecture "On Myself" (first printed in the *Blätter der Thomas-Mann-Gesellschaft*, no. 6 [1966]).

**counterpart to *This Peace*:** trans. H. T. Lowe-Porter (New York: Knopf, 1938). German edition: *Dieser Friede* (Stockholm: Bermann-Fischer, 1938). Thomas Mann, *This War*, trans.

Eric Sutton (London: Secker & Warburg; New York: Knopf, 1940). German edition: *Dieser Krieg!* (Stockholm: Bermann-Fischer, 1940).

**Golo:** at the end of 1939, following the resignation of Ferdinand Lion, Golo Mann and Emil Oprecht had taken over as editors of *Maß und Wert*.

**contribution:** nothing by Heinrich Mann was published in the third and last volume of *Maß und Wert*, edited by Golo Mann.

MAY 5, 1940

*This Peace:* Thomas Mann, "Diese Friede," as first published in excerpts (*Die Zukunft*, November 25, 1938, 2), then under the title "Die Höhe des Augenblicks," in Thomas Mann, *Achtung, Europa!* (Stockholm: Bermann-Fischer, 1938).

*This War:* Thomas Mann, *Dieser Krieg* (Stockholm: Bermann-Fischer, 1940). The edition printed in Amsterdam was never distributed; it was destroyed in the course of the invasion of the German military into Holland.

JULY 23, 1940

**Alfred A. Knopf** (1892–1984): Thomas Mann's American publisher.

**Valeriu Marcu** (1899–1942): historical writer of Rumanian descent. Emigrated in 1933 to the south of France, then to the United States. Among his works: *Schatten der Geschichte, 15 europäische Profile* (1926); *Lenin, 30 Jahre Rußland* (1927; English version, 1928); *Scharnhorsts großes Kommando, Die Geburt einer Militärmacht in Europa* (1928); *Männer und Mächte der Gegenwart* (1930; in English: *Men and Forces of Our Time*, 1931); *Die Vertreibung der Juden aus Spanien* (1934; in English: *The Expulsion of the Jews from Spain*, 1935); *Machiavelli, Die Schule der Macht* (1937; in English: *Accent on Power*, 1939).

**Golo:** Thomas Mann wrote about his son's adventures in a series of letters in August 1940 to Agnes E. Meyer (see *Br.* 2:152–60; *Letters of Thomas Mann*, 342–43, 344–46).

**with his brother's help:** Hans Oprecht (1894–1978). Secretary of the Swiss association of civil servants, president of the Social Democratic Party of Switzerland, member of the national council. Oprecht worked for a period as secretary of the Swiss relief organization for German scholars.

AUGUST 28, 1940

*Testament*

In September 1940, Heinrich and Nelly Mann, Golo Mann, Lion and Martha Feuchtwanger, Franz and Alma Werfel fled by foot over the Pyrenees to Port Bou, Spain, and traveled by train from there to Barcelona, Madrid, and Lisbon. Together with many other German refugees they embarked on October 4 on the Greek ship *Nea Hellas* and reached New York on October 13, 1940. See Heinrich Mann, *Ein Zeitalter wird besichtigt* (Stockholm, 1945), 474–86; and Alma Mahler-Werfel, *Mein Leben* (Frankfurt, 1960), 312–21.

SEPTEMBER 22, 1940

**telegram:** see Thomas Mann's *Tagebuch*, September 20, 1940: "*Telegram from Golo* and Heinrich from Lisbon, where they are waiting [for] a ship. Joy and satisfaction." The present letter was still sent to Lisbon. See also Thomas Mann's letter of September 15, 1940, to Karl Löwenstein.

**Rescue Committee:** at the end of June 1940, following the ceasefire between France and the Third Reich, the Emergency Rescue Committee was founded under the leadership of the president of Newark University, Dr. Frank Kingdon, with the participation of Thomas and Erika Mann, and later Hermann Kesten. The committee worked closely with the president's Advisory Committee on Political Refugees.

**from the Unitarians:** reference is probably to the Unitarian Church, which was active on behalf of refugees at the time.

**from Washington:** Agnes E. Meyer had informed Thomas Mann by telegram that she was making efforts in Washington on behalf of Golo Mann (see *Tagebuch*, August 22, 1940).

**Golo's appointment:** the aim of the "appointment" was to get a visa for Golo Mann. It did not lead to a teaching position at the New School.

**film contract:** the production companies Metro-Goldwyn-Mayer and Warner Brothers offered Heinrich Mann a one-year contract as a scriptwriter. This contract provided the actual basis for an entry visa. Heinrich Mann was paid $6,000 a year to write screenplays, none of which were produced. Warner Brothers did not renew the contract at the end of the year.

**property with seven palms:** on September 12, 1940, Thomas Mann purchased the property at 1550 San Remo Drive, Pacific Palisades.

### NOVEMBER 14, 1940

**your telegram:** after a brief stay in New York, Heinrich Mann went on to Los Angeles, where he, along with numerous other émigrés, took up residence. The telegram has not been preserved. Presumably, it gave notice of the date of Heinrich Mann's arrival with his wife, Nelly, in Los Angeles.

**Beverly and Hollywood:** Beverly Hills and Hollywood.

**Medi:** Thomas Mann stayed with the Borgeses in Chicago from November 14 to 27, 1940. Angelica Borgese, the daughter of Elisabeth (Medi) Borgese-Mann, was born on November 30, 1940.

*election:* reference to the presidential election; on November 5, 1940, Roosevelt became president of the United States for a third time. See *Tagebuch*, November 6, 1940.

**house question:** from September 28, 1938, Thomas Mann lived in Princeton at Mitford House, 65 Stockton Street. From July 5 to October 6, 1940, he rented a house in Brentwood (Los Angeles), at 441 North Rockingham. On October 4, 1940, in a letter to Ida Herz, he reported that he had acquired a piece of property: "We are returning to Princeton for the winter, but have bought a piece of land here with seven palms and a lot of lemon trees, and will probably build." On March 17, 1941, the household in Princeton was finally dissolved, and Thomas Mann moved to California, 740 Amalfi Drive, Pacific Palisades. He settled here on April 8, 1941, to await the completion of his own house. On February 5, 1942, Thomas Mann moved into his home at 1550 San Remo Drive, Pacific Palisades.

### NOVEMBER 16, 1940

**Erik Charell:** director, theater manager, originally dancer. Took over the Großes Schauspielhaus in Berlin from Reinhardt. Directed successful revues and films (*Drei Musketiere, Der Kongreß tanzt*).

**put me properly to work:** Heinrich had signed a one-year contract with Warner Brothers as a scriptwriter at an annual salary of $6,000, which initially secured his livelihood. Since the contract was not renewed, Heinrich Mann found himself compelled to give up the house in

Beverly Hills and move into a small apartment in Los Angeles. From then on he was largely dependent on monthly subsidies from his brother Thomas.

**"novella":** presumably refers to a preliminary sketch of a screenplay for the projected film of *Henri Quatre*.

**Liesl Frank** (1903–): daughter of Fritzi Massary, wife of Bruno Frank. She emigrated to the United States via London with her husband in 1937.

**night of the election:** Franklin D. Roosevelt was elected to a third term as president of the United States on November 5, 1940.

**duchess of Windsor:** the duke of Windsor and his wife sympathized at that time with fascism.

**Princeton:** Thomas Mann had decided to give up his guest professorship in Princeton and settle in California.

**the two Rottenbergs:** Sarah Rottenberg was a friend of Nelly Mann. Further details unknown.

DECEMBER 6, 1940

**the happy event:** the birth of the granddaughter, Angelica Borgese, on November 30, 1940.

DECEMBER 8, 1940

**sacrifices:** probably refers to a report about Great Britain's bad financial condition, which Winston Churchill sent to the American president, Franklin Roosevelt, on December 8, 1940.

**F.D.R.:** Franklin Delano Roosevelt (1882–1945); president of the United States from 1933 to 1945.

FEBRUARY 3, 1941

**this new book:** Thomas Mann, *Die vertauschten Köpfe: Eine indische Legende* (Stockholm: Bermann-Fischer, 1940; in English: *The Transposed Heads: A Legend of India*). With the handwritten dedication: "A minor entertainment for Heinrich and Nelly. Princeton, 9 Jan. 1941. T."

**Bermann-Fischer announces:** Thomas Mann, *Adel des Geistes* was first published by Bermann-Fischer in Stockholm. *Das Problem der Freiheit* (Stockholm: Bermann-Fischer, 1939). *Die schönsten Erzählungen* (Stockholm: Bermann-Fischer; Amsterdam: Querido and de Lange, 1939).

FEBRUARY 4, 1941

**Alfred A. Knopf:** Thomas Mann's New York publisher.

**trip:** Thomas Mann traveled to Washington on January 11, 1942, and was a guest, with his wife Katja, on January 13–14, 1942, of President Franklin D. Roosevelt at the White House. Thomas Mann continued on to Georgia and North Carolina, from January 15 to 18, delivering his lecture "The War and the Future."

**Die vertauschten Köpfe:** Thomas Mann, *Die vertauschten Köpfe: Eine indische Legende* (Stockholm: Bermann-Fischer, 1940; English, *The Transposed Heads*).

**Davidson:** the architect J. R. Davidson (born in Berlin, from Breslau); built numerous villas and apartment houses in Los Angeles and the surrounding area. The house he designed for Thomas Mann is regarded as a particularly successful work.

**rental:** reference to Thomas Mann's temporary residence in Pacific Palisades, California, on 740 Amalfi Drive; see letter of November 14, 1940, s.v. house question.

FEBRUARY 23, 1941

**to Mexico:** in order to get the papers required for immigration, it was necessary to re-enter the United States legally.
**your book:** Thomas Mann, *The Transposed Heads: A Legend of India*.
**birthday:** Heinrich Mann celebrated his seventieth birthday on March 27, 1941.
**Joseph Marie de Maistre** (1753–1821): French philosopher.

FEBRUARY 25, 1941

**affidavit:** see Heinrich's letters of February 23, 1941, and February 28, 1941; letter to Siegfried Marck of March 7, 1941. In his *Tagebuch*, Thomas Mann noted on February 25, 1941: "wrote to Heinrich regarding affidavit, which [I] am refusing for his wife."
**latest *speech*:** in his speech on February 24, 1941, in the festival hall of the Munich Hofbrauhaus, Hitler bombastically announced a new U-boat offensive (for more on the speech, see Max Domarus, *Hitler: Reden und Proklamationen 1932–1945* [Wiesbaden: R. Löwit, 1973], 2:1667–70).

FEBRUARY 28, 1941

**novel:** Frederick Hollander, *Those Torn from the Earth*, preface by Thomas Mann (New York, 1941).
**film-novel:** see Heinrich Mann's letter of November 16, 1940, s.vv. work, novella.

FEBRUARY 29, 1941

**Indian story:** Thomas Mann, *Die vertauschten Köpfe: Eine indische Legende* (Stockholm: Bermann-Fischer, 1940; English, *The Transposed Heads*).
**ashamed of having asked:** see letter of February 4, 1941, to Heinrich Mann.
**Bruno Frank:** see letter to him of February 4, 1941.
*Adel des Geistes:* Thomas Mann, *Adel des Geistes*, first published in 1945 by Bermann-Fischer in Stockholm.
*Das Problem der Freiheit:* Thomas Mann, *Das Problem der Freiheit* had already been published in 1939 by Bermann-Fischer in Stockholm.
*Schönsten Erzählungen:* Thomas Mann, *Die schönsten Erzählungen* (Stockholm: Bermann-Fischer; Amsterdam: Querido and de Lange, 1939).
**your birthday:** Heinrich Mann celebrated his seventieth birthday on March 27, 1941.

MARCH 21, 1941

*Telegram*

Among Heinrich Mann's posthumous papers there is a telegram with the same text dated March 22, 1941.
**birthday dinner:** the birthday celebration eventually took place on May 2, 1941, rather than March 27. Alfred Döblin wrote on July 24, 1941, to Hermann Kesten: "When we recently celebrated H. Mann's seventieth birthday at Salka Viertel's it was like old times: Th.

Mann pulled a manuscript out of his pocket and read his congratulations from it. Then the brother pulled a manuscript out of his pocket and likewise read his printed thanks. We sat over dessert, about twenty men and women, and listened to each other talk about German literature. Feuchtwanger, Werfel, Mehring, the Reinhardts, and a few people from film were there too." Thomas Mann's "Ansprache zu Heinrich Mann's siebzigsten Geburtstag" (Address on Heinrich Mann's seventieth birthday) was intended for Klaus Mann's periodical *Decision* but was not published (manuscript in the Thomas-Mann-Archiv, Zurich); see text in the Documents above. The manuscript of Heinrich Mann's remarks, "Tischrede bei Frau Viertel," is in the Heinrich-Mann-Archiv, Berlin (see *Findbuch*, no. 400; first printed in *Aufbau* 14, nos. 5–6 [1958]).

**will see each other in any case on the 26th:** on March 26 in Los Angeles, Thomas Mann delivered a revised version of the lecture "The War and the Future." He then met with Heinrich Mann and Bruno Frank.

OCTOBER 19, 1941

**one of the stations of our calvary:** major lecture tour from October 14 to the end of November 1941. On October 18, 1941, Thomas Mann delivered his lecture "The War and the Future" (first published in *Decision*, New York, February 1941; reprinted in *Order of the Day*).

DECEMBER 30, 1941

**J. E. Davies** (1876–1958): American diplomat. Ambassador in Moscow from 1936 to 1938.

**my brother-in-law:** Peter Pringsheim (1881–1964), physicist.

**little grandson:** Fridolin Mann (1940–), son of Michael Mann. Model for Nepomuk (Echo) Scheidewein in *Doctor Faustus*.

**broadcast to Germany:** see Thomas Mann, *Deutsche Hörer! 55 Radiosendungen nach Deutschland* (*GW* 11:983–1123) (only twenty-five of the addresses were included in the English version, *Listen Germany!*).

**Schicklgruber:** the name of Hitler's father, the illegitimate son of Maria Anna Schickelgruber, until he reached the age of forty.

APRIL 4, 1942

**checks:** see Heinrich Mann's letter of November 16, 1940, s.v. work.

APRIL 15, 1942

**three unfinished works:** could refer to: Heinrich Mann, *Lidiçe* (Mexico: El Libro Libre, 1943) (notes from 1940 to 1942 have been preserved; manuscript finished on September 27, 1942; see *Findbuch*, nos. 115–17). *Ein Zeitalter wird besichtigt* (Stockholm: Neuer Verlag, 1945) (the date "1940" is written on the file container; notes on the back of letters from the period April 5, 1942, to August 25, 1943; manuscript finished on June 23, 1944; proofsheets dated "Stockholm, May 16, 1945; see *Findbuch*, nos. 222–32). *Empfang bei der Welt* (Berlin: Aufbau-Verlag, 1956) (first draft, April 10, 1941; first revision, April 22, 1941; manuscript finished on June 8, 1945; see *Findbuch*, nos. 98–107, and letter to Karl Lemke of January 1, 1948).

Works first begun at a later date: *Der Atem* (Querido, 1949) (notes on the back of a letter of November 30, 1945; manuscript finished on October 25, 1947; "Reading of proofsheets completed Wednesday, March 2, 1949, at 11:15 A.M."; see *Findbuch*, nos. 1–7). Work on *Die traurige Geschichte von Friedrich dem Großen* probably got underway only in 1947 to 1949 (see *Findbuch*, nos. 65–84).

**Maxim M. Litvinov** (1876–1951): from 1941 to 1943, ambassador from the U.S.S.R. to the United States. He conveyed the honoraria to Heinrich Mann for his publications in the Soviet Union (see *The Story of a Novel*, 10 [11:150]).

OCTOBER 25, 1942

**Your book:** Thomas Mann, *Order of the Day: Political Essays and Speeches of Two Decades*, trans. H. T. Lowe-Porter, A. E. Meyer, Eric Sutton (New York: Knopf, 1942). Contents, among other essays: "Europe Beware!" "A Brother, Niemöller."

**foreword:** dated Pacific Palisades, California, June 11, 1942.

**"Europe Beware!":** the German version, "Achtung, Europa!" first appeared in *Neues Wiener Journal*, November 15 and 22, 1936.

**words about Niemöller:** first published as preface to Martin Niemöller, *God Is My Führer* (New York, 1941). The German version appeared in *Deutsche Blätter*, Santiago, Chile (1943).

***a brother:*** Thomas Mann, "Bruder Hitler." First appeared in *Das Neue Tagebuch* 7, no. 13 (1939).

**Genghis Khan** (1155 or 1167–1227): founder of the Mongolian empire.

**poor Wilhelm:** Wilhelm II (1859–1941), German kaiser from 1888 to 1918. Died in exile in Holland. Further details concerning the context are unknown.

APRIL 6, 1943

**letter from Brazil:** from the Austrian writer Karl Lustig-Prean (1892–1965). The latter emigrated to Brazil in 1939, where he led the movement of the Freie Deutsche. Returned to Vienna in 1948. Among his works: *Der Krieg* (1914); *Kultur* (1916); *Blutgerüst* (1918); *Die Krise des deutschen Theaters* (1929); *Lustig-Preans lachendes Panoptikum* (1952). See Thomas Mann's letter of April 8, 1943 (*Br.* 2:306).

SEPTEMBER 11, 1943, THOMAS MANN ET AL.

*Telegram*

**Elisabeth Bergner** (1897–): actress. Wife of the dramatist and director Paul Czinner. Performed in Innsbruck, Zurich, Vienna, Munich, and Berlin. Emigrated in 1933 to London, then to the United States. Performed again in Germany after the war. Received the Schiller Prize from the city of Mannheim in 1962 and the Bundesfilmpreis in 1963.

**Emil Ludwig** (1881–1948): writer and journalist. Son of the ophthalmologist H. Cohn, who took the name Ludwig in 1883. Went to Switzerland in 1906, then from 1914 in London; correspondent during the First World War in Istanbul and Vienna, later freelance writer in Ascona. Author of novelistic biographies, such as *Goethe* (1920; English version, 1928); *Napoleon* (1925; English version, 1928); *Wilhelm II* (1926; in English: *Wilhelm Hohenzollern*, 1928); *Bismarck* (1926; English version, 1927); *Michelangelo* (1930; English version, 1941); *Lincoln* (and English version, both in 1930); *Cleopatra* (and English version, both in 1937); *Roosevelt* (and English version, both in 1938); *Beethoven* (1943; English version, 1988); *Stalin* (1945; N.B., English version, 1942).

**that letter of Bruckner's:** see Ferdinand Bruckner's letter of November 16, 1943, to Heinrich Mann (printed in Brw. T.—H. Mann, 484):

> In all of our discussions we are naturally very interested in the question of what you and your brother, to whom I'm also writing, would think about the foundation of a Defense League. There is no need to say that it could not fulfill its function without your support. That does not mean that you would be plagued with every detail of the League's work! But if it proves possible to found such an organization, would you be prepared, along with Thomas Mann, to accept the title of honorary president? Your two names would not only lend the League a legitimate character, but would also supply it with a magnificent banner for the time when German writers are able to return home.

**Barthold Fles:** literary agent. Emigrated from Holland to the United States. Active in support of German exile literature after 1933. See Heinrich Mann, *Briefwechsel mit Barthold Fles 1942–1949* (Berlin and Weimar: Aufbau Verlag, 1993).

MARCH 24, 1944

**statement:** Heinrich Mann, "Verehrte Zuhörer!" *The German-American* 2, no. 11 (March 1944), a welcome address to those attending the celebration in New York's Times Hall honoring Heinrich Mann's seventy-third birthday.

**Louis Bromfield** (1896–1956): American writer. Author of the popular novels *Early Autumn* (1926) and *The Rains Came* (1937).

**little daughter:** Domenica Borgese, born March 6, 1944.

**the year 1925:** should probably read 1952.

JULY 29, 1944

**author's copy:** Thomas Mann, *Joseph der Ernährer* (Stockholm: Bermann-Fischer, 1943; in English: *Joseph the Provider*). Heinrich's copy bears the dedication: "to my brother Heinrich, a game in words for hours of rest. Pacif. Palisades, July 30, 1944. T."

**pages about the old and new times:** Heinrich Mann had held a public reading from *Ein Zeitalter wird besichtigt.*

**my musician hero:** Adrian Leverkühn in *Doctor Faustus.*

**Palestrina:** see Thomas Mann's letter of February 18, 1905, s.v.

**Bibi and Gret:** Michael Mann (1919–) and his wife, née Moser, from Zurich.

SEPTEMBER 2, 1944

**Your book:** *Joseph the Provider.*

**"But then there's Widow Pittelkow!":** Heinrich Mann is referring here to Fontane's dedication poem for *Stine* (1890):

> If of the puppets here arrayed
> *Stine* seems not the best displayed,
> Know that I too find her so-so,
> But then there's Widow Pittelkow!
> A count, a baron, and other guests,
> Minor characters are always best,
> Bumpkin comedy, a puppet show,

Not too many pages though.
Whatever flaws might you defile,
Meet with kindness, my poor child!

**the "calm" man:** Mai Sachme, the "governor of the prison" in *Joseph the Provider*, 862 (*GW* 5:1304).

**Eugène Sue** (1803–1857): French novelist. Among his works: *Le Juif errant* (1844f.).

**William Beveridge** (1879–1963): British political economist. The plan he proposed in 1942 became the foundation of British social security legislation in 1948.

**My own book:** Heinrich Mann, *Ein Zeitalter wird besichtigt* (Stockholm: Neuer Verlag, 1945).

SEPTEMBER 7, 1944

**Your letter:** Heinrich Mann's letter to his brother of September 2, 1944. The *Tagebuch* notes on September 7, 1944: "Letter from Heinrich about *Joseph*."

**Lidiçe:** novel by Heinrich Mann, published in Mexico: El Libro Libre, 1943.

**big novel:** Thomas Mann had begun writing *Doctor Faustus* in March 1943.

**reviewer from the *New Leader*:** see the *Tagebuch* entry of July 26, 1944: "*The New Leader* sends pleasing article about Joseph and its critics." The reference is to William E. Bohn's review essay in the column "Home Front," *The New Leader*, July 22, 1944, 10. Thomas Mann responded on grounds of principle to Dr. Bohn, the editor of *The New Leader*, in a letter of July 30, 1944. The letter, without Mann's knowledge, was published on August 8, 1944, in *The New Leader*, under the title "Mann Comments on Critics of Thomas Mann." Although Mann noted in his *Tagebuch* on August 19, 1944, "not pleasant," he restrained himself, responding to Bohn in a friendly tone and without reproach on the same day.

**Book Club:** Book of the Month Club; a book club founded in 1926 by Harry Scherman, which selected the "book of the month." Such a designation prompted large editions and the considerable financial gains that went with them.

**your book on our epoch:** Heinrich Mann, *Ein Zeitalter wird besichtigt* (Stockholm: Neuer Verlag, 1945).

SEPTEMBER 24, 1944

**Martin Gumpert** (1897–1955): Berlin physician and writer. Emigrated to the U.S. in 1936, where he was from time to time a close friend of Erika Mann's in New York. Gumpert appeared as Mai-Sachme in the third and fourth volume of the *Joseph* novels. See 13:435, 436–38.

**F.D.R.'s election speech:** Roosevelt's address to the Brotherhood of Teamsters, Chauffeurs, Warehousemen and Helpers of America, on September 23, 1944, in the Statler Hotel in Washington. See *Tagebuch*, September 23, 1944.

MAY 19, 1945

**Reading your lecture:** Thomas Mann, "Deutschland und die Deutschen," *Die neue Rundschau* (Stockholm) (October 1945). In English: *Germany and the Germans*. An Address Delivered in the Coolidge Auditorium in the Library of Congress, October 13, 1943 (Washington: U.S. Government Printing Office, 1948).

**congratulations:** see Heinrich Mann's letter of June 3, 1945.

**article about you:** Marquis Childs, "Inspiration in Thomas Mann's Career," *St. Louis Post-Dispatch,* June 1, 1945.

**remarks in the *Neue Rundschau:*** Heinrich Mann, "Mein Bruder," *Die neue Rundschau,* special issue for Thomas Mann's seventieth birthday (Stockholm) ( June 1945): 3–12 (preprint from *Ein Zeitalter wird besichtigt*). See text in the Documents above.

JUNE 9, 1945

**essay:** see letters of May 19 and June 3, 1945.

**"play and playing [at] salvation":** see *Joseph the Provider,* 1195 (*GW* 5:1804).

**"Who would have thought it":** *Joseph the Provider,* 1191 (*GW* 5:1798).

SPRING 1946

*Handwritten first draft of a telegram*

**Doctor [Frederick] Rosenthal:** on his advice, Thomas Mann underwent a lung operation in April 1946, in Billings Hospital, Chicago (see his report in *The Story of a Novel,* 165–86; *GW* 11:255–69). When in October 1946 he set about describing the sickness and death of little Echo, he asked Dr. Rosenthal for information about the course of a case of meningitis (see *The Story of a Novel,* 217; *GW* 11:290; and *Doctor Faustus,* 473–79; *GW* 6:627–36).

MAY 22, 1947

**Nietzsche lecture:** Thomas Mann, "Nietzsche's Philosophie im Lichte unserer Erfahrung," *Die neue Rundschau* (Stockholm) (1947): 359–89. Thomas Mann delivered the lecture on May 20 in the Senate House of London University and on June 3 before the XIV international PEN Congress in Zurich.

**Harold George Nicolson** (1886–1968): English diplomat and writer. Member of parliament from 1935 to 1943. Among his works: *Peacemaking* (1919); *Public Faces* (1932); *Curzon, the Last Phase, 1919–1925* (1934); *Diplomacy* (1939); *Some People* (1944); *The Congress of Vienna* (1946); *The English Sense of Humor* (1946); *King George V, His Life and His Reign* (1952); *The Evolution of Diplomatic Method* (1954); *Diaries and Letters 1930–1939, 1939–1945, 1945–1962* (1966–1968).

DEDICATION [N.D., 1948]

***Professor Unrat:*** Heinrich Mann's novel *Professor Unrat, oder Das Ende eines Tyrannen* was first published in 1905 by Langen in Munich. It was filmed in 1930 as *Die Blaue Engel* and since that time has been published primarily under the film title (e.g., by Weichert in Berlin); in English: *The Blue Angel.*

MAY 24, 1949

**news:** Klaus Mann's suicide, on May 21, 1949.

**trip:** Thomas and Katja Mann traveled from London to Sweden and Denmark, from May 19 to 31, 1944. In Stockholm and Copenhagen Thomas Mann delivered the lecture "Goethe und die Demokratie." He was awarded an honorary doctorate at the University of Lund.

**adventure of moving back:** after having been extensively courted—honorary doctorate from Humboldt University (1947); Nationalpreis I. Klasse für Kunst und Literatur der DDR (1949)—Heinrich Mann accepted appointment as the first president of the German Academy of the Arts, to be founded in East Berlin. It would have meant returning to Germany. However, because of administrative difficulties and then, finally, Heinrich Mann's death on March 12, 1950, in Santa Monica, the return did not take place.

*nurse:* Heinrich Mann's nurse, Mrs. Weyl (see Katja Mann's letter of June 24, 1949).

MAY 26, 1949

**sad days:** following Klaus Mann's suicide (May 21, 1949).

**my obligations:** Thomas Mann delivered the lecture "Goethe und die Demokratie" on May 24, 1949, in Stockholm and, the next day, in Copenhagen. He repeated the lecture in June 1949 in Zurich and Bern.

**Academy:** the Swedish Academy organized the lecture delivered by Thomas Mann on May 24, 1949, in Stockholm.

**Oxford:** on May 13, 1943, Thomas Mann had been awarded an honorary doctorate by Oxford University.

JUNE 24, 1949

*Passages marked with an asterisk were underlined by Heinrich Mann.*

**reading:** Thomas Mann read from *Der Erwählte* on June 24, 1949, in Basel Stadtkino.

**Schuls-Tarasp:** the Manns stayed from June 27 to July 18, 1949, in the Schweizerhof Hotel in Vulpera/Schuls to recuperate. Heinrich Mann marked the address in the margin.

**in *Frankfurt:*** after sixteen years, Thomas Mann returned to Germany for the first time, from July 23 to August 3, 1949. He visited Frankfurt on July 25.

**be in California:** the Manns embarked from Le Havre on August 6, 1949, on the voyage to New York. On August 13 they arrived in Pacific Palisades. Heinrich Mann put the word "August" after "middle."

**Mrs. Weyl:** Heinrich Mann's nurse (see Katja Mann's letter of May 24, 1949).

**Viko's Nelly:** Nelly Mann, née Kilian (1895–1962), wife of Thomas Mann's brother Viktor, who had died on April 21, 1949.

***Der Atem:*** Heinrich Mann, *Der Atem*, novel (Amsterdam: Querido, 1949).

JULY 14, 1949

**Weimar:** on August 1, 1949, Thomas Mann delivered his address "Ansprache im Goethejahr" in the Nationaltheater in Weimar (s.v. address, below).

**since "the absence of my son":** Klaus Mann committed suicide on May 22, 1949. Goethe had written to Zelter on December 10, 1830, in reference to the death of his son, "the absence of my son oppresses me."

**address here in Frankfurt:** "Ansprache im Goethejahr," delivered on July 25, 1949, in the Paulskirche. First published in *Neue Zeitung*, July 26, 1949.

**review:** Friedrich S. Großhut, "Heinrich Mann's Senaste," *Expressen* (June 25, 1949); about Heinrich Mann's novel *Der Atem*. The writer Großhut (1906–) emigrated in 1933 to Palestine, spent the period 1948 to 1949 as a journalist in Stockholm, and later lived in the United States.

**something unique and incomparable:** in a letter of September 5, 1949, to A. M. Frey, Thomas Mann wrote about *Der Atem:* "Thank you for the review. My brother already has it and doesn't seem overly delighted. I find, however, that you have expressed yourself with fitting respect, sympathy, and dignity. The overconcentration on language, which, even if one is very careful, often leads to incomprehensibility—of the plot as well—simply cannot be denied. As a public critic I too would have to mention it."

**above languages, of language:** see *The Holy Sinner,* 10; 7:14.

**Georg Lukács** (1885–1971): Hungarian literary historian. Emigrated from Germany to the U.S.S.R. in 1933, later lived as freelance writer in Budapest. The character Naphta in *The Magic Mountain* is partially drawn on his model. See Thomas Mann's essay on Georg Lukács, first printed in *Aufbau* 11, no. 4 (1955) (*GW* 10:545).

# BIBLIOGRAPHY

Banuls, André. *Heinrich Mann. Le poète et la politique.* Paris: C. Klincksieck, 1966 [with chronicle and bibliography].

Bürgin, Hans. *Das Werk Thomas Manns: Eine Bibliographie unter Mitarbeit von Walter A. Reichart und Erich Neumann.* Frankfurt: S. Fischer, 1959.

Bürgin, Hans, and Hans-Otto Mayer, comp. *Thomas Mann: Eine Chronik seines Lebens.* Frankfurt: S. Fischer, 1965 [English edition: *Thomas Mann: A Chronicle of His Life*, compiled by Hans Bürgin and Hans-Otto Mayer, translated by Eugene Dobson (Tuscaloosa: University of Alabama Press, 1969)].

Carlsson, Anni, ed. *Hermann Hesse—Thomas Mann, Briefwechsel.* Frankfurt: Suhrkamp, 1968.

Dietzel, Ulrich, ed. "Heinrich Manns Briefe an Maximilian Brantl." *Weimarer Beiträge* 14, no. 2 (1968): 393–422.

———. *Thomas Mann—Heinrich Mann, Briefwechsel 1900–1949.* 3d ed. Berlin: Veröffentlichungen der Akademie der Künste der Deutschen Demokratischen Republik, 1977 [222 letters]. [Brw. T.—H. Mann]

Eggert, Rosemarie. *Vorläufiges Findbuch der Werkmanuskripte von Heinrich Mann (1871–1950)*, edited and reproduced by the Abteilung Literatur-Archiv der Deutschen Akademie der Künste zu Berlin. Berlin, 1963. [*Findbuch*]

Jasper, Willi. *Der Bruder: Heinrich Mann, eine Biographie.* Munich: Hanser, 1992.

Jonas, Klaus W. *Die Thomas-Mann-Literatur: Bibliographie der Kritik 1896–1975.* Berlin, 1972–1979.

Kantorowicz, Alfred. *Heinrich und Thomas Mann: Die persönlichen, literarischen und weltanschaulichen Beziehungen der Brüder.* Berlin: Aufbau-Verlag, 1956 [42 letters].

———, ed. "Thomas Manns Briefe an Heinrich Mann aus den Jahren 1900–1927." *Geist und Zeit, Eine Zweimonatschrift für Kunst, Literatur und Wissenschaft*, no. 13 (1956) [38 letters and cards].

Mann, Heinrich. *The Patrioteer.* Translated by Ernest Boyd. New York: Harcourt Brace, 1921. Originally, *Der Untertan* (1916).

———. *Berlin: The Land of Cockaigne.* Translated by Axton D. B. Clark. London: Gallancz, 1929. Originally *Im Schlaraffenland: Ein Roman unter feinen Leuten* (1900).

———. *Diana.* Translated by Erich Posselt and Emmet Glore. New York: Coward-McCann, 1929.

———. *The Blue Angel.* London, New York: Hutchinson's International Authors, [1930]. Originally, *Professor Unrat, oder das Ende eines Tyrannen* (1905).

———. *The Little Town.* Translated by Winifred Ray. Boston: Houghton Mifflin, 1931. Originally, *Die kleine Stadt* (1910).

———. *Young Henry of Navarre.* Translated by Eric Sutton. New York: Alfred A. Knopf, 1937. Originally, *Die Jugend des Königs Henri Quatre* (1935).

———. *Henry, King of France.* Translated by Eric Sutton. New York: Alfred A. Knopf, 1939. Originally, *Die Vollendung des Königs Henri Quatre* (1938).

———. "Fünf Briefe an Thomas Mann." *Sinn und Form* 13, nos. 5–6 (1961): 845–51, 959.

———. *Briefe an Ludwig Ewers 1889–1913.* Edited by Ulrich Dietzel and Rosemarie Eggert. Berlin and Weimar: Aufbau-Verlag, 1980.

———. "Briefwechsel mit Julia Mann." In *Ich spreche so gern mit meinen Kindern: Erinnerungen, Skizzen, Briefwechsel mit Heinrich Mann,* by Julia Mann, edited by Rosemarie Eggert, 119–351. Berlin and Weimar: Aufbau-Verlag, 1991.

———. "Briefwechsel mit Lion Feuchtwanger." In *Briefwechsel mit Freunden 1933–1958,* by Lion Feuchtwanger, edited by Harold von Hofe and Sigrid Washburn, 1:297–349. Berlin: Aufbau-Verlag, 1991.

Mann, Klaus. *Briefe und Antworten, 1922–1949.* Edited by Martin Gregor-Dellin. Munich: Spangenberg, 1987.

Mann, Thomas. *Royal Highness: A Novel of German Court-Life.* Translated by A. Cecil Curtis. New York: Alfred A. Knopf, 1916. Originally, *Königliche Hoheit* (1909).

———. *Buddenbrooks: Decline of a Family.* Translated by H. T. Lowe-Porter. New York: Alfred A. Knopf, 1924. Originally, *Buddenbrooks: Verfall einer Familie* (1901).

———. *The Magic Mountain.* Translated by H. T. Lowe-Porter. New York: Alfred A. Knopf, 1927. Originally, *Der Zauberberg* (1924).

———. *Three Essays.* Translated by H. T. Lowe-Porter. New York: Alfred A. Knopf, 1929.

———. *Death in Venice.* Translated by H. T. Lowe-Porter. New York: Alfred A. Knopf, 1930. Originally, *Tod in Venedig* (1913).

———. *Joseph and His Brothers.* Vol. 1, *The Tales of Jacob;* vol. 2, *Young Joseph;* vol. 3, *Joseph in Egypt;* vol. 4, *Joseph the Provider.* Translated by H. T. Lowe-Porter. New York: Alfred A. Knopf, 1934–1944 [Published in one volume by Alfred A. Knopf in 1948]. Originally, *Joseph und seine Brüder: Die Geschichten Jaakobs* (1933); *Der junge Joseph* (1934); *Joseph in Ägypten* (1936); *Joseph der Ernährer* (1943).

———. *Stories of Three Decades.* Translated by H. T. Lowe-Porter. New York: Alfred A. Knopf, 1936.

———. *An Exchange of Letters.* Translated by H. T. Lowe-Porter. New York: Alfred A. Knopf, 1937. Originally, *Ein Briefwechsel* (1937).

———. *The Coming Victory of Democracy.* Translated by Agnes E. Meyer. New York: Alfred A. Knopf, 1938. Originally, *Vom zukünftigen Sieg der Demokratie* (1938).

———. *This Peace.* Translated by H. T. Lowe-Porter. New York: Alfred A. Knopf, 1938. Originally, *Dieser Friede* (1938).

———. *The Problem of Freedom:* An Address to the Undergraduates and Faculty of Rutgers University at Convocation on April the 28th, 1939. New Brunswick, N.J.: Rutgers University Press, 1939.

———. *The Beloved Returns.* Translated by H. T. Lowe-Porter. New York: Alfred A. Knopf, 1940. Originally, *Lotte im Weimar* (1939).

———. *The Transposed Heads: A Legend of India.* Translated by H. T. Lowe-Porter. New York: Alfred A. Knopf, 1941. Originally, *Die vertauschten Köpfe: Eine indische Legende* (1940).

———. *Order of the Day: Political Essays and Speeches of Two Decades.* Translated by H. T. Lowe-Porter, A. E. Meyer, and Eric Sutton. New York: Alfred A. Knopf, 1942.

———. *Listen Germany! Twenty-five Radio Messages to the German People over BBC.* New York: Alfred A. Knopf, 1943. Originally, *Deutsche Hörer! 55 Radiosendungen nach Deutschland* (1942).

———. *Germany and the Germans.* Washington, D.C.: The Library of Congress, 1945. Originally, *Deutschland und die Deutschen* (1945).

———. *Essays of Three Decades.* Translated by H. T. Lowe-Porter. New York: Alfred A. Knopf, 1947.

———. *Doctor Faustus: The Life of the German Composer Adrian Leverkühn as Told by a Friend.* Translated by H. T. Lowe-Porter. New York: Alfred A. Knopf, 1948. Originally, *Doktor Faustus: Das Leben des deutschen Tonsetzers Adrian Leverkühn erzählt von einem Freund* (1947).

———. *The Holy Sinner.* Translated by H. T. Lowe-Porter. New York: Alfred A. Knopf, 1951.

———. *Confessions of Felix Krull, Confidence Man: The Early Years.* Translated by Denver Lindley. New York: Alfred A. Knopf, 1955. Originally, *Bekenntnisse des Hochstaplers Felix Krull* (1954).

———. *Letters to Paul Amann, 1915–1952.* [1959] Translated by Richard and Clara Winston. Middletown, Conn.: Wesleyan University Press, 1960.

———. *A Sketch of My Life.* Translated by H. T. Lowe-Porter. New York: Alfred A. Knopf, 1960. Originally, *Lebensabriß* (1930).

———. *Thomas Mann an Ernst Bertram: Briefe aus den Jahren 1910–1955.* Edited by Inge Jens. Pfullingen: Neske, 1960.

———. *Briefe 1889–1955.* 3 vols. Edited by Erika Mann. Frankfurt: S. Fischer, 1961–1965.

———. *The Story of a Novel: The Genesis of Doctor Faustus.* Translated by Richard and Clara Winston. New York: Alfred A. Knopf, 1961.

———. "Briefe an Heinrich Mann." *Sinn und Form* 19, no. 4 (1967) [10 letters made public in 1965 by the Heinrich-Mann-Archiv der Deutschen Akadamie der Künste].

———. *Letters of Thomas Mann 1889–1955.* Translated by Richard and Clara Winston. New York: Alfred A. Knopf, 1970.

———. *Briefwechsel mit seinem Verleger Gottfried Bermann Fischer 1932–1955.* Edited by Peter de Mendelssohn. Frankfurt: S. Fischer, 1973.

———. *Gesammelte Werke.* 13 vols. Frankfurt: S. Fischer, 1974.

———. *The Hesse-Mann Letters, 1910–1955.* Translated by Ralph Manheim. New York: Harper and Row, 1975.

———. *Tagebücher.* Edited by Peter de Mendelssohn and Inge Jens. Frankfurt: S. Fischer, 1977–.

———. *Reflections of a Nonpolitical Man.* Translated by Walter D. Morris. New York: Frederick Ungar, 1983. Originally, *Betrachtungen eines Unpolitischen* (1918).

———. *Briefwechsel mit Autoren.* Edited by Hans Wysling. Frankfurt: S. Fischer, 1988. [Brw. Autoren]

———. "Dichter oder Schriftsteller? Der Briefwechsel zwischen Thomas Mann und Josef Ponten 1919–1930." In *Thomas-Mann-Studien*, vol. 3, edited by Hans Wysling with assistance by Werner Pfister. Bern: Francke, 1988. [Brw. Ponten]

———. "Briefe an Kurt Martens." In *Thomas Mann Jahrbuch*, edited by Hans Wysling with asssistance by Thomas Sprecher, part 1, vol. 3, 175–247; part 2, vol. 4, 184–260. Frankfurt, 1990–1991.

———. *Notizbücher 1–14.* Edited by Hans Wysling and Yvonne Schmidlin. 2 vols. Frankfurt: S. Fischer, 1991–.

———. "Jahre des Unmuts: Thomas Manns Briefwechsel mit René Schickele 1930–1940." In *Thomas-Mann-Studien*, vol. 10, edited by Hans Wysling and Cornelia Bernini. Frankfurt: Klostermann, 1992. [Brw. Schickele]

———. "'Mit Hauptmann verband mich eine Art von Freundschaft.' Der Briefwechsel zwischen Thomas Mann und Gerhart Hauptmenn." In *Thomas Mann Jahrbuch*, edited by Hans Wysling and Cornelia Bernini, part 1, vol. 6, 245–82; part 2, vol. 7, 205–91. Frankfurt, 1993–1994.

Mann, Thomas, and Agnes E. Meyer. *Briefwechsel, 1937–1955.* Edited by Hans Wysling with assistance by Hans Rudolf Vaget. Frankfurt: S. Fischer, 1992.

Mann, Viktor. *Wir waren fünf: Bildnis der Familie Mann.* 2d rev. ed. Constance, 1964.

Matter, Harry. *Die Literatur über Thomas Mann: Eine Bibliographie 1898–1969.* 2 vols. Berlin and Weimar: Aufbau-Verlag, 1972.

Mendelssohn, Peter de. *Der Zauberer: Das Leben des deutschen Schriftstellers Thomas Mann.* Part 1, *1875–1918.* Part 2, *Jahre der Schwebe: 1919 und 1933.* Frankfurt: S. Fischer, 1975–1992 [posthumous chapters, index, edited by Albert von Schirnding].

Potempa, George. *Thomas Mann—Bibliographie: Das Werk.* With the assistance of Gert Heine. Morsum/Sylt: Cicero Presse, 1992.

Rodewald, Dierk, and Corinna Fiedler, eds. "Briefwechsel mit Samuel und Hedwig Fischer." In *Briefwechsel mit Autoren*, by Samuel and Hedwig Fischer, 394–466, 966–88. Frankfurt: S. Fischer, 1989. [Brw. Fischer]

Schröter, Klaus. *Heinrich Mann in Selbstzeugnissen und Bilddokumenten*, Rowohlts Monographien, 125. Reinbek: Rowohlt, 1967 [with quotations from Heinrich Mann's unpublished works].

Wysling, Hans. "'. . . eine sehr ernste und tiefgehende Korrespondenz mit meinem Bruder': Zwei neuaufgefundene Briefe Thomas Manns an seinen Bruder Heinrich." *Deutsche Vierteljahrsschrift für Literaturwissenschaft und Geistesgeschichte* 55, no. 4 (1981): 645–64 [Thomas Mann's letters of December 5, 1903, and January 8, 1904, and a draft letter by Heinrich Mann].

———. "Heinrich Mann an seinen Bruder: Neuaufgefundene Briefe (1922–1937)." *Thomas-Mann-Studien* (1967–1988): 3:101–46, 196–214 [45 additional letters by Heinrich Mann found by Emmie Oprecht in the Verlagshaus].

———, ed. *Thomas Mann–Heinrich Mann: Briefwechsel 1900–1949.* Frankfurt: S. Fischer, 1968.

Zenker, Edith. *Heinrich-Mann-Bibliographie: Werke.* Berlin: Aufbau-Verlag, 1967.

# CONCERNING THIS EDITION

The present edition publishes all the presently known letters of the Mann brothers. It encompasses a total of 272 letters and drafts of letters, 184 by Thomas Mann, 3 by Katja Mann, and 85 by Heinrich Mann.

The bulk of Thomas Mann's letters were found among his posthumous papers in Prague, in the possession of Leonie Aškenazi-Mann. A portion of them were transferred in the 1950s to the Heinrich-Mann-Archiv der Deutschen Akademie der Künste (see Alfred Kantorowicz, "Briefe an Heinrich Mann," *Aufbau* 11, no. 6 [1955]: 532; Alfred Kantorowicz, *Heinrich und Thomas Mann* [Berlin, 1956], 55; and Hugo Huppert, "Nachgeholte Beiordnungen," *Sinn und Form*, special issue on Thomas Mann [1965]: 118–20). Another portion of the Prague papers ended up in an unknown fashion at a Hauswedell auction in 1957; the sheaf was purchased by the Genevan collector Louis Glatt and sold in 1967 to the Schiller-Nationalmuseum in Marbach. The Akademie der Künste, Berlin/ DDR acquired in the same year ten further letters by Thomas Mann from the private possession of Maria Melichar of Vienna and Munich. The letters of October 24, 1900, and February 11, 1900, are held in a private collection (see Paul Schroers, "Heinrich und Thomas Mann und ihre Verleger," *Philobiblon* 2, no. 4 [December 1958]: 310–14; collection of Dr. Ernst L. Hauswedell, Auction 252, no. 982, May 23–24, 1984). The letters of December 5, 1903, and January 8, 1904, surfaced in 1981 in a secondhand bookstore in Berlin; they were acquired by the Thomas-Mann-Archiv der Eidgenössischen Technischen Hochschule in Zurich. An additional thirty-seven letters by Thomas Mann from the 1930s and 1940s were unexpectedly discovered among Feuchwanger's posthumous papers. Heinrich Mann had thus transferred this part of his papers to Feuchtwanger, rather than his brother. The letters were published in the *Thomas Mann Jahrbuch* of 1988.

Matters concerning Heinrich Mann's letters are less complicated. Among the posthumous papers in Kilchberg were thirty additional letters (1933–1945). In 1973 another forty-six were found in the Verlag Oprecht (1922–1937). They were first published in 1974 in the third volume of the *Thomas-Mann-Studien* of the Thomas-Mann-Archiv in Zurich. The bulk of Heinrich Mann's early letters (prior to 1933) have been lost. Exceptions are one draft letter from the end of 1903 and four letters from the period 1914– 1918.

Two additional letters by Heinrich Mann (December 9, 1939, and May 5, 1940) surfaced in 1985 at the Feuchtwanger Institut. Heinrich Mann's letter of October 23, 1936, along with other correspondence directed to Thomas Mann, was found at the Verlag Oprecht, Zurich, in 1985 and transferred to the Thomas-Mann-Archiv. These letters were also published in the *Thomas Mann Jahrbuch* in 1988.

Previous editions of letters are listed in the bibliography. Spelling and punctuation have been maintained from the originals.

My thanks to Cornelia Bernini, my colleague at the Thomas-Mann-Archiv der ETH in Zurich, for her assistance in the preparation of this new edition.

*H. W.*
*October 1, 1993*

# INDEX

Aboab (bookseller), 181
Adorno, Theodor Wiesengrund, xiii
Africa, 101
Aita, Antonio, 198
Akademische Bühne, 100
Akademischer Verein für medizinische Psychologie, 194
"Altezza Reale" (Caprin), 101
Amann, Paul, 25
America. *See* United States
Amersdorffer, Alexander, 139, 359n
Amsterdam, 129, 131, 229
Andersen, Hans Christian, 2, 322n
Anti-Semitism, xv, 119
*Antony and Cleopatra* (Shakespeare), 93
Aram, Kurt (Hans Fischer), 91, 336n
*Arbeiter-Illustrierte-Zeitung*, 194
Arendt, Hannah, xix
Argentina, 194, 195, 198
Aron, Paul, 160
Aron, Robert, 154, 373n
Arosa, 132, 157, 190, 209, 214
Aryan: professors, 152; race, 149
Aškenazi [Aschermann], Ludvik, 219, 220, 221, 407n
Attersee, 141
Auernheimer, Raoul, 130
Augsburg, 130
*Augsburger Abendzeitung*, 116
Aussee, 132
Austria, 165, 200, 214, 216; bans Heinrich's book, 202; German ambassador protests Thomas's publicity in, 199. *See also* Vienna

Bab, Julius, 21, 30
Baden, 176, 206
Bahr, Hermann, 100; influence on Heinrich and Thomas, 9; interest in producing *Fiorenza*, 76, 77; on *Royal Highness*, 23, 103; summary of life, 323–24n; Thomas on, 70, 110
Balzac, Honoré de, 11, 14, 22, 262

Bandol, 148; Heinrich's letter from, 181–82
Bang, Hermann Joachim, 12
Barbey d'Aurevilly, Jules-Amédéé, 9
Barbusse, Henri, 185
Barcelona, 186
Bari, 231
Basel, 77, 78, 79, 168, 190, 263; Katja Mann's letter from, 261–62
*Baseler Nationalzeitung*, 167, 189
Bauer, Hans, 189
Bavaria, 165
Bayerischen Handelsbank, 110
Beaumarchais, Pierre-Augustin Caron de, 11
Becher, Johannes Robert, 305
Beck, Maximilian, 212
Becker, Carl Heinrich, 138
Beneš, Eduard, 198, 231, 410n
Benn, Gottfried, 145, 146, 147
*Berengaria* (ship): Thomas's letter from, 179–80
Bergner, Elizabeth, 252
Berlin, 90, 105, 111, 134, 148, 162, 181, 183, 187, 236; Heinrich in, 81, 109, 141; Heinrich's bank account impounded in, 148; Heinrich's letters from, 141–47; Thomas in, 68, 70, 82, 100, 117, 129, 138, 323n
*Berliner Tageblatt*, 43, 80, 81, 103, 109, 110, 123
*Berliner Weltspiegel*, 108
*Berliner Zeitgeist*, 81, 267
Bermann Fischer, Gottfried, 167, 174, 179, 201, 203, 253, 258, 261; moves publishing house out of Germany, 192, 194–95, 195–96, 389n; summary of life, 380n; tries to keep German readership, xviii, 153, 185, 191
Bermann-Fischer Verlag, 242, 257
Bern, 176
Bernhard, Georg, 211, 212, 400n
Bernstein, Elsa, 65, 321–22n
Bernstein, Max, 65, 66, 89, 90, 92
Bertaux, Félix, 29, 158, 185, 218, 386n
Bertaux-Piquet, Céline, 147
Bertram, Ernst, 25, 26, 28, 342n

slovakia, 394n; comments on Heinrich's work (negative), xv, xviii, 13–15, 16–17, 19–20, 30, 54–58, 62–63, 123–24, 318n; comments on Heinrich's work (positive), 64, 72, 79, 81, 82–83, 86, 87, 99, 104, 111, 131, 132, 155, 164, 165, 171, 184–85, 190–91, 197, 200–201, 206, 213, 220–21, 222, 227, 255–56, 257, 258, 262, 354n, 385–86n; on communism, 182, 192, 384–85n; compared with Goethe, 29; considered "a Jew" by critic, 119, 348n; considered by Roosevelt for head of postwar Germany, xiii; on death of Klaus, 260–61; decides not to return to Europe (1938), 215; decline in popularity of, xiii, xix–xx; declines to participate in League of Nations meeting, 380n; domestic help problems, 250; emigrates to America, xix, 229; explanation to Heinrich of criticism, 60–61; fairy tales and, 2; on fall of Austria, 214; falls for Katja, 65–66; feels used-up, exhausted, depressed, 46, 49, 83, 118–19; financial difficulties, 44, 52, 122, 123; on formation of German committee, 222–24; on freedom, 64–65; on German emigrés, 191; on greatness, 78–79; on his health, 37, 38, 40, 49, 70, 75, 79, 82, 95, 98, 117, 170, 172, 174, 187, 205, 206, 209, 213, 251, 262, 380n; honorary degrees, 174, 179, 245; identifies with society's pariahs, xiv; on the individual, 292–93; inquires about prospects for return to Germany, 168; on the intellectual, 26; on lack of social criticism in his work, 21, 25; on length of war, 244, 249; letters to Klaus about his books, 396–97n, 408–9n; on literature as death, 19, 46; loans to Heinrich, 101, 104, 106, 112, 113, 116, 117, 122; marriage preparations, 68–69; on *Maß und Wert*, 208–9; Mediterranean voyage of, 357n; as "middling man," 25; in military, 37, 38, 40, 41, 114–15, 309n; Nobel Prize of, xiii, 29; nomination to presidency of the Prussian Academy, 136, 359–60n; obsessed with sister Lula, xv, 16; on organization of Prussian Academy, 137–40, 141–42; parallels and differences in writings compared with Heinrich, xv, xvi, 5–7, 9–10; participates in third war bond drive, 242; photos of, Fig. 1, Fig. 3, Fig. 5–7, Fig. 9–11; plans book on Germany, 376–77n; poems on the sea, 54; portrait painted, 49, 50–51; on possible Argentina trip, 198; on possible Russia trip, 186–87; on psychology, 27; readings/lectures, 53, 54, 65–66, 77–78, 100, 129–30, 171, 194, 198, 199, 215, 222, 232,

261, 412n; reference to Heinrich's motifs, 12–13; requests work for Katja, 87; return to Europe (1947), 259; rivalry/conflict with Heinrich, xiii, xv, 8, 13–28, 29–30; on sexualism, 57–58; sexual orientation, xiv–xv; on Swiss-German conflict, 174–75; tormented by being tied down, 83; on trip to Vienna, 199; uses biographical/historical sources, 12; vacilates about polemic against Germany, 166; on WW I, 121; on writing, 17–18, 53. *See also under* England; France; Germany; Hitler; United States

Mann, Thomas, works:

Articles, Reviews, and Addresses—"The Abject" (planned), 27; "Address on Heinrich Mann's Seventieth Birthday," 291–95; "An die Redaktion des *Svenska Dagbladet,* Stockholm," 24; "Ansprache im Goethejahr," 420n; "The Art of the Novel," 233; "Avenged," 47; "Das beste Buch des Jahres," 389n; "Bilse und ich," 327n, 329n; "The Blood of the Walsungs," 11, 16, 72, 74–75, 76–77, 326–27n; "Dem Fünfundsechzigjährige," 391n; "A Difficult Hour," 16; "The Dilettante," 2, 3, 5; "Europe, Beware!," xiii, 31, 171, 220, 250, 379n, 381n, 396n, 404n; "Felix Krull," 12, 13, 19, 338n; "The Fight Between Jappe and Do Escobar," 345n; "Frederick the Great and the Grand Coalition," 24; "Freiheit und Vornehmheit," 158; "Freud and the Future," 198, 393n, 395n; "Fürsten-Novelle," 7–8, 11, 16; "Gedanken im Kriege," 24, 25, 353n; "Gefallen," 10; "The German Republic," 29, 355–56n; *Germany and the Germans,* 418n; "A Gleam," 317n, 319n, 321n; "Goethe and Tolstoy," 158n10; "Good," 9; "Hoffnungen und Befürchtungen für 1936," 389n; "Der Humanismus und Europa," 394n; "The Hungry," 95; "The Infant Prodigy," 65, 319n, 321n; "Letter on the Death of My Brother Heinrich," 307–8; "Little Lizzy," 5, 47, 90; "The Loved Ones" (planned), 56; "Mass und Wert," 402n; "Ein Nachwort," 327n; "Nietzsche's Philosophie im Lichte unserer Erfahrung," 419n; "Nobelpriset och Carl von Ossietzke," 387n, 389n; "Note on *Die Große Sache,*" 30, 276–80; "On Heinrich Mann's Novel *Der Kopf,*" 271–76; "On the Profession of the German Writer in Our Time," 280–86, 362n, 380n; "Open Letter to Korrodi," 391n; "Peter Schlemihl," 345n; "Railway Accident," 95, 337n; "Report on My Brother,

"Rosen des heiligen Antonius, Die" (Müller), 62
Rosenthal, Frederick, 419n
Rosmer, Ernst. *See* Bernstein, Elsa
Rothschild family, 85
Rottenberg, Sarah, 239–40
Rousseauites, 125, 126
Ruhr, 130
Russia/Russians, 165, 180, 249, 255; Heinrich's success in, 182, 248; Thomas's proposed trip to, 186–87

S. A., 152, 159
Saar, 188
Sahm, Heinrich, 144
Saint-Cloud, 156
Saint-Cyr, 204
Sainte-Beuve, Charles-Augustin, 232
Sainte-Chapelle, 110
St. Gallen, 120
*St. Galler Tagblatt*, 190
St. Gilgen, 132
Sainte-Maxime, 200, 201, 204
St. Moritz, 171
*Salome* (Strauss), 78
*Salome* (Wilde), 55
Salten, Felix, 71, 324
Salus, Hugo, 83
Salzburg, 132, 177, 180, 182, 183, 184
*Sammlung, Die*, xviii, 157, 165, 167
San Antonio, 232, 233
Sanary-sur-Mer, 155, 160, 184, 204
Sand, George, 22
Sänger, Samuel, 98
Sanssouci, 75
Santa Monica, 243
Sauer, Hedda, 103, 341n
Savonarola, Girolamo, 14, 19, 37
Schacht, Hjalmar, 159, 372–73n
Schäfer, Wilhelm, 133, 136, 139, 359n
*Schaubühne, Die*, 111
Schäuffelen, Eugenie, 116
Schaukal, Richard, 51, 57, 58, 61, 98; review of *Fiorenza*, 267–68, 329–30n; summary of life, 311n; Thomas on, 41, 52–53, 267–68; Thomas's quarrel with, 71–72, 80–81
Schauspielhaus: Munich, 52; Zurich, 168
Scheffler, Karl, 98
Schickele, Anna, 204, 372n
Schickele, Hans, 159, 372n
Schickele, René, 102, 137, 159, 161, 204, 224, 372n, 373n, 406n
Schiller, Johann, 12–13, 78, 189, 283, 329n
Schillings, Max von, 362–63n

Schleicher, Kurt von, 367n
Schlumberger, Jean, 208, 398n
Schmied, Ines, 91, 92, 94; conflict with sister Lula, 96–97; Heinrich's relationship with, 16, 20, 332n; Thomas dislikes, 99, 343n
Schmied, Rudolf Johannes, 71, 105, 324n
Schmitz, Oskar A. H., 25
Schnitzler, Arthur, 130, 272–73, 356n
Scholz, Wilhelm von, 134, 137, 360n
Schopenhauer, Arthur, 5, 10, 13, 19, 21, 214, 217
Schrödinger, Erwin, 224
Schuschnigg, Kurt von, 197, 198, 214
Schwabe, Toni, 13, 83
Schwarzchild, Leopold, 191, 192, 210, 211, 399n
*Schwarze Korps, Das*, 223
Seeshaupt: Thomas's letters from, 86–88
Seitz, Karl, 171
Semmering, 130
Servaes, Franz, 100
Settembrini, Luigi, 25
S. Fischer Verlag, 174, 190, 365n. *See also* Fischer, Samuel
Shakespeare, William, 296
Shaw, George Bernard, 102, 131, 162
Sils Baselgia, 204, 216
Sils Maria, 202, 216
*Simplicissimus*, 10, 38, 44, 79
Smith, Edith and Mary, 52, 316n
Southampton, 229, 259
Soviet Union. *See* Russia
Spain, 194, 202, 203, 207, 219, 242
Speidel, Albert Frh. von, 98
Spengler, Oswald, 152, 367n
Spinoza, Baruch, 129
Springer, Idachen, 53, 108, 227
S. S., 159
Stalin, Joseph, 211, 256
Starnberg, 93
Stecker, Karl, 28
Stehr, Hermann, 163, 374n
Sternberg, August, 41, 42
Stifter, Adalbert, 125, 352n
Stilke, Hermann Georg, 90
*Stine* (Fontane), 417–18n
Stinnes-Coupienne, Adeline, 110
Stockholm, 228, 230; Katja Mann's letter from, 259–60; Thomas's letter from, 260–61
Stollberg, J. Georg, 45, 313n
Storm, Theodor, 175
Strasser, Otto, 211, 400n
Strauss, Richard, 44, 78, 146

Wassermann, Jakob, xiii, 61, 83, 190; death, 157, 371n; Schaukal on, 80, 267; Thomas visits, 100, 132

Wassermann-Speyer, Julie, 72

Weber, Hans von, 113

Wedekind, Frank, 20, 57, 75, 327–28n

Week of International Culture, Florence, 271–72

Wegener, Paul, 117

Weill, Kurt, xix

Weimar, 109, 262, 263

Weimar Republic, 206, 211

*weiße Blätter, Die*, 25

Weißer Hirsch, 82

Wells, Herbert George, 131

Werdandi-Bund, 90–91, 336n

Werfel, Franz, 166, 252

West Hollywood: Heinrich's letter from, 247

Weyl, Mrs., 261, 420n

W. Heinemann (publisher), 191, 195

Whitman, Walt, xvi, xvii, xx

Wilhelm, Prince August, 118

Wilhelm II, 251

Windsor, duchess of, 239

Winterstein, Eduard von, 118

*wirkliche Deutschland, Das* (Schmitz), 25

Wolff, Gustav, 92

Wolff, Kurt, 29

Wolters, Wilhelm, 344n

World Committee Against War and Fascism, 185

World Congress of the World Peace Movement, 395n

Wüllner, Ludwig, 44, 77

Würzburg, 205

Wysling, Hans, xv, xvi, xviii

Yale University, 215

Yriarte, Charles, 45

*Zarathustra* (Nietzsche), 10

*Zeit, Die*, 45

Zeppelin, 97

Zitelmann, Hermine von, 70

Zola, Émil, 11, 22

Zsolnay, Paul, 152, 153, 155, 195, 196, 368n

*Zukunft, Die*, 83, 90, 98, 103; Heinrich's contributions to, 72, 331n; Thomas's contributions to, 95, 104

Zurich, 159, 161, 173, 175, 176, 181, 185, 191, 200, 203, 204, 213, 215, 218, 220, 233, 236, 251, 263; Thomas in, 98, 120, 179, 259, 263; Thomas's letters from 69–71, 98–99. *See also* Küsnacht

*Zwanzigste Jahrhundert, Das*, 10

Zweig, Arnold, 161, 373–74n

Zweig, Stefan, 169, 224

| | |
|---|---|
| Indexer: | Andrew Christenson |
| Designer: | Barbara Jellow |
| Compositor: | Prestige Typography |
| Text: | Janson |
| Display: | Janson |
| Printer and Binder: | Edwards Brothers |